HENRY IV

HENRY IV

Chris Given-Wilson

YALE UNIVERSITY PRESS
NEW HAVEN AND LONDON

For information about this and other Yale University Press publications, please contact:
U.S. Office: sales.press@yale.edu   www.yalebooks.com
Europe Office: sales@yaleup.co.uk   www.yalebooks.co.uk

Set in Baskerville by IDSUK (DataConnection) Ltd
Printed in Great Britain by TJ International Ltd, Padstow, Cornwall

Library of Congress Cataloging-in-Publication Data

Given-Wilson, Chris.
    Henry IV / Chris Given-Wilson.
        pages cm
    ISBN 978-0-300-15419-1 (cl : alk. paper)
1. Henry IV, King of England, 1367–1413. 2. Great Britain—Kings and rulers—
Biography. 3. Great Britain—History—Henry IV, 1399–1413. I. Title.
    DA255.G58 2016
                                                                942.04´1092—dc23
[B]
            2015023658

A catalogue record for this book is available from the British Library.

10 9 8 7 6 5 4 3 2 1

For Alice and all our family

TABLE OF CONTENTS

PLATES

13. a and b. Second Great Seal of Henry IV (*c.*1406): (a) obverse; (b) reverse. Courtesy of the Society of Antiquaries. Photos: Michael Bennett.

14. Petitions to the king: from Robert Hallum, archdeacon of Canterbury; Sir Matthew Gournay; and Garcius Arnald of Salins in Guyenne. British Library Add. Ms. 19,398, fo. 23. Copyright © The British Library Board.

15. The Chapel in the Crag, Knaresborough, North Yorkshire, carved by John the Mason in thanksgiving for his young son being miraculously saved from falling rock. Henry IV granted permission for the shrine in 1407. Photo: author

16. Thomas Arundel, archbishop of Canterbury, Lambeth Palace. Nineteenth-century portrait. By permission of the Archbishop of Canterbury and the Church Commissioners.

17. a and b. (a) Battlefield Chapel, near Shrewsbury, dedicated to St Mary Magdalene and founded by Henry IV, *c.*1409, on the site of the battle of Shrewsbury; (b) statue of Henry IV on the east gable of the Chapel. Photos: author.

18. Illustration from Thomas Hoccleve, *De Regimine Principum*, written in 1410–11. British Library Arundel Ms 38, fo. 37. Copyright © The British Library Board.

19. From Henry IV's Great Bible. British Library Royal Ms 1 E IX, fo. 63v. Copyright © The British Library Board.

MAPS AND TABLES

MAPS

TABLES

ACKNOWLEDGEMENTS

Many people have helped me to write this book, some by alerting me to references, some by reading sections, some in fruitful discussions. I hope I have remembered to thank them all at the appropriate point, and if not I apologize.

I have had the good fortune to spend my career in the Department of Medieval History at the University of St Andrews, surrounded by stimulating friends and colleagues, teaching able and interested students, in an environment which, for a medievalist, could hardly be bettered. I am grateful to them all. In 2013–14 I also spent a year working on this book at Fordham University in New York; thank you to Maryanne Kowaleski and her colleagues for making me so welcome there. I am very grateful to Nora Bartlett for her help in compiling the index. The many librarians and archivists who have helped me during the course of researching this book have also been unfailingly helpful; I would especially like to thank the staff of The National Archives at Kew, London, where the majority of the manuscript research for this book was done.

Whenever I go to London, I stay with my sister Rosalind in her house in Clapham, where she and her husband Paul invariably greet me with warmth, good food, good wine and good conversation. I have thought many times how much less pleasant my research would have been without their decades of generous hospitality.

This book is dedicated to Alice, Rachel, Hannah, Paul, Polo, Roxana, Neko, Luna and Cody, in the hope that they will always be safe and happy.

Chris Given-Wilson
St Andrews, March 2015

ABBREVIATED REFERENCES

Titles are given in full in the Bibliography.

All manuscript references are to documents in The National Archives, Kew, London, unless otherwise indicated.

ANLP	*Anglo-Norman Letters and Petitions*
Annales	*Annales Ricardi Secundi et Henrici Quarti*
BIHR	*Bulletin of the Institute of Historical Research*
BJRL	*Bulletin of the John Rylands Library*
Brut	*Brut, or Chronicles of England*
BL	British Library, London
CAD	*Calendar of Ancient Deeds*
CChR	*Calendar of Charter Rolls*
CCR	*Calendar of Close Rolls*
CDS	*Calendar of Documents Relating to Scotland*
CE	*Eulogium Historiarum sive Temporis*, vol. 3
CFR	*Calendar of Fine Rolls*
CGR	*Calendar of Gascon Rolls*
CIM	*Calendar of Inquisitions Miscellaneous*
CIPM	*Calendar of Inquisitions Post Mortem*
CIRCLE CR	*Calendar of Irish Chancery Letters, Close Rolls*
CIRCLE PR	*Calendar of Irish Chancery Letters, Patent Rolls*
Concilia	*Concilia Magnae Britanniae et Hiberniae*, 3 vols
CP	*Complete Peerage*
CPL	*Calendar of Papal Letters*
CPR	*Calendar of Patent Rolls*
CR	*Chronicles of the Revolution*
De Illustribus Henricis	*Johannis Capgrave Liber De Illustribus Henricis*
EETS	Early English Text Society
EHR	*English Historical Review*
Establishment	*The Establishment of the Regime*
Foedera	*Foedera, Conventiones, Letterae*, etc.
Giles	*Incerti Scriptoris Chronicon Angliae*, ed. Giles
Hardyng	*Chronicle of John Hardyng*
HOC	*House of Commons 1386–1421*
HR	*Historical Research*
JGR I and II	*John of Gaunt's Register*
Knighton	*Knighton's Chronicle 1337–1396*
Monstrelet	*Chronique d'Enguerran de Monstrelet*
Ms	Manuscript

ODNB	*Oxford Dictionary of National Biography*
Original Letters	*Original Letters Illustrative of English History*
Polychronicon	*Polychronicon Ranulphi Higden, Monachi Cestrensis*
POPC	*Proceedings and Ordinances of the Privy Council*
PROME	*Parliament Rolls of Medieval England*
Rebellion and Survival	*Reign of Henry IV: Rebellion and Survival*
RHKA	Given-Wilson, *Royal Household and King's Affinity*
RHL I and II	*Royal and Historical Letters of Henry IV,* 2 vols
RS	Rolls Series
SAC I and II	*St Albans Chronicle I (1376–94) and II (1394–1422)*
Saint-Denys	*Chronique du Réligieux de Saint-Denys*
SHF	Société de l'Histoire de France
Signet Letters	*Signet Letters of Henry IV and Henry V*
Traïson et Mort	*Chronique de la Traïson et Mort de Richart Deux*
TRHS	*Transactions of the Royal Historical Society*
Usk	*Chronicle of Adam Usk 1377–1421*
VCH	*Victoria County History*
Vita	*Historia Vitae et Regni Ricardi Secundi*
Westminster Chronicle	*Westminster Chronicle 1381–1394*

INTRODUCTION

On 20 March 1413, the feast of St Cuthbert, King Henry IV of England lay dying in the Jerusalem chamber at Westminster abbey. On a couch beside him was his crown, around him several attendants. Presently his breathing grew so shallow that it was presumed he had died, so a sheet was drawn over his face and the prince of Wales sent for. Believing himself now to be king, the prince gathered up the crown and left the room, but scarcely had he done so when a sigh was heard from under the sheet, and when they drew it back the attendants realized their mistake. Looking about him, the king asked what had become of his crown. 'The prince your son has taken it away,' they replied. They were sent to summon him, and when the prince reappeared Henry asked him to explain himself. 'My lord,' he said, 'these people assured me that you were dead, and since I am your eldest son and it is to me that your crown and your kingdom will descend after your death, I took it away'. 'And how, my son,' asked the king, 'do you have any right to it, for as you well know, I never had any?' 'You held it with your sword, my lord, and for as long as I live I shall do the same,' answered the prince. 'Very well then,' replied the king, 'The rest I leave to God, and I pray Him to have mercy on me.' These were Henry IV's last words. The prince now became King Henry V, and no man gainsaid his right to the kingdom.[1]

Many tales were told of Henry IV's deathbed, most of them, like this one, by people who were not there but who saw it as an opportunity for political point-scoring. Yet the fact that this fable was too good to be true did little to discourage its circulation. Invented or perhaps retailed a quarter of a century after the event by the Burgundian chronicler Enguerrand de Monstrelet, it eventually found its way back to England and was taken up in the sixteenth century by Edward Hall and Raphael Holinshed, through whom it reached Shakespeare and achieved immortality. It was, after all,

---

[1] *La Chronique d'Enguerran de Monstrelet 1400–1444*, ed. L Douët-d'Arcq (SHF, 6 vols, Paris, 1858), ii.338–9.

a good story, and it fitted Shakespeare's image of the king, for it reflected an enduring moral truth of Henry's reign, namely that it was his usurpation of the throne that defined his kingship. Neither at home nor abroad would enemies and detractors permit him to escape from the shadow of 1399. A sense of the displacement of authority rattles around like a pinball in contemporary literature. On the other hand, it does not validate Shakespeare's characterization of the king. The haunted, care-worn, at times almost irrelevant monarch of *Henry IV Parts I and II* bears little resemblance to the man who ruled England between 1399 and 1413, although the tactical 'Bullingbrook' of *Richard II* comes closer to the mark. Peerless poet and dramatist that he was, historically Shakespeare has nothing to contribute to an understanding of Henry or his reign, although his influence on later perceptions of the king was immense.[2]

Better guides are the contemporary chroniclers who, whether or not they liked the king, whether or not they accepted his right to rule, feared and respected his power. Thomas Walsingham, the St Albans monk who wrote the fullest and most informative account of the reign, said that Henry 'reigned gloriously for thirteen-and-a-half years'. Adam Usk praised his 'powerful rule, during which he crushed all those who rebelled against him'. An anonymous chronicler claimed that, despite constantly extorting taxes, Henry was greatly loved by his people, but this was wishful thinking. Most would have agreed with John Strecche, chronicler of Kenilworth priory, who extolled the king's military prowess, but admitted that by breaking his promises he lost the people's trust; nevertheless, he concluded, 'few were his equal, many were his followers, and never was he defeated in battle'. Even Monstrelet, no friend to the Lancastrian dynasty, called him 'a valiant knight, fierce and cunning towards his enemies'.[3] It is difficult to think that they were all wrong.

Compared to the abundance of narratives for the reigns of Richard II and Henry V, that of Henry IV was not well served by the chroniclers. Only the first three years of his reign received comparable coverage, and only Walsingham came close to attempting a consecutive record of its events, although even his (or his assistants') enthusiasm for the task waned as the reign progressed.[4] On the other hand, the fact that those chroniclers

---

[2] Below (Epilogue), pp. 535–41.

[3] *SAC II*, 618–19; *Usk*, 242–3; BL Add. Ms 35,295, fo. 262r; C. Kingsford, *English Historical Literature in the Fifteenth Century* (Oxford, 1913), 277; *Monstrelet*, ii.337.

[4] J. Clark, 'Thomas Walsingham Reconsidered: Books and Learning at Late Medieval St Albans', *Speculum* 77 (2002), 832–60, questions Walsingham's authorship of the whole of the St Albans chronicle.

who saw the reign through from beginning to end, however cursorily, wrote independently of each other, means that they provide complementary information and contrasting points of view. Usk, Strecche, 'Giles' and the Franciscan author of the *Continuatio Eulogii* were not expansive chroniclers, but they were individualistic, opinionated and contemporary. It was not until after the king's death – and more busily after the implosion of Lancastrian kingship in the mid-fifteenth century – that the memory industry set about ironing out the creases to produce the enduring image of the 'unquiet times' of Henry IV.[5]

Yet still Henry remains the most neglected of England's late medieval monarchs. There is, naturally, a contested historiography underlying the opinions expressed in this book, which is discussed further in the Epilogue, but a good number of historians, dazzled by the brilliance of Henry V and the showy self-destruction of Richard II, have allowed their eyes to slip rather hurriedly past the reign that bridged them, viewing Henry IV more as a means (to Richard's overthrow, to Henry V's heroics) than as an end in himself. Much the fullest account of the reign is J. H. Wylie's omnivorous four-volume *History of England under Henry the Fourth*, published between 1884 and 1898, but, despite the remarkable amount of information assembled by Wylie, it is, as its title suggests, a history of early fifteenth-century England rather than a biography of the king. Of modern biographies of Henry, the most balanced is by J. L. Kirby (*Henry IV of England*, 1970), the most readable by I. Mortimer (*The Fears of Henry IV*, 2007), though neither deals adequately with the years after 1406. This imbalance is characteristic of the historiography of the reign almost from the start. Shakespeare's *Henry IV Part II* moves directly from 1405 to 1413, and it was largely through analysis of the parliaments of 1399 to 1406 that Stubbs formulated the thesis that Henry was a constitutional monarch.[6] A rough calculation indicates that the twentieth- and twenty-first-century literature on the years 1399 to 1406 exceeds that on the years 1407 to 1413 by a factor of five or six. It is not hard to see why: the risings of 1400, 1403 and 1405, the Welsh rebellion, French and Scottish hostility and the difficult parliaments of 1401 to 1406 were the crucible of Lancastrian kingship. Moreover, key sources dry up after 1406: 70 per cent of the surviving acts of the Privy Council, three-quarters of Henry's diplomatic correspondence and 85 per cent of his known signet letters belong to the years 1399–1406; six

---

[5] The phrase was coined by Edward Hall, *The Union of the two Noble and Illustre Families of Lancastre and York* (1542).

[6] Below (Epilogue), pp. 538–9.

parliaments were documented during this period, three between 1407 and
1413. Yet there was no slackening in the work of the main departments of
state – chancery, exchequer, law courts. Henry's personal involvement may
have declined along with his health, but government did not, and in fact
the second half of the reign was a time when, secure in the possession
of the throne, the king and his ministers could begin to devise the policy
initiatives denied them by the relentless pressure of the early years.

This book is a political biography, not a history of England in the early
fifteenth century, but some background to the events it describes will
be helpful. England in 1400 was a land of around two-and-a-half million
people. Sixty years earlier the population had been at least double that,
perhaps even six or seven million, but the Black Death of 1348–50 had
halved it and recurrent visitations of the plague blunted recovery. In a
society in which 80 per cent or more of people worked the land for a living,
this demographic catastrophe led to economic and social adjustment: a
surplus of labour became a shortage; more land became available to enterprising peasants; rents, prices and serfdom declined; wages rose. Landlords,
eager to maintain their incomes, reacted with repressive measures, including
labour legislation, but coercion and expectation collided explosively in the
Peasants' Revolt of 1381. Although quickly suppressed, the revolt left the
government and landlords wary of pursuing policies that might lead to
another uprising.
    The pervasive sense of dislocation induced by plague and social unrest
was heightened by military failure and religious divisions. The triumphs of
Edward III and his son, the Black Prince, during the early decades of the
Hundred Years War were becoming a distant, if cherished, memory. Much
of what England had won by the Treaty of Brétigny in 1360 was lost in the
1370s, a decade which also saw the beginning of the Great Schism (1378–
1417), during which rival popes based at Rome and Avignon divided
Europe into opposing camps. It was also in the 1370s that Lollardy, the first
serious outbreak of heresy in England for a millennium, began to trouble
the authorities, as it would continue to do for the next four decades and
intermittently thereafter.
    The fact that policies for the management of the labour force, the
conduct of the war, the healing of the Schism and the suppression of heresy
all came to be seen as the responsibility of royal government reflected the
centralized nature of the English polity by comparison with much of
Europe. The chancery and exchequer were now settled at Westminster,
employing hundreds of clerks who each year despatched thirty or forty

thousand letters in the king's name to all parts of the kingdom.[7] Local administration operated differently, staffed not by graded career officials of the crown but by local men – knights, esquires, gentlemen, merchants – who served limited terms or were appointed to undertake specific tasks such as collecting a subsidy or arraying soldiers for war. Sheriffs, coroners and escheators had for long been the principal royal agents in the shires, but as the demands of the crown increased so did the number of functionaries needed to enforce them, from Justices of the Peace to commissioners of array, customs officers and tax-collectors. Taxation, a *sine qua non* of solvent government by 1400, was deeply disliked and at times violently resisted, but had become familiar enough to most Englishmen to be regularly and efficiently collected. Royal justice by now enjoyed a virtual monopoly of major civil and criminal cases throughout the realm, though not of ecclesiastical or lesser ones. Around three thousand new suits a year were brought to the central law courts, while legislation regulated not just crime and possessory actions but also, increasingly, matters such as work, vagrancy, dress, leisure, and religious and educational practice. Cities and boroughs, of which there were over 600 in the kingdom, had greater licence to regulate their internal affairs, but with the qualified exception of London they lacked the autonomy or political influence of large towns in northern Italy, Flanders, southern France or parts of Germany. Nor were English towns wont to league together in order to achieve their aims, a familiar tactic elsewhere.[8]

Royal government, in short, was not something that Englishmen could ignore, wherever they lived and however great they were. England was not a polity in which kings could rule only by allowing great feudatories a virtually free hand in their own lordships, as was the case in some parts of Europe. One reason for this was because English nobles lacked the large and consolidated blocks of land which made a duke of Brittany or Saxony, for example, the lord of all men within the confines of his duchy and hence, potentially, an alternative rather than an intermediate source of authority to that of the king or emperor. Most English nobles held estates scattered throughout a number of counties, sometimes bearing little relation to the titles they bore.

England's administrative precocity also meant that, generally speaking, men of all sorts and conditions within the English kingdom tended to find that the best way to augment their power was in tandem with the crown,

---

[7] A. Brown, *The Governance of Late Medieval England 1272–1461* (London, 1989), 52.

[8] The Hanseatic and Lombard leagues and the Swiss confederation are the most striking examples; leagues of towns were especially effective in the Empire.

its institutions, and its vast fund of patronage, rather than to set themselves up as rivals to it. This is one reason why, despite dynastic strife, the public authority of the crown expanded so markedly during the later Middle Ages, though it also meant that this was not a public authority simply imposed from above, but exercised in cooperation with the many thousands of landholders and others who, in a myriad of different ways, acted as the crown's agents in the localities. The growth of the crown's authority did not therefore involve a diminution of the authority of lesser polities. The power of noble lordship, the economic and to some extent political influence of merchant elites in the towns, and the control by the gentry of affairs in their localities all increased during the fourteenth century.[9] The raising of contract armies to fight abroad, for example, augmented the military power of the nobility as well as of the crown; the development of the office of Justice of the Peace enhanced the judicial power of crown, lords and gentry simultaneously. If, as is sometimes claimed, the fourteenth and fifteenth centuries witnessed the rise of the state in England (and indeed Europe), it rose through interaction and participation as much as through the stiffening of monarchical institutions, a process of widening cooperation and continuous adjustment punctuated by violent struggle, often for personal or dynastic advancement. That additional (typically financial) impositions by the crown should invite closer scrutiny and provide extra fuel for conflict is hardly surprising. Widening participation in government was bound to throw up more occasions for disagreement, but the only true 'enemies of the state' in late medieval England (as opposed to rebels or adversaries of the king) were hostile foreigners, radical heretics and, when they refused to accept their allotted place in society, as in 1381, the lower orders. Faced with such threats, the establishment closed ranks and entrenched its power.

Widening participation in government is reflected in the ever-expanding role of parliament. Parliament was not an administrative department of the crown, since parliaments were in session only for five or six weeks of the year on average, but it was by now the clearing-house for the great business of the realm, a roughly annual national health check, the outcome of which was not easy to predict. There was always a fair amount of

---

[9] See, for example, R. Davies, *Lords and Lordship in the British Isles, passim*; C. Given-Wilson, 'The King and the Gentry in Fourteenth-Century England', *TRHS* 37 (1987), 87–102. For an analysis of this theme in a Europe-wide context, see J. Watts, *The Making of Polities: Europe 1300–1500* (Cambridge, 2009); for England, see G. Harriss, 'Political Society and the Growth of Government in Late Medieval England', *Past and Present* 138 (1993), 28–57, and G. Harriss, *Shaping the Nation: England 1360–1461* (Oxford, 2005).

criticism, sometimes a great deal, and occasionally parliaments became the stage for bitter infighting, but ideally, and in practice not infrequently, the relationship between king and parliament functioned as a mutually supportive partnership. So too (ideally) did the relationship between the king and the Church, although this was becoming a less equal partnership. The papacy's move to Avignon in 1309, a cause of deep suspicion to a nation engaged in a prolonged struggle with the French, had spawned a more robust attitude to claims of papal sovereignty over Englishmen, leading to increased control by the king and nobility of the large reserves of patronage, from bishoprics downwards, at the Church's disposal. By and large the spiritual jurisdiction of the Catholic Church remained intact, but deep inroads had been carved into what were still nominally its resources. The eventual outcome of this process – the assumption by Henry VIII of supremacy over the *Ecclesia Anglicana* – was far from certain at this stage, but the building blocks were being put in place.

Nowhere did the aspiration of fifteenth-century rulers to act as 'emperors in their own kingdoms' come closer to being realized than in England. This was a functioning state, a vehicle for powerful, potentially predatory, kingship. On the other hand, its dependence on active and cooperative kingship and the power which it invested in the person of the monarch was also its Achilles heel, for it relied disproportionately on the aptitude of each king to make it function in a way that was acceptable to the polity, and aptitude was not something that the lottery of heredity could guarantee.

Table 1 The House of Lancaster and the Crown, 1272–1399 (selective)

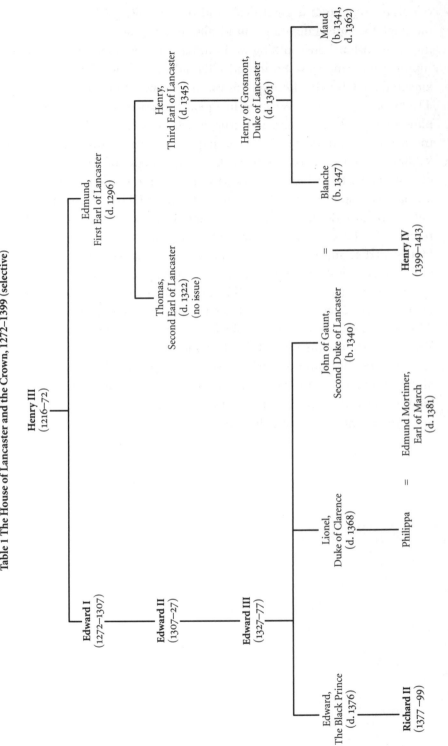

Part One

THE GREAT DUCHY
1267–1399

Table 2 Descendants of John of Gaunt (selective)

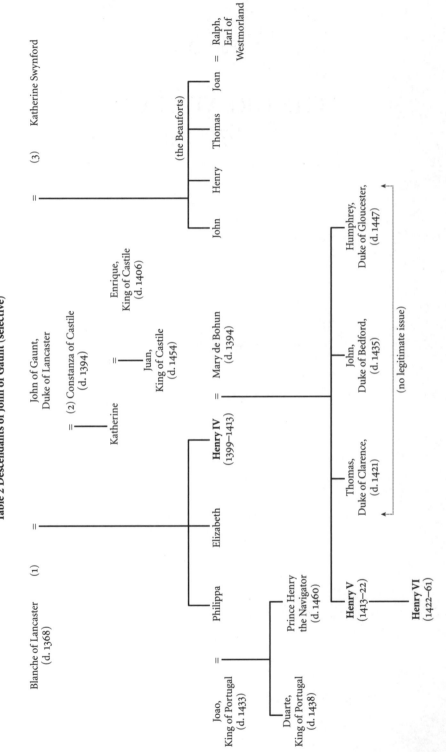

Chapter 1

THE HOUSE OF LANCASTER AND THE CROWN (1267–1367)

The future King Henry IV of England was born on or around 15 April 1367 at Bolingbroke castle, fifteen miles north of Boston on the southern edge of the Lincolnshire wolds, the fifth-born child of John of Gaunt, duke of Lancaster, fourth son of King Edward III, and Blanche, only surviving daughter of Henry of Grosmont, first duke of Lancaster (d. 1361). However, since his older brothers John and Edward had died as infants and his remaining siblings were both girls, he was, from the moment of his birth, his parents' sole and undisputed heir, and the patrimony which he stood to inherit was the greatest in England bar the crown.[1] A century old in the year of Henry's birth, the Lancastrian inheritance had, like most noble estates, been assembled through a combination of aggressive acquisition, royal favour and the misfortunes of others. The prerequisite for its creation was the battle of Evesham in August 1265, at which the baronial coalition that had challenged Henry III's rule for the previous seven years was defeated and its leader Simon de Montfort, earl of Leicester, killed. Two months later the bulk of Montfort's lands, including the castle and honour of Leicester, were granted by the king to his younger son Edmund 'Crouchback', who in 1267 became earl of Leicester. Meanwhile Robert de Ferrers, earl of Derby, who had not been at Evesham but had previously opposed the king, rebelled once more and was defeated at Chesterfield in May 1266; his lands too were granted to Edmund, and in 1267 Henry III also granted his son the castle, honour and county of Lancaster, and the honour of Pickering in Yorkshire.[2] Two years on from Evesham, therefore,

---

[1] For his date of birth, see I. Mortimer, *The Fears of Henry IV* (London, 2007), 364–5, based on E 403/431, Tuesday 1 June, and Henry's later household accounts which record evidence of alms distributed on his successive birthdays. His sisters were Philippa, born in 1360, and Elizabeth, born in 1363/4. For 'Henry of Bolingbroke', see *Brut*, ii.341, and *CE*, 361, 366 (based on a common source).

[2] In 1269 Ferrers was offered the chance to redeem his lands, but the terms demanded of him were extortionate: R. Somerville, *History of the Duchy of Lancaster* (London, 1953), i.3–5; J. Bothwell, *Falling from Grace* (Manchester, 2008), 58, 97; J. Maddicott, *Thomas of Lancaster 1307–1322* (Oxford, 1970), 1, describes it as 'a piece of legal chicanery'.

the foundations of the future greatness of the house of Lancaster had been laid and the disposition of its principal holdings established. Leicester, Kenilworth in Warwickshire (also a former de Montfort castle), and Tutbury in Staffordshire (the Ferrers *caput*) for long remained the principal Lancastrian residences in the Midlands; Pickering marked the first stage of what would later become a dominant, if never unchallenged, interest in Yorkshire; while Lancaster provided Edmund and his descendants with a consolidated block of lands and rights which would one day lead to its elevation to the status of Duchy and County Palatine – as well, of course, as giving them the title by which they would almost invariably be designated. Why that was the case – why, that is, they came to be known as earls of Lancaster rather than of Leicester or Derby – was probably because their claims to the latter two earldoms were less secure, founded as they were upon civil war, disinheritance and legal chicanery. Those whom they supplanted, such as the Ferrers – still peers of parliament even if no longer earls – did not forget this, and continued to nurture their hopes and advance their claims.[3]

The annual value of the lands which Edmund passed on to his son Thomas at his death in 1296 was in the region of £4,500, but more valuable still was Thomas's marriage, arranged by Edmund in 1294, to Alice, daughter and heiress of Henry de Lacy, earl of Lincoln, whose inheritance included the lands of the earldom of Salisbury and was worth a further £6,500 per annum. Thus, following de Lacy's death in 1311, Thomas became the holder of a landed estate the size and value of which – some £11,000 per annum – made him incomparably the richest and most powerful lord in England after the king.[4] Especially useful to Thomas was the fact that the geographical distribution of the Lacy lands tended to augment Lancastrian power in areas where it was already strong, as well as

[3] *CP*, v.313. Since the twelfth century, the trend in England had been in favour of growing security of tenure for landholders, so that many forfeitures proved to be temporary, and those who had profited from political miscalculation knew that there was no certainty that they would hold on to what they had gained. However, the baronial wars of the 1260s proved to be the turning-point of this trend, with the crown henceforward taking a less lenient stance towards treason and rebellion, and a growing number of landholding families suffering forfeiture on a long-term or even permanent basis. Earl Edmund and his descendants would be the first and most notable beneficiaries of this policy, yet neither he nor his eldest son Thomas ever used the style 'earl of Derby'. Thomas even went so far, fifty years after Evesham, as to appoint a chaplain to say masses for Ferrers's soul, apparently some form of expiation or at least 'the product of a guilty conscience': Bothwell, *Falling from Grace*, 92–8; Maddicott, *Thomas of Lancaster*, 320; Somerville, *Duchy of Lancaster*, i.9–10.
[4] Maddicott, *Thomas of Lancaster*, 3, 22; by 1296, Edmund was the lord of 632 separate units of property and 49 demesne manors: R. Davies, *Lords and Lordship in the British Isles* (Oxford, 2009), 159.

to bring in new, often contiguous, centres of wealth and influence. The honours of Clitheroe and Halton were added to Thomas's sizeable possessions in Lancashire; the castle and rich honour of Pontefract significantly expanded his interests in Yorkshire, while the even richer honour of Bolingbroke in Lincolnshire extended his already dominant position in the Midlands towards the North Sea. The lordship of Denbigh in North Wales, also acquired from his father-in-law, was followed seven years later by further substantial lands in the Welsh Marches, for in 1318, following a dispute with John de Warenne, earl of Surrey (who had abducted Thomas's wife Alice the previous year), Warenne was forced to grant him all his lands in North Wales and Yorkshire, as well as some in East Anglia, in return for a number of considerably less valuable manors in Wiltshire, Somerset and Dorset which had come to him through the Lacy inheritance.[5]

Such an unequal exchange, the product of the political circumstances of the moment, might be enforceable in the short term but, like the disinheritance of Robert de Ferrers, was unlikely to remain uncontested. Edmund's accumulation of lands and titles had been his reward for consistent loyalty to the crown; so too had the favours shown to Thomas during his teens and twenties. However, from the winter of 1308–9 (when he was aged thirty), Thomas moved into opposition to the new king, Edward II, a stance which he maintained for the rest of his life, the mistrust and hatred between the two cousins growing ever deeper until, in the autumn of 1321, the civil war which had threatened periodically during the previous decade eventually erupted. The upshot was catastrophic: captured at the battle of Boroughbridge, Thomas was taken to his favourite castle of Pontefract – where, it was rumoured, he had planned to imprison the king had he prevailed – put on trial and, on 22 March 1322, led out to a hillock just below the castle walls and beheaded. Convicted of treason, he also forfeited all his lands and chattels. The Lancastrian inheritance was no more: decapitated and dismembered, it was parcelled out between the king and his supporters, chief among them Lancaster's bitterest enemies, the two Hugh Despensers, father and son.

The road to recovery was not as slow as it might have been, but it required both persistence and good fortune, especially since Thomas had left no son to work his way back into royal favour. His heir was his brother Henry, who had not taken part in the revolt of 1321–2. Yet, although he was restored to the earldom of Leicester in 1324, Henry had to wait until the overthrow of Edward II and the Despensers in 1326–7 before he could

---

[5] Somerville, *Duchy of Lancaster*, i.26, 337; Maddicott, *Thomas of Lancaster*, 234–6.

Map 1 Principle holdings of the duchy of Lancaster

embark with confidence on the process of claiming his brother's inheritance. Even then there were pitfalls to be negotiated: the regime which took
power following Edward II's deposition, led by Queen Isabella and her
lover Roger Mortimer, proved little better than its predecessor, so that once
more an earl of Lancaster (to which title Henry had been restored at the
deposition) found himself in opposition to the crown, or at least to those
who now governed on its behalf. However, once the eighteen-year-old
Edward III asserted his personal authority, did away with Mortimer in
November 1330, and forced his mother into political retirement, relations
between the crown and the nobility improved markedly, so that for the next
thirty years, first under Earl Henry and then, after his death in 1345, under
his son Henry of Grosmont, the house of Lancaster reverted to what it had
been during the first forty years of its existence: a political and military
bloc, the power of which was not to be feared but rather to be augmented
by the king, and one of the chief buttresses of the crown during the harmonious central years of Edward III's reign.

This did not mean, however, that everything once held by Earl Thomas
was regained. John de Warenne's lands in Yorkshire were returned to him
in 1328, never again to pass into Lancastrian hands, while the manors in
Wiltshire, Somerset and Dorset which Thomas had granted to Warenne in
exchange became the subject of a prolonged dispute between the house of
Lancaster and the Montague family, for whom the earldom of Salisbury
was revived in 1337. The title and many of the lands of the earldom of
Lincoln, along with Pontefract and Clitheroe, were not regained until after
the childless death of Alice de Lacy in 1348. By now, the pace of Lancastrian
recovery was quickening, lubricated by the close friendship between Henry
of Grosmont and Edward III and his extensive diplomatic and military
career in royal service.[6] In 1337, while his father was still alive (though by
now largely incapacitated by blindness), Grosmont was created earl of
Derby, the first member of the Lancastrian line to assume that title; by
1349, he could style himself earl of Lancaster, Derby, Leicester and Lincoln,
as well as steward of England.[7] Yet more dazzling honours still awaited
him: on 6 March 1351, as a sign of his pre-eminence among the English
nobility, and in order to enhance his status as a diplomat on the European
stage, he was elevated to the dukedom of Lancaster, only the second person
ever to hold an English dukedom (the Black Prince, Edward III's eldest son
and heir, having been created duke of Cornwall in 1337). In itself, the title

[6] K. Fowler, *The King's Lieutenant* (London, 1969).
[7] Somerville, *Duchy of Lancaster*, i.40.

of duke was honorific, but Edward III simultaneously declared Lancashire
to be a county palatine, in effect devolving the royal administration within
the county into Henry's hands and creating an enclave in which for most
practical purposes the duke could act as sovereign: a county, in contemporary parlance, in which the king's writ did not run. The honour done to
Henry was, and was meant to be, exceptional. It also had financial implications: although the king retained the right to impose taxes in Lancashire as
in the rest of the kingdom, the profits of justice and routine administration
now went directly into the duke's coffers. Thus, whereas his father's landed
income in the early 1330s had amounted to about £5,500 per annum –
only about half of what Earl Thomas had enjoyed – by the time Duke
Henry died in March 1361, his income from his lands in England and
Wales was in the region of £8,380 per annum.[8] Recovery from the disaster
of 1322 had not been complete, but it had been substantial. Once again,
however, the future of the inheritance was under threat: not, on this occasion, because of political miscalculation, but because Henry went to his
grave without having fathered a son.

Henry's heirs were his two daughters, Maud, born in 1341, and Blanche
(Henry of Bolingbroke's mother), born in 1347. Both had been married
during their father's lifetime: Maud in 1352, to William of Bavaria, count
of Hainault, Holland and Zealand, and Blanche in 1359, to John of Gaunt.
By primogenitary custom, the inheritance would be divided between them,
half of it passing under the effective control of each sister's husband. In
April 1362, however, Maud suddenly died, and since she and William had
had no children (he had by this time become insane and was confined in
the castle of Quesnoy), the whole of Duke Henry's inheritance was, fortuitously for Gaunt, reunited in his hands. Later that same year, in the parliament of November 1362, during which Edward III celebrated his fiftieth
birthday, the ducal title which Henry had enjoyed as a lifetime grant was
also conferred upon Gaunt, although he had to wait a further fifteen years
before receiving the same palatinate powers in Lancashire as his father-
in-law. Nevertheless, as the king's son, Gaunt was in a good position to
build upon his inheritance. In 1342, when he was two years old, Edward III
had granted him the earldom of Richmond, and when, in 1372, he agreed
to surrender this to the crown so that it could be used as diplomatic bait for
the duke of Brittany, he made sure that he was well compensated: the
castles and honours of Tickhill and Knaresborough in Yorkshire and the

---

[8] S. Waugh, 'Henry of Lancaster, Third Earl of Lancaster', *ODNB*, 26.569–72; Fowler,
King's Lieutenant, 172, 225.

castle of High Peak in Derbyshire consolidated his already substantial holdings in those counties, while the castle of Pevensey in Sussex gave him a foothold on the south coast. The castle and honour of Hertford, later one of his and his son's favourite residences, had already been granted to him by Edward III in 1360, following his marriage. Lesser additions followed as Gaunt continued to pursue at law his claim to some of the lands forfeited by Thomas of Lancaster in 1322, with varying degrees of success. Gaunt also had great European ambitions, although neither the French possessions which he claimed through Henry of Grosmont, nor the crown of Castile which he claimed through his second wife Constanza brought him much by way of landed income.[9] Nevertheless, by the 1380s, despite the decline in landlords' profits following the Black Death, the gross income from Gaunt's estates in England and Wales was around £12,000,[10] surpassing that of even Earl Thomas at the height of his wealth and power. He was the richest man in England after the king; even his elder brother the Black Prince, before his early death in 1376, had never received more than about £10,000 a year from his English and Welsh estates.[11]

This, then, was the patrimony to which Henry of Bolingbroke was heir: from Dunstanburgh in Northumberland to Pevensey in Sussex, it boasted over twenty castles in England and another half a dozen in Wales. Like the king, the duke of Lancaster could ride from one end of England to the other, passing almost every night under his own roof. Naturally each lord had his favourite residences: for Earl Thomas, it was Pontefract, which he substantially rebuilt and where he spent most of the last five years of his life following his withdrawal from court in 1317.[12] For Duke Henry, whose service to the crown necessitated proximity to London, it was Leicester, with its adjacent game-stocked forests, although how often he was able to stay there is difficult to know: he spent as much time abroad as he did in England, either on campaign or on diplomatic embassies. In his last years, he spent less time at Leicester than he did at the Savoy, the awe-inspiring palace erected during the 1350s on the north bank of the Thames between London and Westminster and said to have cost around £35,000, money which he had plundered from the capture of Bergerac in 1345.[13] During

---

[9] Somerville, *Duchy of Lancaster*, i.51–6.
[10] A. Goodman, *John of Gaunt* (Harlow, 1992), 341, suggests a little under £12,000; Fowler, *King's Lieutenant*, 226, a little over.
[11] D. Green, *Edward the Black Prince* (Harlow, 2007), 63.
[12] Maddicott, *Thomas of Lancaster*, 26, 331.
[13] *Knighton*, 52, 188; Fowler, *King's Lieutenant*, 214.

the 1360s and 1370s, Gaunt also spent much of his time at the Savoy, but following its destruction at the hands of the rebels in 1381 he did not rebuild it but instead used Hertford castle, some twenty miles north of London, as his pied-à-terre when he needed to be in the capital. Much was spent on improving Hertford, although little of it has survived.[14]

It was always in the north Midlands, however, that the heartland of the duchy lay. Southern Yorkshire and Lancashire, Derbyshire, Staffordshire, Leicestershire and Lincolnshire – these were the counties where Lancastrian influence penetrated deepest, where it was possible to ride for two or three days without ever leaving ducal land, where Lancastrian castles stood not simply as the trophies of a great but distant power, but clustered thick upon the ground, in some cases almost visible one from another. Tutbury, perched high on its rock of alabaster above the valley of the Dove on the Derbyshire–Staffordshire border, was the nerve centre of a network of properties whose value was measured by much more than their financial worth, including Kenilworth, Higham Ferrers and Leicester to the south, Melbourne in Derbyshire barely ten miles to the east, and Tickhill, High Peak and Newcastle-under-Lyme to the north; none of them was much more than a day's ride from Tutbury. Kenilworth was a second major administrative centre, especially under Earl Thomas when it served as the headquarters of his receiver-general.[15] Later in the century it was still one of John of Gaunt's favourite residences: he spent some £250 per annum over twenty years constructing a great hall there, ninety feet (27.43 metres) by forty-five (13.72), still mostly standing.[16] Further north lay Pontefract, the focus of the Yorkshire estates and Gaunt's customary base during his northern itinerations, and Lancaster itself, which, although not visited much by fourteenth-century earls or dukes, still housed the headquarters of the duchy administration.[17]

Yet if mighty castles and untold acres were powerful symbols of lordship, in a sense they were just means to an end. Only human beings could translate soil and stone into the political influence to which their lords aspired, and it was thus to the acquisition and retention of servants and supporters that the resources of the Lancastrian inheritance were principally directed. Earl Thomas maintained a peacetime following of between twenty-five and fifty knights, and the total annual cost of his retinue was

[14] Goodman, *John of Gaunt*, 302–3.

[15] Maddicott, *Thomas of Lancaster*, 12.

[16] Goodman, *John of Gaunt*, 305–6; S. Walker, *The Lancastrian Affinity 1361–1399* (Oxford, 1990), 97.

[17] Goodman, *John of Gaunt*, 308–9.

between £1,500 and £2,000, but his *comitiva* was capable of rapid expansion in time of war. The influence which this gave him could be decisive: at the siege of Berwick in 1319, his retinue of some 2,000 men constituted about a fifth of the royal army, so that when he withdrew in a fit of pique, after quarrelling yet again with the king, it proved impossible for Edward II to continue the siege.[18] It is more difficult to establish the size of Henry of Grosmont's peacetime retinue, for few of his indentures have survived, but the number of his permanent retainers was certainly smaller than Earl Thomas's, and with good reason, for Duke Henry was a man almost without enemies in England.[19] What he did need was the capacity to recruit soldiers to serve abroad with him and a personal retinue sufficiently impressive to cut some ice when he served as the king's ambassador to foreign courts, objectives he was well able to meet.[20] With John of Gaunt we are on much firmer ground. His household rolls and registers from the 1370s and 1380s suggest a permanent domestic establishment of between 115 and 130, rising to about 150 by the early 1390s, the annual cost of which varied between £4,200 and £7,100.[21] This, however, did not include the cost of the duke's retainers. A list of his knights and esquires retained in 1382 named seven bannerets, seventy knights, and ninety-six esquires, a figure that continued to rise until his death in 1399, by which time it almost certainly passed 200. So too, naturally, did its cost: by the mid-1390s, he was probably spending about £4,000 a year on his retainers. By contemporary standards, these figures are wholly exceptional (as had also been the £1,500–2,000 spent by Earl Thomas on his retainers). Most fourteenth- and fifteenth-century English magnates spent about 10 or, at the most, 20 per cent of their annual income on retaining fees, and their income was much less than Gaunt's, typically between £2,000 and £4,000.[22] That the Lancastrian affinity under Gaunt was the largest ever recruited in medieval England says much about his political aspirations, as well as

---

[18] Maddicott, *Thomas of Lancaster*, 45–7, 245–9.

[19] Fowler, *King's Lieutenant*, 181–5, 227–9; Walker, *Lancastrian Affinity*, 22.

[20] When he accompanied the king on the six-month 'Reims campaign' of 1359–60, his personal retinue numbered about 1,100 men; when he and the earl of Arundel made their entry to the papal court at Avignon on Christmas Eve 1354 to represent Edward III at the most lavish peace conference of the Anglo-French war so far, they arrived in a convoy of 200 horses, and for the two months that they remained there the hospitality which Lancaster extended was so bountiful that, according to Knighton, 'all the court marvelled': Fowler, *King's Lieutenant*, 201, 290; *Knighton*, 128.

[21] Goodman, *John of Gaunt*, 317, 349; Walker, *Lancastrian Affinity*, 10–14; H. Castor, *The King, the Crown and the Duchy of Lancaster* (Oxford, 2000), 22. Gaunt's daily registers survive for the years 1372–6 and 1379–83 (*JGR I* and *JGR II*).

[22] Walker, *Lancastrian Affinity*, 14–22.

helping to explain why he had little difficulty in assembling 2,000 or even 3,000 men to accompany him on campaign.[23] The only meaningful comparison is with the royal affinity recruited by Richard II during the last decade of his reign, when the king retained 250 or more knights and esquires.[24] The size of the Lancastrian affinity, and Richard II's perception of its threat to his authority, were among the chief reasons why the king chose to retain men on such a scale.

What is more difficult to gauge is the extent to which the Lancastrian affinity provided its lord with the political influence he sought. Under Earl Thomas, at least in his later years as he became increasingly isolated in opposition to the king, it was in large part his affinity which allowed him to ignore his growing unpopularity and to continue his opposition, for although Edward II feared the military power of Thomas's retainers, he could not afford to alienate them, because they formed a bulwark against Scottish incursions. Aware of the leverage that this gave him, Thomas rewarded his retainers handsomely and supported them in their private quarrels. In the end, though, he went too far and, rather than risk their lives in what many of them saw as a failing cause, increasing numbers of his retainers deserted him in the run up to Boroughbridge.[25] It was an important lesson for his successors, and sixty years later, as John of Gaunt relentlessly expanded his affinity – not merely in size but also in geographical scope, recruiting extensively beyond his northern and Midland heartland – it was these events that were remembered.[26] At the same time, Gaunt also found himself attracting the same hostility that Earl Thomas had incurred during his later years. Not that the reasons were the same: Gaunt's unpopularity in the mid-1370s was earned in the cause of *upholding* royal power,[27] which was clearly not the case with Earl Thomas. Nevertheless, there were those who suspected that once Edward III was dead Gaunt might attempt to use his retinue to further his personal ambitions, perhaps even to the point of seizing the crown from his ten-year-old nephew Richard. Viewed in this light, the renewed expansion of the Lancastrian affinity was a cause for alarm.

If this expansion was primarily designed to provide Gaunt with manpower in wartime,[28] social and political developments during the

---

[23] Walker, *Lancastrian Affinity*, 40–1, 248.
[24] *RHKA*, Chapter IV.
[25] Maddicott, *Thomas of Lancaster*, 65, 176–7, 265–96.
[26] Walker, *Lancastrian Affinity*, 32.
[27] Goodman, *John of Gaunt*, 372.
[28] Walker, *Lancastrian Affinity*, 42, 48.

fourteenth century meant that it also gave him greater power in the localities than his predecessors, principally through crown office-holding. It was
during the 1360s that the Justices of the Peace definitively acquired the
dominant role in county peacekeeping that they were to retain well beyond
the Middle Ages, including enforcement of the labour laws as well as felony
and trespass. It was also during the third quarter of the fourteenth century
that local control over the election of sheriffs was finally established, after
many decades of trying, while from the 1370s the commons became more
assertive in parliament, thereby enhancing the authority of MPs as
spokesmen for their shire communities. These were the men – JPs, MPs
and sheriffs, drawn from the upper stratum of the gentry – who figured
prominently in Gaunt's affinity, men with deep roots in local government
through whom it was possible to hitch the authority of the crown to the
coat-tails of the house of Lancaster. As Edward III's winning war of the
1340s and 1350s turned into the losing war of the 1370s, England turned in
on itself, a king too senile to rule gave way to one too juvenile to rule, and
politics at all levels became more divisive. It was against this background
that the chronicler Thomas Walsingham described those who wore Gaunt's
livery in the mid-1370s as men 'whose arrogance the world could scarcely
support', thinking that it entitled them to 'riches before heaven and earth'.[29]

Influence did not mean domination. Only in perhaps three or four
English counties, traditional Lancastrian strongholds such as Derbyshire,
Staffordshire and Lancashire, did the number of men retained and the
extent of the lands held by the duke translate into ascendancy in the region.
Elsewhere, even in counties such as Norfolk or Sussex where he held large
estates, he was one lord among many (albeit the greatest), his lordship
sought and tolerated only as long as he did not overreach his grasp or upset
the equilibrium of local society. Even in the north Midlands, or in Lancashire
where he retained one in three of the knights and esquires in the county, he
still had to be careful not to favour unduly those who accepted fees and
annuities from him, for the county establishment – that indefinable but
pervasive free association of regional gentry bound by personal and familial
connections, the shared concerns of local government, the knightly lifestyle
and a consuming interest in land and lordship – could be just as important
in determining political and social affiliations as the obligations of service
and loyalty to a great lord.[30] Nevertheless, the opportunities and rewards

---

[29] *SAC I*, 92–3.

[30] Walker, *Lancastrian Affinity*, 140–1, 152–3, 192–206, 209, 224; Castor, *King, Crown and Duchy*, 53–8, 193–201; Maddicott, *Thomas of Lancaster*, 60.

which a magnate could offer were a powerful inducement. Ten or twenty
pounds a year, the level of fee customarily offered by Gaunt to his retainers,
was a welcome addition to the income of an esquire with estates worth fifty
or a hundred pounds annually, though perhaps more seductive was the
local standing enjoyed by a man who served the duke of Lancaster, feasted
in his castles and hunted in his chases – a man whose enemies knew that if
they wished to pursue a quarrel with him it might not be with him alone. To
wear the duke's livery badge, the famous **SS** collar, was the outward and
visible sign of this status.

A growing sense of the affinity's history also fostered loyalty and service.[31] St Mary Newark in Leicester, refounded and rebuilt as a college by
Duke Henry in the 1350s, where he and his father were buried on either
side of the high altar, became one focus of Lancastrian devotion. The cult
of Earl Thomas, centred on the richly endowed chapel erected outside
Pontefract castle to mark the spot where he was executed, was another,
although Gaunt himself, knowing that Richard II viewed 'St Thomas of
Lancaster' as no martyr but a traitor, was careful not to encourage this cult
too strongly. Nevertheless, the preservation and repetition in fourteenth-
century chronicles of quasi-hagiographical accounts of Earl Thomas's
'martyrdom' at the hands of a despotic king helped to promote not just a
saintly cult but also a political ideal which tapped into the enduring appeal
of the struggle for liberty against tyranny. Especially influential in this
respect was the vernacular *Brut*, the most widely read and copied chronicle
in late medieval England, which was openly Lancastrian in its sympathies,
drawing on Christ's passion for its account of Earl Thomas's execution
and continuing to recount his miracles long after his death.[32] However
poorly these stood up to scrutiny, they served to identify recognizably
'Lancastrian' values and to create a helpful popular mythology.

There was thus both a cohesive Lancastrian affinity focused upon service
and loyalty to its lord's causes and a Lancastrian affinity which was little
more than the sum of its parts: a congeries of gentry fraternities that found
it convenient to synchronize its fortunes with those of a great lord, provided

---

[31] Walker, *Lancastrian Affinity*, 94–102.

[32] *Brut*, i.207, 216–24, 228–30, 245, 257–63; ii.309, 355. Even more explicitly Lancastrian
in sympathy was the chronicle of Henry Knighton, canon of Leicester abbey, although
readership of his Latin chronicle was much more restricted. Both Knighton and the *Brut*
consistently referred to fourteenth-century earls and dukes as 'good', 'gentle', noble'; cf.
A. Gransden, *Historical Writing in England II* (London, 1982), 72–5; C. Given-Wilson, *Chronicles*
(London, 2004), 36–7.

his interests did not impinge upon theirs. There were always some men prepared to die for their lord, but most retainers were capable of making their own decisions as to where their primary loyalty lay. Every lord, Gaunt famously declared to the commons in the parliament of 1384, was capable of disciplining his own retainers, but the truth fell somewhere short of this, and there were times when the behaviour of his retainers proved an embarrassment to him.[33] Yet the real test of the affinity came at those moments of crisis when its leader set himself on a collision course with the crown. On the first occasion that this happened, in 1322, his retainers failed Earl Thomas and the result was near-obliteration.[34] Despite the steady recovery during the next half-century, the wounds inflicted in the 1320s were hard to heal: the forfeiture of 1322 and subsequent re-grants had established rival claims to much of the Lancastrian inheritance, including those of the crown. To head these off, vigilance and circumspection were required; local disputes must not be allowed to escalate; royal favour must be nurtured, to stop up the mouths of the envious. Much also depended on the character of the man who occupied the throne. Favoured by Edward III, the house of Lancaster was advanced and exalted during the middle years of the fourteenth century, but Edward's death in 1377 brought to the throne a king under whom royal favour was not simply a route to advancement, but also a prerequisite for holding on to what one already had.

[33] *Westminster Chronicle*, 82; Walker, *Lancastrian Affinity* 115, 242–8, 260. Compare Goodman, *John of Gaunt*, 334.

[34] Maddicott, *Thomas of Lancaster*, 295–6; the 'Office of St Thomas of Lancaster', composed shortly after Earl Thomas's execution, claimed that he had been 'abandoned by his company of knights, treacherously deserted by [Robert] de Holland' (*The Political Songs of England from the Reign of John to that of Edward II*, ed T. Wright [Camden Society, London, 1839], 270–1). Holland, one of Thomas's most trusted servants, switched sides just a few days before Boroughbridge and was later assassinated by Lancastrian partisans.

Chapter 2

FATHER AND SON I (1367–1382)

On 12 September 1368, when he was seventeen months old, Henry of Bolingbroke's mother died in childbirth aged twenty-one. Duchess Blanche had been married to John of Gaunt for nine years and borne him six children, three of whom survived her. Commemorated by Chaucer in his *Book of the Duchess* and by Froissart in his poem *Joli Buisson de Jonece* (1373), where he described her as 'young and beautiful ... vivacious, happy, fresh and charming, gentle and sincere, modest in manner', she would not be forgotten by her son, who twenty-four years later named his first daughter after her.[1]

For three or four years after his mother's death Henry was brought up with his sisters in the household of their sexagenarian great-aunt, Blanche Lady Wake, but soon after Gaunt's remarriage in September 1371 to the Castilian princess Constanza, the three children resided for the most part with their stepmother at Tutbury (Staffordshire), the chief Lancastrian stronghold in the Midlands.[2] Their governess here was the duke's mistress, Katherine Swynford, sister-in-law to Geoffrey Chaucer and former lady-in-waiting to Duchess Blanche. It was around the time of his second marriage that Gaunt and Katherine's public affair began, and in 1373 their first child was born, followed by three more in four years. Known as the Beauforts, they became valued friends to Henry, but his closest boyhood companion was probably Thomas Swynford, Katherine's son by her first marriage, who was just a year younger than Henry and was also brought up in the ducal household.[3]

---

[1] J. Palmer, 'The Historical Context of the *Book of the Duchess*: a Revision', *Chaucer Review* 8 (1974), 253–6; *The Register of Thomas Appleby of Carlisle*, ed. R. Storey (Canterbury and York Society, Woodbridge, 2006), no. 166; Chaucer, *The Book of the Duchess*, ed. Helen Phillips (Durham and St Andrews Medieval Texts, 1982), ll. 948–50 (pp. 4, 108).

[2] Goodman, *John of Gaunt*, 48–50; *JGR I*, nos. 299 (dated September 1373, not 1372), 524–5, 535–6, 1236. The three children's household cost 300 marks a year, paid to John Cheyne, treasurer of their chamber.

[3] *JGR I*, no. 1342; for the date of birth of John, the eldest Beaufort, see S. Walker, 'Katherine, Duchess of Lancaster', *ODNB*, 30.888–90. Sir Hugh Swynford, Katherine's first husband, died in November 1371.

In 1374, having reached his seventh birthday and thus, by contemporary reckoning, passed from infancy to boyhood, Henry was given his own governor, the veteran Lancastrian esquire Thomas de Burton,[4] who in 1376 was replaced by William de Mountendre, a Gascon knight who had served in Gaunt's army in France in 1373–4.[5] By this time Henry was increasingly to be found at court with his cousin, the future Richard II, who was three months older than him.[6] On 23 April 1377 they were both knighted, along with another ten scions of the English nobility, by the dying Edward III at Windsor castle during the annual St George's day festivities, with Henry and Richard simultaneously inducted as Knights of the Garter.[7] It was also from this moment that Henry began to be styled as earl of Derby,[8] one of the five earldoms to which Gaunt could lay claim, and it was as earl of Derby that, three months later, he performed his most onerous public duty to date when he bore the principal sword, the Curtana, at his cousin's coronation. Edward III had died on 21 June 1377, and Richard II was crowned on 16 July at a ceremony presided over by Gaunt, the new king's senior uncle since the deaths of his elder brothers Lionel of Clarence in 1368 and Edward the Black Prince in 1376. Gaunt himself carried the Curtana during the coronation ceremony, but for the banquet in Westminster Great Hall which followed he relinquished it to Henry who, throughout the meal, 'standing on the right hand of the king as he sat at table, held in his hand the said principal sword naked and drawn' – a disciplined performance for a boy of ten.[9]

---

[4] *JGR I*, nos. 679, 1614; Walker, *Lancastrian Affinity*, 29 and n. 86.

[5] DL 28/3/1, m. 12; Mountendre was a former retainer of the great Gascon warlord the Captal de Buch (Walker, *Lancastrian Affinity*, 54, 71, and SC 8/258/12863 and 300/14973). In 1376–7 Gaunt allocated separate sums to Henry (£61) and his two elder sisters (£200), indicating that he was being brought up separately from them at least in some respects (DL 28/3/1, m. 5). For other gifts from Gaunt to Henry see *JGR I*, 1342, 1614, and *JGR II*, no. 715.

[6] For £20 allocated to Gaunt's esquire Hugh Waterton to cover Henry's expenses while he was 'staying in the company of the lord prince [Richard]', see DL 28/3/1, m. 12, dated 10 May 1377.

[7] *Anonimalle Chronicle 1333–1381*, ed. V. H. Galbraith (Manchester, 1927), 106; Richard's household account records the purchase for 10s of three swords for this occasion, for himself, Henry, and the son of John d'Arundel, younger brother of the earl of Arundel (E 101/398/9, m. 2), and in 1378 Gaunt levied an aid from his tenants for the knighting of his eldest son (*JGR II*, no. 320). Those knighted with Richard and Henry were Thomas of Woodstock (youngest son of Edward III), Robert earl of Oxford, Lords Beaumont and Mowbray, the sons of the earls of Stafford and Salisbury, the three sons of Henry Lord Percy, and John Sotheray (illegitimate son of Edward III by his mistress, Alice Perrers): E 101/397/20, m. 28.

[8] Somerville, *Duchy of Lancaster*, i.67 and n. 4.

[9] *English Coronation Records*, ed. J. Wickham Legg (London, 1901), 132, 149; *Anonimalle Chronicle*, 114.

Once Richard became king, Henry initially passed more time at court, regularly receiving gifts of robes, cloaks and shoes from the young king for the hunting and hawking seasons, for Christmas and Easter, and for the Garter festivities each April. Garter robes were of scarlet cloth, lined with belly fur and embroidered with garters of blue taffeta inscribed with the motto of the Order, 'Honi soit qui mal y pense'.[10] Henry's courtly upbringing also encompassed occasions such as the wedding of Richard II's half-sister Maud Holand to Waleran of Luxemburg, count of St Pol, celebrated at Windsor during Easter week 1380, when Henry presented the bride with a goblet of gilded silver worth sixty shillings, paid for by his father.[11] The next wedding of comparable significance in England would be Henry's own, and would mark his introduction to the more cut-throat side of court life.

It was Gaunt who arranged Henry's marriage. The object of his attentions was Mary, the co-heiress to Humphrey de Bohun, earl of Hereford, Essex and Northampton, who had died at the age of thirty in January 1373, leaving no sons, two underage daughters, and a very substantial inheritance. The elder daughter, Eleanor (born in 1366), was married to Gaunt's brother, Thomas of Woodstock, earl of Buckingham, probably in 1374.[12] What now happened to Mary (born in 1369–70) was naturally a matter of considerable interest to Buckingham. As long as she remained single, the entire Bohun inheritance would fall to him; were she to marry, he would be obliged to share it with her husband. Inconveniently, other duties now deflected his attention. On 3 May 1380, he indented with the king and council to lead an expedition to Brittany with a retinue of 5,000 men.[13] During the following two months he did what he could to ensure that the

[10] E 101/400/4, mm. 4, 15–18. Liveries to Henry from the Great Wardrobe during the first two years of the reign included a parti-coloured gown and hood of russet and mottled green of the king's livery for the hunting season; a pelisse (fur-trimmed cloak) of grey, decorated with white chevrons and a maunch collar, plus two further long cloaks and doublets for the winter; a robe of gilded blue brocade, two gowns and two cloaks with hoods for Christmas 1377; three coats of blue silk brocade of the king's livery at Easter 1378; a gown 'for hawking' during the winter of 1378–9; another gown 'for the hunting season' during the summer of 1379; and, at various times during these two years, a further fourteen sets of robes, a pair of sheets for his chamber, and several pairs of stockings, slippers, boots, galoshes and gilded spurs. His Garter robes bear witness to his physical development at this time, for in April 1378, when the other Garter knights were each allocated five ells of cloth from which to fashion their robes, Henry, who had just passed his eleventh birthday, received only three ells; a year later, however, he received the full five ells. One ell was roughly 45 inches (114 centimetres).

[11] JGR II, no. 463.

[12] CPR 1374–7, 337.

[13] A. Tuck, 'Thomas of Woodstock, Duke of Gloucester', ODNB, 54.277–83.

Bohun patrimony did not slip from his grasp during his absence: on 8 May he obtained a royal grant of the custody of Mary's share of the inheritance during her minority; on 22 June Eleanor came of age and Thomas performed his fealty to the king for his wife's share of the lands.[14] Shortly before leaving he even took the precaution of bringing Mary to stay with her sister at Pleshey castle (Essex), where he arranged for her to be instructed by nuns with the intention that she should join the order of St Clare. According to Froissart, 'the young lady seemed to incline to their doctrine, and thought not of marriage'.[15]

Hopeful of having ensured the integrity of his inheritance, Buckingham shipped his troops to Calais and, on 24 July 1380, set out with his army on a campaign from which he would not return for nine months.[16] No sooner had he done so than Gaunt made his move. Three days after his brother's crossing, he secured a royal grant of Mary's marriage, 'for marrying her to his son Henry',[17] and shortly after this induced her mother, Joan countess of Hereford, to spirit her away from Pleshey and take her to Arundel, where the young couple were rapidly betrothed.[18] They were married on 5 February 1381 in a service held at Countess Joan's manor of Rochford (Essex).[19] The connivance of the king and council, who would have been aware of the blow this inflicted on Buckingham, is a measure of the financial and political leverage Gaunt exercised in Richard II's minority government. Gaunt attended and presented Mary with a ruby, as well as paying for the festivities; Henry's sisters, Philippa and Elizabeth, each gave their new sister-in-law a goblet and ewer. The king and Edmund earl of

[14] CPR 1377–81, 502; CCR 1377–81, 390–5, 439–40; CCR 1381–5, 269.

[15] Jean Froissart, Chronicles of England, France, Spain and the Adjoining Countries, ed. and trans. T. Johnes (2 vols, London, 1848), i.623–4. This story comes from a variant manuscript of Froissart's chronicles used by Johnes, but subsequently destroyed by fire. Cf. G. Holmes, The Estates of the Higher Nobility in Fourteenth-Century England (Cambridge, 1957), 24 and n. 6.

[16] N. Saul, Richard II (New Haven, 1997), 52–5.

[17] CPR 1377–81, 537 (27 July 1380): her marriage was said to be valued at 5,000 marks (£3,333), but Gaunt paid nothing for it, since it was offset against a larger sum already owed to him for his wages of war. The terms of the grant also included the important concession that if either Henry or Mary were to die without issue before she reached the age of nineteen, Gaunt would be repaid his 5,000 marks.

[18] Froissart claimed that 'the marriage was instantly consummated', but this was precipitate. He also got several other details of the story wrong, such as calling the two sisters Blanche and Isabel and saying that it was their 'aunt' who carried Mary away from Pleshey, but the essentials of his story are corroborated by other sources and undoubtedly correct. Countess Joan was complicit in the plot, presumably hoping to give her daughter a life outside the convent. She probably commissioned a pair of illuminated psalters for the marriage (see below, p. 79).

[19] CCR 1377–81, 439–40; for the 5 February date, see CPR 1381–5, 95; BL Add. MS 5,937, fo. 74.

Cambridge (Gaunt's younger, and Buckingham's older, brother) may also have been there, for ten royal minstrels and four of Cambridge's minstrels received gratuities from Gaunt for enlivening the proceedings.[20] There was nothing hasty or clandestine about the wedding.

Buckingham, meanwhile, was still in France, preparing to withdraw from a frustrating and embarrassing campaign.[21] When he realized that his brothers had colluded against him in the loss of half of his inheritance, 'he became melancholy, and never after loved the duke of Lancaster as he had done hitherto'.[22] In addition to the personal slight, there was also the question of how the details of the Bohun partition would be worked out, an issue which it took fifteen years to resolve, and although Henry and Buckingham would soon demonstrate that they were capable of concerted political action, theirs was a relationship which henceforward seems always to have been tinged by a degree of personal rivalry.

His wedding excepted, there is one other day during the first half of 1381 when Henry's whereabouts are known with certainty. This was Friday 14 June, a day of mortal danger for the young heir to the Lancastrian inheritance, for it was the second of three days during which gangs of rebels from Kent, Essex and London ran amok in the streets of the capital on a scale never seen before and rarely since: the climactic moment of the Peasants' Revolt. Henry was in the Tower of London that Friday morning, along with his cousin the king, Richard's mother Princess Joan, the chancellor and treasurer of England (Simon Sudbury and Robert Hales), and a number of other lords, knights and clerks.[23] Sudbury and Hales had already been singled out by the rebels as objects of special hatred to them; so too had John of Gaunt. The rebels demanded the heads of all three of them, accusing them of treachery to the young king. Fortunately for Gaunt, he was in Scotland at the time, but that was little consolation to those associated with him, some of whom were summarily despatched by the rebels.[24]

Early in the morning of 14 June, the fourteen-year-old king left the Tower with some of his advisers, having arranged to meet the rebel leaders at Mile End, outside the city walls. His reasons for doing so are fairly clear – to

[20] *JGR II*, nos. 556, 688; Gaunt also paid forty shillings 'for that number of pennies placed on the [service] book on the day of the wedding [esposailes]', and for various sums offered in alms. Among the wedding gifts were two gilded cloths later sold by Henry in London for £12: DL 28/1/1, fo. 1.
[21] Saul, *Richard II*, 55.
[22] Froissart, *Chronicles*, ed. Johnes, i.624.
[23] *Knighton*, 210–12.
[24] An esquire of Gaunt's called Grenefeld was beheaded in London that day: Goodman, *John of Gaunt*, 79.

negotiate an end to the violence, to draw the rebels away from the city, and to give those in the Tower who were at risk a chance to escape – but his plan misfired. Sudbury and Hales attempted to flee, but were spotted and forced to retreat; when, around mid-morning, groups of rebels broke into the Tower and began searching it for 'traitors', they were located in the chapel of St John, dragged out to Tower Hill, and immediately beheaded. William Appleton, a Franciscan friar who was also Gaunt's physician, suffered the same fate.[25] Whether Henry was identified but spared on account of his age, or smuggled out of the Tower, or managed to hide from the rebels, is not known, but escape he did, and shortly after he had become king, when a certain John Ferrour rebelled against him, he was granted a pardon by Henry because he had 'wonderfully and gloriously' (*mirabiliter et gloriose*) saved the king's life in the Tower of London nearly twenty years earlier. Ferrour is usually said to have come from Southwark, but there is no record (until 1400) of either Gaunt or his son rewarding him for saving Henry's life.[26]

By the evening of the following day, Saturday 15 June, the revolt in London had been brought under control and the process of suppression began. In the neighbouring counties, however, especially in Essex, Norfolk and Suffolk, the violence barely abated, so that during the last two weeks of June detachments of nobles and gentry were sent out to restore order. Among them was Henry – the first occasion on which he had been involved in military, or at least punitive, action – although there is no indication as to where he went.[27] From October 1381 until September 1382, however, the survival of his first household account makes it possible to trace his activities on a regular, sometimes daily, basis. It also tells us much about the lifestyle of a young nobleman during the later fourteenth century and about the tastes and interests Henry was beginning to develop.

For an earl, albeit a young one, Henry's domestic establishment appears modest. His income for the year totalled £426, his expenses only a little over half that sum, £237.[28] Between ten and twelve horses were stabled in his household, and he had eighteen servants, the most important of whom were Sir William de Mountendre, his 'master'; his receiver Hugh Waterton,

---

[25] R. Dobson, *The Peasants' Revolt of 1381* (London, 1970), 155–208; according to the Westminster chronicler, the executions of Sudbury and Hales took place 'at the eleventh hour' on 14 June (ibid., 201).

[26] E 37/28; he may, however, have been the 'John Ferrour of Rochester', pardoned for homicide in March 1380: *CPR 1377–81*, 456.

[27] E 361/5, m. 19; also sent out were the earls of Buckingham, Kent, Salisbury, Warwick and Suffolk; Cf. *SAC I*, 507.

[28] Waterton's account is DL 28/1/1, a well preserved vellum book of eleven folios.

whose family stood as high as any in Gaunt's confidence; and his chaplain, Hugh Herle. These three had formed the nucleus of Henry's household for at least the past five years.[29] In addition to his boyhood companion Thomas Swynford, Henry also had two esquires ('Arnald and Wynsell') and three clerks to expedite his affairs (William Loveney, John Waterton, and 'Ralph the clerk'). The below stairs component of the household comprised a wardrober (John Dyndon) and his page (Henry), a valet of the chamber (Thomas Totty), a sergeant (Thomas Page), a servant of the kitchen (John Blakedon), a purveyor (William) and three men to care for the horses: John Gysely, keeper of the palfreys, and two sumptermen, Richard and John.

Henry's expenditure fell broadly into two categories: what was needed to keep his household functioning on a daily basis (wages of servants, care of the horses, expenses of messengers, etc.) and what he spent on maintaining the noble lifestyle (clothes, jewels, leisure, gifts, and so forth). About £60 was spent during the course of the year on clothes, textiles, furs and shoes, bought mostly from regular suppliers in London.[30] A further £26 was paid to goldsmiths, some of it for new purchases, some for the repair or refashioning of existing items. For the jousts which followed the wedding of Richard II and Anne of Bohemia in late January, Henry bought 1,000 sequins of gilded copper; a month earlier he had spent £3 on twenty-nine gilded rings from Paris which he distributed as New Year gifts. By contrast, just two rings of gilded silver bought as clasps for a falconer's bag cost over £1.[31] Falconry gloves, hounds for the hunt, gratuities to his father's minstrels for providing entertainment on New Year's Day and a modest four shillings in total for gaming (*ludendum ad tabulas*) all bear witness to his enthusiastic embrace of the noble lifestyle.[32] Also to be expected, although perhaps not in one so young, is the evidence for Henry's jousting, the preferred entertainment of the court as well as vital military training. He took part in at least three jousts during the year: at Smithfield during the festivities following the royal wedding in January, at Windsor during the Garter Day

[29] Herle had bought a missal costing ten marks for Henry's use in 1377: DL 28/1/1, mm. 7, 12; *JGR II*, nos. 93, 206, 308a, 993.

[30] DL 28/1/1, fos. 1r–2v. Special occasions naturally required special garments: for Christmas 1381, Henry had a 'royal cloak' (*clocum regalis*) made for him; for the Garter Day festivities at Windsor in April, he had a 'mantle of St George' costing £4 made from blue brocade, and for Queen Anne's marriage and coronation in London on 22 January 1382 he also had new and ornate robes made up.

[31] Ibid., fo. 3v.

[32] Ibid., fos. 5r–6r.

celebrations, and at Hertford castle on 1 May.[35] Henry also had a bow which had belonged to his mother, for which he bought arrows and bird-bolts.[34] All this suggests an active early interest in martial pursuits; Henry would later acquire something of a reputation for jousting.

Almsgiving and gift exchange accounted for less than £20 of Henry's expenditure in 1381–2. He distributed a regular penny a day to paupers and more when travelling, on feast days, or to mark anniversaries such as those of his grandfathers, Henry of Grosmont and King Edward III. He dried the feet of fifteen paupers on his fifteenth birthday, and on Good Friday gave a penny each to twenty-five indigents at the gate of Hertford castle.[35] Apart from traditional gift-giving occasions such as New Year's Day,[36] he also gave occasional gifts such as wine to his sister Philippa and a horse to the earl of Nottingham.[37] Yet Henry received considerably more in gifts than he disbursed, mainly from his father and Duchess Constanza,[38] on whom he was still financially dependent, because his earldom of Derby was a courtesy title. Most of his income came either from the annual sum of 250 marks which Gaunt had been assigning to him for the past few years, or from the issues of the manors of Soham (Cambridgeshire), Daventry (Northamptonshire) and Passenham (Buckinghamshire), which Gaunt had made over to him, and which yielded a combined total of £192.[39] His reliance on his father is also reflected in his itinerary.[40] Although he visited Pontefract independently in October 1381 while Gaunt was engaged in political matters in the south-east, Henry spent the winter and spring almost constantly with his father, either in the Midlands or at various Lancastrian residences around London, where they attended a succession of court events together.[41] Christmas was spent at

---

[33] Ibid., fos. 4r, 6r–v, 10v. On the latter occasion, he purchased six new lances, while for the jousts at Windsor he bought a new saddle, reins and harness, all gilded and costing 23s; for the Smithfield jousts he acquired two new pairs of spurs as well as the copper sequins noted above. His armour and swords were kept in his wardrobe in Coleman Street, London.

[34] Ibid., fos. 3v, 6r.

[35] Ibid., fos. 4r–v.

[36] Henry also received an *annidonum* (New Year gift) from King Richard, and another from the queen mother, Princess Joan: ibid., fo. 5r.

[37] Ibid., fos. 6r, 10r.

[38] Ibid., 2r, 3r, 5r–v. They gave him material for garments, loaned him their servants and craftsmen, and paid for some of his alms and presents.

[39] Soham yielded £125, Daventry £60, and Passenham just 10 marks: ibid., fo. 1r. For Soham, see the unfinished entry in *JGR II*, no. 706, probably from the spring of 1382, for on 13 April Henry sent his servant William the Purveyor to receive seisin of the manor on his behalf: DL 28/3/1, fo. 8v.

[40] Indications of his whereabouts are scattered throughout DL 28/1/1, indicated with varying degrees of reliability by places where purchases were made (not very reliable), alms and gifts were distributed (more reliable), messengers were despatched, and so forth.

[41] For Gaunt's itinerary in 1381–2 see Goodman, *John of Gaunt*, 89–93.

Leicester, Easter at Hertford. During the summer, Gaunt and Henry toured the Midlands and northern estates of the duchy. June, July and August saw them at Kenilworth, Higham Ferrers and Tutbury, with visits to Beverley in late June and Lincoln in early July; most of September was spent at York and Pontefract, before Gaunt's return to London for the third parliamentary session of the year, which opened on 6 October. The fact that his account fails to include any expenditure on food and drink indicates that Henry and his servants still boarded and lodged in his father's household, of which, in effect, they formed a sub-unit – not so much a separate household as a separate chamber within the ducal household. Nor was Mary de Bohun mentioned in the account: aged eleven, she was still living at Rochford with her mother, Countess Joan, to whom Gaunt granted 100 marks a year for her maintenance.[42] Henry did visit Rochford once, on 18 April 1382, shortly after the birth of a son to his sister-in-law, the countess of Buckingham.[43] He and Mary also doubtless met at court events such as Richard II and Anne's wedding in January 1382, but not until she reached her majority in December 1384 did they begin to cohabit.

Henry's account also provides evidence of his involvement in two controversies. First, it confirms his presence with his father at Lincoln on 11 July 1382, the day judgment was passed by Bishop Buckingham in the cathedral chapter house on the notorious Lollard preacher William Swinderby.[44] Swinderby had been preaching in and around Leicester for several years. Gaunt had initially supported him, granting him an allowance and a hermitage in the woods near Leicester abbey (of which he was the patron); according to the Leicester abbey chronicler Henry Knighton, 'the pious duke of Lancaster always liked to give assistance to the Lollards, for, on account of their appearance and the allure of their sermons, he believed them to be God's saints' – although the chronicler added that 'like many others, he was deceived in this'.[45] Gaunt had certainly acquired such a reputation during the 1370s, not least because of his defence of the

---

[42] *JGR II*, nos. 646, 679, 996; BL Add. MS 5,937, fo. 74.

[43] DL 28/1/1, fo. 5r: he gave 40s to the boy's mistress and 26s 8d to his nurse. He also gave 66s 8d on 16 April to 'an esquire of my lord of Buckingham called Westcombe bringing news to my lord that his lady was delivered of a boy'. This entry has caused confusion in the past, leading to the belief that the 'lady' referred to here was Henry's own wife, Mary, and that this record therefore contains the only surviving evidence of their first child, a boy presumed to have died in infancy. For the correct reading, see Mortimer, *Fears*, 370–1.

[44] DL 28/1/1, fo. 9v: expenses of Hugh Waterton for a journey from Higham Ferrers to Daventry on 4 July, '*et revenit ad dominum apud Lincoln xi die Julii*'.

[45] *Knighton*, 308–9, 312.

controversial Oxford theologian John Wyclif,[46] but by the summer of 1382 his help for men such as Wyclif and Swinderby was becoming an embarrassment. The contentious nature of Wyclif's views, especially concerning the Eucharist, had led to his forced withdrawal from Oxford in the autumn of 1381, and at church councils in London in May and June 1382 several of his opinions were condemned as erroneous or heretical, and a more vigorous process was begun to hunt down and silence his disciples. This was what brought Swinderby to trial.

Among Swinderby's supporters was Philip Repingdon, a canon at Leicester abbey who had studied at Oxford, where he fell under Wyclif's spell. It was probably Repingdon who, with Gaunt's at least tacit support, helped to establish in Leicester the first identifiable Lollard cell outside Oxford University.[47] When Swinderby, following his days as a hermit, expressed an interest in a more coenobitic lifestyle, the canons of Leicester, 'believing him to be the lord's anointed', granted him a chamber in the abbey church along with food and a pension.[48] Swinderby's views were generally more anticlerical than heretical: among the characteristically Lollard themes of his sermons was the idea that tithes were pure alms and could be withheld from an errant priest; that excommunication was a matter for God rather than for the Church; that preaching should not be constrained by episcopal prohibition; that temporal possessions undermined the true work of the Church; and (more riskily) that a priest in mortal sin could not perform the Eucharistic miracle.[49] Nevertheless, the anticlericalism of the 1381 rebels, who some believed to have been inspired by Wyclif, led to an association in the minds of the authorities between anticlericalism, heresy and sedition, and Swinderby was swept up in the net. He was first ordered to stop preaching and appear before Bishop Buckingham's officials on 5 March 1382. This reprimand was ineffective (Swinderby simply 'made his pulpit' between two millstones in the street and continued to preach from there),[50] and on 12 May further investigations were ordered. It was as a result of these that he appeared in Lincoln cathedral on 11 July, where, before an audience including Gaunt, Henry and other notables, he vigorously proclaimed his innocence. However, barely had he begun to purge himself when a number of friars and priests shouted out for him

[46] Goodman, *John of Gaunt*, 241–65.
[47] A. Hudson, *The Premature Reformation* (Oxford, 1988), 77.
[48] *Knighton*, 308.
[49] *Knighton*, 310; *Fasciculi Zizaniorum Magistri Johannis Wyclif cum Tritico*, ed. W. W. Shirley (RS, London, 1858), 337–9; Hudson, *Premature Reformation*, 74–5, 352–3.
[50] *Knighton*, 312.

to be burned and began collecting wood for the pyre, declaring his guilt to be notorious.[51] It was Gaunt who persuaded the bishop to commute the sentence; instead, Swinderby was ordered to recant his views publicly and banned from preaching without licence, but although he moved away from Leicester he did not give up preaching, and nine years later he was again brought to trial for heresy, although once again he escaped with his life.[52]

Like their patron Gaunt, the canons of Leicester were probably a bit coy about their community's early support for 'William the Hermit'. Repingdon himself was not present at his protégé's trial. Following an inflammatory sermon in support of Wyclif at Oxford on 5 June, he had been excommunicated on 1 July and would not be restored to the Church until he recanted in October. Nevertheless, he continued to be much favoured by both Gaunt and Henry, later becoming abbot of Leicester and then bishop of Lincoln, and soon after Henry became king, Repingdon became his confessor – a brave choice, for despite his recantation Repingdon remained equivocal about some aspects of the Church's teaching.[53] Lollardy was still in its infancy at this time, and action such as that taken by Bishop Buckingham helped to dissuade great men like Gaunt from patronizing Lollard preachers, but it would be another thirty years before Lollardy was driven underground. Swinderby's trial had not only brought Repingdon to Henry's attention, it also introduced him to controversies which, by the time he became king, had become much harder to resolve.

The second controversy involved Henry more directly and was the first sign of trouble between him and Richard II. Henry's manor of Passenham, in the north-eastern corner of Buckinghamshire, adjoined Stony Stratford in Northamptonshire, which was held by Sir Aubrey de Vere, chamberlain to the king and uncle of Robert, the nineteen-year-old heir to the earldom of Oxford whose intimacy with Richard II would soon make him almost universally reviled. In the spring of 1382 a dispute broke out between the tenants of Passenham and Stony Stratford,[54] which by 29 May had become serious enough for Henry to despatch sixty valets armed with bows to arrest the malefactors from Stony Stratford. A week later, Hugh Waterton

---

[51] *Registrum Johannis Trefnant 1389–1404*, ed. W. W. Capes (Canterbury and York Society 20, 1916), 238–9; *Knighton*, 312–14; K. McFarlane, *John Wycliffe and the Beginnings of English Nonconformity* (Oxford, 1953), 122–5.

[52] *Registrum Johannis Trefnant*, 231–78, for the full account of his trial in 1391.

[53] S. Forde, 'Repyndon, Philip', *ODNB*, 46.503–5.

[54] Henry initially sent only his servant Thomas Page and his purveyor William to Passenham (in March and April). All the information concerning this episode is to be found in DL 28/1/1, fos. 8r–9r. For 'the battle of Passenham' see K. McFarlane, *Lancastrian Kings and Lollard Knights* (Oxford, 1972), 19–20.

was sent to retrieve a horse stolen from Passenham: here he encountered five hundred esquires and valets from Coventry and its vicinity whom he managed to mollify by offering them breakfast (at a cost to Henry of nearly £2), but a few days later he had to be despatched again to try to reconcile the two sets of tenants. However, even this failed to resolve matters, and in the following month, at his father's suggestion, Henry sent Waterton and William Loveney to tell the king, who was at Easthampstead, that he (Richard) had been misinformed about the dispute, presumably by Aubrey de Vere, or perhaps his nephew.[55] Whatever the outcome, this seems to have settled the matter, but it had afforded an object lesson in curial politics from Gaunt to his son. Henry must have encountered Aubrey and Robert de Vere on a number of occasions, for like him they were both much in evidence at court. Gaunt, too, was well aware of the influence which the de Veres exercised over the young king, but he probably thought Henry's decision to despatch sixty bowmen to Passenham to be an overreaction liable to escalate a dispute between tenants into a dispute between their lords. What Gaunt understood better than his son was the importance of ensuring that the king heard both sides of the story. Sixteen years later, when much graver danger threatened, it was a lesson Henry would act upon.

---

[55] The Latin is unambiguous: Waterton and Loveney were sent to the king *per preceptum domini mei Lancastrie* because *suggestio non vera facta fuit domino nostro regi*.

Chapter 3

THE MAKING OF A DISSIDENT
(1382–1387)

The Passenham dispute was the prelude to Henry's rapid estrangement after 1382 from Richard II's court. Between 1379 and 1381 he had continued to receive winter and summer livery robes from the king, but from 1383 onwards he received no gifts apart from the annual Garter robes which were his entitlement. Richard's household account for the period from September 1383 to September 1384 does not mention Henry once. Those who now clustered around the young king, who had his ear and were the beneficiaries of his generosity, were men such as Robert de Vere, earl of Oxford, Thomas Mowbray, earl of Nottingham, his tutor Sir Simon Burley, and his confessor, the Dominican friar Thomas Rushook.[1] Nor does Henry's name occur with any frequency in the chancery letters for these years. Rarely did he petition the king,[2] and hardly ever was he the recipient of royal favour or associated with Richard in acts of government.

Henry's alienation from the court paralleled the simultaneous collapse of John of Gaunt's relationship with his royal nephew. Gaunt was a proud man who resented being sidelined from the central role in English politics he had enjoyed since the death of his brother the Black Prince in 1376, while Richard was impatient to shake off his uncle's leading reins and to govern in concert with advisers of his own choosing. Military and diplomatic policy was a particular bone of contention.[3] Despite the failure of the 1381 expedition to Portugal led by his brother Edmund, earl of Cambridge, Gaunt still hoped to vindicate his claim to the Castilian throne, and in the parliament of November 1381 he argued that England's (as well as his own) resources should be directed to that end.[4] Others, however,

[1] E 101/400/12, m. 4; E 101/401/6, mm. 19, 23; E 101/401/16, mm. 20, 24 (rolls of great wardrobe liveries 1379–87). The household account book for 1383–4 is E 101/401/2.
[2] For two minor favours granted at Henry's request in November 1380 and February 1384, see *CPR 1377–81*, 561 and *CPR 1381–5*, 374.
[3] Saul, *Richard II*, 108–10.
[4] Goodman, *John of Gaunt*, 96–103.

saw this proposal for what to some extent it was: a strategy for the personal aggrandizement of the duke of Lancaster which would do little to solve England's real problems. Rebuffed and his pride dented, Gaunt accepted defeat for the moment, but continued to press his case, and for the next two or three years the debate over 'the way of Spain' or 'the way of Flanders' was the major fault-line in English foreign policy. In the parliament of February 1383, which sanctioned the despatch of a 'crusade' to Flanders commanded by Henry Despenser, bishop of Norwich, rather than a Lancastrian campaign in Castile, Gaunt was so irritated that he stormed out in disgust.[5]

By 1384–5, the relationship between Gaunt and Richard was so strained that each suspected the other of conspiring to assassinate him. During the Salisbury parliament of April 1384, a mischief-making Carmelite friar called John Latimer was invited to celebrate mass in the king's presence and used the opportunity to launch a tirade against Gaunt (who was not present), accusing him of plotting against the king's life. Richard ordered his uncle to be put to death without further investigation, although he was soon dissuaded from such folly and in the event Gaunt exonerated himself with ease, while Latimer was tortured to death by a group of royalist knights in an unsuccessful attempt to make him divulge his informants.[6] Yet Richard's distrust of his uncle was now plain to all, and incidents multiplied. In August 1384, when Gaunt's protégé John of Northampton, a draper who had been mayor of London between 1381 and 1383, was brought before the king to answer charges laid against him by his enemies in the city, he expressed the opinion that Richard ought not to pass judgment on him in Gaunt's absence; Richard retorted that he was quite competent to sit in judgment on him and on the duke of Lancaster as well.[7] In the following year the tension between them reached breaking-point. At a council meeting at Westminster in early February 1385, Gaunt proposed that Richard should personally lead an English army to France. Although his two brothers supported Gaunt's proposal, the king and his friends were against it, leading to another scene when all three royal uncles walked out. Gaunt declared that he would offer the king no assistance if he would not go to France, while Richard and his friends accused the duke of disloyalty, 'and so', stated the Westminster chronicler, they 'busied themselves about removing him by

[5] *Westminster Chronicle*, 36–7.
[6] *Westminster Chronicle*, 68–80.
[7] *Westminster Chronicle*, 90–6; *SAC I*, 728–30. Northampton was initially condemned to death, but subsequently imprisoned instead following the intercession of Queen Anne.

underhand means'.[8] In other words, they planned to have Gaunt assassinated, apparently with the king's approval. The duke got wind of the plot
on 14 February and fled to Pontefract castle, which he prepared for a siege,
but ten days later he was back and, protected by a breastplate and accompanied by an armed guard, strode into the king's manor-house at Sheen
and upbraided Richard for the company he kept and the shame which he
brought upon himself and the kingdom. Richard was emollient and promised reform, but Gaunt was in no mood to be soothed. Since his life was
not safe at court, he declared, he would absent himself, and withdrew to
Hertford castle. It was left to Richard's mother, Princess Joan, to effect a
reconciliation between them, with Gaunt agreeing to forgive those who had
plotted his death three weeks earlier, identified as Thomas Mowbray, earl of
Nottingham, Robert de Vere, earl of Oxford, and William Montague, earl
of Salisbury.

If Gaunt was still inclined to treat his eighteen-year-old nephew as a
child, there were times when Richard acted the part. A week later, after
a disagreement with William Courtenay, archbishop of Canterbury, at a
council meeting, he happened to encounter Courtenay again while being
rowed down the Thames, whereupon he drew his sword and had to
be restrained from running the archbishop through on the spot.[9] Ten
months later, on 25 January 1386, he punched the earl of Arundel hard
enough to knock him down.[10] Even if those who riled him were far from
blameless – and Arundel was no saint – Richard's propensity for violence
was unnerving, and it is not surprising that within months his reconciliation with Gaunt collapsed. On the campaign to Scotland in August 1385,
Richard's first military command, he and Gaunt quarrelled yet again
when, having reached Edinburgh, Gaunt advised Richard to set off in
pursuit of the Scottish army, but the king, apparently believing his uncle's
advice to be disloyal if not treacherous, decided to burn the city and return
to England.[11] By 20 August the English army had arrived back at Newcastle,

---

[8] For this and what follows, see *Westminster Chronicle*, 110–15, which added that 'these
temporal lords went in constant fear of the duke of Lancaster because of his great power,
his admirable judgment, and his brilliant mind'; Goodman, *John of Gaunt*, 102–3.

[9] *Westminster Chronicle*, 116–17; *SAC I*, 754–6, states that he was so angry with Courtenay
that he wanted to deprive him of his temporalities; when John Devereux, John Trivet,
and the chancellor Michael de la Pole advised him against this, he accused them of
treason.

[10] Trinity College Library Dublin, MS 500, fo. 3. C. Given-Wilson, 'The Earl of Arundel,
the War at Sea, and the Anger of Richard II', in *The Medieval Python*, ed. R. Yeager and
T. Takamiya (New York, 2012), 27–38.

[11] Versions of the dispute differ, with Froissart placing much of the blame on the earl
of Oxford for his insinuations regarding Gaunt's motivation. See *Westminster Chronicle*,

having achieved next to nothing; Richard returned to Westminster, while Gaunt and Henry spent the next two months in Yorkshire and Lancashire.

By now it must have been apparent that the two most powerful men in England found it difficult to work together, and the fear was that, as with Edward II and Thomas of Lancaster seventy years earlier, their mutual distrust might well be leading the realm towards civil war. It was thus fortunate that at the very moment when Richard and Gaunt were quarrelling over strategy in Edinburgh, events at the other end of Europe were conspiring to make Gaunt's claim to the Castilian throne a viable option. The battle of Aljubarrota, fought on 14 August 1385, was a decisive victory for João of Avis, the new Portuguese king, over his great rival Juan of Trastámara, king of Castile,[12] and the weakening of Trastamaran power gave Gaunt his chance. In the parliament of 20 October 1385 (the first parliament to which Henry was summoned) the duke once again requested financial support for an expedition to Spain, and this time king, lords and commons were happy to acquiesce.[13] Whether they truly believed that the Castilian crown could be won is debatable; uppermost in the minds of some, perhaps, was the thought that it would be better if Gaunt left England for a while.[14] An Anglo-Portuguese alliance was thus drawn up, the Roman Pope Urban VI lent his support, and by Christmas 1385 preparations were under way for the duke's *voyage d'Espaigne*. From early April 1386 Gaunt and Henry were at Plymouth,[15] and at the end of June a

---

128–30, and *SAC I*, 762, where Gaunt is said to have advised the king to cross the Firth of Forth; Froissart, *Chroniques*, ed. S. Luce (SHF, Paris, 1869), xi.271–5, said that Gaunt wanted Richard to head south-west to cut off a Franco-Scottish raiding-party in Galloway, but that de Vere warned Richard that Gaunt only wanted to pursue the Scots because he hoped that Richard might be killed, whereupon Gaunt could claim the throne. Cf. Goodman, *John of Gaunt*, 104–5; Saul, *Richard II*, 145. See also Froissart's comment (*Chroniques*, xii.121) about de Vere's influence at this time: 'par celui estoit tout fait et sans lui n'estoit riens fait'.

[12] J. Sumption, *Divided Houses: The Hundred Years War III* (London, 2009), 560–8.

[13] *PROME*, vii.6–7. The amount granted to Gaunt by the commons was £13,300, but it was understood that he would also use his own resources. In February 1386 the king lent him a further £13,300: Goodman, *John of Gaunt*, 115–16.

[14] See the comment by Froissart, *Chroniques*, xii.297: 'Et estoit l'intencion du duc qu'il emmenroit avecques lui femme et enfans et feroit de biaux mariages en Castille et en Portingal avant son retour, car il ne voloit pas si tost retourner, et bien y avoit cause, car il veoit les besongnes d'Engleterre dures et le roy son nepveu jone, et avoit d'en costé lui perilleux conseil, pour quoy il se departoit le plus volontiers'.

[15] Here they remained for most of the next three months, although Knighton says that on 22 April Gaunt and Duchess Constanza paid a final visit to the court to say farewell; they were each presented with a golden crown by the king and queen, and Richard issued an order that Gaunt was in future to be known as 'king of Spain'. Gaunt and Henry also attended the Garter ceremonies at Windsor the following day: *Knighton*, 340; E 101/401/16, m.20 (issue of Garter robes).

Portuguese fleet arrived to bring the English army over to Iberia.[16] On 8 July, while father and son were dining on board Gaunt's ship, a favourable breeze sprang up and the decision was made to sail. Henry returned ashore, and as night fell the fleet slipped out of Plymouth Sound and the duke embarked on a venture that would not see him return to England for three-and-a-half years.[17]

One consequence of the collapse of the relationship between Gaunt and Richard was that from 1382 onwards few of the duke's retainers continued to hold office in the royal household and administration, as several of them had done during the first four or five years of the reign.[18] The Lancastrian affinity was closing in on itself and Henry followed suit, staying almost continuously in his father's company.[19] His first experience of diplomacy, an Anglo-French conference at Leulinghem in November 1383, and his first military venture, the Scottish campaign of August 1385, were both gained while serving in his father's retinue.[20] Henry was also taking on more personal responsibilities. In December 1384, since Mary de Bohun was now fourteen, she and Henry were granted livery of her share of the Bohun inheritance and began to cohabit: their first child, the future Henry V, was born in September 1386, two months after Gaunt left for Iberia.[21] Henry's household expanded accordingly: by 1385 he had a treasurer and steward of his lands, and by 1387 he and Mary had separate

[16] Sumption, *Divided Houses*, 582, says that Gaunt's army of about 5,000 men was transported in a total of 104 ships: 18 from Portugal, 75 English merchantmen, and 11 chartered from Germany or the Low Countries.

[17] *Knighton*, 341.

[18] Walker, *Lancastrian Affinity*, 106.

[19] It is worth noting that when Mary de Bohun came of age in December 1384 and was granted livery of her inheritance, Richard told Gaunt to take Henry's fealty rather than receiving it himself: *CPR 1381–5*, 511–16.

[20] Goodman, *John of Gaunt*, 98–9; *Foedera*, vii.412–14, 418–21. For his presence on the 1385 campaign, see *The Scrope and Grosvenor Controversy*, ed. N. H. Nicolas (2 vols, 1832), i.50; ii.165–6. It has been claimed that Henry accompanied Gaunt on his brief raid into Scotland in April 1384: A .Tuck, 'Henry IV and Chivalry', in *Henry IV: The Establishment of the Regime, 1399–1406*, (York, 2003), 56; J. Kirby, *Henry IV of England* (London, 1970), 22, but there is no contemporary evidence for this. On 19 February 1386, father and son were admitted to the fraternity of Lincoln cathedral, with Sir John Beaufort, his illegitimate half-brother; Sir Robert Ferrers; Sir Thomas Swynford; Sir William Hauley; Thomas Bradley, Edward Beauchamp and Arnald of Gascony, esquires; and Philippa Chaucer, sister of Katherine Swynford and wife of Geoffrey Chaucer: *Chaucer Life-Records*, ed. M. M. Crow and C. C. Olson (Oxford, 1966), 91–3.

[21] *CCR 1381–5*, 511–16; Holmes, *Estates of the Higher Nobility*, 24–5. For the division of the Bohun inheritance see DL 41/240, which assigned lands worth £931 per annum to Eleanor, mainly in England, and lands worth £913 (including the great Welsh lordship of Brecon, said to be worth £624 per annum) to Mary. See below for discussion of Henry's income at this time, pp. 80–1. For Henry V's date of birth, see C. Allmand, *Henry V* (New Haven, 1997), 7; Mortimer, *Fears*, 371.

chambers and wardrobes.[22] His father's departure imposed additional responsibilities. Froissart said that before leaving Gaunt appointed Henry as 'lieutenant of all that he had in England'.[23] No longer could he shelter under his father's wing.

If there were hopes that Gaunt's absence would cool the political temperature, it took less than three months for them to be confounded. The Wonderful Parliament which met at Westminster on 1 October 1386 brought to a head the tensions of the mid-1380s and sparked a political crisis which consumed England for two years and more, and it was a crisis in which Henry played a leading role. Fears of invasion during the summer exacerbated the already febrile atmosphere. At Sluys in Flanders, one of the largest French fleets of the Middle Ages had been assembling since June for an assault upon England, and in mid-September the English government issued a general summons for troops: Henry responded by assembling 47 knights, 203 esquires and 300 archers who remained close to London throughout October.[24] In the event, bad weather prevented the French fleet from sailing,[25] but the panic which gripped the south-east of England during these months – exacerbated by rumours that Richard and his unpopular chancellor, Michael de la Pole, were planning to cede Calais and other lands to the French to secure the peace which they had been seeking for the past few years – set the tone for what followed, and when de la Pole opened the parliament by announcing that the government required four fifteenths and tenths (around £150,000) in taxation to meet its obligations, he was greeted with calls for his dismissal and impeachment.[26] Richard retired to his manor of Eltham (Kent), where he remained for several days if not weeks, refusing to bow to the commons demands until they agreed to grant a tax. Eventually a deputation, led by the king's uncle Thomas (Buckingham, now also duke of Gloucester) and Thomas Arundel, bishop of Ely, arrived to advise the king to return to parliament and accede to the

[22] Somerville, *Duchy of Lancaster*, i.131–2; DL 28/1/2, fo. 1r.

[23] Froissart, *Chroniques*, xii.297; Gaunt certainly made Henry keeper of the duchy and palatinate of Lancaster: Somerville, *Duchy of Lancaster*, i.120; *JGR II*, xlvii; *CIPM 1384–92*, no. 128.

[24] He received £1,902 in wages: DL 28/3/3, m. 2. Henry had been at Monmouth in mid-September for the birth of his first son; *Knighton*, 348–5 ; E 403/534, 22 April; DL 28/1/2, fo. 29.

[25] *Chronique du Religieux de Saint-Denys 1380–1422*, ed. M. Bellaguet (6 vols, Paris, 1839–52), i.458–60, said that the invasion was finally called off around the middle of October.

[26] *PROME*, vii.31–54: Saul, *Richard II*, 157–64; J. Palmer, 'The Parliament of 1385 and the Constitutional Crisis of 1386', *Speculum* 46 (1971), 477–89.

commons' requests; they mentioned the possibility of deposition should he refuse to do so.[27] Chastened, Richard agreed to come back to Westminster, where he was obliged to agree to the dismissal and impeachment of de la Pole. Convicted of peculation and incompetence, the former chancellor was sentenced to imprisonment at the king's mercy, though in fact he spent little time in custody. It was also agreed in parliament that a commission of fourteen lords would be appointed to hold power for one year, beginning on 19 November 1386, with a mandate to effect root and branch reform in all departments of the royal administration, including the king's household. Thus by the time parliament was dissolved on 28 November the nineteen-year-old king had effectively been deprived of executive authority, more or less as if he were still a minor. Power now resided with the Commission of Government, as it was called.

While parliament remained in session, Richard put on a show of compliance, but once it became clear that the Commissioners were in earnest he adopted a policy of non-cooperation.[28] In the second week of February 1387, following an angry meeting of the council at Westminster, he decamped to the Midlands, taking his household with him to evade the Commissioners' scrutiny. Apart from a brief visit to the south-east around the time of the Garter celebrations in late April and early May, Richard and his household remained in the Midlands for the next eight months, while the Commissioners governed the country from Westminster. As the latter's popularity waxed, especially following the earl of Arundel's capture of a Franco-Flemish wine fleet in March, that of Richard and his friends waned.[29] The real butt of popular hatred was Robert de Vere, now duke of Ireland, who in the summer of 1387 compounded his sins by divorcing his wife Philippa, the granddaughter of King Edward III, and abducting one of Queen Anne's Bohemian ladies-in-waiting, Agnes Landskron, whom he married at Chester, probably in mid-July when the king was also there. This insult to the royal family infuriated the king's uncles, especially the duke of Gloucester.[30]

[27] *Knighton*, 354–62.

[28] For example, the Commissioners cut down significantly the flow of cash to the royal household and diverted resources towards a naval campaign against the French commanded by the king's old enemy, the earl of Arundel. For their financial policy, see *RHKA*, 105–6, 118–20.

[29] Arundel sold off some 4,000 tuns of wine in England at rock-bottom prices: A. Bell, 'Medieval Chroniclers as War Correspondents during the Hundred Years War: The Earl of Arundel's Naval Campaign of 1387', *Fourteenth Century England VI*, ed. C. Given-Wilson (Woodbridge, 2010), 171–84.

[30] The Dieulacres chronicler, a royalist sympathizer, described it as the main reason why the duke 'and many others' took up arms against de Vere: M. Clarke and V. Galbraith,

By now Richard's mind had turned to ways of avenging himself on those who had humiliated him. Early in August, while at Shrewsbury, he summoned the royal justices and sergeants-at-law and placed before them a list of ten questions to which he required answers; three weeks later at Nottingham, he repeated the process. Some of these 'Questions to the Judges' dealt in general terms with the king's exercise of his prerogative, others referred specifically to the parliament of 1386. The answers given by the justices, who later claimed coercion but also took their lead from the strongly royalist Chief Justice, Robert Tresilian were precisely those which the king would have wished to hear: they affirmed the king's control over the agenda and proceedings of parliament and declared that the impeachment of de la Pole and the establishment of the Commission of Government had been illegal; those who had been responsible for them deserved to be punished like traitors. So dire were the ramifications of these responses that Richard initially tried to keep them secret, but by October 1387 Gloucester had learned of them and had informed his chief allies among the lords, the earls of Arundel and Warwick.

Events now gathered pace. The Commission of Government's term of office was due to end on 19 November, and Richard, anticipating his resumption of power, returned in splendour to London on 10 November and summoned Gloucester and Arundel to his presence. They refused to come, saying they feared for their lives The king sent the earl of Northumberland to arrest Arundel at his castle of Reigate, but Arundel slipped away and, on 13 November, joined Gloucester and Warwick at Harringay, five miles north of London. Each of the three lords had his retainers with him. On the following day, at Waltham Cross (Hertfordshire), they met a delegation from the king led by the archbishop of Canterbury and the duke of York, where they proclaimed the Appeal of Treason from which derives the name by which they are commonly known, the Appellants or Lords Appellant. The Appeal set out charges of treason against five men close to the king: Robert de Vere, Michael de la Pole, Chief Justice Tresilian, Nicholas Brembre, the former mayor of London, and Alexander Neville, archbishop of York. On 17 November, accompanied by 300 retainers, the three Appellants came before the king in Westminster Great Hall and repeated their appeal. Richard calmly assured them that their accusations would be heard in the next parliament, which would meet on

'The Deposition of Richard II', *BJRL* (1930), 125–81 at p. 167). See also *Westminster Chronicle*, 188; *SAC I*, 823, 829; Froissart, *Chroniques*, xiv.46–7; A. Goodman, *The Loyal Conspiracy* (London, 1971), 25; and Saul, *Richard II*, 183, 471.

3 February 1388; in the meantime, the five accused would be kept in custody and the Appellants' safety was guaranteed.[31] Yet within days it had become apparent that Richard would not keep his word. De la Pole and Neville were allowed to flee, eventually reaching Paris,[32] while Tresilian went into hiding and Brembre tried to rally the Londoners to Richard's cause. Meanwhile de Vere had decided on resistance: armed with letters from the king, he hastened northwards to Cheshire and Lancashire where, together with his agent Sir Thomas Molyneux, constable of Chester castle, he managed within a few weeks to raise some 3,000–4,000 troops.[33] The Appellants were aware of his movements, however, and by early December both sides were preparing for war.[34]

It was at this point that Henry, along with Thomas Mowbray, the young earl of Nottingham, joined Gloucester, Arundel and Warwick, and on 12 December the five Appellants, as they now were, gathered at Huntingdon to plan their campaign.[35] Whether Henry and Mowbray made their decision jointly or individually is not clear. When Gloucester first heard of the Questions to the Judges (in October), he had apparently tried to persuade Henry to join them.[36] If true, this meant that Henry must have weighed up his options for some two months before eventually throwing in his lot with them. As to his reasons for doing so, there must have been more to it than Fovent's belief that Gloucester, Arundel and Warwick made Henry and Mowbray partners in the appeal 'because of affinity', although that may have played a part.[37] For Henry, the deciding factor was probably de Vere's

---

[31] *Westminster Chronicle*, 210–12; *Knighton*, 414–15.

[32] *Saint-Denys*, i.496–8, describes their welcome to Paris.

[33] Richard had appointed de Vere as Justice of Chester on 8 September and North Wales on 10 October, which allowed him to make military arrays there: *CPR 1385–9*, 357; A. Tuck, 'Edmund of Langley, First Duke of York', *ODNB*, 17.762–5. Cf. *CPR 1385–9*, 217.

[34] Arundel's servants at Holt Castle (Clwyd) kept him informed of de Vere's activities: A. Tuck, *Richard II and the English Nobility* (London, 1973), 118; P. Morgan, *War and Society in Late Medieval Cheshire 1277–1403* (Chetham Society, Manchester, 1987), 188.

[35] *Westminster Chronicle*, 218–20; *PROME*, vii.408. Arundel Castle Ms FA. 13, fo. 20, suggests that on 1 December 1387 the earl of Arundel was at his castle of Arundel, in the company of Thomas Rushook, bishop of Chichester, who confirmed the statutes of the earl's college at Arundel. Yet just a few months later Rushook would be accused in parliament of treason by the Appellants.

[36] *SAC I*, 828.

[37] '*racione affinitatis*': *Historia Mirabilis Parliamenti 1386, Per Thomam Fovent*, ed. M. McKisack (Camden Miscellany 14, London, 1926), 18. Mowbray's marriage to Arundel's daughter in July 1384 certainly marked a turning-point in his relations with the court, for before this he had been one of Richard's favourites. After serving as second in command to Arundel on their naval expedition in 1387, he and his father-in-law were snubbed by the king and de Vere despite their success. If de Vere had supplanted Mowbray in Richard's affections, Mowbray may have seen the Appeal as a way of getting rid of the detested favourite: *SAC I*, 814–15.

recruitment of forces in Lancashire and Cheshire, and the consequent undermining of Lancastrian influence there. Gaunt's absence had left his county palatine vulnerable, not just to royal encroachment but also to the local rivalries and ambitions which even the most powerful resident magnate found it hard to keep in check, and there were plenty of men in Lancashire (to say nothing of Cheshire, of which Richard was the earl) who felt themselves excluded from the duke's patronage. Sir Thomas Molyneux, de Vere's chief agent in Cheshire, was a disaffected former Lancastrian retainer who must have relished the chance to strike a blow at Lancastrian influence in the north-west.[38] Richard II had also taken advantage of the week that he spent at Chester from 12–16 July 1387 to bolster his support in the region through the issue of pardons and other favours. The threat to Gaunt's position in the north-west was real enough, and when Henry heard of the musters taken by Molyneux at Flint and Pulford (Cheshire) in the first week of December, it was clear that the defence of his father's interests brooked no further delay.[39] Issuing orders to his servants to send his equipment to Stony Stratford, Henry marched north from London for the 'ricing against the duke of Ireland'.[40]

From Huntingdon, the Appellants could either march south to London to confront the king directly, or west to intercept de Vere's army before it could reach the king. Both options were considered. At their trial in 1397, Gloucester, Arundel and Warwick were alleged to have wanted to depose Richard forthwith, but were dissuaded by Henry and Mowbray from doing so.[41] Henry's own evidence corroborated this: 'Did you not say to me at Huntingdon,' he said to Arundel, 'where we first gathered in revolt, that before doing anything else it would be better to seize the king?' 'You, Henry

---

[38] Sir Ralph Radcliffe, dismissed from the shrievalty of Lancashire by Gaunt, was another disaffected retainer who joined de Vere, as did several who had never looked kindly on Gaunt's ascendancy, such as Gilbert Halsall, Robert Clifton and John Radcliffe of Chaderton: Walker, *Lancastrian Affinity*, 165–70, 176n; *JGR I*, 1237; *Westminster Chronicle*, 222; J. L. Gillespie, 'Thomas Mortimer and Thomas Molineux: Radcot Bridge and the Appeal of 1397', *Albion* 7 (1975), 161–73.

[39] Morgan, *War and Society*, 188; one of the charges later brought against the Appellees was that they planned to arrest Gaunt as soon as he arrived back in England: *Westminster Chronicle*, 261.

[40] 'equitationem contra Ducem Hibernie': DL/28/1/2, fo. 15v.

[41] *PROME*, vii.408. Also accused in 1397, along with Gloucester, Arundel and Warwick, was Sir Thomas Mortimer, illegitimate uncle of the earl of March and steward of the earl of Arundel, the 'sixth Appellant'; he was probably the senior captain, apart from the five lords, in the Appellant army, but did not join in the Appeal of Treason, presumably because he was not a parliamentary peer like the others. He avoided capture in 1397 and died in Scotland in 1399.

earl of Derby, you lie in your teeth', replied Arundel, protesting that he had always sought the king's welfare and honour.[42] These accounts need to be treated with caution (for Henry, in a sense, was also on trial in 1397), but they are far from implausible. Warwick may also have argued that, rather than deposing Richard, they should direct their energies against de Vere, but on balance such sentiments are more in keeping with Henry's and Mowbray's views.[43] Warwick, as far as can be gathered, stood firm with Gloucester and Arundel throughout the crisis: the 'undivided trinity', as Fovent called them.[44]

Yet if Henry and Mowbray acted as a moderating influence on their senior colleagues, this was not the main reason why they joined the Appeal. Both of them, after all, were of an age with Richard and had been brought up with him; both also had private scores to settle with de Vere and may well have believed that, once his influence had been eliminated, the king should be given another chance. Moreover, if Richard were to be deposed, who would replace him? He and Anne of Bohemia had been married for nearly six years but had failed to produce an heir, and the succession was an increasingly live issue in 1386–7. An entail of the crown drawn up by Edward III in 1376–7 had stated that, should Richard die childless, the throne should pass to John of Gaunt and then to his male heirs, failing whom to his other two sons (the dukes of York and Gloucester) successively, and to their male heirs.[45] With Gaunt out of the country, however, his (and thus Henry's) claim might fail by default. Here, then, was another reason why Henry could not afford to remain aloof in 1387, for although the existence of Edward III's entail was not widely known, and there is no evidence that Henry ever cited it, he was probably aware of its terms.

The Westminster chronicler said there were four main reasons for the Appellant rising: first, the rumours that Richard was planning to abandon or sell various English territories and rights in France to the French king; secondly, their belief that England was being misgoverned; thirdly, the incompetence of the king's advisers; fourthly, their fear that the king's counsellors were actively planning their death.[46] Yet if the Appellants

---

[42] CR, 59; Usk, 28–30.

[43] Westminster Chronicle, liv.218–19 (based at this point on a source in Warwick's household); PROME, vii.355.

[44] Historia Mirabilis Parliamenti, 21 (indivisa trinitas).

[45] M. Bennett, 'Edward III's Entail and the Succession to the Throne, 1376–1471', EHR 113 (1998), 580–609. See pp. 96–9 for a fuller discussion of the succession.

[46] Westminster Chronicle, 204–7.

shared a dissatisfaction with the way in which England was being governed, they also feared for their own lands and families should the king and de Vere be permitted to win this trial of strength – and none more so than Henry.

Chapter 4

LORDS OF THE FIELD (1387–1389)

Although the addition of Henry and Mowbray broadened the opposition to the king, it also made it more brittle, for this was a coalition shot through with personal and political differences. Henry and Gloucester had still not resolved the division of the Bohun inheritance; Mowbray and Warwick entertained rival claims to the lordship of Gower (Glamorgan); Mowbray had plotted against Gaunt's life in 1385.[1] However, the real fault-line was how far each was prepared to go to purge the court and reform the royal administration. Gloucester and Arundel pressed throughout the crisis for radical solutions, while Henry and Mowbray – usually portrayed as speaking with one voice, a point difficult to verify – advocated clemency and moderation.[2] Unlike Gloucester and Arundel, Warwick had no history of personal antagonism towards the king, but inclined to stronger measures than did Henry and Mowbray. For the moment, though, once the decision had been taken not to depose the king, the Appellants were united in their aim, which was to neutralize de Vere. The forces they assembled at Huntingdon consisted largely of their private retinues.[3] Although the size of their army is not known, it certainly numbered thousands rather than hundreds, and the largest retinues were probably those brought by Henry and Arundel, the wealthy Appellants.[4] Henry's recruiting agent in December 1387 was Sir William Bagot, a Warwickshire knight retained by Gaunt who also had ties to Henry as well as to Mowbray and Warwick.[5] With many of the Lancastrian retainers abroad with Gaunt,

[1] Above, p. 38.
[2] John Gower, in his *Chronica Tripertita*, ascribed the entire 1387–8 crisis solely to the three senior Appellants, barely mentioning Henry and Mowbray: *The Major Latin Works of John Gower*, ed. and trans. E. W. Stockton (Seattle, 1962), 290–8.
[3] Cf. *Knighton*, 420: they 'sent to every part of the realm to assemble their people'; also *Historia Mirabilis Parliamenti*, 8: 'they raised up the people, each one from his own region'.
[4] When the Appellants divided their forces before Radcot Bridge, the retinues of Arundel and Henry were deployed separately, while those of Gloucester, Warwick and Nottingham combined to form a third 'division'.
[5] Bagot collected £200 on behalf of Henry at Kenilworth castle on 10 December 1387; at Daventry on 15–16 December, cloth was bought to make *signa* (badges) for Henry's retainers

Henry must have relied largely on his own followers, but he had been able to raise 250 men-at-arms and 300 archers at short notice a year earlier, and can hardly have come to Huntingdon with fewer.

The brief military campaign which led to the skirmish at Radcot Bridge, fifteen miles west of Oxford, began with the Appellant forces marching west through Northampton, Daventry and Banbury into north Oxfordshire. Meanwhile de Vere continued southwards from Cheshire through Evesham until he reached Chipping Campden, where he spent the night of 19 December. The Appellants now divided their forces. Gloucester, Warwick and Mowbray took up a position close to Moreton-in-Marsh; Arundel occupied Burford, to prevent de Vere's army crossing the Windrush should he slip past the first Appellant line, while Henry moved south to block the crossing of the Thames at Radcot Bridge.[6] As a result it was Henry who received much of the credit for the rout of the royalist forces, especially, though not exclusively, in the account of the Lancastrian chronicler Henry Knighton. Before de Vere's army even encountered the first Appellant line, his men began deserting, and in a brief engagement with Arundel's men at Burford Thomas Molyneux was killed by Sir Thomas Mortimer. With a second force blocking his retreat, de Vere now pressed on, but when he arrived at Radcot Bridge, eight miles south of Burford, he found some of Henry's forces barring his way, having broken the bridge in three places so that only a single horseman could cross at one time, and the remainder, including Henry himself, fast approaching. Meanwhile Gloucester was coming up from behind. With 'wonderful daring', therefore, he threw off his sword and gauntlets and plunged his horse into the Thames, his only remaining avenue

to wear: DL 28/1/2, fos. 1r, 4v, 13v, 14v, 16r–v, 17v. For Bagot, see L. Clark, 'Sir William Bagot', *ODNB*, 3.242–4, who suggests Bagot may have persuaded Henry and Mowbray to join the older appellants. For Bagot's close involvement with Henry and Gloucester over the division of the Bohun inheritance in early 1388, see DL 41/248, and the petition from Sir John Lestrange preserved as BL Add. Charter 14713. Lestrange and Lord Lovell both claimed the goods and chattels of Sir Nicholas Willy, forfeited for felony, worth about £240. Lestrange claimed to have petitioned Gaunt before his departure for Spain, but 'now in his absence' Lovell had seized them by fraud and with violence. He handed one copy of his bill to Gaunt's council and a second to Bagot for him to give to Henry – an interesting sidelight on Henry's involvement in Duchy affairs during his father's absence. Henry's wife, Mary, was evidently friendly with Bagot's wife, Margaret, to whom she gave a brocade, and in September 1388 one of Bagot's sergeants, John, brought Mary news of the Cambridge parliament. Bagot himself received a gown and a silver livery collar *ad modum de suagg* (a swage) from Henry in 1387 (DL 28/1/2, fos. 21r, 29v).

[6] For these events see J. Myres, 'The Campaign of Radcot Bridge in December 1387', *EHR*, 42 (1927), 20–33; R. Davies, 'Some Notes from the Register of Henry de Wakefield, Bishop of Worcester, on the Political Crisis of 1386–88', *EHR* 86 (1971), 547–58; Morgan, *War and Society*, 188–90.

of escape.[7] Remarkably, he got clean away. That it was a foggy afternoon doubtless helped; when his discarded armour was found the next day, it was initially thought that he must have drowned. In fact, he disguised himself as a groom and managed to reach London for a final meeting with Richard II before crossing to the continent, never to set foot in England again.[8]

Knighton's account is too favourable to Henry. A less partisan reading of the events of 19–20 December might be that, as the least militarily experienced of the Appellants, he had been posted as long stop in the unlikely event that de Vere managed to get as far as the Thames, and that even then he allowed the real prize to slip through his grasp. On the other hand, the Appellants themselves believed that the decisive action of the day had taken place at Radcot,[9] and in fact each of them had played his part in achieving their principal objective, the rout of de Vere's forces.[10] On the following day, 21 December, the victorious 'lords of the field' marched to Oxford, where on Christmas Day they held a masked ball to celebrate their victory.[11] Two days later they reached London and drew up their forces in view of the city walls, while the mayor, Nicholas Exton, handed over the keys of the city to them and distributed ale, wine, bread and cheese to their retainers to discourage them from plundering the city.[12]

Richard meanwhile had taken refuge in the Tower of London, but he soon abandoned hope of holding it against the Appellants and agreed to parley. At a meeting in his chamber on 28 December, he asked them to drop their Appeal; their response was to threaten him with deposition. Next he tried to persuade Henry and Mowbray to break ranks with their senior colleagues, taking Henry up on to the walls of the Tower for a private discussion and inviting him and Mowbray to remain behind when

---

[7] *Knighton*, 420–3. He probably forded the Thames at Bablock Hythe rather than Radcot itself.

[8] He died at Louvain in Brabant five years later.

[9] *Westminster Chronicle*, 268.

[10] According to *Knighton*, 422–5, about 800 of them drowned in the boggy meadows around the Thames, but few others were killed; those who had not already fled were stripped of their arms and sent back to their homes.

[11] For *Domini de Campo* see *De Illustribus Henricis*, 98. Adam Usk, a student at the time, witnessed their entry to Oxford: Warwick and Derby led the vanguard of the army, Gloucester the centre, and Arundel and Nottingham the rearguard (*Usk*, 12–13). Henry bought eighteen masks (*visers*) and gowns 'for the disguising (*degysing*) on the feast of the Lord's birth': DL 28/1/2, fo. 14r. The Appellant army probably spent the night of the 22nd or 23rd at Notley Abbey, between Oxford and St Albans. Henry's wife, Mary, kept in close touch with him during the campaign, sending her messenger Richard Willey from Kenilworth to Notley, Northampton, Daventry, and Chipping Norton for news (ibid., fo. 26r).

[12] *SAC I*, 844.

the others left.[13] But Richard's position was too weak for negotiation, and he and his opponents knew it. To break his resolve, the Appellants (or at least Gloucester, Arundel and Warwick) deposed him for three days, from 29 to 31 December, but according to one account Gloucester and Henry both claimed the right to become king in Richard's stead, so they decided at a council meeting on 1 January 1388 to reinstate him.[14] The idea that Henry would have claimed the throne for himself while his father was still alive is fanciful. If he did favour deposition, he would surely have argued that Gaunt should become king, but the real point at issue between him and Gloucester was probably not who should replace Richard but whether he should be deposed at all.

Now began the cleansing of Richard's court. De Vere, de la Pole and Neville may have fled, and Tresilian was nowhere to be found, but Brembre was quickly seized and on 1 January 1388 orders were issued for the arrest of a further twelve persons, mostly knights of the king's chamber and clerks of his chapel, the inner sanctums of the royal household.[15] The next week also saw the expulsion from court of some fifteen bishops, lords and ladies regarded as undesirable influences and the replacement of various royal officers with the Appellants' nominees.[16] The process of gathering evidence was also set in motion. On 18 January, the earl of Arundel's brother Thomas, bishop of Ely, encouraged an assembly of Londoners at the Guildhall to come forward with any grievances they had against the accused, and on 1 February six of the king's justices were imprisoned in the Tower and replaced by the Appellants' nominees.[17] Two days later the Merciless Parliament opened with the five Appellants, dressed in identical gold robes and walking arm in arm, entering the White Chamber of Westminster

[13] *Knighton*, 426; *SAC I*, 846, says that Richard kept Henry behind 'as a token of love' (*in pignus amoris*). The chroniclers give different dates for this meeting. Saul, *Richard II*, 189, dates it to 30 December.

[14] Clarke and Galbraith, 'The Deposition of Richard II', 157. The chronicler of Whalley abbey (Lancashire) said that Richard was *discoronatus* for three days by Gloucester, Arundel and Warwick (he does not mention Henry and Mowbray) and that the people (*communibus*) wanted Gloucester to become king, but Henry said that since he came from the senior line (elder brother) he should be king. The evidence for Richard's deposition is supported by Gloucester's confession in 1397, and the fact that no royal writs were sealed from 29 to 31 December (ibid., 159-60; *CR*, 81).

[15] *Westminster Chronicle*, 230-1; *SAC I*, 850; *Knighton*, 426-8. Their lists do not tally exactly, but it is reasonably clear that the knights arrested were Thomas Trivet, Simon Burley, John Beauchamp of Holt, James Berners, John Salisbury, Nicholas Dagworth and William Elmham, and the clerks were Nicholas Slake, Richard Medford, Richard Clifford and John Lincoln; John Blake was also arrested.

[16] The lower levels of the king's household had already been purged on 31 December: *Westminster Chronicle*, 228-33.

[17] *Historia Mirabilis Parliamenti*, 14; *Westminster Chronicle*, 232-4.

palace and genuflecting in unison before the king.[18] It was important to project an image of unity: it was also with arms linked that they had confronted Richard in the Tower on 28 December, and whenever charges were read out during the parliament the five Appellants stood together in a line facing the king.[19] They also advertised their solidarity by interchanging liveries, symbolic of political confederacy.[20] Equally important, however, was to emphasize their underlying loyalty to the crown;[21] thus the first thing that they did after genuflecting was to declare that they had never countenanced the king's death either secretly or openly, following which Gloucester made a personal statement that, contrary to rumour, he had never intended to depose Richard or make himself king.[22] Richard had little option other than to excuse his uncle, but whatever the truth of the matter the threat of deposition was not so much lifted as suspended, and it continued to hang over him throughout the session in order to ensure his compliance.

The Merciless Parliament was the longest yet held in England, sitting for four months (3 February–4 June 1388), with a break for Easter from 20 March to 13 April.[23] Its purpose was to try those whom the Appellants accused of treason. Since four of the five Appellees had fled, their cases could be disposed of fairly rapidly, although this did involve some unwelcome (to the Appellants) debate as to the legality of the process of Appeal, which they deflected by declaring that such great matters must be judged not according to legal precedent but by 'the procedure of parliament' – in effect, an assertion of the judicial supremacy of parliament irrespective

---

[18] *Historia Mirabilis Parliamenti*, 14; for the '*parliamentum sine misericordia*', see *Knighton*, 414.

[19] *Knighton*, 426; *Westminster Chronicle*, 310.

[20] Each of the other four lords gave Henry a gold and henna brocade and a long gilded gown of his livery, and Henry reciprocated by giving a blue and gold brocade of his own livery to each of them 'for the parliament': DL 28/1/2, fos. 5r, 11v, 12r. Gloucester also gave Henry two brocades of his livery for the Radcot Bridge campaign. Some of the heraldic images in a richly illuminated psalter and book of hours, BL Egerton MS 3277, may have been commissioned in part 'as a moral justification for the Appellants' cause': L. Dennison, 'British Library, Egerton MS 3277: a Fourteenth-Century Psalter-Hours and the Question of Bohun Family Ownership', in *Family and Dynasty in Late Medieval England: Harlaxton Medieval Studies IX* (Donnington, 2003), 122–55, at p. 149.

[21] For example, when they came into the king's presence on both 17 November and 28 December, they prostrated themselves three times before being bidden by Richard to rise: *Westminster Chronicle*, 212, 226.

[22] *Westminster Chronicle*, 234; *PROME*, vii.64; *Historia Mirabilis Parliamenti*, 14–15.

[23] It is also very well documented. For the chronology, sources and text of the roll, see *PROME*, vii.55–120. Cf. also Saul, *Richard II*, 191–6; Tuck, *Richard II and the English Nobility*, 121–7; Goodman, *Loyal Conspiracy*, 41–8.

of legal niceties.[24] Despite this, by 13 February de Vere, de la Pole, Tresilian and Neville had been convicted of treason *in absentia*, with the first three sentenced to death, Archbishop Neville to exile, and all four to forfeiture of their lands and goods. The one Appellee unfortunate enough not to have escaped was Nicholas Brembre, whose trial began on Monday 17 February. It soon ran into difficulties.[25] He began by asking to be allowed legal counsel, which was refused; he then asked to see a copy of the charges against him, which was also refused; when he attempted to respond to the charges, he was told that he must simply reply 'Guilty' or 'Not guilty'; when he offered to defend himself by battle, this too was refused. Thus passed the first day of his trial. On the following morning, when he was brought in again, the king tried to speak up for him, but in reply several of the lords (not just the Appellants) flung down their gauntlets in affirmation of his guilt. Eventually his case was referred to a committee of twelve lords headed by the king's uncle, the Duke of York, who declared that they found no reason to impose the death penalty. This infuriated the Appellants, but at this point, on the morning of Wednesday 19 February, a diversion occurred: Robert Tresilian was found hiding in sanctuary within the Westminster precinct. Led by Gloucester, the five Appellants strode over from the palace, dragged him from the abbey and, with cries of 'We havet hym! We havet hym!', hustled him into parliament to face his accusers. Having already been convicted, no defence was allowed him, and within a few hours Tresilian had been bound hand and foot, dragged on a hurdle to Tyburn, and there hanged naked before having his throat cut.[26]

As far as Brembre was concerned, however, it was not easy to see how the Appellants would proceed. In the event, they interrogated two representatives from each of the London guilds about their former mayor's guilt, but their answers were inconclusive and they were sent home again. Finally they called in the mayor, recorder and some of the city's aldermen, who stated that they 'supposed' Brembre had been aware of the treachery imputed to him – whereupon, on the afternoon of 20 February, he was taken to the Tower and drawn on a hurdle to Tyburn, his contrition *in extremis* evoking much sympathy from the onlookers. He too was hanged

---

[24] The Questions to the Judges had stated that it was against the king's regality to use impeachment in parliament without the king's consent, to which the use of the process of Appeal was a riposte.

[25] The best accounts of Brembre's trial are in *Westminster Chronicle*, 280–3, 308–13.

[26] *Historia Mirabilis Parliamenti*, 17–18.

and had his throat cut.[27] In the end, then, the Appellants got their way, but already their disregard for legal process was causing unease among the lords and justices – and these, it should be remembered, were the new royal justices, appointed just a few weeks earlier on the Appellants' nomination. The commons, on the other hand, were firm in their support. As the trials unfolded, this division between the lords and the commons would become more marked, one result of which was that for the remainder of the parliament appeal was replaced by impeachment, with the commons as a body acting as prosecutors and the lords as judges. This was how the next two defendants, the lawyer John Blake and the royal sergeant-at-arms Thomas Usk, were dealt with, the former for drafting the Questions to the Judges, the latter for trying to raise the Londoners against the Appellants in the autumn of 1387. Both were executed with the customary embellishments on Wednesday 4 March, 'drenching the streets with their flesh, in the accustomed manner for traitors'.[28]

If there was little opposition to the convictions of Blake and Usk, what followed was more controversial. On trial were four knights of the king's chamber arrested at the beginning of January: Simon Burley, the under-chamberlain; John Beauchamp, steward of the royal household; James Berners; and John Salisbury. It was Simon Burley's trial which revealed the depth of the fracture within the Appellant coalition, indeed it came to be remembered as the cause célèbre of the parliament. Burley was in his fifties, a Knight of the Garter, a former confidant of the Black Prince, and Richard's tutor. His intimacy with Richard was widely attested, as was his habit of making enemies: in 1385 Richard had hoped to elevate him to an earldom, but had had to abandon the idea in the face of opposition.[29]

---

[27] *Westminster Chronicle*, 310–17; *Historia Mirabilis Parliamenti*, 18. As the noose was placed around his neck, the son of Brembre's arch-rival John of Northampton stepped forward to ask him whether he believed he had treated his father fairly. Some claimed that he admitted his vindictiveness towards Northampton, others that he refused to confess to any wrong-doing. Gloucester had clashed with Brembre before, at the parliament of 1378, while Gaunt's support for Northampton in the politics of the city may well have inclined Henry against him as well: P. Nightingale, *A Medieval Mercantile Community: The Grocers' Company and the Politics and Trade of London 1000–1485* (New Haven and London, 1995), 257; *CPR 1385–9*, 158–9.

[28] The *Westminster Chronicle*, 314, says that it took thirty strokes of the sword (*mucronis*) to sever Usk's head; he is better known as the author of the *Testament of Love*.

[29] At Richard's coronation, Burley carried the young king on his shoulders; for the next decade he served as Richard's under-chamberlain and was well rewarded. He was deeply unpopular in Kent, where he held extensive lands (illegally, some thought) and was accused of abusing his position as Constable of Dover castle and Warden of the Cinque Ports. One of the charges against him in 1388 was that he had tried to raise 1,000 men from the Cinque Ports with whom to challenge the Appellants in November 1387: C. Given-Wilson, 'Richard II and the Higher Nobility', in *Richard II: The Art of Kingship*, ed. A. Goodman and J. Gillespie (Oxford, 1999), 107–28, at pp. 117–18.

Three years on, Gloucester, Arundel and Warwick were determined to send him to the scaffold, but their hopes of despatching him speedily were disappointed. Two preliminary hearings on 12 and 17 March proved inconclusive, and the four knights were sent back to the Tower while the parliament adjourned for Easter. When the trials were resumed, the duke of York proved especially resistant, making an impassioned speech on 27 April in defence of Burley's long record of loyalty to the crown and offering to serve personally as his champion; when Gloucester took up the challenge, York 'turned white with anger and told his brother to his face that he was a liar', at which the two royal dukes almost came to blows.[30] Henry too did all he could to save Burley, resulting in a dispute with Gloucester; the king, the queen, Mowbray and many other lords also pleaded for Burley's life, but Gloucester, Arundel and Warwick, supported by the commons, insisted that he must die. The deciding factor was apparently news of a popular rising in Kent in late April in favour of Burley's execution.[31] Yet if Richard had, by now, come to realize that he could not save his friend, it was a humiliation that he never forgot, and the fact that Henry and Mowbray opposed his execution was a critical factor in saving them from the same fate as the three senior Appellants nine years later.[32] The king could at least spare Burley the agony of a traitor's death: citing his membership of the Order of the Garter, he pardoned him the drawing and hanging to which he had been sentenced, so that when he went to his death on Tower Hill on 5 May, he was simply beheaded. A week later, the other three chamber knights followed him, although only Sir John Salisbury suffered the full penalties of treason.

With the execution of Beauchamp, Berners and Salisbury, the bloodletting finally ceased. Eight men had died, five of them suffering the very public torments of a traitor's death. Others, such as the six justices who had answered Richard's Questions and the deeply unpopular royal confessor, Thomas Rushook, had been convicted of treason but were ultimately exiled to Ireland rather than executed, with even Gloucester and Arundel willing to respect Rushook's clerical status and to accept the justices' plea that they had been coerced. Many other matters had also occupied parliament's time – especially foreign policy and crown finance

---

[30] *Westminster Chronicle*, 328–9.

[31] *SAC I*, 852–3; *Historia Mirabilis Parliamenti*, 21; *Westminster Chronicle*, 330–1. The queen went down on her knees to Gloucester and Arundel to beg for Burley's life, but to no avail; he had brought her over from Bohemia at the time of her marriage.

[32] See below, p. 105. In 1392, John of Gaunt contributed £10 to the cost of Burley's tomb (DL 28/3/2, fo. 18v).

– but it was the life and death drama of appeal and impeachment, the scales of retribution and grace, which enthralled and shocked contemporaries: the brutal public executions, the revival of treason as a weapon of political faction, and the open talk of deposition all stirred uncomfortable memories of the dark days of the 1320s. At one level, the Merciless Parliament was a clash of noble, even royal, factions, but it was also a very public and – in the strict sense of the word – popular event, played out in the streets of London and Westminster village as well as in the White Chamber of the palace, and the support of the parliamentary commons, who never wavered in their support for even the most draconian measures,[33] and of the citizens of London, was crucial in allowing the Appellants to get their way, both in December 1387 when they declined to help Richard and again during the parliament itself.[34] One reason for this was because the Appellants had courted public opinion through the circulation of letters and proclamations, but it is also indicative of the profound unpopularity by 1387 of the regime presided over by Richard and his advisers.[35] The Appellants' victims were also well chosen as a focus of popular hatred: Tresilian was not just disliked personally (which he was), he also personified the harshness and venality of the judicial system;[36] Brembre, although not the petty tyrant sometimes portrayed, had plenty of enemies in the city, especially among the non-victualling guilds;[37] while Burley, despite his

[33] According to the *Westminster Chronicle*, 283, no less than 305 gauntlets were flung down as wagers of Brembre's guilt at one point during his trial. *Knighton*, 443–51, preserves a petition from the commons sometimes seen as directed against the Appellants rather than the royal favourites (J. Palmer, *England, France and Christendom 1377–1399* (London, 1972), 136–7, 237–8), but this is difficult to accept: even if it was submitted during the second session and showed some impatience at the length of the parliament, Knighton states clearly that it was directed at the king's advisers, and it raised issues which had been of concern for several years before 1388. *HOC*, i.185–91, analyses the political connections of the knights and burgesses and their 'compliant endorsement' of the attack on the court party.

[34] See, for example, *Knighton*, 407, 427; *CE*, 364–5; *Westminster Chronicle*, 217, 307 (the pardon sought by the Londoners at the end of the parliament); *SAC I*, 844–5, says that while the 'poor' of London supported the Appellants, the wealthier citizens were more fearful; they were certainly divided over Brembre's fate. See also C. Oliver, 'A Political Pamphleteer in Late Medieval England: Thomas Fovent, Geoffrey Chaucer, Thomas Usk, and the Merciless Parliament of 1388', *New Medieval Literatures VI*, ed. D. Lawton, R.Copeland and W. Scase (Oxford, 2003), 167–98; and M. Giancarlo, *Parliament and Literature in Late Medieval England* (Cambridge, 2007), especially 164–9.

[35] For letters and proclamations, see *Knighton*, 411; Goodman, *Loyal Conspiracy*, 41; *SAC I*, 842–3, talks of the 'great delight among the common people' at Radcot Bridge; *Westminster Chronicle*, 211, and *Knighton*, 421, note the numbers of gentry and lesser men who supported the Appellants.

[36] J. Maddicott, 'Law and Lordship: Royal Justices as Retainers in Thirteenth and Fourteenth Century England', *Past and Present Supplement* 4 (Oxford, 1978), 59–68.

[37] For Brembre, see Nightingale, *A Medieval Mercantile Community*, 228–317.

support from the peers, was popularly regarded as unworthy to wield such influence in government.

Popular enthusiasm for the destruction of the king's party may even have broadened the horizon of the Appellants' ambitions: would Gloucester seriously have considered a tilt at the throne if the *communibus* (however defined) had not been behind him? It also showed that they had learned the lessons of the last dozen years or so. As government had grown and politics expanded during the fourteenth century, a larger percentage of the population was affected by what happened at Westminster, and more people took an interest in what was done there.[38] Recent events in England had demonstrated this, notably the Good Parliament of 1376, which had revealed for the first time how effective a force the commons could be, and the Peasants' Revolt of 1381, the first popular uprising in England to be directed principally against royal ministers and the judicial system. The idea that they were in any sense the heirs to Wat Tyler and John Ball would have appalled the Appellants, but the Kentish uprising of April 1388 which sealed Burley's fate was a reminder that public support at any level was worth cultivating. The problem was to ensure that the momentum generated by events did not carry them out of control. Although Henry and Mowbray supported the original Appeal of Treason, as events gathered pace and the net widened, they found themselves being pulled in directions they did not want to go. Henry learned much from his involvement in the political crisis of 1387–8, but most importantly, perhaps, he learned how powerful an agency popular sentiment could be, and how difficult it was, once harnessed, to keep it under control.

While parliament remained in session, the Appellants more or less carried all before them, and before it ended they sought guarantees against future attempts by Richard to exact revenge. Comprehensive pardons were granted to them, to the lords and commons, and to the Londoners; oaths to uphold the acts of the parliament were circulated to the sheriffs of each county; and on 3 June, at high mass in Westminster abbey, the king renewed his coronation oath, the lords renewed their oaths of homage and fealty to him, and William Courtenay, archbishop of Canterbury, pronounced sentence of excommunication on any person who incited the king to reverse the acts of the parliament.[39] Few believed that he would not try,

---

[38] See J. Watts, 'The Pressure of the Public on Later Medieval Politics', in *The Fifteenth Century IV: Political Culture in Late Medieval Britain*, ed. L. Clark and C. Carpenter (Woodbridge, 2004), 159–80; and Watts, *The Making of Polities*.

[39] *PROME*, vii.72–8, 81–2. The commons also granted the Appellants £20,000 for 'saving the king and kingdom' – that is, to pay their retainers for the Radcot Bridge campaign:

however, and Gloucester, Arundel and Warwick were sufficiently appre-
hensive to agree that in future they would never come into the king's presence simultaneously.[40]

Despite his role in the Appeal, Henry had managed to maintain cordial
relations with at least some of those whom the Appellants had dismissed
from the royal household,[41] and for the first time since 1382 he now began
attending court with some regularity and making his voice heard on political matters.[42] Unusually, he spent much of the summer in London. At
some point in the year, probably during the summer, he suffered from a
bout of the pox and, whether because of this or not, he did not take part
in either of the English military ventures of the summer, which was
perhaps fortunate since neither was a success.[43] The earl of Arundel's
expedition to Brittany in June 1388 consumed most of the supply voted by
the commons but achieved little, while an attempt to drive off a Scottish
raiding party ended in English defeat at Otterburn ('Chevy Chase') on
5 August. A week after this, when the king issued a summons for a punitive
expedition to Scotland, Henry transported harness and other equipment
from London to Leicester in preparation for the campaign, but in the event
it was cancelled, it being considered too late in the year to mount an effective response.[44] All this was disappointing, and by the time that another
parliament met at Cambridge on 9 September – barely three months from

---

PROME, vii.67; *CPR 1385–9*, 456. For the schedule of the oath sent to the sheriff of Sussex,
dated 4 June 1388, see C 49/96; 170 Sussex men (thirty-five clerics, ninety-five gentry and
forty burgesses) swore it. On 31 May, Richard invited the lords and commons to his manor
of Kennington for a banquet to celebrate the dissolution of parliament.

[40] *CE*, 367.

[41] Sir Thomas Trivet, who was suspected of having advised the king to lay an ambush for
the three senior Appellants in mid-November, received a cloth of velvet as a gift from
Henry, and Sir Richard Abberbury entertained Henry at his house and was given a livery
gown by him (DL 28/1/2, fos. 5v, 11v, 16v, 5r, 17r).

[42] For example, he began regularly to secure pardons or grants from the king on behalf of
other men: *CFR 1383–91*, 237; *CPR 1385–9*, 368, 406, 409, 439, 452, 461, 510, 531; *CPR 1388–
92*, 7, 29, 41, 100, 128, 150, 177, 449, 463; *CPR 1391–6*, 189, 332, 372. He may also have used
his influence to secure approval for his father's plans to make peace with Juan of Castile,
although it has been argued that this was a betrayal of English interests in the Iberian peninsula: for different views of this see P. Russell, *The English Intervention in Spain and Portugal in the
Time of Edward III and Richard II* (Oxford, 1955), 504–14; Goodman, *John of Gaunt*, 129–30;
Westminster Chronicle, 371. Gaunt sent Sir Thomas Percy to England in the spring of 1388 to
ask for approval for the settlement, and Henry certainly communicated with Percy (DL
28/1/2, fo. 5r). Gaunt was given permission by the king to finalize the settlement on 1 June
1388 (*Foedera*, vii.587–8), but even after this Gaunt may have broken the agreement.

[43] In London, he stayed partly at St David's Inn in Fleet Street. For medicines, smocks
and breeches, and a gilded spike or needle *pro pokkes domini aperiendo* ('for lancing the lord's
pustules'), see DL 28/1/2, fos 15r–v.

[44] Ibid.; *Westminster Chronicle*, 350–1; Goodman, *Loyal Conspiracy*, 50; *CPR 1385–9*, 606, 610.

the dissolution of the Merciless Parliament – public support for the Appellant regime was ebbing; in fact this assembly was to mark the start of the process whereby Richard recovered his authority.

The main concern of the commons at Cambridge was law and order, an issue upon which they and the lords did not see eye to eye. Richard exploited their disagreements, thereby winning back some of that gentry support which he had so conspicuously lacked during the previous year.[45] Yet the real reason for the upturn in the king's fortunes was simply that the death or exile of several of his closest friends had removed the chief reason why the Appellant coalition had come together in the first place. Its fragility now manifested itself. Henry and Mowbray were reconciled to the court during the winter of 1388–9; Gloucester, Arundel and Warwick, however, were not. Mowbray in particular was once again, by the spring of 1389, basking in the royal sunshine that he had enjoyed in the early to mid-1380s.[46] Henry never enjoyed – and never sought – that level of intimacy with Richard. He received one or two relatively minor gifts from the king,[47] but with the resources of the Lancastrian inheritance behind him he felt no need to compete for favours, preferring to cultivate a discreet, though not aloof, distance from the court. He did, however, attend the king's council intermittently, and occasionally witnessed royal charters, which he had never done before February 1388.[48] He was certainly in the council chamber at Westminster on 3 May 1389 when Richard sprang a surprise by announcing that, since he had now reached the age of twenty-two, he proposed to take personal charge of government. Thomas Arundel was dismissed from the chancellorship, Gloucester and Warwick from the council, and the earl of Arundel from the office of admiral; the two chief justices whom the Appellants had appointed were also removed, as were many of those who had been brought into the royal household and administration over the past eighteen months. The council, said Knighton, made no attempt to oppose the king's will, 'but all praised God that He had provided them with so wise a king to watch over them in future'.[49]

[45] *PROME*, vii.121–6; Tuck, *Richard II and the English Nobility*, 134–7; Saul, *Richard II*, 199–201.

[46] C. Given-Wilson, 'Thomas Mowbray, First Duke of Norfolk', *ODNB*, 39.590–5.

[47] In February 1389, for example, a breastplate forfeited by John Beauchamp of Holt, one of the knights executed in the Merciless Parliament (*CCR 1385–9*, 571).

[48] Henry witnessed charters in February, June, October and November 1388: C 53/162; when not at court or in London in 1388–9, he often stayed at Kenilworth (*CPR 1396–9*, 122, 518, 548, confirmations of grants dated 17 and 18 Oct. 1388, 12 June and 1 July 1389).

[49] *Westminster Chronicle*, 391–3, 401: a further wave of dismissals of those associated with the Appellants followed in July; *Knighton*, 528–31; *SAC I*, 866–7, suggests an angrier king than other chroniclers imply. The official proclamation, dated 8 May, is in *CCR 1385–9*, 671,

The royalist revanche of May 1389 was intended to draw a line under the crisis which had engulfed English politics since October 1386. The Appellant coalition had fractured long before this, in fact it barely outlasted the Appeal of Treason; even by the time the second session of the Merciless Parliament began in April 1388, Henry and Mowbray had probably decided, in common with many of their fellow peers, that they wanted no further part in the increasingly grisly spectacle which was unfolding, and eighteen months later the breach was complete. At a council meeting at Clarendon on 13 September 1389, it was reported that Gloucester, Arundel and Warwick (none of whom was present) were anxious to re-establish friendship and concord with the king and council and to abolish the suspicion and mistrust existing between them.[50] Henry was by now a member of that council, as was Mowbray, and both were present at the meeting – a telling indication of the distance that now yawned between them and their former colleagues-in-arms. Two months later Henry was still with the king at Westminster,[51] but by now he knew that his days in the political spotlight were coming to an end: on 19 November 1389, after three years and four months abroad, John of Gaunt landed at Plymouth, declaring his intention to restore peace and harmony between the king and the nobles.[52] Henry was free to step back into his father's shadow – or to embark on new ventures.

676. Richard's inspiration was surely the identical action taken by his near-contemporary Charles VI in November 1388 (Saint-Denys, 555ff.).

[50] POPC, i.12. The last instalment of the £20,000 granted to the Appellants in the Merciless Parliament was paid a month later, on 20 October: Issues of the Exchequer Henry III to Henry VI, ed. F. Devon (London, 1837), 239; CCR 1389–92, 27, 128.

[51] He witnessed two charters dated 14 November 1389 (C 53/162).

[52] Westminster Chronicle, 407–9; SAC I, 891–5.

Chapter 5

THE MAKING OF A HERO (1390–1393)

Despite his failure to curb the cruder instincts of the senior Appellants, Henry's adherence to the opposition in 1387–8 had asserted the untouch-ability of the Lancastrian inheritance without causing an irreparable breach with the crown. At the same time, the credit he won at Radcot Bridge set in motion the process of fashioning for him a reputation for chivalric prowess and military ability which he would never lose, and which would win him admirers at home and abroad and attract able young warriors to his war-band and his causes. The four years following Gaunt's return to England consolidated this reputation, for a number of factors now made it possible for him to fulfil the dream of almost every young nobleman of the age: to joust with Europe's best, to crusade and to visit the Holy Land. First, Henry's father was now one of the richest men in Europe, for the 1388 Treaty of Bayonne between Gaunt and King Juan of Castile stipulated that, in return for renouncing his claim to the throne of Castile, Gaunt would receive a down payment of £100,000 sterling and an annual pension of £6,600 for life: it was Spanish gold – carried to England on the backs of forty-seven mules – which funded Henry's overseas travels between 1390 and 1393.[1] Secondly, the three-year Anglo-French truce of June 1389 opened up the prospect of an extended cessation of hostilities such as often produced an upsurge of crusading activity (as it had in the 1360s); thirdly, the purging of the royal court in 1387–8, followed by the restoration of royal authority in May 1389, had brought a degree of calm to the English political scene. For a twenty-three-year-old with pedigree, means and a thirst for glory, this can hardly have seemed a more propitious time to set out to make a name for himself.

Opportunities to do so abounded. In the autumn of 1389, three French knights, Jean Boucicaut the younger, Renaud de Roye and Jean de Saimpy,

[1] Goodman, *John of Gaunt*, 345; *Expeditions to Prussia and the Holy Land Made by Henry Earl of Derby in the Years 1390–1 and 1392–3*, ed. L. Toulmin Smith (Camden Society, New Series, 1894), lxxxvi; Palmer, *England, France and Christendom*, 142.

sent out heralds to issue a formal challenge to all comers (but especially, it is clear, to the English, whose presumption they resented) to meet them for a friendly trial of arms at St-Inglevert, halfway between English-held Calais and Boulogne. Henry soon made up his mind to attend, a fact which he and Gaunt were keen to publicize, for the St-Inglevert jousts were bound to attract attention.[2] They began on 21 March 1390 and lasted for a month, with Fridays designated as rest days. One hundred and five English knights and esquires made the journey, each of whom took his turn at jousting with one or other of the Frenchmen, but it was Henry who was singled out for his valour.[3] Gaunt had written in advance asking Boucicaut if he would be prepared to run ten rather than the usual five courses with his son, since he knew him to be an exceptionally valiant knight and wanted Henry to learn from him, to which Boucicaut acquiesced.[4] The monk of Saint-Denys, the French royal chronicler, and an anonymous poet who celebrated the gathering both described Henry and his retainers as the bravest of all the challengers. Also noted was the splendour of the gifts he distributed to the Frenchmen.[5]

The core of Henry's retinue at St-Inglevert comprised his eighteen-year-old half-brother, John Beaufort; Sir Robert Ferrers, a long-standing Lancastrian retainer who in 1392 would marry Beaufort's sister Joan; Henry's boyhood companion, Sir Thomas Swynford; Henry Percy ('Hotspur'), the son of the earl of Northumberland; and Sir Thomas Rempston;[6] another group of Englishmen included servants of Henry's

---

[2] According to the chronicler of Bern, Gaunt despatched his herald to various parts of Europe to proclaim the jousts: Froissart, *Oeuvres*, ed. Kervyn de Lettenhove (Brussels, 1867–77), xiv.105–51, 406–20; *Saint-Denys*, i.673–83; English chroniclers were less well informed, but see *Knighton*, 432; *Westminster Chronicle*, 432.

[3] Most of them acquitted themselves respectably, although the anonymous poet named eight Englishmen who 'failed in their duty' and were disgraced; according to Froissart a Bohemian knight in the following of Queen Anne of England, 'Herr Hans', dishonoured himself by striking a foul sideways blow at Boucicaut.

[4] 'Le Livre des Faicts du Bon Messire Jean le Maingre dit Boucicaut', in *Collection Complète de Mémoires Relatifs à l'Histoire de France*, ed. M. Petitot, vols 6–7 (Paris, 1819), vi.430.

[5] 'In sum, so that the truth be known/In all, there jousted one hundred and five/But let it never be forgotten/That the noble earl of Derby/Ran, against each of our men/Five lances, as I myself saw': *Chronographia Regum Francorum*, ed. H. Moranvillé (SHF, 3 vols, Paris, 1891–7), iii.99; Froissart, *Oeuvres*, xiv.417, 419; *Knighton*, 432. Strangely, Knighton did not mention Henry, instead singling out John Lord Beaumont and Sir Philip Courtenay as the Englishmen most deserving of praise. Indeed, Henry's presence at the jousts seems to have gone unremarked in English sources: Richard II's safe-conducts to the French knights were issued at the request of Beaumont, Sir Peter Courtenay, Sir Thomas Clifford, Henry's brother-in-law John Holand earl of Huntingdon, and his former co-Appellant Thomas Mowbray, the earl marshal: *Foedera*, vii.663 (9 March), 665–6 (13 March).

[6] The names of Henry's retainers were so comprehensively garbled by the French chroniclers that most of them are impossible to identify. The monk of Saint-Denys gives the

such as Thomas Totty, John Dalingridge and Ralph Rochford. This impressive Lancastrian showing at St-Inglevert – at least a dozen and probably more – was not merely to allow Henry to cut a figure among European chivalry; it also had a more practical purpose, for Henry had decided by now to go on crusade during the summer, and he was gathering about him like-minded young warriors to form the nucleus of his retinue.

The theatre of crusading to which Henry was initially attracted was the North African or Barbary coastline, where an expedition led by Louis II, duke of Bourbon, had been preparing for several months to besiege the principal Tunisian port of Mahdia.[7] On 9 May 1390, therefore, having been back in England for only two or three weeks, Henry once again crossed to Calais with a retinue of about 120 men and wrote to Paris to seek a safe-conduct from King Charles VI to pass through France to Marseilles, Bourbon's port of embarkation.[8] For some reason, this was refused. Perhaps, despite the truce, the French were still wary of allowing armed retinues led by English nobles to traverse the length of France.[9] On the other hand, John Beaufort was given a safe-conduct, as were several other English knights, and it is difficult to escape the conclusion that there was something personal involved in the rejection of Henry's request, perhaps resentment at the life-grant to John of Gaunt of the duchy of Aquitaine three months earlier, arousing suspicions at the French court that his son's retinue might be diverted on its way to Marseilles.[10] Fortunately

---

following names: Henry Percy, John Courtenay, Robert de Britenac, Herbelain Alain, Thomelin de Fanteston and John Harrington; the anonymous poet has Hervi de Persy (Percy), John Coutenai, Robert Bridelai, Eloi Barclai, Thomelin Nosenton and Jehan Hareton. Despite the variations, these are clearly attempts at naming the same six persons (*Saint-Denys*, i.683; Froissart, *Oeuvres*, xiv.415).

[7] The idea that Henry was already planning in January 1390 to go to Prussia is based on the misdating to 27 January 1390, rather than, correctly, to 27 January 1391, of a letter from Richard II to the king of Poland requesting a safe-conduct for Henry. The letter clearly states that Henry was already (*jam existens*) in Prussia, and that what he sought was permission to venture further into 'very remote parts': *The Diplomatic Correspondence of Richard II*, ed. E. Perroy (Camden Third Series, 48, 1933), no. 116 and p. 218; F. Du Boulay, 'Henry of Derby's Expeditions to Prussia 1390–1 and 1392', in *The Reign of Richard II*, ed. F. Du Boulay and C. Barron (London, 1971), 153–72, at p. 155.

[8] *Westminster Chronicle*, 432–4; DL 28/3/2, fo. 18v; *Expeditions*, xxxix–xlii, 8, 15.

[9] Froissart, *Oeuvres*, xiv.154–5. It is worth noting that Boucicaut was also prevented by the French king from joining Bourbon's expedition; Bourbon's crusade was regarded with a degree of disapproval in Paris.

[10] For the grant to Gaunt, which named Richard II as king of France and thus probably ruffled some feathers at the French court, see Goodman, *John of Gaunt*, 195; it is possible that Richard, jealous of Henry's growing reputation, influenced the decision (C. Tyerman, *England and the Crusades* (Chicago, 1988), 278–9).

for Henry, he had an alternative plan.[11] Returning to England on 5 June, he immediately began preparations to depart for the Baltic. While Henry and Mary (now pregnant with their fourth child) stayed first with Gaunt at Hertford and Leicester and then at Bolingbroke, stores were collected at Boston and two boats were chartered, skippered by Hermann and Hankyn from Gdansk and piloted by lodesmen from the Baltic. Wainscotting was purchased for Henry's cabin and his hammock slung in it. By 19 July all was ready. Henry and his retinue embarked, and the two boats were towed out into the Wash to begin their journey.[12] Three weeks later, on 8 August, Henry stepped ashore at Rixhöft, about thirty miles north of Gdansk.

By the time Henry arrived on the Baltic coast in the summer of 1390, the 'interminable crusade' between the Christian Knights of the Teutonic Order and the kingdom of Lithuania had already endured for over a century and had attracted the service of thousands of Western European knights, including hundreds of Englishmen.[13] Founded in the twelfth century to support Latin crusaders in the Holy Land, the Order had gradually transferred its energy first to the conquest of Prussia and then, once that had been achieved, to the war against Lithuania, upon which its *raison d'être* had come to depend. It was thus inconvenient for the Knights when, in February 1386, King Jogailo of Lithuania, as part of a dynastic arrangement by which he married the Polish Queen Hedwig and became king of Poland too, accepted baptism and proclaimed the conversion of Lithuania to Catholicism, simultaneously adopting the Christian name Wladyslaw. Fortunately for the Order, Jogailo appointed his brother Skirgailo as regent of Lithuania, a decision which alienated their ambitious cousin Vitold, who, in 1389, fled Jogailo's court and asked the Knights for assistance. Anxious to help him, they soon found reasons to do so:

[11] The writ by which Henry appointed his clerk, Richard Kingston, as his treasurer of war, which was dated 6 May 1390 at London, designated Kingston's responsibility as being 'for these journeys which we have arranged to make to the parts of Barbary and of Prussia'. What exactly this tells us about Henry's intentions is, however, far from clear. He may already, on 6 May, have suspected that he might be denied a safe-conduct by Charles VI (*Expeditions*, 1–2, and for Henry's household expenses in Calais, 5–34).

[12] On board were fine spices, fruit and nuts (including 450 lbs of almonds), silver-embossed crockery and jewellery, weaponry, saddles, ropes and cages full of live poultry: *Expeditions*, 23–4, 27, 31–2, 37–8.

[13] T. Guard, *Chivalry, Kingship and Crusade: The English Experience in the Fourteenth Century* (Woodbridge, 2013), 72–97; E. Christiansen, *The Northern Crusades: The Baltic and the Catholic Frontier 1100–1525* (London, 1980), 132; *Crusade and Conversion on the Baltic Frontier 1150–1500*, ed. A. Murray (Aldershot, 2001); W. Paravicini, *Die Preussenreisen des Europäischen Adels* (2 vols, Sigmaringen, 1989–95).

Jogailo may have converted, but many of his subjects were slow to follow suit. Moreover, Samogitia, the 'Wilderness' to the north of the River Neman (or Memel), which had been fiercely contested throughout the fourteenth century, was still openly pagan. This suited Vitold well, for he claimed Samogitia as his: on 19 January 1390, therefore, he made an alliance with the Order providing for a joint campaign, or *reyse*, against Vilnius, Skirgailo's capital, and, as was customary, the participation of Western knights and nobles was invited.[14] What this meant was that the 'crusade' in which Henry participated in the summer of 1390 actually involved taking sides in a Lithuanian dynastic dispute *against* the ruler who had just accomplished precisely what the Order existed in order to achieve: the conversion of Lithuania.[15]

There is no evidence to indicate that Henry or his hosts allowed this fact to trouble them. It is easy to take a sceptical view of the motivation of the Western European reinforcements who arrived almost every year to participate in the *reysen*: the quest for honour and reputation, the desire to cut a figure in the international theatre of chivalric renown, was certainly a powerful driving force for many who chose to make the journey, including, surely, Henry himself.[16] Yet they also sincerely believed that they were defending, even expanding, Christendom. Describing themselves more often as pilgrims than crusaders, some sought spiritual regeneration, others went as an act of expiation, in fulfilment of a vow made at a time of personal danger, or on behalf of a friend or relative unable to go in person. Any or all of these motives might have stirred Henry. Participation in the *reyse* also tended to run in families, and both Henry's grandfather, Henry of Grosmont, and his father-in-law Humphrey de Bohun had campaigned

---

[14] *Expeditions*, xiv–xv; du Boulay, 'Henry of Derby's Expeditions', 157–9.

[15] A. Ehlers, 'The Crusade of the Teutonic Knights against Lithuania Reconsidered', in *Crusade and Conversion*, ed. Murray, 21–44. The crusading status of the expeditions organized by the Knights was open to some doubt, for although terms such as 'pilgrimage' and 'fighting against the enemies of God' were commonly used by Westerners to explain their participation in the *reysen*, there is little evidence of crusade preaching, 'taking the cross', or the issue of crusading bulls by the papacy, as was commonly done for Mediterranean campaigns against the infidel.

[16] What the Order laid on for them has been described alternatively as a 'safari' or as 'a knightly package tour, complete with feasting, hunting, military action, and even a system of prizes to appeal to the most restless and vainglorious noblemen': Christiansen, *Northern Crusades*, 151; Tyerman, *England and the Crusades*, 267. The prizes were awarded at the *Ehrentisch*, the table of honour at which foreign knights were fêted once the *reyse* was over, with those reputed to have performed best being allowed the top places at the table. See Chaucer's comment on the Knight in the *Canterbury Tale* (Prologue, lines 52–4) that 'Ful ofte tyme he hadde the bord bigonne/Above alle naciouns in Pruce./In Lettow hadde he reysed and in Ruce'.

with the Knights in Prussia, in 1351–2 and 1362–3, respectively.[17] John of Gaunt, deprived of the opportunity to crusade himself, certainly encouraged his son to go, and footed the bill.[18] Henry's half-brother, John Beaufort, and his brother-in-law, John Holand, were also enthusiastic crusaders. By the conventions of the time, this was a holy war in a noble and universal cause. Not everyone, it is true, shared that conviction, but the fact that Henry went to Prussia does not mean that he never thought seriously about the issues involved.[19]

Henry remained in Prussia from 8 August 1390 to 31 March 1391.[20] His household consisted of seventy to eighty men, although for the campaign into Lithuania he also recruited locally, bringing the strength of his war-band up to about 150.[21] The *reyse* proper began on 18 August when the company left Königsberg and struck north into 'le Wyldrenesse', a fearsome stretch of heavily forested and waterlogged terrain about a hundred miles wide, where additional horses had to be requisitioned to carry the provisions because the wagons became bogged down in the flooded tracks.[22] Ragnit on the River Neman was reached on 22 August, and here Henry's contingent met up with the Order's main force under Prince Vitold and Marshal Engelhardt Rabe. Hearing that Skirgailo was encamped a dozen miles north-east of Kaunas, the allies crossed the Nerva and, against heavy opposition which claimed several lives including that of the English knight John Loudham, achieved what soon came to be trumpeted as a famous victory. According to the report that reached England, Henry's men captured three or four dukes and killed three others, along with 300 or more of the enemy's finest soldiers.[23] There were, certainly, prisoners and much booty taken, and Skirgailo, who had watched the action from a nearby hilltop, was forced to retreat to Vilnius, pursued by

[17] Fowler, *King's Lieutenant*, 106; Tyerman, *England and the Crusades*, 268; Guard, *Chivalry, Kingship and Crusade*, 144–58.

[18] Gaunt's Iberian expedition of 1386 was, officially, a crusade against the Schismatic Castilians, but not quite the same as 'proper' crusading: Cf. Goodman, *John of Gaunt*, 200–3.

[19] Tyerman, *England and the Crusades*, 264–5; E. Siberry, 'Criticism of Crusading in Fourteenth-Century England', in *Crusade and Settlement*, ed. P. W. Edbury (Cardiff, 1985), 127–34. Wyclif's followers often criticized crusading, yet several of the Lollard knights of the 1380s and 1390s – John Clanvow, William Nevill, Lewis Clifford, John Montague – themselves went on crusade.

[20] His household account for the full eight months is printed in *Expeditions*, 36–142; see also du Boulay, 'Henry of Derby's Expeditions'.

[21] *Expeditions*, xliii–xlvi, 128–42.

[22] *Expeditions*, 49–50; for the climate and terrain, see Christiansen, *Northern Crusades*, 161–5.

[23] *Westminster Chronicle*, 445–9; *SAC I*, 902–3; the two chroniclers clearly used the same source: an eye-witness account written by someone in Henry's following and probably sent across to England once they had arrived back in Königsberg.

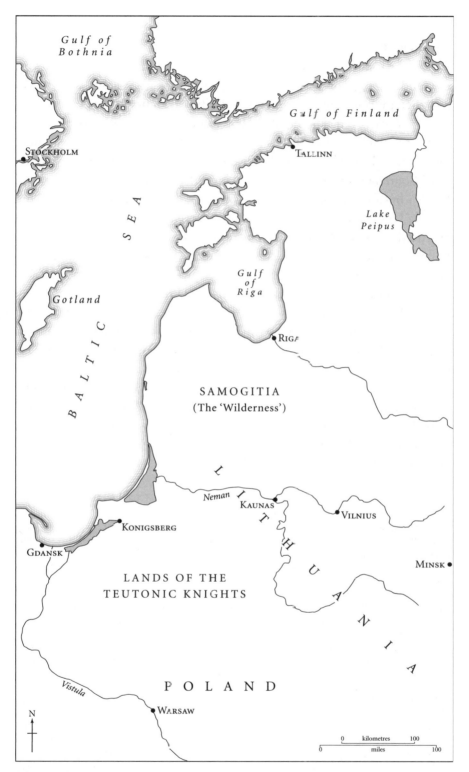

Map 2 Crusading in the Baltic

the Anglo-Prussian forces who, at the beginning of September, laid siege
to the city. Once again the story of their exploits which travelled back to
England grew gratifyingly (for Henry) in the telling. Vilnius was said to
have been taken mainly through the daring of Henry and his men, with
one chronicler even claiming that Henry himself was the first to mount the
walls and place his standard there, while his Prussian and Livonian allies
sat idly by.[24] It was indeed an Englishman in Henry's company, a valet of
Lord Bourchier, who first raised the standard, but it was not on the walls of
Vilnius but on one of its outlying forts, for the city itself withstood the
siege.[25] This was as much success as the allies enjoyed: with winter coming
on and their powder and provisions running low, the drenched and frozen
crusader army abandoned the siege and made its way back to Königsberg,
arriving there on 20 October.[26]

Henry now faced the prospect of two to three months of inactivity
before the frost made the boggy Wilderness tracks passable once more
after the autumn rains.[27] He certainly hoped to campaign again, and on
27 January Richard II wrote at his request to Wladyslaw Jogailo asking for
permission for Henry to travel more widely, but what his plan was is not
clear,[28] and in the event there was no winter *reyse*, so Henry and his retinue
remained at Königsberg until 9 February 1391. It was not a time of hard-
ship. There was plenty of good food, wine and beer to be had; there was
regular jousting, hunting and hawking; beaver and marten fur cloaks were
bought against the cold; Henry's silver dishes were painted with shields of

---

[24] *Westminster Chronicle*, 449; *SAC I*, 903.

[25] Wladyslaw Jogailo wrote to his commander at Vilnius, Clemens of Mostorzow, vice-
chancellor of Poland, in early December, congratulating him on his successful resistance:
Expeditions, cix–cx, 105.

[26] Du Boulay, 'Henry of Derby's Expeditions', 165; *Westminster Chronicle*, 449; *Expeditions*,
cviii, cx.

[27] The winter-*reyse* season might begin in late December, but more often in January or
February; it was shorter than the summer season, usually lasting less than a month, and was
not infrequently cancelled, either because it was too cold or not cold enough: Christiansen,
Northern Crusades, 163–6.

[28] It may have had something to do with the release of two of his knights, John Clifton
and Thomas Rempston, who had been captured during the *reyse*, and on whose behalf
Henry twice sent Derby Herald to parley with Wladyslaw, as well as getting John of Gaunt
to write to the Polish king: *Expeditions*, 108, 111, 139; *Diplomatic Correspondence*, ed. Perroy, 116,
218. Lancaster Herald and the esquire Janico Dartasso were sent back to England with
Henry's letters in November (*Expeditions*, 107–8). According to the report used by the
Westminster chronicler, Marshal Rabe and Henry set off again nine days after arriving
back at Königsberg to intercept an army with which Wladyslaw/Jogailo was planning to
invade Prussia, but this is incorrect. Presumably the author of the report heard rumours of
a planned second campaign, but left for England with his letters before it was cancelled:
Westminster Chronicle, 449.

his arms, and large amounts of fine cloth were purchased, some of it from an English merchant called John Squirrel resident at Königsberg; minstrels, tumblers and dicing provided entertainment. There were also reasons for celebration, for in November news arrived from England of the safe delivery of Henry's fourth son, Humphrey.[29] Naturally it was also important for Henry to advertise his Christianity, which he did by distributing alms to paupers, prisoners and friars, and by capturing or purchasing a number of Lithuanian women and children who were taken back to Königsberg to be converted.[30] The letter describing Henry's exploits which reached England was careful to emphasize this, stating that 11,500 Lithuanian prisoners had been taken back to Prussia or Livonia 'to be made into Christians'.[31] This was, after all, the object of the exercise.

In early February Henry and his household left for Gdansk, where they spent the next six weeks enjoying the amenities and provisions on offer in this vibrant Hanseatic port, the largest and wealthiest town in the eastern Baltic, and preparing for the return journey.[32] As before, two ships were required, both skippered by Germans; three dozen chickens were taken aboard to be fed to the falcons which Henry had recently been given by Conrad von Wallenrod, the Grand-Master of the Teutonic Order in Prussia (he had also been given three young bears and perhaps even an elk).[33] The return journey took a month, reaching Kingston-upon-Hull on 30 April 1391. The first thing Henry did was to make a pilgrimage to the

[29] *Expeditions*, xxxii, 31, 61, 68, 79, 89, 91–2, 100, 103, 107–11, 115. Henry brought six of his own minstrels with him from England; his gambling losses amounted to £69: Guard, *Chivalry, Kingship and Crusade*, 87–9.

[30] The number of 'boys' was probably less than ten; no figure is given for the women: they were lodged with various women at Königsberg and provided with clothes, shoes and food. One of the boys was named after Henry (*Henricus Letoue*): *Expeditions*, 52, 65, 68, 88–9, 90, 92, 110, 113, 116–17.

[31] *Westminster Chronicle*, 449; cf. *SAC I*, 902–3, which gives 'eight' (an error for 'eight thousand') prisoners taken back to Prussia and three thousand to Livonia. Wigand von Marburg said that 7,000 of the enemy were killed or captured, 'most of them pagans' (*Expeditions*, cx).

[32] Henry, his personal servants and close followers took lodgings in a town house belonging to a burgess called Klaus Gottesknecht (which Henry promptly had decorated with a shield of his arms), while his other retainers were accommodated a little outside the city at the bishop's manor: *Expeditions*, xxxii–xxxiv, 72–88, 111. Relations with the local community were not always harmonious: a certain Molwyng Makenhagen, a merchant from Stralsund who had outstanding claims against English pirates, was taken prisoner at one point by some of Henry's men in Gdansk, at which he later protested to Richard II: *Diplomatic Correspondence*, ed. Perroy, p. 213. Pope Boniface IX had declared 1390 to be a jubilee year, so Henry took advantage of the time to gain his indulgence (*absolucione a pena et a culpa*) by offering alms as a pilgrim at each of four churches in Gdansk on seven consecutive days: *Expeditions*, 116–17. It is worth stressing that this was not a crusading but a jubilee indulgence: see Ehlers, 'The Crusade of the Teutonic Knights', 43n.

[33] *Expeditions*, 88, 111.

tomb of John de Thwing, prior of Bridlington (d. 1379), whose canonization he would later support, while his baggage was taken to Bolingbroke
where he arrived on 13 May to be reunited with his family.[34]

Seventeen years later, in conversation with the Hanseatic envoy Arndt
von Dassel, Henry recalled fondly his time in Prussia – his 'gadling days' –
when he had led three hundred men (a pardonable exaggeration) as far as
the 'sacred city' of Vilnius before the onset of winter drove them back to
Königsberg, where the Grand-Master's own physician had tended him
through a serious illness. He was, he declared, a child of Prussia, and there
was no land apart from England that he would rather serve.[35] Diplomatic
niceties apart, he might well have felt nostalgic: for a young man who had
barely been out of England before, he had created a fine impression on the
international stage. English chroniclers declared that 'his pre-eminent
success brought joy to all Christians' and that he had 'fought with the
enemies of Christ's Cross in such a way as to suggest that nothing meant
more to him than to avenge the dishonour of the Crucifix', so that 'his
name was on everyone's lips'.[36] If this was John of Gaunt seeking to carve
out his son's place in history, he seems to have succeeded.[37] Yet it was not
just the English who lauded Henry's deeds. The Prussian chronicler John
von Posilge also praised Henry's performance at the siege of Vilnius,
claiming that he fought most manfully (*gar menlich*) and that it was his perse-
verance which led to the outlying fort being taken.[38] Few qualities were
admired more than manliness, but Richard II had difficulty in persuading
contemporaries that he possessed it, however hard he tried.[39] He could
organize tournaments – as he did at Smithfield in October 1390, during
Henry's absence – but unlike his father, his grandfather and his cousin, he
was not a man who fought real battles.[40] Richard never acquired the chivalric reputation that Henry did, and it piqued him: Henry, after all, had

[34] DL 28/3/3/, m. 3; *Vita*, 126–7, said that several miracles had been reported at Thwing's
tomb in 1389–90; *Expeditions*, 98, 117.

[35] J. Wylie, *History of England under Henry the Fourth* (4 vols, London, 1884–98), iv.8–9. Forty
shillings was paid to a physician from Marienburg who came to visit Henry, probably in late
February: *Expeditions*, 110.

[36] *Knighton*, 537; *Westminster Chronicle*, 458; *De Illustribus Henricis*, 111; BL Add. MS 35,295,
fo. 262r (chronicle of John Strecche).

[37] L. Staley, 'Gower, Richard II, Henry of Derby and the Business of Making Culture',
Speculum 75 (2000), 68–96, at pp. 82, 85, 87.

[38] *Expeditions*, cviii–cix. Wigand von Marburg, the Teutonic Knights' herald, also noted
Henry's participation on the *reyse* (ibid.). I am grateful to Dr Jeff Ashcroft for his help with
medieval German.

[39] C. Fletcher, *Richard II: Manhood, Youth and Politics, 1377–99* (Oxford, 2008).

[40] For the Smithfield tournament, see *Westminster Chronicle*, 450–1 (although neither
Walsingham nor Knighton mentions it); Staley, 'Gower, Richard II, Henry of Derby', 87.

fewer responsibilities. Nor could he have set about the business of acquiring a reputation without his father's money behind him: the cost of his crusade was £4,360, of which £3,542 came from Gaunt, enabling Henry in turn to demonstrate the largesse to his hosts and companions that was expected of him.[41] Doubtless Gaunt considered it money well spent.

Backlit by this glow of chivalric ardour, Henry's fifteen months in England, from May 1391 to July 1392, were the apogee of his gilded youth. He jousted on at least four occasions: at Brambletye in early July 1391, at Waltham in early October, at Hertford around Christmas and at Kennington on some unspecified date. For each of the first two he bought eighteen new lances in addition to other weaponry, armour and harness, some of it from the famous metal workshops of Milan.[42] His taste for spectacle and desire to advertise his wealth and status were the equal of any noble of his time, as witness the £740 which he spent on drapery, mercery, embroidery, furs and jewels during this period.[43] New suits and mantles of silk, satin, velvet or brocade for almost every occasion were made up by his tailor John Dyndon, lined with miniver or ermine by his pelterer William Jakes, and embroidered by his broderer Peter Swan with intricate and costly fringes, sleeves and collars of lace, tissue, taffeta, spangles or gold thread. The livery devices adorning them grew ever more elaborate. One of Henry's velvet mantles had sleeves embroidered with a design of Saint John's wort and his motto 'Soveyne Vous de Moy' (forget me not). Chevrons, wheels, mulberries and flowers were worked into the designs. One of his belts had silver-gilt leaves and fronds hanging from it, weighing nine and half troy marks (just over six pounds). Another gown had sleeves into which were sewn 320 silver-gilt leaves, each one reading 'Soveyne Vous de Moy'. A golden brooch engraved with 'Sanz mal penser' (think no evil) echoed the

[41] The 'gifts' section of Henry's account totals almost exactly £400: *Expeditions*, 3–4, 142, 104–15. It is not clear whether the £3,542 from Gaunt recorded in Henry's account included a sum of £133 6s 8d, which his father also gave him on his return (*pro apparatu suo in primo adventu de Prus*): DL 28/1/3, fo. 1r.

[42] DL 28/1/3, fos. 2v, 3v, 8r, 11r, 13v–14v, 16v, 17r–v, 18r. This is probably Brambletye near Basildon in Essex, although the name also occurs in Surrey and in East Sussex. His agent was 'Francis of Milan', that is, Francis de Courte, later one of his chamber knights. Henry may also have jousted in France, for on 1 January 1392 two French heralds had arrived at Hertford to announce the holding of 'jousts of peace', although when and where are not stated: DL 28/1/3, fo. 20v.

[43] For what follows see especially DL 28/1/3, fos. 2r–16v (William Loveney's account of Henry's great wardrobe May 1391 to May 1392); also the series of accounts of his receiver-general, John de Leventhorpe, for the period from 1 May 1391 to 1 February 1395 (DL 28/3/3 and 4). The two goldsmiths who mainly supplied Henry were called Hermann and Louis.

'Honi soit qui mal y pense' of the Order of the Garter. A silver collar encrusted with eight roundels, each one enclosing a Lancastrian S and the figure of a swan (the livery badge of the Bohuns), cost £23; another, costing £17, had golden locks and keys hanging from it, while one of his brooches was made in the shape of a large letter H on each side of a balas ruby. Friends and followers were also encouraged to advertise his largesse and status: thirty silver-gilt collars of Henry's livery were lined with satin before being distributed to his retainers, while his jousting and crusading companions, Sir Robert Ferrers, Sir John Malet and the Bohemian Herr Hans, each received entire satin livery suits.[44] To his wife, Henry sent a garter with a clasp in the shape of a golden hart set in white enamel with a collar costing £9; Mary responded by sending him six yards of blue velvet. For the christening of their daughter Blanche at Peterborough in 1392, all four of their sons had new shirts of cloth from Champagne, and the elder boys, Henry and Thomas, received silver-gilt Lancastrian livery collars.

By the summer of 1392, however, Henry was ready to return to Prussia. Embarking on 24 July at Heacham in Norfolk, he landed just north of Gdansk on 10 August and reached Königsberg on 2 September, only to discover that Prince Vitold was in the process of making his peace with Jogailo and had dismissed all the Western crusaders.[45] Making a virtue of necessity, therefore, Henry arranged for most of the 150–200 retainers and servants who had accompanied him from England to return home, sent a messenger to his father asking for an exchange of money to be arranged for him at Venice and, accompanied by about fifty friends and servants, set out on 22 September for the medieval equivalent of what would later become known as the grand tour.

Henry's itinerary took him first to Frankfurt-am-Oder, then to Prague, where his party rested for eleven days (13–24 October) before moving on to Vienna for the nights of 4–7 November. Crossing the Julian Alps, he reached Venice at the beginning of December, hired a galley from the Venetian Senate, and on 23 December set sail for Jaffa with about forty servants.

[44] A separate entry mentions twelve silver-gilt collars costing £3, possibly in addition to these thirty.

[45] The accounts for this voyage are printed in *Expeditions*, 145–292; see also du Boulay, 'Henry of Derby's Expeditions', 165–7. The Prussian chronicler John von Polsige said that some of Henry's retainers killed a local man, Hans von Tergawisch, in Gdansk, and were thus in disgrace; there were also rumours of an altercation with the Knights over the right to display the banner of St George, claimed by both the English and the Prussians as their patron saint, but the fact that Marshal Rabe gave Henry £400 towards his expenses belies the suggestion that he parted on bad terms with the Knights: *Expeditions*, xlix–l, cxi, 149, 167, 273.

Sailing via Zara, Corfu, Modon in the Morea and Rhodes, he arrived in the Holy Land in late January and remained there ten days, visiting the Holy Sepulchre and probably the Mount of Olives as well. By 6 February he was back in Jaffa, whence he sailed via Cyprus and Rhodes back to Venice, where he arrived on 20 March. He stayed in Venice for Easter, which fell on 6 April, and then a further two weeks at Treviso (12–28 April) preparing for the return journey to England. Moving at a leisurely pace through Padua, Vicenza and Verona, he spent three or four days in Milan (13–16 May), reached Turin on 21 May, and five days later passed over the summit of Mont Cenis – where, a dozen years later, the chronicler Adam Usk would describe being 'almost frozen to death by the snow', even in the middle of summer – and into Savoy.[46] From here Henry's route took him through Burgundy and Champagne to Paris, barely passing more than one night anywhere until he reached the French capital on 22 June.[47] He crossed from Calais to Dover on 29 June and reached London on 5 July 1393.

Henry travelled in great style. Whenever he moved on, heralds and harbingers were sent ahead to proclaim his imminence and requisition supplies and lodgings. Wherever he stayed more than a night or two, local artisans were hired to paint escutcheons of his arms at the door. Riding his favoured white courser, preceded by Thomas his trumpeter,[48] attended by two dozen knights and esquires on horseback with a baggage train bringing up the rear, his entourage generally covered between fifteen and twenty miles a day but could move faster if required: the 375 miles from Vienna to Treviso took just fourteen days, an average of twenty-seven miles a day, including crossing the Julian Alps by the Predil pass.[49] Local guides and porters were hired when necessary, and between Portogruaro and Venice nine men had to break the ice along the road to ease the convoy's passage.[50] Henry was also accompanied by a small but growing menagerie of curious and exotic beasts: he acquired an ostrich in Bohemia, a 'popinjay' (parrot) in Italy as a gift for his wife Mary, and a leopard, probably a present from the king of Cyprus. For the sea-journey from

[46] *Usk*, 211.

[47] Richard II wrote letters, probably at Gaunt's instigation, to the Grand-Master of the Hospitallers at Rhodes, the king of France, the duke of Burgundy, the duke of Orléans and the lords of Savoy and Piedmont, asking them for safe-conducts to allow Henry and up to 200 of his retainers to pass through their lands in order to accomplish his 'pilgrimages and devotions': *Diplomatic Correspondence*, ed. Perroy, no. 166; *ANLF*, nos. 91–5.

[48] For his courser, see G. Stretton, 'Some Aspects of Medieval Travel', *TRHS* 7 (1924), 77–97 at pp. 80–1. He took six minstrels to Prussia, but sent all except Thomas home from Gdansk: *Expeditions*, xcvi, 269.

[49] G. Parks, *The English Traveller to Italy, I: to 1525* (Rome, 1954), 527–8.

[50] *Expeditions*, 207.

Cyprus to Venice, the leopard had its own cabin and mat to lie on and ate a third of a sheep each day.[51]

Of more lasting value were the contacts established by Henry with European princes, prelates and merchants. At Prague, he spent three days staying with the Holy Roman Emperor Wenzel at his country palace at Bettlern; at Vienna, he was the guest of Albert of Hapsburg, duke of Austria, and paid a visit to Sigismund, king of Hungary, whose palace was on the other side of the Danube.[52] When the Venetian Senate heard that Henry was on his way it voted 360 ducats of public money for his accommodation and put a state galley at his disposal, and on his return from the Holy Land the Grand Council allocated a further one hundred gold ducats for a reception in his honour.[53] At Rhodes Henry was hosted in the castle by the Grand Master of the Knights Hospitaller and at Cyprus by King James of Lusignan. He met the patriarch of Friuli and the archbishop of Milan; while at Milan he was also entertained by the mighty Gian Galeazzo Visconti, count of Vertus and lord (later duke) of Milan, who showed him the tombs of St Augustine, Boethius, and Henry's own uncle Lionel of Clarence.[54] In Paris he was shown around the city by the dukes of Berry and Burgundy. Henry also had regular dealings with some of Europe's foremost banking houses. Thanks to his father having deposited £1,333 at Leicester with Matteo, a partner in the Florentine Alberti bank, Henry was able to withdraw 8,888 Venetian ducats from the Alberti offices at Venice at the beginning of February 1393. Lucchese and Lombard bankers provided a further 4,095 ducats, again in return for Gaunt's deposits, in April and May. International religious orders could also double as banking houses: the Prior of the Hospitallers provided Henry with 1,700 ducats at Venice in exchange for an equivalent sum in sterling made over to the Order in England by Gaunt.[55] Having already availed himself of the

---

[51] The leopard came with a keeper, Mark, and was carried on land in a cage dragged by two horses; at sea, oils and spices were bought for it and fourteen sheep carried aboard to feed it: *Expeditions*, lxv, 194, 229–32, 240, 245–6, 251, 285–6. For Mary's popinjay, see DL 28/1/3, fos. 5v, 16r, 17v; 28/1/4, fo. 20r; 28/3/4, fo. 33r; 28/1/2, fo. 16v.

[52] *Expeditions*, 150, 195, 310.

[53] *Calendar of State Papers Venice I, 1202–1509*, ed. R. Brown (London, 1864), 33–4. This states that the duke of Austria was planning to accompany Henry to the Holy Land, which is doubtless why he sent a knight and an esquire of his with Henry to Venice (*Expeditions*, li, 285), but Duke Albert must have changed his mind.

[54] *De Illustribus Henricis*, 100; Clarence had died in Milan in 1368 shortly after marrying Gian Galeazzo's sister Violanta.

[55] *Expeditions*, liv–lv, 150. John of Gaunt's receiver-general's account itemizes some of these sums; Janico Dartasso was sent to Venice in December 1392 with power to act as Henry's attorney: DL 28/3/2, fos. 12r, 17v, 19v.

services of the Hanseatic merchants in Prussia, Henry's dealings with Italian financiers, who provided the motor for the southern European economy, gave him further connections which he would later find useful. With his reputation as a jouster and crusader preceding him, his *courtoisie* and largesse to recommend him,[56] and a pilgrimage to the Holy Sepulchre furnishing an impeccable pretext for his travels, Henry was feted wherever he went. Six years later, Gian Galeazzo's cousin Lucia would declare that if she could have married Henry, she would have waited 'to the very end of her life, even if she knew that she would die three days after the marriage'. Lucia did come to England, though not to marry Henry. In January 1407 she married Edmund, earl of Kent, and although he was killed in the following year she remained in England until her death in 1424.[57]

Another lasting consequence of Henry's expeditions was the formation of a tight-knit circle of companions who would continue to provide him with service, advice and friendship for the remaining two decades of his life. Fellow travellers such as Thomas Swynford, his chaplain Hugh Herle, and his chamberlain Hugh Waterton had been with Henry since his childhood, but others became attached to him principally because of their shared adventures. Peter Bukton, John Norbury, Thomas Erpingham, Thomas Rempston, Robert Litton, Richard Goldesburgh, Ralph Rochford, Francis de Courte and John Dalingridge would all later become officers of Henry's royal household or knights of his chamber; William Lord Willoughby, who accompanied him on both expeditions, was one of the first lords to join him when he returned from exile in 1399; Richard Kingston, his treasurer while abroad, later served as treasurer of the royal household. Sir John Malet did not live to see the usurpation of 1399, though he too was intimate with Henry in the early 1390s. Young and vigorous, Henry enjoyed the camp-fire camaraderie of these years, and although a man of his means would never have had trouble in finding men to serve him, it is worth remembering that their loyalty to him would be repeatedly tested over the next dozen years and never found wanting.

---

[56] The 'gifts' section of his 1392–3 account totalled £648 (*Expeditions*, 290).

[57] *Calendar of State Papers Milan I, 1385–1618*, ed. A. Hinds (London, 1912), 2; *CP*, vii.161–3. For Henry's wedding gift to her, two gold dishes with sun rays engraved inside and outside, see J. Mackman, 'Hidden Gems in the Records of the Common Pleas: New Evidence on the Legacy of Lucy Visconti', in *The Fifteenth Century VIII: Rule, Redemption and Representations in Late Medieval England and France*, ed. L. Clark (Woodbridge, 2008), 59–72 at p. 71.

The cost of Henry's grand tour of 1392–3 was £4,915, the great majority of which was once again supplied by his father.[58] The return on Gaunt's investment was to see his son's reputation for militant piety enhanced yet further. Fifty years later the Augustinian friar John Capgrave wrote an account of Henry's second expedition almost certainly based on a contemporary newsletter. The emphasis throughout was on godly works, the language quasi-hagiographical. The 'pious and venerable' Henry venerated at the Holy Places 'with great devotion'; he tended to paupers 'with great clemency'; he paid large sums to purchase captives so as to restore them to 'the lands of the faithful'; he gazed upon the tomb of St Augustine 'with great contemplation' and successfully 'found the way of peace' by mediating in a dispute between Gian Galeazzo and the Augustinian friars of Milan; indeed, throughout this year of 'solemn pilgrimage' he bore himself and conducted his men so prudently that he brought pleasure to God, honour to the kingdom, and friendship to all with whom he came into contact.[59] Another piece of the jigsaw of Henry's self-image was slotted into place, and contemporaries were impressed. The original prologue to John Gower's poem *Confessio Amantis* included a dedication to Richard II, but when Gower revised it for the second time in 1392 or early 1393, he replaced this with a dedication to 'mine own lord/Who is called Henry of Lancaster:/The high God has proclaimed him/Full of knighthood and all grace'.[60] Such was the renown to which men of Henry's breeding aspired.

[58] Robert of Whitby, Gaunt's receiver-general, handed over £2,000 to Richard Kingston at King's Lynn in July 1392 as well as the total of £2,341 via bank transfers already noted: *Expeditions*, lxxxvii, 149–51. In fact, the £2,000 from Gaunt handed over in July 1392 was not a gift pure and simple, but differentiated into two parts, a straightforward gift of 1,000 marks (£666) and an 'imprest', or loan, of 2,000 marks (£1,333), to be repaid by Henry to his father, but since it was to be repaid from the receipts of the honours of Bolingbroke and Tutbury, both of which Gaunt now granted to Henry, the effect was not greatly different (DL 28/3/2, fos. 18v, 20r). Marshal Rabe's gift of £400 covered most of the remaining expenses.

[59] *De Illustribus Henricis*, 99–101: due attention is also paid to the numerous great personages by whom Henry was entertained and with whom he mingled. The only evidence of captives in the accounts is a 'Henry the Turk' (or 'Henry the Saracen'), brought back to England, as 'Henry the Lithuanian' had been from Prussia.

[60] John Gower, *Confessio Amantis*, ed. R. Peck (Toronto, 1980), 3, 494–5. He renewed his dedication of the poem to Henry in an *explicit* (ibid., 493). For Gower's allegiance to the House of Lancaster, see N. Saul, 'John Gower: Prophet or Turncoat?', in *John Gower, Trilingual Poet. Language, Translation and Tradition*, ed. E. Dutton, with J. Hines and R. F. Yeager (Woodbridge, 2010), 85–97.

Chapter 6

FAMILY AND LANDS (1391–1394)

By the time Henry returned from Jerusalem in June 1393, he and Mary had four sons and a daughter: the future Henry V, born in September 1386 and named after Henry of Grosmont; Thomas, born in the autumn of 1387, named after Earl Thomas; John, born on 20 June 1389, named after Gaunt; Humphrey, born in the autumn of 1390, named after Mary's father; and Blanche, born in the spring of 1392, named after Henry's mother.[1] The survival of Mary's 1387–8 wardrobe account and a number of her devotional books makes it possible to know considerably more about her than about most aristocratic women of the fourteenth century. In 1387–8 she was based at Kenilworth, but from 1390 onwards Peterborough was her home.[2] Henry spent a good deal of his time at Peterborough in the intervals between his travels and his public engagements, and often sent Mary gifts of cloth or delicacies such as fruit and nuts, oysters, mussels and sprats when he was away.[3] Sometimes she travelled with him,[4] but for the most part her social circle comprised other noble women. She remained close to her mother, Joan countess of Hereford, and her sister, Eleanor duchess of Gloucester, exchanging gifts, livery robes and visits with them, as she did with Gaunt's duchess, Constanza, his mistress, Katherine Swynford, and Katherine's daughter, Joan (Beaufort). A particular friend in 1387–8 was Margaret, wife of William Bagot, a confidence conducive to their husbands' relationship.[5] Mary certainly did not shut herself off from public affairs: she kept abreast of developments during the Appellant rising, and in September 1388 William Bagot sent her a message with news of the Cambridge parliament. She also received messengers from Gaunt

---

[1] *SAC II*, 216–18. Within weeks of Henry's return, Mary was pregnant again.

[2] DL 28/1/2, fos. 19r–29r. See also Henry's wardrobe accounts: 28/3/3, 28/3/4, *passim*.

[3] DL 28/1/3, fos. 5v, 16r, 17v; 28/1/4, fo. 20r; 28/3/4, fo. 23r; 28/1/2, fo. 16v; *CPR 1396–9*, 501, 526.

[4] They visited Lincoln together in July 1390, and regularly spent Christmas and New Year together in the Lancastrian household at Hertford: *Expeditions*, 27.

[5] DL 28/1/2, fos. 17r, 21r, 24r, 25v, 26r.

in Bayonne and his ally the king of Portugal, the husband of her sister-in-law Philippa.[6]

However, it was her musical, artistic and religious interests that are most likely to have influenced Henry, for Mary came from a family more closely identified with the discerning patronage of art and literature than any other in fourteenth-century England. Humphrey de Bohun, earl of Hereford and Essex (d.1361) – 'a retiring, priest-dominated bachelor' – was an early patron of the alliterative revival in English vernacular poetry in the mid-fourteenth century, while his nephew Humphrey (Mary's father) was a patron of Froissart.[7] Mary herself paid for a Latin primer to be bound in London, for strings for a harp (*cithara*), and for a ruler with which to line parchment 'for singing notes to be added', suggesting that she did not just sing and play but also composed music, as Henry may have done.[8] He too owned a harp and bought a 'pipe called a recorder' in the same year. They kept ten minstrels in their household and regularly rewarded itinerant pipers, fiddlers, trumpeters, clarioners, nakerers (cymbal-players). A payment to 'singing clerks' indicates an interest in polyphony as well as minstrelsy.[9]

Yet it was as commissioners of high-quality illuminated prayer-books that successive generations of Mary's family are best known.[10] About a dozen manuscripts – psalters, books of hours and bible leaves – surviving from the second half of the fourteenth century are associated with the Bohuns, usually on the basis of heraldic evidence, although they also conform to a distinctive style of illumination, characterized by their depiction of historical or narrative cycles (generally from the bible), their crowded and small-scale compositions featuring delicate but animated figures with large heads, the proliferation of marginal decoration, much of

---

[6] DL 28/1/2, fos. 26r–v, 29r.

[7] T. Turville-Petre, *The Alliterative Revival* (Cambridge, 1977), 40–2; Given-Wilson, *Chronicles*, 209–11; Davies, *Lords and Lordship*, 74 (quote); J. Catto, 'The Prayers of the Bohuns', in *Soldiers, Nobles and Gentlemen. Essays in Honour of Maurice Keen*, ed. P. Coss and C. Tyerman (Woodbridge, 2009), 112–25, at p. 116. The 'Bridlington Prophecies', written by the Augustinian friar John Erghome around 1370, were dedicated to Mary's father.

[8] DL 28/1/2 (*pro regulando unius pellis pergameni pro cantando supernotando*).

[9] DL 28/1/2, fos. 9v, 15v; 28/1/4, fo. 4v.

[10] 'No other English family of the fourteenth century seems to have taken such an active or personal interest in illuminated manuscripts': L. Sandler, *Illuminators and Patrons in Fourteenth-Century England: The Psalter and Hours of Humphrey de Bohun and the Manuscripts of the Bohun Family* (London, 2014); L. Sandler, *Gothic Manuscripts 1285–1385* (2 vols, Oxford, 1986), i.34–6, and ii.146–65; L. Sandler, 'The Bohun Women and Manuscript Patronage in Fourteenth-Century England', in *Patronage, Power and Agency in Medieval Art*, ed. C. Hourihane (Princeton, 2013), 275–96; Dennison, 'British Library, Egerton MS 3277'. My thanks to Julian Luxford for his help with this topic.

it foliate and sinuous but also at times playful and even irreverent, and a profusion of heraldic devices demonstrating the links between the Bohuns and the English royal family. Most, and perhaps all of them, were executed in the manuscript workshop maintained by the family at Pleshey (Essex), overseen initially by the elder Humphrey's illuminator, the Augustinian friar John Teye, and then from the mid-1380s by Teye's pupil, John Hood.[11] After the second Earl Humphrey's death in 1373, the Bohun tradition of commissioning high-quality manuscripts was continued by his widow, Countess Joan, at Rochford (Essex), by his daughter Eleanor and her husband Thomas of Woodstock at Pleshey, and by Mary.[12] Two richly illuminated psalters, made on Joan's orders to celebrate Mary's marriage to Henry in 1381, contain linked Bohun and Lancastrian heraldic shields; Mary's has a portrait of her, draped in the arms of England and Bohun, kneeling before the enthroned Virgin and Child, while Henry's included his shield of arms in five places.[13] A third psalter showed the tendrils enveloping the Lancaster and Bohun arms touching as if to symbolize Henry and Mary's union, the alliance of two of England's greatest families.[14]

A Book of Hours made for Mary following her marriage indicates the quality of her piety. Its opening folio has a miniature of a praying woman wearing the arms of Bohun and England, while its contents place striking emphasis on the penitential psalms and the saving of sinners.[15] One of the prayers which she added to another psalter asked God to 'breathe into my heart that interior sweetness of spirit with which you inspired your child David [and] open, O Lord, the ear of my soul to the voice of your love . . . a comfort in adversity, a counsel in time of doubt, a caution in time of

[11] In 1384, Teye received permission from the Augustinian prior-general 'to summon Brother Henry Hood for one year only to instruct him in the art of illuminating books': Dennison, 'British Library Egerton MS 3277', 132–3. These manuscripts are now dispersed in a variety of libraries and museums – in Vienna, Edinburgh, Copenhagen, Schloss Pommersfelden, and Lichtenthal abbey near Baden-Baden as well as in London, Oxford and Cambridge.

[12] Edinburgh, National Library of Scotland, MS Adv. 18.6.5, for an illuminated psalter and book of hours made for Eleanor (fo. 148v for the inscription, 'this book belonged to Eleanor de Bohun, duchess of Gloucester, who ordered it to be written').

[13] Oxford, Bodleian Library MS Auctarum D.4.4, fo. 181v; L. Sandler, 'Lancastrian Heraldry in the Bohun Manuscripts', in *The Lancastrian Court: Harlaxton Medieval Studies XIII*, ed. J. Stratford (Donnington, 2003), 221–32; Cambridge, Fitzwilliam Museum MS 38-1950; Sandler, *Gothic Manuscripts*, ii.157–61; cf. also *The Cambridge Illuminations*, ed. P. Binski and S. Panayotova (London, 2005), 189–90. BL Egerton MS 3277 may also include a 'portrait' of Mary (Dennison, 'British Library, Egerton MS 3277').

[14] L. F. Sandler, 'The Lichtenthal Psalter and the Manuscript Patronage of the Bohun Family', *Studies in Medieval and Renaissance Art History*, 38 (2004); see Plate 14 (fo. 8).

[15] Copenhagen, Konigelige Bibliotek MS Thott. 547.4; Sandler, *Gothic Manuscripts*, ii.161–2.

prosperity and a cure in time of sickness'.[16] Such sentiments locate Mary within that stream of late fourteenth-century aristocratic piety which emphasized contemplation and self-examination, a movement owing much to the writings of the hermit and mystic Richard Rolle (d.1349). She probably imbibed this from her mother,[17] but it was a devotional preference which she also shared with members of her husband's family such as Henry's grandfather Henry of Grosmont, who composed the remarkable *Livre de Seyntz Medicines*, a sustained exercise in personal penitence and soul-searching, and his father Gaunt, whose search for a more meaningful form of religious expression had led him to dabble with the Lollards.[18] Mary's household accounts also suggest that her tastes were modest. Her personal servants were not numerous: a receiver (William Burgoyne), a tailor (William Thornby), three ladies-in-waiting (Agnes Burgoyne, Alice Tinneslowe and Mary Hervy), two esquires (Peter de Melbourne and Robert Hartfeld), and an ever-expanding array of nurses and governesses for her family.[19] Her wardrobe expenses in 1387–8 amounted to £202, of which £167 was spent on drapery, mercery and furs; by 1390 she was receiving an annual allowance from Henry of £166 for personal items, and there is no evidence that she exceeded this, although her expenses are not itemized.[20]

This represented less than 10 per cent of her husband's annual income. Thanks to his father's willingness to fund his travels, Henry discovered on his first return to England in April 1391 that his receiver-general John Leventhorpe had accumulated an unspent surplus of £1,574; by early 1393

[16] Catto, 'The Prayers of the Bohuns', 120, 125 (from Bodleian MS Auctarum D.4.4).

[17] J. Catto, 'Religion and the English Nobility in the Later Fourteenth Century', in *History and Imagination*, ed. H. Lloyd-Jones, V. Pearl and B. Worden (London, 1981), 43–55, at pp. 49–51.

[18] Fowler, *King's Lieutenant*, 193–6, and above, pp. 32–4. An illuminated manuscript in the Library of Liverpool Hope University was almost certainly owned by either Henry or Mary; as in the Oxford psalter, the prayers are in Latin and were intended as an aid to meditation: Catto, 'The Prayers of the Bohuns', 120–1 (Liverpool Hope University, Gradwell Collection, MS Upholland College 165). For Henry's piety, see also below, pp. 377–81.

[19] DL 28/3/3, m. 4; 28/1/4, fo. 3, 21r; 28/3/4, fos. 20v, 33v. In 1391–2, Joanna Waryn was nurse to young Henry, Joanna Donnesmore to Thomas and John; by 1393, Mary Hervy had become governess to 'the young lords' (Henry, Thomas and John), but Humphrey (born 1390) and Blanche (born 1392) still had nurses, Margaret and Isabella, respectively. Amy de Melbourne, Katherine Chamberer and Juliana Rockster (a cradle-nurse) are also mentioned in the 1387–8 account; and Juliana and Agneta in 1393–4.

[20] DL 28/3/4, fos. 7r, 20r, 33r; 28/3/3, m. 3.

this still stood at £1,137.[21] Gaunt's generosity apart, Henry's main source of income was, naturally, land. During the early 1390s he normally received £1,800 to £2,000 each year from his estates. Much the most profitable of his possessions was the great Welsh Marcher lordship of Brecon, worth about 60 per cent of this total. He also held a dozen or so manors and seigneurial perquisites, scattered through various English counties.[22] How fortunate Henry was to enjoy this secure landed income can be seen by comparing his situation with that of the duke of Gloucester. Deprived by Mary's marriage to Henry of half of the Bohun inheritance,[23] Gloucester was obliged, in order to support his status as the son of a king, to rely on a series of ad hoc grants and annuities from the royal exchequer, payable from the wool customs or the income from alien priories. In theory, he was meant to receive about £2,500 annually, but only about £1,000 of this (mainly his share of the Bohun inheritance) was secured on land; his exchequer assignments, by contrast, were frequently late, sometimes discounted, and almost invariably involved him having to jostle and plead against others with claims on the ever popular royal purse.[24]

Not that Henry showed any sympathy for the plight of his erstwhile co-Appellant. Wealth on the scale enjoyed by the House of Lancaster translated into power, and during the early 1390s Henry, despite his absences abroad, vigorously pursued all legal avenues available to him to augment his territorial base. To do so, he retained on his council three sergeants-at law (William Gascoigne, John Markham and John Woderove), two apprentices-at-law (Thomas Hornby and John Conyers), and three attorneys to act for him in the King's Bench, the Common Bench and the Exchequer (Thomas Beston, William Armeston and Richard Gascoigne).[25] Initially much of their time was spent trying to maximize Henry's share of the Bohun inheritance, for although an interim partition had been

[21] DL 28/3/3 and 4. Henry's income of £1,740 in 1391–2 included £311 in back payments from the king for his costs in bringing an armed retinue to London in September 1386: DL 28/3/3, m.2, and see above, p. 41.

[22] Over nine months in 1391–2, Henry received £1,429; the annual totals for 1392–3 and 1394–5 were £1,802 and £1,931, respectively. In 1393–4 his landed income dropped to £1,272, mainly because Brecon only yielded £622 instead of its customary £1,100 or so: DL 28/3/4.

[23] See above, pp. 26–8.

[24] A. Tuck, 'Thomas of Woodstock, Duke of Gloucester', *ODNB*, 54.277–83; Goodman, *Loyal Conspiracy*, 87–104.

[25] DL 28/3/3, m. 4; 28/3/4, fo. 9r. Henry did not, however, pay retaining fees to members of the royal judiciary, for after many years of campaigning by the parliamentary commons this practice was prohibited in 1388 on grounds of impropriety: Maddicott, *Law and Lordship*, 59–80.

agreed with Gloucester in 1385, this had never been ratified, and each man had outstanding claims. The situation was complicated by the longevity of Eleanor and Mary's mother, Countess Joan, who held dower rights in her former husband's estates, which meant that the £931 and £913 per annum of lands initially allocated to Eleanor and Mary respectively each represented not a half but one-third of Earl Humphrey's inheritance.[26] Yet it was between Henry and Gloucester that the real dispute lay. Henry's grievances as set out in 1385 were, first, that Gloucester had failed to hand over muniments relating to Mary's share of the inheritance and, secondly, that Brecon should be given to him in full, including the castle and town of Bronllys and certain lands in neighbouring Pencelli which, he claimed, had been an integral part of the lordship of Brecon since the Conquest but had been retained by Gloucester.[27] In fact, this was to make a complicated situation sound deceptively simple, for the lords of Bronllys and Pencelli had enjoyed a large degree of independence from their overlords of Brecon until as recently as the 1350s.[28] Nevertheless, Gloucester had apparently ignored or perhaps even obstructed a royal order of March 1386 assigning Bronllys and the adjoining Cantref Selyf to Henry.[29]

During the fifteen months that he spent in England in 1391–2, Henry despatched a relay of clerks and attorneys to the Tower to search the royal archives for evidence relating to the inheritance. Charters from the reigns of Edward I and II and accounts of long-dead receivers of the lordship of Brecon were copied out, and exemplifications were purchased from the royal chancery and elsewhere. On 17 January 1393, as Henry sailed through the eastern Mediterranean to Jaffa, Gloucester arrived in person in London to rebut his claims. Henry's attorneys immediately sued out a writ of protection for their lord during his absence abroad,[30] but following his return in the summer of 1393 the campaign was renewed. Further writs and pleas, some dating from the thirteenth century, were sought out and copied *pro evidenciam contra Ducem Gloucestrie*. The principal point at issue was still the lands appurtenant to the lordship of Brecon, although there were

---

[26] DL 41/240.
[27] DL 41/140. Henry also demanded from Gloucester a half share in certain properties in Kent, Hereford, Somerset and Oxfordshire, totalling just over six knights' fees, which had not been included in the partition.
[28] R. Davies, *Lordship and Society in the March of Wales 1282–1400* (Oxford, 1978), 92–7.
[29] *CCR 1385–9*, 56–7.
[30] DL 28/3/4, fo. 12r.

a number of other points of disagreement as well.[31] Eventually, early in 1395, a compromise was arranged by John Leventhorpe, Henry's attorney, and John Joy, Gloucester's attorney, and sealed by the two lords in London on 20 June of that year. Gloucester handed over the outstanding muniments (a chest was bought in London to store them), and Bronllys, Cantref Selyf and the adjacent lands in Pencelli were reunited with the lordship of Brecon; in return, Henry made over to Gloucester various portions of land in four English counties. Crucially, however, the agreement stipulated that this compromise was to last only as long as both Henry and Gloucester remained alive; once either of them died, it would be null and void.[32] Each man evidently still felt that he was conceding too much. In the event, although Richard ratified the agreement in July 1396 with only minor adjustments, this stipulation was to serve Henry well, for following the arrest of Gloucester in 1397 it allowed him to reassert his claims to the lands he had reluctantly surrendered two years earlier.[33]

Yet Henry was not content simply to maximize his return from his wife's inheritance. He also set out to recover what he could of the inheritance of Earl Thomas of Lancaster, which involved him and his legal team in two further lawsuits, one with another of his former co-Appellants, the earl of Warwick, over the manors of Warrington (Buckinghamshire) and Long Buckby (Northamptonshire), the other with Elizabeth Nevill over the manors of Sutton and Potton (near Biggleswade in Bedfordshire). In the latter case, it was the death of Elizabeth's husband, John Lord Nevill, in 1388 which presented Henry with his opportunity. Elizabeth was the daughter and heiress of William Lord Latimer (d.1381), through whose family Sutton and Potton had descended since the thirteenth century. In 1315, however, when Thomas of Lancaster's power was at its height, an agreement had been reached that in the event of a failure of heirs in the

[31] For example, rights of presentation to the churches of Barnsley (Gloucs.) and Ystradgunlais in the March of Wales, and the division of Alexanderstown (Gloucs.): DL 41/248; 28/3/4, fos. 24v–25r, 38v.

[32] '. . . and the claims of their heirs will be saved, just as they were before this indenture, and will in no way be prejudiced by this indenture': DL 27/170; see also DL 28/3/4, fo. 39v; CCR 1392–6, 448–9; CIM 1392–9, no. 226, inquisition of November 1397 stating incorrectly that this had been agreed 'about seven years ago'; Holmes, Estates of the Higher Nobility, 24–5; CFR 1391–9, 150–1. William Loveney and William Ferrour went to Wix Priory in Essex 'to take possession and attorney concerning the exchange between the lord [Henry] and the duke of Gloucester', in the late summer of 1395 (DL 28/1/5, fo. 31r). The lands Henry ceded were attached to the manors of Wethersfield (Essex), Nuthampstead (Herts.), Westcott (Bucks.) and Newnham (Gloucs.), along with the advowson of Llanthony by Gloucester priory.

[33] CCR 1392–6, 448–9; CPR 1396–9, 13.

male line the manors would fall by remainder to Lancaster, and it was this
clause that Henry seized upon in 1391 when he petitioned for a writ of *scire
facias* against Elizabeth. Initially this proved successful: on 20 February
1392, following scrutiny of Elizabeth's response, presumably by Henry's
lawyers, it was found that there were inconsistencies between the exemplification which she had procured and its original, dating from the reign of
Edward I, and on account of her 'crafty suit' Richard II's government
ordered the manors to be handed over to Henry.[34] Elizabeth countered by
bringing an assize of *novel disseisin* against Henry, which came before the
justices at Bedford on 25 July 1392, the day after Henry set sail on his
second voyage to Prussia. Several members of the Lancastrian legal team
attended the hearing, including an apprentice-at-law sent by Gaunt, but it
was Henry's receiver-general, John Leventhorpe, who masterminded the
suit.[35] Once again, scribes and attorneys were sent to the Tower and elsewhere to copy out documents bearing on the case, some of them dating
from the reigns of King John and Henry III. A roll of cloth was given to a
certain 'gentleman of the region' (*generoso patrie*), presumably to secure his
favour, and letters patent of the king addressed to the sheriff of Bedfordshire,
William Tyryngton, were seized lest they be tampered with.[36] Careful
preparation and Lancastrian muscle duly reaped their reward: Elizabeth's
assize was defeated, the manors were made over to Henry, and by December
the reeve of Sutton had begun to hand over the profits of his manor to
Leventhorpe.[37] Both manors remained in Lancastrian hands throughout
the fifteenth century and beyond.

Widows were a notoriously soft target in the Middle Ages, and there is
nothing edifying about the sight of Henry waiting until the death of John
Nevill – who had been one of Gaunt's most loyal retainers, and whose son
Ralph, earl of Westmorland,[38] would be one of the first to throw in his lot
with Henry in 1399 – to launch his campaign for the recovery of Sutton
and Potton, but this charge at least could not be laid against him in the case

[34] *VCH Bedfordshire*, ii.247–8; *CPR 1391–6*, 32–3.

[35] Leventhorpe claimed £40 in expenses during the year because he had been so heavily
engaged (*maxime occupatus*) in the lawsuit. Gaunt's apprentice was William Hornby: DL
28/3/3, m. 2, 3, 5, 6; 28/3/4, fo. 11r. The reason why it was Henry rather than Gaunt who
pursued these lawsuits is because Gaunt had only a life estate (tenancy by courtesy) in the
lands formerly possessed by Duchess Blanche, whereas Henry was Blanche's heir and it was
thus up to him to sue for lands to which she had a claim but had not actually possessed. My
thanks to Linda Clark and Simon Payling for clarifying this point.

[36] '*ne mutarentur*': this may be the same William Tyryngton from whom one of Henry's
servants bought nine quarters of corn on 19 July, six days before the assize: *Expeditions*, 152.

[37] DL 28/3/4, fo. 9r.

[38] Ralph was John Nevill's son by his first wife, Maud Percy.

of Warrington and Long Buckby. Originally part of the de Lacy patrimony, these two manors had been forfeited by Thomas of Lancaster in 1322 and held since then by the Basset family.[39] It was the childless death of Ralph Lord Basset of Drayton in May 1390 which supplied Henry with his opening. Although there was some confusion as to who should inherit Basset's lands, both Warrington and Long Buckby soon passed into the earl of Warwick's hands,[40] but even before Henry's return to England in April 1391 he had written to the keeper of the rolls of the royal chancery asking him to search for evidence relating to the ownership of Long Buckby.[41] His claim to Warrington was recognized as early as the winter of 1391–2, although Warwick considered himself to have been unjustly deprived of it.[42] Long Buckby proved a harder nut to crack, for Warwick put up stiff resistance. Eventually Henry brought a writ of *scire facias* against him, and on 16 November 1394 the duke of York, keeper of the realm while the king was in Ireland, ordered the justices to proceed to judgment; the hearing was held at Northampton on 3 December, with Warwick appearing in person to present his evidence.[43] The outcome was a compromise: Warwick retained part of the manor, but Henry did not go away empty-handed, and after he became king continued to claim Long Buckby despite continued resistance from the Beauchamps.[44]

The cost to Henry of pursuing these claims in the years 1391–5 must have been considerably more than the £410 or so itemized in his accounts.[45] Few but the greatest of magnates could have afforded this. In the case of Elizabeth Nevill, Henry's behaviour smacks of predatory lordship, but Gaunt and his son seem to have regarded the defence of what they claimed

---

[39] Somerville, *Duchy of Lancaster*, i.33, 338; *VCH Buckinghamshire*, iv.435–6. Long Buckby adjoined Henry's large and valuable manor of Daventry, which must have made it doubly tempting.

[40] Inquisitions following Basset's death identified Thomas earl of Stafford as his heir, but also named Warwick as having a title by remainder under a deed executed in 1339: *CIPM* xvi (1384–92), nos. 963–75.

[41] DL 28/3/3, m. 5. He also paid 'a certain clerk' for copying out charters relating to the de Lacy inheritance 'in order to have evidence about the same manor' (ibid.).

[42] Henry received income from the manor on 8 December 1392: DL 28/3/3, m. 2; *CIM* 1392–9, no. 298; *VCH Buckinghamshire*, iv.435–6. Warwick's unhappiness explains why Henry's clerks were still gathering evidence about Warrington in the autumn of 1392: DL 28/3/4, fo. 11v. Even after he became king, others were still claiming Warrington (*CAD*, v.A11358; my thanks to Simon Payling for references relating to the Warrington and Long Buckby disputes).

[43] DL 28/3/4, fos. 38v–39v; *CCR 1392–6*, 325–6.

[44] *CPR 1396–9*, 197, 211; Somerville, *Duchy of Lancaster*, i.68, 565. Goodman, *Loyal Conspiracy*, 141, says Henry failed to win Long Buckby, but see *CCR 1409–13*, 129. However, the Beauchamps still claimed it in 1439 (*CIPM*, xv, no. 271; and see *CPR 1396–9*, 197, 211).

[45] DL 28/3/4, fo. 39v. Long Buckby alone cost £116 in 1394.

as their patrimony – including, whenever possible, the recovery of lands
forfeited by Thomas of Lancaster in 1322 – almost as an article of faith.
Given the same resources, it is doubtful whether any of their contemporaries would have acted differently: their opponents, at any rate, had little
compunction in trying to capitalize on Henry's absences abroad to steal a
march on him, but fortunately his father was there to ensure that the army
of Lancastrian lawyers was not outflanked.[46] Whether it was wise of Gaunt
and Henry to revive memories of the great struggle between the crown
and the house of Lancaster during the 1310s and 1320s is another matter.[47]
Richard II would show plainly, once he got the chance, just what he thought
of the parliamentary decisions of 1327 and 1330 which overturned the
judgment of treason against Thomas. For now, however, Richard was still
rebuilding his authority after the trauma of 1387–8, and for now, the house
of Lancaster could continue to flaunt its power with impunity.

Just as these tussles were reaching their climax, tragedy struck: on 24 March
1394 John of Gaunt's wife Constanza died, then three months later Mary
de Bohun also died, giving birth to her sixth child and second daughter,
Philippa, at Peterborough.[48] The last time that Henry saw his wife alive
was probably when he spent a few days at Peterborough in the spring.[49]
Since Constanza's funeral had already been planned for 5 July at the
Lancastrian mausoleum at the Newark in Leicester, it was decided that
Mary would also be buried there on the following day. No record of her
funeral expenses has survived, although the large sum of £608 spent on
Constanza's funeral might have included Mary's service as well.[50] On the
other hand, she may have left instructions to be buried without pomp, for
her religious inclinations were of that stamp. It is difficult to imagine that
Henry did not mourn their unshared future. Although she was no more
than twenty-five, and none of her children was aged more than seven at
the time of her death, between them she and Henry had already succeeded
in instilling in their offspring an inclination towards a reflective mode of

[46] Several of Henry's legal counsel were also retained by Gaunt, who also put his own
lawyers at his son's disposal (for example, Hugh Huls): DL 28/3/2, fos. 13r–v.

[47] In March 1394, Gaunt and Henry even petitioned the king to renounce his right to the
advowson of the church of Owston (Yorkshire) as they wished to grant it to Welbeck abbey
(SC 8/252/12557).

[48] *Westminster Chronicle*, 520–1; Mary died in late June, but the exact date is not recorded.

[49] DL 28/3/4, fos 33r–v: Henry was at Peterborough on 28 and 31 March 1394; by
20 April he was at Pontefract.

[50] DL 28/32/21 (two sums of £544 and £64); *SAC I*, 960. John Strecche said Mary was
buried decently (*honeste*): BL Add. MS 35,295, fo. 262v.

personal religion and a passion for beautiful prayer-books. The fact that three of the Bohun psalters ended up in Germany or Austria and another two in Copenhagen was almost certainly a consequence of the marriages of their two daughters, Blanche and Philippa, to the son of the Holy Roman Emperor and the king of Denmark, respectively: that is to say, they took with them the psalters bequeathed to them by their parents, which suggests that they valued and used them.[51] As to their sons, John and Humphrey were among the most noted bibliophiles of their age, while the future Henry V's literary sensibility and pietistic devotion are well documented.[52] It would be strange to imagine that their upbringing played no part in the development of these traits. Her children certainly did not forget Mary. Nineteen years after her death, when Henry V came to the throne, one of his first acts was to pay a coppersmith to make an effigy of his mother to be placed over her tomb.[53]

---

[51] For the Bohun psalters, see above, pp. 78–80.

[52] John commissioned the magnificent Bedford Hours and purchased 843 books from the French Royal Library following Charles VI's death in 1422 Humphrey's reputation as a patron of humanism has been challenged, but he was certainly a great collector of books and corresponded with Italian humanists: Wylie, *Henry the Fourth*, iv.135; G. Harriss, 'Humphrey, Duke of Gloucester', *ODNB*, 28.787–95; McFarlane, *Lancastrian Kings*, 244; C. Allmand, 'Henry V, King of England', *ODNB*, 26.487–97

[53] E 403/612, 20 May, 17 July 1413. The coppersmith, William Godezer, received £60. This is not the effigy in the Trinity Hospital at Leicester, sometimes claimed to be Mary's, for it is of alabaster, not copper (A. Gardner, *Alabaster Tombs of the Pre-Reformation Period in England* (Cambridge, 1940), 93 and illustration 248. Cf. *John Leland's Itinerary*, ed. J. Chandler (Stroud, 1993), 277–8).

Chapter 7

THE TWO DUCHIES AND THE CROWN
(1394–1396)

In English domestic politics, the early 1390s were characterized by the steady reassertion of Richard II's personal control of government. With the war in abeyance, the crown's financial situation eased, and following his return from Spain, Gaunt's relations with the king improved markedly, at any rate on the surface. In the January 1390 parliament, Richard bestowed two striking favours on his uncle: he converted his life tenure of palatinate powers in the duchy of Lancaster into a hereditary grant, and he endowed him with the duchy of Guyenne for life. Yet Gaunt was not satisfied with this.[1] Despite relinquishing his claim to the Castilian crown in 1387, he still clung to his dream of a great continental *apanage*, not just for the term of his life but one which he could pass on to his heir. In order to realize it, however, he knew he must also win the support of the French, for only if Guyenne were held as a fief of the French crown might such an arrangement be incorporated into a durable peace treaty, and it was this that became his main aim during the series of Anglo-French peace conferences which punctuated the early 1390s, at which he acted as principal English negotiator. Richard, who was eager for peace, initially supported the proposal, even though it meant that the direct link between Guyenne and the English crown which had endured for nearly 250 years would be broken. So, naturally, did Henry, for it meant that after Gaunt's death he would become duke of Guyenne as well as of Lancaster, holding them from the kings of France and England, respectively.

The French were not averse to Gaunt's proposal, reckoning that with time the new duke of Guyenne would become absorbed into the French polity and the troublesome Anglo-Gascon link thus be severed; even Gloucester, normally so resistant to concessions to the French, was prepared to go along with it, albeit reluctantly.[2] To many, however, it was anathema.

---

[1] The two simultaneous grants suggest some give and take between Gaunt and Richard: *PROME*, vii.143–5; *CChR 1341–1417*, 318.
[2] Saul, *Richard II*, 213–14.

The Gascon lords and townsmen, who treasured their freedom from the direct rule of a resident duke and saw their link to the English crown as the best defence against the encroachment of the French monarchy, sent dele-gations to protest to the king and only agreed to admit Gaunt's deputies to Bordeaux if they came 'not as the deputy of the duke of Lancaster, but as the deputy of the king of England'.[3] Gaunt was a persistent man, however, and in June 1393 he negotiated a draft Anglo-French treaty which included the grant of Guyenne to himself, to be held of the French crown, as a condition of lasting peace. To what extent Richard supported this is not clear; there was by now growing tension between the king and his uncle over the peace talks, with suspicion on Richard's part that Gaunt was negotiating more for his own benefit than for that of England.[4] Opposition to the draft treaty also surfaced in Cheshire and Lancashire, led by profes-sional soldiers such as Sir Thomas Talbot and Sir Nicholas Clifton who accused Gaunt, Gloucester and Henry of scheming to deprive the king of his lordship in France and threatened to kill them if they set foot in the north-west.[5] Cheshire contributed a disproportionately high number of men to English armies during the fourteenth century, and the ringleaders of the revolt were men who feared that peace would deprive them of their livelihoods. Gaunt and Henry accordingly went north in the summer of 1393 and managed to pacify the rebels with a mixture of firmness (though very little violence) and promises of future military employment.[6]

Yet this was not the end of the matter: in the parliament which met at Westminster in January 1394, the earl of Arundel launched a scathing personal attack on Gaunt and the king, accusing them of over-familiarity (because Richard wore his uncle's livery collar), of stifling debate in the royal council, and of disregarding the rights of the crown by granting

[3] *SAC I*, 940–3; Goodman, *John of Gaunt*, 195–7. Many Englishmen were equally critical: a council held at Stamford in May 1392 denounced as 'absurd' the idea that Guyenne be lost to the crown 'for the benefit of a single person [Gaunt]': *Westminster Chronicle*, 490–1.

[4] As some had accused him of doing in Iberia. The importance of the draft treaty of 1393 was emphasized by Palmer, *England, France and Christendom*, chapters 2, 8 and 9, but others have questioned its status as a draft treaty, suggesting that it was simply a set of over-ambitious proposals which had little chance of being ratified: see Saul, *Richard II*, 213–24, and C. Phillpotts, 'John of Gaunt and English Policy towards France', *Journal of Medieval History* xvi (1990), 363–86.

[5] *SAC I*, 944–5. There were also local grievances: J. Bellamy, 'The Northern Rebellions in the Later Years of Richard II', *BJRL* 47 (1964–5), 254–74; Morgan, *War and Society*, 193–7, notes the gradual build-up of discontent in Cheshire since 1389–90, centring on the collec-tion of a £2,000 subsidy as well as the threat to the livelihoods of the county's military community.

[6] Some of the rebels were also opponents of Lancastrian dominance in the north: Walker, *Lancastrian Affinity*, 171–4. Henry was at Pontefract on 26 August 1393: DL 28/3/4, fo. 20v.

Guyenne to his uncle.[7] On the latter point the commons agreed with him, describing it as 'ludicrous' for the king of England to do homage and fealty to the French king for Guyenne, whereby the English would 'pass under the heel of the French king and be kept for the future under the yoke of slavery'. The upshot was that both lords and commons rejected the treaty, a decision applauded by the Westminster chronicler, who declared that if anyone less exalted had proposed such terms, he would have been branded a traitor, 'but the duke of Lancaster does as he likes, and nobody brands him' – indeed he had even duped or bribed his brother Gloucester into supporting the plan. The draft treaty, at any rate, was now a dead letter, and by the time Gaunt and Gloucester returned to Leulinghem in late March 1394 to confer once more with the dukes of Berry and Burgundy, hope of a definitive peace treaty had evaporated; instead, the two sides settled on a four-year truce.[8] Henry, meanwhile, toured the north-western shires to suppress the continuing disturbances there, and by mid-July the unrest had subsided.[9]

Yet Guyenne was an itch that Gaunt needed to scratch, and when a revolt broke out in the duchy at the prospect of him holding it even for life, he left England in October 1394 to spend over a year there trying to establish his rule.[10] For much of this time Richard was also out of the country: the truce allowed him to turn his attention to Ireland, whither he departed in September 1394 with an army numbering about 7,500 men, including the duke of Gloucester and four earls.[11] Henry did not accompany the king to Ireland; with Gaunt away, he remained in England to watch over the interests of the Lancastrian inheritance.[12] In fact, with both the king and his uncle out of the country, the winter and spring of 1394–5 proved to be a fallow interlude in English politics, but shortly after Richard's return, at a great council held at Eltham (Kent) in late July 1395, the legality of the

[7] Gaunt was reputedly angry with Arundel for standing idly by in his castle of Holt (Clwyd) during the summer instead of helping to suppress the rising in the north-west: *SAC* I, 956. There were also suspicions that the king made little effort to arrest the ringleaders: *PROME*, vii.258–9, 264–6.

[8] *Westminster Chronicle*, 518–19.

[9] Thomas Talbot gave himself up in May, confessed in Henry's presence to 'manifest high treason', and was committed to the Tower of London. Gaunt was deeply displeased by Richard's later decision to pardon him (he had been retained for life by the king in 1392): *CCR 1392–6*, 294; *CPR 1391–6*, 433; Bellamy, 'The Northern Rebellions', 260, 268.

[10] Palmer, *England, France and Christendom*, 152–65.

[11] Saul, *Richard II*, 277–84.

[12] He accompanied his father to Plymouth in mid-October to bid him farewell, and took the opportunity to visit the putative tomb of King Arthur and Guinevere in Glastonbury abbey. He was back in London by 6 November at the latest: DL 28/3/4, fos. 32v–34r; *CPR 1396–9*, 542.

grant of the duchy to Gaunt was once more brought into question when a delegation from the city of Bordeaux asked the king that it be rescinded, citing letters of Edward III promising that the city would be perpetually annexed to the English crown and never alienated to anyone except the heir to the throne. Two Lancastrian knights who were present responded by justifying the grant (on what grounds is not stated), but five doctors of law declared that the king had no option but to revoke the grant, and the lords of the council agreed with them. This left only the duke of Gloucester and Henry to disagree. Gloucester said that it depended on whether the charter to Bordeaux could be found in the royal archives, but that it would in any case be dishonourable for the king to go back on his grant, but few apart from Henry supported him.[13] Eventually, angry that people were muttering against them, Gloucester and Henry walked out of the chamber and sat down to a meal in the hall, where they were joined by the duke of York (although whether he agreed with them is not clear). Soon after this Gloucester returned to London,[14] but fortunately enough had been done to forestall any decision to revoke the grant, and Richard managed to assuage the fears of the Gascons without depriving Gaunt. However, it had been a close-run thing.[15]

Gaunt, meanwhile, having restored order in Guyenne with promises to respect the Gascons' privileges, was preparing to return to England. In early October he was expected imminently, but instead tarried a while in Brittany before crossing to Dover shortly after Christmas. Henry hurried down from Hertford to meet him, and father and son were reunited at Canterbury on 1 January 1396. However, when Gaunt stopped off at King's Langley (Hertfordshire) a few days later to pay his respects to Richard, the king greeted him coolly, 'with due respect, as was proper, but, as some assert, not with affection'.[16] It was a sign of things to come. Gaunt was now in his mid-fifties, and the restless ambition and sense of duty that had defined his political career were dwindling. Yet his pre-eminent position in the councils of the king had not been relinquished so much as usurped. The earls of Rutland and Nottingham and the chamberlain of the royal household, William Le Scrope, were now the guiding hands behind English foreign policy. While in Brittany in November, Gaunt had

[13] For Froissart's account of the meeting, see *Oeuvres de Froissart*, xv.147–82; for the minutes, see J. Baldwin, *The King's Council in England during the Middle Ages* (Oxford, 1913), 135–7, 504–5.
[14] On 23 July. The council continued until 26 July, when both Henry and the king returned to London (Saul, *Richard II*, 473; DL 28/1/5, fo. 28r; C 53/165).
[15] Palmer, *England, France and Christendom*, 162–3.
[16] *SAC II*, 38–9.

negotiated a marriage between his nine-year-old grandson (the future
Henry V) and Marie, the daughter of the duke of Brittany, and drawn up
a bilateral treaty of alliance with the duke; Richard, when he heard of it,
was furious with his uncle, and nothing came of it.[17] Chastened, Gaunt
retired from court and a few weeks later married his mistress of twenty-five
years, Katherine Swynford, at Lincoln, before embarking with Henry on a
tour of their northern estates.[18] The match was greeted with astonishment,
the great ladies of the court mortified at the idea of having to cede precedence to a woman of such low birth.[19] It was another step in the descent of
Gaunt's political influence.

By early 1396, the House of Lancaster was becoming dangerously isolated
from the levers of power. During Gaunt's fifteen-month absence, Henry
had mostly divided his time between the great Lancastrian strongholds of
Tutbury, Pontefract and Leicester and, when he attended parliament or
the royal council, London and Hertford,[20] but although he did what was
required of him to fulfil his public duties, he had not moved any closer to
either winning or seeking to win the king's confidence. It is worth remembering that not once during Richard's reign did Henry hold any military
command in the royal service, any office in the king's household or administration, or any ambassadorial powers on the king's behalf.[21] The patronage
he received from the king in terms of lands or wardships was negligible.
The contrast in this respect between him and his cousin (also Richard's
cousin) Edward earl of Rutland, the son of the duke of York, is telling.

[17] M. Jones, *Ducal Brittany 1364–1399* (Oxford, 1970), 132–6, and *Recueil des Actes de Jean IV,
Duc de Bretagne*, ed. M. Jones (2 vols, Paris, 1983), ii, nos. 1033–6. The treaty was dated 25
November 1395, and three days later a separate letter of obligation was drawn up whereby
Henry of Bolingbroke was to receive 30,000 francs in return for the hand of his son. In fact,
Marie married Jean, count of Perche, in July 1396, by which time Richard II had already
written to Charles VI suggesting that the young Henry might be betrothed instead to the
French king's youngest daughter, Michelle, but this never happened either (*Diplomatic
Correspondence*, ed. Perroy, no. 229A and p. 253).

[18] Goodman, *John of Gaunt*, 156.

[19] *Annales*, 188; *Oeuvres de Froissart*, xv.238–9.

[20] The charters Henry witnessed in 1395 were dated 26 July at Eltham, 11 and 26 Sept. at
Westminster and 22 Sept. at Windsor; he occasionally sought a royal pardon for a follower,
as on 12 June (*CPR 1391–6*, 577). He attended parliament in Jan.–Feb. 1395 and was at
Tutbury for several weeks in the spring and again in August before journeying on to
Pontefract; he visited Leicester for the anniversary of Mary de Bohun's death in late June
and was at Hertford or in London from October to December: *PROME*, vii.287, 304; DL
28/3/4, fos. 32v–34r. Details of his movements in 1395 are taken from his great wardrobe
account, DL 28/1/5 and charter witness lists (C 53/165).

[21] Except in 1383, when he was sixteen and simply accompanying his father: see above,
p. 40.

Some seven years younger than Henry, Rutland during the 1390s acted as constable of England, admiral of England, constable of the Tower of London, constable of Dover castle and warden of the Cinque Ports, and keeper of the king's forests south of the Trent. By way of reward, he was granted the castle and lordship of Oakham (Rutland), the lordship of the Isle of Wight along with Carisbrooke castle, and a clutch of lucrative wardships.[22] Henry's brother-in-law (and Richard's half-brother) John Holand, earl of Huntingdon, was similarly lavishly rewarded with offices, lands and other favours in the 1390s, during which he was chamberlain of England. The chamberlain of the household from 1393–9, William Le Scrope, and Henry's former co-Appellant Thomas Mowbray, captain of the town and castle of Calais, also received much from the king during these years.[23]

Henry's measured degree of distance from the royal court might be explicable in personal terms, by Richard's mistrust of his cousin, Henry's reluctance to involve himself too deeply in politics while his father was still alive, or Gaunt's desire to protect his heir from the potential consequences of his opposition to the king in 1387–8. Yet the problem went deeper than this, for by now an element of open rivalry between the crown and the house of Lancaster had begun to manifest itself, a rivalry all too reminiscent of the decade-long struggle between Edward II and Earl Thomas which had so nearly led to the extinction of the Lancastrian inheritance seventy years earlier, and which in certain respects had its roots in that earlier conflict. At the local level, Richard still nurtured a desire to clip his uncle's wings in the north-west, a region with which, as earl of Chester, he tried to develop a special relationship.[24] De Vere's attempt to boost royal support there in 1387 may have backfired, but during the 1390s Richard made a more determined effort to assert his authority, as a result of which both king and duke expanded their affinities in Cheshire and Lancashire significantly, apparently, though not overtly, in competition with each other.[25] The visible manifestation of this arms race was the livery badge. In the winter of 1389–90, to please his uncle, Richard had sported a

[22] Jean Creton said that 'the king put more trust in him [Rutland] than any of his friends': *CR*, 138; *RHKA*, 166–7; R. Horrox, 'Edward of Langley, Second Duke of York', *ODNB*, 17.801–3.

[23] Saul, *Richard II*, 226–7.

[24] Cf. T. Thornton, 'Cheshire: The Inner Citadel of Richard II's Kingdom?', in *The Reign of Richard II*, ed. G. Dodd (Stroud, 2000), 85–96.

[25] See Walker, *Lancastrian Affinity*, 174–81, for Richard's 'assault upon his uncle's lordship' in the north-west at this time, rejecting the idea of cohabitation between the two affinities in the 1390s.

Lancastrian collar, but within a few months he began distributing his own
badge of the white hart, not just as a way of augmenting his following
among the gentry in the aftermath of the crisis of 1386–9, but also to try
to counter the appeal of the **SS** collars distributed by Gaunt and his son,
which had acquired something of the cachet of a chivalric order. Both
sides were criticized for the gang culture which livery badges induced: to
the commons they were a source of sufficient unease to require legislation,[26]
while chroniclers and poets anthropomorphized them as the medieval
antecedents of animated cartoon warriors battling it out for control of the
kingdom. Richard's white hart badges, wrote one poet, 'swarmed so thick
throughout the length and breadth of his land' that he came to believe in
the infallibility of his power, and if 'the good greyhound' had stood idly by
there would have been no stopping him. The greyhound was Henry,
'because of his livery of linked collars of greyhounds', according to Usk;
the Dieulacres chronicler's image of a pack of hounds driving 'that hated
beast the white hart' from the land appealed to a society addicted to the
chase.[27]

Livery badges might only be symbols, but their connotations reverber-
ated. So too did the implications of Richard's attempts to secure the
canonization of Edward II. He had been pressing for this since the early
1380s, and in 1395 a book of Edward's miracles, compiled at Richard's
request, was despatched to Rome to speed up the process. Even his bid to
make a saint of his great-grandfather had something of the character of a
duel with the House of Lancaster, since for much of the fourteenth century
it was not Edward II but Thomas of Lancaster who had seemed more
likely to be canonized, and 'Saint' Thomas's cult had a good deal more
popular support than 'Saint' Edward's. Indeed it was probably Richard's
enthusiasm for Edward's cult which sparked the late fourteenth-century
revival of Thomas's cult, with Walsingham declaring that in 1390 'Saint
Thomas of Lancaster was canonized'. In fact, Thomas never was canonized, although he continued to be popularly venerated into the early

---

[26] Walker, *Lancastrian Affinity*, 94–6; *RHKA*, 238–43; Saul, *Richard II*, 200–1, 263–4, 440; D.
Fletcher, 'The Lancastrian Collar of Esses. Its Origins and Transformations down the
Centuries', in *The Age of Richard* II, ed. J. Gillespie (Stroud, 1997), 191–204.

[27] 'Then were those royal badges both of the hart and of the crown hidden away, so that
some said that the esquires of the duke of Lancaster, wearing their collars, had been preordained by a prophecy to subdue like greyhounds in this year the pride of that hated beast
the white hart': *The Deposition of Richard II*, ed. T. Wright (Camden Society, Old Series,
1838), 8–12; *Usk*, 52; *CR*, 155; and see P. Strohm, 'The Literature of Livery', in P. Strohm,
Hochon's Arrow: The Social Imagination of Fourteenth-Century Texts (Princeton, 1992), 179–83.
Henry's gift to Queen Isabella on her arrival in England in 1396 was a necklace with a
golden greyhound set with a ruby and a pearl (*Traïson et Mort*, 110).

sixteenth century, while the cult of Edward II barely outlived Richard's deposition.[28] In the 1390s, however, there was a real danger that this competition for divine favour might escalate, for Richard regarded his great-grandfather's deposition as the great stain on the history of the English crown and was determined to rehabilitate Edward's reputation. The idea that Earl Thomas, a rank traitor in his eyes, should remain forever vindicated, let alone canonized, while Edward and his loyal supporters remained eternally damned, was anathema to Richard, and if Edward were to be canonized it would not be inconceivable, indeed it might well be seen as logical, for Richard to declare the acts accompanying his deposition, including the judgments of 1327, to be annulled.

These rival cults thus had the potential to dig deep into the bedrock of noble power, which was always land; and if it came to a trial of strength between the crown and the house of Lancaster, it was always likely to be land that lay at the heart of the matter. Disputes over land might fall into abeyance for generations or even centuries in the Middle Ages, but rarely were they forgotten entirely, with each turn of fortune's wheel liable to bring renewed claims from those whose ancestors had lost out, and renewed insecurity for those who had benefited from their misfortune. It must have been with trepidation, therefore, that Gaunt and Henry viewed the rise to royal favour in the mid-1390s of a number of young men whose forefathers had once held estates now possessed by the house of Lancaster – men such as Thomas Despenser, the great-great-grandson of the infamous Hugh Despenser the Younger who had profited so hugely, if briefly, from the forfeiture of Earl Thomas, or John de Montague, the nephew and heir of that William earl of Salisbury who, in the 1360s, had been pressurized into acknowledging Gaunt's claim to a number of properties in Wiltshire.[29] The greatest danger, however, came from the crown itself, for it was Edward II who had been the principal beneficiary of Earl Thomas's forfeiture until its restoration to his brother in 1327.[30] That the reversal of the 1327 judgment, leading in all probability to the reclamation by Richard of the Lancastrian estates, would require a political upheaval of seismic proportions was self-evident, and Richard would have to believe himself to

[28] *SAC I*, 896; for these competing cults see C. Given-Wilson, 'Richard II, Edward II, and the Lancastrian Inheritance', *EHR* 109 (1994), 553–71; the two cults sprang up in the 1320s (to some extent as rivals from the start) but had waned since the mid-century. The immediate cause of Walsingham's remark was the death in 1389 of the young earl of Pembroke, whose ancestor Aymer de Valence had sat in judgment on Thomas of Lancaster in 1322.

[29] Somerville, *Duchy of Lancaster*, i.35–6.

[30] Given-Wilson, 'Richard II, Edward II, and the Lancastrian Inheritance', *passim*.

be strong enough to contain the resulting fall-out. The problem was that his grip on power was tightening almost by the month. This is what made the accelerating rivalry between crown and duchy and the decline of Lancastrian influence so dangerous.

In addition to this there was the matter of the succession to the throne, a question made doubly urgent by the death of Richard's queen, Anne of Bohemia, on 7 June 1394. Twelve years of childless marriage meant that the succession had been working its way up the political agenda for some time now. Some believed that should the king fail to have issue, the throne would devolve by hereditary right to Roger Mortimer (b.1374) or, in the event of his death, upon his younger brother Edmund (b.1376).[31] The Mortimer brothers were the sons of Edmund, earl of March (d.1381), who had married Philippa, the daughter of Lionel, duke of Clarence. They were thus descended from the second son of Edward III, albeit through a female line, whereas Gaunt was the third son of Edward III. It was even asserted later that Richard had declared in the parliament of 1386 that Roger was his heir, although there is no mention of this in the official records.[32] In January 1394, however, Gaunt is alleged to have petitioned that Henry be acknowledged as Richard's heir, at which Roger Mortimer protested, claiming seniority. Gaunt's response was to cite the so-called Crouchback Legend, which had it that Edmund, first earl of Lancaster, rather than Edward I, had in reality been the elder son of Henry III, but that he had been passed over for the crown on account of his crooked back, although its reversion had been vested in his heirs (the house of Lancaster). Roger replied, quite correctly, that this was simply false, and the king ordered them to drop the matter.[33] That Gaunt used the Crouchback Legend to assert the Lancastrian claim – as Henry would later do – is beyond doubt, and he was even said to have forged a chronicle

[31] *Westminster Chronicle*, 194.

[32] So said the authors of the *Brut* (ii.341) and the *CE* (iii.361). One of them clearly copied from the other, or else they used a common source; the latter is perhaps most likely. The *Brut* says that Richard made Roger his heir apparent (*heyre parant*), but this cannot be correct, for this would have implied that he would take precedence, even if Richard and Anne produced a son. For the re-dating of this episode to the parliament of 1386 rather than 1385, and the argument that it was linked to talk of Richard's deposition and that Richard was reminding parliament that if he were dethroned they would get a twelve-year-old in his place, see I. Mortimer, 'Richard II and the Succession to the Crown', *History* (2007), 320–36.

[33] *CE*, iii.369–70. The nineteen-year-old Roger succeeded to his earldom of March and was granted livery of his lands during the January 1394 parliament (on 25 February), which might have occasioned a debate about the succession: *CP*, viii.448–9. He had not been formally summoned to this parliament, but he witnessed his first charter on 13 March, a week after it ended (C 53/164).

to try to prove his point, although it needs to be remembered that all these accounts were written after 1399 and thus influenced by Henry's usurpation.[34] They are, however, independent of each other, and the likelihood is that a discussion of the succession did take place at the time of the 1394 parliament, probably in the context of the Anglo-French negotiations. After all, the fundamental objection of the Gascons to Gaunt's appointment as duke of Guyenne was that they did not want to accept anyone as their duke 'unless he be the king or the king's heir'. One obvious solution to this problem was that either Gaunt or his son be recognized as Richard's heir – which, given Edward III's entail of 1376, they may well have regarded themselves as entitled to in any case in the event of Richard dying childless.[35] Yet if this self-evidently appealed to Gaunt, it was hardly likely to have been Richard's way of solving the Gascons' problem. In fact, the king had no wish to air the question of the succession, and he would not have thanked Gaunt for raising it, although he must have known perfectly well that others were discussing the possibility of the crown passing to the house of Lancaster. After all, unless Richard had a child, Gaunt and then Henry were his next heirs in the direct male line, and this was a kingdom in which the majority of great estates had been entailed upon male heirs during the course of the fourteenth century, as indeed the crown had been in 1376.[36] Yet Richard did not want Henry to succeed him, as he made clear a few years later.[37] Here, then, was another issue threatening to open a fissure, not just between the crown and the house of Lancaster but also between the house of Lancaster and other members of the royal family.

This was still a fissure, however, not a rupture. If Richard were to produce an heir, much of the tension would be taken out of English politics, and it was partly to this end that the king's foreign policy was directed in 1395–6. Gaunt and Henry played virtually no part in this, indeed Henry, still

[34] Hardyng and Usk both corroborate the use of the Crouchback Legend, the first by Gaunt 'in order to supply his son Henry with a title to the crown', the second by Henry: *CR*, 195–7; *Usk*, 64–7.

[35] *SAC I*, 962–3; Palmer, *England, France and Christendom*, 152–9; Bennett, 'Edward III's Entail'. In *CE* (369–70), the chronicler's account of Gaunt's claim in the January 1394 parliament comes between a discussion of Gaunt's thwarted ambitions in France and his appointment as duke of Aquitaine; although the chronology of this chronicle is often confused, the context is suggestive.

[36] Bennett, 'Edward III's Entail; C. Given-Wilson, 'Legitimation, Designation and Succession to the Throne in Fourteenth-Century England', in *Building Legitimacy. Political Discourses and Forms of Legitimacy in Medieval Societies*, ed. I. Alfonso, H. Kennedy and J. Escalona (Leiden, 2004), 89–105.

[37] *CR*, 202.

dreaming of foreign fields, was sorely tempted by an offer from William, count of Ostrevant, to join him on a campaign in Friesland (or Frisia), the rebellious and inaccessible northernmost region of his father the count of Holland's domains, but both Gaunt and the king advised him not to go.[38] Gaunt may have thought it irresponsible of Henry to wish to be off seeking fame abroad when his own powers were on the wane, and although it had no discernible effect on their relationship, this is the first and only hint of a disagreement between father and son. They spent the spring of 1396 in Yorkshire together, doubtless attending to Duchy business.[39]

By this time, the king's foreign policy had borne fruit. On 3 March 1396, a twenty-eight-year truce with France was concluded, including an agreement that the English king would marry Charles VI's daughter, Isabella, at a grand ceremony to be held in the autumn.[40] In August, Gaunt and the king crossed to Calais for a meeting with Duke Philip of Burgundy to finalize the arrangements.[41] Henry did not accompany them, but he and his eldest son, now ten, both attended the summit between Richard II and Charles VI at Ardres, eight miles south of Calais, in late October,[42] a courtly extravaganza comparable to the Field of the Cloth of Gold of June 1520, not simply because of its extraordinary cost but also because it was held on the same site. Four days of talks between the two monarchs culminated in the little Isabella, now almost seven years old, being handed over to her twenty-nine-year-old husband on 30 October, and five days later they were married at the church of St Nicholas at Calais. This union apart, the diplomatic achievements of the summit were not impressive: an agreement to try to bring an end to the Papal Schism and some vague promises to try to resolve Anglo-French disputes without resort to arms and to continue the search for a final peace between the two kingdoms. Richard also promised to aid his new father-in-law against all men in future – an

[38] The invitation is further evidence of Henry's reputation abroad: 'If you can persuade your cousin the earl of Derby to join your company', Count William was told, 'your expedition will be more worthy and your enterprise more renowned.' According to Froissart, 'everyone knew that [Henry] would willingly have gone, if the king had not prevented him at the request of the duke of Lancaster' (*Oeuvres de Froissart*, xv.228–9, 269–71). For this episode see also Tuck, 'Henry IV and Chivalry', 67.

[39] They witnessed royal charters when the king visited York in late March: C 53/165 (29 March and 1 April); Saul, *Richard II*, 473.

[40] The earls of Rutland and Nottingham served as proxies to plight Richard's troth in Paris, the latter placing the ring on Isabella's finger and occupying the seat normally reserved for the groom (*Saint-Denys*, ii.363–5, 413–15).

[41] Henry witnessed a charter at Westminster in late July (C 53/165), but apart from this not much is known about his movements during the summer of 1396.

[42] For the young Henry's presence at Ardres, see DL 28/3/5, fo. 14r.

undertaking which Charles may have interpreted more literally than the English king intended. Equally important for Richard was the opportunity the summit afforded him to project an image of kingship in keeping with his conception of his office. The gifts which he and Charles exchanged, the banquets they hosted for each other, their gorgeous apparel and enormous, richly caparisoned retinues excited the amazement of contemporaries and must have set the English exchequer back by a minimum of £10,000 and quite possibly a lot more.[43] Gaunt and Henry played a full part in the proceedings: together with the duke of Gloucester and the earls of Rutland, Nottingham and Northumberland, they escorted the French king to Richard's pavilion on the opening day of the summit, all six of them decked out in full-length suits of red velvet with a white heraldic bend of the livery of the former Queen Anne.[44] By 15 November, however, Henry was back at Dover, and on 22 November he reached London. He and Gaunt spent Christmas at Hertford and paid a brief visit to Tutbury early in 1397 before returning to Westminster for the opening of the parliament, the first for two years, which had been summoned for 22 January.[45]

[43] Saul, *Richard II*, 229–34; Palmer, *England, France and Christendom*, 176–7; *Saint-Denys*, ii.451–67; J. Stratford, *Richard II and the English Royal Treasure* (Woodbridge, 2012), 57–64.

[44] *SAC II*, 38–51. Despite Froissart's assertion to the contrary, Henry's kitchen journal (DL 28/1/9) makes it clear that he went to Calais; the duke of York remained in England as keeper of the realm (*Oeuvres de Froissart*, xv.298; *Foedera*, vii.841). Henry's household was based at Guines, just west of Ardres, for his two weeks in France. Gaunt paid £200 for accommodation at Calais on 16 October, but probably moved closer to Ardres once the summit began (DL 28/1/9, fo. 4v; DL 28/3/5, fo. 12r).

[45] *CCR 1396–9*, 73; DL 28/1/9, fos. 2v, 5r, 6v, 7r–v.

Chapter 8

RICHARD RESURGENT (1397–1398)

The early 1390s had seen the house of Lancaster at the height of its power. Rich, renowned and resented, it threw its weight around a realm whose king was still feeling his way back from the humiliations inflicted on him in 1387–8. By the beginning of 1397 it had lost some of its swagger. Gaunt's credibility at home and abroad was irretrievably damaged by the Cheshire and Gascon risings, while his and Henry's inclination towards parallel rather than integrated development with the crown was viewed with increasing suspicion at a court now dominated by a new constellation of royal favourites. The conclusion of the Anglo-French negotiations marked another step-change in Richard II's kingship: freed for the foreseeable future from the prospect of war with France, he could focus on domestic politics. He also reaped significant financial benefit from the marriage – a dowry of 800,000 francs (£133,333) of which 300,000 francs were handed over on the day of the wedding.[1] Politically and financially, therefore, the truce put Richard in a stronger position vis-à-vis his subjects, and it must have been with trepidation that those who had formerly crossed him gathered at Westminster in mid-January.

Although only revealed in its fullness from July 1397 onwards, and even then merely by stages, the clenched resentment of a decade is clearly detectable in Richard's actions from the time of the January 1397 parliament onwards. The mainsprings of the king's policy were twofold: the desire to avenge himself on his foes, and the achievement of that unchallenged authority within his realm which he had always regarded as his due but which had hitherto been denied him. When the commons submitted a bill criticizing the cost of the royal household and the 'multitude of bishops and ladies with their followers' who hung about the court, Richard demanded to know the identity of the individual responsible for introducing it. The unfortunate culprit, the clerk Thomas Haxey, was condemned to death as a traitor and only pardoned following a grovelling

---

[1] Palmer, *England, France and Christendom*, 171–4.

apology from the house.[2] Richard was making it clear that he was not going to countenance a return to the parliamentary politics of the 1380s, with the government constantly on the back foot fending off criticisms of royal extravagance and favouritism. Parliament was cowed, petitioning closely controlled.[3] Yet the king did not have everything his own way. When he unveiled a plan to accompany his new father-in-law Charles VI on a military expedition against Gian Galeazzo Visconti, the duke of Milan, it met with no favour from the commons, and it was only the arrival of news that the French had decided not to proceed with the expedition which permitted Richard to climb down without losing face.[4] Henry would have been relieved: Gian Galeazzo was a friend with whom he continued to maintain regular contact through messengers, shared servants, and gift-exchange.[5] Nor, on the French side, did Charles VI's brother, Louis duke of Orléans, support the proposal, since he was married to Valentina, Gian Galeazzo's daughter. Their attachment to the Visconti cause was one of the factors that drew Henry and Louis together in the late 1390s.[6]

One of the last acts of the January 1397 parliament was the legitimation of Henry's half-siblings, the four Beaufort children of John of Gaunt by Katherine Swynford. Gaunt had already secured a papal decree legitimizing them in the eyes of the Church, but their secular legitimation on 6 February was necessary to enable them to inherit lands, titles and offices in England 'as if born in wedlock'.[7] Henry witnessed both this ceremony and the promotion to an earldom four days later of John Beaufort, indicating that he remained at Westminster until the dissolution of parliament on 12 February. However, the duke of Gloucester and the earls of Arundel and

[2] *PROME*, vii.305–30.

[3] G. Dodd, 'Richard II and the Transformation of Parliament', in *The Reign of Richard II*, ed. G. Dodd, 71–84.

[4] *PROME*, viii.313; D. Bueno de Mesquita, 'The Foreign Policy of Richard II in 1397: Some Italian Letters', *EHR* 1941, 628–37. It was the disastrous defeat of the crusading army at Nicopolis in September 1396, news of which reached Paris on Christmas Eve, that forced the French to change their plans.

[5] DL 28/1/5, fos. 9r, 21r; 28/3/5, fo. 13v; 28/1/6, fo. 8v. For Franco-Milanese hostility, see *Oeuvres de Froissart*, xv.352. Cf. Tuck, 'Henry IV and Chivalry', 62. Francis de Courte, Gian Galeazzo's esquire, had been staying with Henry more or less continuously since 1393: DL 28/1/5, fos. 3r, 10v, 20r; 28/1/6, fo. 24r; 28/1/9, fos. 6r, 21r.

[6] Bueno de Mesquita, 'Foreign Policy of Richard II', 634–7. In March 1398, there was a rumour in Italy that Henry was on the point of marching down to the peninsula with 200 lancers and 500 archers, marrying Gian Galeazzo's cousin Lucia (whom he had met in 1393) and joining the duke in an attack on Florence.

[7] *PROME*, vii. 322–3 (correctly, 6 February). This later became a contentious issue: see below, p. 306.

Warwick left early,[8] and Gloucester and Arundel then infuriated the king by refusing to attend a council meeting, claiming that they were ill.[9] The rekindled tension between the king and the three senior Appellants also manifested itself in the decision to deprive Warwick of his manor of Bishopston on the Gower peninsula (Glamorgan), for his allegedly illegal occupation of which he was obliged to make a public apology to the king and fined for contempt. What was disturbing about this, and about Richard's decision to allow the earl of Salisbury to challenge the earl of March's right to the great Marcher lordship of Denbigh (Clwyd), was that the king was indicating his willingness to re-examine land claims dating back to the early years of the fourteenth century.[10] There was no suggestion for the moment that this process would involve the Lancastrian inheritance, but it was probably not coincidental that Gaunt chose this moment to draw up the first of a series of dispositions aimed at ensuring the safe passage of his lands to those for whom he intended them following his death.[11] He also secured a new charter from the king confirming his rights within the Duchy of Lancaster and elsewhere in England.[12]

Henry spent the spring of 1397 jousting at Windsor (in early March), with his father at Tutbury (for Easter), and visiting his daughters, now five and two, at Eaton Tregoz in Herefordshire, where they were being cared for by Hugh Waterton, before returning to London in mid-May.[13] Then, on 6 July 1397, he and six of his servants took up residence in the king's household.[14] By now Richard, never a man to forget where he had buried the hatchet, had made up his mind.[15] Warwick, having accepted an invitation

[8] All three were appointed triers of petitions (as was Henry), but none of them witnessed the promotions of Beaufort and Thomas Mowbray on 10 February (*PROME*, vii.311).

[9] *Vita*, 137. Gloucester and Arundel were said to be unhappy with the French truce and royal marriage.

[10] *PROME*, vii.320–1.

[11] On 11 February 1397 he created a jointure entailing his castles and honours of Tickhill, High Peak and Knaresborough, together with other lands, upon himself and Katherine Swynford, the effect of which was to grant her secure possession of them after he died (*CPR 1396–9*, 76).

[12] John Casemaker was paid 4s 6d to make a strong-box covered with black leather 'bound in iron, with keys and locks' to store these documents (DL 28/3/5, fos. 13v, 15r).

[13] DL 28/1/6, fos. 4Ar, 25v, 30r and v, 37r; DL 28/1/9, fos. 9v, 12r, 15r. Goodman, *John of Gaunt*, 159; Henry was at Hertford with his father on 10 June (Whit Sunday): DL 28/1/9, fo. 15r.

[14] DL 28/1/9, fo. 16r. Thomas Young and John Atherton, clerks of Henry's chapel, and his servants, John Young, John Wilbraham and John Bernard, each received four pence a day for 'staying with the lord [Henry] in the household of the king from the sixth day of July until the first day of August'.

[15] The French chroniclers said that Henry, together with Gloucester, Arundel, Warwick, Nottingham, Archbishop Arundel, the prior of Westminster abbey and the abbot of

to dine with the king, was arrested on 10 July at the bishop of Exeter's house outside Temple Bar and sent to Tintagel (Cornwall).[16] Arundel was persuaded by his brother to surrender himself, the king having sworn to Archbishop Arundel that no harm would befall the earl; he was sent to Carisbrooke castle on the Isle of Wight. To apprehend Gloucester, Richard gathered a force of men-at-arms and rode through the night to Pleshey castle, seizing the duke at dawn, despite the lamentations of Duchess Eleanor (Henry's sister-in-law). Gloucester was taken to Dover and thence to Calais.[17] It was at least fifteen years since Henry had lodged in Richard's household, and there can only have been one reason why he did so now: because he was complicit, willingly or unwillingly, in the king's attack on the three senior Appellants. So too, doubtless, was his father: on the same day that Henry moved into Richard's household, the king confirmed Gaunt's tenure of the Duchy of Aquitaine.[18] The true extent of their complicity is unclear, and if Henry and Gaunt wanted to save themselves from a similar fate they arguably had little option but to feign support for Richard; it may also be significant that at times they were permitted a degree of detachment from the ensuing process. Yet there is no suggestion that Henry protested at what was being done, at times quite the contrary.

Parliament was summoned to Westminster on 17 September, and in early August the king and his supporters gathered at Nottingham castle to draw up the charges, which, mimicking the procedure used in 1387–8, were presented in the form of an Appeal of Treason. The essence of the accusations was that the three lords had traitorously usurped royal authority in 1386–8 and acted to the prejudice of the king's regality. Those who

St Albans, became involved at around this time in a conspiracy to kill or imprison Richard II, John of Gaunt and Edmund, duke of York, and to put the remaining lords on the royal council to death. The details of this 'St Albans Plot' vary, but it originated with the pro-Ricardian author of the *Traïson et Mort*, who said that it was Mowbray who disclosed the plot to the king, leading to the arrest of Gloucester, Arundel and Warwick. For the improbability of the story, see J. Palmer, 'The Authorship, Date and Historical Value of the French Chronicles on the Lancastrian Revolution', *BJRL* (1978–9), 145–81, 398–421; *CR*, 7–8; *Traïson et Mort*, 121–7; *Saint-Denys*, ii.477; *Chronographia Regum Francorum*, iii.144.

[16] *PROME*, viii.55; the pressure on Warwick had ratcheted up in May when the king ousted him from Gower and ordered him to pay thirteen years' arrears of the profits of the lordship (£5,333) to Mowbray, adjudging that the latter's father had been unjustly deprived of it in 1353: C. Given-Wilson, *The English Nobility in the Late Middle Ages* (London, 1987), 169; *CCR 1396–9*, 123–5.

[17] *CR*, 54, 64–5, 71–2.

[18] R. Mott, 'Richard II and the Crisis of July 1397', in *Church and Chronicle in the Middle Ages: Essays Presented to John Taylor*, ed. I. Wood and G. A. Loud (London, 1991), 165–77, at p. 172. A royal proclamation of 18 July stressed that Gaunt, Henry and York had consented to the arrest of the three senior Appellants, which, strictly speaking, was probably true: *Foedera*, viii.6–7.

formally presented the Appeal to the king – the 'Counter-Appellants' – were the earls of Rutland, Kent, Huntingdon, Salisbury, Nottingham and Somerset, William Le Scrope and Thomas Despenser. The inclusion of Thomas Mowbray, an Appellant in 1387–8, indicates that this was not the reason why Henry did not join the Counter-Appeal; nor was it because he was Gloucester's nephew, for so too was Rutland. Perhaps the king did not regard Henry as reliable enough, or perhaps Henry asked to be excused, or even refused to present the Appeal. Either way, it made it imperative for him to cooperate with the king in other ways, and he was present at Nottingham in early August, lodging with his household at Dale abbey, seven miles west of the city.[19] Henry, Gaunt and the duke of York were also licensed to bring their retinues to parliament 'for the comfort of the king': 300 men-at-arms and 600 archers for Gaunt, 200 and 400, respectively, for Henry, and 100 and 200 for York. This was a small army, and suggests that Richard felt that he had nothing to fear from them, although naturally the Counter-Appellants brought their retinues as well, and the king also summoned 2,000 of his Cheshire archers to serve as his bodyguard.[20] London in September was a city under occupation.

Following the Nottingham council, which deferred the Appeal of Treason to parliament, Henry spent time at Leicester and Kenilworth before returning to London early in September. Richard had ordered his retainers to join him early on the morning of Saturday 15 September at Kingston-upon-Thames (Surrey) to ride with him on a 'great justice' to Westminster palace – a symbolic reclaiming of his capital.[21] Henry had hired a house in Fleet Street, and on the evening of Sunday 16 September, the eve of the parliament, he held a banquet there which the king attended.[22] For the opening of parliament the following morning, Monday

---

[19] DL 28/1/6, fos. 15v, 20v, 30v. The fact that Henry later sought a charter of pardon from the king for the gathering together (*adunacione*) of men-at-arms and archers at Nottingham should not be taken to imply that he had any intention of resisting Richard, which would have been tantamount to suicide; this pardon was the result of a petition from Gaunt, York and Henry to the king, asking for permission to bring men into the king's presence; it was endorsed with the king's licence, authorizing them to bring the numbers of men specified in his writ of 28 August cited below (SC 8/221/11038).

[20] *CR*, 73; *CCR 1396–9*, 210.

[21] *CCR 1396–9*, 210; *The Historical Collections of a Citizen of London*, ed. J. Gairdner (Camden Society, New Series, 17, 1876), 96; BL Harleian Ms 3775, fo. 86r. The author of the *CE* (p. 373) described the king 'riding fearsomely (*terribiliter*) through the middle of London'.

[22] *Historical Collections*, 96; called 'John Rotes Inne in Fleet Street' in BL Harleian Ms 3775, fo. 86r; DL 28/1/9, fo. 18v. Henry hired three boats with sixteen bargemen for the use of his followers; six of his bargemen had formerly served Gloucester, but now sported gowns of Henry's livery. His six minstrels were at the banquet, as were his two older sons Henry and Thomas, both of whom received gowns for the occasion, while the court painter John

17 September, a marquee had been erected in Westminster palace yard, around which were ranged hundreds of the king's Cheshire archers. The speaker of the commons was Sir John Bussy, who had served both Gaunt and Henry for a decade or more but was now bound fast to the king; no one can have been in doubt about the agenda.[23] The Commission of Government of 1386 was revoked and declared to have been treasonable, and the charges against Gloucester, Arundel and Warwick read out. Arundel was brought to trial first, on Friday 21 September, and immediately claimed the benefit of two royal pardons granted to him in 1388 and 1394. John of Gaunt, presiding as steward of England, told him, 'That pardon is revoked, traitor!' 'Never was I a traitor,' rejoined Arundel, 'and to be sure, when it comes to treason, you are in greater need of a pardon than I am.' When Bussy informed him that it was the king, the lords 'and us, the faithful commons' who had revoked his pardons, Arundel retorted that the faithful commons, his supporters, were not present, only 'you and your crew, who have always been false'.[24] Yet it was Henry who provided the most damning piece of evidence against his former ally, asking him:

'Did you not say to me at Huntingdon, where we initially gathered in rebellion, that before doing anything else it would be best to seize the king?' 'You, earl of Derby, you are lying through your teeth', replied [Arundel]. 'I never considered any action against our lord the king except what was in his interests and to his honour.' Then the king himself said to him, 'Did you not say to me in the bath-house behind the white hall, at the time of your parliament, that there were a number of reasons why my knight Sir Simon Burley deserved to die? To which I replied that I could see no reason why he should die – but even so you and your fellows treacherously put him to death.'[25]

This was safe ground for Henry. The seizure of the king and the death of Burley were precisely the issues that had divided him and Mowbray from the other Appellants ten years earlier, and Richard knew this. Turning to Gaunt, the king ordered him to pass sentence: Arundel was adjudged a traitor and

Prince had been employed to paint thirteen curlews, thirteen doves and thirteen popinjays 'in gold, silver and other colours for the entertainment (convivio) put on for the king at the time of the parliament' (DL 28/1/6, fos. 3r–v, 4Ar, 26r–v, 28r, 30r, 36v; DL 28/1/9, fo. 18v).
    [23] PROME, vii.331–428.
    [24] CR, 59. It was later alleged that at least some of the MPs had not been fairly elected but appointed at the king's will (SAC II, 78, 186–7).
    [25] Usk, 30–1.

condemned to death, with the forfeiture of all his lands and possessions. He was beheaded that afternoon on Tower Hill, where Burley had died.

Two days later, on Sunday 23 September, it was Gaunt's turn to host a banquet at the bishop of Durham's house in London,[26] then on the Monday Thomas Arundel, the archbishop of Canterbury, was also convicted of treason, deprived of his see and exiled for life, on the grounds that he had supported the 1386 Commission.[27] The real drama, however, was yet to come. Around mid-August, rumours had begun to circulate that the duke of Gloucester had died. In fact the king had ordered Mowbray to have him killed at Calais, but Mowbray hesitated, fearful of committing so dreadful a crime, and it was not until three weeks later, on the night of 8 September, that Gloucester was murdered, suffocated or strangled in a back room of the Princes Inn at Calais.[28] However, his death was not yet public knowledge, and for the moment Richard and Mowbray colluded in a public charade to mask their crime. When formally requested by the king to produce Gloucester for trial, Mowbray announced that he was unable to do so, since 'I held this duke in my custody in the lord king's prison in the town of Calais, and there, in that same prison, he died'.[29] Within a few months of the parliament, the suspicions aroused by Gloucester's death would begin to tear great cracks in the fabric of Richard's new political order, but for the moment it remained only to pass posthumous sentence of treason on the king's uncle and to declare his lands and possessions forfeit to the crown.[30] Four days later, on 28 September, the earl of Warwick was also put on trial, and although his confession of the treasons imputed to him was widely derided, it did save his life: 'moved to pity', the king commuted his death sentence to life imprisonment on the Isle of Man.[31] Two years later, in Henry's first parliament, when Warwick, 'blushing with shame', denied having ever publicly admitted his treason, Henry told him to be quiet since everyone knew he had.[32] Neither as earl of Derby nor as

[26] *Historical Collections*, 96; BL Harleian MS 3775, fo. 87r.

[27] *PROME*, vii.350–1.

[28] *CR*, 219–21; Given-Wilson, 'Richard II, Edward II and the Lancastrian Inheritance', 562–3.

[29] *CR*, 79; *PROME*, vii.411–12.

[30] *CR*, 78–83. A confession which Gloucester had written 'by his own hand' at Calais on the afternoon that he died was read out on the Tuesday in order to provide further justification for his conviction, although it was abbreviated; the true date of his death was concealed and his pleas for mercy omitted (*PROME*, vii.413–14).

[31] *CR*, 61; *PROME*, vii.415–16. 'By St John the Baptist,' Richard declared, 'this confession of yours, Thomas of Warwick, is worth more to me than the value of all the lands of the duke of Gloucester and the earl of Arundel.'

[32] *SAC II*, 252–5.

king of England did Henry shed many tears over the fate of his former co-Appellants.

Henry's acquiescence in Richard's coup brought instant rewards. On the Saturday, the day following Warwick's trial, the king pardoned him and Mowbray for their role in the events of 1387–8.[33] They also shared in the most lavish bestowal of new titles ever seen in England. Five dukes, one duchess, one marquess and four earls were created, among whom Henry became duke of Hereford. He was the only one of the new dukes not to have acted as a Counter-Appellant,[34] and on Monday 1 October he celebrated his new status by hosting a requiem mass and dinner, attended by the king and queen, at the Carmelite friary between Fleet Street and the Thames, at which the bones of Thomas Mowbray's father, John Lord Mowbray, who had died on crusade in 1368, were ceremonially reinterred, having been brought back in a jar from Constantinople.[35] A goodwill gesture towards his fellow survivor, Mowbray, the occasion must also have been tinged with relief, although both men knew that it was far from over. Parliament had been adjourned, not dissolved, and would reconvene at Shrewsbury in late January to consider the 'weighty causes and matters . . . which cannot be decided at this time',[36] a form of words unlikely to soothe fears.

The king now moved to Windsor,[37] accompanied by Gaunt and Henry. According to Henry, Mowbray told him two months later that 'if other people had not been there', he and Gaunt would have been either seized or killed when they came to Windsor, but this may have been a stretch of the imagination on the part of Mowbray, who by now was a man living in fear on account of the rumours circulating about his involvement in Gloucester's murder. The ubiquitous Bagot told him of the rumours in October 1397, to which Mowbray 'swore great oaths' that he had in fact saved Gloucester's

[33] PROME, vii.354–5. The pardon stated that in 1387–8 they had 'come to [the king] as loyal lieges, away from the company of the said duke [of Gloucester] and the earls of Arundel and Warwick, and had remained with our lord the king since'.

[34] Apart from Henry, the new promotions were: Edward earl of Rutland to duke of Aumale; John Holand earl of Huntingdon to duke of Exeter; Thomas Holand earl of Kent to duke of Surrey; Thomas Mowbray earl of Nottingham to duke of Norfolk; Margaret Marshal to duchess of Norfolk; John Beaufort earl of Somerset to marquess of Dorset; Thomas Despenser to earl of Gloucester; William Le Scrope to earl of Wiltshire; Thomas Percy to earl of Worcester; Ralph Nevill to earl of Westmorland. The Counter-Appellant to miss out was John Montague, earl of Salisbury, who had only inherited his earldom two months earlier.

[35] DL 28/1/6, fos. 7v, 8r, 15v; E 326/9376. Henry paid for 'regal canopies' to be made for the king and queen.

[36] PROME, vii.359.

[37] CPR 1396–9, 207, 210–12.

life for more than three weeks and only eventually did the deed 'out of
dread of the king and fear of his own life'.[38] This was probably true, yet
herein lay his dilemma, for his initial hesitation had also angered Richard,
and before long the strain would become too much for him to bear alone.
Henry, meanwhile, was undertaking a progress to the seat of his new
duchy.[39] Leaving London around 20 October, he visited his three younger
children at Eaton Tregoz, then moved on via Hereford to Brecon, where on
6 November he presided over the chief court of his lordship of Brecon,[40]
before returning to Woodstock, where he spent one or two nights with the
king.[41] From Woodstock, Henry made his way unhurriedly back to London,
but as he passed through Brentford on his way to the city, sometime during
the first week of December 1397, he met Thomas Mowbray.

From the moment Mowbray began speaking to him, Henry would have
been aware of the magnitude of the events unfolding ahead of him and
the possibility that they would lead to the destruction of the house of
Lancaster. Unfortunately there is no surviving record of Mowbray's side of
the story; the words and sentiments attributed to him were written by
Henry, whose first consideration was to ensure that nothing he said would
be self-incriminating. There is, nevertheless, plenty of evidence to support
the essential points of Henry's story, and no reason to suppose that he
would have invented it. As he told it, he was riding between Brentford and
London when Mowbray unexpectedly came upon him and declared, 'We
are about to be undone'.[42] When Henry asked why, Mowbray replied,
'because of what was done at Radcot Bridge'. When Henry protested that
they had been pardoned by the king, Mowbray told him the king had
decided to 'annul that record'. He went on to tell Henry about the plot to
seize or kill him and Gaunt when they came to Windsor in early October,
adding that those responsible for it were the duke of Surrey and the earls
of Wiltshire, Salisbury and Gloucester (four of the eight Counter-
Appellants), whereas the dukes of Aumale and Exeter, the earl of Worcester
and Mowbray himself had sworn not to allow any lords to be destroyed

---

[38] *PROME*, vii.369; *CR*, 211.

[39] For Henry's itinerary in October–November 1397, see DL 28/1/10.

[40] For this privilege the tenants and residents of Brecon, Hay and Cantref Selyf had to
give him a 'gift' of £1,233, the first instalment of which (£530) was handed over to Henry
that same day: SC 6/1157/4. This was separate from the rents and other perquisites of the
lordship which, as already noted, frequently yielded over £1,000 a year.

[41] Richard was at Woodstock from 15–21 November: Saul, *Richard II*, 473; Henry and his
servants stayed 'in the household of the lord king' on 19 November (DL 28/1/10, fo. 9r).

[42] *PROME*, vii.369–70.

without just cause; in other words, that the latter four were the 'other people' who had saved Gaunt and Henry at Windsor – and not just Gaunt and Henry for, as Mowbray went on to explain, he and Aumale and Exeter, as well as John Beaufort earl of Somerset, were also in danger of being 'undone' by Surrey, Wiltshire, Salisbury and Gloucester. Yet this was not all: the conspirators were also intent on reversing 'the judgment concerning earl Thomas of Lancaster', and the king himself was a party to this plot. 'God forbid!' replied Henry, adding (for public, and especially Richard's, consumption) that it would be a 'great wonder' if the king were to assent to such a scheme, since he had sworn to be a good lord to him. Yet if what Mowbray said were true, 'we could never trust in them'. 'Certainly not,' agreed Mowbray, 'since even if they are unable to achieve their purpose at present, they will be intent on destroying us in our homes ten years hence.'

Mowbray's revelations placed Henry in a quandary. Whatever the precise details of the plot or the factions involved, the idea of a conspiracy to bring down the house of Lancaster was credible, and the four lords identified by Mowbray as being behind it – Surrey, Wiltshire, Salisbury and Gloucester – plausible conspirators. Greedy for greatness, harbouring claims from bygone generations against Gaunt and his heirs, they were men who had nailed their colours unequivocally to Richard's mast.[43] It is in fact difficult to believe that Henry was as innocent as he pretended to be of any suspicions as to Richard's intentions. Yet what was he to do? And what, he must have wondered, did Mowbray hope to achieve by telling him all this? Was Mowbray really in league with the king (as another account of the anti-Lancastrian conspiracy alleged),[44] and setting a trap for Henry? If that were the case, and if Henry simply remained silent, he would lay himself open to a charge of misprision. If, on the other hand, he revealed to the king what Mowbray had said to him, there was no telling how Richard might react. In fact he did what he had usually done when in trouble: he turned to his father. He told Gaunt about Mowbray's revelations, and together they decided that the least dangerous option was to tell the king.[45] Exactly when Gaunt told Richard is difficult to say, but it must have been by mid-January.[46] Shortly after New Year, despite the midwinter

[43] Given-Wilson, 'Richard II, Edward II, and the Lancastrian Inheritance', 555–7.
[44] Ibid., 559.
[45] CE, iii.379.
[46] Richard stayed in the Midlands in December and January, while Henry spent most of December in London before travelling to Leicester to spend Christmas with his father and then on to Framlingham castle (Suffolk), the home of Margaret Marshal, newly created duchess of Norfolk, where he spent New Year (DL 28/1/6, fos. 5v, 24v; Saul, Richard II, 473).

conditions, Henry went north to the shrine of John of Bridlington, where he had prayed at moments of danger or deliverance in the past; he also commissioned a London goldsmith to make him a chain for a medicinal stone to counter the effects of poison.[47] On his return, he was informed that he had been summoned to Richard's presence.

Richard was staying at Great Haywood in Staffordshire between 18 and 23 January 1398, awaiting the resumption of parliament at Shrewsbury.[48] When Henry arrived,[49] he was asked by the king to tell him what had transpired between him and Mowbray. Richard then asked him to write it down, which Henry did, 'on the understanding that I may enlarge upon or abridge any of the following at any time that it should please me or seem necessary to do so, always saving the substance of my accusation'. He also secured another pardon from the king for any treason or other crime he might have committed in the past.[50] Mowbray was not at Great Haywood, but he must have heard about Gaunt's and Henry's revelations within a day or two, and reacted with fury. He laid an ambush for Gaunt, apparently intending to kill him on his way to the parliament, but Gaunt was forewarned and reached Shrewsbury unscathed.[51] Panicking, Mowbray now fled, leaving Henry a free hand to present his side of the case, which he did on Wednesday 30 January, the third day of the parliament. Richard immediately stripped Mowbray of his office of Earl Marshal, and four days later issued orders for his arrest. Meanwhile, on 31 January, the last day of parliament, Richard announced that he did not for the moment intend to reach a decision regarding Henry's allegations, but that the matter would be referred to a commission of eighteen members of the lords and commons which included many of those mentioned in Henry's schedule, such as Gaunt, the dukes of Aumale, Surrey and Exeter, and the earls of March, Salisbury and Gloucester.[52]

On the same day, Henry secured yet another pardon from Richard after kneeling before the throne and confessing his part in the 'uprisings, troubles

[47] Nor did he omit to send the king an Epiphany gift, a gold tablet with an image of John the Baptist, and to Queen Isabella a hart of gold with pearls for its crown (DL 28/1/10, fos. 12r, 22v, 24r; *CPR 1396–9*, 571).

[48] Saul, *Richard II*, 473.

[49] He came with an impressive retinue: he paid £27 for the wages of the knights, esquires and archers who accompanied him to Shrewsbury for the parliament (DL 28/1/10, fos. 3v, 32v).

[50] *PROME*, vii.370; Henry's pardon was dated 25 January at Lilleshall (Shropshire), indicating that he probably remained with Richard, who was at Lilleshall that day, until parliament met (*CPR 1396–9*, 280).

[51] *Usk*, 48–9; *Traïson et Mort*, 16–17.

[52] *PROME*, vii.370.

and misdeeds perpetrated in your kingdom'.[53] Whether this made him feel more secure may be doubted. Before bringing the session to a close, Richard once again indicated his willingness to reconsider land claims dating from the reign of Edward II. The judgments against the Elder and Younger Despenser in 1321 and 1327 were overturned, and Thomas Despenser, the new earl of Gloucester, given permission to sue for recovery of their lands. So far-reaching were the ramifications of this decision that Thomas was obliged to swear on the cross of Canterbury that he would not attempt to recover any of these properties, either from Richard himself or from any of ten named lords of the realm, including Gaunt and Henry.[54] Yet such judgments created uncertainty, and rumours now abounded. Adam Usk, a protégé of the Mortimers, said that Richard and his friends were also conspiring to entrap the earl of March and divide up his lands between them, but March bore himself with enough circumspection to avoid the trap.[55] Seeking reassurance, Henry and Gaunt secured from the king on 20 February a quitclaim and release of any rights which Richard might have in the lands or properties formerly held by Earl Thomas of Lancaster by reason of the latter's treason, sedition or forfeiture; in other words, Richard now promised not to do precisely what Mowbray had said that he and his friends had planned to do.[56]

The next eight months of Henry's life were dominated by the unravelling of his dispute with Mowbray. On 23 February, by which time Mowbray had either surrendered or been arrested, he and Henry appeared before the king at Oswestry, where it was agreed that their case would be referred to a meeting of the royal council in late April. In the meantime, both men were imprisoned at Windsor, although Henry was promptly bailed by a consortium of lords headed by his father and remained at liberty throughout the spring and summer.[57] Mowbray, on the other hand, was detained in

[53] *PROME*, vii.387.

[54] *PROME*, vii.386–9. Richard accomplished much else at Shrewsbury, including a grant of the wool subsidy for life, the annulment of all the acts of the Merciless Parliament, the reaffirmation of the Questions to the Judges of 1387, and the trial of John Lord Cobham, an elderly peer whose crime was to have been involved in the setting up of the Commission of Government in 1386. Although convicted of treason, Cobham was sentenced, like Warwick, to exile for life rather than to death.

[55] C. Given-Wilson, 'Chronicles of the Mortimer Family, 1250–1450', in *Family and Dynasty in Late Medieval England*, ed. R. Eales and S. Tyas (Donington, 2003), 67–86, at p. 75; *CR*, 60, 62; *Usk*, 38–40. Usk said that it was in order to prevent the loss of Denbigh that March had come over from Ireland, of which he was lieutenant, to attend the Shrewsbury session of parliament.

[56] *CPR 1396–9*, 285; Gaunt had a copy made and kept in the Duchy archive (DL 10/363).

[57] *Traïson et Mort*, 142; *CCR 1396–9*, 249; *ANLP*, no. 56. Henry's household account (DL 28/1/10) also makes it clear that he remained at liberty.

prison for several months.[58] Thus far, Richard's behaviour had suggested a presumption of Mowbray's guilt, and things continued for the moment to go Henry's way. At the beginning of March, William Bagot was obliged to seal two recognizances in which he swore neither to disinherit nor to make any attempt on the life of Gaunt, his wife or his children, on pain of being put to death without further process.[59] Then on 19 March came a setback: the parliamentary committee appointed at Shrewsbury met at Bristol and decreed that unless sufficient proof could be found one way or the other the dispute between Henry and Mowbray would be tried by battle.[60] Henry probably felt reluctant to commit his cause to the hazard of a duel; true, he was an experienced and successful jouster, but so was Mowbray.[61] He thus brought further charges, more susceptible to proof, against Mowbray. At a council meeting at Windsor on 29 April,[62] he made three new accusations: first, that Mowbray was guilty of peculation with respect to his custody of Calais; secondly, that he was 'the cause of all the treason committed in your realm these last eighteen years'; thirdly, that Mowbray had murdered the duke of Gloucester. This last charge must have been especially unwelcome to Richard. Simply to talk of Gloucester's murder was, in a sense, to point the finger at the king, for it was his contention that Gloucester had died a natural death. Henry may have hoped that Richard would take fright and proceed to judgment against Mowbray forthwith, hoping to avoid any further discussion of the question, but would Mowbray then plead that he had been acting on the king's orders? It was to neither man's advantage to have the matter discussed, and for Henry to have raised it was a dangerous, though calculated, gamble.[63] In the event, Mowbray admitted receiving large sums for the custody of Calais but denied peculation, admitted having once planned to kill Gaunt but insisted that Gaunt had pardoned him, but of Gloucester's death he said nothing, and no more was heard of it. Richard asked both men if they would agree to be reconciled, but when they replied that they would not, he set a day for their combat: it would take place at Coventry on Monday 16 September. The

---

[58] He was held first at Windsor and later in the great wardrobe at Baynard's castle in London: *Usk*, 48.

[59] *CCR 1396–9*, 291–2; *CPR 1396–9*, 317. Bagot was also suspected of being involved in the anti-Lancastrian plot. He later admitted, in the October 1399 parliament, that he had once planned to put Gaunt to death, despite his years of service to the house of Lancaster (Given-Wilson, 'Richard II, Edward II and the Lancastrian Inheritance', 559).

[60] *PROME*, vii.422–3; Given-Wilson, 'Richard II, Edward II and the Lancastrian Inheritance', 564–5.

[61] *Westminster Chronicle*, 437.

[62] *Traïson et Mort*, 13–17 (the author was an eyewitness); *CR*, 99, 103–4.

[63] That Henry accused Mowbray of Gloucester's murder is confirmed in *CE*, 379.

five-month delay was intended as a cooling-off period, but may also have been designed to give Richard time to consider his options.

Henry remained at liberty throughout these months.[64] His household accounts convey a sense of restlessness. He was continually on the move, to Yorkshire, Lincolnshire and Norfolk in the early summer, London at the beginning of July and various places in the west Midlands in August and September.[65] The main purpose of this itineration of the Lancastrian heartlands was probably to show himself to his people, to remind them where, should it become necessary, their allegiance lay.[66] He distributed over fifty livery collars in 1397–8,[67] while his small band of personal friends, most of whom had been with him for many years, gathered close about him, accompanying him on his travels and directing his affairs. Peter Bukton and Robert Litton, steward and controller respectively of his household, Thomas Erpingham, the Watertons, Thomas Rempston, John Tiptoft, the Milanese esquire Francis de Courte, John Pelham and John Norbury were regularly, in some cases almost continuously, with him during 1398.[68] Messages also passed between Henry and several of the French princes during the summer of 1398, indicative of foreign interest in the upcoming duel.[69] Gian Galeazzo Visconti sent Henry a new suit of Milanese armour, accompanied by four of his armourers to ensure that it was properly fitted, since 'he loved him so greatly'.[70] In early August, the king made a final attempt to reconcile the two men, without success.[71] On 23 August Henry's half-brother, Henry Beaufort, now bishop of Lincoln,

[64] He also received some grants from the king, notably the reversion of the properties which he had surrendered to Gloucester for life in 1395 (Westcott, Wethersfield, Nuthampstead and Newnham), restored to him in May 1398 as part of Mary de Bohun's inheritance (CCR 1396 9, 246, 266, 269), and a gift of £300 from the king, part of an unspecified larger sum which Richard ordered to be paid to Henry 'for certain reasonable causes particularly moving the said lord king' (E 403/559, 24 July 1398).

[65] On 19–20 June he visited the shrine of St Mary at Walsingham (Norfolk), praying, perhaps, for a resolution to his predicament (DL 28/1/10, fos. 29r–v).

[66] Walker, Lancastrian Affinity, 204 ('this great circular tour of his father's dominions'); Davies, Lords and Lordship, 90.

[67] DL 28/1/6, fos. 22r–23r (some of these collars included his favoured motto, Souvenez vous de moi).

[68] DL 28/1/10, fos. 29v–34r; 28/1/6, fos. 22r–24r.

[69] The duke of Brittany sent two men to Henry at Hertford in May, the steward and three knights of Charles VI of France stayed with him at Birmingham on 5 August, and in September messengers arrived from the dukes of Burgundy and Orléans; Henry sent his old jousting companion Marshal Boucicaut a saddle (DL 28/1/10, fos 14v, 23r, 25r, 31r; 28/1/5, fo. 24v; 28/1/9, fos. 6v, 7r).

[70] Oeuvres de Froissart, xvi.95–6; DL 28/1/5, fo. 21r. In return he sent the duke a saddle. Mowbray ordered a suit of armour from Germany, probably Bohemia. Francis de Courte liaised between Henry and Gian Galeazzo.

[71] CCR 1396–9, 324.

ordered prayers and processions for the justice of Henry's cause to be held throughout his diocese.[72] By 31 August, when Richard issued a general invitation to the contest, it must have become apparent that this eagerly awaited combat really was about to take place.[73]

By the afternoon of Sunday 15 September the king had arrived at Baginton, the tower-house belonging to William Bagot halfway between Kenilworth and Coventry, where, after dinner that day, Henry came to pay his respects to Richard. At daybreak on the Monday, Mowbray did likewise.[74] An enormous crowd had gathered, including a delegation of French lords led by the Count of St Pol and representatives from Scotland and Germany. Henry, as the appellant, arrived at the lists at nine o'clock with six or seven splendidly caparisoned horses,[75] and was formally charged to state his purpose. 'I am Henry of Lancaster, duke of Hereford,' he replied, 'and I have come here to do my duty in combat with Thomas Mowbray, duke of Norfolk, a false and disloyal traitor to God, the king, his kingdom and myself.' Then, raising his shield, which was silver with a red cross like the arms of St George,[76] he closed the visor of his helmet, made the sign of the cross, and entered the lists, where he rode straight to a seat decorated with red flowers, dismounted and entered his pavilion. Next to appear was the king, accompanied by lords, ladies and a great host of archers and men-at-arms; once Richard had taken his seat, a herald called upon Mowbray to come forward and do his duty. He too rode to his pavilion and dismounted. The two men's lances were measured by the constable and marshal to ensure that they were the same length, and handed back to them. When everything was ready, the herald ordered the pavilions to be taken down, the seconds were instructed to remove the horses' restraints,[77] and Henry and Mowbray were bidden to do their duty.

Henry promptly raised his lance and advanced seven or eight paces, while Mowbray 'neither moved nor made any attempt to defend himself'. However, before anything else could happen Richard rose from his seat

---

[72] M. Bennett, *Richard II and the Revolution of 1399* (Stroud, 1999), 132.

[73] E 403/559, 31 August.

[74] On 12 August Henry had had his armour moved to Kenilworth, and here he based himself for the next few weeks, although he did twice visit nearby Coventry, presumably in preparation for the combat; he also made brief visits to London and Hertford in late August or early September (DL 28/1/6, fo. 42v; 28/1/10, fos. 23–8). What follows is based primarily on the eyewitness account in *Traïson et Mort*, 17–23, 149–58.

[75] *Usk*, 50–1.

[76] 'dargent a une croix rouge pareille aux armes Saint George' (*Traïson et Mort*, 19).

[77] Henry's second at the duel was his esquire Robert Waterton (*CPR 1396–9*, 514). Mowbray was attended by the Bohemian esquire Jacques Felm (*Traïson et Mort*, 149).

and cried out that the two men be escorted back to their places.[78] Two hours now passed before John Bussy emerged to announce the king's decision. Although he stressed that Henry and Mowbray had both defended their honour, the issue between them was so grave a matter that the king had decided to banish the duke of Hereford from the realm for a period of ten years. This caused uproar, for despite Richard's announcement it was assumed that Henry must have forfeited his honour. Eventually, when the crowd had been quieted, it was announced that Mowbray too would be banished, in his case for life. Richard justified his decision on the grounds that he wished to avoid the dishonour that would befall the loser of the duel, since both men were so closely related to the king, and that he needed to guard against the possibility of quarrels breaking out between them or their followers in future. The more severe sentence on Mowbray he explained by the fact that at the Windsor council on 29 April he had confessed to 'certain civil points' (presumably his attempt to ambush Gaunt), that he had failed to support the repeal of the acts of the Merciless Parliament, and that his misgovernance of Calais had placed the security of the town in jeopardy. He was thus ordered by the king to make his way to Germany, Bohemia or Hungary, or to go on pilgrimage to Jerusalem, but not, under pain of treason, to live in any other part of Christendom. No such geographical limits were placed on Henry; he and Mowbray were, however, strictly ordered not to communicate with each other while in exile or to have any contact with Thomas Arundel, the exiled archbishop of Canterbury. Both men were to leave the realm by 20 October.[79]

The chroniclers did not believe Richard's explanation: some thought he was punishing Henry for opposing him in 1387–8, others that he had simply been waiting for an opportunity to destroy him.[80] However, they were writing in the aftermath of the revolution of 1399, which also helps to explain their almost unanimous dislike of Mowbray.[81] Impetuous and mercurial Mowbray may have been, but he took a more principled stance than Henry in 1397–8, as witness his insistence on the validity of the 1388 appeals, to which he and Henry had both been parties. Moreover, if Henry's

---

[78] *Traïson et Mort*, 21; *CR*, 63, 68, 97. *Usk*, 50–1, said that the two dukes actually began the combat, but when 'it seemed to [the king] that the duke of Hereford was going to win', he ordered a halt to the proceedings, but this is contradicted by all other accounts.

[79] *CR*, 89–92.

[80] *Usk*, 50–1; *CR*, 63; *SAC II*, 108–9, 120–3.

[81] The Kirkstall chronicler, for example, wrote of the worthy (*venerabilis*) duke of Hereford appealing the frightful (*horrificum*) duke of Norfolk (*Kirkstall Abbey Chronicles*, ed. J. Taylor, Thoresby Society Publications, 1952, 120); Usk (pp. 50–1) claimed that Richard planned to recall Mowbray as soon as possible.

story of their encounter in December 1397 was true, then Mowbray had every right to feel betrayed. Had he not been trying to warn Henry of the danger to his life and his inheritance, to which Henry responded by breaking his confidence and denouncing him as a traitor?[82] Nevertheless, the anger felt by many contemporaries at Henry's treatment was understandable: this was a man, after all, against whom nothing had been proven, and who – if his story is to be believed – had been trying to warn the king about the covert disaffection of a magnate who was apparently on the closest of terms with Richard.[83] The revival of exile as a political punishment for opponents of the crown suggests indecision on Richard's part: fearful of allowing either Henry or Mowbray to be proved right, he chose instead to inflict unmerited but harsh punishment on at least one of them.[84]

The five weeks allowed to Henry before his departure he spent with his father at Leicester and visiting Eaton Tregoz.[85] A major preoccupation was the care of his children, who by now ranged in age from four to twelve. Humphrey, Blanche and Philippa remained at Eaton in the care of Sir Hugh Waterton during Henry's exile.[86] The three older boys had begun to be moved around more, their range of contacts expanding as they matured. John spent most of his father's absence in or around London, with his tutor Thomas Rothwell.[87] The young Henry, the heir, was retained – or perhaps

[82] The comment of the author of *CE* that Mowbray spoke to Henry 'secretly and in total confidence' is easy to believe (*CR*, 68).

[83] The French chroniclers reflected this dismay, but included some strange and implausible additions. The *Chronographia Regum Francorum* (iii.165) said that when Richard announced his decision to halt the combat and exile Henry and Mowbray, John of Gaunt tried to dissuade him, saying 'I know them better than you; they are both worthless, and as for my son, I assure you that he will enrage and confound you again and again to an extent that you have never been enraged or confounded. Let them fight for God's right and die in the duel, nothing withstanding', to which Richard simply replied that he intended to keep a close eye on Henry. *Saint-Denys* (ii.670–4), in contrast, said that Gaunt advised the king to forbid the combat, asking Richard what he would do should Henry lose. 'I will have him drawn to the gallows,' replied the king, adding that even if it were Gaunt himself who was involved he would do exactly the same.

[84] Froissart's belief that Richard reduced Henry's term of exile to six years has no basis in fact, although Henry did have two more meetings with the king before he left England: at Nuneaton on 20 September and at Windsor on 3 October (*Oeuvres de Froissart*, xvi.109–10; *CPR 1396–9*, 417, 514). Cf. *Traïson et Mort*, 23, 158, where 'Nonetes' is wrongly taken to be Leicester.

[85] DL 28/1/10, fo. 30r; Goodman, *John of Gaunt*, 165.

[86] Richard Chalons was 'esquire of the lord's daughters'; two grooms and two ladies-in-waiting, Katherine and Marie, were responsible for their daily care. The seven-year-old Humphrey had the esquire William Gyse to attend him, and was occasionally taken to Tutbury or Kenilworth to spend time with his grandfather. Humphrey had his own goat, which his maid Lucy Salmay was paid sixpence to milk for eight weeks (DL 28/1/6, fo. 11r; 28/1/9, fos. 13r, 15v, 19v–21r; 28/1/10, fos. 11v, 31r, 34r; SC 6/1157/4, m. 4r).

[87] DL 28/4/1, fos. 13v–14v. When Gaunt died in February, a boy was sent from London to Eaton Tregoz with black livery robes for the three younger children.

detained – at court by the king, and accompanied him on campaign to Ireland in May 1399; although he was apparently well treated by Richard, he must have felt that he was in some sense a hostage for his father's behaviour. The only one to accompany their father into exile was his second son Thomas, said to have been Henry's favourite.[88] Richard had done what he could to forestall any challenge by Henry or Mowbray to the judgment given at Coventry, forbidding them under pain of treason even to request the reversal of his decision or to sue for permission to return.[89] However, Henry was allowed to appoint attorneys to act on his behalf while abroad and to sue for livery of any inheritance which might fall to him during his exile, an obvious reference to the fact that Gaunt was not expected to live for another ten years. Seventeen named companions also received letters of protection to accompany him into exile: they included stalwarts from his crusading days such as Erpingham, Rempston and Norbury, men who had served him since his childhood such as William Loveney and Thomas Totty, and the constable of Bordeaux and future archbishop of York, Henry Bowet, who was given permission to accompany Henry to 'Lombardy and elsewhere in those parts', an indication of Henry's uncertainty about his intentions.[90] Gaunt is said to have advised his son either to go to Paris or to visit his sisters in Iberia. He certainly departed in style: he was licensed to travel with up to two hundred servants, £1,000 in cash, and whatever he needed in terms of plate, jewels, horses and other baggage.[91] He spent his last week in London, confirming grants to his servants and retainers, settling his affairs and borrowing money.[92] On 8 October he appointed attorneys to act in his absence: these included a number of familiar servants – John Leventhorpe, Hugh Waterton, his household treasurer Simon Bache, his steward Peter Bukton, and Mary de Bohun's

[88] *Historical Collections*, 101, says that Thomas returned from exile with his father in the summer of 1399 (cf. G. Harriss, 'Thomas, Duke of Clarence', *ODNB*, 54.284–5; DL 28/1/10, fo. 28r; *CR*, 35). Richard knighted the young Henry in Ireland (Allmand, *Henry V*, 12).

[89] *PROME*, vii.424–5.

[90] SC 8/332/15718A and B: the full list was: Erpingham, Rempston, Norbury, Totty, Loveney, John Dabrichecourt, John Cokeyn, Henry Bowet, John Payn, Robert Chalons, Esmond Bugge, John Knyveton, John Multon, Henry Longdon, Ralph Ramsey, John Topcliff of Kent and William Pomfreit. Totty was licensed to impress 'sufficient vessels . . . called *passageres*' for Henry's channel crossing *(CPR 1396–9, 417, 425, 440)*.

[91] Richard also gave instructions allowing Henry to stay at Calais for a month with twelve persons or at Sangatte castle (Pas-de-Calais) with his household (*CPR 1396–9*, 440, 470, 499, 537; *CCR 1396–9*, 339).

[92] Among the sums he borrowed were 100 marks from the abbot of Gloucester, £40 from the archdeacon of Leicester, £100 from the bishop of Durham and 100 marks from Thomas Hardwick, clerk; these were repaid in November 1399 (DL 42/15, fo. 74v).

former receiver William Burgoyne – along with magnates such as the duke
of Aumale, the archbishop of York, the earls of Northumberland,
Worcester and Wiltshire and, surprisingly, the earl of Salisbury, a slippery
parvenu with a claim to several Lancastrian properties.[93] On 13 October,
the feast of the Translation of Edward the Confessor, Henry crossed from
Dover to Calais and headed straight for Paris.[94]

---

[93] *Foedera*, viii.48–50.

[94] Mowbray made the parallel crossing from Lowestoft to Dordrecht six days later; he
never set foot in England again, dying of the plague at Venice on 22 September 1399
(*PROME*, vii.425).

Chapter 9

'A MANIFEST MIRACLE OF GOD'
(1398–1399)

For most of the eight months he spent in Paris, Henry was based at the Hôtel de Clisson, at the heart of the city near the Temple. The welcome he received from King Charles VI and the princes of the blood was generous, and there was even talk of a possible marriage between him and Mary, the widowed daughter of the duke of Berry.[1] Richard, alarmed, sent the earl of Salisbury to Paris to remind the French king that Henry was a traitor, and when Duke Philip of Burgundy repeated Salisbury's words in Henry's hearing it caused a row between them, although Charles protested that Henry had been treated unfairly.[2] Yet if the French took a dim view of Richard's machinations against Henry, accusing him of secretly coveting the Lancastrian estates, the English king could point out that Henry's failure to disentangle himself from the undergrowth of factionalism which had sprung up around the intermittently insane Charles did little to smooth the path of Anglo-French diplomacy.[3] Whether or not it was Henry's decision to stay at the Hôtel de Clisson, it was a decision with implications: its builder, Olivier de Clisson, one of the towering figures of French politics during the last thirty years of the fourteenth century, was the inveterate foe of England's ally John de Montfort, duke of Brittany; as one of the 'Marmousets' who had excluded the royal uncles from power between 1388 and 1392, he was also hated by the dukes of Berry and Burgundy, who toppled him from power following Charles's first attack of madness in

---

[1] *Saint-Denys*, ii.674 ('as long as he remained there, he was lodged in royal residences, lavishly provided for, along with his retinue, at the king's expense, and loaded with gifts'). *Chronographia Regum Francorum* (iii.166) said that Henry also visited Meaux, just east of Paris, at some point.

[2] *Oeuvres de Froissart*, xvi.141–9; Salisbury was in Paris from late October to early December 1398: E403/561, 18 October; J. Laidlaw, 'Christine de Pizan, the Earl of Salisbury and Henry IV', *French Studies* 36 (1982), 129–43.

[3] The chronicler of Saint-Denis said Henry befriended the duke of Berry, but Berry was not in Paris for much of the time Henry was there: from early August 1398 until 9 February 1399 he remained on his estates in Berry and Auvergne. Nor did he favour Henry's marriage to his daughter (F. Lehoux, *Jean de France, Duc de Berri* (3 vols, Paris 1966), ii.394–407).

1392.[4] This, however, only drove Clisson into the arms of the king's brother Louis, duke of Orléans, with whom he concluded a pact in October 1397 – in reality, a pact against Philip of Burgundy and his clients, who by now dominated the royal council. Philip was the English king's main ally at the French court and the architect on the French side of the twenty-eight-year truce of 1396. Louis of Orléans, by contrast, advocated a more robust cross-Channel policy, drawing into his orbit men such as Clisson who had waged decades of often successful warfare against the English.

Clisson was only rarely in Paris these days, but he and Henry were in contact.[5] Around Christmas time, there was a rumour that the two of them, together with Louis of Orléans and John, count of Nevers, were planning an expedition to Avignon and Milan where, with the help of Duke Gian Galeazzo (Louis's father-in-law), they would effect a reconciliation between the Roman and Avignonese popes.[6] Henry's friendship with Orléans was also well known: they often supped together, and in late January 1399 Louis entertained Henry and Mary de Berry at his castle of Asnières (Normandy), apparently to encourage their relationship.[7] Yet their alleged initiative on the Schism, the most contentious issue in French politics and one of the many which divided Orléans and Burgundy, can hardly have received the blessing of either the French or the English king,[8] and it is easy to see why Richard felt constrained to take counter-measures. Salisbury's mission to Paris was one such move; another was Richard's decision in October 1398 to retain a man whose reputation for thuggery outstripped even that of

[4] The Hôtel de Clisson, built around 1370, was a monument to the wealth and power of this former constable of France: J. Henneman, *Olivier de Clisson and Political Society in France under Charles V and Charles VI* (Philadelphia, 1996); Lehoux, *Jean de France*, ii.201.

[5] He was in Paris in April 1399, however, at the *Parlement* (Henneman, *Olivier de Clisson*, 171, 191, 304).

[6] Note Henry's earlier request to take Henry Bowet to Lombardy, above, p. 117. P. Pietresson de Saint Aubin, 'Documents inédits sur l'installation de Pierre d'Ailly à l'évêché de Cambrai en 1397', *Bibliothèque de l'école des Chartes* (1955), 121–2, 138–9; *CR*, 26–9. John of Nevers was the son of Philip, duke of Burgundy; it was said that Burgundy and Orléans had settled their differences, but this was optimistic. The possibility of a marriage between Henry and Lucia Visconti, Gian Galeazzo's cousin, was also still being discussed as late as May 1399.

[7] *Oeuvres de Froissart*, xvi.116, 137; E. Collas, *Valentine de Milan, Duchesse d'Orléans* (Paris, 1911), 253; BL Add. Charters 3066, 3404. Duchess Valentina gave Henry a diamond and a set of seven enamels on this occasion, costing 862 francs; she also gave two diamonds worth 30 francs each to two of Henry's esquires with him at Asnières on 27 January. See also 'Histoire de Charles VI, Roy de France, par Jean Jouvenal des Ursins', in *Choix de Chroniques et Mémoires sur l'Histoire de France*, ed. J. Buchon (Paris, 1838), 323–573, at pp. 405–7.

[8] H. Kaminsky, 'The Politics of France's Subtraction of Obedience from Pope Benedict XIII, 27 July 1398', *Proceedings of the American Philosophical Society* 115 (1971), 366–97. Orléans supported Benedict XIII, who supported Orléans's ambitions in Italy: B. Schnerb, *Jean Sans Peur, Le Prince Meurtrier* (Paris, 2005), 164.

Clisson. Pierre de Craon, Lord of Ferté-Bernard, had fled France following a bungled attempt to assassinate Clisson in the rue de Saint-Pol, just yards away from the royal palace, in June 1392 and eventually made his way to England where, on 15 October 1398, two days after Henry left Dover to begin his exile, the English king retained him at the extravagant price of £500 a year for life.[9] His infamy notwithstanding, Craon still had powerful friends at the French court, and they were not the same men as those whom Orléans or Clisson counted as their friends. In February 1399 Richard sent Craon and the royal under-chamberlain, Sir Stephen Le Scrope, to Paris on 'secret affairs', that is, to assess the state of French politics.[10]

If Richard made sure to keep abreast of developments in France, Henry also kept in touch with events in England. He exchanged letters with his father, who continued to offer him advice until, around Christmas, the fifty-eight-year-old Gaunt fell ill.[11] He died on 3 February 1399 at Leicester castle, deeply depressed on account of the uncertainty surrounding his son's future and that of the Lancastrian inheritance.[12] His will included the unusual provision that his body should remain unburied for forty days after his death, and thus it was not until 16 March that he was interred next to the high altar in St Paul's cathedral in London beside Henry's mother, Duchess Blanche.[13] This was, Henry knew, a pivotal moment both for Richard and for himself: would the king keep his word and let him sue for livery of his father's estates, or would he succumb to the temptation to sequester the Lancastrian inheritance? The answer was not long in coming. A week before the funeral, at a council meeting at King's Langley (Hertfordshire), Richard made the decision to extend Henry's ten-year

[9] Henneman, *Olivier de Clisson*, 153–4, 169–71; *Foedera*, viii.52; Craon received £666 13s 4d of this (E 403/561, 6 November, 8 January; E 403/562, 2 May, 13 May, 9 July), and accompanied Richard to Ireland (*CPR 1396–9*, 553).

[10] E 403/561, 21 February.

[11] Henry's ministers' accounts show constant messengers between England and Paris (DL 28/4/1, fos. 2r, 4v, 6r, 7r). When Marshal Boucicaut invited him to join an expedition against the Turks to avenge the disastrous defeat by a crusading army at Nicopolis in 1396, Henry sent Sir Thomas Dymmok to ask Gaunt if he ought to go. Gaunt advised against it, saying that if he felt the urge to travel, he would be better advised to visit his sisters in Portugal and Castile. Dymmok took the opportunity to visit Henry's children and make a tour of his English estates (*Oeuvres de Froissart*, xvi.132–7).

[12] Goodman, *John of Gaunt*, 168, 174, quoting the Kirkstall chronicle. Gaunt had secured a pardon from the king for all his debts on 30 December, and £1,000 in restored tallies on 8 January (*CPR 1396–9*, 467; E 403/561, 8 January).

[13] 'My beloved consort Blanche', he called her in his will. J. Post, 'The Obsequies of John of Gaunt', *Guildhall Studies in London History* (1981), 1–12, at pp. 2–4, suggests that Henry may have slipped across from Paris for the funeral, but this is most unlikely; several of Henry's letters were dated from London in the spring of 1399, for he had left a seal in the hands of his chief ministers while he was abroad (DL 28/4/1, fos. 2–7).

exile to a life sentence, and take possession of his father's lands. William Bagot, who was there, promptly sent a messenger to Paris informing Henry of the king's decision and advising him to 'help himself with manhood',[14] so that by the time it was announced publicly on 18 March it is likely that Henry already knew his fate. Richard's pretext was that Henry's request to be permitted to sue for livery of any lands that might fall to him, granted to him in the aftermath of the judgment at Coventry, had been contrary to the terms of that judgment, which had forbidden him to petition for any mitigation of his sentence.[15] Two days later, on 20 March, Richard also denied Henry the stewardship of England, an office held by the house of Lancaster for over a hundred years.[16]

Thus began the final crisis of Richard's reign. Popular support for his regime had been eroding for some time. Demonstrations of loyalty for victimized magnates – by the Mortimer retainers, for example, who turned out in their thousands to greet the earl of March on his arrival at Shrewsbury, all dressed in his livery, or by the one thousand and more well-wishers who gathered on the quayside at Lowestoft to give Thomas Mowbray a rousing send-off in October 1398, or by Thomas Geldesowe of Witney, one of the leaders of an uprising in the Thames Valley in the spring of 1398, who adopted 'Thomas, the young earl of Arundel' as his *nom de guerre* – were matched by local opposition in Warwickshire, Gloucestershire and else-where to upstart royal favourites such as Thomas Holand, the newly created duke of Surrey, and Thomas Despenser, now earl of Gloucester.[17] Shortly

---

[14] In other words, to take whatever measures he deemed necessary, force included. The messenger was Roger Smart. According to Bagot, Richard vowed that as long as he lived Henry would never return to England. C. Fletcher, 'Narrative and Political Strategies at the Deposition of Richard II', *Journal of Medieval History* 30 (2004), 323–41, has questioned whether Richard did extend Henry's sentence of exile from ten years to life, correctly pointing out that this is not specifically stated in the Record and Process. Yet it is mentioned by two contemporary chroniclers as well as by Bagot, and it seems fairly clear that this was Richard's intention (*CR*, 75, 97–8, 211–12; *Chronicles of London*, ed. C. L. Kingsford (Oxford, 1905), 53). Richard retained Bagot that day as a member of his council with an annual fee of £100: *CPR 1396–9*, 494.

[15] *CR*, 92; identical letters granted to Mowbray in October 1398 were revoked the same day, so when Margaret, duchess of Norfolk, died on 24 March, Richard seized her estates, although Mowbray was her heir.

[16] *CPR 1396–9*, 490 (grant of the stewardship to the duke of York).

[17] *Usk*, 38–9; Usk says 20,000 turned out to greet March, but this is hard to believe (*PROME*, vii.425; Davies, *Lords and Lordship*, 71; Saul, *Richard II*, 442–4; *CPR 1396–9*, 350, 365). The son of the decapitated Earl Richard of Arundel was called Thomas. For the rising, see *Oxfordshire Sessions of the Peace in the Reign of Richard II*, ed. E. G. Kimball (Oxfordshire Record Society 53, Banbury, 1983), 82–9; Bennett, *Richard II and the Revolution of 1399*, 123–4. The rising took place in the same area as the battle of Radcot Bridge a decade earlier.

before the aborted duel at Coventry, Richard issued orders to deal severely with any persons found defaming the king or his royal dignity.[18] His body-guard of Cheshiremen, the archers and yeomen of the crown who by early 1399 numbered at least 760 and possibly up to 2,000, were especially disliked, not just for their wanton violence but also for their unbefitting inti-macy with the king: for every livery badge of the white hart that the king handed out, punned the author of *Richard the Redeless*, he lost ten loyal hearts.[19] The blank charters which the king demanded from London and the seventeen counties closest to the capital aroused suspicion and dismay: the Londoners, said one citizen, were all 'indicted as rebels' by being forced to seal admissions of guilt accompanied by pleas for forgiveness, 'and no man knew what it meant'. The day after seizing Henry's inheritance, the king issued a general prohibition against letters being sent out of the realm.[20]

Richard knew that it was in Paris that the likeliest threat to his kingship lay, and initially he tried to mollify Henry, allowing him to collect his income from Mary de Bohun's lands and promising him £2,000 a year from the treasury.[21] When Gaunt died, he sent an esquire to Paris to inform him.[22] Yet all this was as nothing when set against the blows the king inflicted on him in March 1399. To many, Richard's decision confirmed that it was his purpose all along to bring down the house of Lancaster, thus allowing Henry to present himself as the champion of property rights against a perjured regime.[23] A contemporary poet excoriated Richard's cronies as 'gentlemen from the dung (*de stercore*)' and called on 'the eagle duke ... Henry of Lancaster, our light, our glory, our friend' to return and, together with Christ, save the people and 'have the villains drawn and

---

[18] *CPR 1396-9*, 505 (repeated a few months later: *CCR 1396-9*, 505).

[19] *CR*, 31-2; Bennett, *Richard II and the Revolution of 1399*, 123.

[20] *Historical Collections*, 98-101. The blank charters were stored in the royal chancery (*CCR 1396-9*, 488, 503).

[21] Most of this was paid, up until 20 June 1399, plus a gift of 1,000 marks to help him move to Paris. The future Henry V was also given £500 a year plus £148 to pay for his equipment in Ireland (E 403/561, 14 November, 7 December, 21 February, 5 March; E 403/562, 2 May, 6 May, 20 June). Mowbray got £1,000 a year during his exile.

[22] The esquire was Peter Breton. This entry appears in the exchequer issue roll under 8 January (E 403/561), but another entry under the same date records payments to messen-gers to summon lords to Gaunt's funeral, and since Gaunt did not die until 3 February these entries must have been inserted under the wrong date.

[23] Richard never got the chance to reveal his plans for the Lancastrian patrimony. In the short term, Gaunt's vast estates were parcelled out between the king's favourites among the higher nobility – the dukes of Aumale, Surrey and Exeter and the earls of Wiltshire and Salisbury – but the door was left open for the young Henry to enter into his inheritance in due course: A. Dunn, *The Politics of Magnate Power* (Oxford, 2003), 168-77. In April, Henry sent his esquire, Esmond Bugge, to Windsor to try to persuade the king to relent (DL 28/4/1, fo. 6r; *CR*, 97).

beheaded' – the villains being Bussy, Bagot, Green and Le Scrope.[24] Henry must have been aware of such sentiments. Letters passed regularly between him and his council in London, and he knew that Richard was planning to go to Ireland, taking with him not only the hated Cheshire bodyguard but also several of his leading supporters among the remodelled upper nobility. His opportunity would come.

A concatenation of events in the early summer strengthened Henry's hand: Thomas, the son and heir of the earl of Arundel, escaped from the custody of the duke of Exeter and fled abroad to join his uncle, the exiled archbishop of Canterbury.[25] After leaving England in October 1397, Archbishop Arundel had initially made his way to Ghent, then to Rome, where he incurred Richard's wrath by asking the pope to restore him to his see, and then, by January 1398, to Florence, where he remained for a year or so before returning north and spending time at Cologne and Utrecht.[26] By early June at the latest, uncle and nephew had moved to Paris to join Henry. This was an act of defiance in itself, for Henry's sentence of exile had forbidden him any contact with the former archbishop. Richard had a healthy respect for Arundel,[27] a man of nimble intellect and sharp tongue: he had berated the king to his face at least twice in the past, and would do so again.[28] Yet it cannot have been an easy moment: the last time Henry and Arundel had met was at the September 1397 parliament, where Henry had helped to secure the conviction for treason of Arundel's brother and Gaunt had pronounced sentence of death on him. Walsingham reckoned that the archbishop's willingness to forgive if not forget must have required supernatural intervention.[29] In the event, Henry and Arundel's reunion in Paris marked the forging of a partnership not merely for a revolution but for a reign.

[24] *Political Poems and Songs*, i.366–8 ('On the Expected Arrival of the Duke of Lancaster').

[25] *CPR 1396–9*, 214; Thomas was 17 and had been mistreated in Exeter's household, especially by 'John Schevele' (Sir Thomas Shelley), who made him perform menial tasks. He escaped with the help of a London mercer, William Scott, and joined the archbishop in Cologne or Utrecht: *Historical Collections*, 101; *CR*, 116.

[26] *Diplomatic Correspondence*, ed. Perroy, 238, 240; D. Carlton, *The Deposition of Richard II* (Toronto, 2007), 75–86; A. Brown, 'The Latin Letters in MS. All Souls 182', *EHR* 87 (1972), 565–73. Arundel thought Florence 'an earthly paradise' and struck up a friendship with the Florentine chancellor and humanist Coluccio Salutati.

[27] Note John Bussy's comments on Arundel's ingenuity and cunning (*SAC II*, 80).

[28] *Knighton*, 354–60; *CR*, 68; *CE*, iii.382.

[29] According to Walsingham, on the night that Gaunt died, his penitent spirit appeared in a vision to Arundel while he was at Utrecht and begged forgiveness for the injustices which he had inflicted upon the archbishop and his kinsfolk; Arundel, moved by such contrition, promised the spirit to pray to God for his soul (*SAC II*, 122–3).

Events in France also moved in Henry's favour. The dukes of Burgundy and Berry both moved out of the city before the end of May, either to escape an outbreak of plague or in frustration at the behaviour of the duke of Orléans. The latter's influence at the French court was now paramount.[30] On 17 June, by which time news would have reached Paris that Richard had crossed to Ireland, Henry and Orléans drew up a treaty of alliance.[31] On the face of it, this infamous (as it became) document appears unexceptionable. It bound Henry and Louis by mutual oaths to support each other's friends, oppose each other's enemies, uphold each other's honour and well-being, and come to each other's help in times of war or unrest, for as long as the Anglo-French truce remained in place. The exclusion of named individuals, including the kings of France and England and the duke of York,[32] sought to allay any suspicion that it was a treaty directed against any of those persons. Yet suspicion there was, and given the timing that is not surprising. Henry would later claim that he had revealed his plans in full to Orléans, who had approved them and promised aid against Richard, and there were many in France who believed him, for the alliance seemed to guarantee, at the minimum, French connivance at the enterprise he was about to undertake. Orléans's reasoning is less easy to explain, but he probably found his territorial ambitions in southern France thwarted by the Anglo-French truce and hoped to foment trouble for the English king and the duke of Burgundy.[33] Whether he truly believed that Henry would succeed in overthrowing Richard is another matter, although he must have realized that it was a possibility; while it is unlikely that Henry was actively aided by Orléans or anyone else in France, relations between the French and English courts had already cooled markedly since the heady days of 1396.[34] Nevertheless, Henry covered his tracks: stopping off at Saint-Denis on his way to the coast, he let it be known that he was

[30] Burgundy was in the Low Countries from May until August. Berry, having quarrelled violently with Orléans, retired to his castle of Bicêtre; Charles VI, apparently, 'could no longer refuse anything that the duke of Orléans requested' (Lehoux, *Jean de France*, ii.414–18).

[31] *CR*, 109–14.

[32] As Henry must have known, York had been appointed keeper of England during Richard's absence in Ireland.

[33] Saul, *Richard II*, 406–7, where it is argued that English diplomacy in Italy also hindered his ambitions.

[34] Orléans may have acted in a fit of pique, for it was at just this time that some twenty domestic servants of the young Queen Isabella, including her governess, Margaret de Courcy, and her secretary, arrived in Paris, having been deported from England on Richard's orders; this aroused great anger in France and infuriated Orléans, who had a particular affection for his niece. They were given £465 for removal expenses (*CR*, 110: E 403/562, 10 June).

planning to travel to Spain. As far as can be gathered, he was allowed to board an English merchantman at Boulogne without any attempt being made to stop him.[35] Within two weeks of sealing his alliance with Orléans he was back in England.

The success of the revolution of 1399 is explicable in part by the absence of the king, his Cheshiremen and his magnates in Ireland, and in part by the element of surprise Henry achieved.[36] It was much more than a personal triumph: it was the vindication of the Lancastrian affinity, of loyalties and affiliations which had been nurtured and tautened for decades and generations to the point where they were able to withstand both the blandishments and the bullying of a king such as Richard. Since taking control of the duchy, Richard had done what he could to break the nexus between the affinity and its lord. Annuities paid by Gaunt to some ninety of his former retainers were not confirmed unless they agreed to 'stay with the king only', while the duke's estates were placed in the hands of those whom the king regarded as his most dependable supporters, although it soon became apparent that they had failed to inspire any personal allegiance among their new tenants.[37] The investment which successive earls and dukes had ploughed into the Lancastrian corporation – an ongoing process, for Henry distributed 192 livery collars and 27 crescent badges in the summer of 1399 – now paid its dividend.[38] Richard could neither buy nor command its defection.

It was doubtless the confidence he placed in his father's affinity that persuaded Henry to land in Yorkshire.[39] Putting in first at Cromer in

---

[35] *CR*, 25–31, 111, 116–17. One French source said that Charles VI permitted him to leave the realm because he said he was going to England to discuss 'matters concerning peace' with Richard II (*Chronographia Regum Francorum*, iii.169). He was carried to England by Thomas Gyles of Dover, who was rewarded with the office of bailiff of Rye for life (*HOC*, iii.258; *CPR 1399–1401*, 35). *Saint-Denys*, ii.706, said that Burgundy heard about unusual maritime traffic around Boulogne and tried to discover what was going on, but Henry avoided detection.

[36] E 403/562, 13 May, 12 July: £2,639 for the war wages of 120 men-at-arms and 900 archers from Cheshire going to Ireland with the king (*CCR 1396–9*, 489–90; D. Biggs, *Three Armies in Britain* (Leiden, 2006), 65–80).

[37] *RHKA*, 216, 310 (these 90 included 36 of Gaunt's knights and esquires); Dunn, *Politics of Magnate Power*, 171–2, who suggests that some of Gaunt's ministers may have been transferring duchy revenues surreptitiously to Paris via Lucchese merchants; Walker, *Lancastrian Affinity*, 177, 231.

[38] DL 28/4/1, fo. 15v; these livery badges cost £83.

[39] Walsingham said he initially sailed up and down the coastline to test the defences, and a small party of men under John Pelham was landed at Pevensey in Sussex (a duchy castle), where they were still being besieged by a royalist force three weeks later: S. Walker, 'Letters to the Dukes of Lancaster in 1381 and 1399', *EHR* 106 (1991), 68–79.

Norfolk (a duchy property) to pick up supplies, then around 30 June at Ravenspur, an abandoned settlement at the mouth of the Humber where a hermit was later permitted to build a chapel to mark the spot, he eventually disembarked at Bridlington or a point close by, hoping presumably to enlist the aid of his favourite saint for his enterprise.[40] Among the first to join him were Robert Waterton, steward of Pontefract, bringing with him 200 foresters from Knaresborough, and the Yorkshire knight Sir Peter Bukton, former steward of his household.[41] The force Henry had brought with him from France consisted of a few dozen persons at most, and although it included experienced soldiers such as Erpingham, Rempston, de Courte and Norbury, it was in no sense an army of invasion. As a banner to rally the discontented, however, it served its purpose admirably. Henry himself, Archbishop Arundel, and the son of his beheaded brother were potent symbols of the warped judgments of Richard's later years. That the Lancastrian affinity would rally to Henry's cause might have been expected, but equally reassuring to Henry must have been the speed with which magnates such as the earls of Northumberland and Westmorland and Lords Willoughby, Greystoke and Roos came out against the king, and the fact that the citizens of York and Hull loaned him money to pay his troops. By the middle of July, the platoon-sized force which had beached at Ravenspur at the end of June had been transformed into an army several thousand strong.[42]

Although localized acts of resistance to Richard's regime broke out with remarkable speed,[43] Henry remained wary during the first two weeks after his landing, moving from one duchy castle in Yorkshire to another (Pickering, Knaresborough, Pontefract); only once his level of support

---

[40] *CPR 1399–1401*, 209; DL 42/15, fo. 69v; Biggs, *Three Armies*, 105–9; *CR*, 133; the hermit was Matthew Danthorpe.

[41] *Usk*, 52–3; *Chronica Monasterii de Melsa*, ed. E. Bond (3 vols, RS, London, 1866–8), iii.298–9. Some of Henry's retainers may have had advance notice of his intentions: John Davy, a Lancastrian servant, hastened from London to Dover 'on hearing of the lord's arrival at the end of [June]', presumably the landing of Pelham and his men at Pevensey (DL 28/4/1, fos. 7v, 15r).

[42] Claims that up to 200,000 men joined him are implausible: for the size of Henry's force see *CR*, 35, 126, 252–3 (to the list on pp. 252–3 should be added the names of John Langford and William Bromfield): (DL 29/728/11987, m. 10, and E 403/564, 28 November). Henry's second son Thomas, aged twelve, was also with him. The 51 men who received around £5,000 of wages for joining him were only the captains of companies, some of whom brought scores and even hundreds of men. For the loans from York and Hull, totalling £433, see *CPR 1399–1401*, 354.

[43] So at least it was later claimed by, for example, the garrisons of Dunstanburgh and Kenilworth, who claimed to have held them in Henry's name from 1 and 2 July; partisans of the earl of Warwick claimed to have seized Warwick castle on 4 July (DL 29/728/11987, mm. 5, 10; DL 42/15, fo. 71r; Mott, 'Richard II and the Crisis of 1397', 176).

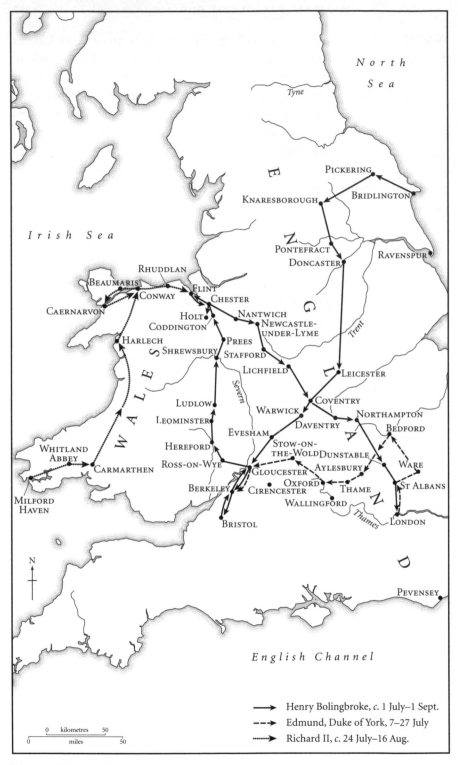

Map 3 The revolution of 1399

became apparent did he advance more rapidly southwards. At Leicester, around 20 July, he recruited followers from his father's Midland honours and from the retainers of the earl of Warwick.[44] So far, he had encountered little resistance,[45] but what the keeper of the realm would do was unclear. News of an impending invasion had reached Westminster on 28 June, prompting the duke of York to order the sheriffs to raise troops and join him at Ware (Hertfordshire) as soon as possible.[46] As yet, York had little idea where the danger lay – the south coast and the west country both featured in his earliest plans – but by 7 July, when he left London for St Albans, he knew that Henry had landed in Yorkshire. On 12 July he moved to Ware to collect his troops, and by 16 July he had arrived at Oxford, where further contingents joined him.[47] At its peak, his army consisted of around 3,000 men, but his position was weak. News of the 'wondrous events' in the north filled the land. 'The eagle is up and has taken his flight', enthused one poet, and 'with him he brings the colt of the steed' (the son of the earl of Arundel); the bush would be cropped (Bussy), the grass mown (Green) and the 'great bag' cut down to size (Bagot).[48] The author of *Richard the Redeless* characterized Henry alternately as the eagle, the falcon or the greyhound. The poem opened in July at Bristol, where the author was praying in the church of the Trinity when rumours began to circulate that, while Richard 'warred in the west', Henry, a man whom 'all the land loved throughout its length and breadth', had landed in the east 'to right his wrong, so that he should later do likewise for [the people]'. 'Now, Richard the Redeless (ill-advised)', chided the author, 'take pity on yourself, you who led your life lawlessly and your people as well', for Henry 'has entered into his own', and 'covetousness has crushed your crown forever'.[49] Sympathy for Henry's cause could also be found among the duke of York's troops, some of whom bluntly informed him that they would not partake in an attack on Henry, while York himself is said to have declared that he had no intention of attacking someone who had come to

[44] Biggs, *Three Armies*, 189–94.

[45] Although he had some trouble gaining entry to Knaresborough castle (*CR*, 133).

[46] E. H. Pearce, *William de Colchester, Abbot of Westminster* (London, 1915), 76–7; E 101/42/12; *CR*, 111.

[47] *CR*, 247–51; Biggs, *Three Armies*, 139–40.

[48] *Political Poems and Songs*, ed. T. Wright (2 vols, RS, London, 1859–61), i.363–6 ('On King Richard's Ministers'). Such anthropomorphic livery imagery would have been instantly recognizable: one of the Arundel livery badges was a horse. Likewise, Gloucester was the swan, the earl of Warwick the bear-keeper, and so forth.

[49] *Political Poems and Songs*, i.368–417. Although begun in early July, the poem was not completed until several months later, for Henry had assumed the rule of the kingdom, although Richard is referred to as still alive.

ask for the restoration of his rightful inheritance.[50] Thus even as his army was mustering, it began to disintegrate, desertions multiplying as the invader approached. Money was not York's problem: he handed out over £2,000 to his captains and promised a good deal more. Yet there were many, as Walsingham put it, who, having accepted payment, 'set off to find the duke of Lancaster and to fight with him at the wages of King Richard'.[51] By about 20 July the keeper's position was becoming untenable. Hoping to make contact with Richard's army when it returned from Ireland, he sent his fellow councillors (Bussy, Le Scrope, Green, Bagot and John Russell) to Bristol, while he himself moved northwards via Stow-on-the-Wold to Gloucester and Berkeley, a route designed to effect a meeting with Henry.

Meanwhile Henry had arrived at Warwick castle on 24 July to discover that the duke of Surrey had placed a crowned hart of Richard II's livery and a white hind of his own livery atop the castle gate, both of which he demolished – the clearest signal yet that his ambitions extended beyond the restoration of the duchy of Lancaster.[52] Publicly, Henry claimed that he had returned merely to claim his rightful inheritance, a cause which he knew would unite support behind him, and it was later asserted that he had sworn 'upon the relics of Bridlington', as well as at Doncaster when he was joined by the Percys, that this was all he would claim.[53] Yet it is hard to believe that it did not cross the minds of those who marched with him in the summer of 1399 that their support was likely to have more thorough-going consequences. Left to rule, Richard might bide his time, but ulti-mately he would seek revenge, as he had in 1397–8; despite claims to the contrary later made by the Percys and others, his deposition was surely seen as the likeliest outcome of a successful military campaign by Henry. More contentious was the question of who would succeed him, to which Henry probably gave answers that were at best ambiguous and more likely mendacious.

Crossing the Severn at Gloucester,[54] Henry arrived on Sunday 27 July at Berkeley, where he and York 'came to an agreement' in a chapel outside the castle.[55] Exactly what this entailed is not recorded, but the outcome is clear: York abandoned his attempt to resist Henry's progress by force. Henry may

[50] CR, 118, 127 (Walsingham was at St Albans and in a good position to know).
[51] CR, 118–19, 247.
[52] CR, 135–6.
[53] CR, 192–3; he was said to have sworn similar oaths at Knaresborough and at Chester (J. Sherborne, 'Perjury and the Lancastrian Revolution of 1399', Welsh History Review (1988), 217–41).
[54] Henry was at Gloucester on 25 July (DL 28/4/1, fo. 2r).
[55] 'because the duke of York did not have the strength to resist him' (CR, 127).

have been asked to give certain undertakings in return, but it was probably too late for that by now. A few Ricardian die-hards such as Henry Despenser, bishop of Norwich, were placed under arrest, and on the following day the two dukes moved on to Bristol. Bagot had escaped to Ireland, but Le Scrope, Bussy, Russell and Green were still in the castle. Surrendered by the garrison, they were kept in custody overnight and tried before a military court on the morning of 29 July. Russell was spared, feigning insanity, but Le Scrope, Bussy and Green were convicted and beheaded; had they not been, it was said that the mob would have 'broken them into little pieces'.[56] In Henry's eyes they were guilty specifically of betraying him and his father, for Le Scrope came from a family with a tradition of service to the dukes of Lancaster, while Bussy and Green had both been Gaunt's retainers for nearly two decades, yet all three had been accomplices to the seizure of his inheritance.[57] York's role at Bristol was telling: as keeper of the realm, he not only attended the execution of the king's councillors but used his authority to order the surrender of the castle.[58] Indeed it was probably on his formal authority that they were tried, although in practice it must have been Henry's decision. From now onwards, Henry increasingly acted as if he were already king of England, even if he continued to preserve the fiction that he was acting in Richard's name. Yet by 2 August, when Henry appointed the earl of Northumberland to be keeper of Carlisle castle and warden of the West March of Scotland, offices manifestly in the gift of the crown, and sealed the appointment with the duchy of Lancaster seal, the line separating his de facto and *de jure* authority must have seemed to many to have faded almost to vanishing point.[59]

The fact remained, however, that Richard was still at large and, so far as Henry knew, in possession of an army. The king had arrived back from Ireland at Milford Haven (Pembrokeshire) around 24 July. A week later he had reached Carmarthen and made contact with some of the duke of York's officials, who probably told him of the startling transformation in his and Henry's fortunes. Deciding that he could not risk an armed confrontation – for the army which he commanded was but a shadow of the force which he had led to Ireland two months previously, storms and

[56] Ibid., 120, 128. They were not convicted of treason, but of misleading Richard II, and their possessions were seized by Henry 'through conquest': see below, p. 442.

[57] Walker, *Lancastrian Affinity*, 266, 270.

[58] *CR*, 120.

[59] E 404/15/46. On 31 July, as duke of Lancaster and steward of England, Henry also granted John Norbury all the lands in England of John Ludwyk – a grant in the king's gift (BL Add. Charter 5829).

delays having scattered his fleet to a variety of ports – he made instead for North Wales, whither he had already despatched the earl of Salisbury to raise support and which was sufficiently close to Cheshire to offer the chance of a counter-attack or at least a refuge.[60] In the interests of speed, he left his army behind, slipping away with just a dozen followers on the night of 31 July, dressed as a priest according to one account.[61] When Aumale and Worcester awoke to find him gone, they disbanded the royal household, dismissed the army and made their way to Chester to submit to Henry.[62]

Henry's decision to make for Cheshire, Richard's inner citadel, made good sense. Marching along the Anglo-Welsh border during the first week of August, a route parallel to that of the king about sixty miles to the west, he encountered isolated pockets of resistance, but nothing to slow his progress apart from the daily influx of renegades from Richard's Irish army such as Robert Lord Scales, Thomas Lord Bardolf and (once he reached Chester) Aumale, Worcester, and Lords Lovell and Stanley.[63] Yet according to Adam Usk the most welcome recruit to Henry's cause was no earl or peer but a greyhound, credited by the chronicler with an unerring instinct for the mutability of political fortunes. After the death of its first master, the earl of Kent, in 1397, the dog had found its way by instinct to Richard, with whom it remained day and night for two years, but when the king abandoned his army at Carmarthen it promptly deserted him and 'once again by its own instinct, alone and unaided', made its way to Shrewsbury, where it 'crouched obediently before Henry, whom it had never seen before, with a look of the purest pleasure on its face'. Delighted at such a happy augury, Henry allowed it to sleep on his bed, and later, when brought once again

---

[60] D. Johnston, 'Richard II's Departure from Ireland, July 1399', *EHR* 98 (1983), 785–805.

[61] *CR*, 139.

[62] *CR*, 122, 129, 141. On their way home, the royalist soldiers were harried and despoiled by the Welsh; if they tried to attack Henry's strongholds in Wales and the March, they would have found them well defended. The gates, moat, walls and drawbridge of Brecon castle had been strengthened; the keeper of Kidwelly castle had brought in oil and rocks to hurl at any who might be rash enough to try to assault it, and Hay-on-Wye castle was also reinforced; a detachment of horsemen was sent from Cantref Selyf to Gloucester 'to defend their lord against his enemies' (DL 29/548/9240; SC 6/1157/4, mm. 3–4; Davies, *Lords and Lordship*, 84–5).

[63] The intrepid Adam Usk claimed to have persuaded the people of Usk not to harry Henry's army, and to have persuaded Henry to set free and promote Thomas Prestbury, a monk of Shrewsbury whom Richard had imprisoned in Ludlow castle for subversive preaching. Usk provides a vivid day-by-day account of Henry's route-march, noting that he and his followers 'partook liberally' of the wine which they found stored along the way. It was Eleanor Holand, Richard's niece and lady of Usk, who tried to organize resistance there (*Usk*, 52–6; *CR*, 128–9).

into Richard's presence, it failed to recognize him.[64] Also at Shrewsbury, where he spent the nights of 5 and 6 August, Henry received the submission of Chester, conveyed to him by Sir Robert and Sir John Leigh, members of the family which more than any other had been influential in promoting the king's interests there.[65] For Richard, this represented the closing of the last window of hope, but it also disappointed some of Henry's own followers, whose hatred for Cheshire and its people had encouraged them to join him in the hope of plundering the county, but who now returned to their homes. In fact they were over-hasty. Despite promising to spare Cheshire, Henry was either unable or unwilling to prevent it being ravaged once his army entered the county on 8 August: crops were wasted, booty seized, chapels stripped of their valuables and exemplary retribution exacted. Three days after his arrival, Perkyn Leigh, a hero to many Cheshiremen and the leading royalist in the city, was summarily beheaded and his head set up on a stake outside the east gate of the town.[66] For two weeks Henry's army occupied Chester, destroying houses and looting whatever weapons or provisions they cared to seize. The city chamberlain's account claimed that his men had seized 400 bows, large quantities of arrows, bowstrings, lance-heads, crossbows, baldrics and quarrels from the castle, along with substantial quantities of wine and salt.[67]

Meanwhile, the king and his small band of devotees had made their way northwards from Carmarthen, keeping close to the coast, and arrived at Conway castle around 6 August, but no army awaited him, only the hundred or so men who had accompanied Salisbury from Ireland.[68] 'Downcast and miserable', Richard had with him the dukes of Exeter and Surrey, the earl

[64] *Usk*, 86–7. A story that so perfectly personified (or at least caninified) the English people's transfer of allegiance from one ruler to another might be dismissed had not Froissart also heard it, although he heightened the drama of the greyhound's defection by placing it at the moment of Richard's capture (Froissart, *Chronicles*, ed. G. Brereton (Harmondsworth, 1968), 453).

[65] *CR*, 128–9.

[66] When Usk went to Coddington chapel on the morning of 9 August, hoping to say mass, 'I found nothing there except doors and chests broken open, and everything carried off' *(Usk*, 56–8; *CR*, 153–4; Clarke and Galbraith, 'The Deposition of Richard II', 163–4).

[67] SC 6/774/10, mm. 2d, 3d (items were also taken from Flint and Rhuddlan). The garrison was paid to defend Chester from 3 July to 5 August, 'on which day the aforesaid castle was, under certain conditions, delivered and handed over to the said duke [Henry]'.

[68] For the last two weeks of Richard's freedom, we are largely dependent on the 'Metrical Chronicle' of Jean Creton, a *valet-de-chambre* at the French court who came to England in the spring of 1399 to join the king's expedition to Ireland. When news came of Henry's landing, Creton was sent back to North Wales with the earl of Salisbury and was with the king when he surrendered. For extracts from Creton's chronicle, see *CR*, 137–52; the whole text is translated in 'Metrical History of the Deposition of Richard the Second', ed. J. Webb, *Archaeologia* (1823).

of Gloucester, three bishops including Thomas Merks of Carlisle, and half
a dozen or so servants and soldiers including the redoubtable Navarrese
esquire Janico Dartasso. In the hope that something short of unconditional
surrender might yet be negotiated, Exeter and Surrey were sent to parley
with Henry. Exeter advised Richard to confront Henry directly, to offer him
his inheritance and remind him of the shame which would fall upon his
head should he depose a lawful king. There was apparently still a belief, or at
least a hope, that the army left behind at Carmarthen might rejoin them in
the north, but within a further day or two a messenger arrived from South
Wales to inform the king that his Irish army had disbanded, which plunged
Richard into another slough of despond. Believing Conway to be threatened, he decamped, first to Beaumaris on Anglesey, then to Caernarvon,
possibly thinking to escape by ship, possibly searching for the safest refuge.
The castles were unfurnished and unprovisioned: there was only straw to
sleep on and barely enough to eat. Richard, 'his face often pale', cursed the
day that he had decided to go to Ireland, but if he seriously thought of
fleeing overseas, which he probably could have done, something or someone
persuaded him not to; by 15 August at the latest, he was back at Conway to
await the return of Exeter and Surrey.

They never did return. On arrival at Chester, Exeter began confidently by
urging Henry to beg Richard's pardon for his 'outrage' in returning from
exile, which, he assured Henry, would be freely granted, but he was quickly
brought down to earth.[69] Cutting off his brother-in-law almost in mid-
sentence, Henry told the two dukes that he had no intention of allowing
them to return to Conway. Surrey was locked away in Chester castle,
Exeter detained in Henry's household, although when he pleaded too
insistently to be allowed to leave, Henry banished him from his presence.
The next day or two were spent conducting a lightning raid on Holt castle,
eight miles south of Chester, a former Arundel castle which was now the
king's principal treasury in the north-west, where Henry seized at least
some of the very substantial quantities of money and plate.[70] Returning to

---

[69] 'Metrical History', 121: Creton said that Exeter spoke 'quite boldly' to Henry 'for he had
married his sister', but Creton was not there (Exeter's wife was Elizabeth, Henry's elder sister).

[70] For the treasure at Holt, see below, p. 175. Walsingham said Richard also went to Holt
at this time, presumably to recover his treasure, but it seems unlikely that the king could
have reached the castle and Creton does not mention it (*SAC II*, 154–5). Part of Henry's
thinking was doubtless to prevent the treasure there from being looted by others under
cover of the disturbances; some £20,000 of the Despensers' and Baldock's personal wealth
was looted during the revolution of 1326–7, and took twenty years to recover (M. Ormrod,
Edward III (New Haven, 2011), 47).

Chester around 12 August, he despatched the earl of Northumberland and, possibly, Thomas Arundel, to Conway to lure Richard out of the castle.[71] What happened next was disputed at the time and still is. The Lancastrian version of events was that Richard, while still at liberty at Conway, promised Northumberland and Arundel that he was willing to abdicate and asked them to set up a committee to determine how this might best be done.[72] Creton, however (who fails to mention Archbishop Arundel's presence at Conway), said that Northumberland tricked Richard out of Conway by swearing on the host that he would not be deposed as long as he agreed to restore Henry to his inheritance and to the stewardship of England, and to submit five of his councillors to trial in a parliament at which Henry, by virtue of his office as steward of England, would act as 'chief judge'; having thus inveigled the king out of Conway, the earl ambushed him (he had concealed his troops behind an outcrop a few miles down the road) and led him to Flint to await Henry's arrival.[73]

Creton's story is surely closer to the truth. That Richard willingly agreed to abdicate at Conway is most unlikely, although it is possible that he agreed to remain king in name while effective power would be devolved to Henry. Equally problematical is Northumberland's role: he later claimed that Henry had deceived him, having initially sworn that Richard would not be deposed but would remain king 'under the direction, and by the good advice, of the lords spiritual and temporal'.[74] Northumberland's feelings towards the house of Lancaster were ambivalent: he had quarrelled bitterly with Gaunt in 1381 and resented the duke's interference in the affairs of the Anglo-Scottish Marches. More to the point, perhaps, his son Hotspur was married to Elizabeth, aunt of Edmund Mortimer, whom many regarded as the rightful heir to the throne should Richard be deposed; if Henry made any promises to Northumberland, they are more likely to have concerned the succession than the question of whether or not the king had to go. Like Henry, Northumberland knew that sooner or later Richard would seek revenge. Realistically, Northumberland, Henry, and perhaps Arundel must all have told a succession of lies in order to get their hands on the king – although there was probably no other way that

[71] The archbishop may or may not have gone to Conway: see Sherborne, 'Perjury and the Lancastrian Revolution', and Saul, *Richard II*, 413–16, who thought that he was not there but that 'a role was created for the prelate in the later narratives to lend a measure of legitimacy to the proceedings'.

[72] *CR*, 169–70.

[73] The five councillors to be submitted for trial were the dukes of Exeter and Surrey, the earl of Salisbury, the bishop of Carlisle, and the clerk Richard Maudeleyn.

[74] *CR*, 38–9, 194–5.

they could have done so, and according to Creton Richard also lied, consoling his followers that he would never allow them to be brought to trial in parliament and would assuredly be avenged upon his enemies. Within another few hours, however, by late morning on Friday 15 August, he had fallen into Northumberland's hands, and his assurances counted for nothing.[75]

When he realized he had been led into a trap, Richard asked to be allowed to return to Conway, but the earl would have none of it: 'Now that I have you here,' he replied, 'I will take you to Duke Henry as soon as I can, for you must know that I promised this to him ten days ago.'[76] After a midday meal at Rhuddlan, the party moved on to Flint on the estuary of the Dee, where they spent the night. Henry arrived the following day, his army 'marching along the sea-shore, drawn up in battle array', while Richard stood on the battlements and watched them approach. A small detachment including Archbishop Arundel, Aumale and Worcester broke off from the main host and came up to the walls; Aumale and Worcester, Richard could not help noticing, no longer wore his livery but Henry's. The archbishop entered the castle first. Descending from the keep, Richard greeted him in the courtyard and the two men had a long conversation. Creton said that Arundel comforted the king and told him no harm would come to him, but another account of their exchange stated that Arundel told Richard he was 'the falsest of all men', that he had sworn upon the host that no harm would come to his brother the earl, and that 'You have not ruled your kingdom but ravished it [and] by your foul example you defiled both your court and the kingdom.'[77] Henry, meanwhile, had ordered his troops to surround Flint, but agreed to wait until the king had dined.[78] Eventually, fully armed apart from his bascinet, he passed through the gate and Richard came out to speak to him. Both men removed their headwear, and Henry bowed twice 'very low'. Richard spoke first: 'Fair cousin of Lancaster, you are right welcome.' Henry's reply was to the point: 'My lord, I have come sooner than you sent for me, and I shall tell you why: it is commonly said among your people that you have, for the last twenty or twenty-two years, governed them very badly and far too harshly,

[75] CR, 146–8.

[76] What follows is mainly from Creton's account (CR, 147–51).

[77] CE, iii.382; the author thought Henry was already in the castle, and only when he cried 'Enough!' did Arundel relent.

[78] Creton and his companion took the opportunity to present themselves to Henry at the gate, explaining that they had been sent by the king of France to accompany Richard to Ireland. Henry replied in French, 'My young men, do not fear, nor be alarmed at anything you might see. Keep close to me and I will answer for your lives.'

with the result that they are most discontented. If it please Our Lord, however, I shall now help you to govern them better than they have been governed in the past'; to which Richard answered, 'If it please you, fair cousin, it pleases us as well.' These were, according to Creton, their exact words,[79] and for the moment there was no more to be said. Henry called out ('in a stern and savage voice') for horses, whereupon two derisory little nags were brought forward, one for Richard, the other for the earl of Salisbury, to whom Henry, remembering his visit to Paris a few months earlier, refused to speak. Leaving Flint two hours after midday, they reached Chester before nightfall, where the king was jeered by the mob before being locked in the keep with a few close friends, including Salisbury and the bishop of Carlisle. No one else was permitted to speak to him; it was the evening of Saturday 16 August, and his reign had effectively ended. It had taken Henry less than fifty days to conquer both king and kingdom, exulted Walsingham, 'a manifest miracle of God'.[80]

[79] 'the very words that they exchanged, no more and no less, for I heard them and understood them perfectly well' (CR, 149–51).
[80] SAC II, 156, 234.

Chapter 10

THE MAKING OF A KING (1399)

There were many, not all of them supporters of Henry, who believed that the triumph of the house of Lancaster in the summer of 1399 had been foretold, whether by Merlin, by John of Bridlington, or even by Bede. Froissart claimed to have been told as much thirty years previously; Adam Usk could not decide whether Henry was the eaglet prophesied by Merlin to overthrow the White King, or the greyhound prophesied by Bridlington to subdue the hart; even the Ricardian author of the Dieulacres Chronicle reported rumours that Henry's victory had been preordained.[1] Creton was more sceptical: on the ride from Flint to Chester, he fell in with an elderly knight in Henry's retinue who told him that both Merlin and Bede had prophesied Richard's fall 'in the parts of the north, in a triangular place', and that Conway was that place; although Creton agreed that Conway was triangular, he thought the English far too credulous of prophecies, phantoms and witchcraft, a characteristic which he believed to indicate 'a great want of faith'.[2] He was right, though, to say that the English put great store by prophecies, and it was particularly at times of crisis or upheaval that people recalled them. Prophecies not only explained events, they justified them, and the events people were witnessing required justification. Whether or not Henry himself circulated prophecies in the summer of 1399 to justify his hounding of the king, he would certainly do so soon.[3]

For the moment though, as July turned to August, as the royalist armies evaporated, and especially once the king had been captured, the need to

[1] Froissart, *Chronicles*, ed. Brereton, 470–1; *CR*, 155. *Usk*, 50–2, thought Henry might be the greyhound 'because he came in the dog-days [of summer], and because he drove utterly from the kingdom countless numbers of harts'. References to the eagle derived from the *Prophecy of the Eagle*, and ultimately the Merlin prophecies. Of the king's capture at Flint, Usk (58) said it fulfilled the prophecy about the White King. Cf. L. Coote, *Prophecy and Public Affairs in Later Medieval England* (York Medieval Press, 2000), 63–4, 167; M. Bennett, 'Prophecy, Providence and the Revolution of 1399', *Prophecy, Apocalypse and the Day of Doom: Harlaxton Medieval Studies XII*, ed. N. Morgan (Donington, 2004), 1–18.

[2] 'Metrical Chronicle', 168–70.

[3] *Traïson et Mort*, 180–7, said Henry sent out 'a hundred and fifty pairs of letters' containing 'artful fabrications' about Richard, but these have not survived; see also *CE*, 381, and *Saint-Denys*, ii.704; and cf. Given-Wilson, *Chronicles*, 38–48.

restore a sense of normality became increasingly urgent, for the country was in turmoil. Law courts had ceased to function, government was paralyzed, robbers and highwaymen went about their business unchecked, and rumour spiralled out of control.[4] On 11 August, a report that Richard had returned from Ireland brought a crowd of Londoners to Westminster abbey to search for him, and although they failed to find him they did arrest a number of his supporters whom they imprisoned in Ludgate.[5] The overthrow of the king was in danger of escalating into a popular uprising, and the sacking of Cheshire was not something which Henry could afford to see repeated elsewhere; it was just such popular fervour which, at the time of the Merciless Parliament, had hijacked the relatively limited political programme to which he had subscribed. A series of measures during the week following Richard's capture thus attempted to reassert control. Parliament was summoned to meet at Westminster on 30 September, justices and keepers of the peace were told to resume their sessions, and the sheriffs were ordered to proclaim the restoration of law and order; the current lawlessness, they were told, was contrary to both Henry's and Richard's wishes.[6] To avoid plundering on the way to London, Henry dismissed most of his supporters at Chester, retaining only a select band of knights, esquires and valets who would remain with him for the duration of the upcoming parliament.[7] Before leaving Chester, he also despatched Henry Dryhurst to Dublin to bring his eldest son back to England.[8]

---

[4] *Chronica Monasterii de Melsa*, ed. E. Bond (3 vols, RS, London, 1866–8), iii.254; *CCR 1396–9*, 513; *CPR 1396–9*, 597.

[5] BL Harleian Ms 3775, fo. 87v; *Historical Collections*, 101; *Usk*, 60–1; Pearce, *William of Colchester*, 77. The riot was called a 'hurlyng', a word also used to describe the 1381 revolt. Joan, the daughter of Richard II's unpopular justice Robert Tresilian, was later granted an annuity of £5 as compensation for damage she suffered from looters in 1399 (E 404/24, no. 514).

[6] *CCR 1396–9*, 512, 521–2; these were still sent out in Richard's name, but with Henry's endorsement.

[7] Walsingham says that he kept 'only' 15,000 men with him, while Creton says he kept thirty or forty thousand with him, figures which are not credible; Creton adds that this was to spare the countryside 'for it had already been considerably devastated during their advance' (*CR*, 123, 151, 252–3). Those who were dismissed were probably paid from the treasure seized at Holt castle. Richard had deposited £43,964 along with jewels and other treasure at Holt in the keeping of his clerk, John Ikelyngton (much of it probably seized from the earl of Arundel); Henry later acquitted Ikelyngton, acknowledging that he had made 'certain payments' out of this hoard to Henry both before and after he came to the throne (Creton said that Henry made off with all the money he found at Holt, but Ikelyngton's acquittance gives the lie to this: *Foedera*, viii.162–3; 'Metrical Chronicle', 124–5). In addition, John Leventhorpe collected £1,586 from the exchequer on 20 June and £1,733 from Westminster between 19 and 21 August, indicating that news of Richard's capture must have reached the capital by then (E 403/562, 20 June; DL 28/4/1, fo. 15r).

[8] Dryhurst, who was from 'West Chester', also retrieved the ornaments of Richard's chapel which had been left there, as well as eight tuns of red wine; he was paid £69 (E 403/569, 5 March).

The journey to London took twelve days, with Henry and Richard reaching Westminster on Monday 1 September. At Lichfield, on either 23 or 24 August, the king tried to escape by lowering a rope from his window, but the attempt was foiled and henceforward he was guarded more closely; Walsingham reported that at St Albans about a thousand men were set to watch over him each night.[9] Yet Henry continued to act with deference towards the king, always standing behind him, 'resplendent in his armour', waiting until proper respect had been shown him and refusing to allow any undue ceremonies to be performed in his own honour. Written instruments continued to be issued in Richard's name up until the moment when he was deposed.[10] From mid-July until mid-August, Henry had shown less regard for legal niceties, as witness the executions of Le Scrope, Bussy and Green at Bristol, or Perkyn Leigh at Chester, but once he had the king in his grasp he demonstrated a judicious awareness of the need to act in accordance with the law – not because the throne might slip from his grasp, which was unlikely, but with an eye to what might later be said about how he had acquired it. That Richard would be deposed was by now widely accepted. While Henry was still in Cheshire, a deputation of Londoners had offered the city's submission to him, and Salisbury, Norwich and King's Lynn soon followed suit.[11] On his arrival at the capital, he was greeted as a conquering hero. The first thing he did was to make his way to St Paul's to pray at his father's tomb, a grateful son to the last.[12] Richard, after being allowed to hear mass at Westminster on the morning of 2 September, was despatched to the Tower, where he would spend the next two months. Henry tactfully eschewed Westminster palace or any of the other royal residences in the vicinity of London, instead taking up his lodgings first at the bishop of London's palace by St Paul's and then at the Hospitaller priory at Clerkenwell.[13]

It took a month to devise and implement a formula for replacing the king. The committee charged with drafting it consisted of lawyers, prelates and

[9] *CR*, 152; there may also have been an attempt by some of the Cheshiremen to rescue Richard at Cholmondeston, near Nantwich: Morgan, *War and Society*, 204.

[10] *CR*, 124; however, these instruments were often issued 'by the assent' of Henry, Archbishop Arundel, or others: *CPR 1396–9*, 589–98 for examples. Henry also ceased to date his duchy letters by Richard's regnal years from 10 September 1399 onwards: Somerville, *Duchy of Lancaster*, i.138, n.3.

[11] *CR*, 159; 'Metrical History', 176–7; Bennett, *Richard II and the Revolution of 1399*, 173, 233; K. Parker, 'Politics and Patronage in Lynn, 1399–1416', in *Rebellion and Survival*, 210–27 at p. 212.

[12] 'Metrical Chronicle', 180–1; Creton says he 'wept very much' on seeing Gaunt's tomb.

[13] 'Metrical Chronicle', 181; he may also have spent some time at Hertford: *Traïson et Mort*, 215 n. 1.

nobles, and included Adam Usk as one of its doctors of laws; monks were ordered to bring all their chronicles to Westminster to be scrutinized for precedents, and a range of evidence was assembled.[14] The obvious precedent was the deposition of Edward II in 1327, but the bull of 1245 by which Pope Innocent IV had deposed Emperor Frederick II was also consulted, and Usk's assertion that the 'perjuries, sacrileges, sodomitical acts, dispossession of his subjects, reduction of his people to servitude, lack of reason and incapacity to rule' cited by Innocent were taken as sufficient to justify deposition is up to a point borne out by the thirty-three charges against Richard set out in the Record and Process, the official account of the proceedings.[15] The accusation of perjury was repeated ten times in the Record and Process, while the formal sentence of deposition recalled the king's 'many perjuries, his cruelty, and his numerous other crimes'. As this indicates, the central thrust of the charges was a sustained denunciation of Richard's character: evil, wicked, deceitful, faithless, crafty, overbearing, vainglorious, foolish, unbridled and cruel are just a selection of the adjectives used to blacken his name. He bore hatred in his heart, employed fear and threats to bend others to his arbitrary will, and acted as though 'the laws were in his mouth, or in his breast'. A more specific list of crimes welded this character assassination to constitutional issues: Richard had violated his coronation oath, imposed extortionate and unwarranted financial burdens upon his subjects, and undermined the liberties of the Church, the realm and parliament. Such claims were validated by reference to his harsh and unjust treatment of his opponents (especially Henry himself, Archbishop Arundel and the duke of Gloucester), to his unruly Cheshiremen, and to the blank charters and novel oaths he forced upon his subjects and ministers.

The Record and Process thus set out both a moral and a legal case for Richard's deposition. Distorted and exaggerated as they were, the charges against him contained recognizable elements of truth, and they chimed well with contemporary belief in the correlation between a ruler's ability to govern himself and his ability to govern his kingdom.[16] To focus on the

[14] The order specified 'all of their chronicles which touched upon the state and governance of the kingdom of England from the time of William the Conqueror until the present' (*CR*, 124; E 403/564, 1 December).

[15] *Usk*, 62–3. For the Record and Process, see *The Deposition of Richard II*, ed. D. Carlson (Toronto Medieval Latin Texts, Toronto, 2007), translated in *CR*, 168–89.

[16] The ultimately Aristotelian idea that a king who was unable to control his own passions and impulses was incapable of governing his kingdom well was almost an axiom of political thought at the time – as expressed, for example, in the works of Gower (Saul, 'John Gower: Prophet or Turncoat?', 90–1).

process by which Richard was deposed is, however, to miss the main point of the Record and Process, the full title of which was 'The Record and Process of the Renunciation of King Richard the Second since the Conquest and of the acceptance of the same renunciation, together with the deposition of the same King Richard'. As this makes clear, the crucial stage in the procedure by which Richard ceased to reign was his renunciation of the crown. The Record and Process is in fact a carefully structured and worded document. Beginning with Richard's 'voluntary' resignation of his crowns to Northumberland and Archbishop Arundel at Conway; progressing via his 'cheerful' and 'willing' confirmation of this resignation, symbolized by his 'public' removal of the royal signet ring from his finger, in the Tower of London on 29 September; continuing thence to the public reading of his renunciation in both Latin and English before the 'estates and people' of the realm in Westminster Great Hall, and their unanimous acceptance of this, 'without dissent', on 30 September; it makes it clear that the process of unkinging Richard was in effect complete before a single charge had been publicly read against him. Only after the acceptance of his resignation did the assembly agree, 'in order to remove any scruple or malevolent suspicion', to read out the many 'wrongs and shortcomings [which] rendered him worthy of deposition'. As Usk stated, the additional sanction of deposition was simply 'a further precaution' (*pro maiori securitate*); even the formal sentence of deposition questioned its own necessity, stating that it was 'beyond what was strictly required' since it was unclear as to whether, following his resignation, Richard had 'any royal dignity or honour left in him'.[17]

This point was of central importance. It was not simply that there was widespread unease about the legality of deposing an anointed king, although that was certainly the case. Equally germane was that, as king-in-waiting, Henry had no wish to concede at the outset that it was lawful for the estates of the realm (let alone parliament) to depose a king contrary to his wishes; hence the insistence on the voluntary nature of Richard's resignation, although, as is made clear by an independent eyewitness account of the meetings in the Tower and at Westminster on 28–29 September, this was a fiction. According to this source, 'The Manner of King Richard's Renunciation', when asked if he was willing to abdicate, the king became 'greatly incensed' and refused utterly to do so, declaring that 'he would like to have it explained to him how it was that he could resign the crown, and

[17] *Usk*, 62–3; *Deposition of Richard II*, ed. Carlson, 57.

to whom'.[18] Later, confronted by Henry in person, Richard agreed to resign on certain conditions; only when told that this was impossible, and that 'he must do it simply, without any conditions', did he read out the act of renunciation prepared for him. On the following day, when this was read to the estates and they were asked whether they accepted Richard's resignation, they cried out, 'Yes, yes, yes'; the notary John Ferriby then proceeded to a reading of the articles of deposition, which was followed by another cry of 'Yes, yes, yes' to the king's deposition. The first and fundamental stage in the process was thus securing the king's resignation; as Usk put it, the king 'self-evidently deposed himself'.[19]

'The Manner' amply exposes the lies which underpinned the Record and Process, as well as explaining why it was the latter which was circulated to monasteries and other interested parties, although even before this was done the text was further sanitized, with some of the charges being amplified and one or two inconvenient truths excised.[20] Walsingham, for example, stated that after the decision of the estates had been conveyed to Richard in the Tower on 1 October and proctors had renounced their homage and fealty to him, the king replied that 'he did not wish to renounce those special dignities of a spiritual nature which had been bestowed upon him, nor indeed his anointment; he was in fact unable to renounce them, nor could he cease to retain them'.[21] Nor was it true that he had admitted in his act of renunciation to being unworthy or unable to govern, 'it was simply that his government had not been acceptable to the people'. When Chief Justice Thirning, principal proctor for the estates, refuted this, 'the king simply smiled and asked to be treated accordingly, and not to be deprived of the means with which to sustain himself honourably'.[22] Thus only once it was clear that further negotiation was futile did Richard bow to the inevitable, but even then he refused to hand his symbols of office to Henry, instead 'simply placing his crown upon the ground, he resigned his

---

[18] *CR*, 162–7. Its author may have been Thomas Chillenden, prior of Christ Church, Canterbury, who was present in the Tower; it was used by the author of *CE* (382–4) as the basis for his account of these events.

[19] Before the articles were read, the archbishop of York gave a sermon on the theme of Isaiah 51:16 ('And I have put my words in thy mouth' – misconstrued in 'The Manner', but cf. *Usk*, 68–9); whether anyone noticed the irony is not recorded.

[20] *The Deposition of Richard II*, ed. Carlson; Given-Wilson, *Chronicles*, 70–2.

[21] Walsingham may have derived this from the 'Protestation of King Richard before Resignation', printed in *The Deposition of Richard II*, ed. Carlson, 69–70, and used by the author of the *Vita* (p. 159).

[22] *CR*, 187–9. Compare the 'Protestation': 'he did not wish nor intend to renounce the qualities [*carecteris*] impressed upon his soul by his anointing'; he did, however, go on to renounce the 'rule of the realm' (*regimen regni*) to Henry, 'inasmuch as he could'.

rights to God'. Usk confirmed this, pointing out that his signet ring was not handed over willingly (as per the Record and Process), but removed and given to Henry later.[23]

By this time Henry had been chosen as king. The fourth stage of the procedure described in the Record and Process – following Richard's resignation, its acceptance by the estates, and his deposition – was Henry's 'challenge' to the throne and his acclamation as king. This was presented in strikingly different style and language from the rest of the document. The language of Richard's renunciation and deposition was punctiliously formal, inflated and legalistic. The use of Latin rather than the customary Anglo-Norman of the parliament rolls was a statement of gravity, the prose verbose and repetitive, frequently using several words where one would have sufficed.[24] Those present in the Tower and their representative capacities were carefully enumerated, as in a charter witness list. The intention, clearly, was to elevate it to a precision of meaning that could not fail to be understood.[25] Henry's challenge, by contrast, was brief and imprecise, and it was delivered and recorded in the vernacular, the first such formal declaration by a king in the English tongue.[26] It being apparent, as the Record and Process put it, that 'the realm of England with its appurtenances was vacant', Henry rose from his seat, made the sign of the cross, commended himself to God, and read from a script as follows:

'In the name of fadir, son, and holy gost, I, Henry of Lancastre, chalenge this rewme of Yngland, and the corone with all the members and the appurtenances, als I that am disendit be right lyne of the blode coming fro the gude lorde kynge Henry therde, and thorgh that right that god of his grace hath sent me, with helpe of my kyn and of my frendes, to recover it; the whiche rewme was in point to be undone for defaut of governance and undoing of the gode lawes.'

Usk said that Henry read this from the throne, but he is surely wrong; both the Record and Process and 'The Manner' were at pains to emphasize that right up until the moment of his acclamation as king, he remained seated

[23] *CR*, 155 (Dieulacres Chronicle); *Usk*, 68–9.
[24] Thus the king's act of renunciation was called his 'Renunciation, Resignation, Demission and Cession'.
[25] *The Deposition of Richard II*, ed. Carlson, 8.
[26] W. M. Ormrod, 'The Use of English: Language, Law and Political Culture in Fourteenth-Century England', *Speculum* 78 (2003), 750–87, at p. 750.

in 'his proper and accustomed place', the seat formerly occupied by his father. Details which might have implied presumption on Henry's part were omitted from the official version.[27]

The blunt, unvarnished English of Henry's claim was a statement in itself, an implicit rejection of the language of majesty and distance which Richard had cultivated during the later years of his reign and a signal that Henry intended to practise an accessible style of kingship.[28] It was nevertheless a carefully worded statement and behind it lay a good deal of discussion. Henry's initial instinct had been to claim the kingdom by conquest, but Chief Justice Thirning advised him that this might imply that he could disinherit landholders at will.[29] Vestiges of a claim by conquest were nevertheless retained in Henry's challenge, dangling unobtrusively from the idea that God had seen fit to favour his cause and, along with 'my kin and my friends', to help him 'recover' the kingdom. 'Default of governance' and 'undoing of the good laws' provided a second line of justification, but the crux of Henry's claim was, as it had to be, blood-descent. This was not justified by the Crouchback Legend, which had been rejected at a meeting of the committee held on 21 September following a search of the chronicles assembled at Westminster,[30] but a more generalized manifesto probably intended to incorporate both the idea that Henry had royal blood on both sides of his pedigree and that he was, after Richard, the heir to the throne in the uninterrupted male line. Indeed, 'The Manner' stated that he claimed the kingdom as the 'nearest male heir' to Henry III, and this may well be correct, with the words attributed to him in the Record and Process being inserted later as a suitably ambiguous compromise.[31]

Yet if he could present himself with confidence as heir to the throne in the direct male line, everyone knew that Henry was not the primogenitary heir: that position was occupied by the eight-year-old Edmund, son of Roger, earl of March, who had been killed in battle against the Irish in July 1398. In 1403, when the Percys rebelled, they claimed that Henry had sworn neither to depose Richard nor to claim the throne for himself, but

[27] Thus 'The Manner' suggests that on his arrival at Westminster at nine o'clock he had been treated like a king-in-waiting, being greeted at the cemetery gate by the abbot and monks and escorted in procession to the abbey, and that when he entered the Great Hall (between twelve and one) he was preceded by Sir Thomas Erpingham 'carrying his splendidly decorated and bejewelled sword' (CR, 164–5, 172; Usk, 68–9).

[28] N. Saul, 'Richard II and the Vocabulary of Kingship', EHR 110 (1995), 854–77.

[29] CR, 186–7. He had seized the lands of Le Scrope, Bussy and Green by right of conquest, but his right to do so was later challenged (below, p. 442).

[30] CR, 195–6; Usk, 64–7; Given-Wilson, Chronicles, 71–2; and see above, p. 141.

[31] CR, 166. Alternatively, the author of 'The Manner' may have interpreted Henry's words as being less ambiguous than they were intended to be.

had then promptly deprived Edmund of his birthright. However, there is
no credible evidence that they or anyone else opposed Henry's challenge at
the time he made it.[32] There were in fact several good reasons to prefer
Henry's claim in 1399. Edmund's youth was crucial: England needed unity
in the aftermath of Richard's misrule, and the succession of a child was
unlikely to achieve this. Also, the majority of English nobles had by this
time made settlements of their estates in tail male, thereby excluding
female descendants, and in 1376 Edward III had in effect extended this
custom to the crown, even if the fact was not widely known. What was
certainly well known was that in France the nobility had decided to exclude
females and their descendants from the succession, making it arguable that
only a descendant through the male line would stand a chance of enforcing
the Plantagenet claim to the French throne. Henry did not deploy such
arguments in 1399, or at least not in public, but one further argument he
did use was that by (allegedly) handing over his signet ring to Henry,
Richard had effectively designated him as his successor.[33] Since Richard
had been asked on at least one occasion to choose between Lancaster and
Mortimer, this was a point worth making.[34]

Henry's claim was, at any rate, sufficient unto the day: each of the lords
was asked if he would accept it, and each gave his assent. Henry then rose
from his seat to say: 'My lords spiritual and temporal assembled here, we
beg you not simply to speak these words with your mouths if they do not
come from your hearts, but to agree to them with your hearts as well as
your mouths. Nevertheless, should it happen that some of you do not in
your hearts assent to this, that would be no great surprise to me.'

If this sounded slightly defensive, Henry was soon reassured: another
loud cry of 'Yes, yes, yes' greeted his words, whereupon the archbishops of
Canterbury and York led him to the throne and kissed his hands. Kneeling
for a moment to pray, he made the sign of the cross on the front and back
of the throne, and then, 'to the great joy of the people', seated himself on
the cloth of gold draped across it. Once the acclamation had subsided,
Archbishop Arundel preached a sermon on the theme 'A man shall rule

[32] *CR*, 193–5; for the 1403 rebellion, see below, pp. 216–32. It was John Hardyng, writing
in the mid-fifteenth century, who reported the Percys' objections in 1399. Hotspur, the
husband of Edmund Mortimer's aunt, may well have hoped that Edmund would be made
king, but whether he said as much in 1399 is another matter.

[33] This helps to explain the prominence accorded to the signet in the Record and Process
and the chronicle of a knowledgeable commentator such as Usk (*CR*, 186).

[34] See above, pp. 96–7. Despite the uncertain status of the idea of royal designation of a
successor, it was often claimed by usurpers (Given-Wilson, 'Legitimation, Designation and
Succession to the Throne', 89–105).

over the people',[35] emphasizing Henry's maturity and manliness in contrast to Richard's childish wilfulness, following which Henry gave an undertaking (once again in English) that even though conquest had played a part in his claim to the throne, he would not disinherit anyone apart from 'those persons that have acted contrary to the good purpose and the common profit of the realm'.[36] Fears were thus calmed that other supporters of the deposed king might be treated as Le Scrope, Bussy and Green had been.

The proceedings now drew to a close. The chancellor, treasurer, constable and marshal formally surrendered their symbols of office (seals, mace and baton) and were reappointed as the new king's ministers.[37] Parliament was scheduled for Monday 6 October and Henry's coronation one week later, but for the moment it was time to celebrate. It was between three and four o'clock in the afternoon when Henry rose from his throne and, 'looking at the people with a glad and kindly countenance', withdrew to the White Hall of the palace of Westminster, where a banquet had been prepared.[38]

Parliament duly opened on 6 October, but remained in session no longer than it took for Archbishop Arundel to deliver a sermon, for a speaker to be elected, and for triers and receivers of petitions to be appointed, before being adjourned.[39] Henry's choice of Monday 13 October (the Translation of Edward the Confessor) for his coronation might have been a way of signalling his appropriation of the saint who had become the talisman of English monarchy, but it was also an auspicious date, for it was a year to the day since he had crossed to France to begin his exile.[40] Although suffused with centuries-old religious and political symbolism, the English coronation ceremony was not set in stone, and around its spiritual nucleus there had grown up over the years a panoply of political and social rituals giving expression to notions such as continuity, renovation, reconciliation, orderliness and hierarchy. Henry added several elaborations of his own, the first of which was the dubbing of forty-six new knights who joined the king in

[35] I Samuel 9:17.
[36] CR, 186.
[37] CR, 166–7. Henry began to use the royal style immediately: further appointments were made later that day (E 404/15, nos. 1–17).
[38] SAC II, 210.
[39] PROME, viii.9–11. For more details, see below, pp. 366–7.
[40] Traditionally, coronations were on a Sunday, but Richard II's was on a Thursday, perhaps because it was felt that he needed to be crowned quickly (C. Given-Wilson, 'The Coronation of Richard II', Ceremonial de la Coronacion, Uncion y Exequias de los Reyes de Inglaterra, ed. E. Ramirez Vaquero (Pamplona, 2008), 195–227, at p. 201).

the Tower two days before the coronation, spent the night maintaining a
vigil, were ritually bathed as a sign of purification (thus mimicking Henry's
own preparations for his coronation, which also entailed an all-night vigil
and a purifying bath), and were then knighted during mass on the Sunday
morning before accompanying Henry in procession to Westminster later
in the day, dressed in identical long green robes and hats trimmed with
miniver and embellished with cords and tassels of white silk.[41] The existing
royal order of knighthood in England, that of the Garter, was restricted by
its statutes to twenty-six members and included many who, as Richard's
nominees, were politically unreliable. Henry's new knights, by contrast,
were mostly staunch Lancastrians and would form a chivalrically bound
fraternity of young braves, dedicated by their act of creation to the personal
service of the new sovereign.[42] As the creation of a king who had won a
name for himself on crusade and was the companion of famous knights
such as Marshal Boucicaut and Louis of Orléans (both of whom had
recently founded orders of knighthood), Henry was expressing the intention to raise the reputation of English knighthood from its currently rather
anonymous level. His inspiration may have been the order of *La Banda* (the
Sash), created in 1332 by Alfonso XI of Castile when he dubbed 112 knights
at his coronation to provide him with a corps of chivalric companions to
prosecute the war against the Moors.[43]

[41] Dubbings had taken place at coronations in the past, but never on such a scale or in
such conspicuous fashion: nine new knights were created at Richard's coronation, but not
until the banquet with which the ceremony concluded (ibid., 199–200). Also in the Tower
at the knighting ceremony on Sunday were Henry Green, king of the heralds of Scotland,
and other heralds from England and abroad (E 403/565, 21 November: *Oeuvres de Froissart*,
xvi.204–5).

[42] As well as the king's three younger sons (Prince Henry having already been knighted),
they included the heirs to the earldoms of Arundel, Warwick, Stafford and Devon, John
Pelham, Ralph Rochford, John Tiptoft, Robert Chalons and Thomas Dymmok (*Chronicles
of London*, ed. Kingsford, 48; *Traïson et Mort*, 224–5; *Usk*, 70; R. Strong, *Coronation. A History
of Kingship and the British Monarchy* (London, 2005), 162; BL Harleian Ms 1386, fo. 18). Despite
a belief that this marked the foundation of the Order of the Bath, it was more in the nature
of a fellowship, being limited neither by statutes nor in number, although it did inaugurate
a tradition of creating 'Knights of the Bath' on the eve of the coronation. There are references to 'the order of knighthood of the Bath' in the fifteenth century (M. Keen, 'Treason
Trials under the Law of Arms', *TRHS* 1962, 85–103, at p. 90), but it was not formally
founded until 1725. Froissart stated merely that each of the knights 'had his chamber and
his bath where they were bathed that night' (*Oeuvres de Froissart*, xvi.205). The great wardrobe livery roll of the coronation, which listed forty-six knights, included *milites de balneo*, but
in a later hand: *The Coronation of Richard III*, ed. A. Sutton and P. Hammond (Gloucester,
1984), 92; see also F. Pilbrow, 'The Knights of the Bath: Dubbing to Knighthood in
Lancastrian and Yorkist England', *Heraldry, Pageantry and Social Display*, 195–218; J. Risk, *The
History of the Order of the Bath* (London, 1972), 6–9.

[43] P. Linehan, *History and the Historians of Medieval Spain* (Oxford, 1993), 584–601; Henry's
sister Katherine was married to Juan I of Castile.

The main event on the afternoon of Sunday 12 October was the procession through London from the Tower to Westminster palace. Despite the rain, Henry rode bare-headed on a white charger, wearing a short doublet of cloth of gold, a blue garter on his left leg, and the badge of the king of France around his neck, a reminder of the Plantagenet claim to the French throne. He was accompanied by over 2,000 lords, ladies, knights, clerks and household servants, all wearing newly made robes, and perhaps three times as many horses.[44] The mayor and citizens of London were arrayed in fur-trimmed scarlet liveries and sported their company badges. Those who rode closest to the king such as Thomas Erpingham, who carried Henry's sword, and Thomas Percy, who bore the steward's baton, wore red velvet or silk, and the streets were decked out with gorgeous hangings and punctuated with conduits dispensing free wine.[45]

Following his vigil and bath, Henry began the day of the coronation by confessing himself and hearing three masses.[46] Shortly before nine o'clock the monks of Westminster and other prelates crossed the yard from the abbey to the palace, where they waited outside the royal chamber. Barefoot apart from his sandals, Henry emerged to be first purified by the archbishops of Canterbury and York with holy water and incense, and then conducted by the monks and bishops back to the abbey; four citizens of the Cinque Ports held above him a canopy of blue silk supported by silver rods attached to which were 'four jingling golden bells', while the bishop of London carried the holy sacrament and sang the mass.[47] On one side of him walked the thirteen-year-old Prince Henry, on the other the earl of Northumberland. Four swords were borne around the king rather than the usual three: Prince Henry carried the Curtana, the coronation sword which Henry himself had borne at Richard's banquet twenty-two years earlier, while the earls of Somerset (John Beaufort) and Warwick (released from exile on the Isle of Man) each bore a sword wrapped in red and bound with golden straps to symbolize twofold mercy. The additional sword, carried by the earl of Northumberland, was the one Henry had

---

[44] The livery roll (*Coronation of Richard III*, 92–9) lists 85 lords, 62 ladies, 64 clerks, 197 knights, 230 esquires of the body, 225 'other esquires', 416 valets, 573 yeomen, 208 grooms, 25 minstrels and 25 bargemen. Strong, *Coronation*, 142, doubted Froissart's figure of 6,000 horses, but it is not impossible.

[45] *SAC II*, 224–5; *Chronicles of London*, 48; *Usk*, 70.

[46] The scribe of one Froissart manuscript added cattily, 'for he had great need of it [confession]': *Oeuvres de Froissart*, xvi.206.

[47] *Traïson et Mort*, 226; *SAC II*, 226–7.

with him at the time of his landing at Ravenspur three months earlier and was known as Lancaster sword.[48]

Much of the ceremony in the abbey followed established custom. On entering the church, the procession advanced towards an elevated platform covered with crimson cloth set up between the transepts, on top of which was the throne draped in cloth of gold. Henry mounted the steps and sat on the throne. Archbishop Arundel ascended with him before turning to the congregation to ask if they wanted Henry as their king. 'Yes' they cried, stretching out their hands towards him as a sign of faith and allegiance.[49] Turning back to Henry, Arundel read out the four articles of the coronation oath, which the king swore to uphold.[50] The two men then descended from the platform and approached the high altar, where another cloth of gold had been spread over the paving stones, and here, while the congregation sang *Veni Creator Spiritus*, Henry's clothes were stripped from his upper body and he was anointed on his hands, chest, shoulders, upper back, arms and head.[51] Unction was the transcendental moment of the coronation, by which the new king was invested with quasi-sacerdotal qualities and raised, as The Lord's Anointed, above other mortals. What is more, it was indelible, as Richard had reminded those who came to the Tower on 1 October to inform him of his deposition – his point being that Henry's enthronement in Westminster Hall the previous day might have made a king of him, but not an anointed king.[52] Henry's way of trumping his predecessor was to have himself anointed with a new, miraculous, holy oil. This, it was claimed, had been given to Thomas Becket during his exile in France in the 1160s, when the Blessed Virgin appeared and had handed

[48] Adam Usk, who was there, said that it was unsheathed but without a point, to symbolize the execution of justice without rancour, but the symbolic meaning of these swords was interpreted variously: the London chronicler stated that the Curtana 'betokened peace', while one of Froissart's scribes asserted that it was the sword of the Church and that Northumberland's was the sword of justice, but another reversed this (*Oeuvres de Froissart*, xvi.206 and n; *Usk*, 72–4; *Chronicles of London*, 49; *Foedera*, viii.90–1). Walsingham said it was decided that four swords would be carried in future (*SAC II*, 262; *Coronation of Richard III*, 237–44).

[49] *Oeuvres de Froissart*, xvi.207. See the Illustration in Strong, *Coronation*, 160. It would be another three weeks before Arundel was formally restored by Pope Boniface IX to the see of Canterbury, but neither Arundel nor Henry recognized Roger Walden, intruded to the see by Richard II, and Arundel had simply resumed the archbishopric after Richard's capture, presenting the pope with a fait accompli (cf. *Usk*, 78–82).

[50] Usk (p. 73) said: 'I heard the king swear to my lord of Canterbury that he would strive to rule his people with mercy and truthfulness in all matters'. Richard took the oath *before* the acclamation, thus rendering any vestige of the 'elective' process virtually redundant, but Henry reverted to the correct order as set out in the coronation *ordines*.

[51] Froissart says he was anointed in six places; the *Chronicles of London* (p. 49) in four.

[52] *CR*, 188; above, p. 143.

him a figurine of a golden eagle enclosing an ampulla which contained the oil with which future kings of England should be crowned; the first king to be crowned with it, she said, would be a champion of the Church, recover the lands held by his forefathers in France, and drive the infidel from the Holy Land. Brought to England in the early fourteenth century, the ampulla was unearthed in the 1390s by Richard while rummaging through some old chests in the Tower; when he read about its miraculous properties, he asked Archbishop Arundel to anoint him with it, but Arundel refused, saying that unction was not a rite that could be repeated. Thus it was that Henry became the first king to be anointed with St Thomas's oil, as a result of which, declared Walsingham, it was believed that he had been chosen by God to accomplish greater deeds than any king before him.[53] The French ambassadors to whom Henry proudly showed the ampulla a few weeks after his coronation were struck by his confidence that St Thomas's oil would give him victory over his enemies; it also placed English coronations on a par with those of the French kings, who were traditionally anointed with chrism brought from heaven by an angel at the baptism of King Clovis in 496 and kept ever since in the *Sainte Ampoulle*.[54] Unfortunately the effects of Henry's anointment were not all beneficial, for according to Usk the new oil caused his head to be so infected with lice that his hair fell out, so that for months afterwards he was obliged to keep his head covered.[55]

Unction was followed by crowning. Dressed in his coronation robes 'like a deacon', Henry was now invested with the regalia: slippers of red velvet, rebated spurs, sword, bracelets, pallium, the crown itself (placed upon his head by the two archbishops) and the ring taken from Richard in the Tower. According to Froissart, the crown used was St Edward's and was arched in the shape of a cross – in other words, a closed ('imperial') rather

---

[53] There are several versions of this story; one of them relates that Richard took the ampulla to Ireland in 1399 and was relieved of it by Archbishop Arundel at Chester (*SAC II*, 236–41; *CE*, iii.380, 384; Strong, *Coronation*, 116–18). Before 1399, kings were anointed with two oils, those of St Mary of Sardinia and St Nicholas; Becket's oil was regarded as both holier and more exclusive, and continued to be used throughout the fifteenth century: C. Wilson, 'The Tomb of Henry IV and the Holy Oil of St Thomas at Canterbury', in *Medieval Architecture and its Intellectual Context: Studies in Honour of Peter Kidson*, ed. E. Fernie and P. Crossley (London, 1990), 181–90. John Gower noted: 'H[enry] the eagle has captured the oil, by which he has received the rule of the realm' (*The Minor Latin Works of John Gower*, ed. R. F. Yeager (Kalamazoo, 2005), 46–7).

[54] *Saint-Denys*, ii.732–3.

[55] This is quite plausible, since after his anointing a cap was placed on the king's head and not removed for a week, allowing any infection to fester: *Usk*, 242.

than an open crown.[56] If he was right, then it must have been made during Richard's reign, for Richard had certainly used an open crown in 1377. That it was his supplanter who benefited from Richard's desire to elevate the symbolism of the coronation ceremony with new oil and a new crown was ironic.[57] Wearing his crown, Henry now took the sceptre in his right hand and the coronation staff in his left and was blessed by the archbishop, kissed by each of the bishops, and escorted back up to the throne while the prelates sang *Te Deum Laudamus*; this was followed by the coronation mass and a final blessing, after which the royal party processed back to the Great Hall, his four sons riding ahead of the new king while the Constable and Marshal cleared a way through the throng.[58]

The day ended with a banquet in the Great Hall, newly rebuilt with its intersecting arch-brace and hammer-beam roof designed by Richard's master-carpenter Hugh Herland. The menu has survived.[59] There were three courses, each one accompanied by *soteltees* (delicacies, often spiced). The first included sturgeon, heron, pheasant, boar's head, brawn, capon and other 'great meats' and 'royal viands'; this was followed by venison, crane, bittern and pullet, more brawn *fryez* and 'great tarts'; finally there was rabbit, egret, curlew, partridge, peewit, quail, eagle, snipe and other small birds, along with apples and *doucettys* (sweetmeats). Henry and the prelates sat at a table on a high platform against the south end of the building. Behind him stood his eldest son and the earl of Northumberland holding their swords, while the earl of Westmorland and Lord Furnivall held the sceptre and staff. Coronation duties had been allocated at the Court of Claims on 4 October: the earl of Arundel acted as butler, the earl of Oxford as ewerer, Lord Grey of Ruthin as naperer, Thomas Erpingham as chamberlain, John Lord Latimer as almoner, William Venour as waferer and Edmund de la Chaumbre as lardiner; William d'Argentan carried the

---

[56] *Oeuvres de Froissart*, xvi.207: this has *archie en trois*, probably a scribal error for *archie en croix*, although the meaning would be much the same: P. Grierson, 'The Origins of the English Sovereign and the Symbolism of the Closed Crown', *British Numismatic Journal* 33 (1969), 118–34, at p. 129, n.2.

[57] Anne of Bohemia, the daughter of Emperor Charles IV, might have encouraged its use, for Holy Roman Emperors usually wore a closed rather than an open crown. Although there is little before the sixteenth century to indicate any widespread association in England between a closed crown and imperial pretensions, Henry V and his successors did use a closed crown (Strong, *Coronation*, 120–2; Grierson, 'The Origins of the English Sovereign', 130–3).

[58] It had been usual since Edward I's time for new kings to receive homage from the nobility during the mass, but Henry delayed this until the parliament the next day, perhaps because it had in effect been done on 30 September (Given-Wilson, 'Coronation of Richard II', 206–7; *Chronicles of London*, 50; *Usk*, 76–7).

[59] BL Harleian MS 1386, fos. 17–18.

king's golden goblet and the mayor of London poured his wine. The dukes of Aumale, Surrey and Exeter and the earls of Somerset and Warwick helped to carve and serve the king's food.[60] Seating was arranged according to precedent, with the barons of the Cinque Ports and the mayor and aldermen of London occupying tables just below the king's, and further tables reserved for the dukes and earls of the realm and for the newly created knights.[61]

Halfway through the meal the great north door opened to reveal Sir Thomas Dymmok, the king's champion, armed from head to foot, bearing a sword sheathed in black with a golden hilt and sitting astride one of the king's best war-horses. Flanked by two mounted knights, one bearing his spear and the other his shield, he rode up the hall before approaching a herald and handing him a scroll on which were written the following words: 'If there is any man high or low, of any estate or condition, who says that Henry, king of England, here present and crowned this day, is not the rightful king nor rightfully crowned, I will either now, or whenever our lord king determines, offer him battle with my body and prove that he is a false liar.'[62]

Circling to each corner of the hall, the herald repeated the challenge four times in English and French. The predictable silence was broken only when Henry himself remarked bullishly, 'If need be, Sir Thomas, I shall personally relieve you of this task,' releasing Dymmok to ride out into the night again, taking with him the horse and its trappings as his fee. 'And after he had voided the hall,' states the London chronicler, 'the revel ended'.[63] There was, after all, a parliament due to meet in the morning.

---

[60] *Usk*, 72–3; *Foedera*, viii.90–1; *Chronicles of London*, 49. There were always disputes over the right to perform these offices. Thomas Mowbray's attorneys claimed the office of marshal, but in his absence it was assigned to Westmorland; Aubrey de Vere, as earl of Oxford, claimed the office of chamberlain, but was made ewerer instead, Erpingham's claim being preferred; Ivo FitzWarin challenged d'Argentan's right to carry the golden goblet, and the mayor of London challenged Arundel's right to be butler, but was asked instead to pour the wine; John Drayton unsuccessfully challenged Lord Grey's claim to be naperer. For the proceedings of the Court of Claims, which was presided over by the earl of Worcester as deputy for the steward of the realm, the king's son, Thomas, see BL Add. MS 35,861, fos. 5–43, BL Lansdowne Ms cclxxx, BL Cotton Vespasian C.xiv, fos. 149–56, and BL Stowe MS 579, fos. 24–40.

[61] *Oeuvres de Froissart*, xvi.208. The *Traïson et Mort* said that a few servants of the dukes of Berry and Orleans attended, but that other foreigners were excluded; this, however, is implausible.

[62] Sir Thomas's father had acted as champion at Richard's coronation, although the family's right to the office was challenged both in 1377 and 1399 by the Freville family; Adam Usk drafted the petition on behalf of Dymmok for the Court of Claims on 4 October, and preserved it in his chronicle (*Usk*, 74–5).

[63] *Usk*, 72–3; *Chronicles of London*, 49–50.

The twin ceremonies of enthronement on 30 September and coronation on 13 October had marshalled every available argument to emphasize
that Henry was as rightful a king as any who had come before him: descent
through blood, the designation of his predecessor following his voluntary
abdication, popular acclamation, divine favour as demonstrated by his
virtually bloodless triumph, the explicit intervention of the Blessed Virgin
Mary and the implicit sanction of England's two most famous saints,
Thomas Becket and Edward the Confessor. For the future, Henry had
stressed that, although he would uphold knightly values, he was not going
to let the fact of his conquest lead him to abuse his powers: he would
respect both property rights and the will of the people, and would temper
his justice with mercy.

It would be a matter of no more than a few days before such undertakings began to be put to the test.

Part Two

A KING AT WAR, 1399–1405

Chapter 11

'IN THIS NEW WORLD' (1399–1400)

Despite the undoubted popular support for Richard II's deposition, what Henry effected in 1399 was less of a revolution than a *coup d'état*. Westminster-based offices such as the chancery and exchequer had by now developed a civil service ethos allowing them to bridge royal minorities and political crises with a minimum of disruption, and apart from some changes at the higher levels, government could be expected to continue much as before. Moreover, since England was the most centralized and manageable large kingdom in fourteenth-century Europe, control of Westminster went a long way towards ensuring control of the country. Yet this coup was more than a dynastic side-step. The Lancastrian affinity, having delivered the throne to Henry, now became the dominant power-network in the kingdom, and one of the questions facing the new king was the extent to which he could afford to allow others to share that power. Allegiance to the Lancastrian regime was the challenge that Henry's usurpation set to the English polity, and it entailed acceptance of the Lancastrian affinity.

It was certainly the question of allegiance that dominated the proceedings of the parliament that reassembled at Westminster on 14 October, the day after the coronation. United by a sense of shared complicity in the overthrow of Richard's regime, the knights and burgesses seem to have been almost more Lancastrian than the king.[1] While Henry sought reconciliation and a springboard to launch his rule, the commons and some of the lords saw the parliament as an opportunity to avenge themselves on the former king's chief abettors, and as a result the focus of the assembly was more retrospective than constructive. The tone was set from the start. John Doreward, a former retainer of the duke of Gloucester who would shortly be appointed to the Privy Council, was chosen as speaker;[2] the acts of the 1397–8 parliament were repealed and its victims or their heirs restored to

---

[1] *HOC*, i.209–18. Although Henry kept with him many of the troops who had marched with him between July and September, there is nothing to suggest that they were needed.

[2] For the resignation of the initial choice as speaker, John Cheyne (also Gloucester's retainer), see below. pp. 366–7.

their lands and titles; and the decisions of the Merciless Parliament were reaffirmed. Then, on Thursday 16 October, the fury erupted. William Bagot, shipped back in chains from Ireland, was brought in and asked, under interrogation, whether he stood by a bill he had drawn up. He replied that he did, thereby pointing the finger directly at the duke of Aumale as the former king's chief accomplice in both the murder of the duke of Gloucester and the confiscation of the Lancastrian estates following Gaunt's death. Aumale vehemently denied any involvement in Gloucester's death, hurling down his hood as a gage of battle against anyone who so accused him. Henry told him to retrieve it, but not in time to prevent Walter Lord FitzWalter from taking up the challenge. Yet if the lords and commons really wanted to know what had happened to Gloucester, said Bagot, they should interrogate a valet called John Hall who was currently being held in Newgate prison.

Manacled and shackled, Hall was brought into parliament on Saturday 18 October. The details which he revealed of Gloucester's murder – suffocated under a featherbed by half a dozen esquires and valets in a back room of the Princes' Inn at Calais – were shocking enough, but equally so was his unequivocal testimony that the men behind it were Richard II and the dukes of Aumale and Norfolk.[3] Aumale's life now hung by a thread: 'You, Aumale, were responsible for the death of the duke of Gloucester! You were midwife to his murder!' cried FitzWalter, casting down his hood as he did so. Some twenty other lords followed suit, and there was 'such a mighty tumult and clamour from the commons offering battle on this point that the king was afraid that the duke was about to be put to death before his very eyes'. It was the first real test of Henry's authority. Crying out for restraint, 'he first begged, then warned, and finally ordered them not to do anything which was against the law, but to act legally and only after proper discussion'.[4] Order was eventually restored, but only on condition that Aumale and the other Counter-Appellants be put on trial. Meanwhile John Hall, who had admitted being present at Gloucester's death (though only, he claimed, because forced to by the duke of Norfolk on pain of a similar fate), was adjudged to suffer 'the harshest death to which he could possibly be sentenced, since the duke of Gloucester was so great a personage'. He was drawn on a hurdle from Tower Hill to Tyburn that

---

[3] *PROME*, viii.87–9; A London chronicler said he was strangled 'with two towels made in snare wise and put about his neck': *A Chronicle of London from 1089 to 1483*, ed. N. Nicolas and E. Tyrell (London, 1827), 82.
[4] *Chronicles of London*, 54–5; *CR*, 207–8.

same afternoon and there disembowelled, hanged, beheaded and quartered.[5]

The next week was devoted to drawing up indictments against the six surviving Counter-Appellants, and debating the fate of the former king. On Tuesday 21 October the commons asked that Richard be brought into parliament to stand trial. This Henry was reluctant to do, partly for fear that it would stir up further division between the lords (how far, after all, might the guilt be held to have spread?), but also on constitutional grounds: could parliament try a king, even a deposed one?[6] Instead the lords were asked individually what they thought should be done with Richard, for, Henry declared, he did not wish to deprive him of his life. It was agreed that he be imprisoned for life, and on 29 October the former king was removed from the Tower. Although his destination was initially kept secret, by Christmas it had become known that he was being held in Pontefract castle.[7]

The trial of the Counter-Appellants also began on 29 October. The charges against them were essentially threefold: that they had presented the appeals in the 1397–8 parliament, consented to Gloucester's murder, and assented to the confiscation of Henry's inheritance. The second charge they denied absolutely – on this their lives depended. The first and third they could scarcely deny, but pleaded coercion by the king and William Le Scrope. Once again parliament erupted, with gages and accusations hurled across the chamber. Thomas Lord Morley challenged the earl of Salisbury to a duel; FitzWalter once again challenged Aumale. But Henry had no desire to see further blood spilt, and when, on Monday 3 November, Chief Justice William Thirning delivered judgment on them, it spoke more of mercy than of vengeance. Aumale, Surrey and Exeter were stripped of their ducal titles; John Beaufort lost his marquisate of Dorset; and Thomas Despenser his earldom of Gloucester. The lands and goods which any of them had acquired since September 1397 (chiefly the forfeited estates of the three Appellants) were confiscated. As security for their future behaviour, they were also prohibited from distributing livery badges and told that if they tried to restore Richard to the throne, they would *ipso facto* be guilty of treason.[8] Nor did it end there, for a proclamation was made throughout the realm inviting anyone who wished to complain of their misdeeds to

[5] Usk saw 'the quarter of his body which included the right hand' placed on a stake near London bridge; his head was sent to Calais, the scene of his crime (*Usk*, 78; *CR*, 221).

[6] There may well have been some debate about this before a decision was made (*SAC II*, 818–25).

[7] *SAC II*, 264–5.

[8] For the Statute of Liveries, see below. pp. 393–6.

come forward and justice would be done to them. The earl of Salisbury was excluded from the judgment since, having accepted Morley's challenge, his case had been referred to the Court of Chivalry. This met on 9 December and decreed that they should fight a duel at Newcastle in February.[9]

Parliament remained in session for a further two weeks, until 19 November, but made disappointingly little provision for the future. The wool subsidy was renewed for three years, but tunnage and poundage and direct taxation were neither requested nor granted. Instead, Henry was exhorted to recover the former king's jewels and other moveable wealth, which were believed to be of great value, although he was also encouraged to settle Richard's debts and repay his loans.[10] Titles were heaped upon the thirteen-year-old Prince Henry, who became prince of Wales and duke of Guyenne and Lancaster. Once the former king and his chief accomplices had been dealt with, however, the momentum of the session ebbed away. Punishing the Counter-Appellants was doubtless a cathartic and bonding process, but it also threatened new divisions, for there was a widespread feeling that they had been treated too leniently, with some even alleging that Henry, Archbishop Arundel and the earl of Northumberland had been bribed to spare the lives of men 'whom the common people thought evil and who deserved to die'. Just as the king was about to dissolve parliament, a letter was found in his chamber threatening a rebellion if he allowed the Counter-Appellants to live. The lords and commons denied all knowledge of it, but Henry's desire for reconciliation evidently did not chime with the mood of the country.[11] Whether it would win over Richard's supporters also remained to be seen. Publicly humiliated and widely reviled, only by pleading cowardice had they succeeded in saving their skins – at least for the moment. Whatever he might have hoped, Henry's expectations of their future allegiance are unlikely to have been high.

The revanche – the 'Epiphany Rising', a plot to assassinate the new king and his sons and restore Richard to the throne – probably came sooner

---

[9] Salisbury was the only Counter-Appellant who had not been given a new title in September 1397, which afforded less justification for demoting him. Aumale had also accepted FitzWalter's challenge, but the king had declared that he wished to hear the evidence of the duke of Norfolk (Mowbray) before deciding what to do; in fact, Mowbray had died at Venice on 22 September, and the dispute between Aumale and FitzWalter was shelved until the parliament of 1401 when they were (at least nominally) reconciled (*PROME*, viii.110; *Great Chronicle of London*, 80–1).

[10] *PROME*, viii.30, 62–4; see below, pp. 175–6.

[11] *SAC II*, 276–9.

than expected, but there was nothing unexpected about the revanchists. The chief lay conspirators were the earls of Kent and Huntingdon (demoted from the dukedoms of Surrey and Exeter, respectively); Thomas Despenser (demoted from earl of Gloucester); William Montague, earl of Salisbury; two of Richard's chamber knights, Thomas Blount and Benedict Cely; and the obscure but obviously disaffected Ralph Lord Lumley and his son Thomas. Several of the former king's clerks were also implicated, including Thomas Merks and Henry Despenser, the bishops of Carlisle and Norwich; William Colchester, abbot of Westminster; Roger Walden, the intruder appointed by Richard II to the see of Canterbury during Thomas Arundel's exile; and two of Richard's household clerks, Richard Maudeleyn and William Ferriby. As for the earl of Rutland (Aumale), no one seemed very sure what role if any he played in the rising; he may initially have joined the conspiracy but later betrayed it, he may have played a double game from the start, or perhaps it was only his detractors (of whom he had many) who claimed that he was involved. The prominent part he played in suppressing the rising indicates that Henry gave him the benefit of the doubt. The sixth Counter-Appellant, Henry's half-brother and childhood companion John Beaufort, was certainly not involved; despite being deprived of his marquisate for failing to stand up to Richard's machinations in 1398–9, he had made his peace with Henry and was now fully committed to the new regime. He too took a leading role in the suppression.[12]

Henry, who was recovering from food poisoning, had spent Christmas at Windsor with a smaller than usual household and was planning to round off the seasonal celebrations with a day of masques and jousts on 6 January, the Epiphany. It was under cover of these festivities that the rebels, who had been conspiring together since mid-December, planned to strike, but before the day arrived they were betrayed, possibly by a London prostitute, whose clients included both a loose-tongued conspirator and an esquire of the royal household, possibly by the earl of Rutland, or possibly simply through carelessness.[13] At any rate, by the time the rebel lords met as arranged at Kingston-upon-Thames (Surrey) on Sunday 4 January, the

[12] For a summary of the events of the rising see A. Rogers, 'Henry IV and the Revolt of the Earls', *History Today* (1968), 277–83. The main contemporary accounts are in *SAC II*, 284–98; *Traïson et Mort*, 229–51; there are extracts from these and other sources in *CR*, 47–50, 224–39. For Rutland's and Beaufort's role in the suppression, see E 403/564, 20 March.

[13] *SAC II*, 283; *Giles*, 7, says that the mayor of London heard about the plot from some indiscreet Londoners and hurried to Windsor to advise the king to come to London at once.

king knew of the plot and was hurrying back to London, summoning his retainers as he went.[14] Thomas Knolles, mayor of London, raised the citizens, while Henry sent a message to Archbishop Arundel, warning him just in time ('as we were approaching Kingston') of the danger.[15] Arundel, who had also been marked out for execution, retired to Reigate castle. The rebels, realizing they had been unmasked, nevertheless rode to Windsor where once more they vainly proclaimed Richard II king, then to Sonning (Berkshire) where Richard's child-queen Isabella's household was lodged. Kent, Salisbury and Lumley then rode westwards, perhaps trying to reach Shrewsbury or Cheshire, perhaps to flee abroad. By the evening of 6 January they had reached Cirencester. The townspeople, alerted to their intentions, arrested them, locked them in the abbey, and summoned Thomas Lord Berkeley to conduct them to the king, but this proved unnecessary: two days later, when they tried to flee – apparently by starting a fire in order to cover their escape – all three were dragged out into the marketplace and beheaded. Meanwhile Huntingdon had made his way into Essex hoping to flee by boat to the continent; found hiding in a mill at Prittlewell, he was taken to Pleshey castle and handed over to Joan countess of Hereford, Henry's mother-in-law. Accounts differ as to whether she hastened him to his execution or the popular clamour obliged her to hand him over to the mob, but the upshot was that he was beheaded outside the castle gate by 'plebs and mechanics' on the very spot where, two-and-a-half years earlier, the duke of Gloucester had been arrested by Richard II.[16] Thomas Despenser also tried to flee abroad from his castle of Cardiff, but he was betrayed by the captain of the ship he chartered and taken instead to Bristol, where once again lynch law prevailed: he was beheaded in the marketplace on 13 January.[17]

Meanwhile the king had set off with a mixed force of retainers and Londoners in pursuit of the ringleaders, but by the time he reached Oxford on 11 January he was able to despatch letters to the sheriffs telling them the danger was over.[18] Most of the remaining suspects were brought here, and at Oxford castle on 12 January Henry presided over their trials. The charge, inescapably, was treason. Some ninety men stood accused, most of whom were quickly pardoned since they were menials press-ganged into joining

---

[14] Henry was still at Windsor on 3 January (DL 42/15, fo. 69r).

[15] CR, 236–7; E 403/565, 4 February (Knolles's reward).

[16] Usk, 88–9; SAC II, 290–7; BL Add MS 35, 295, 262r.

[17] CR, 238–9; Giles, 9, said the mayor was forced by the townspeople to hand him over for execution.

[18] The Black Book of Winchester, ed. W. Bird (Winchester, 1925), 6–7.

the rising, although twenty-seven were convicted and adjudged to a traitor's death. Most of these were simply beheaded since, as Henry put it: 'the
sight of so many people being put to such a death would be quite horrid,
and the sound of it most odious, and lest they should, on account of the
great pains they would suffer, deny God their Creator or fail to keep their
Creator properly in mind at the going forth of their souls'.[19]

The most fortunate rebel was John Ferrour, who was pardoned and
released because he had saved Henry's life in the Tower at the time of the
1381 Revolt. Four of the ringleaders, however – the knights Thomas Blount
and Benedict Cely and the esquires John Walsh and William Baldwin –
suffered the full penalty of drawing, hanging, beheading and quartering.
Adam Usk, who had an eye for such details, recalled seeing their bodies
being carried to London 'chopped up like the carcasses of beasts killed in the
chase, partly in sacks and partly on poles slung across pairs of men's shoulders, where they were later salted to preserve them [for display]'.[20] Rumours
of the rising had also spread north, sparking disturbances in Derbyshire and
Cheshire among opponents of the Lancastrian regime, but these subsided
once news arrived from Cirencester and Oxford.[21] By 15 January Henry was
back in London where, on the following day, Archbishop Arundel led a
procession through the city chanting the *Te Deum* in thanksgiving for the
king's deliverance.[22] Maudeleyn and Ferriby were caught and executed three
weeks later, but the higher-ranking churchmen escaped with their lives, even
if the bishop of Carlisle was initially condemned to death.[23]

There remained one possible conspirator. According to one account,
Richard II confessed that the rebels had been acting on a plan devised by
him at Conway castle.[24] Although it is far from impossible that schemes
of a general nature were discussed during those desperate August days
in North Wales, it is difficult to believe that Richard, closely guarded at
Pontefract castle, could have been involved in any detailed planning.[25]
What was clear, however, was that as long as he remained alive, he was an
incentive to treason, and in this sense the rising was the catalyst for his

---

[19] E 37/28.
[20] *Usk*, 89.
[21] P. McNiven, 'The Cheshire Rising of 1400', *BJRL* 52 (1969–70), 375–96; D. Crook,
'Central England and the Revolt of the Earls', *HR* (1991), 403–10.
[22] Wylie, *Henry the Fourth*, i.107.
[23] Sir Bernard Brocas and Sir Thomas Shelley were also executed on 5 Feb.; for Carlisle,
see below, pp. 349–50.
[24] *CE*, 387.
[25] His gaolers were Robert Waterton, constable of Pontefract castle, and Thomas
Swynford, now a royal chamber knight (DL 42/15, fo. 70v; E 403/564, 20 March).

death. The minute of a great council meeting held on 8–9 February recorded cagily that if he were still alive, 'as it is supposed that he is', he should be securely guarded, but that if he were dead this should be demonstrated to the people. By 17 February it was known that he was dead and an esquire was sent to bring his corpse from Pontefract to London.[26] The date often given for his death is 14 February. It was not a violent death: when his body was examined in the nineteenth century, no wounds were found on it.[27] The chroniclers stated either that Richard was so despondent at the failure of the rising and the death of his friends that he starved himself to death, or that his gaolers starved him to death. The former is possible, but the latter is a good deal more likely, as is the supposition that they were acting on Henry's orders. For the moment, however, the fact of Richard's death was more important than the manner of it, which is why Henry had his body brought down to London slowly and publicly exhibited at the major towns en route, 'or at least that part of the body from which his face could be recognized, that is, from the forehead to the throat', as Walsingham, who saw the corpse at St Albans, explained. Two days of exequies attended by Henry were observed at St Paul's on 6–7 March before the body was taken to King's Langley (Hertfordshire) 'at dead of night' for burial.[28] Not everyone was convinced: rumours surfaced periodically for nearly twenty years that Richard was still alive, although how many people truly believed them is not clear. More damaging initially was that, already a usurper, Henry was now also a regicide, a taunt which his enemies lost no time in seizing upon.

And enemies he had: many of them, as the rising had demonstrated. As far as committed Ricardians were concerned, Henry's policy of reconciliation had not worked. Whether it would be more effective in persuading others remained to be seen, but the February great council decided not to take any chances. 'In this new world', it advised the king, he should retain 'a certain number of the more sufficient men of good fame' in each county, appoint them to the commissions of the peace and entrust them with 'saving the estate of the king' in their localities. He should also ensure that

---

[26] *POPC*, i.107, 111–12; E 403/564, 17 February (the esquire was William Pampilion).

[27] D. W. Dillon, 'Remarks on the Manner of the Death of King Richard II', *Archaeologia* (1840), 75–95. The simplest way to kill him would probably have been poison, but this is not mentioned by any writer. The story told in the *Traïson et Mort* that Richard was hacked to death at Gravesend castle by eight henchmen of Henry's led by Sir Peter Exton is clearly false (*CR*, 233–4).

[28] *SAC II*, 298–9. Richard had built a tomb for himself next to Anne of Bohemia in Westminster abbey; when Henry V came to the throne in 1413, he had Richard's body exhumed and moved there (below, p. 521).

his servants were well armed and select a number of 'sufficient armed esquires and archers' from each county and keep them near him so that they could guard him night and day.[29] The royal household and affinity were to be both expanded and militarized; the new regime's grip on the kingdom was to be tightened.

The threat to Henry's throne came not just from England, a point which the king was quick to stress: the ports were closed during the Epiphany Rising and the rebels accused of plotting to bring Charles VI of France into the realm.[30] Convenient as this was, it was not simply propaganda, for Anglo-French relations during the first few months of Henry's reign were unpredictable. It was, after all, Charles's son-in-law whom Henry had deposed, thereby humiliating his ten-year-old daughter, and to make matters worse he now appeared unwilling to return either Isabella or her dowry to Paris. This was not an attempt to provoke the French – in fact it was linked to Henry's desire for an Anglo-French peace – but it gave the French royal family a personal stake in the fallout from Richard's deposition and a focus for their animosity towards the English usurper. Men such as Waleran, count of St-Pol, the widower of Richard II's half-sister, and the king's brother Louis of Orléans (Isabella's uncle) felt a sense of familial betrayal which made them honour-bound to take action.[31] It was under St-Pol's command that a French invasion fleet was said to be gathering at Harfleur in late January 1400, and two weeks later the great council expressed the view that war with France seemed more likely than either peace or the confirmation of the 1396 truce. In fact, the French king had issued an undertaking on 29 January to respect the truce, although this did not stop him detaining an English herald in Paris, declining to grant Henry's ambassadors an interview, or continuing to address him as 'he who calls himself king of England'.[32] Henry for his part had welcomed Charles's ambassadors to his court in October 1399 and wrote on 29 November to 'our dearest kinsman of France', proposing a marriage

[29] POPC, i.107–10.

[30] CPR 1399–1401, 385; E 403/565, 21 Feb.

[31] C. Taylor, 'Weep Thou for Me in France. French Views of the Deposition of Richard II', Fourteenth Century England III, ed. W. M. Ormrod (Woodbridge, 2004), 207–22, at pp. 214–19; see below, p. 236.

[32] Foedera, viii.123–4; Henry also confirmed the truce at this time (Saint-Denys, ii.744–6); POPC, i.102–4; Usk, 94; S. Pistono, 'The Diplomatic Mission of Jean de Hangest, Lord of Hugueville, October 1400', Canadian Journal of History 13 (1978), 193–207; S. Pistono, 'Henry IV and Charles VI: The Confirmation of the Twenty-eight-year Truce', Journal of Medieval History (1977), 353–65.

alliance between the prince of Wales and one of Charles's daughters.[33] Since Richard II was still alive at this point, he could hardly have been referring to Isabella, but once Richard had been buried Charles VI became fearful that she would be forcibly remarried to one of Henry's sons, something he was determined to avoid. Nevertheless, the predominant mood in Paris – heavily influenced by Philip, duke of Burgundy, whose rich county of Flanders depended on English wool exports for its cloth industry – was of reluctance to embark on another round of open warfare. It was at Henry himself rather than at England that French threats were targeted, accompanied by a propaganda war against the 'infamous traitor' designed to blacken his reputation at the courts of Europe.

One way to counter French propaganda was to cultivate good relations with other European powers, and here a number of factors worked in Henry's favour. The reputation he had gained as crusader and pilgrim in the early 1390s, the personal contacts he had made then, and the belief that he had been unjustly treated in 1398–9 were all cards that might be played to advantage; four sons and two daughters also represented a healthy hand with which to bid in the international marriage market. One priority was reassuring England's major trading partners. Four days after taking the throne, Henry wrote to the Doge of Venice assuring him that Venetians would always be treated 'like our own lieges' in England; the privileges of other foreign merchants were also confirmed.[34] Envoys were despatched to Rome, France, Hungary, Germany, Spain, Ireland and elsewhere to explain the 'horrible causes' for Richard II's deposition – presumably a catalogue of his misdeeds – and, whether on account of this or for pragmatic reasons, hostility throughout much of Europe was muted.[35] In Scandinavia, the Italian peninsula, the Holy Roman Empire and Iberia (where one of Henry's sisters was queen of Castile, another queen of Portugal) rulers rapidly accepted the usurpation as a fait accompli, and negotiated with the new English king much as they had done with his predecessors.[36]

However, this was not the case in Scotland, France's long-standing ally: England's confusion was Scotland's opportunity. Since the 1370s, crossborder warfare had been driven mainly by Scottish aggression, resulting in

---

[33] *Saint-Denys*, ii.730–2. He also restored the English lands of alien priories dependent on French houses (*Foedera*, viii.101–9).

[34] *Calendar of State Papers Venice I*, 39 (4 October); *Foedera*, viii.112–13; E 28/7, no. 17 (15 November).

[35] *Chronicles of London*, 61; SAC II, 278–9.

[36] A. Tuck, 'Henry IV and Europe: A Dynasty's Search for Recognition', in *The McFarlane Legacy. Studies in Late Medieval Politics and Society*, ed. R. Britnell and A. Pollard (Stroud, 1995), 107–25.

the recovery of substantial areas of land north of the Tweed–Solway line, the English response to which had generally been reactive and ineffective.[37] The chance to capitalize on political upheaval south of the border was thus tempting, although it was not the Scottish king who decided policy. Robert III, who had ruled in name since 1390, was ill and ageing, and had been effectively sidelined at a general council held at Perth in January 1399. In his place, his twenty-year-old son David, duke of Rothesay, was appointed lieutenant of the realm for three years, but to exercise power Rothesay had to feed the ambitions of his uncle Robert, duke of Albany, and of Archibald the Grim, third earl of Douglas, who controlled much of the north and south of the kingdom, respectively.[38] It was this shifting, but for the moment stable, triumvirate which was responsible for the more aggressive policy towards England which marked the early months of Henry's reign.[39] Letters in King Robert's name addressed Henry as 'duke of Lancaster, earl of Derby and steward of England', Wark castle in Northumberland was raided in mid-October (possibly on the day of Henry's coronation, something of a Scottish tradition), and fears of a Scottish invasion were rife at Westminster, leading to calls for a punitive expedition by the king.[40] The earl of Northumberland and his son Hotspur, wardens of the west and east marches, respectively, also favoured a campaign, for they had ambitions north of the border, although whether they wanted the king to come north in person is questionable. Henry assured parliament on 10 November 1399 that his plan to invade Scotland, approved that day, had not been conceived at the instigation of the northern magnates but was born of his own desire to defend his realm from the 'great wickedness and rebellion of the Scots', but his defensive tone hinted at unease about Percy influence on his decision.[41]

News had also reached Henry of the disaffection of George Dunbar, earl of the Scottish March, whose daughter Elizabeth had been betrothed to the duke of Rothesay in 1395, but then jilted in favour of Douglas's daughter Mary, leaving him feeling 'gretly wrangit'. Dunbar was one of the finest

[37] A. Macdonald, *Border Bloodshed. Scotland, England and France at War, 1369–1403* (East Linton, 2000), 5–8 and the maps on pp. 12 and 16.

[38] S. Boardman, *The Early Stewart Kings: Robert II and Robert III, 1371–1406* (East Linton, 1996), 214–15.

[39] Macdonald, *Border Bloodshed*, 133–6.

[40] *RHL I*, 4, 8 (the truce had expired on 29 September; the letters were dated 6 October and 2 November); E 403/565, 17 December; *SAC II*, 278–80; Boardman, *The Early Stewart Kings*, 226. Edward III's coronation day (1 February 1327) had also been marked by a cross-border raid: Ormrod, *Edward III*, 64–5.

[41] *PROME*, viii.36–7.

soldiers of his age, until now an implacable enemy of the English who more than any other had been responsible for the Scottish recovery of the 1370s and 1380s.[42] As the holder of much of East Lothian, his defection to the English cause would open up the prospect of recovering lands the English had claimed since the 1330s. On 2 December 1399, Henry sent Dunbar a gift of £100, an opening gambit which within two months had him negotiating to switch to the English allegiance.[43] This was a coup for Henry, not just symbolically in that a great Scottish magnate publicly acknowledged his legitimacy as king of England, but also in terms of the experience Dunbar brought to English campaigning in the north. With Dunbar's secession, the tone of Scottish diplomacy softened. A placatory letter of Robert III to 'our dear cousin of England' dated 14 March proposed urgent talks to confirm the truce.[44] Henry, however, continued to exploit divisions north of the border. Donald, lord of the Isles, and his brother John, still smarting from the campaign which Albany and Rothesay had mounted against them in the late summer of 1398, were invited to England to speak with Henry's envoys. On 4 June, summonses were sent out to retainers of the crown and the duchy of Lancaster to join the king at York ready to cross the border.[45] By this time the Scots knew that Henry was in earnest. Despite a frustrating delay of several weeks while provisions were assembled, by 25 July the English king was at Newcastle, where Dunbar swore within a month to withdraw his allegiance from 'Robert that pretends himself king of Scotland', and on 7 August Henry resuscitated the ghost of the mythical, but still resonant, Brutus, 'first king of Albion' to demand that King Robert and the Scottish magnates come to Edinburgh to perform homage to him. A week later he crossed the border at the head of an army of some 13,000 men.[46]

Henry's Scottish campaign offered him a chance to demonstrate greater commitment than Richard to the integrity of his realm and the plight of

[42] A. Macdonald, 'George Dunbar, Ninth Earl of Dunbar or March', *ODNB*, 17.207–10; R. Nicholson, *Scotland: The Later Middle Ages* (Edinburgh, 1974), 218.

[43] E 404/15, no. 107; *Foedera*, viii.131–3; Boardman, *The Early Stewart Kings*, 226–7; Walter Bower, *Scotichronicon*, ed. D. Watt, viii (Aberdeen, 1987), 30–3.

[44] *Foedera*, viii.144; *RHL I*, 25–7. Having ratified the Anglo-French truce in May, Henry was confident that the French would not aid the Scots, and he made sure the Scots knew this; on 18 June he ordered that French shipping was not to be molested, although Scottish shipping might be (*Foedera*, viii.144, 147).

[45] E 403/567, 4 June.

[46] *Foedera*, viii.153–7; Wylie, *Henry the Fourth*, i.133–4. For the campaign, see A. Brown, 'The English Campaign in Scotland', in *British Government and Administration: Studies Presented to S. B. Chrimes*, ed. H. Hearder and H. Loyn (Cardiff, 1974), 40–54; and A. Curry, A. Bell, A. King and D. Simpkin, 'New Regime, New Army? Henry IV's Scottish Expedition of 1400', *EHR* 125 (2010), 1382–1413.

his northern subjects, to seal the defection of Dunbar, and to show that he was serious about restoring at least part of south-eastern Scotland to English allegiance. To lead his nation in war must have been an attractive prospect to a king who had already intimated his desire to polish up the chivalric lustre of a tarnished English crown. There may also have been fears, perhaps shared by the king himself, that the Percys were becoming a little too presumptuous and usurping royal jurisdiction in the northern counties.[47] Yet there were also broader considerations. The political configuration of the British Isles was not set in stone, and English imperialism, which a hundred years earlier had seemed as if it might define the future shape of Britain, continued to exercise a hold on the nation's imagination.[48] The emphasis which Henry placed upon his own Scottish ancestry, as well as upon the claims to ancient English overlordship of which Edward I had made so much during the 1290s, suggest that, whether or not he truly believed that he could unite Britain under his kingship, Henry was not insensible to the possibilities which history presented.[49] This also helps to explain why, in contrast to the devastation wreaked by Richard II's army in 1385, Henry earned plaudits from the Scottish chroniclers for the restraint shown by his soldiers on their march through Berwickshire and Lothian.[50] This was Dunbar's 'country', and if his defection was to bear fruit his tenants needed incentives to follow his lead.

To judge by the course of the campaign, its symbolic significance mattered as much to Henry as any prospect of short-term political gain. Despite its size and cost, the English army spent just two weeks in Scotland, basing itself at Leith to maintain contact with the sizeable fleet which had also been mobilized.[51] No serious attempt was made to dislodge the duke of Rothesay from Edinburgh castle, and unsurprisingly he declined a second invitation to perform homage to Henry.[52] Henry did, however, secure an undertaking

    [47] C. Neville, 'Scotland, the Percies, and the Law in 1400', in *Establishment*, 73–94.
    [48] P. Crooks, 'State of the Union: Perspectives on English Imperialism in the Late Middle Ages', *Past and Present* 212 (2011), 3–42.
    [49] Bower, *Scotichronicon*, viii.34–7; Given-Wilson, *Chronicles*, 65–9; for 'muniments concerning the subjection of the king of Scots along with a bag of various chronicles' taken north in the summer, see *Antient Kalendars and Inventories of the Treasury of His Majesty's Exchequer*, ed. F. Palgrave (3 vols, London, 1836), ii.62–3.
    [50] Boardman, *The Early Stewart Kings*, 230; R. Cox, 'A Law of War? English Protection and Destruction of Ecclesiastical Property during the Fourteenth Century', *EHR* 128 (2013), 1381–417.
    [51] Curry, Bell, King and Simpkin, 'New Regime, New Army', *passim*; documents bearing on the claim to overlordship, plus provisions and £5,780 in coin were taken north: (E 403/567, 13 July, 25 Sept.)
    [52] *Foedera*, viii.157–8 (21 August).

from the Scottish leadership, via Sir Adam Forrester, a knight of the duke of
Albany, that consideration would be given to his claim to overlordship. Later,
he would claim to have been deceived by Forrester into leaving Edinburgh
sooner than he would have,[53] yet if Henry really did hope to have his overlordship recognized by the Scots (and he continued to press the point), a
more prolonged and destructive campaign was unlikely to achieve that end.
By 29 August, at any rate, the English were back in England, where popular
opinion was distinctly unimpressed by the king's foray.[54] Far from establishing English lordship in south-eastern Scotland, the defection of Dunbar
had aggravated tensions. Cross-border raiding intensified, with a retaliatory
Scottish force driven back from Reidswire (near Carter Bar) just one month
later, while the deadly feud between Dunbar and the Douglases regularly
spilled over into the northern English counties.[55] Meanwhile, Henry had to
raise the money for his soldiers' wages, but scarcely had writs been issued for
a parliament to meet at York in late October (suggesting that Henry planned
to remain in the north, presumably to monitor the situation on the border),
when news arrived of an uprising in Wales.[56]

There was little at this stage to indicate that the revolt of Owain Glyn Dŵr,
a descendant of the princes of Powys and Deheubarth, would be one of the
defining events of Henry's reign. The immediate cause of Glyn Dŵr's disaffection was said to be the withholding by his neighbour, the Marcher Lord
Reginald Grey of Ruthin, of a writ summoning him to perform military
service in Scotland, the last straw in a bitter personal rivalry that had been
simmering for some time.[57] Violence erupted on 16 September when a
group of Owain's kinsmen and friends gathered at his manor of Glyndyfrdwy
near Llangollen in north-east Wales and proclaimed him prince of Wales.
For the next nine days, about 300 of his followers attacked and burned

[53] POPC, i.169; PROME, viii.163; see below, p. 214.
[54] Vita, 167; Usk (p. 100) said the Scots inflicted more harm on the English than vice versa;
cf. Curry, Bell, King and Simpkin, 'New Regime, New Army', 1413.
[55] The battle of Reidswire was on 29 September (Usk, 101 and n.4). Archibald the Grim
died around Christmas 1400, but his son and heir Archibald was equally hostile to Dunbar.
For the West March, see H. Summerson, Medieval Carlisle. The City and the Borders from the Late
Eleventh to the Mid-Sixteenth Century (Cumberland and Westmorland Antiquarian and
Archaeological Society, 2 vols, Kendal, 1993), 395–7.
[56] PROME, viii.93. The writs to meet at York were issued on 9 September, although
Henry also seems to have considered holding the parliament at Westminster (Wylie, Henry
the Fourth, i.146).
[57] Vita, 167–8; Giles, 20–1; Walsingham attributed their enmity to a land dispute (SAC II,
304–5). See R. Davies, The Revolt of Owain Glyndŵr (Oxford, 1995), 102–3, for the outbreak
of the revolt.

Ruthin and another half a dozen towns in east Wales, but on 24 September they were routed at Welshpool by Hugh Lord Burnell with a force raised in the English border counties, so that by the time Henry arrived at Shrewsbury two days later Owain was already a fugitive.[58] Nevertheless, since there had been a simultaneous, presumably coordinated, uprising in Anglesey under the brothers Rhys and Gwilym ap Tudor, Henry postponed parliament and, like Edward I more than a century earlier, marched his army along the north coast of Wales as far as Caernarfon before returning via Welshpool to Shrewsbury on 15 October. At least nine rebels were executed and garrisons installed in Caernarfon, Harlech, Criccieth and Beaumaris.[59] Henry could not be accused of failing to take the revolt seriously, but he was also careful not to overreact. A pardon was offered to any rebel who submitted to the king, and many did so, including one of Glyn Dŵr's sons.[60] Owain himself spent the winter on the run, 'hiding away on cliffs and in caverns with no more than seven followers'.[61] It seemed as if the rebellion was over, and Henry could be forgiven if, after a brief council meeting at Worcester on 18 October, he set off back towards London believing that it had been, quite literally, a nine days' wonder.[62]

Waiting for the king in London was Jean de Hangest, lord of Hugueville, ambassador of the French king, on a mission to secure the repatriation of Queen Isabella, preferably accompanied by her jewels and 200,000 francs (£33,333) of the dowry paid to Richard II following their marriage in 1396. With the truce confirmed, Isabella's fate had become the fulcrum upon which Anglo-French diplomacy turned. A meeting of the council in the spring had advised Henry that he was obliged to return Isabella and her jewels to France 'unless it should prove possible to obtain remission (*faire mitigacion*) by means of marriage or otherwise', but the question of the 200,000 francs was deferred.[63] Realistically, Henry could not afford to repay the money. Meanwhile, Charles VI was determined that his daughter would marry neither Prince Henry nor any of the Lancastrian usurper's other

[58] Llinos Smith, 'Owain Glyn Dŵr', *ODNB*, 22.516–22. Henry was between Northampton and Leicester when he heard of the rising. The response to his new summons for service was impressive: John Warwick, the sheriff of Northamptonshire, claimed to have raised 40 men-at-arms and 600 archers from the knights, esquires and valets of the county to accompany the king to Shrewsbury (E 28/23, no. 9).

[59] E 403/569, 4 December; E 404/16, nos. 370, 452 (a garrison of 100 at Caernarfon, 30 at Criccieth).

[60] Davies, *Revolt*, 102.

[61] *Usk*, 100–1.

[62] *Vita*, 108–9 (Henry was at Evesham from 19 to 21 October).

[63] *POPC*, i.118.

sons. Months of ambassadorial talks at Calais while Henry campaigned in
Scotland yielded a promise from the English to return Isabella before
2 February 1401, but the financial impasse prompted a different approach.
Following his capture at Poitiers in 1356, King John II of France had agreed
to pay Edward III a ransom of £500,000, only about 60 per cent of which
had been paid. If Isabella's dowry could be offset against this much larger
sum, Henry could claim some justification for withholding it. The French
quite reasonably argued that outstanding claims from John's ransom had
been superseded by subsequent agreements, notably the truce of 1396,
when it had not been mentioned. Nevertheless, a list of questions was
drawn up and distributed to lawyers at Oxford and elsewhere in England
for their opinions. That Henry would get the response he sought was virtually a foregone conclusion: legal justification was required primarily in
order to put pressure on the French king to grant him an acquittance for the
200,000 francs, so that once Isabella was back in Paris Henry's evasion
would not be used as a pretext to reopen the war.[64]

Experienced negotiator as he was, Hangest's diplomatic skills were
tested to the limit in October 1400. Forbidden by Charles VI to address
Henry as king of England, he was nevertheless expected not only to secure
the return of Isabella and her dowry, but also to try to see the young queen
in person.[65] A difficult task was made harder when his fellow ambassador,
Charles VI's secretary Pierre de Blanchet, fell ill and died in London on
19 October. Nevertheless, Hangest managed, with the help of Thomas
Percy, earl of Worcester, to secure a brief interview with Isabella at
Havering-atte-Bower (Essex) at which she assured him that she would
not enter into any contract of marriage in England. Hangest was then
summoned to Windsor to meet Henry. Their first discussion on 26 October
was not a success. Although he addressed Henry as 'sovereign of England',
the ambassador emphasized that he did so in a personal capacity; when
Henry then asked him for his diplomatic credentials, he replied that he
had none – none at any rate that referred to Henry as king. At this point
Henry dismissed him, but after consulting his councillors he agreed to
meet him again the next day, and again on 28 October, an indication of his
eagerness to maintain the Anglo-French truce. Indeed he even entertained
Hangest to dinner on 27 and 28 October. However, his formal response,

[64] E 28/8, no. 9; *Usk*, 100–15, includes the questions to which as a crown lawyer he
had to respond before 29 September; Oxford University was asked for its response on
12 November (*Foedera*, viii.164).

[65] Pistono, 'The Diplomatic Mission of Jean de Hangest'; if possible, he was also to travel
to Scotland to reassure Robert III of continuing French goodwill.

communicated through the earl of Worcester, would have been less pleasing to French ears. He would restore Isabella with her jewels, he declared, but not the 200,000 francs; in return he expected Charles VI to hand over a waiver for the money before his daughter was repatriated. This was his final offer, and in early November Hangest crossed back to France.

The matter of Isabella's return continued to subvert hopes of Anglo-French rapprochement for another eight months. She eventually left England on 31 July 1401, escorted from Calais to Leulinghem by the earl of Worcester, and there was handed over, together with her jewels but without her dowry, to Waleran, Count of St-Pol, who conducted her back to Paris to be reunited with her father.[66] Five years earlier, as a six-year-old bride, she had stood amid dazzling pomp on the same spot, the personification of a hoped-for new era of Anglo-French concord. Now, 'dressed in black and scowling with deep hatred at King Henry',[67] she seemed to presage the onset of a new war, for despite the almost funereal splendour accompanying her return no one doubted that the fate of the twenty-eight-year truce – sealed with a marriage so rudely ruptured, ratified by two kings neither of whom recognized the other, disowned by allies with whose interests it conflicted, and openly challenged by some of the most powerful men in Paris – hung in the balance.[68] Meanwhile, in Scotland, the revival of English claims to overlordship and Henry's invasion in August 1400, intended as the showpiece of his first year on the throne, had infuriated the Scots, while the defection of Dunbar allowed the belligerent new earl of Douglas to achieve an unparalleled degree of domination of southern Scotland. In short, Henry had antagonized both the French and the Scots, and he would pay the price.

[66] Her jewels, gold and silver were valued at £9,364, and she had much else of value besides; these were returned, though not the gifts she had received in England since 1396, which included a greyhound made of gold set with a balas ruby and a large pearl given to her by Henry (Stratford, *Richard II and the English Royal Treasure*, 65, 117). For an inventory used by the French, see *Choix de Pièces Inédites Relatives au Règne de Charles VI*, ed. L. Douët d'Arcq (2 vols, Paris, 1863), ii.273–9; their acquittance was lodged in the treasury (*Antient Kalendars*, ii.64).

[67] *Usk*, 133, who added that she burned with desire to avenge Richard's death.

[68] C. Phillpotts, 'The Fate of the Truce of Paris, 1396–1415', *Journal of Medieval History*, 24, 61–80. For the ceremony on 31 July, *Saint-Denys*, iii.3–5; *POPC*, i.130–6, 143–4.

Chapter 12

THE PARLIAMENT OF 1401

Fifteen months into his reign, Henry's need for money was acute. Having laid such stress on the 'insupportable burdens' Richard had needlessly imposed upon his subjects, he had forborne from requesting either a direct subsidy or tunnage and poundage in October 1399.[1] Perhaps as a result of this, or perhaps in consequence of assurances it was later claimed he had given during the revolution, there had arisen a popular belief that he had undertaken not to raise taxation. In fact, he had promised no more than to avoid raising taxes unless it proved necessary to do so, in which case he would seek the consent of parliament, which was little different from what had happened hitherto.[2] There was certainly no undertaking to 'live of his own', or to refrain entirely from demanding direct taxation, despite the popular appeal of such notions.[3] Nevertheless, Henry had raised expectations. When he asked Londoners for a loan in 1400, they replied that he had promised to 'abstain from loans and tallages of this sort'; early in 1401, the citizens of Bristol refused to pay money overdue from Richard's reign 'because of the king's pardon, so they claimed, at his first arrival in the kingdom'. Around the same time an unlucky collector of ulnage (cloth tax) was beaten to death by drapers at Norton St Philip (Somerset) because his demands were 'contrary to the promise excusing them from such payments which the king had made to them at the time of his happy return'; another tax-collector barely escaped the same fate at Dartmouth (Devon).[4]

---

[1] *PROME*, viii.15, 18–20.

[2] Cf. the Percy manifesto of 1403: Thomas Gascoigne, *Loci e Libro Veritatum*, ed. J. Rogers (Oxford, 1881), 229–30; *Hardyng*, 352–3; *PROME*, viii.30; *SAC II*, 222. Henry was probably referring inter alia to the grant of the wool subsidy for life in 1398.

[3] Cf. Thomas Hoccleve, *The Regement of Princes*, ed. F. Furnivall (EETS, London, 1897), 174, who thought a king should 'live of your own good, in moderate rule'.

[4] *CE*, 387; *Usk*, 131. Usk said that it was the women of Bristol who led the protest; the sum involved may have been the £333 from the citizens of Bristol recorded as having been paid into the royal chamber on the same day that the sergeant-at-arms was paid (E 403/569, 27 March). Those who had lent Henry aid in the summer of 1399, such as the citizens of York with their loan of 500 marks, may have believed that they especially would be relieved of further demands under the new regime: C. Liddy, *War, Politics and Finance in Late Medieval England: Bristol, York and the Crown 1350–1400* (Woodbridge, 2005), 214–15.

The fact that Henry had inherited the duchy of Lancaster which, together with his own Bohun inheritance, was worth between £12,500 and £14,000 a year, also served to frame the terms in which debate over the king's financial needs was conducted.[5] Might not the income from the duchy help to alleviate the king's needs? Henry made it clear from the start that the answer was no. The day after his coronation, a charter was drawn up declaring the duchy to be entirely separated from the crown, 'as if we had never assumed the ensign of royal dignity', and the creation of Prince Henry as duke of Lancaster a month later theoretically sealed this separation by excluding the duchy's resources from the king's direct control.[6] In practice this made it more amenable to the king's will, and the duchy did make a small contribution to crown income, but no more than about £1,120 a year on average. The majority of its revenue was used to pay the annuities assigned on its lands (£8,000–9,000 a year) and the wages and other administrative costs of the estate.[7] There were good reasons for Henry to insist on this detachment of duchy from crown. It was a way of emphasizing the distinction between his private lordship and his public governance, and a guarantee to the duchy's annuitants, who included many Lancastrian stalwarts, that its revenues would continue to be used to reward them rather than being swallowed up by the greedy maw of the state – and, conversely, that the situation would not arise whereby the duchy might be suspected of being a charge on the exchequer. It was also (though Henry would not have said so) an attempt to ensure that, should he suffer the same fate as Richard, the duchy would remain with his children rather than fall to his supplanter.

Another factor raising expectations was the belief that Richard had amassed great wealth during the later years of his reign and that his hoard had fallen into Henry's hands. There was some truth in this. There was, for example, the £43,964 which Richard had stored at Holt castle, at least some of which Henry had seized in August 1399; part of this was used on the spot to pay his army while the remainder was probably drawn upon periodically as a source of ready cash over the next three years, for not until November 1402 was John Ikelyngton, the clerk entrusted by Richard with safeguarding it, acquitted of the full sum. As the spoil of conquest it

[5] J. Nuttall, *The Creation of Lancastrian Kingship* (Cambridge, 2007), 75–93. However, the well-informed Philip Repingdon said nothing about promises to restrict taxation in the letter he wrote to Henry in the summer of 1401 (*Usk*, 136–43).

[6] Castor, *King, Crown and Duchy*, 27; *PROME*, viii.37; DL 28/4/1, fos 13v, 31v.

[7] Castor, *King, Crown and Duchy*, 29; DL 28/4/1, fo. 25r. The annuities which Henry had been paying from his own (Bohun) estates before 1399 were also now paid from the duchy (DL 42/15, fo. 75r).

would presumably have passed through the king's chamber, for which few accounts survive.[8] There was also the latest instalment of Queen Isabella's dowry that Henry had been so reluctant to return to Charles VI; the £14,664 paid into the exchequer in French crowns on 10 December 1399 doubtless came from this.[9] Exhorted by parliament to recover whatever he could of Richard's cash, jewels and moveable goods, Henry certainly made an effort to do so, but how much of this found its way to the exchequer is not clear. Like kings before him, Henry had a keen appreciation of his right to retain windfalls for his personal use.[10] Yet if he could justifiably claim to be acting according to the mores of his predecessors, that was probably not perceived to be good enough for a king who had so stridently criticized the financial policies of his predecessor, and successive parliaments continued to question him about Richard's 'missing money'.[11]

These windfalls went a long way towards helping Henry to navigate his first year, for his only other major source of real (as opposed to borrowed) income was the wool customs, which brought in some £40,000. Apart from this the exchequer fed off scraps, such as the ornaments of Richard's chapel royal, abandoned by him at Haverfordwest in July 1399, or the forfeited goods of Le Scrope, Bussy, Green, and the rebel earls of January 1400, which yielded a little over £2,000.[12] By the autumn of 1400 there were signs of imminent financial collapse. Fictitious loans (assignments of revenue by tallies which turned out to be uncashable) totalled over £25,000 between Easter 1400 and Easter 1401.[13] In February 1400 Henry had secured an aid from the great council 'in order to avoid the summoning of any parliament',[14] yet between April and July relays of sergeants-at-arms

[8] *PROME*, viii.163–4; *Foedera*, viii.162–3 (Ikelyngton's acquittance, wrongly dated to Nov. 1400). For Richard's wealth and Holt castle, see *RHKA*, 89–90.

[9] A. Steel, *Receipt of the Exchequer 1377–1485* (Cambridge, 1954), 81–2; E 403/564, 1 Dec.; above, pp. 171–2.

[10] *PROME*, viii.62–4. Exchequer officials spent three days valuing the jewels and plate which had once belonged to Edward III, Richard II, Queen Anne, the duchess of York and the duke of Gloucester (whose wife and son had both died), as a result of which 340 items, some of considerable value, were passed by them to the king's chamber on 20 November 1399 (*Antient Kalendars*, iii.313–58). Yet Henry also passed about £10,000 from the chamber to the exchequer between Oct. 1399 and Jan. 1401 (*RHKA*, 88–91).

[11] Nuttall, *Creation of Lancastrian Kingship*, 79–83. The 1,000 marks which Londoners gave him as a coronation gift must also have gone to the chamber, since it is not noted in exchequer records: C. Barron, *London in the Later Middle Ages: Government and People, 1200–1500* (Oxford, 2004), 12.

[12] *Antient Kalendars*, iii.358–61; DL 28/4/1, fos. 5r, 18r, 19r; E 403/565, 1 Dec., 16 Jan., 7 April; E 404/15, nos. 455, 459; Steel, *Receipt*, 83.

[13] Steel, *Receipt*, 83–4.

[14] *POPC*, i.102–9: the thirteen bishops in attendance agreed to advance him a clerical tenth from their dioceses and to ask the religious houses to do likewise, while twenty

were despatched to monasteries, prelates and laymen seeking loans.[15] As a result, the exchequer borrowed more than £20,000 during the year, the most generous individual lender being Richard (Dick) Whittington, the London mercer and both former and future mayor of the city.[16] It was probably to facilitate borrowing from the city that Whittington and two of his fellow Londoners, John Shadworth and William Brampton, were retained as members of the king's council on 1 November 1399.[17]

Yet even extensive borrowing could not bridge the gulf between income and expenditure. The cost to Henry of his campaign to regain the throne, plus the liabilities of one sort or another which he inherited from Richard, amounted to at least £35,000 and probably a good deal more.[18] A memorandum drawn up early in 1401 estimated that Calais and its ring of protective bastions cost £13,333 a year, Ireland £5,333, and Guyenne, 'in the event that men are sent there', £10,000.[19] Scotland was not mentioned, but the wardenships of the northern marches held by Northumberland and Hotspur cost at least £15,000 a year; nor was a figure given for the cost of defending English ports and shipping, although this too absorbed several thousand pounds a year.[20] All in all, around £50,000 a year, and at times a good deal

---

temporal lords promised to provide a total of 146 men-at-arms, 352 archers and ten fully equipped ships of war for three months at their own expense. In return, Henry undertook to ensure that the buyers for his household paid for what they purchased rather than abusing the royal right of purveyance.

[15] E 403/ 569, 9 May, 13 July; E 404/15, no. 172; E 28/7, nos. 62, 63.

[16] Whittington loaned £1,666 and was probably instrumental in persuading the city to loan the king £1,333 on 6 July 1400: Steel, *Receipt*, 82–4, 113; E 403/565, 10 December (1,000 marks from Archbishop Arundel); E 403/567, 15 July, 27 September (days when large loans were received); E 403/569, 7 February.

[17] E 403/569, 5 November; E 404/15, no. 477. The only occasion when Whittington and Brampton were recorded as attending the council was in June 1400 (*POPC*, i.122).

[18] Wages totalling about £5,000 were paid to Henry's supporters in 1399 (*CR*, 252–3). Richard's household debts were around £12,000, unpaid wages for the Calais garrison £6,664 (*RHKA*, 96, 101; E 403/565, 1 December); Queen Isabella had over fifty servants, and many household debts; the cost of conveying her to France was estimated by the council at £8,242 (*CPR 1399–1401*, 323; E 404/16, nos. 219, 273; *POPC*, i.154); there were back payments to annuitants and debts to London drapers and goldsmiths to be cleared; £1,000 was given to the executors of Henry's old foe Thomas Mowbray to clear his debts at Venice (E 403/565, 17 December, 1 March; E 403/569, 26 March; *CPR 1399–1401*, 231, 307); the widows of those whom Henry had executed needed to be supported, such as Henry's sister Elizabeth, countess of Huntingdon, given 1,000 marks a year for life, her daughter Constance and Isabel, widow of William Le Scrope (E 404/16, no. 219; *CPR 1399–1401*, 201, 285).

[19] *POPC*, i.154; it also included sums of £16,000 'for the recent loan made to the king's use' and £8,242 for the return of Queen Isabella. When Prince Thomas became lieutenant of Ireland in July 1401 he was promised £8,000 a year (E 404/16, no. 728).

[20] J. Bean, 'Henry IV and the Percies', *History* 44 (1959), 212–27. Thomas Percy was given over 1,400 marks to raise a fleet to counter French piracy in November 1399 (E 403/565, 28 November; C 49/48/1).

more, was required to service England's ongoing military commitments, and this at a time of nominal truce with France, which for much of the fourteenth century had formed the principal item of military expenditure.

Domestic expenditure consisted principally of the royal household, the running costs of the administration, and crown annuities. The annuities bill had risen during the latter part of the fourteenth century as it became more common for the king to retain knights and esquires for service in peace and war. For Henry, who felt bound to continue retaining those who had served his father and himself before 1399 but equally could not afford to cut off those whom Richard had retained, annuities were financially embarrassing but politically necessary: as the council reminded him in February 1400, the security of his throne depended upon it.[21] During the first seven months of his reign he retained more than a hundred knights and esquires with annuities ranging in value between £20 and £100, although much larger annuities were paid to some members of the aristocracy.[22] Recruitment continued thereafter, and by late 1400 the recurrent annuities bill assigned from crown revenues was reckoned by the council to amount to £24,000, in addition to the £8,000 or more assigned on the duchy lands.[23] The parliament of 1399 had pleaded with the new king to restrain his generosity when making grants, but it was not easy to do so.[24]

In the royal household, it should have been easier to make economies. During the last four years of his reign, Richard had spent an average of £53,200 on his wardrobe, great wardrobe and chamber, the three principal spending departments of the household (compared with £22,000 during his first fifteen years). This was mainly due to the king indulging his penchant for luxury and display and the inflated size of the household, whose permanent staff grew from 396 in 1383–4 to 598 in 1395–6.[25] Here, surely, was an opportunity for Henry to demonstrate his commitment to a thriftier form of rule, but he failed to do so. The first year of the reign saw massively increased expenditure in the great wardrobe (£17,717) and overall spending in the three main household departments which, at

---

[21] *POPC*, i.109–10; *RHKA*, 203–57.

[22] Thus Thomas Percy, earl of Worcester, was given 500 marks a year for life in December 1399, in place of lands granted to him by Richard II following the 1397 forfeitures which he had been obliged to return to Arundel's and Gloucester's heirs (*CPR 1399–1401*, 178). The duke of York had an annuity of 1,000 marks dating from 1385.

[23] *POPC*, i.154; *RHKA*, 135–6; A. Rogers, 'The Royal Household of Henry IV' (unpublished PhD thesis, University of Nottingham, 1966), 71–2, counted annuities totalling £22,351 on crown revenues during the first year of the reign, excluding grants of land, offices, wardships, etc.

[24] *PROME*, viii.48–9.

[25] *RHKA*, 94, 278.

around £53,000, almost exactly matched Richard's later years. By March 1401 the household treasurer, Thomas Tutbury, had run up debts of £10,300, and his failure to make prompt payment for provisions purveyed for the household was becoming a scandal.[26] The exceptional costs of the great wardrobe in 1399–1400 could be explained as a new king refurbishing his court,[27] but Henry's unwillingness or inability to rein in his household spending was widely perceived to betoken corruption, incompetence, or an inexcusable failure of the will to implement reform. When he spent £460 on jewellery and silver plate for himself and Prince Henry on the same day that he sent messengers around the country begging loans from any who might be persuaded to lend, it is perhaps not hard to see why the commons in the parliament of January 1401 were perplexed.[28]

When the Byzantine emperor Manuel II arrived at Dover on 11 December 1400 for a state visit which would last nearly two months, it was thus not an unalloyed blessing, although a blessing it was, for here was a potentate – an emperor, no less – only too happy to acknowledge the English king's regality and sprinkle some imperial stardust on his court. With his empire crumbling around him and Constantinople blockaded by the Turks, Manuel was on a tour of Western European rulers trying to persuade them to contribute men or money to a crusade to save Byzantium.[29] Everywhere he went – Venice, Milan, Paris – he was feted as befitted his status and given promises of aid, and Henry could scarcely do less. King and emperor spent Christmas together at Eltham, where Henry organized splendid entertainments for his guest, including a great mumming put on by the aldermen of London, before loading him with gifts at his departure.[30] In return, Manuel presented Henry with a literally priceless piece of the seamless tunic woven by Christ's mother for her son with her own hands, which delighted the king.[31] An effusive letter from Manuel also described Henry ('the king of

[26] *RHKA*, 79, 87, 112.

[27] Rogers, 'Royal Household', 347–8.

[28] E 403/567, 13 July 1400.

[29] D. Nicol, 'A Byzantine Emperor in England: Manuel II's Visit to London in 1400–1401', *University of Birmingham Historical Journal* 12 (1969–70), 204–25. He had been waiting to cross to England since September: E 403/567, 13 August, 25 September; *Saint-Denys*, ii.774; *RHL*, i.39–40. He visited Becket's shrine and was greeted by Henry at Blackheath on 21 December.

[30] Wylie, *Henry the Fourth*, i.163; *SAC* II, 306–11; *Usk*, 118–21; *CE*, 388. For his time in Paris, see *Saint-Denys*, ii.754, 774–5.

[31] Lambeth Palace Ms 78. Henry later divided the piece of tunic into two, gave one to Westminster abbey and the other, 'because of his great trust and close friendship', to Thomas Arundel, who in turn gave it to the high altar of Canterbury cathedral, where it was placed in a silver-gilt reliquary which also contained a thorn from the crown of thorns and a drop of the blood shed by Becket during his martyrdom. My thanks to Rob Bartlett for this reference.

Britain the Great') as willing to provide men-at-arms, archers, money and
ships for a crusade, but if Henry really made such promises – and he doubtless wanted to help Manuel, for crusading was close to his heart – the reality
was different.[32] The cost of entertaining him and his fifty-strong household
for two months was a heavy burden, and in the end the emperor departed
with no more than the £2,000 Richard II had promised to his envoy some
years earlier but never paid. In exchange, Henry kept for himself the money
donated to the crusade in collecting-boxes set up in churches around
England, the sum of which probably exceeded £2,000 even if gathering it
in was no easy matter.[33]

By the time Manuel left in early February, the parliament postponed from
the autumn had been in session for two weeks or more. That the commons
would be asked for taxation was clear from the start; equally clear was that
they would not sell their assent cheaply. Uppermost in the minds of those
who gathered at Westminster on 20 January 1401 were three issues: the
financial competence of the government, the authority of the Church and
the condition of Wales. The commons' speaker, Sir Arnold Savage of
Kent, was ideally suited to the task: upright and forthright, praised for his
resistance to the king's financial demands, he was (unlike John Cheyne in
1399) a man to whom not a hint of Lollard contamination attached itself.[34]
Keen not to be rushed into making decisions, he requested from the start
that the commons be given answers to their petitions before deciding
how much taxation to grant (an idea later enshrined in the call for redress
of grievances before grant of supply). This was unacceptable to Henry,
and he told the commons so,[35] but by the time parliament ended on 10
March the king had been obliged to give ground, most notably in relation
to his choice of councillors and ministers. Those whom Henry had
appointed in September 1399 to run his household were men who had
served his father or himself, but had little experience of royal government
and its network of interdepartmental routines: Thomas Tutbury (keeper
of the wardrobe and household treasurer), the esquire Robert Litton
(financial controller of the royal household) and Sir Thomas Rempston
(steward of the royal household). All three were, at the insistence of the

[32] J. Barker, *Manuel II Palaeologus (1391–1425): A Study in Late Byzantine Statesmanship* (New
Brunswick, 1969), 178–80.
[33] E 403/569, 26 March.
[34] *HOC*, iv.306–10. He had been a knight of Richard II's chamber during the 1390s.
[35] Although he waited until the last day of the session to refuse Savage's request, which
rather defeated the point of it (*PROME*, viii.101, 106).

commons, replaced during the first nine days of March, as was the chancellor, John Scarle, former chancellor of the Palatinate of Lancaster.[36]
Those who replaced them were former ministers of Richard II: Thomas
More, Thomas Brounfleet and the earl of Worcester (Thomas Percy)
became treasurer, controller and steward of the household, respectively,
while Edmund Stafford, bishop of Exeter, resumed the chancellorship
which he had held from 1396 to 1399. Three months later, Henry's friend
John Norbury was replaced as treasurer by Laurence Allerthorpe, an
exchequer baron of twenty-five years' standing. The only one of the chief
officers of state to retain office was Richard Clifford, keeper of the privy
seal, who had been appointed in 1397.[37]

Henry's ministers were not replaced because of their political sympathies. Rempston and Norbury remained close to the king and continued to
serve as privy councillors, as did John Scarle for the remaining two years of
his life.[38] Nor was political affiliation the salient factor in the choice of their
replacements. What the commons wanted was financial experience and
proven competence.[39] Nevertheless, the enforced reshuffle of March 1401
was bound to be seen as a public questioning of the king's judgement, as was
a bill drawn up during the last week of the parliament asking that members
of the commons be present when the king named his councillors and that
those appointed should not be replaced before the next parliament.[40]
Several of those who attended council meetings in 1399 and 1400 were
Lancastrian knights and esquires whose qualifications for the task were not

---

[36] *PROME*, viii.94–5, 132, 139; A. Rogers, 'The Political Crisis of 1401', *Nottingham Medieval
Studies* 12 (1968), 85–96; *RHKA*, 107–8. Tutbury had been keeper of Gaunt's wardrobe in the
early 1390s, Litton controller of Henry's household in the late 1390s, and Rempston Henry's
standard-bearer and companion in exile, 1398–9.

[37] The commons commended Clifford's talents to the king (*PROME*, viii.111–12).

[38] A. McHardy, 'John Scarle: Ambition and Politics in the Late Medieval Church', in
Image, Text and Church, 1380–1600. Essays for Margaret Aston, ed. L. Clark, M. Jurkowski and
C. Richmond (Toronto, 2009), 68–93, at p. 89.

[39] For evidence of confusion in household finance see the pardons for 'missing
money', cited in Rogers, 'Royal Household', 652–3, and 'Political Crisis of 1401', 90; on
26 March 1401 the officers and chamberlains of the exchequer were paid for having
spent three days at Westminster 'arraying and amending' various records of the treasury
(E 403/569, 26 March; and for evidence of confusion in the Duchy accounts at this time,
with conflicting orders as to where receivers were supposed to present their accounts,
DL 42/15, fos. 75r–v).

[40] *PROME*, viii.152; A. Brown, 'The Commons and the Council in the Reign of Henry
IV', *EHR* 79 (1964), 1–30; G. Dodd, 'Henry IV's Council', in *Henry IV: The Establishment of
the Regime 1399–1406* (York, 2003), 95–115, p. 110, argues that this was presented to the king
shortly after parliament was dissolved, but it clearly envisages that the commons would still
be at Westminster.

fully evident.[41] This was not a wholesale attack on the council, but neither was it a ringing endorsement of the king's choices.

There was also a wider context for these concerns, one that may well have troubled some of the lords more than the commons: the 'Lancastrianization' of the English polity. The royal household was staffed almost entirely by former servants of Henry or his father.[42] Most of the sheriffs and justices of the peace appointed during the early years of the reign were known supporters of the new regime, as were many of the knights elected to the parliament.[43] In a sense this illustrated the strength of Henry's position, for although there was plenty of hard bargaining in 1401, it was conducted within recognized parameters and between men most of whom were fundamentally on the same side. The aim of the commons was not to undermine Henry's rule or make it more difficult for him to govern, let alone to replace the Lancastrian dynasty, but to work out ways to help him to govern better and thus restore to the regime the popularity it had forfeited since the early months of the reign.[44] Henry tolerated their criticism, a sign that he did not regard it as a threat to his rule. On the other hand, the Lancastrianization of the English polity was also evidence of Henry's failure during the first eighteen months of the reign to rise above the factionalism which had swept him to power. The fact that he had militarized his household early in 1400, retained over 200 knights and esquires during the first fifteen months of the reign, continued to distribute Lancastrian livery badges to his followers, and had insisted on his right to recruit an affinity on a scale that dwarfed any other in the realm – all this laid him open to the charge of acting more like a usurper than a king.[45] It was a narrow circle of men upon whom Henry had relied thus far, a habit which he would find hard to break.

---

[41] For example, the esquires John Doreward, John Frenyngham and Thomas Coggeshall (sometimes called John in council documents) (E 404/16, no. 550; E 403/569, 5 Nov., 21 Nov.).

[42] Only about 10 per cent of the 600 or so members of Richard II's household in 1396 were still in the royal household in 1402, compared to over 40 per cent of Edward III's household servants in 1376–7 still employed in Richard II's household in 1383 (RHKA, 56; dates based on surviving wardrobe account books).

[43] D. Biggs, 'The Reign of Henry IV: The Revolution of 1399 and the Establishment of the Lancastrian Regime', Fourteenth Century England I, ed. N. Saul (Woodbridge, 2000), 195–210, at pp. 207–9.

[44] G. Dodd, 'Conflict or Consensus: Henry IV and Parliament, 1399–1406', in Social Attitudes and Political Structures. The Fifteenth Century Series 7, ed. T. Thornton (Stroud, 2001), 118–49; Dodd, 'Henry IV's Council', 113.

[45] Castor, King, Crown and Duchy, 7–21. For livery badges and livery legislation, see below, pp. 393–5.

The picture that emerges from this is of six weeks of hard bargaining followed by ten days at the beginning of March in which compromises were hammered out. So it was too with the issue of ecclesiastical authority. The king's influence over ecclesiastical affairs had grown markedly since the second half of the thirteenth century, but with influence came responsibility. Confronted by the challenge of John Wyclif and his followers since the 1370s to the Church's spiritual authority, it was to the crown that the ecclesiastical hierarchy looked for protection. Simultaneously, however, it was to the crown that would-be reformers looked for encouragement. The parliament and clerical convocation of January–March 1401 marked an important moment in this struggle.[46] Adam Usk, who was present, said that 'the Lollards, assembling in London from every part of the kingdom, intended utterly to destroy the clergy'; this was alarmist, but petitions from the commons relating to alien priories, tithes, appropriations, parochial non-residence and provisors indicate a significant reformist element among the commons.[47]

Yet parliament also witnessed a powerful assault on the Church's critics. It was customary under Richard II for the opening speeches to include an undertaking on the king's behalf to maintain the Church and its liberties as his progenitors had done, but in 1401 Chief Justice Thirning added to this the words 'and as has been approved by the holy fathers and doctors of the holy church and by holy scripture'.[48] Such self-consciously orthodox language was echoed by the speaker. Savage addressed the assembly on several occasions, once comparing the three estates of the realm to the Trinity, another time likening parliament to the Catholic mass and quoting Thirning's words that it was the Church approved by patriarchs, doctors and scripture that was to be upheld.[49] Arundel's opening address to convocation on 29 January also made it clear that its primary task was to discuss heresy, and later that day an imposing royal delegation arrived at St Paul's to assure him that firm measures to eliminate heresy would not fail for lack of royal support.[50] Arundel thus knew that he was pushing at an open door, and decided to test the king's and the laity's resolve. One way to do this was to draft a petition outlining measures the clergy wished to see adopted to counter heterodoxy, which was duly done, but another option offered the

---

[46] Convocation met on 27 Jan. at St Paul's.

[47] *Usk*, 8; *PROME*, viii.105, 118–19, 125–6. For these issues, see below, pp. 352–60 and 368–9.

[48] *PROME*, viii.98. This was the only time that this phrase was included in the opening sermon.

[49] *PROME*, viii.110, 121.

[50] *Records of Convocation*, ed. G. Bray (10 vols, Canterbury, Woodbridge, 2006), *IV*, 214–15. The delegation was led by Northumberland, Erpingham and Norbury; the quid pro quo was that the clergy were expected to grant a tax.

chance to make the point more compellingly. Lurking in the archbishop's prison was a chaplain, William Sawtre, who in the spring of 1399 had been tried for heresy and had publicly recanted, but subsequently relapsed. Arundel decided that the moment had come to try him again. Brought before convocation on five occasions during February, Sawtre was interrogated but failed to exculpate himself. On 26 February he was declared incorrigible (primarily on account of his views on the Eucharist), degraded and passed over to the lay powers to be punished as a heretic.[51] True to his word, the king drafted a writ that same day to the mayor and sheriffs of London empowering them to burn Sawtre, although it was not yet handed over to the city officers, probably to allow time for the interrogation of a more prominent heretic, John Purvey.[52] In the event, Purvey's trial had to be postponed, since Arundel was required in parliament, and on Wednesday 2 March it was decided to go ahead with Sawtre's execution. Defiant to the last, hurling abuse at the archbishop and prophesying the ruin of the kingdom, he was taken to Smithfield and there bound, standing upright, to a post set in a barrel with blazing wood all around, 'and thus reduced to ashes'.[53] This was enough for Purvey, who by the end of the week had recanted his former beliefs at St Paul's Cross, acknowledging the sacrament of the Eucharist.[54]

The emphasis on the Eucharist in both these trials justified the decision to resort to what had been widely accepted since the twelfth century as the appropriate penalty for relapsed heretics. The statute passed by parliament eight days after Sawtre's death, based on the petition drafted in convocation, has come to be known as *De Heretico Comburendo* ('For the Burning of a Heretic'), and is often said to have introduced the death penalty for heresy to England. In fact heretics had been burned in England in the thirteenth and fourteenth centuries, and their fates recorded in thirteenth-century legal treatises as common law precedents, although it was about seventy years since the last occasion.[55] Nor did the statute claim to be introducing

---

[51] *Records of Convocation IV*, 216–26; P. McNiven, *Heresy and Politics in the Reign of Henry IV* (Woodbridge, 1987), 81–6. When first questioned on 12 February, Sawtre tried to conform, but as the trial progressed he adopted a more aggressive, even impertinent, tone.

[52] *Foedera*, viii.178; *PROME*, viii.108–9. A. McHardy, 'De Heretico Comburendo, 1401', in *Lollardy and the Gentry in the Later Middle Ages*, ed. M. Aston and C. Richmond (Stroud, 1997), 112–26, at p. 115 (where she points out that there is no evidence that heresy was discussed in parliament before 2 March). Purvey had been Wyclif's secretary and had translated the Lollard Bible into English.

[53] *Usk*, 122–3; *CE*, 388.

[54] *Records of Convocation IV*, 226–9.

[55] A. E. Larson, 'Are all Lollards Lollards?', in *Lollards and Their Influence in Late Medieval England*, ed. F. Somerset, J. Havens and D. Pitard (Woodbridge, 2003), 59–72, at p. 61;

the death penalty. Its principal provisions were to restrict as far as possible opportunities for the spread of suspect ideas through Lollard schools, books and conventicles, and to reinforce the powers of the secular authorities to help the Church to eliminate heresy.[56] Those who ignored these warnings would be punished by imprisonment and fines; if obdurate, they would be 'burned in a high place', which was, as the king's writ of 26 February ordering Sawtre's execution had stated, 'customary in such cases'. Twenty years earlier, standing trial in Lincoln cathedral, William Swinderby had been saved from the flames only by Gaunt's intervention.[57]

De Heretico Comburendo – retrospectively and misleadingly so called – appealed to different people for different reasons. Majority opinion among the commons was reassured that the king was serious about dealing with out-and-out heresy, for to the common law precedents for burning heretics he had added statutory authority. The faith, declared Savage in his closing speech, had been 'on the point of annihilation by evil doctrine', but thanks to Henry 'this doctrine and its sect' had been destroyed, for which the commons should give thanks to God (*Deo gratias*) thus bringing the

P. Cavill, 'Heresy, Law and the State: Forfeiture in Late Medieval and Early Modern England', *EHR* 129 (2014), 270–95, at p. 274 (citing Bracton and Britton).

[56] *PROME*, viii.122–5.

[57] A petition in French from the archbishops and bishops addressed to parliament and preserved in Thomas Hoccleve's formulary reminded the king that 'in other realms subject to the Christian religion when any persons are condemned by the church for the crime of heresy they are promptly handed over to secular judgment to be put to death and their temporal goods confiscated', and went on to ask for help from the 'secular arm' in the campaign to eliminate heretics 'so that those who are unwilling to be corrected and amended by spiritual discipline should be punished by temporal punishment'; this 'help' was to be 'by way of a statute' (H. G. Richardson and G. Sayles, 'Parliamentary Documents from Formularies', *BIHR* (1934), 152–4; BL Add. MS 24.062, fo. 189v). This does not quite amount to requesting the introduction of the death penalty for heresy in England, although there is no doubting the implication. However, the fact that the archbishops should ask for this power to be set down in a statute does not mean that they were asking for a new type of punishment for heresy to be introduced (as noted above, heretics had been burned in England before), but rather that this was something which they felt should be confirmed by being enshrined in statute form. However the petition does not seem to have been actually submitted to parliament, for it is not recorded on the parliament roll. Richardson and Sayles dated this to January 1397, which has generally been accepted, but the evidence for this is inferential and it seems just as likely that it was intended for the parliament of January 1401, as a supplementary petition to the clergy's petition on Lollard schools and conventicles which, as frequently noted, was in Latin, which was very unusual for parliamentary petitions. If so, it was presumably in response to this that the final paragraph of the king's reply detailing the secular punishments for heretics was added; this was incorporated in the statute, although the petition itself had said nothing about forms of secular punishment. It is worth noting Usk's comment (p. 8) that 'my lord of Canterbury, forewarned of [the Lollards'] evil schemes, had prepared suitable counter-measures'.

parliament (qua mass) to a conclusion.[58] According to Walsingham it was the commons who were behind the statute, but although they did submit a petition requesting that Lollards 'have such judgment as they deserve', it was the more specific petition of the clergy which provided the basis for the statute.[59] Arundel saw it as a way of confounding those who had converged on London to lobby for reform and of steering marooned souls back towards orthodoxy, while to Henry, Lollardy was a threat to law and order as well as to souls. There is little to indicate that he felt any urgent desire to introduce more salutary forms of punishment for heresy to England; nothing had been said about heresy during his first parliament eighteen months earlier. He did, however, need to clamp down on public disorder, and in this context Sawtre was a particularly apposite victim, for in February 1400 he had been suspected of treason and felony, probably resulting from involvement in the Epiphany Rising.[60] The king's support for the statute also helped him to secure his taxes – a point made implicitly by the commons when they granted a tenth and fifteenth on 10 March, and explicitly by convocation when it granted a clerical tenth the next day, even if it was only with 'dark mutterings' that the taxes were voted.[61]

Dark mutterings were also heard about the Welsh. Usk, hearing that 'all sorts of rigorous measures' were being planned against his countrymen, awoke in great agitation from a dream on the night before parliament was dissolved and, fearing ruin, committed himself to the protection of the Holy Spirit.[62] His apprehension was justified, for despite the stifling of Owain Glyn Dŵr's uprising in September 1400, the principality was seething. Welsh scholars were deserting Oxford and Cambridge to return to their native land, and Welsh labourers had fled homewards to arm themselves. If strong measures were not taken, the commons informed the king, a new rebellion seemed imminent.[63] When John Trevaur, bishop of St Asaph, cautioned against dealing too severely with Glyn Dŵr lest the Welsh rise up, the knights and burgesses are said to have replied that they 'cared naught for barefooted buffoons (*scurris nudipedibus*)'.[64]

---

[58] *PROME*, viii.121.

[59] *SAC II*, 308; *PROME*, viii.122–5, 139.

[60] *CPR 1399–1401*, 190; McNiven, *Heresy and Politics*, 82. McHardy, 'De Heretico Comburendo', 118. See also *CCR 1399–1402*, 185, an order from the king to the sheriffs to clamp down on unlicensed preaching dated May 1400.

[61] *Records of Convocation IV*, 233–6; *PROME*, viii.121; *Usk*, 126–7.

[62] *Usk*, 126–7.

[63] *PROME*, viii.104; *Original Letters*, i.8–9.

[64] *CE*, 388.

This was unwise, for Wales around 1400 was a country which neither the English nor the Welsh could quite feel was theirs.[65] Sparsely populated and with poor communications, especially in the mountainous north-west, its landmarks to an outsider were the formidable castles and walled towns built by English colonists and maintained under their control. For most of the fourteenth century these settlers had kept the land quiescent, helped by its political fragmentation. The north and west (Pembrokeshire excepted) comprised the principality of Wales, the domain of the English crown, conquered in the late thirteenth century. The south and east, broadly speaking, were divided into about thirty major and a few minor Marcher lordships, nearly all of which by this time were held by the great aristocratic families of England, most notably the Mortimer earls of March, the Fitzalan earls of Arundel and the house of Lancaster. Brecon, Henry's most valuable possession before 1399, was perhaps the greatest of these.[66] It was thus English aristocrats, through their stewards, receivers and lesser officials, who ruled Wales and were the major beneficiaries of its fruits, and they ruled it with a strong hand, very largely through Englishmen, and with an eye to extracting as much as they could from it. So too the Church in Wales: of the sixteen bishops appointed to Welsh sees between 1372 and 1400, only John Trevaur was a Welshman. Poor and remote, the Welsh sees were usually seen by English carpetbaggers as stepping-stones to something better across the border.

Bearing the weight of this superstructure was another Wales, a native people united by kinship, custom, a shared culture and history, and an abiding resentment at being made to feel – as the scribe of Hopkin ap Thomas, patron of Welsh poets and adherent of Glyn Dŵr, put it – like exiles in their own land. The barriers dividing English Wales from Welsh Wales were legal, ethnic and historical. Royal and burghal legislation regulating matters such as residency, trade, office-holding and law-worthiness, broadly designed to keep the Welsh in their place, had since the late thirteenth century created a parallel world of allegiances and hierarchies within native Welsh society. The leaders of this community of the excluded were the *uchelwyr*, men descended from the native Welsh princes of former times who were barred by English laws from reaching the highest rungs of the administrative ladder by which their land was governed, but in whose persons rested the aspirations of their people. Owain Glyn Dŵr, Rhys ap Tudor and his brother Gwilym were *uchelwyr*, their lineage, prowess and

---

[65] Davies, *Revolt*, 5–93.
[66] Brecon had been a Bohun, not a Lancaster, lordship.

hospitality celebrated by the bards, expectations of them shaped by the ubiquitous prophets and poets. Without the cooperation of such men, English rule was unenforceable.

As the fourteenth century drew to a close, political developments in England brought change to Wales. Peace with France during the 1390s deprived Welsh esquires and archers of one of the few means available to them of achieving near equality with their English counterparts. The deaths of the earls of Arundel and March in 1397–8 disrupted long-standing ties of patronage (Glyn Dŵr himself had served in the earl of Arundel's retinue), as did the fall of Richard II, not only in Wales itself but also in the border counties, for Richard had favoured Cheshiremen and retained an abnormally high proportion of the Herefordshire gentry.[67] In 1398, he had also retained Gwilym and Rhys ap Tudor as king's esquires. The hunting down of a king in North Wales in the summer of 1399 must also have raised doubts about royal authority, as must the lawlessness in England which followed it. It did not require hindsight to assert that Wales at the outset of the fifteenth century was ready to explode.

Eleven petitions concerning Wales were submitted to the 1401 parliament. Some related to breaches of cross-border security such as cattle-rustling.[68] Others were retrospective, such as the request that no Welshman who had taken part in the rebellion be pardoned until he had paid compensation. More insulting, especially to the many Welsh who had remained loyal to the crown, were petitions which reinforced their exclusion from equal status in the legal and economic life of the country. One requested that they be barred from acquiring property or burgess status in English towns in Wales, another that no full-blooded Englishman be convicted in Wales except by the verdict of English justices or burgesses. And when the royal council met at Coldharbour House on the Thames a week after the parliament ended, it issued a supplementary and more stringent set of ordinances.[69] As a perpetual reminder of their insubordination, the Welsh were now made to contribute financially towards the English garrisons in their castles; gatherings of Welshmen were prohibited without the permission of their lord's officers; minstrels, bards, rhymers, 'wasters and other Welsh vagabonds', often suspected of spreading sedition, were forbidden to take payment for their entertainment; further restrictions were placed

[67] *RHKA*, 217–23.

[68] *PROME*, viii.136, 140, 144–5.

[69] *CPR 1399–1401*, 469–70; *Foedera*, viii.184. Davies, *Revolt*, 287–8, and *PROME*, viii.96–7, argue that Henry tried to moderate the commons' demands, but the council ordinances had the opposite effect.

on office-holding by Welshmen; and judicial cooperation between Marcher lords was stepped up to ensure that offenders were caught and punished.

The Marcher lords came in for a good deal of criticism during the parliament, the commons evidently believing that they did not take their duty seriously enough to defend the English from Welsh incursions; they were now enjoined to place their castles in better repair and to see that the law was enforced. Nor did the king escape censure. Henry, said Arnold Savage, had appointed 'people born in the same country' to be his officers in Wales, which was contrary to the ordinances of 1295 and likely to result in mischief; he advised the king to search out Edward I's ordinances to see if they required strengthening.[70] The result was the Coldharbour meeting on 18 March. Its reconstitution of the legal and ethnic screen dividing English and Welsh was against the grain of history. Through the four-teenth century, as Anglo-Welsh worlds slowly meshed – an almost inevi-table process over time, despite attempts to prevent it – the laws separating them had come to be seen as increasingly outdated and, to the Welsh, irksome. Now they were not merely confirmed but extended.[71] There is no doubting the virulence of anti-Welsh sentiment at Westminster in early 1401, and little to suggest that Henry did not share it.

One further decision was arguably very costly. On 10 March, the last day of the parliament, the king issued a general pardon to those who had rebelled in September, but with three named exceptions: Owain Glyn Dŵr and Rhys and Gwilym ap Tudor.[72] It was the Tudor brothers who, three weeks later, launched the assault on Conway which reignited the rebellion and realized the commons' worst fears. The main reason why they did so was to pressurize the crown into pardoning them in return for surren-dering the castle.

---

[70] *PROME*, viii.104–5, 144–5.
[71] For the anti-Welsh legislation and its context, see Davies, *Revolt*, 284–92.
[72] *CPR 1399–1401*, 451; *Foedera*, viii.181–2.

Chapter 13

THE PERCY ASCENDANCY (1401–1402)

It was the combination of rebellion in Wales and intensified hostility on the Anglo-Scottish border during the early years of Henry IV's reign that led to the augmentation of the power of the Percys. No family apart from the king's had profited more from the deposition of Richard II. Before 1399 was out, Northumberland had been made constable of England for life and warden of the West March for ten years, granted the Isle of Man, and put at the head of a consortium which farmed the Mortimer inheritance during the young earl's minority. His son Hotspur became warden of the East March, also for ten years, sheriff of Northumberland, justiciar of Chester and North Wales, and sheriff of Flintshire; he was granted the lordship of Anglesey and custody of the Mortimer lordship of Denbigh. Father and son thus secured a virtual monopoly of civil and military power on the Scottish marches and in North Wales. Meanwhile Thomas Percy, the earl's brother, was one of only two men permitted to keep the title to which he had been promoted in 1397 (earl of Worcester); became admiral of England for life; and was appointed to head the negotiations with the French over Queen Isabella's return.[1] This cascade of offices and favours was not simply reward for the Percys' help in 1399, crucial as that was. It also recognized the long and lauded careers of all three of them as soldiers, diplomats, Knights of the Garter and supporters and kinsmen of the House of Lancaster.[2]

Probably by design, the roles adopted by the Percys during the early years of Henry's reign were demarcated. Hotspur, first and foremost a

---

[1] J. Bean, 'Henry Percy, first Earl of Northumberland', *ODNB*, 43.694–70; A. Brown, 'Thomas Percy, Earl of Worcester', *ODNB*, 43.737–9; S. Walker, 'Sir Henry Percy (Hotspur)', *ODNB*, 43.702–4.

[2] Hotspur and Worcester had been Gaunt's fee'd retainers, while Northumberland and Gaunt, despite a famous quarrel in 1381, subsequently cooperated without obvious difficulty (K. Towson, '"Hearts Warped by Passion": The Percy-Gaunt Dispute of 1381', *Fourteenth Century England III*, ed. M. Ormrod (2004), 143–52). Northumberland and Worcester, born in 1341 and 1343, respectively, were the sons of Mary, daughter of Earl Henry of Lancaster (d.1345); Northumberland spent much of his youth in the household of the first duke of Lancaster, Henry of Grosmont (d.1361).

soldier, took charge of the defence of the northern border and the pacification of Ricardian Cheshire, and was rarely in London. Worcester, except when abroad on embassies or supervising naval operations, remained with the king. Northumberland stayed for the most part at Westminster, the leading lay magnate on the council, involved in planning of all kinds, although he did not entirely delegate his responsibilities in the north to his son.[3] The parliament of 1401 and its aftermath saw a further increase in their responsibilities.[4] In March, Worcester became steward of the royal household, and in October he was appointed to be Prince Henry's governor; in the same month, the farm of the Mortimer inheritance was granted to Northumberland alone. However, with the seizure of Conway by the Tudor brothers, it was the brilliant and unpredictable Hotspur who was catapulted to the forefront of the nation's affairs, for it was to him that the king entrusted its recapture.

Gwilym Tudor was the leader of the forty or so men who infiltrated Conway castle on 1 April 1401, choosing a moment when the captain was away and all bar five defenders were attending a Good Friday service in the town.[5] Hotspur swiftly invested the castle, but it took four weeks for Prince Henry to come to his help.[6] By this time negotiations were under way for it to be surrendered, as eventually happened in late May: in return for vacating the castle, the rebel leaders received pardons for everything they had done hitherto (including their devastation of Conway town), but were obliged to hand over nine of their party to the prince, who promptly executed them with predictable savagery – 'a most shameful thing for [Gwilym and Rhys] to have done', in Usk's view, 'and an act of treachery against their fellows'.[7] Nevertheless, the psychological boost of the Conway escapade – an exploit which, had it been performed by Englishmen in France, would have found its way into annals of chivalric heroism – was widely felt. Conway castle was reckoned to be almost impregnable. It was where Richard had taken refuge

---

[3] No one attended more council meetings or witnessed more charters during the first three years of the reign than Northumberland: Brown, 'The Commons and the Council', 30; D. Biggs, 'Royal Charter Witness Lists for the Reign of Henry IV, 1399–1413', *EHR* 119 (2004), 407–23, at p. 418; Worcester also attended the council regularly when not absent from Westminster.

[4] Rogers, 'Political Crisis of 1401', 91–3, argues that the Percys manipulated the 1401 parliament to augment their powers.

[5] K. Williams-Jones, 'The Taking of Conwy Castle, 1401', *Transactions of the Caernarvonshire History Society* 39 (1978), 7–43 at p. 13.

[6] E 403/573, 19 April 1402: Hotspur 'remained at the said siege for four weeks at his own expense without help from anyone apart from his own men'.

[7] *Usk*, 129.

in August 1399, just a year after retaining Rhys and Gwilym.[8] If the brothers' primary aim in capturing it was to secure pardons, they must also have enjoyed cocking a snook at the man who had deposed their former patron. Glyn Dwr himself played no part in their exploit, and they sought no pardon for him; indeed it may be that at this stage they saw themselves more as rivals to Owain for leadership of the Welsh cause than as his adherents. Yet the consequence of their audacity, intentional or otherwise, was to galvanize Owain into action once more, perhaps in the hope that he too might secure a pardon. This was precisely what the king had feared. While Hotspur questioned the wisdom of the anti-Welsh ordinances and grew testy about Henry's failure to send him sufficient funds, Henry's main concern was the precedent set by offering such lenient terms to rebels.[9] Not the least of the brothers' achievements was to sow seeds of mistrust within English ranks.

Summer 1401 saw the revolt spread into Central Wales and even to Carmarthenshire and Brecon.[10] By early June the king was sufficiently worried to advance as far as Worcester, planning to lead an army into Wales himself, although on this occasion, hearing news of some minor English successes and believing the remaining rebels to be 'only of little reputation', he decided to turn back.[11] By the autumn, however, the situation had worsened, with Harlech under siege and Aberystwyth threatened, and at the beginning of October Henry and the prince led a sizeable army into Wales, arriving before Caernarfon on 8 October and then moving south to vent their fury on the Cistercian monks of Strata Florida, who were believed to be in league with the rebels.[12] Owain could not be found, however, despite spies and messengers being sent out to hunt him down.[13] When Llywellyn ap Gruffudd Fychan of Caio, who had offered to lead the king to the Welsh leader but knowingly misled him, was interrogated by

---

[8] Davies, *Revolt*, 79; the English were the 'undisputed April Fools' of 1401 (Allmand, *Henry V*, 20).

[9] *POPC*, i.147–53; *RHL I*, 69–72; E 28/9, no. 2, lists 35 men to be pardoned (these pardons were confirmed on 4 July). Prince Henry received £300 for his expenses at Conway in July 1401, but Hotspur had to wait until April 1402 to receive payment of £200 (E 404/16, no. 739; E 403/573, 19 April).

[10] *RHL I*, 152–3; Davies, *Revolt*, 105; on 30 August 1401 the king ordered Prince Henry to go to *South* Wales to suppress rebellions there (E 404/16, no. 766).

[11] *POPC*, i.133–5 (dated at Worcester, 8 June).

[12] *Usk*, 144; *Vita*, 170. The royal army stabled their horses in the church and it was said that not a monk remained at the abbey. Many Welsh Cistercian houses had close links with the native population and were centres of Welsh culture and sentiment. See *CPR 1401–5*, 61, which blamed the devastation of the abbey on Welsh rebels as well as on the English army.

[13] DL 29/548/9241, m. 2.

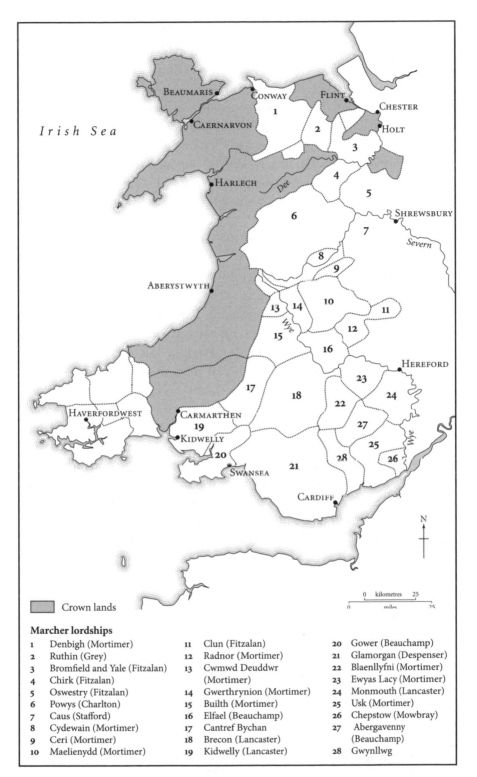

Crown lands

Marcher lordships

1	Denbigh (Mortimer)	11	Clun (Fitzalan)	20	Gower (Beauchamp)
2	Ruthin (Grey)	12	Radnor (Mortimer)	21	Glamorgan (Despenser)
3	Bromfield and Yale (Fitzalan)	13	Cwmwd Deuddwr (Mortimer)	22	Blaenllyfni (Mortimer)
4	Chirk (Fitzalan)			23	Ewyas Lacy (Mortimer)
5	Oswestry (Fitzalan)	14	Gwerthrynion (Mortimer)	24	Monmouth (Lancaster)
6	Powys (Charlton)	15	Builth (Mortimer)	25	Usk (Mortimer)
7	Caus (Stafford)	16	Elfael (Beauchamp)	26	Chepstow (Mowbray)
8	Cydewain (Mortimer)	17	Cantref Bychan	27	Abergavenny (Beauchamp)
9	Ceri (Mortimer)	18	Brecon (Lancaster)		
10	Maelienydd (Mortimer)	19	Kidwelly (Lancaster)	28	Gwynllwg

Map 4 Wales and the Glyn Dŵr Revolt

Henry as to why he had done so, he replied that he would prefer to lose his
head rather than betray Glyn Dŵr's counsel. His wish was granted, but his
example applauded. 'We English could learn a lesson from this', wrote the
Evesham chronicler, 'to keep our counsels and secrets faithfully between
ourselves even unto death'.[14] Yet Owain had not gone far, and as soon as
Henry returned to Shrewsbury on 15 October, after barely two weeks in
Wales, he emerged from hiding, sacked Welshpool, then marched his men
to Caernarfon where, on 2 November, he raised his princely standard, a
golden dragon on a white field, although on this occasion he was beaten
off by a sortie from the garrison.[15]

Shortly before this, perhaps while the king was still in Wales, Glyn Dŵr
let it be known through the Percys and Edmund Mortimer (Hotspur's
brother-in-law) that like the Tudor brothers he would be prepared to
submit to the king in return for a promise to spare his life, but when this
was put to the council at Westminster in November 1401 it declined to
accept his plea.[16] With hindsight, it is easy to recognize that passing up this
opportunity came back to haunt the English, but there was nothing
straightforward about the decision. The revolt was still some way short of
a national uprising, royal agents were busily accepting submissions and
obligations from former rebels, a formidable series of military commands
had just been set up throughout Wales, and Henry probably reckoned that,
having allowed thirty-five rebels to walk out of Conway unscathed, any
further sign of weakness would simply provide encouragement to others.[17]
Nor was it clear that Owain's surrender would bring the revolt to an end;
the pardon of the Tudor brothers had not done so. Owain's offer of
submission tells us as much about his own problems as about the English
crown's. His leadership of the revolt was not yet secure, and for the moment
his defiance seemed to have been checked.

That soon changed, however, as 1402 began with a raid on Ruthin, the
lordship of Owain's old enemy Reginald Grey, enabling the rebels to
replenish their stock of cattle.[18] In April, Grey learned that the Welsh
leader was once again in the vicinity of Ruthin: setting off in pursuit with
a small force, he ventured into unfamiliar territory, only to find himself

---

[14] *Vita*, 170, which adds that two of Llywellyn's sons were with Owain at the time.

[15] *Usk*, 147.

[16] *POPC*, i.173, ii.59–60; *ANLP*, no. 244; Wylie, *Henry the Fourth*, i.246.

[17] Davies, *Revolt*, 106; *POPC*, i.173; E 403/571, 9 December 1401 (payment to Master John
Barell for spending 20 days in Wales and the Marches securing obligations and submissions
in the military court to secure peace and tranquillity in Wales).

[18] According to *Usk*, 147, the raid took place on 30 January.

ambushed and led away to Snowdonia 'bound tightly with thongs'.[19] Then, on 22 June, at the battle of Bryn Glas or Pilleth, just south of Knighton (Powys), Owain secured an equally notable and ultimately more significant triumph when his forces overcame a levy from Herefordshire led by Edmund Mortimer, capturing Mortimer himself and killing several hundred of his men. Stories of the mutilation of the corpses by Welsh women aroused indignation in England, but more corrosive of English morale were the rumours of treachery among Edmund's followers and even of collusion in his own capture by Mortimer himself, rumours which the king and his advisers at Westminster believed. From this time onwards, wrote the Evesham chronicler, 'Owain's cause began to flourish greatly, and ours to fail'.[20] Prevented by the king from ransoming himself – a source of real controversy, especially since Reginald Grey ransomed himself for £6,666 and was free by the end of the year – Edmund married Glyn Dŵr's daughter Catherine on 30 November 1402 and two weeks later wrote to his vassals announcing that henceforth he would strive to vindicate his father-in-law's rights in Wales.[21]

Especially disturbing for the king was the commonality of interests now building up between Glyn Dŵr, the Percys, and followers of the Mortimers. Edmund was not just a major landholder in Wales and the Marches, he was also the uncle of that other Edmund Mortimer, earl of March, now aged ten, whom some believed to have a better title to the throne than Henry, and his renunciation of allegiance to Henry in December 1402 was accompanied by a public exhortation to his supporters ('unless King Richard is alive') to place his nephew on the throne. The elder Edmund's sister Elizabeth was married to Hotspur, who was strongly in favour of ransoming him.[22] Hotspur had other grievances too: frequently obliged to fund his operations from his own resources, he was becoming alienated from the king's policy in Wales. His unease at the ordinances of March 1401, his parleying with the captors of Conway and the negotiations with Glyn Dŵr in late 1401 all bespeak a belief in conciliation and negotiation

[19] *Vita*, 172.

[20] *SAC II*, 323–5; *Vita*, 172–3; Wylie, *Henry the Fourth*, i.250, notes that it was believed that after capturing Grey in April, Owain had spared the Mortimer lands: H. Watt, 'On Account of the Frequent Attacks and Invasions of the Welsh: The Effect of the Glyn Dŵr Rebellion on Tax Collection in England', in *Rebellion and Survival 1403–13*, ed. G. Dodd and D Biggs (York, 2008), 48–81, at p. 72.

[21] *Original Letters*, i.24–5; R. Davies, 'Sir Edmund Mortimer', *ODNB*, 39.375–6; Foedera, vii.279; *Usk*, 158–60; *Hardyng*, 359; *CPR 1401–5*, 176, and E 403/574, 19 Oct., for Edmund's lands being granted away and his goods seized by the king in mid-October 1402.

[22] Davies, *Revolt*, 179–80.

rather than the hard-line approach adopted by the king.[23] It must have
been with misgivings, therefore, that Hotspur went north in the autumn of
1402 to join his father in resisting a Scottish invasion of Northumberland,
leaving the king to take an army once again into Wales. First planned in
late June, Henry's campaign was delayed until the beginning of September,
by which time the weather had turned. Rain battered the royal army for
more than a fortnight, with some English soldiers perishing from the cold.[24]
A particularly violent storm on the night of 7 September flattened the
king's tent and might have killed Henry himself had he not gone to bed in
his armour. Some in England believed that the appalling weather had been
conjured up by Owain's magicians, others that it was by the evil arts of the
Franciscan friars, who, like the Cistercians, were suspected of complicity
with the Welsh. What is clear is that Henry's third campaign to Wales
within twenty-four months was widely seen as a personal humiliation for
the king.[25]

    The Welsh war was a battle against geography, the elements, guerrilla
tactics and a hostile native population, and it took Henry a while to learn
its lessons. Armies of invasion could wreak damage, seize much-needed
resources and exact reprisals, but what was needed against an enemy who
simply retreated to the muscular outcrops of the north-west and waited
until the English went home was a network of permanent garrisons. From
late 1401, probably under the influence of Hotspur and Thomas Percy (the
latter having now added the lieutenancy of South Wales to his array of
responsibilities), these had begun to be established, but they suffered from
chronic shortage of cash and its backwash: indiscipline and desertion.[26]
Here, too, a change of policy was needed. The king had hoped in 1401–2
that as much as possible of the cost of the war could be borne by the
revenues of the principality of Wales – in effect by the prince, its lord, from
his own resources – but this was quite impractical, for as the rebellion
spread the revenues of the principality dwindled, until by 1403–4 they had
virtually vanished.[27] This caused tension between the king and his son as

    [23] *Giles*, 30–2, believed that Hotspur argued the case strongly to the council for offering
Owain the pardon he sought, and when this was refused he left Wales for the north.
According to *POPC*, ii.59, the Welsh leader also had 'great affection and affinity' with the
earl of Northumberland.
    [24] *POPC*, i.185.
    [25] *SAC II*, 324–7; *CE*, 394; *Vita*, 174; Clarke and Galbraith, 'Deposition of Richard II'
(*Dieulacres Chronicle*), 176.
    [26] R. Griffiths, 'Prince Henry and Wales', in *Profit, Piety and the Professions in Later Medieval
England*, ed. M. Hicks (Gloucester, 1990), 51–61 at pp. 54–9. For garrisons set up in November
1401 see *POPC*, i.173–7.
    [27] Allmand, *Henry V*, 23–8; Griffiths, 'Prince Henry and Wales', 55.

well as between the king and Hotspur. In May 1402, Prince Henry wrote to the council saying that if money to pay his soldiers were not found soon he would be obliged to retreat to England, to his eternal dishonour.[28] As the inefficacy of the English response became apparent, so support for Glyn Dŵr continued to grow.

The simultaneous escalation of hostilities on the northern border was to some extent a riposte to Henry's foray into Scotland in August 1400, and to some extent driven by the Percy–Douglas rivalry. The Douglas and Percy families had much in common. Both had augmented their lands and influence spectacularly during the fourteenth century, mainly through the opportunities afforded by a century of near-continuous cross-border warfare, but since the 1370s the advantage had lain with the Scots, making it impossible for the Percys to realize their long-nurtured territorial ambitions north of the border.[29] By the time Earl Archibald the Grim died around Christmas 1400, he had achieved a position of dominance in Scotland south of the Forth, his hold over the west march now securely established and his following in East Lothian expanding almost daily following George Dunbar's defection.[30] No respite followed his demise. His son and heir, Archibald the fourth earl, already the possessor of a fearsome reputation, soon busied himself with the organization of a programme of cross-border raids. Not all of these met with success, for in Hotspur and Dunbar he was pitted against two of the finest soldiers of their age, although he did manage to chase them back to England when they advanced into Lothian in February 1401.[31] Yet if his military domination of the south was not disputed within Scotland, Douglas had not yet secured control of diplomatic policy towards England, which, guided by the dukes of Albany and Rothesay, appeared during the spring and summer of 1401 to be moving in the direction of a settlement with Henry IV.[32]

Partly by luck and partly by design, events now conspired to remove this restraining hand on Douglas's rough inclinations. In early October 1401,

---

[28] *POPC*, ii.62–3.

[29] J. Bean, 'The Percies and their Estates in Scotland', *Archaeologia Aeliana* 35 (1957), 91–9.

[30] Given-Wilson, *English Nobility*, 132–5; M. Brown, *The Black Douglases 1300–1455* (East Linton, 1998); Dunbar castle, Earl George's ancestral stronghold, was delivered by its keeper to Douglas in July 1400.

[31] A. Macdonald, 'George Dunbar, Ninth Earl of Dunbar or March', *ODNB*, 17.207–10; Brown, *Black Douglases*, 145–7.

[32] Macdonald, *Border Bloodshed*, 143–5; *POPC*, ii.52 ('the earl of Douglas and other young lords are not in favour of a treaty of peace, but the king of Scotland, his son of Rothesay, the duke of Albany and other prelates and lords of substance of Scotland are desirous of peace, so it is said').

Rothesay, the heir to the throne and lieutenant of the realm, was arrested
near St Andrews (Fife) on the orders of Albany, who was becoming alarmed
at his nephew's growing challenge to his authority. Albany and Douglas
now struck a deal: in return for supporting Albany's coup, Douglas was to
be given a virtually free hand, not only to dismember George Dunbar's
earldom in favour of himself and his supporters but also to pursue his own
policy towards England. Rothesay disappeared into Falkland castle, where
he was almost certainly murdered,[33] while Douglas hurried south to Kirk
Yetholm in the borders, where the latest round of Anglo-Scottish peace
talks opened on 17 October. His aim was to ensure that they did not interfere with his plans, especially now that his designs on Dunbar's earldom
had received official sanction, for any lasting agreement with the English
would probably have entailed the defector's return to the Scottish fold.

Douglas's fears were not misplaced: the reinstatement of Dunbar was
indeed one of the conditions advanced by the English at Kirk Yetholm.
The record of this meeting is instructive.[34] On the one hand, Henry was
still keen to secure formal recognition of his overlordship of Scotland (a
matter on which he claimed to have received assurances in August 1400)
and once again he had assembled a mass of evidence going back to the
mythical Brutus, eponymous first king of Britain, to justify his claim. In
return, his envoys offered the Scottish king (who was not present) an
annuity or land worth up to £1,000 a year in England.[35] On the other
hand, Henry was also eager to secure a truce for as long as possible – even,
he suggested (on the model of the Anglo-French truce of 1396), for up to
thirty years, to be accompanied by one or more marriages between the
royal houses of each kingdom. However, this was to be accompanied by
guarantees from the Scots that Berwick, Roxburgh and Jedburgh would
remain unmolested, that the Scots would not ally with the French, and that
George Dunbar would be welcomed back to East Lothian.[36] If this proved
unacceptable, a truce for one year might be agreed, with the same conditions; otherwise the commissioners should simply agree a two-month

[33] He died in March 1402. The official line, which even his father King Robert
sanctioned, was that he had contracted dysentery: Boardman, *Early Stewart Kings*, 238–46.

[34] *POPC*, i.168–73 (Henry's instructions to his commissioners); *Anglo-Scottish Relations 1174–
1328: Some Selected Documents*, ed. E. Stones (Oxford, 1965), 346–65 (report of the meeting by
an English clerk).

[35] It is worth noting that the Scots had said in August 1400, when Henry was in Edinburgh,
that they would consider the question of homage (above, p. 170).

[36] £500 had recently been spent on strengthening the defences of Berwick and Roxburgh
(E 28/8, 10 Dec. 1400, 19 March 1401).

extension to the truce.[37] Douglas and the Scottish commissioners 'utterly refused' every one of these proposals – a rebuff accompanied, according to the English account, by 'some very undiplomatic language'. When the English asked whether the Scots would be prepared to submit their differences to arbitration, the bishop of Glasgow asked whether Henry would be equally willing to submit his claim to the kingdom of England to arbitration; whereupon, after three days, the meeting broke up in acrimony. Sweeping up his retainers, Douglas hurried to Dunbar castle to put his stamp on his new lordship by issuing a number of land grants before crossing the Tweed 'with banner displayed' – in effect a declaration of war – ravaging Northumberland and burning Bamburgh.[38]

That each side should blame the other for the renewal of hostilities was to be expected,[39] but on the English side a gap was also opening up between the aims of the king and those of the Percys and Dunbar. Henry, preoccupied with disorder in England and Wales, needed a respite from war in the north. Dunbar, on the other hand, needed to maintain the pressure on the Scots if he was going to regain East Lothian, as did Northumberland and Hotspur in pursuit of their own claims north of the border.[40] Nor did Douglas need any encouragement, and he now launched a multi-pronged offensive against the Lancastrian regime, apparently with Albany's support. Beginning with the invention of a pseudo-Richard II, this included Franco-Scottish naval cooperation and attempts to assist Welsh and Irish enemies of the English crown, but the main thrust was delivered in a series of raids into the northern English counties.[41] June 1402 witnessed at least three Scottish forays into Cumberland and Northumberland, one of which led to the killing of Sir Patrick Hepburn at Nesbit Muir (Roxburghshire) by Dunbar.[42] Undeterred, Douglas and Murdoch Stewart (son and heir of the

[37] The English commissioners were also instructed to raise the question of the outstanding sums still due from the ransom of David II, but were told this was to be done amicably and not stand in the way of any agreement.

[38] Nicholson, *Scotland*, 219–22; Macdonald, *Border Bloodshed*, 146–7; Boardman, *Early Stewart Kings*, 239–40.

[39] *RHL I*, 52–65. Chroniclers on each side did likewise: Bower, for example, claimed that Douglas aggression was a legitimate response to attacks by Dunbar and the English (*Scotichronicon*, viii.43).

[40] Dunbar was said to have saved Hotspur's life at Otterburn in 1388 (A. Macdonald, 'George Dunbar, Ninth Earl of Dunbar or March', *ODNB*, 17.207–10).

[41] For the ghost of Richard II, see below, p. 209. Macdonald, *Border Bloodshed*, 145–6, 150; Boardman, *Early Stewart Kings*, 240. For fleets to counter Scottish piracy, see E 403/571, 14 March, and E 403/573, 4 April. It is possible that Glyn Dŵr's letter asking Robert III for help found its way to the Scottish court (*Usk*, 149 and n. 6).

[42] Hepburn's force might have included men returning from a raid on Carlisle (*SAC II*, 323); Macdonald, *Border Bloodshed*, 152–3.

duke of Albany) assembled some 10,000 men, including thirty French knights and esquires, and in early September crossed the Tweed and set out to harry Northumberland.

Having raided up to the gates of Newcastle without encountering resistance, the Scots turned homewards, but when they reached Wooler, ten miles south of the Tweed, on 14 September, they found their path blocked by an English force under the command of Dunbar and the Percys. Taking up a defensive position on Humbleton Hill overlooking Glendale, the Scots prepared for battle. Hotspur wanted to charge the Scottish formation, but Dunbar persuaded him to hold back until the English archers had had a chance to prove their worth.[43] It was sound advice. A hailstorm of arrows pinned the Scots down 'like fallow deer or penned up mules' until they 'bristled like hedgehogs' with English shafts. The bravery of Sir John Swinton, who led a counter-attack, met only with death. Douglas himself sustained five wounds, including the loss of an eye. In little more than an hour the battle was over and the Scots were in flight, pursued by the jubilant English as far as the Tweed, where many drowned trying to ford the river.[44] 'May God be blessed in all things', exulted Walsingham, 'who gave us the victory, not through the actions of the nobles and lords, but of the unremarkable poor and serfs, for there was not a single lord, knight or esquire who took any action against the enemy until they had been crushed by the archers.' With the men-at-arms barely engaged, English losses were minimal.[45]

Along with Bannockburn (1314), Halidon Hill (1333) and Neville's Cross (1346), Humbleton Hill marked a watershed in Anglo-Scottish warfare. A harvest of around 1,000 prisoners included Douglas, Murdoch Stewart, the earls of Angus, Moray and Orkney, a further eighty or so Scottish knights – 'the flower of the fighting men of the whole realm of Scotland' – and several French knights and esquires.[46] Douglas would remain a prisoner for seven years, Murdoch for thirteen. The removal at a stroke of so many great men left a political vacuum in Scotland, especially in the south, where not just Douglas but many of the other prisoners held the majority

[43] For accounts of the battle see *Scotichronicon*, 43–9; *SAC II*, 328–35; *Vita*, 174–5; Clarke and Galbraith, 'Deposition of Richard II' (*Dieulacres Chronicle*), 177; Macdonald, *Border Bloodshed*, 153–4. The Evesham chronicler put the English army at 12,000 men-at-arms and 7,000 archers, but this sounds too high.
[44] *CPR 1401–5*, 121; Walsingham said 500 Scots drowned, the Evesham chronicler 1,000.
[45] *SAC II*, 332–3; the king was told that only five English were killed (*CDS*, iv.402–3).
[46] *Scotichronicon*, viii.49 (quote), and *SAC II*, 333, give contemporary lists; see also Macdonald, *Border Bloodshed*, 154–5, who adds the names of some French knights accompanying the Scots.

of their lands. In the longer term, Humbleton made the Scots more wary of raiding into England, but for the moment their thoughts turned mainly to defence, since for the English the prospect now opened up not just of an end to thirty years of attrition but of an undefended Scottish March ripe for exploitation or even annexation.[47] The triumphant return of George Dunbar probably seemed to many a foregone conclusion, while the Percys greedily eyed the Douglas patrimony. For King Henry, Humbleton was a welcome relief, although in one sense its timing – coinciding with his own ignominious withdrawal from Wales – left much to be desired. Yet he was determined to wring whatever benefit he could from the victory, and it was to this end that on 20 September, as soon as he was informed of what had happened, he wrote to Hotspur, Northumberland, Dunbar and the other English captains prohibiting the ransoming of their prisoners without his permission.[48] Instead, they were to be brought to Westminster, where a parliament had been summoned to meet in a week's time.

---

[47] Macdonald, *Border Bloodshed*, 158–9; Boardman, *Early Stewart Kings*, 246–7.
[48] SC 1/57/122A and B, written at Daventry; *CDS*, iv.402–3; *Foedera*, viii.278–9.

Chapter 14

PIRACY, RUMOUR AND RIOT (1401–1402)

The presence of a French contingent in the Scottish army at Humbleton Hill would not have surprised the English, for Franco-Scottish collusion against the Lancastrian usurper had been growing for over a year, orchestrated by the self-appointed archpriest of Gallic Anglophobia, Duke Louis of Orléans.[1] Around Christmas 1401, Orléans concluded an alliance with the earl of Crawford at Paris, which led to both the despatch of French knights and esquires to Scotland (including those who fought at Humbleton) and the waging of virtually open warfare on English shipping in the Channel and the North Sea. Although attacks had taken place during the previous two years, this heralded a marked escalation of the war in the Channel and North Sea: at least twenty-five English vessels were seized between March and July 1402. The English were far from passive victims, capturing at least forty-eight French ships during the summer. The fleets responsible for this were under the command of the royal admirals, Richard Lord Grey and Sir Thomas Rempston, but they were captained by men such as John Hauley of Dartmouth, Mark Mixto of Fowey, John Brandon of Lynn, Henry Pay of Poole and Richard Spicer of Southampton, whom the French had no hesitation in labelling as pirates, but who in fact operated for much of the time as privateers.[2]

That the English government was using these men to attack French and Scottish shipping is clear; less so is the extent to which it was able to control their activities. This was especially the case with neutral vessels suspected of carrying enemy cargoes. Castilian merchants complained of seventeen incidents in which either their ships or their cargoes had been seized, the

---

[1] M. Nordberg, *Les Ducs et la Royauté* (Uppsala, 1964), 171; *Saint-Denys*, iii.9; *POPC*, i.128–9; G. Pepin, 'The French Offensives of 1404–1407 against Anglo-Gascon Aquitaine', in *Soldiers, Weapons and Armies in the Fifteenth Century*, ed. A. Curry and A. Bell (Woodbridge, 2011), 1–40, at pp. 2–3.

[2] C. Ford, 'Piracy or Policy: The Crisis in the Channel, 1400–1403', *TRHS* 29 (1979), 63–78; *Saint-Denys*, iii.153. By early July 1402 the French were thought to be about to invade England: E 403/573, 3 and 4 July.

Flemings twenty-seven. Worst affected, however, were the Hanseatics, who between 1402 and 1404 suffered the loss, destruction or pillage of at least fifty-nine ships. By the winter of 1404–5, the Hanse was trying to organize a general boycott of English trade.[3] Henry's increasingly urgent orders to Hauley, Pay, Spicer and their fellows to make restoration or pay compensation to the victims strongly suggest that he was losing control of the situation, but it would take years rather than months to repair the damage to England's trading relations. 'May God sink all pirate ships!' wrote one Florentine merchant to a colleague.[4] Meanwhile, the Anglo-French truce became ever more precarious.

Simultaneously with the Pirate War, the French and the Scots stepped up their attempts to discredit Henry and undermine his rule in England. From the French side, this took the form of public challenges to personal combat. The chronicler of Saint-Denis explained it thus: having conceived 'an implacable hatred' of the English because of their treatment of Richard II and Isabella, yet being unwilling to attack them openly lest they appear as truce-breakers, 'they sought an honourable pretext to avenge these intolerable injuries', and found it in the chivalric challenge.[5] These challenges began in 1400, but initially the lords followed the advice of the commons in 1401, who recommended that they be ignored because of the risk and expense involved.[6] In May 1402, however, the earl of Rutland, now serving as lieutenant of Guyenne, unwisely accepted a challenge from a group of Orléanistes to a seven-a-side combat at Montendre (between Bordeaux and Angoulême). Orléans's aim was to demonstrate French military superiority over the English, and this, in the estimation of his compatriots, he succeeded in doing.[7] One English knight was killed, the other six surrendered and returned to England 'covered in shame and confusion', while the victorious French, led by Guillaume de Chastel, one of Orléans's chamberlains, made their way in triumph to Paris, where Christine de Pizan composed ballads in their honour and Charles VI gave each of them 1,000 francs for vindicating French arms. Emboldened by success, Orléans now decided to challenge the English king directly, and on 7 August wrote to Henry proposing that a hundred Frenchmen should do battle against a

[3] T. Lloyd, *England and the German Hanse 1157–1611* (Cambridge, 2002), 111–16.

[4] H. Bradley, 'The Datini Factors in London', in *Trade, Devotion and Governance: Papers in Later Medieval History*, ed. D. Clayton, R. Davies and P. McNiven (Stroud, 1994), 55–79, at p. 63.

[5] *Saint-Denys*, iii.30–4.

[6] *PROME*, viii.102–3.

[7] C. Given-Wilson, 'The Quarrels of Old Women: Henry IV, Louis of Orléans, and Anglo-French Chivalric Challenges in the Early Fifteenth Century', in *The Reign of Henry IV: Rebellion and Survival, 1403–1413* (York, 2008), 28–47.

hundred Englishmen, led by himself and Henry, respectively, until one side
forced the other into surrender, whereupon the defeated would become the
prisoners of the victors. He cannot have believed for a moment that a
reigning monarch would accept such a challenge: his letter was intended as
an insult and was taken as such. Henry's reply, dated 5 December 1402,
expressed wonderment at Orléans's temerity, advised him to know his
place and mind his manners better in future, and formally annulled the
personal alliance which the two men had concluded in June 1399. Around
the same time, the earl of Northumberland received a similar letter from
Guillaume de Chastel, to which he replied in equally brutal terms, ridi-
culing his presumption and informing him that if he wished to engage in
combat with the earl he could find him on the Scottish march, where 'you
will behold the quivering sword of our office, which we wield against your
execrable vow and your accomplices'.[8]

Further letters followed, two more from Orléans and one from Henry,
progressively more unchivalric in their language. Louis accused Henry of
being a usurper and a regicide; Henry called Louis a liar, a coward and a
fomenter of discord within the French kingdom.[9] Crude as such taunts
were, they chafed at the ever-exposed nerve of great men's honour. It was
the cruelty Henry had displayed towards his niece Isabella which, claimed
Louis, left him honour-bound to act as her champion; Henry retorted that
although it was beneath him to reply he would do so since it was a matter
which concerned his honour. Yet Orléans's intemperance irritated many
people in France. The monk of Saint-Denis compared their insult-trading
to the bickering of old women and deemed the letters unworthy of inclusion in his chronicle, while the clerk who enrolled them in the register of
the French *parlement* (apparently at Orléans's request) described them as
'verbose and windy, without consequence or prudence'.[10] Honour must be
upheld, to be sure, and Orléans clearly believed that he was defending not
just his niece's honour but that of France; nevertheless there was genuine
fear in Paris that his bombast would lead to open warfare.

The Scots, too, sought ways to undermine Henry, and during the winter
of 1401–2 began to disseminate a rumour that Richard II, having escaped
from Pontefract, had been recognized while working as a kitchen-boy for
Donald, Lord of the Isles, by a woman who had met him in Ireland. With

[8] *Monstrelet*, i.43–66; Given-Wilson, 'Quarrels of Old Women', 42–5.
[9] These letters were dated 26 March and 14 October 1403 (from Louis) and 30 May 1403
(from Henry); Louis's final letter is in BL Add. Ms 30,663, fos. 281–6.
[10] *Saint-Denys*, iii.61; Lehoux, *Jean de France*, ii.523, n. 8: 'He littere verbose et ventose,
absque fructu et discretione'.

the earl of Douglas now in the ascendant, this was too good an opportunity
to miss, and the impostor – whose real name was Thomas Ward of
Trumpington, and who was sometimes called the Mammet (puppet) – soon
found himself brought before King Robert. Also at the Scottish court at this
time was William Serle, an esquire of Richard's chamber who had fled north
in 1399, forged the royal signet, and begun sending letters into England
proclaiming the imminent return of the former king.[11] By April 1402 the
rumour had reached the ears of Charles VI of France, who despatched Jean
Creton (Richard's companion in North Wales in August 1399) to discover the
truth of it, but although Creton soon satisfied himself that the Mammet was
a fraud, this did little to dampen what was becoming an improbably successful
propaganda war.[12] 'Richard' was sighted at Berwick, in Wales and even at
Westminster, belief in his continued existence nourished by a seditious
undercurrent of prophecy and hearsay which, by the summer of 1402, was
no longer the preserve merely of the dispossessed and the marginalized.

The seedbed in which these stories took root was growing disillusion with
Henry's rule during the first three years of his reign, not simply as a reaction
to his inability to cope with England's enemies, but also to government insolvency and the prevalence of disorder. Naturally, these problems were linked.
It was resistance to English rule in Wales, Ireland and Guyenne which, from
1401 onwards, obliged the king to make much more generous financial provision for their governance, while simultaneously reducing almost to vanishing
point the crown's income from its dominions; the Pirate War reduced
customs revenues by disrupting trade, but necessitated much increased
expenditure on the defence of the sea;[13] the fees due to the Percys for keeping
the Scottish marches during the first three years of the reign amounted to
some £40,000, but Scottish devastation and the need to provide manpower
for border defence meant that the three northern counties had to be
exempted from paying taxes.[14] Nor was there any relief from the demands

[11] *Scotichronicon*, viii.28–9; *RHKA*, 181–2; S. Walker, 'Rumour, Sedition and Popular Protest
in the Reign of Henry IV', *Past and Present* 166 (2000), 31–65; P. Morgan, 'Henry IV and the
Shadow of Richard II', in *Crown, Government and People in the Fifteenth Century*, ed. R. Archer
(Stroud, 1995), 1–32, at pp. 8–10; *Select Cases in the Court of King's Bench VII*, ed. G. Sayles
(Selden Society, London, 1971), 126–7, 212–15. Thomas Ward was maintained for nearly
two decades at the Scottish court.
[12] *CR*, 52, 244–5; for Creton, see above, p. 133.
[13] Below for Ireland and Guyenne; Wales should have yielded £12,000–£14,000 a year to
the crown, but by 1403 produced practically nothing, whereas the network of garrisons
established there, if properly maintained, would have cost at least £13,000 a year: Davies,
Revolt, 252, 258–9; *POPC*, i.173–4, ii.64–7.
[14] Bean, 'Henry IV and the Percies', 222–4; *PROME*, viii.152.

of annuitants, for domestic unrest militated against any reduction in the size of the royal retinue. Signs of strain soon appeared. Failed assignments totalled some £34,000 between April 1401 and September 1402; hectoring letters to the council bemoaned the inability of the king's lieutenants and officials to carry out the tasks entrusted to them owing to lack of funds.[15] Between May and July 1402, more than £16,000 was borrowed by the exchequer, much of it loaned by Londoners, to whom royal plate and crown jewels were handed over as security. Yet when Henry wrote to the treasurer, Laurence Allerthorpe, in July 1401 enclosing a list of some 300 lords, knights and esquires to be summoned to a great council, Allerthorpe replied that he did not have enough money to pay the messengers charged with bearing the summonses.[16] The one hopeful development was the fall in expenditure on the royal household from the altogether excessive £53,000 which it had cost during the first year of the reign, but even this was to some extent deceptive, for it was achieved in part by increased abuse of purveyance.[17] 'Around this time,' wrote Walsingham, 'grumbling broke out among the people against the king, mainly because he received provisions but paid nothing for them'; the 1402 parliament agreed, claiming that there was 'great clamour throughout the realm' at the household's failure to pay its debts.[18]

Such concern was sharpened by fear of a repetition of the mob violence which had accompanied the 1381 revolt. The revolution itself saw widespread looting, barely brought under control before the lynching of the rebel earls at Cirencester, Pleshey and Bristol in January 1400.[19] Although necessary in the circumstances, declared Adam Usk, this 'fury of the common people (*plebeiorum*)' was 'contrary to the natural order' and 'might at some future time embolden them to rise up against the lords'.[20] The

---

[15] *POPC*, i.152; ii.57, 62; *RHL*, i.73, 85.

[16] Steel, *Receipt*, 86–7 (borrowing); *POPC*, i.155–64; *ANLP*, 331; *Usk*, 144–5. Kirby, *Henry IV*, 128, implies that the budgetary calculations in *POPC*, i.154 were presented at this council, but the figures given for Ireland and Guyenne appear to predate the appointments of Thomas of Lancaster in May and Rutland in July.

[17] *RHKA*, 94, 116, 271, 278; *POPC*, i.181–2; *CPR 1399–1401*, 445, 475, 489–90, 504, 513, 515, 536. Economies were achieved mainly by establishing tighter exchequer supervision of household accounting procedures, by ring-fencing sources from which the household could draw cash, and by cutting back on courtly extravagance. There may also have been a reduction in the number of household staff, although this still stood at 528 in 1402. Yet the fall in household expenditure was partly offset by the fact that Prince Henry now had his own household which needed to be funded: in 1402–3 the prince's household treasurer, Simon Bache, received £3,025 and spent £2,963 (E 101/404/23).

[18] *SAC II*, 314; *PROME*, viii.208, 216; Steel, *Receipt*, 85–7; *RHKA*, 112; *An English Chronicle 1377–1461*, ed. W. Marx (Woodbridge, 2003), 29.

[19] Above, p. 162.

[20] *Usk*, 88–91.

council which met in early February thought likewise: while rewarding the men of Cirencester for their loyalty, it forbade people to take the law into their own hands and threatened exemplary punishment (even the penalties for treason) for those who disobeyed. Sheriffs and justices of the peace were ordered to suppress unlawful gatherings, and in order to discourage malicious accusations of involvement in the rising a general pardon was proclaimed for crimes committed before 2 February.[21] Yet further violence soon followed. In April 1400 an outbreak of fighting between gangs of London apprentice-boys caused numerous deaths, prompting the king's intervention with the city authorities.[22] Frome, the nodal point for the Somerset cloth industry, had been restless since the summer of 1399, when the townspeople took advantage of the confusion to imprison the king's ministers and destroy the town's guildhall. The chief justice of the King's Bench, Walter Clopton, was sent to quell the riots, but not until November 1400 did the citizens sue for pardon.[23] Here and at Bristol, which also saw disturbances, anger focused especially on the cloth tax the king was believed to have rescinded.[24] It was while attempting to collect this that the unfortunate Thomas Newton was hacked to death in the marketplace at Norton St Philip (Somerset) 'with more than a hundred mortal wounds', prompting the king to visit the town in person, although on this occasion he opted for leniency.[25] South Wales also saw attacks on royal officials, possibly linked to the new outbreak of revolt in the north; at Usk, in April 1401, the burgesses broke into the town gaol to release a prisoner, while a month later at Abergavenny the sheriff of Hereford, Sir William Lucy, was lynched just as he was about to hang three robbers, and the lord, Sir William Beauchamp, briefly besieged in his castle.[26] Around London and in the West Midlands, bands of highwaymen were terrorizing travellers and threatening royal officials.[27] A gang led by one John Garbour broke into the precinct of

---

[21] *POPC*, i.107–13, 118–19; E 404/15, no. 143; *CPR 1399–1401*, 183; *Foedera*, viii.124. The general pardon excluded the county of Chester, and certain individuals to be named by the king. For examples of malicious accusations of involvement, see *Foedera*, viii.168–9, 176, and *CCR 1399–1402*, 137–8.

[22] *Usk*, 94–6; *SAC II*, 301; *Foedera*, viii.139.

[23] *CPR 1399–1401*, 267; E 28/8, no. 19; Walker, 'Rumour, Sedition and Popular Protest', 49–50.

[24] E 403/569, 27 March; *CPR 1399–1401*, 315; Wylie, *Henry the Fourth*, i.198; *PROME*, viii.58, and *Vita*, 163 (relaxation of the cloth subsidy in 1399); *PROME*, viii.104–5, for Bristol and Frome as centres of unrest.

[25] *Usk*, 128–31; *CPR 1399–1401*, 516–17, 520–1.

[26] *Usk*, 132–3.

[27] *CPR 1399–1401*, 413, 418, 552; Wylie, *Henry the Fourth*, i.191–8; *Crime, Law and Society in the Later Middle Ages*, ed. A. Musson with E. Powell (Manchester, 2009), 92–4, 147–8.

Ramsey abbey and killed one of the monks and several of the abbot's servants.[28] An epidemic of plague and widespread harvest failure in the autumn
of 1400 exacerbated the sense of insecurity, while 1402 saw a catastrophic
fall in wool production owing to flooding and disease.[29]

Early in May 1401 the collapse of order persuaded Philip Repingdon –
abbot of Leicester, close friend and future confessor of the king – to send
Henry a stark admonition about his failure to uphold the law. The great
hopes he had raised in 1399, wrote Repingdon, were quite dashed: law and
justice were exiles from the kingdom, while murder, robbery, persecution of
the poor and outrages of all kinds abounded, so that the will of the tyrant
had replaced the rule of law. As a punishment, God had permitted the
common people to usurp the natural authority of their superiors and
become 'senseless and uncontrollable like wild beasts', and if the king
failed to curb this insubordination, a more terrible and comprehensive
divine vengeance would shortly follow, similar to that which had befallen
Richard II. Quoting copiously from the bible, Repingdon apologized for
his bluntness but reminded the king that it was better to be told the truth by
a loyal friend than 'betrayed with flattering kisses like the traitor Judas',
which (he implied) was what other courtiers did. It was a letter that a king
might expect to receive from his confessor – his 'conscience' – but that does
not make the sentiments Repingdon expressed less authentic.[30] The appointment two weeks later of powerful new commissions of the peace suggests
that Henry took the advice to heart, but silencing the 'lies, so light of foot,
they leap to the skies', was harder.[31] The brutal execution of William Clerk,
a scribe from Cheshire who was sentenced in the Court of Chivalry to have
his tongue cut out for speaking ill of the king, his hand severed for committing his thoughts to parchment, and his head cut off because he was unable
to prove his allegations, was one way to tackle the problem, but aroused
indignation at the extension of the court's jurisdiction.[32]

---

[28] KB 9/186, no. 76 (and no. 78 for a similar 'insurrection' against Muchelney abbey in
Somerset).

[29] *Great Chronicle of London*, 84; *Usk*, 98; Bradley, 'The Datini Factors in London', 60–1.

[30] *Usk*, 136–43. Repingdon was certainly Henry's confessor three years later, and may well
have been acting in that capacity already; P. Strohm, *England's Empty Throne 1399–1422*
(London, 1998), 174–8, emphasizes the deference displayed in his letter, despite its overtly
admonitory subject-matter.

[31] For the commissions, see *CPR 1399–1401*, 556–67, and Rogers, 'Political Crisis of 1401',
90; for the quote, *Mum and the Sothsegger*, 67–8.

[32] *Usk*, 122–3. Cf. the commission to Northumberland, the constable and thus president
of the Court of Chivalry, to hear cases touching the 'estate, fame and condition of the
king's person and the dignity of the crown' on 4 February 1401; Clerk was executed eleven
days later (*CPR 1399–1401*, 458). For concern about the Court of Chivalry in the parliament
then meeting, see *PROME*, viii.143.

A flurry of rumours, prophecies and portents around this time reflected the pervasive sense of foreboding.[33] The appearance of the devil at Danbury (Essex), of an evil spirit and an apocalyptic thunderstorm at Hertford, and of the *cometam terribilem* which evoked so much speculation as it blazed across the European sky during the spring of 1402 all indicated that the times were out of joint.[34] Even the weather was seen as evidence of God's displeasure with Henry: since he had come to the throne, according to the wife of a tailor from Baldock (Hertfordshire), there had been barely seven days of seasonable weather, the moral of which was that the earl of March was the rightful king of England, Owain the rightful prince of Wales (and Cornwall), and Henry himself a changeling. The pope, she declared, supported the claims of both March and Glyn Dŵr.[35] The power of supernatural 'signs' to shape actions should not be underestimated: Henry's own confidence in the miraculous qualities of Becket's oil did nothing to discourage belief in the validity of prognostication.

By the spring of 1402, popular and political discontent had found a common focus in the belief that Richard II was still alive in Scotland and awaiting the opportunity to return and claim his rightful inheritance. On 9 May, Henry told the authorities in the northern counties to try to stop the story filtering southwards, but just two days later commissions were issued to all the English sheriffs ordering the suppression of alehouse gossip to the effect that Henry had not kept the promises he made at his coronation.[36] Yet far from subsiding, the rumours now reached a crescendo: Richard, it was believed, would time his reappearance in England for the feast of the Nativity of St John the Baptist (24 June), whereupon Henry would flee across the Channel and marry the duchess of Brittany, a voyage for which he was already believed to be preparing.[37] As with so many rumours there was a kernel of truth to this, for Henry was indeed planning to marry Joan, dowager duchess of Brittany, but needless to say Richard failed to make his appearance at midsummer.[38]

---

[33] Given-Wilson, *Chronicles*, 29–32.

[34] *SAC II*, 317, 321–5; *Usk*, 116, 154–6; *CE*, 389. The comet of 1402 was Halley's comet.

[35] *Select Cases in King's Bench VII*, ed. Sayles, 123–4. The tailor's wife is not named, but John Sparrowhawk of Cardiff, who repeated the rumours publicly, was condemned to a traitor's death in April 1402. The accusation of being a changeling, the son of a butcher from Ghent, was originally made against Gaunt himself (*SAC I*, 60).

[36] *Foedera*, viii.255, 261–2; *CPR 1401–5*, 126: 'gatherings in taverns and other congregations of the people' were to be monitored.

[37] *Select Cases in King's Bench VII*, ed. Sayles, 126–8; *CPR 1401–5*, 99–100.

[38] For Henry's marriage to Joan, see below, pp. 234–5.

The grid along which these stories travelled comprised mainly Franciscan and Dominican friars, whose itinerant lifestyle and confessional rapport with both rich and poor provided them with the opportunities to disseminate them. Why they wished to do so is less clear, although one Franciscan from Aylesbury (Buckinghamshire), when interrogated by Henry, maintained that his order had enjoyed the special favour of King Richard.[39] In fact, during the first two years of his reign Henry had shown considerable goodwill to the friars, taking them under his protection, prohibiting slander against them, and granting alms to a number of friaries.[40] Nevertheless, by the spring of 1402 friars from many parts of England – Winchester, Cambridge, Norfolk, Nottingham, Stamford, Leicester, Northampton – were alleged not only to be claiming that Richard was alive but raising money to be sent to Glyn Dŵr and plotting to kill the king.[41] At least eleven of them, mainly Franciscans from Leicester, were arrested at the beginning of June, among them their warden, Roger Frisby, whom the king interviewed before his trial. Frisby, a master of theology and casuistry, stated that Richard's return was foretold in the Bridlington Prophecy.[42] 'Do you say that Richard is alive?' asked the king. 'I do not say that he is alive,' replied Frisby, 'but I say that if he is, he is the rightful king of England.' When Henry pointed out that Richard had abdicated, Frisby responded that he had not been at liberty at the time and thus his abdication was not lawful, which made Henry a usurper. 'I did not usurp the crown, I was properly elected,' rejoined Henry. 'That election means nothing if the rightful incumbent is alive,' retorted Frisby, 'and if he is dead, then you killed him, and if you killed him you lose any title or right you have to the kingdom.' 'That is a lie. Be gone!' concluded Henry. A few days later, Frisby and his fellows were drawn from the Tower to Tyburn and there hanged and beheaded, along with various others caught up in the web of speculation, including Walter of Baldock, former prior of the Augustinian house at Launde (Leicestershire), and Sir Roger Clarendon, a renegade bastard of the Black Prince (and thus half-brother to Richard II), along with two of his servants.[43] In total, the Ricardian fever of April/May 1402

---

[39] CE, 390.

[40] Although the Franciscans of Llanfaes (Anglesey) had been driven out or executed for supporting Glyn Dŵr in September 1400, Henry took the view that this had more to do with their Welshness than their fraternal profession: Foedera, viii.189; CPR 1399–1401, 65, 199, 289, 418 (Llanfaes), 485; CE, 388–9; E 403/571, 21 November, 15 December (50 marks a year to the Oxford Franciscans, £20 a year to the London Dominicans).

[41] Wylie, Henry the Fourth, i.269–79.

[42] CE, 391–2.

[43] C. Given-Wilson, 'Sir Roger Clarendon', ODNB, 11.770.

claimed around twenty victims before Henry had it proclaimed on 18 June that the ringleaders had been dealt with and that he did not intend to proceed against those who had heard or repeated their stories without seditious intent.[44]

The bushfire of rumours clearly unnerved the king. The burgeoning belief in the possibility of Richard's restoration was an indication of the failure of the Lancastrian regime to secure the popular legitimacy it craved. The friars' exhortations were not accompanied by any political programme. What they offered was simply an alternative version of legitimate government, one which evidently still commanded loyalist sympathies.[45] The original jury before which Frisby and his fellows appeared, composed of citizens of London and Holborn, refused to serve, so new jurors had to be brought in from Islington and Highgate, and even they later apologized in tears to the Franciscans, insisting that had they not returned guilty verdicts they would have lost their own lives.[46] It was not just armed insurrection that Henry had to fear: passive resistance, rumour and gossip could also make his kingdom ungovernable. Popular unrest, stirred up by the revolution of 1399, the defiance of local interest groups, the bad harvests and the high price of grain, was increasingly sidling up to high politics to present a threat the government could not ignore. The amnesty proclaimed by Henry on 18 June sounded more edgy than authoritative. Nor did it quell the rumours, which before long found expression in the mouths of men far more influential than friars, men such as Edmund Mortimer and Hotspur, and echoes of which would continue to reverberate not just until the end of Henry's reign but into his son's as well.[47]

It was the twin issues of insolvency and lawlessness that dominated the proceedings of the parliament that met at Westminster on 30 September 1402. That the commons would be asked to grant taxation was a foregone conclusion, and they duly did so, though not without 'great difficulty', nor without concessions from the king. The king's friend Henry Bowet, who had replaced Allerthorpe as treasurer in February 1402, was in turn

[44] *Foedera*, viii.262.

[45] Walker, 'Rumour, Sedition and Popular Protest', 46. Another friar, when asked by Henry, 'And what would you do with me if you triumphed over me?', replied, 'I would make you duke of Lancaster'.

[46] *CE*, 393–4.

[47] For Edmund Mortimer, see above, p. 195 Rumours that Richard was alive were last heard in 1417: P. McNiven, 'Rebellion, Sedition and the Legend of Richard II's Survival in the Reigns of Henry IV and Henry V', *BJRL* 76 (1994), 93–117; Walker, 'Rumour, Sedition and Popular Protest', 41–2.

removed on 24 October and replaced by Guy Mone, bishop of St David's, making 1402 a year of three treasurers; as in 1401, the commons were showing their preference for a tried and tested minister of Richard II over a Lancastrian protégé.[48] There were predictable, though doubtless heart-felt, pleas to the king to restrain his generosity, to pay for his household provisions, to resume more alien priories so that their revenues could be used to pay his debts, and to introduce a more equitable system for priori-tizing the payment of annuities according to length of service, a conse-quence of the over-assignment with which all exchequer creditors had to contend.[49] The speaker, Sir Henry Retford, then once again asked the king what had become of Richard II's treasure: the response, according to one chronicler, was that it had been given to the earl of Northumberland 'and others'; when the commons asked the king whether, 'since much had been handed over to him but he himself had nothing', they could question his ministers, Henry refused.[50] In the end, however, a fifteenth and tenth was granted, and with convocation also granting one and a half clerical tenths the exchequer could anticipate receiving around £60,000 during the course of the winter.

Prioritization of the question of law and order was signalled from the outset of the session in the sermon delivered by the chancellor, the bishop of Exeter, the theme of which was 'Great peace have they which love the law'.[51] Every man must keep the law, he declared, and he who does not must be punished; it was the 'importunate and insatiable greed and avarice of the common people, as well as of other great men' which had destroyed Rome. That great men were as guilty of law-breaking as common people was not a fact of which the commons needed to be reminded, for it was principally against noble and gentry gang-masters that the livery laws of 1399 and 1401 had been aimed, prohibiting lords of any degree from giving out livery badges.[52] Yet to hold high-born offenders to account was never easy, so it is not surprising that when an opportunity now arose to bring one notorious offender to justice, it was seized upon. Sir Philip Courtenay,

---

[48] *Vita*, 175; *PROME*, viii.175–6 (154–220 for the full proceedings); E 403/574, 24 Oct. The wool customs and tunnage and poundage were also renewed for three years. Mone had served as treasurer in 1398.

[49] *PROME*, viii.171, 188, 208, 210, 216; Henry agreed that older annuities should be paid before more recent ones, but that assignments for the household should be paid before either.

[50] *CE*, 395.

[51] Psalm 119: 165; *PROME*, viii.158.

[52] *RHKA*, 236–43; N. Saul, 'The Commons and the Abolition of Badges', *Parliamentary History* 9 (1990), 302–15.

fifth son of the earl of Devon, was a man who believed in conciliation only once the alternatives had been exhausted, and had for some time been waging a campaign of intimidation against his Devonshire neighbours, including the sheriff, Sir Thomas Pomeroy.[53] Pomeroy was no innocent himself and had employed similar tactics to enforce his claims elsewhere, but on this occasion was probably more sinned against than sinning. Their quarrel centred on the Chudleigh inheritance, for Pomeroy and John Courtenay, Sir Philip's second son, had both married into the family and claimed rights in Joan Chudleigh's dower.[54] Waiting until Pomeroy was in Wales with the king, the Courtenays took twenty or so armed accomplices and ejected his family and servants from half a dozen properties in and around Exeter, carrying off the deeds and muniments relating to them so that Pomeroy could not defend himself at law. Nicholas Pontington, a local esquire, was another man whose estates Courtenay coveted: denouncing his father as a bastard (and thus unable to inherit), Courtenay packed the jury empanelled to hear the case and secured a release of the property by going to the house of Pontington's cousin Thomas as he lay on his deathbed. Then, in June 1401, Courtenay led sixty men to the Cistercian abbey of Newenham, near Axminster, imprisoned the abbot for two weeks and abducted two of his monks whom he forced to become his huntsmen, which was contrary to Cistercian rules. His objective was to be recognized as patron of the abbey, and probably to overturn the election of the abbot, who denied his claim to patronage. In the 1402 parliament his victims teamed up, each presenting a petition which was forwarded by the commons to the lords. The problem, as the abbot explained, was that Sir Philip was 'so powerful in his lordship and in his maintenance in the said county [Devon]' that the common law was impotent against him. The same could doubtless have been said of many such men in many counties. The abbot might have added that much tended to be forgiven Sir Philip because of his usefulness to the government: he was a former admiral and lieutenant of Ireland, and was now actively engaged in helping to suppress rebellion in Wales. And so it was again: confronted by his victims, Courtenay admitted his crimes and was sent to the Tower, but three weeks later, on the

---

[53] *HOC*, ii.670–3 ('his predilection for violence and thuggery was extreme even by medieval standards'). Philip's father, Edward, earl of Devon, was accused of intimidatory violence against Sir William Esturmy in 1392: *Select Cases before the King's Council 1243–1482*, ed. I. Leadam and J. Baldwin (Selden Society, London, 1918), 77–81.

[54] *HOC*, iv.109–10; E 28/23, no. 68. Pomeroy was knighted on the 1400 Scottish campaign and given lands in Devon for his service (*CPR 1399–1401*, 390; *CPR 1401–5*, 44). He was sheriff of Devon in 1401–2, but removed after six months in office.

final day of the parliament, the king agreed at the request of the lords to release him on surety of £1,000. Men of his experience were too valuable to be locked away for long.[55]

Friars and Welshmen were easier to deal with, provided they could be caught. A further nine anti-Welsh statutes were passed (most of which simply gave statutory authority to the ordinances issued by the council of March 1401), and a statute against Glyn Dŵr's alleged accomplices, the mendicants, set a minimum age of fourteen for entry into the fraternal orders. Although there had long been suspicions that the friars enticed children to join them, what they were really being held to account for was the treason of some of their members earlier in the year. The provincials of the four mendicant orders were brought into parliament and, 'placing their right hands on their breasts', swore to uphold the new law.[56] At the same time, Archbishop Arundel was given notice that if he could not find a solution to the age-old problem of benefit of clergy – the right of felonious clerics not to suffer corporal or capital punishment – before the next parliament, Henry would do it himself 'in such a way as shall become evident'.[57]

Even the one piece of good news, the victory of the Percys at Humbleton Hill, turned sour on the king. On Friday 20 October, three weeks into the session, four Scottish and three French prisoners taken at the battle were led into the White Chamber and paraded before the lords and commons before bowing three times to Henry and 'most humbly' begging him to treat them according to the law of arms. Chief among them was Albany's son, Murdoch Stewart, but it was Sir Adam Forrester – the man who had assured Henry in Edinburgh in August 1400 that consideration would be given to his claim to overlordship of Scotland – who acted as their spokesman: if the king wished to avoid the spilling of more Christian blood, he declared, this was an ideal moment to conclude a truce or perhaps even a final peace. This clearly riled Henry – and perhaps not surprisingly, given the hawkishness of Scottish policy during the past year. Forrester, he declared, had 'by many white lies and subtle promises . . . suddenly caused the king to leave the said land of Scotland' [in August 1400], and had he known Sir Adam then as well as he did now he would certainly not have withdrawn so hastily. To this Forrester could only

[55] PROME, viii.165–70, 176.

[56] PROME, viii.156–7, 195–6, 208–11; Davies, Revolt, 285. Anti-Welsh sentiment was high, with reports of men alleged to be Welsh killed around Oxford and in the border counties (SC 1/43/61).

[57] PROME, viii.177–9. See below for benefit of clergy, pp. 348–52.

apologize, and once he had done so Henry's tone softened markedly, even
to the point of inviting the prisoners to dine with him in the Painted
Chamber.[58]

Too sensitive to be recorded officially was the absence of the earl of
Douglas. Bridling at Henry's injunction against ransoming his prisoners,
Hotspur had remained in the north and was refusing to hand over his prize
captive. Yet he was certainly not absent from the thoughts of those present,
or at least not those of Dunbar, who submitted a petition asking Henry
whether, 'if you, or other lords of the realm on your behalf, should conquer
all or part of the realm of Scotland, that the said supplicant [Dunbar] can
have and enjoy all his castles, lordships and lands which are in the aforesaid
realm of Scotland, should you or any other person whatsoever conquer the
said castles, lordships and lands, or any of them'.

Henry was quick to reassure him, emphasizing that if he or anyone
under his command conquered any of Dunbar's castles or lordships, they
would be returned to him 'to be held of our said lord the king as of his
crown'.[59] If one implication of this carefully worded petition was that the
English were now planning the annexation of southern Scotland, another
was that Dunbar wished to ensure that others – and he can only have
meant the Percys – would not be given licence to hold on to whatever they
might conquer. As in 1399, the king was proclaiming his determination to
keep an eye on Percy ambitions.

Despite Hotspur's absence, he and Henry did apparently meet soon
after parliament ended, and although Henry assured the Percys that their
rights in their prisoners would be respected, the encounter was a stormy
one. According to Hardyng, Hotspur accused the king of dishonouring
himself by not ransoming Edmund Mortimer, while Henry blamed
Hotspur for not seizing Glyn Dŵr when he had had the chance and
refusing to hand over Douglas. A more theatrical version of the meeting
had Henry calling Hotspur a traitor and threatening him with a dagger, to
which Hotspur replied 'Not here, but on the battlefield'. It is a story redolent with hindsight, but nevertheless indicative of the breakdown in their
relationship. Their next meeting would be at the battle of Shrewsbury.[60]

---

[58] *PROME*, viii.162–3.
[59] *PROME*, viii.174–5. For the commons' support for Dunbar, see *SAC II*, 338.
[60] *Hardyng*, 360–1; *CE*, 396; *English Chronicle*, 33. For discussion, see R. Ambuhl, *Prisoners of War in the Hundred Years War: Ransom Culture in the Late Middle Ages* (Cambridge, 2013), 58–61. The fact that Hotspur sent Henry a horse (*cursorem*) as a gift at this time suggests that their relationship had not yet broken down completely (E 101/404/21, fo. 49r).

Chapter 15

FROM HUMBLETON HILL TO
HATELEY FIELD (1403)

For the next few months, the disagreement with Hotspur over his prisoner remained in abeyance. Following the dissolution of parliament on 25 November, Henry spent Christmas and New Year at Windsor before setting off in mid-January 1403 to greet his new queen, Joan of Navarre, the widow of the duke of Brittany. They were married on 7 February in Winchester cathedral, and on 26 February Joan was crowned as queen of England at Westminster abbey.[1] Barely had the celebrations finished before Henry was back at work. Among those who attended the coronation was the earl of Northumberland, who four days later received a grant from Henry, the scope of which matched the Scottish pretensions of Edward I or Edward III in its audacity. For his victory at Humbleton Hill and other 'great labours' in Scotland, Northumberland was given the earldom of Douglas in its entirety, including Eskdale, Liddesdale, Lauderdale, Selkirk, Ettrick Forest and Teviotdale, all of which were simultaneously annexed to the English crown. Northumberland was thus to hold everything currently held either by the earl of Douglas or by his mother.[2] Neither of them, it can safely be assumed, had been consulted; nor had the Scottish king. A week after this, on 9 March, Henry set up a commission to decide all outstanding claims relating to the prisoners taken at Humbleton Hill. Northumberland and Hotspur were not appointed to this, on the grounds that 'they cannot act honestly on account of their own interests'. This may well have piqued them, although the earl of Westmorland was also

---

[1] For the king's second marriage, see below, pp. 234–5; M. Jones, 'Joan of Navarre, Queen of England', *ODNB*, 30.139–41; Kirby, *Henry IV*, 150. For Joan's escort from Brittany, see E 403/574, 27 and 30 October 1401; for £23 worth of cloth used to pave Winchester cathedral for the wedding, E 101/404/21, fo. 40v; BL Harley MS 279, fos. 45–6, reproduces the menu at the wedding banquet. The coronation was followed by jousts at which Richard Beauchamp, the twenty-one-year-old earl of Warwick, acted as Joan's champion.

[2] *Foedera*, viii.289–90. The grant, dated 2 March at Westminster, excluded Galloway and Annandale, Roxburgh and any other lands previously granted to the Neville family.

excluded, apparently at his own request. It indicates at any rate that the matter was far from resolved.[3]

The grant had a twofold objective: to seize the initiative by reasserting long-standing English territorial claims north of the Tweed–Solway line, and to mollify Northumberland at a time when relations with the Percys were becoming strained. His family had long nurtured ambitions to extend its territorial power north of the border. Northumberland's grandfather (Henry Lord Percy, d.1352) was one of only three English magnates whose rights to their Scottish lands were recognized by Robert Bruce in 1328, a concession which Percy surrendered to Edward III six years later in return for the castle and forest of Jedburgh, 500 marks a year from the customs of Berwick-upon-Tweed, and the keeping of Berwick castle.[4] Jedburgh yielded little to the Percys during the fourteenth century (save to provide another cause of dispute with the Douglases), but they continued to claim their 500 marks annuity from the Berwick customs.[5] The transfer by Northumberland of his rights in Jedburgh and of this annuity to his brother Thomas in October 1397, just three weeks after the latter became earl of Worcester, gave another Percy a stake in the politics of the Scottish border, which as a younger son he had hitherto lacked, but the grant of the Douglas earldom in March 1403 raised Percy – and by extension English – ambitions in the southern uplands to a different level.[6] With Earl Archibald a prisoner in England and George Dunbar acknowledging the lordship of the English crown, Henry IV now had the chance to impose a degree of control over the border region such as Edward III had briefly achieved seventy years earlier. That the prospect of such a radical reordering of territorial interests in the region should generate rivalries is hardly surprising. Dunbar clearly felt uneasy about the potential impact of Percy expansion on his own earldom (which bordered Lauderdale); one chronicler even thought that he desired Hotspur's death 'so that he could more easily reign in Northumbria'.[7] Meanwhile, the transfer in March 1402 of Roxburgh castle from Hotspur's hands to those of Westmorland (with the

[3] *CPR 1401–5*, 213.

[4] Stones, *Anglo-Scottish Relations*, 342–5; Bean, 'The Percies and their Estates in Scotland', 91–9.

[5] See, for example, *CDS*, iv, no. 281 (1379).

[6] *CPR 1396–9*, 223 (19 October 1397); A. L. Brown, 'Thomas Percy, Earl of Worcester', *ODNB*, 43.737–9. However, Northumberland did not transfer the captaincy of Berwick castle to his brother.

[7] *Giles*, 33. See also the comment of Dunbar's wife shortly after the battle of Shrewsbury, that people 'bear us great enmity for the death of Sir Henry Percy' (*RHL I*, 301).

strikingly generous fee of 4,000 marks a year) added fuel to a rivalry which until now had largely been contained.[8]

There was little to be gained by waiting, and in April 1403 Hotspur crossed the border into Teviotdale and laid siege to Cocklaw Tower near Hawick.[9] The garrison proved hard to dislodge, however, and after a few weeks he agreed with the captain, John de Grymslaw, to suspend the assault, but that if a Scottish force did not arrive to relieve Cocklaw before 1 August it would be surrendered. News of Hotspur's compact reached London in early June, by which time the duke of Albany, with his and the realm's honour at stake, was already making plans to raise a relief force. On the English side, said Walsingham, there was scarcely a magnate, not even the king, who did not wish to take part in what promised to be a grand chivalric encounter.[10]

For the moment, though, Henry had much else to occupy him, especially Owain Glyn Dŵr, whose followers were harrying English garrisons throughout Wales.[11] For the past two years, Henry had relied principally on the Percys to coordinate the English military response, with Hotspur serving as lieutenant in North Wales and Worcester in South Wales, but on 1 April 1403 Prince Henry, now sixteen, took up office as royal lieutenant throughout Wales with an annual fee of £8,108, sufficient to maintain a force of 500 men-at-arms and 2,500 archers.[12] April and May saw him achieve some military successes: forces were sent to relieve Harlech and Aberystwyth, and Glyn Dŵr's estates at Sycharth and Glyndyfrdwy were laid waste, but by the time the prince returned to his headquarters at Shrewsbury in mid-May, Owain was already gathering a new force said to be 8,240 men strong. At the beginning of July, he marched triumphantly down the Tywi valley, precipitating the collapse of English administration in the region.[13] Dryslwyn, Newcastle Emlyn, and even Carmarthen fell to his men, and Dinefwr, Kidwelly, Llandovery and Brecon were besieged. On 5 July, John Skidmore wrote from Carreg Cennen saying that 'all of Carmarthenshire, Cydweli, Carnwyllian and Iscennen yesterday swore themselves to Owain'. Three days later Richard Kingston wrote to the

[8] E 403/571, 1 March; E 403/574, 9 Dec.; Bean, 'Henry Percy, First Earl of Northumberland', *ODNB* 43.694–702.

[9] *Scotichronicon*, viii.49–53, said he was confident of rapidly conquering southern Scotland.

[10] *SAC II*, 356–7; *POPC*, i.203–4; Boardman, *Early Stewart Kings*, 270–1.

[11] Davies, *Revolt*, 111–13.

[12] E 101/404/24 (roll of the prince's household), fo. 1, records his receipt of £2,666 on 12 June. Payments of over £7,000 to the prince are recorded on the exchequer issue rolls, but these included several failed assignments (E 403/574 and 576, 22 Feb., 26 March, 12 June).

[13] Davies, *Revolt*, 112; *Original Letters*, i.11–12.

king from Hereford telling him that if he did not come to Wales at once the whole country would be lost, adding ominously that 'people talk very unfavourably'; he advised Henry to march day and night to get there, 'for if you come yourself with haste, everything else will follow from that'.[14]

It was not the king who was making his way towards Wales, however, but Hotspur. Leaving affairs in the north in his father's hands, he came south 'with a small following, feigning peace' during the first week of July, but having arrived at Chester (of which he was still justiciar) on Monday 9 July, he set about proclaiming that Richard II was still alive and that all those who wished to overthrow King Henry should make their way to Sandiway, a dozen miles east of Chester, where the former king would be arriving, along with the earl of Northumberland and a large army, on 17 July.[15] A 'multitude of fools of both sexes' – the Dieulacres chronicler's words – duly made their way to Sandiway, but once again Richard failed to appear and instead they found themselves conscripted (some, but by no means all, unwillingly) into an insurrectionary army. For Hotspur to recruit the bulk of his forces in Cheshire made good sense. The favoured status the county had enjoyed under Richard II had not been forgotten; nor had the pillaging of Henry's troops in August 1399.[16] Cheshiremen, especially Cheshire archers, also enjoyed a high military reputation. Hotspur's next move, which was to march his army, now several thousand strong, southwards along the Welsh border to Shrewsbury, also made good sense. His aim was to confront what he believed to be the only significant royalist force in the Midlands, the 3,000 or so men with Prince Henry, and to overwhelm it before the king had a chance to react.

It was widely believed that Hotspur was acting in collusion with Glyn Dŵr and Edmund Mortimer, an impression not dispelled by the coincidence of timing between his arrival from the north and Owain's march down the Tywi valley at the beginning of July.[17] On the other hand, the fact that Glyn Dŵr was marching westwards towards Pembrokeshire during the second week of July, *away* from the English border, indicates either that

[14] *Original Letters*, 14–20.

[15] Clarke and Galbraith, 'Deposition of Richard II' (*Dieulacres Chronicle*), 177–8; Hotspur spent the night of 9 July with Petronilla Clerk of Chester, who later lost her property for harbouring him: E. J. Priestley, *The Battle of Shrewsbury 1403* (Shrewsbury, 1979), 8.

[16] Above, p. 133. Morgan, *War and Society*, 212–18. Yet Cheshire was by no means solidly for the revolt; Sir John Stanley, for example, former lieutenant of Ireland, fought for the royalist side at Shrewsbury.

[17] *SAC II*, 359; *CE*, 396; *CPR 1401–5*, 391, records the forfeiture of William Lloyd, a Denbigh esquire said to have acted as a messenger between Hotspur and Glyn Dŵr; he fought and died with Hotspur at Shrewsbury; Hotspur may also have tried to raise Anglesey against the king: R. Griffiths, *Conquerors and Conquered in Medieval Wales* (Stroud, 1994), 126.

something had gone awry with their plans or that they were predicated not on a rendezvous but on diversionary activity.[18] Hotspur did, however, meet up with his uncle Thomas, earl of Worcester, Prince Henry's governor and second-in-command of his army. Worcester's decision to join his nephew was evidently not a spur of the moment decision.[19] Like Hotspur, he may have resented having to cede control of operations in Wales to the sixteen-year-old prince. As Hotspur led his troops towards Shrewsbury, Worcester slipped away to the north of the town; by 20 July at the latest he had joined the rebel army, taking with him many of the 260 men-at-arms and archers he had retained for the prince's campaign and perhaps other disaffected soldiers as well.[20]

Yet there was one eventuality which Hotspur and Worcester had overlooked: the arrival in the Midlands of the king. Since his wedding in February, Henry had remained close to London, staying mainly at Eltham and Windsor, keeping in touch with the Anglo-French negotiations at Leulinghem. These were concluded with a truce on 27 June.[21] A few days before this Henry had written to inform Northumberland that he did not plan to come north for the anticipated battle against the Scots at Cocklaw. The earl was probably relieved to hear this, and when he replied to Henry on 26 June from Heelaugh (Yorkshire), it was not to try to change his mind but to request money with which to pay his own troops; indeed Walsingham claimed that Northumberland discouraged Henry from coming north, since it would not be advisable for him to 'desert his country'.[22] Yet within a day or two of receiving the earl's letter, Henry had changed his mind,

[18] P. McNiven, 'The Scottish Policy of the Percies and the Strategy of the Rebellion of 1403', *BJRL* 62 (1969–70), 498–530, at pp. 518–20. It may have been the military check suffered by Owain's followers on 11–12 July, when Baron Carew intercepted and slaughtered about 700 of them, that persuaded him to change his plans (*Original Letters*, i.21–2). It was also said that while at Carmarthen (5–6 July) Owain sent for Hopkin ap Thomas, a 'Master of Brut' (scholar of prophecy), to ask him to predict his future; Hopkin told him that he was shortly going to be captured, between Carmarthen and Gower, under a black banner. Given Owain's predilection for prophecy, this might have induced him to change his plans (although Shrewsbury was obviously not between Carmarthen and Gower).

[19] Walsingham said Worcester brought money with him from London to pay his nephew's troops (*SAC II*, 359).

[20] For Thomas Percy's retinue, see E 101/404/24, fo. 4 and roll 2: he was contracted to bring 40 men-at-arms and 200 archers, but seems to have had 48 men-at-arms and 212 archers. The scores of men listed on fos. 8–10 who received no wages after 24 June *pro prodicione* ('for treason') probably include many of his retainers, although others were paid up to 17 July, indicating that they declined to join the earl in abandoning the prince.

[21] For the king's movements, see E 101/404/21. A great council was summoned to Westminster on 28 May to discuss the Anglo-French talks: E 403/576, 25 May.

[22] *SAC II*, 357; *POPC*, i.204–5.

presumably as a result of the conclusion of the French negotiations.[23] It was certainly a hasty decision, leaving him no time to raise an army of any size. On 1 July he was still in London. By 9 July – the day Hotspur arrived at Chester – the king had reached Higham Ferrers (Northamptonshire), whence he wrote to London asking the council to send Prince Henry £1,000 as soon as possible while he continued northwards 'in order to give aid and comfort to our very dear and faithful cousins the earl of Northumberland and his son at the battle honourably undertaken by them for us and our realm against our enemies the Scots', after which he planned to proceed directly to Wales.[24]

For two more days Henry continued north, reaching Nottingham on 12 July. It was here that he heard of Hotspur's revolt, and on the following day turned sharply west to Derby and then Burton-on-Trent, despatching messengers to the prince and writs to sheriffs, magnates and royal annuitants ordering them to come immediately to the king 'to resist the malice of Henry Percy, who is referring to us merely as Henry of Lancaster and is issuing proclamations throughout Cheshire that King Richard is still alive'. The council was told to raise as much as it could in loans to pay the royalist troops, and a royal sumpterman was sent to spy on Hotspur's movements.[25] The 17 and 18 July were spent at Lichfield and the next night at St Thomas's priory near Stafford, probably to allow time for Henry's supporters to join him, but thoughts of further delay were dispelled by George Dunbar, who told the king that if he did not act swiftly Hotspur's army was only likely to grow.[26] By 20 July both armies had arrived outside Shrewsbury.

Henry's rapid advance surprised Hotspur, who had been preparing to besiege Prince Henry in Shrewsbury but now retreated a few miles

---

[23] Added, perhaps, to the fact that he was quite incapable of providing the earl with the £20,000 he had requested in order 'to preserve the good name of the chivalry of your realm'.

[24] *POPC*, i.206–7.

[25] *POPC*, i.207–9; *Foedera*, viii.313–14. A group of London merchants loaned £1,000 almost immediately: £666 was delivered to the king at Burton and £666 to the prince at Shrewsbury. On the same day, £666 was also sent to Northumberland and Hotspur for the wages of their northern retainers, although presumably it was actually despatched a few days before this: E 403/576, 17 July, E 101/404/24, fo. 1, fo. 49r (John Clynke, messenger to the prince); E 403/578, 10 Dec. (Hugh Malpas, the royal sumpterman). Henry also borrowed 2,500 marks from Lewys de Portico, a merchant of Lucca, whom he met 'sur notre chemyn vers la bataille de Salobirs', perhaps an arranged, rather than a chance, encounter (E 404/22, no. 278, writ of repayment, dated 1 March 1407).

[26] *SAC II*, 363–5. Although he had accompanied Hotspur to Cocklaw, Dunbar seems to have been back in London in early July, where he collected assignments for his exchequer annuity (E 403/576, 2 and 6 July)..

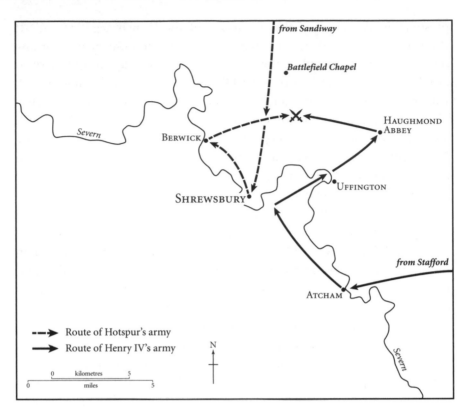

Map 5 The battle of Shrewsbury

north-west to the hamlet of Berwick.[27] The royal army, which had approached the town from the south-east, spent the evening crossing the Severn near Uffington before camping in the vicinity of Haughmond abbey. The early morning of Saturday 21 July saw both sides advance, Hotspur's eastward and the king's westward, then draw up within sight, but not bowshot, of each other two or three miles north of Shrewsbury. Several hours of talks followed, accounts of which vary.[28] The Dieulacres chronicler stated that Henry had written 'amicable' letters to Hotspur from Burton on 16 July offering to discuss his grievances, but had been

---

[27] The Shrewsbury burgesses later claimed to have burned the suburb on one side of the town (presumably the north) 'in order to save the town' (*PROME*, viii.443).

[28] For the battle, see Clarke and Galbraith, 'Deposition of Richard II' (*Dieulacres Chronicle*), 178–9; *SAC II*, 359–73; *Hardyng*, 351–3, 361–2; *CE*, 396–7; and *Usk*, 169. *Scotichronicon*, viii.57–9, and *A Collection of the Chronicles and Ancient Histories of Great Britain, by Jean de Wavrin*, ed. W. Hardy (6 vols, RS, London, 1864–91), i.58–67, are hopelessly misinformed.

rebuffed. Generally speaking, the chroniclers also credited Henry with taking the initiative to try to avoid bloodshed on the morning of the battle, although since they were in most respects sympathetic to the king's cause this is to be expected. One point on which they agreed was that Worcester took charge of the negotiations from Hotspur's side, and several of them blamed him for misrepresenting the king's emollient replies to Hotspur and thus scotching any chance of arbitration.[29] In reality, there was little chance of compromise, for Hotspur's fundamental grievance, on which all the sources concur, was his assertion that Henry had usurped the throne, a point Henry was never going to concede without a fight. Set against this simple unconquerable fact, the other accusations levelled against Henry – that he had raised excessive taxes, surrounded himself with evil counsellors, overridden the law, packed parliament, or failed to ransom Edmund Mortimer – were incidental to the negotiations on the morning of 21 July.[30]

Having come this far, Hotspur and Worcester had little option but to insist on Henry's removal: this was after all the basis on which they had recruited their army. What had brought them to this point was a good deal more complex, but tension between the king and Hotspur had been growing for at least two years. Wales was one source of contention, with Hotspur advocating a more conciliatory policy towards Glyn Dŵr (perhaps in order to free up men and money with which to defend the Scottish border), and the king accusing Hotspur of inappropriate, arguably treasonous, contact with the Welsh.[31] Another was Henry's failure to make adequate funds available to Hotspur and his father, either in Wales or, more importantly, on the Scottish marches, although given his financial problems the king actually seems to have tried quite hard to keep them

---

[29] *Brut*, ii.363; *Giles*, 33; *SAC II*, 373. From the king's side, the negotiations were led by the abbots of Shrewsbury and Haughmond, and the keeper of the privy seal, Thomas Langley.

[30] The manifesto which Hardyng claimed was presented to the king 'in the field' by two of Hotspur's esquires focuses overwhelmingly on Henry's perjury in 1399 towards both Richard II and the Percys themselves, although its authenticity is questionable. Hardyng had not included this manifesto in the first ('Lancastrian') version of his chronicle, only adding it after a Yorkist king came to the throne in 1461; he said that it was addressed to Henry by the earl of Northumberland, who was not there, as well as Hotspur and Worcester. Hardyng also claimed to have seen letters in Warkworth castle bearing the seals of lords who had promised to join Hotspur in revolt but then let him down, but if these existed they have not survived (*Hardyng*, 362). For someone who claimed to be at the battle, his account of it is remarkably brief; see also Bean, 'Henry IV and the Percies', 216–17 (although Bean's similar criticisms of the Dieulacres chronicler are less justified).

[31] Messengers seem to have passed regularly between Hotspur and Glyn Dŵr (*Giles*, 30–1; *Original Letters*, i.9).

supplied.[32] Events during the autumn of 1402 had brought these tensions close to breaking-point, especially the king's refusal to allow the Percys to ransom Edmund Mortimer or to put the earl of Douglas to ransom, both of which Hotspur regarded as slights upon his family's honour. The favours shown by Henry to Westmorland and George Dunbar during 1402 also probably rankled. In sum, by the summer of 1403 Hotspur had come to believe that his expectations were unlikely to be fulfilled as long as Henry remained king and that only by gaining control of the crown and its resources could this be achieved. With his eleven-year-old nephew, the earl of March, on the throne, such control would have seemed assured.

Worcester must also have been tempted by this prospect. He had assumed such a range of responsibilities between 1399 and 1402, and was so well trusted by Henry, that he too may have come to believe that all that stood between the Percys and an unchallengeable ascendancy in the kingdom was the House of Lancaster.[33] On the other hand, he had lost the stewardship of the household in the spring of 1402 and the lieutenancy of Wales shortly afterwards, and perhaps sensed that the Percy star was on the wane. Like his nephew, he also questioned the king's policy in Wales.[34] Unlike his nephew, he was evidently capable of hiding his true feelings, and his decision to rebel was a shock to all, especially the king and the prince, not least because his enviable military reputation must have attracted recruits to the rebel army. Also in the rebel ranks was Hotspur's prisoner the earl of Douglas, for whom victory offered the prospect of turning the tables on his arch-enemy Dunbar, whereas defeat was unlikely to lead to disaster since he could not be accused of treason against the English king and was in any case too valuable a hostage.[35] Yet it was the battle-hardened Dunbar who proved the greater asset on the day, his influence on the outcome of the battle thought by some to have been pivotal. With the negotiations between the two sides dragging on into the after-

---

[32] Northumberland's claim in June 1403 that the king owed them £20,000 was an exaggeration (Bean, 'Henry IV and the Percies', 222–4); Steel, *Receipt*, 133–4, shows that others suffered from uncashable tallies considerably more than they did. For Hotspur's complaints, see Dunn, *Politics of Magnate Power*, 100–1, who points out that both he and his father also profited considerably from their wardship of the Mortimer estates in England and Wales. However, they did sometimes have to pay troops from their own resources, as the king acknowledged (*CDS*, v, no. 915).

[33] The French royal chronicler, poorly informed about the Percy rebellion, believed that he was 'tormented by his notorious betrayal of King Richard, his natural lord' and motivated by 'tardy remorse' *(Saint-Denys*, iii.111).

[34] Davies, *Revolt*, 181–2, 242.

[35] Boardman, *Early Stewart Kings*, 269. Archibald was now calling himself 'earl of Douglas, lord of Galloway and Dunbar' *(RHL I*, 56).

noon of 21 July, Dunbar warned the king that the rebels were only playing for time and advised him to attack.[36] Henry had come to the same conclusion: 'as the day slipped away towards the hour of vespers', wrote the Dieulacres chronicler, the king began to realize that what his enemies really wanted was to make Hotspur or his son king: 'As long as I remain alive,' exclaimed Henry, 'I swear that that will never be. In the name of God, take the banners forward!'[37]

The battle which followed was the first in which the massed formations of English and Welsh bowmen which had terrorized French and Scottish armies during the fourteenth century found themselves pitted against each other, and it would long be remembered as one of the bloodiest battles fought on English soil.[38] Henry deployed his army in three divisions, with the vanguard under the command of the twenty-five-year-old earl of Stafford (appointed constable in place of Northumberland a few hours before the battle) and the rearguard under the sixteen-year-old prince. The king kept Dunbar, who had fought many times both with and against Hotspur and Douglas, close by him in his own division. Hotspur's divisions were commanded by Douglas, Worcester and himself. He took up position on a gentle ridge overlooking farmland thick with peas, which he hoped would encumber any royalist advance, thereby nullifying the slight numerical advantage in the king's favour. Contemporaries referred to it as Hateley, Hussey, or Hinsey field.[39] The opening phase of the battle saw the two vanguards led by Stafford and Douglas advance towards each other before firing volley after volley of lethal arrows. Initially it seemed as if Hotspur's bowmen had secured the advantage, for the royalist vanguard, numbering some 4,000 men, broke and fled under the onslaught and the earl of Stafford was killed.[40] When the archers began to run short of ammunition,

[36] SAC II, 369; Usk, 169. Dunbar was later permitted to call his herald 'Shrewsbury herald' in recognition of his role there (A. Macdonald, 'George Dunbar, Ninth Earl of Dunbar or March', ODNB, 17.207–10; CDS, iv.148).

[37] Dieulacres Chronicle, 179. Hotspur's son Henry was born in 1393; his mother was aunt to the earl of March.

[38] M. Strickland and R. Hardy, The Great Warbow (London, 2005), 262–5; Priestley, The Battle of Shrewsbury, 10–16.

[39] Or occasionally Bull field or Old field; I am grateful to Philip Morgan for information on this. The royal wardrobe account refers to it as 'the field of Hynsifeld near Shrewsbury' (E 101/404/21, fo. 49r).

[40] SAC II, 371. One indication of the number of arrows used at the battle of Shrewsbury is the despatch of four cartloads of bows, arrows and bowstrings from the Tower a few days later to replenish the royal army's stock (E 403/576, 20 July, 4 Sept.). Some of the payments entered under 17 and 20 July on this exchequer issue roll were entered several days or even

Hotspur and Douglas, eager to press home their advantage, led a frontal assault on the division commanded by the king. It was a gamble born of desperation: Henry could not be allowed either to live or to escape. The fact that his standard-bearer, Sir Walter Blount, one of two knights wearing the royal arms as decoys, was killed, is an indication of how near Henry came to losing his own life; as the hand-to-hand fighting grew fiercer around him, he was persuaded by Dunbar to move to a safer position. Not so Prince Henry, who, despite being struck by an arrow which lodged in a bone just below his eye, refused to leave the field, instead leading the royalist rearguard in a counter-attack which broke through enemy lines before turning to encircle Hotspur's division. This was the decisive moment of the battle. At some point during the close-quarter fighting which ensued, Hotspur was killed, by whom is not known, and although some of his supporters set up a cry of 'Henry Percy king!', when they heard the king's answering shout of 'Henry Percy is dead!' their spirit broke and they began to flee. The pursuit was brutal but brief, for by this time darkness was encroaching. The eclipse of the moon which followed was providential, for the crescent moon was the Percy livery badge.[41]

Casualties were heavy on both sides (unusually so for a victorious army), principally as a consequence of the murderous arrow-storm with which the engagement began. This was, said the Wigmore chronicler, a tragic and utterly lamentable battle (*bellum dolorissimum ac multum lamentabile*), in which 'father killed son and son killed father, kin slew kin and neighbour slew neighbour'. Around 2,000 bodies, perhaps more, were buried in a mass grave on the site of the battle, others up to three miles distant; a further 3,000 or so were wounded, some of whom subsequently died. This probably represents about a quarter, perhaps a third, of the number who took part on both sides. Particularly shocking to contemporaries was the high proportion of men of gentle birth who perished at the hands of those undiscriminating reapers of late medieval English armies, the longbow-men.[42] Of the six divisional commanders, two were killed (Hotspur and

---

weeks later: for example, the king's proclamation announcing the death of Hotspur and capture of Worcester is entered under 17 July, four days before the battle.

[41] Also providential, according to Walsingham, was the fact that Hotspur had spent the night before the battle at Berwick, since it was rumoured that he had once been told he would die at Berwick, which he naturally thought meant Berwick-upon-Tweed (*SAC II*, 367).

[42] The names of about fifty of the dead are known. The Dieulacres chronicler said that 1,847 died on the field, a Durham chronicler 2,291. The Wigmore chronicler's statement that 3,460 bodies were buried in the mass grave is probably an exaggeration: he stated that the grave was 100 feet long, 24 feet wide and 12 feet deep (Bodleian Library, Oxford, Ms Film 54, fos. 39–40). I am grateful to Philip Morgan for allowing me to read his chapter

Stafford) and another two wounded (Prince Henry and the earl of Douglas, who was struck in the groin and lost a testicle before being captured by Sir James Harrington).[43] The account by the royal surgeon, John Bradmore, of the process by which he extracted the arrowhead buried in Prince Henry's face, which includes a drawing of the instrument which he designed to do so, provides graphic evidence of the potentially lethal nature of arrow-wounds.[44] Having removed the shaft, he wrote, 'the head of the aforesaid arrow remained in the furthermost part of the bone of the skull for the depth of six inches'. To draw it out, Bradmore fashioned some probes from

> the pith of old elder, well dried and well stitched in purified linen cloth the length of the wound. These probes were infused with rose honey. And after that I made larger and longer probes . . . until I had the width and depth of the wound as I wished it. . . . [Then] I prepared anew some little tongs, small and hollow, with the width of an arrow. A screw ran through the middle of the tongs. . . . I put these tongs in at an angle in the same way as the arrow had first entered, then placed the screw in the centre and finally the tongs entered the socket of the arrowhead. Then, by moving it to and fro, little by little, with the help of God, I extracted the arrowhead.[45]

To stop his patient going into spasm, Bradmore massaged the prince's neck every morning with a muscle relaxant and placed a hot plaster on it to soothe him. With the arrowhead removed, he used a syringe to cleanse the wound with white wine before inserting wads of flax soaked in a purifying solution of white bread, barley flour, honey and turpentine oil. Every two days he shortened the wads, and within twenty days the wound had healed and a 'dark ointment' was applied to regenerate the flesh. Given the depth of the wound, the prince's courage in remaining on the field and

---

'The Days of the Dead' from his forthcoming book on the battle, where he argues that the armies were probably rather smaller than the 10,000–12,000 often suggested. Cf. Mortimer, *Fears*, appendix 4.

[43] *CDS*, iv.136.

[44] Strickland and Hardy, *Great Warbow*, 284–5; Bradmore received £2 for buying medicines in the wardrobe account for 1402–3: E 101/404/21, fo. 40v.

[45] Presumably the tongs were pushed into the socket from which the shaft had been drawn, then the screw inserted to push them apart until they held fast against the sides of the socket, allowing the arrow-head to be pulled out. The operation must have been excruciatingly painful.

leading a counter-attack was as remarkable as was Bradmore's ingenuity in curing him.

Upon the outcome of the battle of Shrewsbury turned the future not just of Henry IV's reign but of the Lancastrian dynasty. Had the king been captured, he would assuredly have been either executed as a traitor or quietly done away with in some dismal dungeon, his brief 'interregnum' as a usurper vilified under the new order, his family and principal supporters driven into exile or worse, while the crown reverted to its 'rightful' line under the earl of March, subject to the overweening direction of the Percys. Henry's fate, in other words, would have been that of Richard II, his place in history that of Richard III. Yet there was little joy to be had from victory. When shown Hotspur's body, the king is said to have wept, although he had no compunction in displaying the corpse seated upright between two millstones at Shrewsbury for a few days, so that there could be no doubts as to his death, before having it taken down and quartered, the head impaled at York atop one of the city gates.[46] Worcester also wept when he saw his nephew's body; Henry wanted to spare Worcester's life, but the king's followers were so incensed by his treachery (he was a Knight of the Garter, as was Hotspur) that he was quickly tried and executed in Shrewsbury, along with two prominent Cheshire rebels, Richard Venables, baron of Kinderton, and Sir Richard Vernon, baron of Shipbrook, an example to the restive county.[47]

These executions took place on the morning of Monday 23 July, following which the king left Shrewsbury; there was still the earl of Northumberland to be dealt with. The previous day, Henry had written to Westmorland, Robert Waterton and other loyal northern lords, ordering them to suppress the army of 'traitors' the earl had assembled in Yorkshire.[48] By 4 August the king had reached Pontefract, gathering men and money as he went, issuing threats against those who persisted in maligning him, and attempting to prohibit the plundering of Percy properties.[49] Meanwhile

[46] Immediately after the battle Hotspur's body was interred for the night at Whitchurch (Shropshire) before being brought back to Shrewsbury; his other quarters were sent to London, Bristol, Newcastle and Chester to be displayed there (*CPR 1401–5*, 299; Wylie, *Henry the Fourth*, i.364).

[47] The *Brut* (ii.549) records that when Sir John Stanley, wounded on the king's side at Shrewsbury, was asked what advice he had for Cheshire, he told the king 'Burn and slay, burn and slay!' Thomas Percy's head was displayed on London Bridge (*SAC II*, 377; *Foedera*, viii.320; *CPR 1401–5*, 293).

[48] *Foedera*, viii.319.

[49] *CPR 1401–5*, 292–3; *Foedera*, viii.321; E 403/576, 17 July.

Northumberland, hearing that Westmorland was moving against him, backed away to Newcastle, where he was coolly received, then after a few days to his northern stronghold of Warkworth.[50] Here he was brought an invitation from the king: if he would come in peace, without his retainers, and submit himself to Henry's mercy, his life would be spared. The interview took place on 11 August at York, where the pale, severed head of his son now crowned the city's gate. To what extent the earl shared Hotspur's and Worcester's guilt was unclear. Hardyng believed that he did, claiming that their manifesto was presented to the king by all three Percys.[51] This would mean (if it is authentic) that the manifesto had been drawn up in the north and brought south by Hotspur, which might help to explain the movements of the earl of Douglas, who was in Edinburgh on 10 July yet fought with Hotspur and Worcester at Shrewsbury eleven days later.[52] If Douglas had been paroled by Hotspur to enable him to fight against Henry – presumably in return either for a measure of freedom or for concessions in relation to his earldom – the rebellion must have been a less hasty affair and Northumberland's involvement more likely. However, Walsingham thought it possible that Northumberland was moving southwards to promote peace between Hotspur and the king, and when he appeared before parliament in February 1404 to account for his actions the commons also gave him the benefit of the doubt.[53] That the earl knew of his son's resentment towards the king is certain; how much he knew of Hotspur's plans is less certain, but it is possible that his advance southwards was part of a strategy for him to challenge the king directly while Hotspur dealt with Prince Henry. Glyn Dŵr was wreaking havoc in Wales and the king had little more than his household troops with him. It was a plan that could well have succeeded, and it nearly did.

Although the king almost certainly believed Northumberland to be guilty of misprision, if not treason, there was nothing easy about the decision to be made, for he can hardly have viewed with equanimity the prospect of a power vacuum in the north. However, he was not in forgiving mood. Also at York was the ascetic and prophet William Norham, who had once been imprisoned by Richard II for his indiscretions; he now repeated

[50] The citizens of Newcastle refused to allow the earl's troops in the town, although they allowed him to enter with a few servants; when his troops tried to force an entry the next day, they were beaten off (SAC II, 377–8).

[51] According to Hardyng (361) the earl had agreed to come south to join Hotspur, but 'failed him foul without witte or rede'.

[52] Boardman, Early Stewart Kings, 270.

[53] SAC II, 377.

his mistake, and Henry had him beheaded.[54] When Northumberland arrived, he was treated as guilty until proved innocent, despite disclaiming any foreknowledge of Hotspur's rebellion.[55] Addressed but briefly by Henry, he was taken into custody and sent to Baginton (Warwickshire) to await trial in parliament; his lands were placed under the administration of William Heron, Lord Say, steward of the royal household; and he was made to seal orders to his retainers to hand over his castles in the north, some of which they were still holding in his name.[56] The subsequent attempts to eject them confirmed the king's fears: for more than a year after Shrewsbury, a group of knights and esquires, some of them renegades from Shrewsbury, others with a lifelong attachment to the Percys, continued to gather in Northumberland, 'the crescent [badge] on their sleeves', refusing to surrender their castles to Henry's commissioners.[57] Their leader was Sir William Clifford, testimony to whose temerity survives in a memorandum of the conditions which he demanded in return for surrendering Berwick: namely, that he and his garrison would receive back payment since Hotspur's death and a full pardon, and that Hotspur's ten-year-old son, now heir to his grandfather's earldom, should be promised all of his father's inheritance once he came of age, and in the meantime should remain in Clifford's guardianship.[58] At its heart lay a desire for the continuation of Percy hegemony in the north.

Nor was it just his own retainers who continued to offer comfort to Northumberland. When parliament met in January 1404 the speaker, Arnold Savage (by now also a royal councillor), petitioned for the earl to be brought into parliament, granted a charter of pardon and restored to all his lands, even hinting that upon the king's mercy depended the grant of a subsidy by the commons. To bargain thus on behalf of a man widely

---

[54] *SAC II*, 381; *CE*, 397.

[55] *CE*, 398; *SAC II*, 381.

[56] His seal was brought to him from London to do this: E 403/578, 9 Nov. His keeper at Baginton was Henry's esquire, Thomas Totty: E 101/404/21, fo. 40v; A. King, 'They Have the Hertes of the People by North: Northumberland, the Percies and Henry IV, 1399–1408', in *Henry IV: The Establishment of the Regime*, ed. G. Dodd and D. Biggs (York, 2003), 139–59.

[57] *POPC*, i.209–17; *Foedera*, viii.322–3; *RHL I*, 204. The castles were Berwick, Alnwick, Warkworth, Prudhoe, Langley and Cockermouth. Scottish prisoners from Humbleton Hill were still held in some of them.

[58] *POPC*, ii.79–80. Clifford proposed to use those of Hotspur's valuables which were in his possession to maintain the boy. The king believed these were worth at least £2,666, Clifford much less. For his betrayal of William Serle, see below, pp. 263–4.; A. King, 'Sir William Clifford: Rebellion and Reward in Henry IV's Affinity', in *The Fifteenth Century IX: English and Continental Perspectives*, ed. L. Clark (Woodbridge, 2010), 139–54 at pp. 148–9. By December 1404 Clifford was once again being paid his royal annuity of £40 (E 403/580, 2 Dec.).

suspected by the king and his followers of treason was audacious, yet the support which Northumberland received from both the lords and the commons indicates genuine uncertainty as to the degree of his collusion in his son's rebellion. Like the king, they too must have feared a collapse of authority in the north. In the event, Northumberland was found guilty (by the lords) not of treason but of the much less heinous charge of contravening the Statute of Liveries, the fine for which was promptly pardoned. Thanking 'my friends the commons', he renewed his oath of allegiance on 8 February and was restored to his inherited lands, though not to those which he had been granted since 1399, nor to the constableship of England, nor to the wardenship of either of the Marches.[59] It was a compromise which, in the end, probably suited the king: although not destroyed, the earl had been put on notice. Yet there was no doubting his humiliation, and the erosion of his influence in Anglo-Scottish affairs, the springboard for his family's power for over a hundred years, was confirmed in July 1404 when he was obliged to surrender his family's claim to Jedburgh and Berwick. A month later, he handed over three of his grandchildren as hostages for his good behaviour.[60] Despite Henry's show of clemency, he had not left the sexagenarian earl with many options.

It is easy to accept the Dieulacres chronicler's comment that the general pardon proclaimed by Henry shortly after the battle was granted more out of fear than love.[61] If the king and his son had avoided disaster at Shrewsbury, it had been a chastening experience for both of them. Deserted by his governor and second-in-command, Prince Henry had come (probably literally) within an inch of losing his life. For the king, one of the lessons of the revolt was how many people in England (to say nothing of the Welsh and the Scots) had come to believe that he deserved the same fate as his predecessor. On the other hand, the rapid response to his summons for help must have given him encouragement. There were plenty of men prepared to fight for, as well as against, him, and indeed to die for him, such as Sir John Luttrell, a life retainer of the king whom he had created a Knight of the Bath in 1399, who received Henry's summons at his manor of East Quantoxhead (Somerset), hastily dictated a will declaring that he was 'going with all possible speed to join his most dread

---

[59] *PROME*, viii.222, 231–3, 279; *CE*, 400; for his mainpernors, see C 49/48, no. 5; three weeks after his pardon he was receiving new tallies for failed assignments for £786 dating from 1401–2 (E 403/578, 26 Feb.).

[60] *CPR 1401–5*, 412; Bean, 'Henry Percy, Earl of Northumberland', *ODNB*, 43.694–702; *SAC II*, 417.

[61] Clarke and Galbraith, 'Deposition of Richard II' (*Dieulacres Chronicle*), 176–7.

lord the king . . . to resist the malice of the false traitor Sir Henry Percy',
and never returned.[62] If the king might argue that the outcome of the
battle demonstrated divine favour for his cause and his dynasty, what it also
demonstrated was that it was still upon the Lancastrian affinity that his
survival depended.

[62] Philip Morgan, personal communication.

Chapter 16

LOUIS OF ORLÉANS AND OWAIN GLYN DŴR (1403–1405)

Although it removed the threat from the Percys, the battle of Shrewsbury did little to alleviate Henry's problems elsewhere. Indeed, even the humbling of the Percys was a mixed blessing, for the question now arose as to how to govern the north without them. The king's answer was to appoint his fourteen-year-old son John as his lieutenant: for the remainder of the reign Prince John and the earl of Westmorland divided the East and West Marches between them, but their ability to conciliate disaffected Percy supporters was limited, especially in Northumberland, where there were many such as William Clifford who yearned for the restoration of Percy power.

Nor did Hotspur's death do anything to check Glyn Dŵr; on the contrary, the following eighteen months would see his rebellion reduce still further the effective sphere of English authority in Wales. Following his interview with Northumberland at York in mid-August 1403, Henry had made his way back to Wales to try to repair the damage done by the rebels over the previous few months.[1] By now, the annual autumn exercise in not finding Glyn Dŵr was acquiring a familiar, if depressing, rhythm, although since Henry's campaigns were essentially reactive there were always variations. On this occasion, his principal objective was the relief of Carmarthen, the major royal stronghold in South Wales. Arriving on 24 September, he spent five days there, reinforcing the garrison with 550 men and restoring the town's defences, before returning to Hereford on 3 October.[2] He remained close to the border, mainly at Gloucester, Bristol and Cirencester, for over a month, despatching orders to the sheriffs and nobles of the south-west to array troops to come with him 'to meet the traitor and with the aid of God destroy him', but if this gave the impression that he planned to re-enter Wales in person it was misleading; by the middle of November

---

[1] A council was held at Worcester to raise loans (2–10 September). Henry reached Brecon by 21 September (E 101/404/21).
[2] Davies, *Revolt*, 113–14; *POPC*, i.217–18.

he was on his way back to Westminster and, yet again, barely had he left before Glyn Dŵr's followers renewed their attacks.[3] Cardiff, Kidwelly and Caernarfon were all besieged in November 1403, and at the latter two the besiegers included Frenchmen and Bretons.[4]

The threat from France was growing apace. Until now, the attempts of Louis of Orléans and his acolytes to undermine Henry had consisted of semi-covert attacks on English shipping, the despatch of a small expeditionary force to Scotland, and increasingly abusive letters of defiance. The latter were certainly an irritation and threatened to become more than that: in the spring of 1403, Henry delayed the ratification of the truce of Paris until he had received assurances that they had been written without the consent of Charles VI or the French council, and that they did not constitute a disavowal of the truce.[5] In practice, however, the extension of the truce heralded not a diminution but a sharp escalation in Anglo-French hostilities.

Anglo-French relations had not been improved by Henry's decision during the winter of 1401–2 to open negotiations for the hand of Joan, duchess of Brittany, the widow of Duke John IV (d.1399).[6] There were obvious strategic reasons to recommend an Anglo-Breton alliance, and equally obvious reasons for the French government to oppose it. Civil war in Brittany had crucially undermined the French crown between the 1340s and the 1370s, and the prospect of reviving the influence which Edward III had put to such good effect there was tempting. Moreover, Henry and Joan had met on several occasions and seem to have got on well. Joan certainly wrote warmly to Henry in February 1400, and she did not hesitate before accepting his proposal, despite knowing that the French royal family and a fair proportion of the Breton nobility would oppose it. Thus on 2 April 1402, after hasty and secretive negotiations, she and Henry were married

---

[3] *CPR 1401–5*, 439–40.

[4] This was not the first time that the French had come to the aid of the Welsh: see *RHL I*, xxxiii, for French adventurers in Wales in March and July 1403. In late February 1404, six French ships laden with wine and spices appeared off the Llyn peninsula; if seized, wrote the lieutenant of Conway, they would bring 'great profit': *Original Letters Illustrative of English History*, ed. H. Ellis (4 vols, London, 1824–7) i.30–5; *RHL II*, 15–17, 22–4; E 403/579, 17 June (Harlech); Davies, *Revolt*, 192.

[5] On the day the truce was confirmed, 27 June 1403, the French council handed over a notarial instrument to this effect (F. Wilson, 'Anglo-French Relations in the Reign of King Henry IV of England, 1399–1413', unpublished PhD thesis, McGill University, 1973, 208–9; *SAC II*, 379).

[6] Messengers went to Brittany in December 1401 (E 403/571, 15 Dec.), but the negotiations were kept secret.

by proxy.[7] When news of the match reached Paris the reaction was swift, and by October Duke Philip of Burgundy was in Nantes, where he imposed a settlement on Joan: she was allowed to take her two daughters to England with her, but her sons, including her thirteen-year-old heir, were removed to Paris, and Philip himself assumed the regency of the duchy until the boy came of age. The episode is instructive: Burgundy remained opposed until his death to Orléans's undermining of the Anglo-French truce, but he would not tolerate any attempt by Henry to weaken French authority in what the Valois regarded as their sphere of influence.[8]

Burgundy's intervention in Brittany irritated Orléans, who shared his rival's desire to negate Henry's influence there but had hoped to install Olivier de Clisson as the young duke's guardian.[9] Elsewhere, too, their antipathy helped to smooth the course of Henry's diplomacy. This was certainly the case in Germany following the deposition in August 1400 of the Holy Roman Emperor Wenzel (Richard II's brother-in-law) in favour of Rupert of Wittelsbach, the Elector-Palatine. Orléans supported Wenzel's efforts to regain his crown, hoping to exploit the imbroglio in the Empire to realize his ambitions in the Rhineland and the Low Countries; Burgundy, though more even-handed, inclined towards Rupert.[10] Thus when Rupert, who craved international recognition as much as Henry did, wrote to the English king in January 1401 proposing a marriage between his son Louis and Henry's daughter Blanche, it was seized upon with alacrity, and on 14 February it was agreed that the marriage would take place the following year.[11] The only obstacle was the £5,333 required for the first instalment of Blanche's dowry, for which Henry resorted to the almost obsolete expedient of a feudal aid,[12] but eventually the money was collected and in June 1402, magnificently escorted, the ten-year-old Blanche departed for Cologne. Henry never saw his eldest daughter again: she died of a fever in

[7] Joan was the daughter of Charles the Bad, king of Navarre, and granddaughter of John II of France (d.1364): M. Jones, 'Joan of Navarre', *ODNB*, 30.139–41. For her letter to Henry, see *RHL I*, 19 20.

[8] Duke John IV, Joan's first husband, had been brought up at Edward III's court and the result for the French was disastrous. Philip was called in by members of the Breton nobility who opposed the match (Henneman, *Olivier de Clisson*, 193–6).

[9] *Saint-Denys*, iii.41; F. Autrand, *Charles VI: La Folie du Roi* (Paris, 1986), 392–3. Clisson was the inveterate foe of the Breton ducal family.

[10] Nordberg, *Les Ducs et la Royauté*, 152–77; G. Small, *Late Medieval France* (Basingstoke, 2009), 140.

[11] E 28/8, no. 40; *Foedera*, viii.170–81.

[12] *Foedera*, viii.232–3 (December 1401). The final instalment of the dowry (totalling £13,333) was not paid until 1446 (Tuck, 'Henry IV and Europe', 115–19).

May 1409, aged seventeen.[13] Her marriage had, however, helped to counter
the machinations of Louis of Orléans, for despite his domestic problems
Rupert proved a faithful ally, writing to Henry to reassure him that although
Orléans had tried to recruit followers in Germany for an expedition against
England, he had forbidden his vassals from taking part in it. Henry, for his
part, sought a full treaty of alliance with Rupert, although this never materialized.[14] Henry's search for a suitable match for his younger daughter,
Philippa, also benefited from irresolution in France. Margaret, queen
dowager and regent of Denmark, Norway and Sweden, had initially
sought the hand of a French princess for her son and heir, Eric, but she was
rebuffed, and late in 1402 agreement was reached on a marriage between
Eric and Philippa.[15] With the kings of Castile and Portugal married to two
of Henry's sisters, there was thus a respectable level of diplomatic support
in Europe to set against Franco-Scottish hostility.[16] The French had failed
to leave the English king isolated.

Yet hopes of peaceful coexistence with France seemed doomed to failure.
By the summer of 1403, Burgundy's influence on French policy was weakening, perhaps on account of his failing health, perhaps because of the
unquenchable ambition of Orléans. Duke Louis's hostility towards
England, and towards Henry in particular, stemmed from three factors:
first, his high conception of France's place in Europe and his sense of
personal responsibility for its destiny during the tragedy of his brother's
reign; secondly, his competition with Burgundy for control of the resources
of the French monarchy in order to prevent them being used to fund the
ambitions of a dynasty which he believed, rightly or wrongly, not to have
the interests of the French state at heart; thirdly, that Henry, his friend and
ally in 1398–9, had duped him, or at any rate that he needed to give that
impression, for Louis was much criticized in France for his part in

---

[13] Wylie, *Henry the Fourth*, i.255–6. Her husband was 23 and much impressed with his wife,
as were many other Germans. Her bejewelled crown is still in the royal treasury at Munich.
The earl of Somerset led the delegation to Cologne, which cost at least £10,000 and probably quite a lot more: E 101/404/11 (expense account); E 403/573, 11 May, 15 and 21 July,
26 September (9,500 marks for her expenses).
[14] Nordberg, *Les Ducs et la Royauté*, 175–6; Tuck, 'Henry IV and Europe', 118; *Foedera*,
viii.253–4 (Henry's proposal for a treaty, 28 April 1402).
[15] Tuck, 'Henry IV and Europe', 119–20; *RHL I*, xl–xliv; *Foedera*, viii.257, 265; *POPC*, i.222.
A second marriage between Prince Henry and Eric's sister Katherine was mooted, but later
dropped (E 403/573, 27 June 1402). The initial reluctance of the English council was overcome when Eric agreed not to seek a dowry. He and Philippa eventually married in 1406.
[16] *RHL I*, xlvi–vii; *Foedera*, viii.345, 347; E 101/404/21, fo. 40r (Spanish ambassadors in
London, Dec. 1402).

facilitating Richard II's downfall. There was thus an element of posturing in his defiance of Henry, although there was no doubting the threat it posed to the maintenance of the truce. From the summer of 1403, what had previously been a war of words and fleets metamorphosed into a war of conquest in Guyenne and a campaign of brutal coastal raids in the north.[17] Each side blamed the other for starting it. The French royal chronicler said that shortly after the truce was ratified on 27 June the English raided Brittany, to which the Bretons responded in mid-August by attacking Plymouth, Jersey and Guernsey. The raid on Plymouth was led by Guillaume de Chastel, the hero of Montendre, and resulted in the looting and burning of the town and the seizure of several ships. Walsingham said that it was the Breton raid that came first, sparking English retaliation led by William Wilford, the mayor of Exeter, who assembled a fleet from Bristol, Plymouth and Dartmouth and systematically ravaged the Breton coastline, destroying forty ships and capturing the same number; Brittany, claimed the chronicler, was left 'in a state of mourning'.[18]

Orléans's growing influence was also seen in the decision in November 1403 by Waleran, count of St-Pol, to challenge Henry openly. Back in 1380, while staying in England, St-Pol had married Richard II's half-sister, Maud Holand, and had developed a close relationship with the deposed king. Like Louis of Orléans, he believed his family's honour to have been impugned by Richard's deposition, and on 9 November 1403, a month after the third and last of Orléans's missives to Henry, he too sent the English king a letter of defiance. The imputations were predictable (usurper, regicide), but the threat of hostile action more urgent: he planned, so he said, to devote his energies to the task of avenging Richard in any way that he could, by land or sea, although he was careful to emphasize that his quarrel with Henry was a personal one and that his letter did not constitute an official rupture of the Anglo-French truce.[19] Since Waleran was a vassal of Burgundy, he needed to tread carefully, for Duke Philip was increasingly concerned at the drift to war, and during the summer of 1403 had sought permission from Charles VI to negotiate a separate

[17] For Guyenne, see below, pp. 253–9.
[18] *Saint-Denys*, iii.109–13; *SAC II*, 384–7. 'Rebels' in the Channel Islands may also have been French sympathizers (*Foedera*, viii.303).
[19] St-Pol had conceived a particular hatred for the earl of Rutland, who he believed to have betrayed Richard II in 1399. He had an effigy of him suspended upside down outside Calais as a mark of disgrace (*Monstrelet*, i.67–8; for the date see Lehoux, *Jean de France*, ii.524, n.1; Given-Wilson, 'Quarrels of Old Women', 36–7). Henry did not reply, saying he 'took little account' of the letter.

commercial agreement with the English on behalf of his Flemish subjects.[20] By this time, however, St-Pol was more inclined to look to Orléans for leadership, and soon cast caution to the winds. In December 1403, he led 1,600 men on a raid on the Isle of Wight, although he was soon forced to retire, 'covered with ignominy' according to the Saint-Denis chronicler, and in February 1404 the Calais garrison took revenge by devastating the count's lands in Picardy.[21] Two months later Duke Philip died, following which St-Pol concluded an alliance with Orléans in return for an annuity of 6,000 *livres tournois*.[22]

Little now stood in the way of Duke Louis and those who shared his instincts. The real French target in the north was Calais, and soon after Philip of Burgundy's death the French council decided to besiege the town. Nothing came of this, in part because Henry's sister Catherine, the Castilian queen, persuaded her husband not to give the French the naval assistance they requested to blockade the town, but England's bridgehead in France was chronically vulnerable and before long the French would try again.[23] In the meantime, seeking alternative ways to strike at Henry, the French council made contact with Glyn Dŵr, who on 15 May 1404 had written to Charles VI proposing a treaty of alliance. Composed in formal Latin and diplomatic protocol – 'Owain, by the grace of God Prince of Wales, to all those who shall see these our letters, greetings' – his letter informed the French king that he was sending as his special nuncios Master Griffith Young, doctor of laws, 'our chancellor', and his kinsman, John Hanmer, to conclude a permanent or temporary Franco-Welsh alliance.[24] The French were delighted: feted as plenipotentiaries, Young and Hanmer were given a gilded helmet, breastplate and sword to present to their

[20] Schnerb, *Jean Sans Peur*, 146; Wilson, 'Anglo-French Relations', 222–3; *Choix de Pièces Inédites*, i.249–51. At a French council meeting in January 1404 this agreement was confirmed, but Philip had to promise that Flanders would fight the English when required to do so and allow French armies to use Flemish ports; this was confirmed by his widow Margaret after Philip's death. The agreement was both confusing and extremely difficult to enforce, for the Four Members of Flanders (the body representing the Flemish merchants) wanted Flemish ports to be open to all commerce, while the English wanted Flanders to declare its neutrality: Philip's compromise failed to satisfy the Flemings and alienated many people in Paris, especially Orléans, who was bitterly opposed to allowing separate Anglo-Flemish talks to take place. I am grateful to Dr Chris Ford for his thoughts on this topic.

[21] *Saint-Denys*, iii.117–21; *SAC II*, 391. For possible links with the countess of Oxford's conspiracy, see below, pp. 262–3.

[22] On 9 July 1404 (Schnerb, *Jean Sans Peur*, 167).

[23] *Saint-Denys*, iii.157–9.

[24] BL Add. MS 38,525, fo. 8; dated 15 May 1404 at Dolgellau. For a note of Owain's seal, showing him seated on a throne on one side and a horse on the other, see *Choix de Pièces Inédites*, i.286.

master and promised help in the shape of an expeditionary force. Within two months a pact had been drawn up announcing that, united and bound in true friendship, the king of France and the prince of the Welsh would do their utmost to destroy Henry of Lancaster, his adherents and supporters. Before departing Young and Hanmer compiled a memorandum of the best harbours, most practicable routes and most fertile regions in Wales.

Thus far, French attempts to strike at the English had met with little success. Following St-Pol's humiliation on the Isle of Wight, the year 1404 saw attacks on Portland, Dartmouth, Falmouth, Southampton, the Isle of Wight and even Hornsea on Humberside, some by Flemish or Normans but most by Bretons, envied by many of their compatriots as the only ones permitted to break the truce. More often than not these ended badly.[25] The Norman raid on Portland left many of them drowned or captive, and when Guillaume de Chastel attacked Dartmouth in April he was killed and several of his captains taken prisoner. The attempt to coordinate hostilities with the Welsh was another fiasco. True to his promise to Owain, Charles VI authorized the count of La Marche to raise a force of 1,000 men-at-arms and crossbowmen to take to Pembrokeshire, and by mid-August sixty vessels had been assembled at Brest (Brittany), but La Marche, detained in Paris by (it was alleged) a love affair, did not reach Brest until mid-November, by which time it was too risky to round Land's End. Instead, he made for Falmouth (Cornwall), where he was driven off by the local levies, several of his men drowning as they retreated. The princes of the lily were furious, accusing the count of 'forgetting that he was the issue of royal blood' and sullying French honour. English retaliation was swift, with privateers and freebooters from the Channel ports infesting the coasts of Normandy, Brittany, Picardy and Flanders 'like a swarm of insects'. The indomitable Henry Pay, having narrowly escaped execution at the hands of a crew from Normandy, sailed up the Seine almost as far as Paris, seizing several ships on his way home.[26] Even the monk of Saint-Denis conceded that the English usually had the better of these exchanges. French mercenaries continued to find their way to Wales to fight the English, but Glyn Dŵr would have to wait a little longer for his promised expeditionary force.[27]

---

[25] Saint-Denys, iii.161, 169, 171, 223–7, 259, 317–21; SAC II, 399–405, 437.

[26] SAC II, 407; Saint-Denys, iii.181, 197.

[27] For the treaty, dated 14 June, see Foedera, viii.365–6; Saint-Denys, iii.164–7, 197, 223–7. 'John Spaigne of France' commanded ships at the sieges of Harlech and Caernarfon, summer 1404 (E 403/579, 17 June).

Yet as matters stood it hardly seemed as if Owain needed outside help, for 1404 marked the high-water mark of the Welsh revolt. In the north, isolated coastal garrisons clung on in the face of unremitting pressure, their plight typified by a letter from Reynald Baildon, keeper of Conway, to his superiors at Chester on 10 January: the rebels, he wrote, were planning to cross to Anglesey to seize all the men and cattle there and take them to Snowdonia; the French were once more besieging Caernarfon castle, 'since it is now more feeble than when they last attacked it'; the constable of Harlech had been kidnapped and taken to Glyn Dŵr, raising doubts about his loyalty, and many of his soldiers were dead or sick with the plague while others had tried to flee but been killed by rebels. A second letter written by the deputy constable of Caernarfon a few days later and delivered 'through a woman, since he had no man who dared to come', added that Glyn Dŵr and the French had now brought siege engines and scaling ladders up to the castle, which was defended by a garrison of just twenty-eight men, eleven others having been killed.[28] Remarkably, Caernarfon held out, though not so Harlech or Aberystwyth, both of which had fallen to the Welsh by the end of the year, and this time (unlike Conway in 1401), they had no intention of bargaining away what they had won in return for pardons – a measure of Glyn Dŵr's burgeoning confidence.

It was also during 1404 that Owain held his first parliament (at Machynlleth in Powys), and that the first Welsh bishop, John Trevaur of St Asaph, defected to his cause, followed a few months later by Lewis Byford, recently provided to the see of Bangor. No longer could Owain simply be dismissed as a guerrilla leader: he was beginning to look like a true prince of the Welsh people.[29] In central and south Wales too, 1404 was a grim year for the English of Wales. Kidwelly was captured and looted in August; Cardiff and Coety were eventually relieved, but only after prolonged sieges and costly expeditions. Rebel incursions into the English border counties also intensified, with Shropshire particularly hard hit. One indication of the economic destruction caused by these raids is the level of exemption from taxation granted by the crown between 1404 and 1407, which in Shropshire averaged more than 25 per cent and in Herefordshire around 10 per cent.[30] In August 1404, Henry permitted the people of Shropshire

---

[28] *Original Letters*, 33–6. Baildon added optimistically that if 200 men could be sent to Conway and 200 to Caernarfon, the land could soon be pacified, for apart from 4 or 5 individuals 'and some vagabonds' the gentlemen of Merionethshire and Caernarvonshire wanted peace with the English.

[29] Davies, *Revolt*, 116.

[30] Watt, 'The Glyn Dŵr Rebellion and Tax Collection', 56–66, 77–81; *POPC*, ii.77–8.

to make a local truce with the rebels for three months; humiliating as it was, he probably had little option. From Wales itself, needless to say, the revenues of both the crown and the marcher lords could scarcely be collected at all: a letter from the constable and receiver of Bromfield and Yale to their lord, the earl of Arundel, described the lordship as 'void and desolate of tenantry for the most part' and men from Cheshire were planning to loot and waste it. The king, they added, had 'cried havoc throughout Wales', a pardonable exaggeration.[31] Yet by early 1405 English hegemony in Wales hung by a thread.

The government's failure to make headway in Wales in 1403–4 was due in part to Prince Henry's long convalescence following his injury at the battle of Shrewsbury – he did not return to Wales until July 1404 – and partly to lack of money to fund operations.[32] Between 1401 and early 1404, the exchequer had contributed around £4,000 a year to the suppression of the revolt, but during the following year Prince Henry received less than £1,000. After this, however, things improved rapidly: from the winter of 1404–5 until the summer of 1408, an annual average of some £12,000 was passed to the prince.[33] The renewal in the spring of 1405 of his appointment as the king's lieutenant in Wales was also ominous for the Welsh, indicating that after eighteen months during which the English crown had been restricted to a policy of containment, it was now moving on to the offensive. The effect was soon felt. In April 1405, a large company of Owain's partisans was surprised in the act of burning Grosmont (Monmouthshire) by an English force led by Gilbert Lord Talbot and Sir John Greyndour. According to a letter from the prince to his father, the rebel contingent numbered 8,000 men, about one in ten of whom were killed and a 'great chieftain' taken.[34] The numbers doubtless grew in the telling, but it was a significant check to the revolt in the south-east and was followed two months later by a still more damaging defeat at Usk, where Owain's brother was killed, his eldest son Gruffudd captured, and their 'great host' driven off from the castle with substantial losses. The

---

[31] *POPC*, i.236; *ANLP*, no. 308 (dated 1400–9, but probably from the middle years of the decade).

[32] The prince's household account records that he was 'in the march of Wales' from 1 to 20 July 1404, then either at Hereford or at Leominster until 21 November (E 101/404/24, fos. 14r–v; Davies, *Revolt*, 118–19, 233).

[33] R. Griffiths, 'Prince Henry, Wales and the Royal Exchequer', *Bulletin of the Board of Celtic Studies* 32 (1985), 202–15.

[34] *Original Letters*, i.37; *Foedera*, viii.390. This was on Wednesday 11 March; the prince said he would have sent the chieftain to the king except that the captive 'still could not ride easily'.

victorious English commanders (Greyndour again, with Richard Lord Grey) then beheaded 300 of their captives before the castle, although not Gruffudd, who was led away to London where he later died in the Tower. Then in June, Owain's brother-in-law and envoy John Hanmer was captured. Relief was also at hand for the beleaguered English castles, where garrisons were strengthened, preparations begun for the recapture of Harlech and Aberystwyth, and plans laid for another royal expedition to Wales in May or June.[35] 'And from this time onwards,' wrote Adam Usk, 'Owain's fortunes began to wane in that region.'[36] Perhaps the successes of the previous two years had made the rebels a little overconfident. It was guerrilla tactics that suited them; when they confronted English forces in open battle they were always likely to come off second best. Nor did the renewal of the crown's commitment to restoring control in Wales go unheeded. Prominent supporters of Owain's in both the north-east and the south-east sought terms in return for abandoning his cause. A contingent of Dubliners landed in Anglesey and 'did much hurt to the Welshmen'.[37] The arena of defiance was shrinking, and by the summer Owain was once again thinking in terms of making a treaty with the English king.[38]

Ironically, it was at this moment that the Franco-Welsh alliance concluded in the previous year delivered on its promise. In August 1405, a French force some 2,600 strong landed at Milford Haven (Pembrokeshire); its leaders were the marshal and admiral of France and the vastly experienced Jean de Hangest, lord of Hugueville, last seen by Henry when he came to England in October 1400 to negotiate Queen Isabella's return. Yet if there was no doubting the symbolic significance of the moment, the achievements of the joint Franco-Welsh force were more questionable.[39] Its only tangible success was the capture of Carmarthen, and even that was achieved by negotiation rather than assault. A part of the army, though probably not all of it, penetrated into England, arriving in late August at Woodbury Hill, a few miles from Worcester where Henry was holding a council. The Burgundian chronicler Monstrelet claimed that the English

---

[35] *CPR 1405–8*, 6 (indentures for 1,000 men-at-arms and 5,500 archers, including 864 members of the king's retinue, for service in Wales, March 1405).

[36] This was the battle of Pwll Melyn (*Usk*, 212–13; Davies, *Revolt*, 231; *SAC II*, 435).

[37] *Ancient Irish Histories: The Works of Spencer, Campion, Hanmer and Marleburrough*, ed. J. Ware (2 vols, Dublin, 1809), 19. They also carried off the shrine of St Cybi from Llangiby to Dublin.

[38] *RHL II*, 76–9.

[39] *Saint-Denys*, iii.322–9; *Monstrelet*, i.81–4; *SAC II*, 463–5; Davies, *Revolt*, 193–6. For Hangest in 1400, see above, pp. 171–3.

and Franco-Welsh forces confronted each other across the valley for a week before deciding against battle, but his story lacks corroboration. At any rate, within a few weeks the French had retired to Pembrokeshire; some of them returned to France immediately, others remained in Wales until early in the new year, possibly because a dozen or more French vessels on their way to Wales were seized by the admiral Thomas Lord Berkeley, and Sir Thomas Swynburn, acting in conjunction with Henry Pay.[40] The council in Paris was disappointed with the campaign, and it seems to have made little impression in England. Doubtless it helped Owain to consolidate his hold on Pembrokeshire, at least temporarily, and he assuredly hoped that it heralded the start of an era of Franco-Welsh cooperation, for in March 1406 he wrote to Charles VI to tell him that to reinforce their alliance he was transferring the allegiance of the Welsh Church from Rome to Avignon.[41] In fact, the 1405 expedition marked both the beginning and the end of meaningful Franco-Welsh military cooperation, and did little to revive Glyn Dwr's fortunes.

Elsewhere too the year 1405 marked a perceptible shift of momentum in Henry's favour. The Pirate War was tailing off, leaving England's ports and shipping a good deal less vulnerable than they had been two or three years earlier, as is reflected in the recovery of wool and cloth exports, which by 1405-6 were back to their 1398-9 levels.[42] In May 1405, Waleran of St-Pol covered himself with shame once again when he tried to seize the castle of Marck, one of the Calais bastions, but was forced to beat such a hasty retreat that he left behind his armour, pennon and siege engines; a month later he was relieved of his command in Picardy and ordered by the French council not to retaliate. Not so the English, who sent a punitive fleet under the king's second son Thomas and the earl of Kent, which raided Sluys in Flanders, burned half a dozen towns in Normandy and captured three carracks on the way home.[43] For the moment, the threat to Calais was once again dispelled, although Henry knew it was only a matter of time before the French would try again. The problems involved in paying a garrison numbering over 500 men meant that wages were invariably in arrears, creating an atmosphere of discontent leading to rumours of treason and

[40] SAC II, 465.

[41] For Owain's letters to Charles VI, dated at Pennal on 31 March 1406, see T. Matthews, Welsh Records in Paris (Carmarthen, 1910), 40-54, 83-99; Davies, Revolt, 169-72.

[42] Wilson, 'Anglo-French Relations', 280; SAC II, 407; Saint-Denys, iii.181, 197, 228; E. Carus-Wilson and O. Coleman, England's Export Trade 1275-1547 (Oxford, 1963), 122, 138. January 1405 saw the first direct Anglo-Burgundian talks for a mercantile truce.

[43] Saint-Denys, iii.258-63, 317-21; SAC II, 437-9, 460-1; Foedera, viii.397.

betrayal. The debts of the town's treasurer were over £11,000, and the
English ambassadors who spent much of the year there negotiating with
French and Flemish envoys complained that they could not even cover
their living expenses.[44] The coming and going of foreign envoys also
aroused suspicions of spying, and the negotiations made slow progress.
Yet, remarkably, throughout these two years of effectively open warfare
between the summer of 1403 and the summer of 1405, the fiction of an
Anglo-French truce was maintained – and that, in a sense, was the point of
the negotiations: by simply continuing to talk about the truce, the English
and French governments colluded in confirming that it remained in existence. Stillborn they might have appeared, but the talks served a purpose.[45]

[44] D. Grummitt, 'The Financial Administration of Calais during the Reign of Henry IV,
1399–1413', *EHR* 113 (1998), 277–99, at p. 285. For rumours of treason at Calais, see *SAC II*,
388–9; *RHL*, i.xc–xcii, 284–93. In May 1403, the victualler of Calais, Reynald Curteys, was
imprisoned for debt by the king's council (C 49/48, no. 4).
[45] Phillpotts, 'Fate of the Truce', 69–72.

Chapter 17

AN EMPIRE IN CRISIS: IRELAND AND GUYENNE (1399–1405)

Challenges to Henry IV's rule during the early years of his reign came from every part of the king's dominions, including the lordship of Ireland and the duchy of Guyenne. Both of these had been claimed by the English crown since the mid-twelfth century, but they were very different. Guyenne, inherited rather than conquered, had barely been settled by English land-holders, and its native Gascon lords and townsmen were described as 'the king's loyal subjects'; they in turn expressed a consistent desire to maintain their attachment to the English crown, partly for commercial reasons and partly for fear of domination from Paris. The native or Gaelic inhabitants of Ireland, in contrast, were 'the king's enemies' or 'the wild Irish', an inferior and semi-barbaric people who stubbornly refused to accept the reality of conquest and settlement by English landholders.[1] To make matters worse, their obduracy seemed to be paying off. During the thir-teenth century, English rule in Ireland had expanded to include half or more of the surface area of the island, but since then a slowdown in the rate of emigration from England, a succession of political checks and lengthy minorities among Anglo-Irish landholders, and a vigorous Gaelic counter-offensive had eroded the settlers' position. Dazzled by visions of continental glory, neither the king nor the great English lords who held estates there prioritized Ireland; absenteeism became endemic and the task of upholding English rule was increasingly left to men of lesser rank.[2] Meanwhile, those Anglo-Irish families which had made Ireland their home and had few remaining interests in England, such as the Geraldine earls of Desmond and Kildare and the Butler earls of Ormond, became increas-ingly acculturated to the local way of life, a tendency condemned as degen-erate in the 1366 Statute of Kilkenny, which forbade intermarriage between native Irish and English settlers and prohibited the latter from using the

---

[1] For a 'wild Irishman', see *Select Cases Before the King's Council*, ed. Leadam and Baldwin, 86.

[2] In the 1360s, however, a period of peace with France, Edward III gave his son Lionel of Clarence large resources to try to re-establish control of Ireland.

Irish language, dress or pastimes. At the same time, intercourse between Westminster and the 'English of Ireland' grew more peevish, with much talk in the Irish parliament of the 'liberties of Ireland' and many unofficial treaties made with Gaelic lords.[3] 'Liberties' certainly did not mean separatism, however: the Anglo-Irish needed the king of England as much as he needed them, and the earls of Ormond in particular were adept at securing privileges from the English monarchy, especially when they feuded with the Geraldines, as they often did.[4]

Power struggles in England exacerbated these problems.[5] Richard II's 1394–5 campaign, the first by an English king in Ireland for nearly 200 years, was notable for its attempt to bring the native Irish lords into a more direct relationship with the crown and thus to establish a more inclusive framework for relationships between the competing polities on the island (although it naturally also aimed to reassert English control), but its achievements were largely undone by what followed.[6] When Richard left Ireland in April 1395, he appointed Roger Mortimer, the twenty-one-year-old earl of March and Ulster, as his lieutenant there, but on 27 July 1398 Roger, having fallen under suspicion in England, was abruptly replaced by one of the rising stars of Richard's court, Thomas Holand, duke of Surrey. In fact, unbeknown to the king, Roger had been killed just one week before this, in a skirmish with the O'Byrnes at Kellistown (County Carlow).[7] Yet another Mortimer minority (no earl of March since 1330 had lived beyond the age of 31) necessitated a second royal campaign, but the foreshortened fiasco that was Richard's 1399 expedition was the starkest reminder yet that policy towards Ireland was at times but a reed in the crosswinds of English factional rivalries.

Given that Roger's son and heir Edmund was not only earl of Ulster, lord of Connacht, Trim and Leix and the holder of half of Meath, but also had a plausible claim to Henry's throne, it would be surprising if his

[3] P. Crooks, 'Representation and Dissent: 'Parliamentarianism' and the Structure of Politics in Colonial Ireland', *EHR* 125 (2010), 1–34 at p. 28.

[4] R. Frame, 'Lordship Beyond the Pale: Munster in the Later Middle Ages', in *Limerick and South-West Ireland: Medieval Art and Architecture* (British Archaeological Society Transactions 34, Leeds, 2011), 5–18.

[5] *A New History of Ireland II: Medieval Ireland 1169–1534*, ed. A. Cosgrove (Oxford, 1987), 545; P. Crooks, 'Factions, Feuds and Noble Power in the Lordship of Ireland, c.1356–1496', *Irish Historical Studies* 35 (2007), 425–54.

[6] R. Frame, *The Political Development of the British Isles* (Oxford, 1990), 216; J. Lydon, 'Ireland: Politics, Government and Law', in *A Companion to Britain in the Later Middle Ages*, ed. S. Rigby (London, 2009), 335–56, at p. 347; Crooks, 'State of the Union', 35–8.

[7] Roger was in Irish dress and was thus not recognized by his killers (R. Davies, 'Roger Mortimer VII, Fourth Earl of March', *ODNB*, 39.403–4.

exclusion from the succession in 1399 was not greeted with some disquiet in Ireland. However, it was probably caution, or perhaps merely a break-down in communications, which was responsible for the fact that two-and-a-half months on from Henry's coronation the chancellor and treasurer in Dublin were discovered still to be issuing writs in the former king's name and were crisply ordered to substitute HENRY for RICHARD.[8] Yet Henry could hardly be faulted for not appointing the eight-year-old Edmund as his lieutenant. Perhaps more indicative of his intentions was the fact that the man he did appoint, Sir John Stanley, although well versed in Irish affairs, was only given £5,333 a year, more than half of which was to be raised from revenues within Ireland, which were always at the mercy of events. Royal lieutenants between 1361 and 1399 had usually been given between £6,000 and £8,000 a year and sometimes more.[9] The reissue in December 1399 of the 1380 statute ordering absentee English landlords to return to Ireland or forfeit two-thirds of their profits was a further attempt to make the colony self-financing, but was largely unworkable because of the number of exemptions granted.[10] Henry, it seemed, was intent on governing Ireland on the cheap, but, as his financial embarrassments mounted, even the relatively small amounts that the lieutenant was meant to receive from the English exchequer proved hard to secure.[11]

Aside from the retinue of 100 men-at-arms and 300 archers stipulated in Stanley's indenture, the defence of the 'four loyal counties' (Dublin, Kildare, Meath and Louth) was entrusted to Sir Edward Perers, who had been appointed as marshal of the armed militia of Ireland by Richard II, but proved a stalwart upholder of Lancastrian rule there. James Butler, earl of Ormond, who since the death by drowning of his rival, the earl of

---

[8] *Foedera*, viii.114-15 (15 December 1399); P. Crooks, 'Factionalism and Noble Power in English Ireland, *c.*1361-1423' (unpublished PhD thesis, Trinity College, University of Dublin, 2007). I am grateful to Dr Crooks for his advice on Anglo-Irish history in Henry's reign.

[9] *CPR 1399-1401*, 92; E 404/15, no. 133 (Stanley's appointment, 10 December). As deputy to Robert de Vere, duke of Ireland (1386-8) and justiciar of Ireland (1389-91), Stanley had gained a reputation for administrative competence and a disregard for the claims of the native Irish (M. Bennett, 'Sir John Stanley', *ODNB*, 52.226; E. Matthew, 'The Financing of the Lordship of Ireland under Henry V and Henry VI', in *Property and Politics in Later Medieval English History*, ed. A. Pollard (Gloucester, 1984), 97-115, at pp. 98, 109; Thomas Holand was promised £7,666 a year in 1398, all from the English exchequer (Saul, *Richard II*, 287-8).

[10] A point noted by the council (*POPC*, i.182-3, April-May 1401, not 1402).

[11] See, for example, £1,400 worth of uncashable tallies exchanged in November 1400: E 403/569, 21 November (also 26 October, 4 November, 9 December and 26 February); Steel, *Receipt*, 133, counted uncashable tallies to Stanley of £4,405, but some of these doubled as replacements for each other.

Map 6 Ireland in Henry IV's reign

Desmond, in 1399 had emerged as the leader of the Anglo-Irish nobility, also showed himself more than willing to cooperate with the new regime.[12] Yet the lieutenant's resources were woefully inadequate to his task. Despite attempts to pacify Art MacMurrough, the 'chief captain of his nation and of all the Irish in Leinster', he openly defied English authority in County Carlow and the northern part of the liberty of Wexford. In Ulster, meanwhile – where the discontinuity of Mortimer leadership had for years allowed the O'Neills of Tyrone to raise black-rent (protection money) almost at will, intermittently enforcing their demands with devastating raids – matters were further complicated during the summer of 1400 by the arrival of a Scottish fleet at Strangford Lough (County Down), which routed an English force led by the constable of Dublin castle.[13] Stanley was eventually recalled by the king on 18 May 1401, less than halfway through his agreed three-year term, and was followed back to England by Thomas Cranley, archbishop of Dublin and former chancellor, who, in an interview with the king on 30 June, gave Henry a chilling account of the decay of English lordship in Ireland.[14]

The king responded decisively, committing the lieutenancy to his second son Thomas – an attempt (despite the fact that Thomas was only thirteen years old) to demonstrate a more serious commitment to the colony by giving it a figurehead to act as a focus of loyalty for the Anglo-Irish, and perhaps for the Gaelic lords as well. As an earnest of his intentions, the king also promised Thomas £8,000 a year, all of which was to be drawn from the English exchequer.[15] This striking change of direction was an acknowledgement not simply of the fact that his hope of making the English colony in Ireland largely self-supporting had failed, but also of the danger that the rapidly escalating Welsh rebellion might light a similar fire across the Irish Sea. Owain Glyn Dŵr had the same thought, and wrote to the Scottish king and the Irish lords in November 1401 to invite them to support his struggle against 'our mortal enemies, the Saxons', appealing to the kinship which bound the Celtic peoples and the fact that their eventual triumph had been foretold by Merlin, and adding pointedly that the longer the Welsh revolt continued, the longer would be the respite enjoyed by the

---

[12] E 403/565, 16 December; *CIRCLE PR 1 Henry IV*, nos. 70, 127, 155 (Perers), 94 (Ormond); *CIRCLE PR 2 Henry IV*, nos. 24, 29, for Ormond, 'the king's beloved cousin'.

[13] *Ancient Irish Histories*, 17.

[14] *CPR 1399–1401*, 397; *CCR 1399–1402*, 338; *Ancient Irish Histories*, 17; Wylie, *Henry the Fourth*, i.228–9; *POPC*, ii.43–52. Cranley was accompanied by the archbishop of Armagh; Usk heard them 'complaining vehemently' to the king (*Usk*, 134–5); D. Johnston, 'Thomas Cranley', *ODNB*, 14.10–11.

[15] E 404/16, no. 728; Matthew, 'Financing', 98.

Irish from the unwelcome attentions of the English. Calls for common
action between England's Celtic neighbours had been issued before, and
the threat of Ireland providing a base for Welsh rebels, to say nothing of
the threat to the English colony there, became graver still with the defection of Edmund Mortimer in the summer of 1402.[16] Edmund had acted as
governor of Ireland in 1397–8, and if the foremost adult representative of
the greatest English family in Ireland had decided to throw in his lot with
the king's enemies, who was to say which way its clients and well-wishers
would turn?

Prince Thomas thus stood in need of wise heads about him, and he was
not disappointed. Archbishop Cranley, a man much praised by contemporaries, was reappointed as chancellor, and the Lancashire knight Sir
Laurence Merbury as treasurer; both remained in office until 1406.[17]
Edward Perers stayed on as marshal, but overall responsibility for defence
(under the prince's authority) was given to Sir Stephen Le Scrope, who was
appointed deputy lieutenant and 'governor of the wars'. The Navarrese
esquire Janico Dartasso, who like Le Scrope had distinguished himself in
Ireland under Richard II, also returned with Prince Thomas and would
spend much of the reign there, serving as justiciar, mediator, army
commander and admiral.[18] Thomas and his deputies also established a
good working relationship with the earl of Ormond, who in turn looked to
the prince not to obstruct his attempts to expand his influence in Munster
at the expense of the Geraldines.[19]

Ormond was not disappointed, for the prince needed whatever help he
could muster. Before his arrival in Dublin in November 1401, a number of

---

[16] Owain's letter to the Irish lords, dated 29 Nov. 1401, did not reach its destination, since
his messengers were beheaded (*Usk*, 148–53); cf. Lydon, 'Ireland: Politics, Government and
Law', 345.

[17] *CIRCLE PR 3 Henry IV*, no. 30; Cranley had also been chancellor in 1398–9; Merbury
replaced him in July 1406. For Cranley, see the fulsome obituary in *Ancient Irish Histories*,
26–7.

[18] *CIRCLE PR 3 Henry IV*, nos. 84, 137, 222, 251. Both Dartasso and Scrope had shown
conspicuous loyalty to Richard II in 1399, accompanying him to Conway, where Dartasso
refused to discard the king's livery badge; Le Scrope (the brother of William, executed at
Bristol in July 1399) was suspected of involvement in the Epiphany Rising, but exonerated:
S. Walker, 'Janico Dartasso: Chivalry, Nationality and the Man-at-Arms', in S. Walker,
Political Culture in Later Medieval England, ed. M. Braddick (Manchester, 2006), 115–35;
E. Curtis, 'Janico Dartas: Richard II's "Gascon Esquire": His Career in Ireland, 1394–
1426', *Journal of the Royal Society of Antiquaries of Ireland* 63 (1933), 182–205; A. Dunn, 'Loyalty,
Honour and the Lancastrian Revolution: Sir Stephen Scrope of Castle Combe and his
Kinsmen, *c*.1389–*c*.1408', *Fourteenth Century England III*, ed. W. M. Ormrod (Woodbridge,
2004), 167–83.

[19] Crooks, 'Factionalism and Noble Power', 257–64; *CIRCLE PR 3 Henry IV*, no. 112 (grant
to Ormond of custody of Desmond lands in Tipperary), 192, 212.

Gaelic lords had promised allegiance to his father's crown, and a brief foray in January 1402 secured the submission of others, but the protection of English enclaves was a Sisyphean task and often enough the best that could be offered to beleaguered towns was permission to make truces and trade with their Irish neighbours.[20] In July 1402 the mayor of Dublin, John Drake, led a force of Dubliners to Bray (in the medieval county of Dublin) where they slew 493 Irish rebels, 'all men of war',[21] but by February 1403 Janico Dartasso was reporting that he dared not proceed from Leinster into Ulster because the roads were too dangerous.[22] The problem was not just the native Irish but also members of the Anglo-Irish gentry, one group of whom abducted the chief baron of the Irish exchequer, Richard Rede, while another murdered John Dowdall, the sheriff of Louth, in September 1402.[23] This was the prelude to the revolt that broke out in Ulster in May 1403, which was supported not just by Scottish galloglass but also by Anglo-Irish knights and esquires. Carrickfergus was 'totally burned' and Sir Walter Bitterley, the royally appointed steward of Ulster during the earl of March's minority, killed. Initially the English government reacted with fury, but within a few years the perpetrators had been pardoned. Although this revolt preceded and was thus not a consequence of the Percy rebellion in England, it may well have been fomented by disgruntled supporters of the Mortimers, and was exactly the type of ripple effect the king must have feared following his usurpation and Edmund Mortimer's defection the previous year.[24]

It was shortly after this that Ormond, perhaps taking advantage of the disturbance, launched a 'great war' against the Geraldines to assert his superiority in Munster, for which he was scarcely reprimanded, let alone punished. Indeed he may have had covert official sanction, because he was

---

[20] CIRCLE PR 3 Henry IV, nos. 232–6 (indentures with Irish lords), 154; CIRCLE PR 4 Henry IV, no. 197 (making truces).

[21] The king rewarded Drake by granting the city one of his personal swords as a special mark of favour; known as the Great Sword, it is still regularly used for its original ceremonial purpose: C. Blair and I. Delamer, 'The Dublin Civic Swords', Proceedings of the Royal Irish Academy (1988), 87–142.

[22] New History of Ireland II, ed. Cosgrove, 544; Walker, 'Janico Dartasso', 123; Ancient Irish Histories, 18; CIRCLE PR 4 Henry IV, no. 93.

[23] CIRCLE PR 3 Henry IV, no. 15; CPR 1399–1401, 519. Rede's kidnappers were pardoned, as were some but not all of those who murdered Dowdall; without their cooperation the county could not be defended: B. Smith, Crisis and Survival in Late Medieval Ireland (Oxford, 2013), 94–102; CIRCLE PR 4 Henry IV, nos. 48–59.

[24] New History of Ireland II, ed. Cosgrove, 581; K. Simms, 'The Ulster Revolt of 1404 – An Anti-Lancastrian Dimension?', in Ireland and the English World in the Late Middle Ages: Essays in Honour of Robin Frame, ed. B. Smith (Basingstoke, 2009), 141–60; CIRCLE PR 4 Henry IV, no. 241; PROME, viii.261–2, 301–2.

high in Prince Thomas's favour, and in May 1403 had been deputed to
open and adjourn the Irish parliament at Waterford.[25] Such partisanship
made it difficult for the lieutenant and his deputies to claim to be governing
on behalf of all the English of Ireland, but by this time the prince was
wearying of his task. Lack of money had undoubtedly hampered his effectiveness. In August 1402 Archbishop Cranley wrote to the king informing
him that his son 'has not a penny in the world . . . [and] his soldiers are
departed from him, and the people of his household are on the point of
departing'. In total, during the two years that Thomas remained in Ireland,
only about 50 per cent of what his father had promised him was actually
paid, and by the summer of 1403 his accumulated arrears stood at £9,156.[26]
On 1 September, with his sixteenth birthday approaching, his father gave
him permission to return to England.[27] He sailed from Dublin in November,
and would not return for five years.

Thomas's departure left his deputy, Stephen Le Scrope, as the effective
governor of Ireland, and it was clearly a surprise when two months later
Le Scrope followed the prince back to England without making arrangements to cover his absence. A great council thus met in March 1404 to
choose an acting governor, and although it was said – doubtless correctly
– that the earl of Ormond was elected by the assembly, his appointment
must have met with official approval, for he continued to hold office until
Le Scrope's return and was reappointed when the deputy crossed to
England a second time.[28] The earl's first task was to suppress the continuing revolt in Ulster, for which he was granted a subsidy. During the next
eighteen months he also took the opportunity to secure favours and promotions for a number of his friends,[29] a policy resented by Desmond, Kildare

[25] Crooks, 'Factionalism and Noble Power', 280–92; CIRCLE PR 4 Henry IV, no. 192.
[26] RHL, i.74; Wylie, Henry the Fourth, i.232–3. About £8,900 was sent across to him in
1402–3 (E 403/573, 21 July; E 403/574, 9 Dec.; E 403/576, 12 June). The figure of £18,000
for uncashable tallies given in Steel, Receipt, 133–4, conflates several attempts to replace the
same assignments and thus exaggerates the level of crown default. See also B. Blacker,
'A Lancastrian Prince in Ireland', in History Ireland (1998), 22–6. In March 1403 a new indenture granted Thomas all the profits of the Irish administration without obligation to
account to the English exchequer, but in return he was expected to sustain all the expenses
of ruling the lordship, and in practice he found the revenues hard to collect (Foedera, viii.293).
[27] CPR 1401–5, 188.
[28] CIRCLE PR 5 Henry IV, nos. 35, 131; CIRCLE PR 6 Henry IV, no. 30; RHL, ii.29–35 (1404,
not 1405); Le Scrope left 'suddenly', perhaps in connection with the talk in the January 1404
parliament of replacing Prince Thomas as governor (PROME, viii.279). Ormond's letters to
the king dated 18 March ostensibly asked to be excused from office, but in reality were probably a plea for adequate funds to be made available to him.
[29] One of Ormond's first acts was to pardon himself and his mistress, Katherine of
Desmond, for having alienated and acquired lands without licence: Crooks, 'Factionalism
and Noble Power', 264–9; CIRCLE PR 5 Henry IV, no. 118.

and others, although to Prince Thomas it was a price worth paying for the political support he could offer. However, on 7 September 1405, aged around forty-five, Ormond suddenly died at Gowran (County Kilkenny). His death, said a Gaelic annalist, left the English of Ireland 'very power-less'; it also threatened to unravel the prince's policy for governing his father's colony.[30]

Henry's approach to governing Guyenne reveals both similarities and differences from his approach to Ireland. The traditional oaths of homage and allegiance extracted from towns and nobles at the outset of the reign reflected the feudal, and thus in practice more conditional, basis of his rule in the duchy, as did the efforts made to consolidate the support of vassals with a history of loyalty such as the lords of Duras, Caumont, Montferrand and Lesparre.[31] Nonpar de Caumont was confirmed as seneschal of the Agenais and received many favours, but it was the appointment of Gaillard de Durfort, lord of Duras, as seneschal of Guyenne which was especially noteworthy, for it was nearly a century since a native Gascon had held the post.[32] His appointment was also a money-saving measure, for as in Ireland the king seems initially to have hoped to make the rule of Guyenne largely self-financing. The English officials upon whom he relied were of respect-able but not exalted rank, such as Sir John Trailly, who was confirmed as mayor of Bordeaux, and his constable, the trusted Henry Bowet, but more influential than either was the experienced Francesco Ugguccione, arch-bishop of Bordeaux since 1384, a cleric of international stature and a future cardinal. Nevertheless, as the supplanter of a king born in Bordeaux and the son of John of Gaunt, whose pretensions there had aroused such hostility in the early 1390s, Henry's acceptance as king-duke was never going to be a formality.[33] It was in the cities of Bordeaux and Bayonne that opposition to the new king was most vociferous, although only in the latter, where there was a brief takeover by an anti-Lancastrian faction, did it merit description as a rebellion.[34] This was doubtless what prompted Durfort and

[30] Crooks, 'Factionalism and Noble Power', 293–4 (quote).

[31] C 47/25/6, nos. 28–9 (oaths of allegiance in 1399–1400; the Black Prince secured more than 1,000 oaths of homage when he became prince of Aquitaine in 1363); CGR 1399–1400, nos. 8–28; E 404/15, no. 161 (Caumont's indenture, 24 Feb. 1400). My thanks to Guilhem Pepin for his help with Guyenne in Henry's reign.

[32] CGR 1399–1400, no. 53; Durfort's appointment concerned some on the king's council (POPC, i.181).

[33] M. Vale, English Gascony (Oxford, 1970), 27–54; for Gaunt in Guyenne, see above, pp. 89–92.

[34] CGR 1400–1, no. 10. Froissart, perhaps overstating the case, said Richard's deposition was greeted in Bordeaux with 'great sorrow' (Oeuvres de Froissart, xvi.211–21).

Map 7 The duchy of Guyenne

Caumont to visit England in the spring of 1400, and to the appointment in May of Sir Hugh Despenser as the king's envoy to the duchy.[35] A firm but tactful visitation of Bayonne during the summer of 1400 sufficed to restore order there, and in the spring of 1401 both cities received pardons.[36]

By this time, however, a mixture of bad luck (John Trailly and Nonpar de Caumont both died in 1400–1), rumblings of aggressive intent from Paris, and pleas from English supporters persuaded Henry that the retention of his duchy required the commitment of greater resources. Almost inevitably, it was Louis of Orléans who was the spearhead of French aggression. In January 1401 he persuaded Charles VI to make the dauphin duke of Guyenne, thereby signalling French intent to recover it.[37] Three months later the powerful Archambaud de Grailly, Captal de Buch, was tempted by the offer of the county of Foix to abandon his family's customary attachment to the English cause: on 28 March 1401 he swore allegiance to Charles VI, and a week later did liege homage in person to Orléans. Henry had done what he could to retain Archambaud's loyalty, either pretending or convincing himself that this was merely a temporary deviation from his 'natural' English allegiance, and his consistent refusal to condemn the count was probably a factor in the latter's unwillingness to commit himself irretrievably to Orléans's camp.[38] But meanwhile Duke Louis was busy staking his own claim in the duchy: already (since 1394) count of Angoulême, he was also granted the county of Périgord in May 1400 following the banishment and flight to England of the former count.[39] The possession of these two counties meant that Orléans's personal domain now marched with the Bordelais, and a raid into Périgord in June 1401 left any remaining English supporters there in no doubt as to what the future held for them.[40] Henry and his envoys expressed outrage at what they saw as Orléans's unprovoked attacks on English jurisdiction in Guyenne, but to Duke Louis, whose maximalist view of the French state saw the treaty of Brétigny as an aberration, the very presence of Englishmen claiming sovereignty within the borders of the French kingdom was a provocation.

[35] CGR 1399–1400, no. 146; CPR 1399–1401, 271.
[36] CGR 1400–1, no. 10 (pardon to Bayonne, 14 March 1401); E 28/8 (pardon to Bordeaux, 9 May 1401); CGR 1400–1, nos. 26, 34, 49 (confirmation of trading and other privileges).
[37] Pepin, 'The French Offensives of 1404–1407', 1–3. This provoked an angry response from Henry, who had appointed Prince Henry as duke of Guyenne in October 1399 (Lehoux, Jean de France, ii.216).
[38] CGR 1399–1400, no. 172; CGR 1400–1, 113; Pepin, 'The French Offensives', 37–9.
[39] Henry IV welcomed the count of Périgord and offered him money and help, but he failed to regain his county: Usk, 134; E 403/571, 28 October 1401 (gift of £120); E 404/16, nos. 773–4.
[40] Vale, English Gascony, 46.

Early in 1401 Archbishop Ugguccione wrote to Henry begging him to
send the earl of Rutland, 'the person who, after my lords your sons – who
are still too young to labour thus far – is closest to your blood and to your
heart', and on 5 July the king's cousin was duly appointed lieutenant of
Guyenne for three years at an inflated annual fee of £16,666.[41] He arrived
in September accompanied by an impressive retinue: Robert Lord Scales,
the veteran Matthew Gournay, seneschal of Les Landes, Edmund Thorpe
as mayor of Bordeaux, and William Farrington, who replaced Henry
Bowet as constable and would remain in the duchy for the rest of the reign.
The new ruling council in Guyenne also included Guilhem-Amanieu, lord
of Lesparre, and Bertrand de Montferrand, who along with Ugguccione
and Durfort provided a solid wedge of local support.[42] Yet despite his semi-
royal status and impressive list of powers, there is little to suggest that
Rutland succeeded in imposing his authority in the duchy. Richard Ashton,
keeper of the great stronghold of Fronsac on the Dordogne, proved reluctant to hand it over to him, and in May 1402 the English knights whom he
led on to the field at Montendre were soundly beaten, even if the lieutenant himself did not take part in the combat.[43] By September 1402
Rutland was thinking of returning to England, probably in order to ensure
his inheritance of the dukedom of York following his father's death, but by
November he had changed his mind; within another month he had fallen
out with William Farrington and imprisoned the constable in his own
castle of Bordeaux.[44] In mitigation, Rutland could plead that he had great
difficulty in securing cash from the English exchequer, and by May 1403 he
had changed his mind once more and was on his way back to England,
having (like Stanley in Ireland) completed barely half of his three-year
term and received less than half of the amount promised to him. Meanwhile
Orléans cemented the allegiance of the two greatest nobles in Guyenne,
his cousin Charles, lord of Albret, whose appointment as constable of

[41] Rutland's indenture stated that if Henry could send one of his sons to Gascony (which
was evidently to be desired), Rutland would relinquish his post and return to England
(C 47/24/9, no. 6; E 404/16, no. 738; Vale, *English Gascony*, 31, 39–40, 43, 45, 48; E 403/565,
7 April, E 403/567, 11 June).

[42] *CGR 1400–1*, nos. 31, 54, 79, 92 (Rutland's powers as lieutenant), 101, 113 (the council).

[43] For Montendre, see above, p. 203. *CGR 1400–1*, no. 111; *CGR 1401–4*, no. 79; Given-
Wilson, 'Quarrels of Old Women', 31–2. Hugh Despenser also died in 1401.

[44] Vale, *English Gascony*, 246; *CGR 1401–4*, no. 94 (September 1402), where Rutland was
'former lieutenant' and Fronsac was committed to Farrington. This may have been the
source of their dispute; by November Rutland was 'lieutenant' once again (*CGR 1401–4*,
no. 96). Given his slippery reputation and the fact that he had been deprived of the
dukedom of Aumale three years earlier, he might not have thought his inheritance assured.
Edmund duke of York died on 1 August 1402.

France he secured in February 1403, and Bernard, count of Armagnac, who (like Waleran of St-Pol) became his vassal in return for an annuity of 6,000 *livres tournois*. Brutal and feared, Bernard would support Duke Louis until his death, later giving his name to the Armagnac party.[45]

This was the prelude to a succession of French assaults on English-held towns and castles in Guyenne, combined with a coordinated attempt to cut naval supply lines and disrupt maritime trade between England and the duchy. The latter was always one of the aims of the attacks on English shipping. The sack of Plymouth by Guillaume de Chastel on 10 August 1403 owed much to its role as the principal port of embarkation for Guyenne.[46] During the winter of 1403–4 naval blockades of Bordeaux and Bayonne were established.[47] It was the land war, however, upon which the main French effort was focused, and it was Orléans, nominated as captain-general in Guyenne in March 1404, who orchestrated it.[48] The main offensives were launched in mid-August and lasted for three months. To the east of Bordeaux, Constable Albret led a force of 1,500 men into the Limousin and Périgord, where a dozen English strongholds either surrendered or were stormed, including Courbefy, the most important Anglo-Gascon castle in the Limousin. Meanwhile Jean, count of Clermont, and Jean de Grailly, the sons of the duke of Bourbon and the count of Foix, respectively, led a campaign in the south of the duchy, first against Lourdes in the foothills of the Pyrenees and then into the southern Landes, some ninety miles south of Bordeaux, capturing another ten castles.[49]

On 22 July 1404, presumably having heard that a French assault was imminent, Henry wrote some two dozen letters to lords, prelates and towns in Guyenne, thanking them for their support and reminding them of their allegiance to the crown. One of these, couched in the friendliest terms, was to the count of Foix, suggesting that his son's adherence to the French party was contrary to the count's wishes and asking him to restrain his activities. This had some effect, for Archambaud, ambivalent as ever about

[45] *Saint-Denys*, iii.69, commented on Albret's unsuitability as constable, since he was lame, short and feeble. For Armagnac, see Nordberg, *Les Ducs et la Royauté*, 75, 120.

[46] Wilson, 'Anglo-French Relations', 190; for the Plymouth raid, above, p. 237.

[47] Pepin, 'The French Offensives of 1404–1407', 3–10; Vale, *English Gascony*, 48–53; *Foedera*, viii.336 (expected invasion of Oct. 1403); *POPC*, ii.81 (escort for Anglo-Gascon wine convoy, Dec. 1403).

[48] Autrand, *Charles VI*, 402.

[49] *Saint-Denys*, iii.205, said Clermont took 34 strongholds and was much praised in Paris. He also said (iii.201) that many of the Bordeaux citizens hated Henry, so Albret tried to take the city by treachery; the execution in London of 'traitors from the city of Bordeaux' in 1403–4 lends this some support (*CE*, 399).

his own allegiance, did attempt to limit the extent of his son's assaults.[50] Yet his performance of homage to Louis of Orléans in 1401 had undoubtedly damaged the English cause. Around this time, an English clerk in Bordeaux drew up a list of the nobility of Béarn and Les Landes, estimating the number of English and French supporters in each region. In Les Landes it was said that the nobility were English to a man, but in Béarn (held by the count of Foix) only sixteen noble houses were reckoned to be reliable while three were sympathetic to the French, seven were split between English and French allegiance, and two had declared their neutrality. Given that no one seemed very sure which side their lord supported, such liquid loyalties are not to be wondered at.[51]

Meanwhile, loyal Gascons did what they could to repel the French onslaught: Gaillard de Durfort moved into the Agenais to defend Port-Sainte-Marie and a column of men from Bordeaux raided Albret's lands to the south of the city. However, the vacancy left by Rutland's departure in 1403 had not been filled, so that, encouraging letters apart, help from England did not stretch much beyond the modest retinues commanded by Sir William Farrington and Sir Matthew Gournay (the latter by now a septuagenarian), along with large quantities of wheat despatched from England between October 1403 and the summer of 1405 to relieve scarcity in the duchy, a measure of the efficacy of the French blockade.[52] Yet although the French successes of 1404 had failed to deliver a decisive blow to the English and their supporters, the capture of over twenty strongholds to the south and east of Bordeaux, many of them surrendered in return for financial inducements, left the city dangerously exposed to future onslaughts. With many of Albret's troops wintering in Cognac, less than sixty miles to the north, matters did not bode well for the new year.

To counter the threat, Henry turned in early 1405 to one of his most trusted knights, Sir Thomas Swynburne, appointing him mayor of Bordeaux; it would be he and Farrington, along with the loyal Gascon

---

[50] E 28/14, *passim*. For the confusion over the allegiance of the Count of Foix, see the letters in *RHL I*, 438–57; Pepin, 'French Offensives of 1404–1407', 8–9, 37–9. Henry wrote to Archbishop Ugguccione on 16 August 1404 apologizing for being so taken up with domestic problems that he had not had time to deal with overseas affairs, but now that the Scottish marches were peaceful he hoped soon to suppress the Welsh rebellion and intended to help the archbishop (*CDS*, v.281).

[51] Vale, *English Gascony*, 154–5, 165–70; Pépin, 'The French Offensive', 36–9.

[52] *CGR 1401–4*, nos. 110–13, 118, 121, 128–42, 149, 151, 158–61, 168; *CGR 1404–5*, nos. 2–4, 7–8, 17, 49, 52; *POPC*, i.222. Gournay may have been in his eighties rather than in his seventies: M. Jones, 'Sir Matthew Gournay', *ODNB*, 23.86–7. Hugh Luttrell was appointed mayor of Bordeaux to replace Edmund Thorpe in May 1404, but since he was MP for Somerset in the same year he may not have visited the duchy.

lords and the citizen militias of Bordeaux, Bayonne and other towns, who for the next seven years would take responsibility for the defence of the duchy. Swynburne and Farrington, both by now middle-aged, belonged to that cadre of seasoned royal deputies who had spent much of their lives circling the perimeter of England's reach, learning to govern different outposts of the empire – a proto-colonial service.[53] Farrington had been seneschal of Saintonge in the 1370s, lieutenant of the captain of Calais in the 1390s, and had taken part in both of Richard II's Irish expeditions. He had also served as an ambassador to Rome and Portugal, and was an experienced naval commander and an expert on the law of arms. Swynburne had served since the 1380s as keeper of Roxburgh castle, captain of Guines and then Hammes in the march of Calais, and most recently, in 1404, as ambassador to the Burgundian court. He was well known to the king, for he had jousted at St-Inglevert in 1390 and visited the Holy Land at the same time as Henry in 1392–3. Following his arrival in Bordeaux in May 1405 with a retinue of fifty men-at-arms and a hundred archers, he immediately set about strengthening the defences of the city and its outlying forts – and none too soon, for the summer of 1405 witnessed the most direct assault yet on the heartland of England's duchy. In mid-August, 1,300 men led by Bernard of Armagnac made their way down the Garonne, capturing half a dozen strongholds before arriving in late September before the walls of Bordeaux. His advance was timed to coincide with the arrival in the Gironde estuary of three Castilian galleys led by Louis of Orléans's ally Don Pero Niño, count of Buelna, in the hope that a joint blockade of the city by land and sea would force its surrender.[54] Niño did manage to sail to within two miles of Bordeaux, doing a good deal of damage along the way, but he was driven off by the citizens on 26 September and a few days later Armagnac withdrew.[55]

Yet if Bordeaux and its hinterland had been saved, the survival of English Guyenne was in the balance. The crown's influence in Saintonge and the Agenais was dwindling, fighting in Périgord was almost continuous, and a French offensive in Les Landes led to the loss of Aire-sur-l'Adour. Bayonne was also threatened, and Gaillard de Durfort was

[53] M. Labarge, 'Thomas Swynburne', *ODNB*, 53.527–8; S. Walker, 'William Farrington', *ODNB*, 19.130–1; *CGR 1404–5*, no. 12 (Swynburne's appointment, 14 March 1405).

[54] Niño had been taken into Orléans's household earlier in the year: Wilson, 'Anglo-French Relations', 267.

[55] *Saint-Denys*, iii.357–9, credits Armagnac with the capture of twenty strongholds, and said that he was paid by the citizens to abandon the siege of Bordeaux.

sent to take control of the city.[56] The Bordelais was becoming ever more isolated. Once again, however, the lethal power struggle at the heart of France's royal family came to the rescue of the Anglo-Gascons. After two years, during which Orléans's ascendancy had remained almost unchallenged, the new duke of Burgundy, John the Fearless – a 'stunted, stern, suspicious man' – chose the summer of 1405 to start asserting himself. Once again France was brought to the brink of civil war, and although on this occasion Orléans and Burgundy managed, just in time, to pull back from the edge, their mutual hatred made it almost impossible to coordinate French policy. It was, as ever, the Lancastrian usurper who was the chief beneficiary.[57]

Henry's imperial policy thus went through three phases between 1399 and 1405. At first he seems to have been reluctant to commit resources to the defence of his dominions. Financial caution, distrust of some members of the aristocracy, and the nonage of his sons must all have played a part in his thinking. By mid-1401, two factors in particular made him change his mind: the spread of the Welsh rebellion, which also posed a threat to Ireland, and the likelihood of war with France following the dauphin's creation as duke of Guyenne.[58] His response – the second phase – was to look to the royal family for lieutenants, as his predecessor Edward III had done.[59] Prince Henry, aged fourteen, was sent to his principality of Wales to exercise command; his brother was despatched to Ireland; the king's cousin, Rutland, was sent to Guyenne, and his half-brother John Beaufort was made captain of Calais. These appointments were not merely symbolic, although the symbolism of England's dominions under unitary family governance, each with its own great Plantagenet as the king's alter ego, was certainly important. Yet great men could not be fobbed off with inadequate resources, and Henry also made extravagant funding promises to his new viceroys. Here lay the catch, for the exchequer was quite unable to honour them, and Prince Thomas and Rutland both came home within two years. Their frustration is understandable, but compares unfavourably with Prince John's equally cash-starved ten-year tour of duty in the north.

[56] *POPC*, i. 250.

[57] *Saint-Denys*, iii.331–45; Autrand, *Charles VI*, 404–7; Wylie, *Henry the Fourth*, ii.82 (quote). Orléans and Burgundy clashed in mid-August, only agreeing to be reconciled in mid-October.

[58] See the opening speech in the 1401 parliament (*PROME*, viii.99).

[59] Ormrod, *Edward III*, 414ff. Richard II made Gaunt duke of Guyenne in 1390. He also made Robert de Vere duke of Ireland in 1386, and his nephew, Thomas Holand, lieutenant in 1398, both of whom he was said to wish to make king of Ireland (*Usk*, 76–7).

Nor were they replaced, despite Rutland demitting office and Thomas not returning to Ireland for five years. Instead – the third phase – the king now decided to rely on deputies, who might not have carried the inherent authority of a royal lieutenant but whose experience and local contacts were invaluable, as was the support of Gascon or Anglo-Irish nobles such as Durfort and Ormond, and of Archbishops Cranley of Dublin and Ugguccione of Bordeaux.

Nevertheless it proved difficult to stem the tide. By 1405, it was clear that Louis of Orléans had set his heart on the recovery of Guyenne and that Glyn Dŵr, despite recent reverses, had rekindled a fire long smouldering. A hundred years earlier, the British Isles had seemed on the verge of becoming the English Isles: the principality of Wales had been annexed, administrative structures were being created to service English rule in Ireland, and most of the Scottish nobility had submitted to Edward I. Just forty years earlier, in the 1360s, Guyenne had stood at the heart of a vast English domain encompassing between a quarter and a third of the French realm. By September 1405, the view across Henry's empire was a study in disintegration: one French army lay before Bordeaux; another marched through South Wales. Wherever Henry looked, he saw a landscape of castles and towns surrendered, raids, destruction and defection. The 1406 parliament was told by the speaker, Sir John Tiptoft, that no less than ninety-six strongholds in Guyenne had fallen to the French in the course of the previous year.[60] The death of the earl of Ormond and the dalliance of Prince Thomas left a power vacuum in Dublin, as did the destruction of Percy power in the Scottish marches. Calais and its satellite fortresses were under constant threat of attack, their garrisons underpaid and restless. Here, as in Wales, Ireland and Guyenne, the balance of financial profit and loss had tipped unsustainably towards the latter. In sum, the English king simply did not rule the majority of what he claimed to rule, and he was beggaring himself in the attempt. The very survival of England's empire was in question.

[60] *PROME*, viii.339.

Chapter 18

THE DEATH OF AN ARCHBISHOP
(1404–1405)

The resistance Henry encountered from every corner of his dominions in the years 1403–5 might not have surprised him greatly; that those who were not English but over whom the English claimed to rule should seek to exploit upheaval in the imperial heartland was to be expected. Within England, on the other hand, the king must have hoped that his victory at the battle of Shrewsbury would cause his opponents to think again. Three times during the autumn and winter of 1403–4, 'in order to abolish all ambiguity or evil intention', the lords were obliged to renew their oaths of allegiance to Henry and the prince. Yet rumour would not be silenced, and in February 1404 even Archbishop Arundel had to ask Northumberland to assure parliament that neither he (Arundel) nor the duke of York had in any way colluded with Hotspur and Worcester. York – the former Rutland – was ever the object of suspicion, but that Arundel's loyalty might be in doubt is an indication of the fevered speculation at Westminster.[1] Spies were said to be about the king's person, some of his councillors were openly denounced as having 'evil intentions', and his ministers were accused of submitting fraudulent accounts.[2]

Nor was this simple scaremongering, for plots continued to be hatched, such as the rather opaque conspiracy in Essex and Suffolk headed by Maud, countess of Oxford, and the abbots of Beeliegh, St Osyth and St John's, Colchester. Countess Maud was the mother of Richard II's former favourite, Robert de Vere, and seems genuinely to have believed that the former king was alive and planning to return to England. Whether or not Louis of Orléans and Waleran of St-Pol also believed this, they too were said to be in on the plot, and there was hope that St-Pol would follow up his descent on the Isle of Wight in December 1403 by landing on the Essex coast to support the rising. White hart badges were duly distributed, letters

---

[1] *PROME*, viii.233–4; Northumberland provided the required assurances, which was a little ironic since he himself had just denied any foreknowledge of his son's conspiracy.

[2] *PROME*, viii.239, 243, 255, 279, 312–13; Wylie, *Henry the Fourth*, i.411.

purporting to come from Richard (though in fact sealed by William Serle in Scotland) were circulated, and beacons along the coast of Suffolk and Essex broken down 'for the riding and coming of the Frenchmen'.[3] The ex-queen Isabella, it was said, would land at Harwich on 28 December and go from there to Northampton to be reunited with her husband. She did not do so, of course, and by April 1404 the chief conspirators had been arrested. Given that one of their alleged aims was to kill the king, they were treated with uncommon leniency: the countess and the three abbots had all been pardoned by mid-November, and although some of the lesser conspirators stood trial, almost all of them were acquitted.[4] It is unlikely that they had ever been seen as a serious threat: the real culprit, as Walsingham pointed out, was William Serle, and although what Countess Maud and her accomplices had planned could undoubtedly be construed as treason, Henry evidently preferred to see them as dupes.[5] Their willingness to pay heavy fines to regain their freedom doubtless helped sway the king, but his decision to pardon them may also have been influenced by the fact that the real culprit had by now been caught.

Serle's undoing was his misplaced trust in the integrity of a fellow-conspirator. In June 1404, with the Percy castellans in the north still refusing to surrender to royalist agents, he crossed the border, looking for support from William Clifford, captain of Berwick, only to find himself detained and escorted to Pontefract where, in return for a royal pardon, Clifford handed him over to the king. Neither man could have been in doubt as to the fate that awaited Serle: as well as committing numerous acts of treason by forging letters under the royal signet, he was also wanted for the murder of the duke of Gloucester in 1397. Taken initially to Southwark, where he confessed under interrogation that the Scottish impostor was just that, he was sent back to Yorkshire to begin a prolonged and excruciating death. Repeatedly drawn on a hurdle, hanged, then cut down while still alive in each of the major towns along the route from Pontefract to the Tower, including York, Doncaster, Lincoln, King's Lynn, Norwich and Colchester,

---

[3] J. Ross, 'Seditious Activities: The Conspiracy of Maud de Vere, Countess of Oxford, 1403–4', in *Fifteenth-Century England III: Authority and Subversion*, ed. L. Clark, (Woodbridge, 2003), 25–41 (quote at p. 31). New beacons to warn of invasion had recently been set up: *Giles*, 35–6. A letter purporting to come from Richard was also sent to the parliament of January 1404, but its bearer hastily denied that the former king was alive and the matter seems to have been dropped (*CE*, iii.400).

[4] It is possible that one conspirator, William Blithe, was executed: Ross, 'Seditious Activities', 35.

[5] *SAC II*, 414; *CE*, iii.401–2; *Select Cases in the King's Bench VII*, ed. Sayles, 151–5. It was also alleged that the Scots and the Welsh were involved in the conspiracy.

he was finally disembowelled, decapitated and quartered at Tyburn and his head set on top of London bridge. To Henry, Serle's drawn out passion was a calculated act of political theatre, intended to remind successive audiences of the corresponding procession of Richard's corpse from Pontefract to London four-and-a-half years earlier – the soon-to-be-dead Serle in the footsteps of the assuredly dead king – and of the fate awaiting those who stubbornly continued to defy the evidence of their own eyes and ears.[6]

Walsingham claimed that after Serle's death the rumour that Richard was alive ceased, but such optimism was premature, for two years later it was still causing sufficient concern to be the subject of parliamentary legislation.[7] It was the Mortimer claim to the throne, however, which thrust itself to the fore in the early months of 1405. Edmund and Roger Mortimer, the thirteen- and eleven-year-old sons of the former earl of March, had been kept since Henry's accession in close, but not harsh, custody at Windsor and Berkhamstead and brought up alongside the king's younger children, their claim to the throne never officially discussed despite being much talked about in the country at large.[8] However, in mid-February 1405, an attempt was made to abduct them from Windsor castle, apparently with the intention of taking them to Wales to join their uncle Edmund and Glyn Dŵr. Behind this plot was Constance, Lady Despenser, sister of the duke of York and widow of the Thomas Despenser who had been lynched at Bristol in January 1400 after joining the Epiphany rising. Somehow she managed to persuade a locksmith to make duplicate keys to Windsor castle: spirited away during the night of 13 February, the boys were hurried westwards, but recaptured within a day or two in a forest near Cheltenham and returned to custody. The locksmith lost his head, and four days later Lady Constance was brought before the lords of the realm at Westminster.[9] Without denying her own part in the affair, she sought to throw the blame on others. The 'principal instigator of the kidnapping', she declared, was the duke of York, adding improbably that he had also planned to assassinate the king by climbing over the walls of

---

[6] *SAC II*, 417; *CE*, iii.402; *Usk*, 176; *English Chronicle*, 35, 123; BL Add. Ms 24,512, fo. 119, for Serle's interrogation at Southwark and the death of his accomplice, Richard Tighler (who was executed at Pontefract), and the distribution of his body parts. Details of Serle's fate differ slightly, but Henry himself commented that he 'endured great number of pains, more severe than other traitors heretofore' (*CCR 1402–5*, 203, 352–7; *CPR 1401–5*, 441).

[7] *PROME*, viii.362; Walker, 'Rumour, Sedition and Popular Protest', 39–41, 60.

[8] *CP*, viii.450–1; *CPR 1401–5*, 406 (£200 a year annually for their maintenance); Given-Wilson, *Chronicles*, 200–1.

[9] W. Dugdale, *Monasticon Anglicanum* (6 vols, London, 1846–9), vi (Part 1), 355 (Wigmore Chronicle); *SAC II*, 431–3.

Eltham palace while Henry was spending Christmas there two months earlier. Her animosity towards her brother might be explained by the rumours that it was he who had betrayed the Epiphany rising, thus causing her husband's death, but may equally have been prompted by the knowledge that the duke was a man against whom much tended to be insinuated and a good deal of it believed. On the other hand, both Prince Henry and the commons in the October 1404 parliament praised York's service in Wales over the past eighteen months.[10] Perhaps this is what saved him, for he confessed to the council that he had indeed known about the kidnap plot, although he claimed to have forewarned Henry about it.[11] The plot to assassinate the king he strenuously denied, and Henry evidently chose to believe him. He was nevertheless imprisoned in Pevensey castle for around ten months, and his lands and goods seized into the king's hands, before being pardoned in December 1405; his sister was also imprisoned, at Kenilworth, but by mid-1406 she too had been pardoned, a considerable act of grace on Henry's part.[12] Others too were alleged to have been implicated. Thomas Mowbray, the nineteen-year-old earl marshal, admitted having known about the plot, but claimed not to have approved of it and was given the benefit of the doubt. For the second time in a year, whisperers were also at work against Archbishop Arundel, who once again had to clear his name in the king's presence, this time on bended knee, although exactly what was being alleged against him is unclear.[13] Whether the two boys were complicit in their own abduction is also unclear, but it is difficult not to think that their uncle, Edmund Mortimer senior, and Glyn Dŵr were parties to it. Had the boys been brought safely into Wales, it was to Glyn Dŵr and his son-in-law that they would assuredly have been taken.[14]

---

[10] *PROME*, 291, 302–3; R. Horrox, 'Edward of Langley, Second Duke of York', *ODNB*, 17.801–03. £3,445 was assigned to York from the exchequer the day after Constance made accusations against him (E 403/580, 18 February 1405).

[11] *Foedera*, viii.386–7; *CE*, iii.402.

[12] *CP*, iv.281; E 403/580, 2 March; for petitions from York and his wife in June 1405, see *Foedera*, viii.387–8.

[13] *SAC II*, 433–5, said that 'he was excused for the arrest of the duke [of York] and of the aforesaid lady [Constance] and all the others', which might imply that he was alleged to have been a party to their conspiracy but might equally imply that he was involved in their arrest; he went on to deny that he had ever communicated 'anything sinister' to anyone about the king, at which Henry expressed delight. Around this time Arundel's sister, Joan, countess of Hereford, wrote to Hugh Waterton complaining that she and her brother were being slandered to the king: *ANLP*, no. 334 (dated 28 October, either 1404 or 1405).

[14] On 1 March 1405 the council advised the king to keep Edmund and Roger with him at all times, and if he campaigned in Wales, they should be placed in a secure marcher fortress, but no further action was taken against them (*POPC*, ii.105–6).

Whether or not the earl of Northumberland knew about any of these
plots, he was by this time almost certainly planning once again to overthrow Henry.[15] Notwithstanding his pardon in the January parliament,
1404 had been a chastening year for him: excluded from the council, on
which he had once enjoyed such a prominent role, forced to surrender his
castles, his lands in Scotland, and three of his grandchildren as hostages to
the king, even within his northern heartland his influence was marginalized. It was the fifteen-year-old Prince John, now constable of England as
well as warden of the East March, and his mentor, the king's brother-
in-law, Ralph earl of Westmorland, warden of the West March, who now
exercised public authority over the borders.[16] Walsingham said Westmorland displayed 'hatred and ingratitude' towards Northumberland and his
men, and given his role in subduing the Percy retainers in the aftermath of
Shrewsbury this ill-feeling was surely reciprocated, with the two earls' stagy
parliamentary reconciliation in February 1404 little more than a charade.
Westmorland must surely have felt that Northumberland and his son had
exercised excessive influence on the marches during the first few years of
the reign, and this was his chance to even things up.[17]

The early months of 1405 saw Northumberland carefully trying to allay
any suspicion that he had not returned to the fold. Writing to Henry from
Warkworth on 12 January to excuse himself from attending a council
meeting at Westminster because of his 'great age and debility, and the long
and arduous journey in wintertime', he signed himself 'Your Humble
Matathyas', as he had in June 1403, a reminder of the history of successful
cooperation between him and the king. Two months later, after an absence
of a year, he was once again attending meetings of the council.[18] The earl's
reappearance at Westminster may have been designed to give him the
opportunity to acquaint himself with the king's plans, and perhaps to test
the waters with others sympathetic to his cause. What he would have discovered was that the king was planning soon to campaign in Wales; at the
beginning of May, Henry moved to Worcester, then on to Hereford. Like
Hotspur two years earlier, Northumberland probably hoped that the king's
preoccupation with Glyn Dŵr would allow him time to gather support, but

---

[15] It is possible that the Tripartite Indenture dates from February 1405: below, p. 317.

[16] It was to these two that northern rebels had to sue for pardon after the battle of
Shrewsbury (*PROME*, viii.244, 277–8).

[17] *SAC II*, 435; *PROME*, viii.234–5; A. Tuck, 'Ralph Neville, First Earl of Westmorland',
ODNB, 40.516–21.

[18] *POPC*, i.244, 250; ii.98, 103–4; J. Nuttall, '*Vostre Humble Matatyas*: Culture, Politics
and the Percys', in *The Fifteenth Century V*, ed. L. Clark (Woodbridge, 2005), 69–83.
Northumberland was aged 64.

first he had to neutralize the earl of Westmorland, and it was thus against his chief northern rival that his first move was directed. Hearing that Westmorland was staying with Sir Ralph Eure at the latter's castle of Witton-le-Wear near Bishop Auckland (Durham), he took four hundred of his retainers to surround it, only to discover that Westmorland had got wind of the plan and escaped to Durham. Frustrated, he instead (on 6 May) seized Robert Waterton, whom Henry had sent to parley with him, and retreated to where he felt safest – the far north.[19] Crossing the Tyne, issuing orders to his retainers for his principal strongholds (Prudhoe, Alnwick, Langley, Cockermouth, Warkworth) to be garrisoned and provisioned, he made his way, accompanied by Thomas Lord Bardolf, to Berwick, where, after taking possession of both town and castle, they ensconced themselves behind its massive walls and awaited the outcome of events.[20]

Initially they may have felt encouraged, for by about 20 May the authority of the king and his officers was being challenged in much of Yorkshire. In Cleveland, local gentry, including prominent Percy retainers such as Sir John Fauconberg and Sir John Colville del Dale, were said to have assembled 7,000 or 8,000 followers, whom they were encouraging to press for the redress of 'troubles and failings' in the kingdom. This uprising was halted in its tracks, however, when a royalist force commanded by Prince John and Westmorland arrived near Topcliffe, captured the leaders and dispersed their followers. But in the city of York more serious trouble was brewing.[21] Here the protesters were led by Richard Scrope, archbishop of York, and Thomas Mowbray, the earl marshal. Scrope was a man more closely associated with the previous than the current regime. Sent to Rome by Richard II in 1397 to seek the canonization of Edward II, he was rewarded with his archiepiscopal see on his return, and although he

---

[19] *SAC II*, 435; J. R. Whitehead, 'Robert Waterton', *ODNB*, 57.576–7; Henry knew of Waterton's seizure by 22 May (*Signet Letters*, no. 370).

[20] Whether Bardolf joined the raid on Witton-le-Wear is not clear; he was due to accompany the king to Wales but secretly slipped away from London, probably during the second week of May 'towards the parts of the north'; astonished and fearing trouble, the council despatched William Lord Roos and Chief Justice William Gascoigne to follow him (*POPC*, i.262). Walsingham (*SAC II*, 456–9) said that Northumberland and Bardolf were admitted to Berwick after telling the mayor that they remained loyal to the king, and when the mayor found out the truth he begged forgiveness from Henry, but according to the indictment in the 1406 parliament the earl took it by force and allowed the Scots to loot the town and carry off the mayor (*PROME*, viii.410). On 9 June, Prince John wrote to his father from Durham saying that he had been informed by the mayor of Newcastle (Roger Thornton) that Bardolf, Northumberland, and 'a great company of Scots', including the earl of Orkney, had taken over Berwick town and castle (*RHL II*, 61–3). For the Scots looting Berwick, see also *POPC*, ii.xiii.

[21] *PROME*, viii.407–8.

acquiesced in Henry's usurpation there is no evidence of a personal rapport between him and the new king. Between 1399 and 1405 he kept his distance from the court, encouraging the northern convocation to prevaricate and negotiate over the king's demands for clerical taxation.[22] It was a sermon he gave in York Minster which galvanized the citizens into action, probably on Sunday 17 May. He and Mowbray also drew up a list of grievances which they posted on the gates of the city, the doors of religious houses, and elsewhere along 'highways and byways', not just in York itself but in surrounding villages, where the archbishop was also said to have preached.[23] By 27 May some 8,000–9,000 people, mostly citizens and clergy of York and its environs but also including gentry such as Sir William Plumpton, had gathered on Shipton Moor, just north of the city. Here they waited for three days – hoping, perhaps, that Northumberland and Bardolf might join them – but instead, on 29 May, they found themselves confronted by the army led by Prince John and Westmorland.

'And thus, arrayed for battle,' read the indictment later presented to parliament, 'the said Richard [Scrope] and Thomas [Mowbray] and their other accomplices were captured on the same day on the said moor.'[24] The truth, however, was not so straightforward. Negotiations were opened, during which Westmorland assured the archbishop and earl marshal that he would do his best to persuade the king to remedy their grievances. Apparently satisfied with this, Scrope and Mowbray encouraged their supporters to disband, but were then promptly arrested and taken to Pontefract castle. Henry, meanwhile, had left Hereford on 23 May, abandoning his campaign in Wales. On 28 May he was at Derby, whence he wrote to the council to say he had just heard that Northumberland, Bardolf and Mowbray (he did not mention the archbishop) had 'risen against our royal majesty' and telling them to meet him at Pontefract. Yet by 1 June, at Nottingham, he was already envisaging 'the next archbishop of York', and when he reached Pontefract on 3 June he apparently refused to speak to Scrope and ordered Sir John Stanley, steward of the royal household, to

[22] *Calendar of the Register of Richard Scrope, Archbishop of York 1398–1405*, ed. R. Swanson (Borthwick Texts and Calendars, 2 vols, 1981, 1985), ii–iii, 19–22 (the grant of a tenth by the northern convocation in June 1404 was made conditional on receipt of letters from the king promising a cessation of royal commissions prejudicial to Church liberties, and immunity from the subsidy granted at the last parliament; only after these letters were received was collection of the tenth authorized); M. Ormrod, 'The Rebellion of Archbishop Scrope and the Tradition of Opposition to Royal Taxation', in *The Reign of Henry IV: Rebellion and Survival, 1403–1413*, ed. G. Dodd and D. Biggs (York, 2008), 162–79, at pp. 172–3.
[23] *Giles*, 44.
[24] For these events, see *SAC II*, 440–59, and *CE*, 405–8; *PROME*, viii.407–13 (indictments).

seize the city of York into the king's hands.[25] The king's fury, plain to all, was soon communicated to Thomas Arundel, who hastened northwards to intercede for his fellow archbishop. In the meantime Henry had moved on to York. Here the terrified citizens streamed out to meet him, 'barefooted and bareheaded, wearing filthy rags, and, carrying swords in their hands [to surrender], they pleaded for pardon, weeping and wailing miserably'.[26] Henry 'rebuked them fiercely' and ordered them back into the city to await his pleasure.

This was on Saturday 6 June. Early on the Monday morning, having ridden through the night, Thomas Arundel arrived at York; on seeing him, one of Henry's knights allegedly told the king that if Scrope were allowed to live, his supporters would abandon him. Arundel responded by warning Henry of the dire consequences of executing an archbishop, and advised him to submit Scrope to the judgment of either the pope or parliament. Affecting concern at Arundel's exhaustion, the king assured him that nothing would be done without his advice and told him to go and rest. Accounts differ as to what happened next, one asserting that Scrope was tried while Arundel was taking breakfast, another that Arundel was present at the trial but that Henry told him plainly that nothing he might say would save his fellow primate. Apparently not present at the trial was William Gascoigne, who walked out after insisting that the commission appointed by Henry had no authority to pass judgment on an archbishop.[27] Deflecting his Chief Justice's scruples, Henry ordered the remaining members of the commission to proceed, and Scrope, Mowbray and Sir William Plumpton were speedily condemned to death, placed on scrawny nags, and taken outside the city where the York citizenry had been ordered to assemble. The spot chosen for their execution was in a field of barley beneath a windmill.[28] When the nineteen-year-old Mowbray trembled at the sight of the sword, the archbishop comforted him and assured him that they would shortly be reunited in Paradise. According to one source, Scrope's last words were: 'It is for the laws and good government of England that I die.'

---

[25] *POPC*, i.264–5; *Foedera*, viii.398; *Signet Letters*, no. 376. An alternative version of Walsingham's chronicle stated that Henry had a brief conversation with Scrope at Pontefract (*SAC II*, 807–11).

[26] *SAC II*, 451; *Usk*, 203, added that they took off their trousers and prostrated themselves naked on the ground, 'almost as if it were another judgment day'; Strecche said they were 'naked, in rags, prostrating themselves like humble beggars' (BL Add. MS 35,295, fo. 263v).

[27] Wylie, *Henry the Fourth*, ii.233–6; for the commission, see *CPR 1405–8*, 65; *SAC II*, 453, 809, named Sir Thomas Beaufort, the king's half-brother, and the earl of Arundel as the prime movers in the trial, whereas *Giles*, 45, named William Fulthorpe and Sir Ralph Eure.

[28] BL Add. MS 35, 295, fo. 263v; *Usk*, 202.

His afterlife as a miracle-worker began almost immediately, and some believed that soon after this Henry contracted leprosy. Never before had an English king dared to execute a bishop, let alone an archbishop.[29]

Further executions followed, of townsmen, clergy and gentry, although the hundreds of pardons issued dwarfed the few dozen beheadings. York's liberties were suspended and a fine of 500 marks imposed on the city.[30] Henry's main task now, however, was to deal with Northumberland and Bardolf, and this time he was determined that the northern strongholds would yield. By the evening of 9 June, the day after Scrope's execution, he was already at Ripon planning his campaign: a large army was gathered, ships were sent with supplies from the coastal towns of Yorkshire to await the king's arrival at Berwick, and an impressive array of guns and siege-engines assembled, one of which, according to Walsingham, was so huge that no fortification could withstand it.[31] There may have been a last-minute attempt at negotiation, but although Northumberland agreed to release Robert Waterton, it soon became clear that the time for forgiveness was past.[32] By 21 June the king was at Newcastle. Langley, Cockermouth and Prudhoe castles surrendered, and by 1 July the royal army stood before Warkworth. According to Henry's own account, the captain initially refused to deliver the castle to him, whereupon the cannons were hauled up and seven shots fired at the walls, enough to bring the captain to his senses and 'submit to our grace, high and low'.[33] The garrison was allowed to depart, and five days later the king was before Berwick. Northumberland and Bardolf had fled to Scotland, promised refuge by Sir David Fleming, but even so the garrison of Berwick castle initially refused to surrender, so once again the cannons were brought up – this time including 'the great

[29] For hagiographical accounts of Scrope's last moments, see *Giles*, 46–7, and S. K. Wright, *Martyrium Ricardi Archiepiscopi* (Catholic University of America, 1997: http://english.cua.edu/faculty/wright/latmaidston.cfm).

[30] *CPR 1405–8*, 67–79; *SAC II*, 457; Wylie, *Henry the Fourth*, ii.245. For pardons issued, see A. Dunn, 'Henry IV and the Politics of Resistance', in *Fifteenth-Century England III*, ed. L. Clark (Woodbridge, 2003), 5–23, at pp. 19–22, and *Signet Letters*, no. 381. The total fine paid by the citizens of York was over £500: £200 was taken by the royal household as a contribution to its expenses (BL Harleian Ms 319, f. 5v).

[31] *SAC II*, 457, says Henry's army was 37,000 strong, surely an exaggeration; for shipping, see *CPR 1405–8*, 74. In June 1404, Henry had brought his cannons as far as Pontefract, but Northumberland and Clifford submitted before they were used; he may have left them there, just in case: E 403/579, 17 June (1404). Westmorland suggested in late 1403 that cannon be brought north to subdue the Percy strongholds (*POPC*, i.210).

[32] Not least because, on 11 June, Northumberland had sought help from the French and Scots; and he only agreed to release Robert Waterton if his brother, John, replaced him as a hostage (*PROME*, viii.409–13).

[33] *POPC*, i.275.

gun' – and after one man had been killed by a ball which struck a tower the remainder surrendered. At least eight of them were beheaded, including William, son of Lord Greystoke, and the young Sir Henry Boynton of Acclam in Cleveland.[34] Only Alnwick, under the command of the wily William Clifford, still held out, but when he heard the news from Berwick even he agreed to surrender, just in time to receive his customary pardon.[35] With the fall of Alnwick, the Percy *caput*, on 14 July, the rebellion was over: Northumberland and Bardolf were adjudged traitors by the Court of Chivalry and the process of distributing their lands and goods began. At Durham on 20 July six of the ringleaders of the Cleveland uprising were condemned and executed, their heads despatched about the region. By the time Henry passed southwards into Nottinghamshire on 25 July, on his way back to Wales, the leathered and weathered features of some three dozen traitors crenellated the town gates of Richmond, Jarrow, York, Scarborough, Bishop Auckland, Helmsley, Yarm, Newcastle, Guisborough, Barmpton, Darlington, Barnard Castle, and doubtless elsewhere.[36] And so the land grew quiet.

One of the purposes of the indictment presented to parliament a year later was to demonstrate a link between the various uprisings in the north during the summer of 1405. Northumberland, it was alleged, was 'conspiring, plotting and conniving' with Scrope and Mowbray 'and also with my lords John Fauconberge, Ralph Hastings [leaders of the Cleveland rising] in their treasons and rebellions'.[37] Initially, as he hastened north in late May 1405, Henry may have believed this to be the case, but the peers of parliament were not convinced.[38] Northumberland and Bardolf, they eventually agreed, had acted treasonably and if caught would suffer the full penalties

[34] *CE*, 408; *SAC II*, 460–3; *Duo Rerum Anglicanum Scriptores Veteres viz Thomas Otterbourne et Johannis Whethamstede*, ed. T. Hearne (2 vols, Oxford, 1732), 257 (Otterbourne mainly copied Walsingham's account, but added Greystoke's name). The will of Boynton's father, Sir Thomas, dated 28 July 1402, hints at his impetuosity: he was forbidden to sell or disparage (*calumniare*) any of the principal items at Acclam and ordered upon his father's blessing to make a reasonable settlement for his mother Margaret's dower (Borthwick Institute, *Facsimiles of York Wills 1389–1514*, iii, fo. 97v).

[35] Clifford had already agreed to surrender Alnwick once Berwick fell (A. King, 'Sir William Clifford: Rebellion and Reward', in *The Fifteenth-Century IX. English and Continental Perspectives*, ed. L. Clark (Woodbridge, 2010), 150–1.

[36] *CPR 1405–8*, 68–74. But not Scrope's head, which had been allowed honourable burial, along with his body, in York Minster.

[37] *PROME*, viii.409.

[38] See Henry's letter of 28 May, above, p. 268. For what follows, *PROME*, viii.411–13; S. Walker, 'The Yorkshire Risings of 1405: Texts and Contexts', in *Establishment*, 161–84, at pp. 164–6.

of the law, but the behaviour of Scrope and Mowbray, while it 'seemed
to be' treasonable, they declined to pass judgment on.[39] Nor could the
chroniclers agree on the extent of collaboration between the various
risings. The closest that Walsingham came to depicting the four chief rebel
lords as acting in concert was in his later, abbreviated account of the
risings, when he said that 'it was alleged (*ut fertur*)' that the citizens of York
'expected some encouragement (*confisi solatio*)' from Northumberland and
Bardolf; in his earlier and fuller account of the rising he distinguished
quite carefully between the armies raised by Scrope and Mowbray 'on
the one hand' and Northumberland and Bardolf 'on the other'.[40] John
Hardyng also wrote two accounts of the risings: his first version (presented
to Henry IV's grandson, Henry VI, in 1457) made no connection between
Northumberland's acts of rebellion and the archbishop's protest movement, whereas his second (presented to the Yorkist king Edward IV six
years later) claimed that Scrope and Mowbray were joined by a contingent
of Percy retainers on Shipton Moor and that the gentry leaders of the
Cleveland rising were beheaded 'for the earl of Northumberland'; his
intention being, apparently, to portray the cause for which Northumberland
claimed to be fighting, the restoration of the 'Yorkist' line to the throne, as
receiving the blessing of the martyred archbishop. The other contemporary chronicles, including the *Continuatio Eulogii*, 'Giles', and a northern
account, treated Scrope's and Northumberland's rebellions as separate
events and any link between them as little more than a coincidence of
timing.[41]

Yet to imagine that two, or even three, uprisings in the same region
within the same month were quite unrelated, stretches credulity. There
must have been, at the least, a degree of revolutionary contagion, with
news from different parts of the north-east being carried back and forth,
stirring new outbreaks of discontent and putting heart into those who, for
one reason or another, felt aggrieved with Henry and his regime. Moreover,
Percy retainers were certainly involved both in the Cleveland rising and at

[39] Initially, the lords asked for more time to consider the question, but then appear to have
dropped it. The commons raised the question again towards the end of the 1406 session,
but Scrope and Mowbray were never convicted of treason in parliament.

[40] Simon Walker ('The Yorkshire Risings', 168) thought differently, arguing that
Walsingham's earlier account suggested that the four leaders had raised '*an* army' (his
italics), but the Latin is *congregassent exercitus* – the plural, not the singular *exercitum* – which
makes the implication of the sentence quite different. It is thus Walsingham's second, rather
than his first, account which goes further in implying (though rather hesitantly) a connection between the risings (*Historia Anglicana*, ii.269; *SAC II*, 448–9; *Annales*, 407).

[41] Walker, 'The Yorkshire Risings', 168–71; *Hardyng*, 362–3; *CE*, 405–8; *Giles*, 42–7;
Kingsford, *English Historical Literature*, 282–3 (Appendix II: 'A Northern Chronicle').

Shipton Moor, although it does not necessarily follow that they were acting on the earl's orders.[42] The different groups of rebels also shared certain grievances – especially, perhaps, resentment at the growing power of the earl of Westmorland. In Northumberland's case this is self-evident, but several chroniclers also placed Mowbray's dislike of Westmorland at the start – and thus, arguably, at the heart – of his alliance with Scrope, claiming that 'ancient envy' induced Mowbray to complain to the archbishop that Westmorland had deprived him of his family's traditional office of marshal of England and the lands that went with it, and that the archbishop began his rabble-rousing sermon on Shipton Moor by deploring the rift between Westmorland and Mowbray.[43]

Yet if Westmorland – brother-in-law to the king, regional lieutenant for an unpopular regime, and the man who had intervened decisively to halt Northumberland's move southwards in July 1403 – probably had little difficulty in attracting enemies in the north-east,[44] there is little to suggest a deeper common purpose or shared ideology between Scrope and Mowbray on the one hand and Northumberland and Bardolf on the other. Northumberland's discontent requires little explanation. His humiliation in 1403–4, the loss of his son, and the surrender of much of his power in the north had left him isolated and bitter. His aim, as he made clear to Owain Glyn Dŵr, to Robert III of Scotland, and to Louis of Orléans, was to remove Henry from his throne. Bardolf's behaviour indicates that he shared this aim, although why he did so is far from clear; according to Walsingham he had opposed the king at two recent councils, but on what grounds the chronicler did not explain. It may have been family ties that brought him into the circle of disaffection: Northumberland acted with him as executor of his mother's will, and his daughter Anne was married to Sir William Clifford.[45] In Mowbray's case, family ties were crucial. Aged thirteen at the time of his father's banishment in 1398 (a humiliation for

---

[42] For the Percy (and other) connections of executed rebels, such as Plumpton, Persay, Colville, Fauconberg, Lamplugh, Hastings and FitzRandolph, see P. McNiven, 'The Betrayal of Archbishop Scrope', *BJRL* 54 (1971), 173–213, at pp. 176, 190–1, and Walker, 'The Yorkshire Risings', 180.

[43] *CE*, 405; J. Raine, *Historians of the Church of York and its Archbishops* (3 vols, RS, London, 1879–94), iii.288; *Giles*, 43–4.

[44] Although his hold on his Richmondshire heartland remained solid throughout the disturbances: M. Devine, 'The Dog that Did Not Bark: Richmondshire and the 1405 Rebellion', in *Richard Scrope: Archbishop, Rebel, Martyr*, ed. P. J. Goldberg (Donington, 2007), 45–63.

[45] *SAC II*, 440–1; H. Summerson, 'Thomas Bardolf, Fifth Baron Bardolf', *ODNB*. 3.791–2. *Giles*, 42, claimed that Bardolf had been involved in treasonable activities earlier in Henry's reign.

which he would have held Henry responsible), he was subsequently brought up in the household of Queen Isabella, an establishment unconducive to the fostering of sympathy for the Lancastrian cause. Having lost the marshal's office, Mowbray was already implicated in plotting against the king in February 1405, before a dispute over precedence with the earl of Warwick was decided in the latter's favour in the following month, adding to his sense of grievance.[46] Like Bardolf, he was meant to go to Wales to serve against Glyn Dŵr in the spring of 1405, but instead of mustering with the king at Hereford he made his way to York and confided in Scrope.

Mowbray's input to the articles which he and Scrope distributed in York and its vicinity was probably not as extensive as the archbishop's, but it was not negligible. Several versions of their manifesto survive, the most authentic of which is that preserved by Walsingham, which he claimed to have translated 'almost word for word' from the English in which it was broadcast. This and the summary version in the *Continuatio Eulogii* both included clauses stating that lords who had been deprived of their inheritances should be restored to them, as was their birthright, a demand not restricted to Mowbray but very probably inspired by him.[47] Three other themes are prominent in the manifesto: first, that the financial impositions of the crown on both laity and clergy were excessive – not just the frequent tenths and fifteenths but also the customs and subsidies which impoverished merchants, 'confiscations in the guise of loans', and the abuse of the royal right of purveyance; associated with this was the fact that these levies were not put to the purposes for which they were raised but were squandered or appropriated by the 'greedy and covetous' councillors surrounding the king, who should be replaced. The second main theme was parliament: a meeting was urgently requested in which grievances could be remedied, and it was to be conducted in the proper manner, that is to say, knights and burgesses should be freely elected rather than nominated by the king, lawyers should not be excluded, and the assembly should be held in London, 'which is a more public place, and where these matters can best be corrected'. Thirdly, Walsingham emphasized that the liberties of the Church should be upheld, although this was not a point especially emphasized in the *Continuatio Eulogii*. The manifesto ended with the claim that once the realm was thus reformed, the Welsh would soon return to their accustomed obedience to the English crown, an indication (were it needed)

---

[46] *POPC*, ii.104; R. Archer, 'Thomas Mowbray, Second Earl of Nottingham', *ODNB*. 39.595–6, comments that Henry had not treated Mowbray ungenerously, but that he was 'a headstrong youth with unrealistic expectations'.

[47] *SAC II*, 442–5; *CE*, 405–6.

1 Henry IV, alabaster effigy on his tomb in Canterbury Cathedral, commissioned by his widow in circa 1425. Joan of Navarre's effigy was added after her death in 1437.

2 Richard II, the 'Coronation Portrait', Westminster Abbey, shows him in full regal attire with crown orb, sceptre, robes and slippers. Although commissioned *c*.1395, it presents a youthful Richard, perhaps intended to suggest his appearance at his coronation in 1377.

3 The Lichtenthal Psalter, Lichtenthal Abbey, Baden-Baden, commissioned by Henry's mother-in-law Joan, countess of Hereford, to celebrate his marriage to Mary de Bohun in February 1381. This is the opening to Psalm 1. The arms of Lancaster and Bohun in the left margin are linked by tendrils to symbolize their union.

4 Pontefract castle, West Yorkshire: the remains of the Gascoigne Tower, where Richard II was imprisoned following his deposition in 1399, and where he died in February 1400, probably on Henry's orders.

5 Warkworth castle, Northumberland: the keep, built by the earl of Northumberland at the end of the fourteenth century. Henry IV besieged it in July 1405, when 'seven shots' from the king's cannon forced the captain to surrender it.

6 Lancastrian livery collar of linked **SS**, silver, fifteenth century. The **SS** collar was the chief livery badge of the Lancastrian dynasty, and hundreds were worn by its supporters both before and after 1399.

7 Sycharth, Powys: the mound beyond the farmhouse was the site of Owain Glyn Dwr's moated mansion, 'utterly destroyed' in a raid led by Prince Henry in May 1403.

8 The royal surgeon John Bradmore's description of his 'cura domine principis wallie' (cure of the lord prince of Wales) and his drawing (centre right) of the instrument he designed to extract from Prince Henry's face an arrow-head which, he said, had penetrated 'the bone of the skull for the depth of six inches' at the battle of Shrewsbury in July 1403.

9a Lancaster castle: the gatehouse, statue of John of Gaunt flanked by shields of the arms of Henry IV and Henry V as prince of Wales, erected by Henry IV as a monument to Lancastrian dynastic power.

9b Lancaster castle: the gatehouse, construction of which was begun on Henry IV's orders in 1399 and completed under Henry V.

10 'Saint' Richard Scrope, archbishop of York, executed by Henry for treason in June 1405, holding the windmill under which he was beheaded. The popularity of his martyr-cult obliged the king to forbid access to his tomb within a few months of his death.

11 King James I of Scotland
(1406–37), captured in the
North Sea in March 1406,
remained a prisoner of the
English until 1424. This
sixteenth-century anonymous oil
painting on panel in the Scottish
National Portrait Gallery is
said to have been based on a
fifteenth-century original.

12 Thomas, duke of Clarence, second son
of Henry IV, born 1387, died 1421, his
tomb effigy with SS collar in Canterbury
cathedral. Next to him lay the effigy of his
wife, Margaret Holand, whom he married in
1412; on Margaret's other side was the effigy
of her first husband, John Beaufort, earl of
Somerset (d.1410).

13a and b Second Great Seal of Henry IV (*c*.1406), (a) obverse. 'Iconographically the finest great seal of the late middle ages in England', it shows Henry in the centre of a perpendicular screen flanked by SS Michael, George, Edward and Edmund, and above him the Virgin and Child. It also incorporated the change in the French arms from France Ancient to France Modern and Prince Henry's arms as prince of Wales, duke of Cornwall and earl of Chester.

(b) reverse: the king as warrior.

14 Petitions to the king from (top) Robert Hallum, archdeacon of Canterbury; (middle) Sir Matthew Gournay; (bottom) Garcius Arnald of Salins in Guyenne. Each one is endorsed at the top in Henry's hand. On the petition from Hallum, he has written 'H. R. volons et avons grante toute ceste bille qil soit fet' ('We King Henry wish and have granted this entire bill so that it be done').

15 The Chapel in the Crag, Knaresborough, North Yorkshire, a wayside shrine carved out of the cliff above the River Nidd by John the Mason in thanksgiving for his young son being miraculously saved from falling rock. Henry IV granted permission for the shrine in 1407.

16 Thomas Arundel, archbishop of Canterbury, Lambeth Palace. This nineteenth-century portrait is said to be based on a fifteenth-century original, but is unlikely to have pre-dated Holbein and may be even later. Arundel was vilified for his 'heretic-burning' during the Reformation, but this more sympathetic portrayal suggests a revival of his reputation.

17a Battlefield Chapel, near Shrewsbury, dedicated to St Mary Magdalene and founded by Henry IV *c*.1409 on the site of the battle of Shrewsbury as a house of prayer for the souls of those who had died at the battle.

17b Statue of Henry IV on the east gable of the church.

The text within the manuscript image reads:

ȝe noble and myȝtty Prince excellent
My lorȝ the Prince · o my loȝȝ gracious
A humble seruant and obedient
On to ȝour estate hye and glorious
Of which I am ful tendȝe and ful ȝelous
At recommaunde ȝn to ȝour worthynesse
With herte enteer and spirit of meeknesse

18 Thomas Hoccleve, poet and clerk of the privy seal, presents his *Regement of Princes*, written in 1410–11, to Henry, Prince of Wales, 'hye noble and myghtty prince excellent/My lord the prince and my lord gracious'.

19 Henry IV's Great Bible, at 63 x 43 cm. the largest illuminated bible made in medieval England.
The illuminated initial portrays St Jerome in his study, showing desks similar to the 'great desk' on
two levels built for the king's study at Eltham, in which he kept his books.

of the disastrous impact of the continuing revolt in Wales on Henry's reputation.[48]

Several further versions survive of what were alleged to be Scrope's complaints against Henry and his supporters, although their authenticity is questionable.[49] Especially dubious is the claim that Scrope 'desired that the crown of England should be restored to the right line or descent'. Had Scrope and Mowbray expressed such a wish publicly, it would have been manifest treason and would have aligned their declared aims more closely with those of Northumberland and Bardolf, but the assertion that they did so is almost certainly a later, Yorkist-inspired gloss associated with the hagiographical tradition which grew up around Scrope's martyr cult. The more reliable accounts of Walsingham and the *Continuatio Eulogii* author point instead to a series of demands broad enough to appeal to a range of interests in the kingdom, both popular and elite, without presenting a direct threat to the regime. Taxation, needless to say, was never popular, and the previous six months had seen unusually heavy impositions, with an almost unprecedented two lay tenths and fifteenths (in addition to other fiscal novelties) granted at the parliament of October 1404, the level of taxation on customs higher than at any time since the 1340s, and the northern and southern convocations providing at least two clerical tenths, each within less than a year. Scrope's York convocation would have felt especially aggrieved, for between 1399 and 1403 they had only granted one clerical tenth, but in 1404 not only were they pressurized into granting one in June and another in December, but also, for the latter, into abolishing the traditional exemption threshold of £10, thus bringing even the poorest benefice-holders within its ambit. Then in early May 1405 Scrope attended the council held by the king at Worcester, where it was decided in addition to oblige stipendiary chaplains (also formerly exempt) to contribute to these demands. This may have been the trigger for his sermon in York minster two weeks later.[50] Unlike the southern convocation, which almost invariably met at the same time as parliament, the northern clergy did not

---

[48] See also the hexameter inscribed on the wall of the monks' choir at St Albans abbey, which dates from around this time: 'Christe Dei splendor, supplico tibi, destrue Gleendor' (*Original Letters*, i.43).

[49] Walker, 'The Yorkshire Risings', 171–5; *Historians of the Church of York*, ed. Raine ii.292–311, 428–33; iii.288–91; Wright, *Martyrium Ricardi Archiepiscopi*. These include the accusation that Henry had committed perjury in 1399; that sheriffs had not been freely elected; and that Henry had put to death a number of notable lords such as the earls of Huntingdon, Gloucester and Salisbury, Hotspur, Worcester and Sir Roger Clarendon.

[50] Ormrod, 'The Rebellion of Archbishop Scrope', 162–79; Walker, 'The Yorkshire Risings', 183; *Signet Letters*, no. 328; *Register of Richard Scrope*, ii.993.

benefit from regular opportunities to present their complaints to a wider audience in the form of gravamina. Scrope's emphasis on parliament as the fount of remedies would thus have resonated with many of the clergy who were so prominent among his followers, just as his emphasis on the burden of customs duties and the plight of the merchants would have struck a chord with the citizens of York, many of whom also supported him.[51] To contemporaries, his unhappiness at the conduct of parliament had unmistakable relevance to the moment, for the October 1404 assembly was not held in London, lawyers were excluded from it, and there were accusations that the elections had been rigged.[52] Yet by couching his grievances in the customary language of reform and correction – of estates and liberties, the concept of fiscal proportionality and the salvation of the realm and the faithful community – Scrope was also appealing to a well-established audience for the expression of 'loyal opposition' to the crown, a stage on which English archbishops had always played a leading and, at times, tragic role.

What soon became all too clear to him and Mowbray was that the king saw their protest movement in a very different light. The enthusiastic response to their exhortations probably exceeded their expectations and may have contributed to their downfall, for whatever Henry believed their motives to be, the appearance on Shipton Moor of 8,000 or 9,000 men, some armed, was too threatening to be regarded as a loyal or peaceful movement. The composition of their host must also have irritated the king. The level of clerical involvement, recalling the treasonable activities of Richard II's chaplains in January 1400, of dissident friars in 1402 and of Maud de Vere's fellow-conspirators in 1403–4, probably persuaded the king that if an example was not made there would be no end to priestly sedition. He also seems to have interpreted the mass resistance of the citizens of York – the only major town openly to defy Henry during his reign – as a challenge to his support for William Frost, the cooperative but lofty mayor who had been ousted in February 1405 after five consecutive years in office.[53] Armed urban uprisings were common enough on the continent, but remarkably rare in England and to be firmly discouraged.

Yet if all this goes some way towards explaining why Henry was prepared to risk such a disproportionate reaction to the northern rebellions of May 1405, there is still something puzzling about the king's ferocity. The

[51] Walker, 'The Yorkshire Risings', 177–9; C. D. Liddy, 'William Frost, the City of York and Scrope's Rebellion of 1405', in Goldbergh, ed., *Richard Scrope*, 64–85.

[52] *PROME*, viii.281–2.

[53] Liddy, 'William Frost', 77–82; and see below, p. 429.

degrading submission ritual performed by the massed ranks of York citizenry (not just a representative group of them, which was customary), the
harvest of heads across the north-east, the deployment of cannon for the
first time on English soil, and the first judicial execution of an English
bishop were clearly Henry's way of signalling that enough was enough. Yet
despite the allegation that the rebel hosts had arrayed themselves for war,
with banners unfurled, it is worth remembering that neither at Topcliffe
nor at Shipton Moor was there any suggestion of armed resistance to
Westmorland and Prince John, nor was a single life lost on the royalist side.
The result was a propaganda coup for Henry's opponents – already a regicide, this was a king who also executed archbishops – and ecclesiastical
censure was bound to follow, as it duly did a few months later when the
pope excommunicated all those involved in the archbishop's death
(although without naming them).[54] Yet, although Henry would later be
made to pay for his show of force, it would be difficult to deny that it
worked in the short term. The earl of Northumberland was now a broken
reed, his followers cowed into submission, and the spate of domestic rebellions that had plagued the king since the start of his reign at last abated.

By the summer of 1405, it must have seemed as if Henry had perfected the
art of falling and falling without ever quite hitting the ground. He had led
campaign after campaign – to Scotland, to Wales, to Shrewsbury, to the
north – but what they had achieved was no more than a measure of
containment, although given the odds he faced this was no small feat.
Looking back a few years later, however, contemporaries would have identified 1405 as the turning-point of the reign. The commitment to suppressing the Welsh rebellion had begun to pay off, and the English Channel was
a good deal safer than it had been a year or two earlier. It was within
England itself, however, with the brutal crushing of the northern risings,
that this year really marked a watershed. Henceforward, England was not
a land at war with itself, and in this convalescent nation there was time to
make plans for the future.

---

[54] *SAC II*, 470–1; Wylie, *Henry the Fourth*, ii.346; M. Bennett, 'Henry IV, the Royal
Succession and the Crisis of 1406', in *The Reign of Henry IV: Rebellion and Survival, 1403–1413*,
ed. G. Dodd and D. Biggs (York, 2008), 16–27.

Part Three

RECOVERY AND REFORM 1404–1410

Chapter 19

THE SEARCH FOR SOLVENCY
(1404–1406)

By early 1404, it was clear that more systematic ways of addressing the crown's financial problems had to be found. Thus far, it had survived – just – by supplementing unpopular taxation with equally unpopular loans, padded out by windfalls, forfeitures, and the forbearance of those who used their private resources to pay their soldiers' wages, but patience was becoming exhausted, the exchequer's and household's debts were spinning out of control, annuities were not being paid, and as the theatres of war and rebellion fanned out, obligations continued to mount.[1] On top of this, piracy and a succession of wet summers had by 1403 caused English wool and cloth exports, the revenues from which constituted the exchequer's primary source of recurrent taxation, to shrink from an annual average of £39,000 in 1399–1402 to just £26,000.[2] Yet the parliament which met on 14 January 1404 at Westminster was determined that if the king was to be granted taxation he would have to agree to structural reform.[3] There were a number of ways in which this might be achieved: if household expenditure could not be reduced, then the household could be starved of cash; new and more acceptable forms of taxation could be devised; restrictions could be imposed on royal grants and annuities; greater efforts could be made to assign specific revenue streams to specific areas of expenditure, thus ensuring prioritization according to needs (although needs might be

---

[1] The discharge of John Ikelyngton in Nov. 1402 probably marked the end of substantial windfalls (*PROME*, viii.163). For the Percys paying their forces from their own revenues, see *CDS*, v, no. 915. For a commission to raise loans in October 1403, see *POPC*, ii.72–6 (not 1402). Despite heavy borrowing in the autumn of 1403 the incidence of failed assignments once again rose alarmingly during the winter, amounting to some £15,000 in the Michaelmas term, which saw paltry cash receipts (Steel, *Receipt*, 89–90).

[2] Wool exports fell from 16,400 sacks in 1401–2 to 10,200 sacks in 1402–3, the lowest export total for 60 years, and did not recover until 1405–6; cloth exports (less valuable for taxes) fell from 47,000 cloths in 1401–2 to 27,000 cloths in 1402–3: Carus-Wilson and O. Coleman, *England's Export Trade*, 55–6, 122, 138; A. R. Bridbury, *Medieval English Clothmaking: An Economic Survey* (London, 1982), 119.

[3] Parliament was first summoned to Coventry on 3 Dec. 1403, but postponed on 24 Nov (*PROME*, viii.221).

perceived differently); the king could also be encouraged to maximize his ordinary revenues, for example the yield from crown lands. One way or another, each of these expedients was tried, but the results were not encouraging.

As their speaker, the commons chose the straight-talking Arnold Savage, but although he was now a privy councillor and can hardly have been unaware of the crown's predicament, he went straight on to the attack.[4] The king, he declared, made 'undue and unwise' grants; the royal household was badly managed and overstaffed; ministers could not be trusted with taxes; purveyance was continuously abused. When Henry asked him why the commons were so 'ill-disposed and discontented' with him, Savage replied that it was no wonder, considering the burdens he placed on his people; if reform was not implemented, 'we do not see how your realm will be well governed'. At this point the king retired to Windsor for a few days, where he pardoned the earl of Northumberland – for Savage had even had the audacity to hint that unless the earl was restored the commons might not make any kind of grant.[5] In the end they did make a grant, but not of a fifteenth and tenth: the 'new and extraordinary (*novam et exquisitam*)' tax they sanctioned was a nominal 5 per cent levy on landed or moveable income.[6] Behind this lay a desire to shift the burden of taxation from the poor to the king's wealthier subjects, but the reluctance with which it was agreed makes it clear that it was not motivated by any spirit of philanthropic self-sacrifice, rather on account of fear of the popular backlash likely to follow the grant of another lay subsidy. The commons insisted that no mention of the tax be made on the parliament roll and that all records relating to its collection be destroyed, so that it could not be used as a precedent. How much they thought it would yield is not clear: £12,000 of the proceeds were to be given to the king to clear his debts, with the remainder being paid not into the exchequer but to four war-treasurers who would be responsible for ensuring that it was spent entirely on defence rather than being diverted by the king and his ministers to other purposes. If by 15

---

[4] *CPR 1401–5*, 236. He attended the great council held at Sutton (Surrey) on 11 Jan., called presumably to prepare a case for taxation to be presented to the parliament. He had also been speaker in January 1401 (above, p. 180).

[5] *PROME*, viii.222–3, 230–1, 239, 242, 279 (the 'Durham Newsletter', an independent account of the exchanges between Henry and Savage).

[6] *SAC II*, 394–7. Each holder of a knight's fee was to pay twenty shillings; landholders who did not hold by knight service were to pay one shilling for each twenty shillings per annum they held; those with less than twenty shillings of land but moveable goods valued at twenty pounds would also pay one shilling in the pound.

May the king had not raised an 'army on the sea' to defend the realm, the entire grant would be null and void.[7]

What soon became apparent was that the cost of this naval force alone, estimated at £9,546, was likely to exceed the entire proceeds of the tax. Shrouded in confusion from the start, its lack of transparency was a powerful inducement to evasion and it appears to have yielded no more than about £9,000, of which at least £6,526 went directly to the war-treasurers.[8] The appointment as war-treasurers of three London citizens and a chamberlain of the exchequer was most unwelcome to the king. An expedient last tried in the 1380s, it had the effect of depriving the crown of the flexibility to distribute income as it wished, which was in fact precisely what it was designed to do, thereby ensuring that taxes voted for war were spent on war.[9] In practice, however, it threatened even the routine obligations of government, including annuities. Payment of the £20,000 and more of exchequer annuities promised by Henry or his predecessors was a running sore. Parliament had stipulated in 1401 that customs revenue should not be used for this purpose and that new annuitants must declare the value of grants they already held from the crown. In 1402 the over-assignment of shrieval revenues led to Henry agreeing that those whose grants bore the earliest dates should be preferred over those with more recent grants, but that precedence should be given to paying the debts of the royal household. Now, however, the king declared that although certain ordinary sources of revenue should be reserved for the household, those who held annuities assigned on them should nevertheless be paid in full.[10] This was unrealistic. In fact, crown revenues came under such pressure in 1404 that by July the king had to put a complete stop on the payment of exchequer annuities, an embarrassment acknowledged in the October parliament when it was agreed to suspend them retrospectively for a year

[7] The figure of £12,000 was not the expected yield of the tax, but the amount to be handed directly to the king: cf. M. Jurkowski, C. Smith and D. Crook, eds, *Lay Taxes in England and Wales 1188–1688* (Kew, 1998), 74–5. The details were duly omitted from the parliament roll, but preserved by Walsingham and on the subsidy roll: S. Chrimes and A. Brown, *Select Documents of English Constitutional History 1307–1485* (London, 1961), 212–14; *SAC II*, 394–7; *CFR 1399–1405*, 251–4.

[8] *PROME*, viii.226; E 403/579, 17 June. Parliament had failed to specify the process by which the tax was to be levied, so the justices had to be called in to do so (*POPC*, ii.270).

[9] The war-treasurers were John Hadley, Thomas Knolles, Richard Merlawe (all Londoners) and John Oudeby (*RHKA*, 121–30).

[10] *PROME*, viii.105, 107, 210, 240. For the compilation of a 'great roll' of royal annuitants in January 1401 for inspection by the king and the barons of the exchequer, see E 403/569, 5 Feb. 1401.

from Easter 1404.[11] This was a decision fraught with political danger.
Henry had relied on the unpaid service of his annuitants to suppress rebellions and campaign in Wales and Scotland during the early years of the
reign, but the longer annuities remained unpaid the fewer were likely to
respond. After 1404, Henry's military summonses ceased to refer to his
annuitants and referred only to his retainers or retinue, a presentational
strategy shifting the emphasis from financial obligation to loyalty.[12]

Unfortunately the stop on annuities did little to improve the situation in
the household either, despite the fact that expenditure in the great wardrobe
dropped from an annual average of £11,100 between 1399 and 1403 to just
£2,800 between 1403 and 1406 – the main reason why the overall cost of
the household departments fell from £41,700 during the first four years of
the reign to £32,300 over the next three years.[13] Thus the commons did
(through the war-treasurers) succeed in one of their main objectives, which
was to squeeze the household's sources of supply, but any expectation that
annual expenditure in the wardrobe could be kept to £12,100 (the upper
limit, or *certum*, proposed in January 1404) was hopelessly unrealistic. In fact
the wardrobe spent almost exactly double this during the following year, so
that by January 1405, when wardrobe keeper Thomas More demitted office
after four years, he left debts totalling some £12,000, of which £7,000 had
been incurred during the previous fifteen months.[14] Most of these were
purveying debts, the inevitable safety valve for a household starved of ready
cash, but a deeply unpopular expedient cited by Archbishop Scrope and
others as a prime cause of disaffection with Henry's kingship.[15]

Thus while 1404 proved to be a year of relief for lay taxpayers, the
impact on annuitants and household creditors of the measures adopted in

[11] *PROME*, viii.294; *RHKA*, 129, 136.

[12] Compare E 403/567, 4 June 1400 and *POPC*, i.121 (service in Scotland), *POPC*, i.185
and E 403/573, 4 July 1402 (service in Wales) and E 403/579, 8 April 1404 (to resist French
'malice'), all of which summoned both annuitants and retainers, with E 403/589, 24 Oct.
1406 (the rescue of Calais), E 403/591, 1 June 1407 (service in Wales) and E 403/608, 28
Aug. 1411 (for service 'over the sea'), which referred only to the king's retainers. The distinction between the king's annuitants and his retainers is not clear, and the change probably
mainly a matter of presentation. In 1404–5, the payment of annuities became a matter of
grace rather than right. When the king's esquire, John Golafre, received his annuity it was
made clear that it was because he had accompanied the king to Wales and the north: E
159/182, rot. 3d; cf. G. Harriss, *Cardinal Beaufort* (Oxford, 1988), 13; A. Brown, 'The
Authorization of Letters under the Great Seal', *BIHR* 37 (1964), 125–56.

[13] *RHKA*, 94.

[14] *PROME*, viii.240–2: it was agreed in January 1404 that the household's revenues were
to be taken from the sheriffs' farms, the petty custom, the profits of the hanaper, escheats,
the alien priories, ulnage duties on cloth and the ancient custom on wool (*RHKA*, 108, 129).

[15] *RHKA*, 112; above, p. 274.

the January parliament was severe. In addition, Henry found it impossible to fund any sustained military activity. During the five months that Prince Henry spent on the Welsh border between 1 July and 21 November 1404, just £934 was passed to him; the king failed for the first time since 1400 to campaign in Wales in person, and Glyn Dŵr duly enjoyed his most successful year thus far.[16] Naval operations, thanks to the conditions attached to the commons' grant, were better supported, but Guyenne and Ireland were more or less left to fend for themselves.[17]

A letter from the council to the king in early June 1404 revealed the scale of its task. Henry had asked his councillors to send money urgently to the prince, who was on his way to Wales. Their response was to itemize with rueful clarity the crown's obligations.[18] First, £900 of loans raised during the January parliament, mainly to pay Welsh garrisons, had not yet been repaid. Secondly, £2,000 of the subsidy granted by parliament had been earmarked to repay a loan from the city of London. Thirdly, members of the council had advanced a total of £533 which would have to be repaid.[19] Fourthly, the king had ordered the war-treasurers to send £333 to Prince Thomas to clear his debts, £866 to three London merchants to repay loans, and £200 to the great wardrobe to cover the cost of St George's Day liveries. With their fifth point, the scale of the councillors' problem became grimly apparent. For the promised naval force of 600 men-at-arms, 1,200 archers and forty-two ships, the two admirals were owed £9,546, some of which had been paid, and more, 'God willing', would be paid this week, thanks to the archbishop of Canterbury, the chancellor (Henry Beaufort), Hugh Waterton, John Norbury, Thomas Knolles and 'the good people of London', all of whom had advanced unspecified sums, but a further

---

[16] E 101/404/21, fos. 14–16 (prince's household account). See the prince's letter to Thomas Arundel begging him to intercede with the king to send him funds, as he had nothing with which to pay his soldiers and had had to pawn his plate; and the king's letter to the council, 29 August, saying he 'cannot at present be honourably accompanied' to Wales – that is, that he could not afford a retinue to go with him (*ANLP*, no. 296; *POPC*, i.234). When Cardiff was besieged in December, its citizens begged Henry for help, but he 'neither came nor sent help', and the town was burned (*CE*, 401).

[17] Of £6,526 disbursed by the war-treasurers in summer 1404, around £4,000 went to the two royal admirals, Thomas Beaufort and Thomas Lord Berkeley (E 403/579, 17 June).

[18] *POPC*, i.265–70 (1404, not 1405, for York was in prison in June 1405; Henry was at Nottingham on 31 May in both 1404 and 1405).

[19] £333 from Lord Lovell (assigned to him on the subsidy in Wiltshire), £100 from Henry Bowet, bishop of Bath and Wells, and £100 from Hugh Waterton. This money had been sent to Carmarthen, but it had in addition been necessary to assign £636 from the subsidy in Somerset towards the payment of the South Wales garrisons' wages for June, which was proving a problem since only £200 had been collected in Somerset.

£2,348 would have to be borrowed within the next six weeks. Sixthly, £666 of the subsidy in Norfolk was needed for the expenses of the royal household. Seventhly, Prince John had been promised £4,000 for the keeping of the East March, a part of which had been assigned to him from the subsidy in Yorkshire and Lancashire, but for the rest 'he can have no payment'. Eighthly, £533 of the £1,000 promised to the earl of Somerset as captain of Calais was still due to him; a further £200 was needed for the repair of ships, and £100 for the expenses of the king's envoys at Calais. In summary, the amount needed simply to cover the most pressing of the crown's commitments was around £20,000, and the councillors had no idea where they might borrow this. Worse still, they had heard reports from several counties that the subsidy granted in January was going to raise less than had been hoped, while the wool and cloth customs were so overburdened with assignments that 'little of them remains'. And thus, they concluded, they had no idea what to do next but to await the 'most excellent and wise advice' of their sovereign lord.

Yet if the council's letter demonstrated the disparity between the crown's revenue and its commitments, embedded in it were pointers to the way forward, notably a detailed analysis of obligations and priorities, and a policy of trying to match specific sources to specific requirements. The latter was not new – the wool customs of Hull and Boston, for example, had been ring-fenced for the payment of the Percys as March wardens in 1401–3, and up to a half of the wool subsidy had been regularly reserved for Calais since 1390 – but its application would become more systematic and provide a greater level of security for vital areas of expenditure during the second half of the reign.[20] For the moment, however, it was clear that a breakdown of government credit had occurred, and although Henry's loyal backers in London had not forsaken him,[21] in the short term the exchequer was largely reliant on a diminishing circle of the faithful such as Thomas Arundel, Hugh Waterton, John Norbury, Henry Bowet, John

---

[20] CDS, v, no. 893; E 28/8, no. 69; cf. E. Wright, 'Henry IV, the Commons and the Recovery of Royal Finance in 1407', in *Rulers and Ruled in Late Medieval England*, ed. R. Archer and S. Walker (London, 1995), 72; Grummitt, 'Financial Administration of Calais', 298; Harriss, *Shaping the Nation*, 64–5. A letter from Richard Aston, lieutenant of Calais, dated 17 August, said the garrison's wages were 'two entire years and more' in arrears (*RHL* I, 287).

[21] It was often to Londoners that Henry turned in a crisis. As he hastened towards Shrewsbury in July 1403 to confront Hotspur, a group of London merchants (John Woodcock, John Walcott, Thomas Knolles, Richard Whittington, John Hende and Richard Merlawe) almost instantaneously raised nearly £1,000 to send to him. Almost exactly the same group of Londoners raised over £3,000 in July 1405 as he raced north to face Northumberland and Bardolf (E 403/576, 20 July, 4 Sept.; E 403/582, 18 July; E 403/585, 9 Nov.).

Lovell, the earl of Westmorland, the chancellor (Henry Beaufort) and treasurer (William Lord Roos), many of them privy councillors.[22]

There was still the option to put pressure on the Church to grant more, especially tempting in 1404 since clerical tenths would come directly to the exchequer rather than to the war-treasurers, but risky in view of the already high incidence of clerical discontent. At the council held at Worcester in September 1403 Henry had rebuked the clerics for 'enjoying peace at home' while he criss-crossed the country putting down rebellions, where-upon a pack of royalist knights and esquires suggested that all the bishops present be stripped of their treasure and horses and sent home on foot. Arundel's indignation persuaded the king to call them off on that occasion, but only on condition that the archbishop summon convocation and try to convince his suffragans of the king's necessity. The result, however, was no more than a half tenth along with a few hundred pounds in loans, so in the summer of 1404 the archbishops were once more induced to summon their convocations, and this time each granted a whole tenth, although both imposed conditions.[23] Yet clerical tenths would not solve the king's problems: their combined yield was around £16,000, less than half that of one lay fifteenth and tenth, and by August it had become clear that the hand-to-mouth measures of the past six months could be sustained no longer. On 25 August, therefore, at a great council at Lichfield, writs were issued for parliament to meet on 6 October.

The second parliament of 1404 – nicknamed 'Unlearned' (*Illiteratum*) because the writs of summons forbade the return of lawyers as MPs – met not at Westminster but at Coventry. The reason why lawyers were excluded was because it was thought that they spent too much of their time on their clients' business and not enough on that of the realm. There were suspi-cions that Henry had gone further than this and told the sheriffs whom they should return as knights of the shire; true or not, such gossip was

---

[22] Steel, *Receipt*, 127, 138. Councillors might also waive their fees and expenses: Richard Clifford, bishop of Worcester and keeper of the privy seal, agreed to accept £50 for conducting Princess Blanche to Cologne, 'freely and gratuitously' writing off the remainder of the £111 owed to him (E 403/578, 20 Oct. 1403).

[23] *SAC II*, 381–3, 410–11 and n. 583; Ormrod, 'The Rebellion of Archbishop Scrope', 168–71; the Canterbury convocation insisted in May that the Church's liberties be confirmed and its goods be exempt from purveyance, but granted an additional sum of two shillings in the pound on normally exempt benefices valued at over five pounds. For the negotiations with the York convocation in June, see above, p. 275.

uncomfortable for a king who had levelled precisely the same charge against his predecessor.[24]

The main topic, inescapably, was finance, for it was clear that different measures were required from those adopted in January. Two proposals were discussed, one targeting the wealth of the Church, the other that of lay landholders. The first came from the parliamentary knights and certain 'leading men' of the realm, described by Walsingham as 'less knowledgeable than heathens', who proposed that the temporalities of the Church be confiscated for one year.[25] Their spokesman was the privy councillor and diplomat John Cheyne, a known critic of the Church who represented a powerful body of opinion, and the upshot was a 'mighty altercation between clerics and laymen', with the laity claiming that while they risked their lives and emptied their coffers to defend the realm, the clergy 'had been sitting at home doing nothing, being no help to the king at all'.[26] Once again this provoked a furious response from Arundel, who pointed out (correctly) that the clergy had granted more tenths than the laity had granted fifteenths and tenths, and that they also prayed ceaselessly for the king and the realm. Cheyne professed himself underwhelmed by the latter point, but Arundel was undeterred. Supported by Archbishop Scrope and, significantly, by a number of temporal lords including Edward, duke of York, he reminded the knights that they had recently (in 1401) persuaded the king to confiscate the lands of the alien priories on the grounds that this would increase the crown's revenues, yet in reality it was they, not the king, who had benefited from the seizures. 'While you grow proud and enrich yourselves on these things,' Arundel went on, 'the king is in need and suffers penury, as he did before'; and when a copy of Magna Carta was produced to show that those who threatened the liberties of the Church were liable to excommunication, the plan was dropped.[27] In a sense, though, the pressure worked, for ten days after parliament adjourned,

---

[24] *PROME*, viii.281–2; lawyers had been excluded from parliament once before, in 1372. For the nickname, see *SAC II*, 419; for interference in elections, see *CE*, 402; *CR*, 178; and above, pp. 275–6. In fact the number of royal retainers elected in October, sixteen, was actually six fewer than had been elected in January (*HOC*, i.164–5).

[25] Walsingham has two accounts of this episode, with differences of emphasis (*SAC II*, 419–25, 795–803).

[26] Cheyne was not speaker of the commons, as Walsingham says (the speaker was Sir William Esturmy), nor was he an elected MP; he presumably attended parliament as a privy councillor.

[27] It was Richard Young, bishop of Rochester, who threatened the knights with Magna Carta; he was known as 'Canterbury's Mercury' because he gave voice to Arundel's thoughts (*SAC II*, 422–3). Walsingham said Arundel was inspired by reading a passage from the life of St Edmund of Abingdon (d.1240). Papal bulls concerning alienations of land by the king and magnates prejudicial to the crown were sent to Coventry to be consulted (*Antient Kalendars*, ii.70). It was also during this parliament that Arundel complained to

Arundel convened the southern convocation, which voted to grant one-and-a-half tenths, followed two weeks later with a tenth from the northern convocation.

Although Walsingham presented the clash at Coventry in terms of clergy versus laity, he also pointed out that the reason why some of the lay lords supported the bishops was because when, earlier in the parliament, the knights had proposed a resumption of crown lands granted out during the last forty years, a measure which would have seriously affected the incomes of many members of the nobility, the bishops had vigorously opposed the idea.[28] The idea of resuming the royal patrimony, the second main proposal discussed, had been gaining ground for several decades and was acquiring quasi-constitutional status: if the king were to take back the lands which had formerly belonged to the crown and use the revenues from them to support his wars and other expenses, rather than granting them to his supporters, then it was possible to envision a future in which he would no longer need to come cap in hand to parliament for taxation.[29] Unfortunately, there were too many vested interests involved for this to be a realistic proposition, although Henry did show some interest in the idea, agreeing to resume for one year the profits of royal lands granted out since 1377. He also promised to set up a commission to examine all grants made by him and his predecessors since 1366, and it was probably on this basis that the commons granted taxation, although if that was the case they were to be cruelly disappointed: opposed by the lords and barely encouraged by the king, the commission proved a dead letter and the plan was shelved.[30]

This was ungrateful of Henry, for the Unlearned Parliament was in the end as open-handed as its predecessor had been tight-fisted. It granted the king two full lay fifteenths and tenths, one to be collected before Christmas, the other during the course of 1405; it extended the wool customs and tunnage and poundage until September 1407; and it repeated the attempt to raise more from the wealthier members of society, first as noted by allowing the king to take one year's profits from royal lands granted out since 1377, and secondly by granting him 5 per cent of the value of all

Henry about some household knights, whom he called Lollards, who turned their backs on the Eucharist; see below, pp. 418–19.

[28] *SAC II*, 798–9; *PROME*, viii.291–5.

[29] *RHKA*, 137–8; B. Wolffe, *The Royal Demesne in English History* (London, 1971), 76–86. The 1399 parliament made such a proposal in general terms (*PROME*, viii.49).

[30] Only about twenty cases of resumption followed (Wright, 'Recovery of Royal Finance', 70), although the idea did not submerge: when John Beaufort was promised £1,000 of land in 1406, they were to be from those *que non sunt parcella corone* (E 403/585, 26 March 1406).

lands and rents worth more than £333 a year.[31] Naturally such generosity came at a price: once again, Henry had to agree to the appointment of war-treasurers, and once again he was told that if within three months he had not raised adequate forces for the defence of the sea, the Scottish and Welsh marches, and Guyenne, then the parliamentary grant would be null and void. Lest there be any misunderstanding, the terms of the grant also included the draconian threat that anyone who tried to cite royal or exchequer authority to use these subsidies to pay for debts already incurred, rather than for 'the defence of the realm in time to come', would be guilty of treason.

Nevertheless, the combined total of between £90,000 and £100,000 from the lay and clerical subsidies allowed military operations to resume in the spring of 1405, although the unremitting military commitments, the legacy of debt from the previous year, and the successful operation of the war-treasurers system, which continued to deprive Henry of the freedom to determine his own financial priorities, meant that there was also still much resort to borrowing.[32] Yet Henry was learning his lessons: the new war-treasurers appointed in the Coventry parliament were Thomas Lord Furnivall, a privy councillor whom Henry shrewdly appointed as treasurer of the exchequer three weeks after parliament was dissolved, presumably in an attempt to blur the line between his twin responsibilities, and Sir John Pelham, an utterly dependable chamber knight who had shared Henry's exile in 1398–9 and had custody of the Mortimer brothers from 1406 to 1409. Sympathetic to the king's problems, they were prepared at times to advance substantial sums to him.[33] Even so, by August 1405, with the north barely subdued and a French army in Wales, Henry felt obliged to call another great council to Worcester.[34] Despite the alarm bells so recently

---

[31] *PROME*, viii.288–90, 294–5. Members of the royal family and holders of coastal or marcher castles were excluded from the grant of one year's profit from royal lands, the assessment of which ran from Easter 1404 to Easter 1405; it was extremely difficult to enforce and seems to have raised very little. The 5 per cent tax on lands over £333, granted by the temporal lords and ladies, yielded just £997 (Jurkowski, Smith and Crook, eds, *Lay Taxes*, 75–6).

[32] Loans to the exchequer and uncashable tallies between April and November 1405 each amounted to around £10,000, as did the debts of the new wardrobe keeper, Richard Kingston, over two years, despite the fact that he received £5,445 from the king's chamber (E 403/585, 27 Oct., 10 Dec.; Steel, *Receipt*, 90–3; *RHKA*, 107–8; BL Harleian MS 319, Kingston's account book from Jan. 1405 to Dec. 1406).

[33] They loaned the exchequer at least £5,500 between June and November 1405: E 403/582, 18 July; E 403/585, 27 Oct., 10 Dec. For Pelham, see J. Roskell, *The Commons in the Parliament of 1422* (Manchester, 1954), 210.

[34] John Darell, the treasurer's clerk, brought to Worcester rolls, memoranda and other documents *predicti thesaurarii intime tangentis*, as well as tallies relating to the taxes granted in 1404 (E 403/582, 18 July).

sounded by Scrope's rebellion, it was once again to the clergy that he turned, and once again a bitter row ensued, but on this occasion no clerical tenth was forthcoming. Henry was paying the price for his duplicity, and to make matters worse, on the return from Wales the royal wagon train was caught in a flood which swept away carts, treasure and even, it was said, some of the king's crowns.[35]

Following the Worcester council of September 1405, Henry spent a month in the Midlands, mainly at Kenilworth, before returning to London. He remained in the vicinity of the capital for the next eight months.[36] The country was uneasy, with rumours of an imminent Scottish invasion and continuing disturbances in the north, Breton and Norman pirates circling for prey, and the French expeditionary force wintering in Pembrokeshire. Early in December a parliament was summoned, initially to Northampton, then to Coventry, then to Gloucester (in order to support Prince Henry in Wales), but in February a French fleet was spotted gathering at the mouth of the Thames and it was decided to switch it to Westminster.[37]

Although the Long Parliament of 1406 met on 1 March and was not dissolved until 22 December, it spent less than four months of that time actually sitting. Its deliberations reflect the rapidly developing situation through the year, with priorities changing from one session to the next and decisions made in March or June being reversed in November or December, and only at the very end was a compromise worked out. The issues which concerned it were a mix of the old and the new. Finance, the role of the council and the need to protect English shipping and to prosecute the wars in Wales and Guyenne were by now standard fare, but to these were added the (unexpectedly difficult) question of ratifying the sentences against the lords who had rebelled in 1405 and the settlement of the order of succession to the crown.[38]

---

[35] Walsingham said that the king's advisers again proposed that the bishops be obliged to hand over their treasure and horses without further ado, but he may have confused this with the September 1403 council; he described the treasure lost in the floods as the king's *thesauro impreciabili et coronis suis*, but the incident is not mentioned in the wardrobe account book (*SAC II*, 462–3).

[36] For Henry's itinerary, see BL Harleian Ms 319, fos. 6–38. He spent Christmas, New Year and Easter at Eltham, late April at Windsor, and three spells totalling around four weeks at Hertford castle.

[37] There was also a suggestion in December that Henry might go to Bordeaux, but as usual this came to nothing: *Signet Letters*, nos. 514, 523; *POPC*, ii.280; *PROME*, viii.319; *Foedera*, viii.414–15 (Scottish invasion). For rumours in the north, see C 49/48, m. 6, discussed by Walker, 'Rumour, Sedition and Popular Protest', 31–2.

[38] For the official record, see *PROME*, viii.318–416.

The first session lasted for five weeks before adjourning on 3 April for Easter. As their Speaker, the commons chose Sir John Tiptoft, a young knight of the king's chamber with impeccable Lancastrian credentials and an abundance of political talent. Despite Henry's apparent enthusiasm for the choice it is difficult, given the language used by Tiptoft, to believe that he acted as a royal stooge, although at times the opinions he expressed were probably less his own than those of the members who had elected him. Indeed it was the king's trust in him which allowed him to be so outspoken.[39] There was, at any rate, a good deal of plain speaking from the start, focused principally on the household, the keeping of the seas, Wales and Guyenne. As usual, Henry wanted taxation, but this the commons would not grant without receiving assurances in return. All that the king was prepared to concede for the moment was that a date be set for the expulsion of some French and Bretons (mainly servants of Queen Joan) thought to be inflating the cost of the royal household. The real issue of the moment, however, was the defence of English shipping, for which it was agreed that the merchants and ship-owners of the realm would receive the proceeds of tunnage and poundage, plus one-quarter of the wool subsidy, for seventeen months from 1 May, in return for which they would fit out a fleet to patrol the seas. Agreeing even this much evidently involved some harsh words, and on the last day of the first session Tiptoft rose to deny a rumour that certain members had spoken about the king 'other than they should have', as a result of which Henry bore a 'heavy heart' towards the commons. Henry graciously reassured them that he still thought of them as his loyal subjects.[40]

By the time the second session was due to begin on 26 April events had moved on. On 22 March James, earl of Carrick, the heir to the Scottish throne, was seized by English privateers off Flamborough Head (Yorkshire) on his way to France, and brought to London. Two weeks later his father, Robert III, died, apparently of grief, whereupon the eleven-year-old became King James I of Scotland, but it would be another eighteen years before he was sent back to his kingdom.[41] Fortune also favoured the English

[39] Tiptoft was born around 1378, had been in Henry's service since 1397, and may have shared his exile in 1398–9: L. Clark, 'John Tiptoft', *ODNB*, 54.832–3; and A. Pollard, 'The Lancastrian Constitutional Experiment Revisited: Henry IV, Sir John Tiptoft and the Parliament of 1406', *Parliamentary History* 14 (1995), 103–19.

[40] *PROME*, viii.331–4. The agreement with the merchants stipulated that their fleet(s) should be manned by 2,000 fighting men from 1 May to 1 November, and 1,000 men from 1 November to 1 May.

[41] *Scotichronicon*, viii.60–3; Walsingham reported that when Henry heard that James was being sent to France to learn French and courtly etiquette, he dissolved into laughter and

counter-insurgency in Wales: in January troops were landed on Anglesey, the start of a campaign to slip a noose around Snowdonia and strangle Glyn Dŵr into submission; during the spring, the remaining French troops in Pembrokeshire departed; and on 23 April, St George's Day, a fierce encounter left around 1,000 Welsh rebels dead, including one of Glyn Dŵr's sons.[42] Meanwhile, Bishop Beaufort had been sent to Calais on 26 March to discuss a lasting Anglo-French peace sealed by a royal marriage.[43] It was thus with cautious optimism that the lords and commons reconvened at Westminster, but at this point the king's health collapsed. Early on the morning of 28 April, he wrote from his lodge in Windsor Great Park informing the council that 'an illness has suddenly affected us in our leg', causing him such pain that his physicians had advised him not to travel, especially on horseback; nevertheless he hoped to come to London in three or four days. A few hours later he wrote again to say that his condition had worsened and advised the council to proceed without him.[44] This may have been the prolapsed rectum of which it was later claimed that he had been cured with a treatment devised by the fourteenth-century physician John of Arderne (Adam Usk also said that Henry suffered from 'rupture of the internal organs'). Both the condition and the treatment were painful: the remedy advocated by Arderne recommended first bleeding the leg before concocting an ointment called *unguentum apostolorum*, so named because it included twelve principal ingredients. When this was heated and applied to the prolapsed part of the rectum, 'it schal entre agayn', whereupon it should be dressed to prevent it protruding once more. If necessary, the procedure could be repeated several times.[45] Presumably this was not necessary, or at least not immediately, for Henry left Windsor the next day, travelling by water to Kingston and then on to Westminster, and on 1 May the royal household took up residence at the bishop of Durham's inn at

---

declared, 'Well, if gratitude were a Scottish trait, they would have sent this youth to me to be brought up and educated, for I too know the French language' (*SAC II*, 472-3). Henry Sinclair, earl of Orkney, was captured with him, by men of Great Yarmouth and Cley.

[42] *SAC II*, 470-1; Davies, *Revolt*, 121-3; eight of a squadron of twenty-eight ships presumably sent to bring the French back from Pembrokeshire were also captured by the English (*SAC II*, 474-5).

[43] The English ambassadors remained there from 26 March to 22 May: E 404/22, no. 239; Nordberg, *Les Ducs et la Royauté*, 127; *Foedera*, viii.432-5.

[44] *POPC*, i.290-2.

[45] John Arderne, *Treatise of Fistula in Ano*, ed. D'Arcy Power, EETS 139 (London, 1910), xii, 74, 130; *Usk*, 247. The principal ingredients of the 'green ointment of the Twelve Apostles' were white wax, pine resin, aristolochia, incense, mastic, opoponax, myrrh, galbanum and litharge. Arderne wrote his treatise in 1376 and died soon after, but a post-1413 translator of his work added in the margin 'With this medicine was King Henry of England cured of the going out of the lure' (prolapsed rectum).

Dowgate, where it remained until 6 July.[46] It took months, however, for the king to recover, and from now on his energy declined.

Parliament thus initially (on 30 April) reconvened without the king, and although he was fit enough to attend sittings on 15, 22 and 24 May, and on 7 and 19 June, at other times he was absent (for example, on 8 and 25 May) and messengers had to be sent back and forth between Westminster and Dowgate.[47] Yet few allowances were made for Henry's health. Returning initially to the question of aliens, the commons obliged him to agree to the deportation within three weeks of forty-four named Bretons and Frenchmen. This was followed by a request that the king nominate his councillors in parliament and agree to a bill defining their role, one aim of which was to furnish them with the power to monitor royal grants. Although not intended as criticism of the individuals concerned (since the seventeen councillors whom Henry nominated on 22 May were largely the same men who had served on the council over the previous few years), the bill was designed to reassert the independence of the council from the court and, given the king's health, to establish its powers on a formal basis. Behind such moves, as ever, lay a desire to reduce spending and bring order to crown finances, fundamental to which was the cost of the royal household. The latter, Tiptoft told the king, was 'full of rascals (*de raskaille*) for the most part', while his ministers 'wickedly deceived' him. When asked whether a parliamentary committee would be permitted to audit the accounts of the war-treasurers appointed at Coventry, Henry replied that 'kings were not wont to render account'.[48] Yet in the end he yielded – the first time that the principle of parliamentary audit of ministerial accounts had been conceded. His reward, if such it was, was the addition of 12d in the pound to tunnage and poundage paid by alien merchants, though only for a year. This would not do a great deal to relieve the exchequer.

By this time Henry Beaufort and his fellow commissioners had returned (on 22 May) from Calais, and in the light of their discussions and of the unpredictability of the king's health an act was passed for the succession of the crown. The main English proposal at Calais was for Prince Henry to marry one of Charles VI's daughters (the ex-queen Isabella seems still to have been the bride of choice).[49] Should the king die and the prince marry,

---

[46] BL Harleian Ms 319, fos. 21–6.

[47] *PROME*, viii.335–53.

[48] *PROME*, viii.347; *CE*, 409 (*reges non solebant compotum dare*).

[49] *Foedera*, viii.435. *Monstrelet* (i.126) added that if an Anglo-French marriage were concluded, Henry might agree to allow the prince to succeed him forthwith; Monstrelet's account has a number of errors, however, placing the talks in Paris and naming Francis de

but then himself die before fathering a son, there was thus a possibility that the throne would pass to his (hypothetical) daughter rather than to one of his three adult brothers. Such a risk to the dynasty's recently won throne was not one with which the lords and commons were comfortable, especially since the succession of a Lancastrian princess was bound to reopen the question of the earl of March's claim through a daughter of Edward III. It was therefore decided, in the 'Act for the Inheritance of the Crown' passed by parliament on 7 June, to entail the crown in the male line, meaning that Prince Henry's heir, should he fail to produce a son, would be his brother Thomas.[50] Doubtless the act was designed to double as retrospective legitimation of Henry's claim through the male line in 1399, although this was not made explicit. The main purpose was to provide a greater degree of security for the future of the dynasty and the peace of the realm, although it would not have escaped notice that unquestionably legitimate kings with unquestionably legitimate heirs had no need for parliamentary legislation on the succession; and within six months it would be reversed.

Ratifying sentences of treason against convicted rebels should have been more straightforward, but when, on the last day of the second session, Henry invited the lords to affirm the guilt of Northumberland, Bardolf, Scrope, Mowbray and their adherents, they proved surprisingly reluctant to do so, preferring instead to offer Northumberland and Bardolf another three weeks to make their submission, and postponing any decision on Scrope and Mowbray.[51] Wariness about extending the scope of treason and lingering unease at the king's execution of the archbishop probably explains their hesitancy. Those responsible for Scrope's death (which can only have included Henry) were, after all, under sentence of excommunication, even if Archbishop Arundel had as yet declined to publish Pope Innocent's bull.[52] News may also have arrived that Northumberland and Bardolf were by now in Wales, having fled Scotland in the spring after being warned that they were about to be betrayed. After being worsted by Edward Lord Charlton in a skirmish in June 1406 they slipped across the

---

Court (called 'earl of Pembroke') as chief English ambassador, and an offer by Henry to abdicate is very unlikely. Yet Henry was serious about an Anglo-French marriage for the prince, and in mid-May wrote in support of the idea to Charles VI and his council (E 403/587, 18 May).

[50] *PROME*, viii.341-7, 358-60; if Thomas then died without a son, Prince John would succeed, then Humphrey. The duchy of Lancaster was excluded and would remain heritable by the king's heirs general.

[51] *PROME*, viii.411.

[52] Bennett, 'Henry IV, the Royal Succession and the Crisis of 1406', 16-17.

Channel, where they spent several months failing to drum up support in
Paris for an invasion of England.[53]

By 6 July, nearly three weeks after the second session ended, Henry was
at last fit enough to leave Bishop Langley's hostel, and by the end of the
month he was at Walsingham priory – 'England's Holy Land' – where he
spent two days, presumably praying at the healing shrine of the Virgin,
before moving on to Lynn for a week (4–11 August) to bid farewell to his
daughter Philippa before she left for Denmark. Her retinue, as befitted a
queen-in-waiting, numbered nearly 150, headed by Bishop Henry Bowet
and Richard, brother of the duke of York, all clad in green and scarlet
livery.[54] Such obligatory splendour did not come cheap – at least £4,200,
and probably a good deal more, was needed to pay for Philippa's send-off –
and even before parliament's adjournment the exchequer had launched a
borrowing campaign which, by 28 July, had raised over £16,000 in loans,
secured on the tenths granted by York and Canterbury convocations
during the summer; in addition, a subsidy of half a mark was granted from
normally exempt clergy such as mendicants, chantry priests and stipendiary vicars.[55] Yet no sooner was money raised but it was spent: between
mid-May and mid-August £11,500 was disbursed to the three elder
Lancastrian princes for Wales, Ireland and the Scottish marches, and a
further £4,600 to support the royal household's summer itineration.[56] That
accounted for the clerical tenths.

As summer passed, however, it became increasingly apparent that it was
from France that the real threat would come. Having teetered on the brink
of civil war in October 1405, Louis of Orléans and John of Burgundy had
managed to bury the hatchet for long enough to agree on a twin-pronged
offensive in the autumn of 1406, with John besieging Calais and Louis
Bordeaux, and by the time Henry returned to London in mid-September

[53] Usk, 214–15; Davies, Revolt, 123; Saint-Denys, 426–32 (but the French chronicler's subsequent report of a great victory for the Percys over the king and Prince John is fantasy).
    [54] Wylie, Henry the Fourth, ii.442–9; for Philippa's expenses, see E 101/406/10 and E
101/405/10.
    [55] The tax on unbeneficed clergy was deeply unpopular and raised little, though £1,694
was received from it on 12 July: E 403/587, 18 May, 7 June (orders to speed up collection of
customs); E 401/638, 12 and 28 July; SAC II, 470–3; Steel, Receipt, 94, mentions £12,000 of
loans, but there are additional sums on the issue rolls.
    [56] Around £4,500 was passed to Prince Henry for operations in Wales, £4,300 to Prince
John and the earl of Westmorland for the Scottish marches, and £2,720 to Prince Thomas
for Ireland (E 403/587, 18 May, 6 Aug., 14 Aug.; for household receipts, see BL Harleian MS
319, fo. 2v).

preparations for both were well in hand.[57] To accompany these assaults, a letter written by Charles VI on 2 October called upon the English people to rise up against 'he who now holds the rule of England' and restore the crown to its 'true heirs', promising them such help as he had already given the Welsh – although whether many Englishmen read the letter is doubtful.[58] Alarmed, Henry tried to head off the French with another embassy to Paris offering Prince Henry's hand in marriage (though not to Isabella, who on 29 June had married Charles, son of Louis of Orléans), redress for past injuries and security for French, Flemish and Breton fishermen, but it was in vain, and by 20 October the council was impressing ships and summoning royal retainers to join the army which the king proposed to lead 'to the rescue of Calais'.[59] It would be difficult in such circumstances to conduct business as normal, and although the third session of parliament did eventually begin on 18 October, and sat for at least five days, it was probably suspended shortly after this and did not meet again until 18 November.[60]

By this time the crisis at Calais had passed. As before, it was no royally led expeditionary force but the ungovernable enmity of Burgundy and Orléans which saved the town. Despite their show of amity over the past twelve months, the stranglehold which Louis had established over the French treasury since 1404 was making John the Fearless's position financially untenable, and it was imperative for him to increase his revenues from Anglo-Flemish trade. This, however, meant making a mercantile truce between England and Flanders, a policy towards which Louis was always opposed.[61] The Burgundians had in fact been conducting negotiations to this end (not always openly) for the past three years, and the impressive army which John mustered to threaten Calais in October 1406 was to

[57] On 21 April, John the Fearless replaced Louis as captain-general of French forces in Picardy and West Flanders, while Louis became captain-general of Guyenne: Pépin, 'The French Offensives of 1404–1407'; Schnerb, *Jean Sans Peur*, 194–201; R. Famiglietti, *Royal Intrigue: Crisis at the Court of Charles VI* (New York, 1986), 54–60; Nordberg, *Les Ducs et la Royauté*, 127–51. The Channel Islands were raided in late July (*RHL II*, 115).

[58] BL Add Ms 30,663, fos. 277–9 (partly reproduced in *Saint-Denys*, iii.428–30): Henry is *ille qui modo regimini Angliae occupat*, who had lost any right to the throne he might have had *ex tam multiplicibus ab eo commissis criminibus*; the letter was given to the earl of Northumberland to take back to Scotland with him.

[59] *Foedera*, viii.451–6 (5 Oct.); E 403/589, 7 Oct., 24 Oct.; *Monstrelet*, i.126, said the reason why Orléans opposed the Henry–Isabella marriage proposal in the spring was because he intended to marry her to his son.

[60] *PROME*, viii.322, 350, 353.

[61] Philip the Bold had regularly extracted between 100,000 and 200,000 *livres* a year from the French royal treasury; during 1406 John received no more than 37,000 *livres*: Autrand, *Charles VI*, 407–8.

some extent an exercise in pressurizing Henry to accept his terms –
although that does not mean that he would not have used his army if he
felt that he had a chance of taking the town. Around 11–12 November,
however, with winter approaching, he abandoned the siege and returned
to Paris, complaining that Louis – who had left for Bordeaux in mid-
September – had starved him of the funds needed to complete the task. By
the time Louis returned to Paris on 18 February 1407, the Anglo-Flemish
mercantile truce had been concluded (30 November) and ratified by
Charles VI (15 January 1407).[62]

The collapse of the Anglo-French marriage talks was one reason why
parliament decided in December to annul the Succession Act passed in
June and revert to the traditional order of inheritance by heirs general
rather than restricting it to heirs male. Whether Prince Henry had fully
acquiesced in the June act may be doubted, and with his authority growing
following the king's illness he was probably keen to assert the right of *any*
of his children to inherit the crown.[63] The second Succession Act was one
of a number of compromises agreed during the third session of parliament, although the fact that it lasted for five weeks (18 November to 22
December) indicates that there was much hard bargaining. The king had
already decided on his return to London on 14 September to relieve the
merchants of the task of safeguarding the sea, which, he claimed, was not
working, and thus, from 22 October, to cancel the additional 12d on
tunnage and poundage paid by alien merchants since mid-June.[64] This
may be an indication that alternative sources of revenue were under
discussion, but if so further concessions would be required from Henry,
principally in relation to conciliar control of expenditure. The nomination
of a council of sixteen on 27 November was a step in this direction, but
within three weeks it had been superseded by a new and different list of
councillors. Whereas the 27 November list still included the knights who

[62] BL Add. Charter 58,420; *POPC*, i.292–4; *Foedera*, viii.469–76 (published in England on
10 March 1407). John got no further than Saint-Omer, about 35 kilometres from Calais, in
October; here his army mustered, cut down 32,000 oaks to construct siege engines, then
disbanded.

[63] His agreement to the June act is emphasized a little too insistently (*PROME*, viii.342,
354–61). For a statement of the 'traditional' view, see *RHL I*, 20. 'Two great letters patent'
containing the Succession Act were delivered to the treasury on 20 May 1407, consulted by
Henry V in May 1413, and 'shown' to Henry VI in June 1453, before being returned to the
treasury in October 1454 (*Antient Kalendars*, ii.84).

[64] *PROME*, viii.389, 404–6. Henry may have been diverting their revenues. By mid-
October he wished to impress their ships for his planned expedition to Calais; however, the
merchants were permitted to receive part of the wool subsidy until 24 Nov. to cover their
outlay (*CCR 1405–9*, 156–7).

had attended over the previous few years (Hugh Waterton, Arnold Savage, John Cheyne), the council nominated in December was aristocratic in composition, including no one below the peerage apart from (ex officio) the steward of the royal household, Sir John Stanley, and the new keeper of the wardrobe, Sir John Tiptoft, appointed on 8 December. Tiptoft's first act as keeper was to persuade the king to agree, once the Christmas festivities were over, to retire to 'some convenient place' where, with conciliar advice, a programme would be drawn up to ensure that in future the household was under 'moderate governance . . . to the pleasure of God and of the people'.[65] The most significant change in conciliar personnel, however, was the fact that Prince Henry now began to attend more regularly. The first few months of the parliament had seen the commons urging the prince to hasten to Wales to take command of operations there, but by the autumn there was a growing sense that he was needed at Westminster.[66] However, it would be a few years before Prince Henry became dominant, for on 30 January Archbishop Arundel was reluctantly persuaded to replace Thomas Langley as chancellor, and with the prince still much occupied in Wales in 1407–8 it was the archbishop who assumed leadership of the council.[67]

The reconstituted council was strong throughout on both military and administrative experience, with the duke of York, the earl of Somerset, Richard Lord Grey and Hugh Lord Burnell having played leading parts in the French and Welsh wars, and each of the three current chief ministers (Thomas Langley, Lord Furnivall and John Prophet) chaperoned by his predecessor (Henry Beaufort, William Lord Roos and Bishop Bubwith).[68] John Stanley also boasted a wealth of governmental experience; not so Tiptoft, although he would amply repay the faith placed in him. Yet it was not merely its composition but also the power entrusted to it that marked the dawn of a new era in the history of Henry's council. Thirty-one articles, drafted by the lords and presented by the commons, formed the basis of a fundamentally altered relationship between king and council.[69] Henry

[65] POPC, i.295–6. Thomas Brounfleet, a household administrator for twenty years and formerly Richard II's butler, was chosen as the king's controller (in effect the deputy treasurer of the household).

[66] PROME, viii.330, 347.

[67] SAC II, 498–9.

[68] Brown, 'Commons and Council', 24–6; PROME, viii.323. Prophet had replaced Bubwith as keeper of the privy seal on 4 October 1406, though Bubwith was retained on the council (E 404/22, nos. 159, 273).

[69] PROME, viii.366–75; POPC, i.296–8 (amendments by the council to an earlier draft); G. Dodd, 'Patronage, Petitions, and Grace: The Chamberlains' Bills of Henry IV's Reign',

was now to govern 'entirely and in all cases' by the council's advice, and a number of councillors were to remain with him constantly; they were to oversee household finance; no new royal grants which diminished the crown's revenues were to be made; the king was only to hear petitions on Wednesdays and Fridays and members of the council were to be present; if courtiers or others tried to sway his mind, the council was to be consulted before any action was taken; councillors themselves were not to show favour to friends or suitors, and as far as possible were to act honestly and in unison; departmental heads were to initiate enquiries into their offices. All this the new councillors swore in parliament to uphold, although Arundel stressed that only if adequate revenues were granted by the commons would they be able to fulfil their side of the bargain. Henry also swore in parliament to abide by the articles, though only 'saving his estate and the prerogative of the crown', and only until the next parliament.

Further concessions on either side cemented the deal: there would be no new war-treasurers, but the accounts of earlier ones would be audited; in allocating royal revenues, priority would be given to annuities – many of the lords and commons being themselves annuitants, for whom the virtual stop on payments over the past two or three years had become a test of loyalty; and Northumberland and Bardolf were duly convicted of treason, although tellingly nothing further was said about Scrope or Mowbray. All this was agreed by 17 December, following which the king was granted one tenth and fifteenth and the wool subsidy was renewed until September 1408.[70] At the last minute, a suggestion from the commons that 'certain lords' should be personally responsible for repaying the tenth and fifteenth, should it not be spent correctly, threatened to derail the settlement; the king was furious, the lords 'refused point blank' to admit such liability, and the commons backed down. Four days before Christmas, at the conclusion of a sitting which dragged on deep into the night, the deal which had taken nearly ten months to broker was struck.[71]

Yet three years of conflict, debate and experimentation had brought no structural reform. Since January 1404, the search for solvency had thrown up proposals for ecclesiastical disendowment, the resumption of crown lands, new forms of taxation, the appointment of war-treasurers and

in *The Reign of Henry IV: Rebellion and Survival, 1403–1413*, ed. G. Dodd and D. Biggs (York, 2008), 126–31; Wright, 'Recovery of Royal Finance', 71–2.

[70] *RHKA*, 136–7; *PROME*, viii.369–70 (for 17 Dec.); 363–5 (for audit of Pelham's and Furnivall's accounts; war-treasurers would not be appointed again until 1449).

[71] *SAC II*, 480–3.

parliamentary auditors, the suspension of annuities, the imposition of a *certum* on the wardrobe, the expulsion of aliens, the devolution of naval defence to merchants, and an about-turn from extreme niggardliness in March 1404 to uncommon liberality eight months later. By December 1406, almost every one of these experiments had been shelved (although some would be revived), and parliament had returned to the tried and tested route of direct and indirect subsidies, placing its faith in a privy council backed by statutory powers to enforce royal compliance. The answer, it seemed, lay not in new remedies but in making the existing system work, and no one knew more about the existing system than Archbishop Arundel, who now entered upon his third term as chancellor of the realm.

Chapter 20

ARCHBISHOP ARUNDEL AND THE
COUNCIL (1407–1409)

For ten months following the dissolution of the Long Parliament Henry was less active in government, perhaps because his health was still recovering but also because the thirty-one articles were strictly enforced. Initially he remained in London, where on 24 January he attended the wedding of the earl of Kent to Lucia Visconti, before retiring to Hertford for most of February and March.[1] When the great council scheduled by parliament eventually met in London in mid-April, it lasted nine weeks, but although the king attended some of the sessions it was Arundel, Tiptoft, and Bishop Bubwith, the treasurer, who drew up new financial guidelines. One of its first acts, on 20 April, was to send a copy of the thirty-one articles to the exchequer, attaching to it a writ saying they were to be implemented without fail, even if Henry himself were to send them an order to the contrary; that this was sent in the king's name was perhaps rather humiliating. In the following month he was obliged to ask the exchequer to deliver money to his chamber 'without any kind of difficulty or delay'.[2]

Yet Henry's confidence in his archbishop meant that he was content for the moment to leave day-to-day government in his hands. The number of surviving signet letters of the king fell from an average of over a hundred a year between 1399 and 1406 to about fifteen a year thereafter. Once the council was over, in mid-June he set off for the Midlands and Yorkshire, passing through Leicester, Nottingham and York to the shrine of John of Bridlington, presumably to pray for his health, while Prince Henry returned to Wales to besiege Aberystwyth. Adrift and becalmed, the king nevertheless hoped that his campaigning days were not over. Early in the year he was planning to go to France, and in May and again in

---

[1] A decade earlier, Lucia had thought about marrying Henry. He now gave her away at the church door and gave her a wedding gift of a pair of gold dishes 'engraved with sun rays inside and out' (Mackman, 'Hidden Gems', 71); in Nov. 1408, Henry redeemed silver vessels worth £200 for her (*CPR 1408–13*, 147).

[2] E 175/11/32 (*aliquo mandato nostro vobis in contrariam directo non obstante . . . per ipsum regem*); E 403/591, 1 June (*absque dilatio aut difficultate quacunque*).

September he declared his intention to march against Glyn Dŵr in person, but no royal campaign materialized, though whether this was because he was denied money or because his health prevented him is not clear.[3] Nevertheless, Henry continued to keep a close eye on mercantile disputes and negotiations with the French and the Scots, and to impose his will on both the archbishop and the pope in the matter of episcopal appointments,[4] and before long he began to chafe at the restrictions imposed upon him. When the thirty-one articles had been drawn up, it was agreed that they would remain operative only until the end of the next parliament; by late August, Henry had decided that parliament should meet at Gloucester on 20 October.

The Gloucester parliament proved a good deal more obliging than its predecessor. The commons chose as their speaker the butler of the household, Thomas Chaucer, son of Geoffrey – the first of five occasions that he held the office – but when Chaucer began by criticizing the council which had governed for the previous ten months he was put firmly in his place by Arundel's vigorous defence of both its policies and its integrity, for which, he added, it had received scant gratitude. Between them, the king and the archbishop also secured a grant of one-and-a-half fifteenths and tenths, although not without an 'altercation' when Chaucer objected to the fact that the sum requested had been presented to the commons as a fait accompli following negotiations between the king's ministers and the lords. Although the king had to agree that this was not the way things were usually done – that is to say, that the right to determine the level of taxation belonged to the commons, the role of the lords being limited to assent – the sum granted was what the government requested.[5] However, probably the most important outcome of the parliament from the king's point of view was the dismissal (with royal gratitude) of the council established in December 1406 and the jettisoning of the thirty-one articles. Not that Arundel was dismissed; with Henry's blessing, he retained the chancellorship for two more years, having evidently overcome his reluctance to do so. The difference was that the king was now free to exercise his prerogative.

There were also signs that his strength was returning. When told in early February that Northumberland and Bardolf were back in England and raising another insurrection, he immediately made plans to challenge

---

[3] Probably the latter, for on 2 June he was promised £2,000 for his retainers and given £1,236 of it: although received in his chamber, it was lay subsidy money (E 403/591, 1 June, 2 June; E 403/593, 3 Oct.; *Foedera*, viii.466).

[4] Below, pp. 354–60; *Foedera*, viii.466, 478–9; *Signet Letters*, nos. 688–706.

[5] *PROME*, viii.417–18, 422, 425–9.

them. In fact the rapid response of his Yorkshire retainers deprived him of the chance to lead an army in the field. Led by the sheriff, Thomas Rokeby, they blocked the path of the rebel army at Grimbald Bridge near Knaresborough, forcing the earl to make a detour via Tadcaster, where on 19 February his force was encircled by loyalists. A brief fight ensued on Bramham Moor, a few miles to the west of the town, in which Northumberland was killed and Bardolf so severely wounded that he died soon after. Their heads were brought to the king at Stony Stratford and that of Northumberland, 'with its fine head of white hair', impaled on a lance and sent south to be placed on London Bridge.[6] Henry went north anyway to supervise the mopping-up operation, despite it being one of the harshest winters in living memory. Leaving London at the beginning of March, he spent twelve days at Wheel Hall, a few miles south of York, sentencing or pardoning rebels, and then three weeks, including Easter, at Pontefract. By the end of May he was back at the Tower of London, whence he travelled upriver to stay with Archbishop Arundel at Mortlake. Here, towards the end of June 1408, he suddenly collapsed.

It was immediately apparent that what the king had suffered was a good deal more serious than what had afflicted him two years earlier; for a while he was even thought to have died.[7] Henry's illness defies precise diagnosis, but it is safe to say that it was not the leprosy claimed by those contemporaries, French and Scottish as well as English, who believed that the king was being punished for the death of Archbishop Scrope. On the other hand, his symptoms evidently did include a disfiguring skin disease, variously reported as a burning sensation, as 'great pustules' on his face and hands, or by Adam Usk as 'festering of the flesh [and] dehydration of the eyes'.[8] He had suffered from the pox aged twenty, and his skin probably became more prone to rashes, or perhaps psoriatic, as he grew older. Yet this cannot have been the whole story. He remained at Mortlake for nearly a month, only resuming work in mid-July, and for the rest of his life his health remained precarious. He now travelled more by water and often preferred the seclusion of friends' houses to royal residences.[9] In September

[6] *SAC II*, 530–5.

[7] *SAC II*, 534–7. He was at Mortlake from 19 June to 12 July.

[8] *Usk*, 247; *CE*, 405–8, 421 and *Giles*, 47, both claimed that leprosy afflicted him immediately after Scrope's beheading, but he was riding and campaigning again within a week; cf. Mortimer, *Fears*, 300–3; P. McNiven, 'The Problem of Henry IV's Health', *EHR* 100 (1985), 747–72. The examination of Henry's face in 1832 (see pp. 523–5) showed his nasal cartilage still intact, most unlikely for a leper.

[9] Among those in whose houses he stayed during 1408–9 were Hugh Waterton, Henry Beaufort, Henry Bowet and John Fordham, bishop of Ely: D. Biggs, 'An Ill and Infirm

he engaged an Italian physician, David Nigarellis of Lucca, but although he was fit enough to preside over debates about the Schism in July and October, by early December it was thought prudent to recall Princes Henry and Thomas to Westminster.[10]

In mid-January 1409 the king suffered a relapse and believed himself to be dying: on 21 January he made a will regretting his 'misspent life' and four days later issued a general pardon to those who had rebelled against him. The grooms of his chamber who now cared for him, 'sleeping around the king's bed at night', featured prominently in his will. By this time he had been moved to Greenwich, whence he wrote on 1 March to the duke of Berry saying he had been seriously ill for six weeks.[11] By mid-March the crisis had passed, but despite Henry's protestation to Arundel on 31 March that he was no longer ill, in fact his health was from now on a constant concern.[12] Clearly this was something more disabling than a skin condition: perhaps a circulatory problem which weakened his heart, perhaps a chronic intestinal condition following his prolapsed rectum. His collapses were not strokes, for his brain seems to have been unaffected and his resolve to govern insofar as he could was undimmed. He was later reported to have told his son on his deathbed that his illness had made his mind stronger and more devout.[13] That is quite plausible, but it inevitably placed strains on England's polity.

In such a crisis, those who expected, and were expected, to assume the burden of rule were the great lords of the realm, but as events in France demonstrated this was never straightforward. In Henry's case, however,

---

King: Henry IV, Health, and the Gloucester Parliament of 1407', in *The Reign of Henry IV: Rebellion and Survival*, ed. G. Dodd and D. Biggs (York, 2008), 180–209; Wylie and Waugh, *Reign of Henry IV*, iii.159, 246.

[10] E 403/596, 4 Dec., although Thomas only arrived in March. On 30 Nov. the king was looking forward to the festive season, ordering 1,000 marks to be set aside 'for the array of our person' for Christmas (E 404/24, no. 252).

[11] J. Nichols, *A Collection of all the Wills of the Kings and Queens of England* (Society of Antiquaries, London, 1780), 203–7; E 403/596, 13 February (the general pardon was extended in May: E 403/599, 23 May); *Signet Letters*, no. 952. The grooms and other personal servants who he asked his executors to reward were Wilkin, John Warren, William Thorpe, Thomas de la Croix, Jacob Raysh and Halley. The *garciones vigilatores circa lectam domini in noctibus* named in the 1408–9 great wardrobe account were John Halley, John Warren, William Thorpe, John Burford and William Wardell (E 101/405/22, fo. 31).

[12] *SAC II*, 564–5; *Signet Letters*, nos. 735–6. Henry often commented on his health in his letters; Prince Henry apparently liked to be reassured about his father's health (*ANLP*, 286–7, 405, 465; *CDS*, v.917). Letters saying he was 'in good health' are thus not evidence that he had been ill, although in 1409 this was certainly the case. In October 1409 a royal sergeant, Henry Fowler, had permission to go on pilgrimage to the Holy Land for 'the convalescence and health of the king's person' (*CPR 1408–13*, 113).

[13] *De Illustribus Henricis*, 111.

there were compensating factors. First, unlike Charles VI, he remained sane at all times and capable of ruling much of the time; secondly, he had a large family; thirdly, the tight group of advisers on whom he relied had always been small and they were accustomed to working together, although naturally there were rivalries and individuals' influence fluctuated. For instance, once Arundel assumed control of the administration, that of the Beauforts certainly diminished. John Beaufort also suffered bouts of ill health from 1407 onwards, while his younger brothers were not fully trusted by the archbishop, who did not look kindly upon either the worldly and ecclesiastically uninterested Henry Beaufort or the conspicuous role his brother Thomas had played in Richard Scrope's trial. When John Beaufort, perhaps afflicted by illness, requested in February 1407 that the act legitimating him and his siblings ten years earlier be confirmed, it was probably at Arundel's prompting that its wording was altered to exclude any possibility that they might in future claim the crown. To be sure, such a possibility seemed remote at the time, for the king's sons and arguably several others stood between them and the throne, but this only made their exclusion seem gratuitous.[14] There was no public falling-out with Arundel, and John and Henry Beaufort remained on the council through 1407 and beyond, but they were not the dominant force they had been or would again be.

In their place it was the king's sons who now came to the fore. Fortunately – though not fortuitously – by the time Henry became seriously ill his three elder sons all had several years' experience of military command and the financial responsibilities that came with it. As children, he had taken care to educate them, giving them personal tutors and ensuring they were schooled in Latin and music as well as leadership and swordplay; once he became king he tried to make time to spend with them.[15] Barely had they reached adolescence when great responsibilities were thrust upon them. Henry became prince of Wales at the age of thirteen, Thomas lieutenant of Ireland and John warden of the East March at fourteen. Their role as

---

[14] *CPR 1405–8*, 284. This was done by inserting the words *excepta dignitate regali* in the clause specifying the inheritances to which they were entitled; the duke of York and his brother, to say nothing of the two Mortimer boys, would certainly have been considered closer to the throne than the Beauforts (McNiven, *Heresy and Politics*, 134).

[15] Prince Henry's tutor in 1398–9 was Peter Melbourne, Thomas's was Winslow Dorstayner, and John's was Thomas Rothwell: Henry bought 'seven books of grammar in one volume', costing four shillings, for Henry, a Latin grammar for John, and 'two books of ABC' for his daughters; also swords, bucklers, hauberks, daggers and horses (DL 28/1/10, fo. 2v; 28/1/6, fo. 11r, 36v; 28/1/5, fo. 34r; 28/4/1, fos 13–14; 29/1/9, fos 2v, 3v, 14v, 22v; *ANLP*, 404).

imperial viceroys was a way of testing their suitability for kingship as well as underlining the primacy of the king's family, just as the increasing use of phrases such as 'our dearest brother' or 'our most beloved son' during the second half of the reign underlined its unity.[16] After 1406, especially after 1408, Henry's kingship gradually shaded into Lancastrian family government.

Yet although he groomed his sons for power, Henry did not indulge them, a point that did not pass unnoticed. In 1407, and again in 1410, the commons reminded the king that none of his younger sons had been granted the titles and lands that befitted their status and asked him to rectify the situation, but he was in no hurry to do so. Financial considerations doubtless played a part in this; as he told the commons in 1410, he would promote and endow his younger sons 'as soon as it could well be done'.[17] But there was also method in the king's meanness: he wanted to keep his sons hungry, and he wished to reserve for himself the option of using their marriages for diplomatic advantage.[18] He also knew better than most that their characters and capabilities were very different: the impolitic and restless Thomas was said to make hard war on those who crossed him, but was a great promoter of those loyal to him; John was dutiful and upright, a man of good habits and a worker for peace; Humphrey was 'most learned'.[19] Yet it was Prince Henry, the heir to the throne, who was naturally the focus of attention. The 1406 parliament marked the prince's entry into politics, and from now on he was frequently listed as a member of the council and a witness to royal charters.[20] However, it was only from the winter of 1408–9 that his mission in Wales allowed him to devote the

[16] His plans for Humphrey, twenty-two at his father's death but less dashing than Thomas and less politic than John, are not clear: G. Harriss, 'Humphrey, Duke of Gloucester', *ODNB.* 28.787–93. Humphrey may have chafed at the lack of responsibility, but there is no evidence of disloyalty to his father, although he was involved in a property dispute with the duke of York in 1409, which the king decided in York's favour; Humphrey's 'warden' at this time was John Hartlepool (*CPR 1408–13*, 150; Biggs, 'Witness Lists', 414–15).

[17] *PROME*, viii. 427, 482. In fact he did begin to provide for them, perhaps in response to parliament: Humphrey received 5,000 marks to purchase the reversion of the lands of Sir Matthew Gournay in November 1407, and John was given the remaining lands of Northumberland and Hotspur in the king's hands in July 1410: E 403/593, 16 Nov., 4 Dec. (Humphrey's treasurer, 'Arkesworth', was given 2,000 of the 5,000 marks straight away); *CPR 1408–13*, 212.

[18] In January 1410, it was suggested that John might marry a daughter of the duke of Albany (*POPC*, i.326.)

[19] *De Illustribus Henricis*, 109. Thomas's men twice became involved in affrays with the Londoners in 1410–11, once in association with John's men (*Chronicle of London 1089–1453*, 93).

[20] After November 1406, the prince witnessed 57 per cent of royal charters (Biggs, 'Witness Lists'), 415.

majority of his time to English affairs; until then it was Archbishop Arundel who continued to drive the policy agenda at Westminster.

Nor was there any doubt about what Arundel placed at the top of that agenda; the outstanding achievement of his administration was the restoration of solvency to crown finance. Insofar as this was done, it was principally by orthodox means such as restricting expenditure, improving cash flow to the exchequer, establishing priorities and appointing competent officers subject to conciliar supervision. The experiments of 1404–6 were mostly jettisoned. In certain respects Arundel was fortunate, for improved security in the Channel and the North Sea led to a surge in wool exports, to 13,000 sacks in 1406–7, 15,000 in 1407–8, and 17,000 (the highest total of the reign) in 1408–9.[21] Yet the policy also bore its maker's hallmark, for Arundel's instincts were conservative and he had made it clear during his terms as chancellor in the 1380s and 1390s that his understanding of the idea of reform was not innovation but a return to first principles.[22] This began straight after Christmas 1406 with a moratorium on payments from the exchequer. The first two months of 1407 witnessed no issues of either cash or assignments, despite the fact that the exchequer was open on eight days between 19 January and 4 March. Meanwhile, the proceeds of the lay subsidy granted in December were allowed to accumulate, and by 23 April, when the last substantial payment arrived, more than £30,000 had been amassed.[23] The moratorium on assignments meant that this was almost entirely in cash, a deliberate policy of channelling revenues through the exchequer rather than allowing them to be anticipated at source through the issue of tallies. The collection and disbursement of revenues was to be controlled from the centre, thereby enabling effective planning and prioritized allocations. The sum of £40,025 received in cash at the exchequer during the Michaelmas 1406–7 term – nearly all of it in February and March – was twice as much as it had received in cash in any term of the reign hitherto.[24]

It was soon needed, for around Christmas time a crisis developed at Calais when the garrison, despairing of being paid, seized the wool in the

[21] Carus-Wilson and Coleman, *England's Export Trade*, 122–3.

[22] M. Aston, *Thomas Arundel* (Oxford, 1967), 351–2, 377.

[23] Most of the lay subsidy, due for collection on 14 February, was received from 22 February to 4 March: E 403/589 and 657 (issue rolls, showing no payments from 13 December to 4 March); E 401/639, 22 Feb., 1 March, 4 March; E 401/641, 4, 13, 15, 22 and 23 April (receipt rolls).

[24] Steel, *Receipt*, 94–5.

town's warehouses in the hope of selling it to recoup their arrears. Finding the £18,000 a year which the garrison cost in time of war was never easy, but following the dismissal of the war-treasurers in the 1406 parliament the system of reserving a portion of the wool subsidy for Calais more or less broke down, and by 1407 the town's treasurer, Robert Thorley, was £30,000 in arrears.[25] The government's initial reaction was to offer the mutineers just £5,000 in assignments, but in early March a more realistic agreement was drafted, perhaps as a consequence of a new threat to the town (real or imagined) from Burgundy.[26] The London merchant and former war-treasurer Richard Merlawe became treasurer of Calais, the stapler merchants upon whom its prosperity depended were given a greater say in running its finances, reservations on the wool subsidy were renewed, and in April the great council arranged for £19,500 to be sent across the Channel during the next two months.[27] This calmed the situation, although it added fuel to the debate over the long-term funding of the garrison, a question that later proved divisive.

This injection of cash to Calais meant, however, that less was available to distribute to others. This was the task of the great council which met in London in mid-April.[28] Allocations were made in cash, thus reducing the risk that sources of revenue would become over-committed, leading to uncashable tallies and the creation of fictitious loans. In 1406, only 47 per cent of all issues were in cash; in 1407, the figure was 83 per cent. Control over the exchequer was also tightened by limiting the ability of regular spenders such as royal lieutenants or the household to use recurrent writs to secure funds: specific writs authorizing one-off issues and their sources were now more widely (though not exclusively) needed to secure payments, for the open-ended nature of recurrent writs created uncertainty about which revenues had been tapped. The most difficult task, however, was to decide on the order of priorities between spenders. Military and defence expenditure topped the list: £12,086 was allocated to Prince Henry for operations in Wales in addition to the £19,543 sent to Calais, but the decision to return to the system whereby half of the wool customs was reserved

[25] The system of reservation had worked reasonably well since 1390, but in 1406 the pressure on the exchequer was too great: Grummitt, 'Financial Administration of Calais', 277–99; £30,000 was Thorley's debt in June 1407, but he ceased to be treasurer in March; see the letter from the garrison to the king in January 1407 (*RHL*, ii.145–8).

[26] *Foedera*, viii.466; the French took Oye castle round this time; the English responded, taking Pouille (*SAC II*, 516).

[27] E 403/589, 11 Dec.; E 403/591, 9 and 24 May, 12 and 23 June; Tiptoft went to Calais to supervise the payments.

[28] Wright, 'Recovery of Royal Finance', 72–81.

for Calais left dangerously little for Scotland, Guyenne, Ireland or sea-defence; until the next crisis, they would simply have to make do.[29] A further complication was the king's desire to lead his own campaign to Wales. Bowing to his wishes, the council allocated him over £10,000 from the lay subsidy; when the royal campaign was abandoned, some £5,000 of this was instead used to finance the royal household.

Although this use of the lay subsidy to fund the household was noted on the exchequer receipt roll, such had not been the intention of the council; misappropriation of taxation granted for defence was after all contrary to one of the commons' cherished principles, which the appointment of war-treasurers in 1404 had been explicitly intended to uphold and the thirty-one articles implicitly confirmed.[30] On the other hand, it had been agreed in parliament that £6,000 from the wool subsidy would be given directly to the king to be spent as he wished, the expectation presumably being that at least part of this would be spent on the household, so the council in 1407 had already begun to retreat from the principle of using taxation only for purposes of defence. This retreat would not be confirmed for another year, but it is noteworthy that no complaint was heard in the Gloucester parliament about what would assuredly have been deemed misuse of taxes two or three years earlier.[31] There were three main reasons for this. The first was that the king had been obliged to surrender his power to authorize payments from the exchequer: in other words, he had agreed that his right to make grants should be subject to conciliar supervision, something which the commons had been urging on him since the start of the reign.[32] The second was because under the eye of its new treasurer, John Tiptoft, household spending was being brought under control. Between December 1406 and July 1408 (Tiptoft's period of office) the annual average expenditure of the wardrobe was £20,446, about four-fifths of what it had been between 1399 and 1406.[33] There were doubtless many who still regarded this as

[29] £1,000 was allocated to Scotland, but nothing for Ireland or the sea: Wright, 'Recovery of Royal Finance', 78; Griffiths, 'Prince Henry, Wales and the English Exchequer', 214; Grummitt, 'Financial Administration of Calais', 298.

[30] E 403/591, 2 May; Wright, 'Recovery of Royal Finance', 76–7.

[31] *RHKA*, 130; cf. *CPR 1405–8*, 297.

[32] G. Harriss, 'Budgeting at the Medieval Exchequer', in *War, Government and Aristocracy in the British Isles c.1150–1500: Essays in Honour of Michael Prestwich*, ed. C. Given-Wilson, A. Kettle and L. Scales (Woodbridge, 2008), 179–96, at p. 189. Hence Henry's writ to the exchequer in April 1407 (above p. 302). The commons alleged tactfully in 1401 that people took advantage of Henry's 'kindness and generosity' (*PROME*, viii.150).

[33] *RHKA*, 76–94, 271–2. The cost of the household thus fell to £30,300 a year, despite increased exchequer issues to the chamber, up from £4,300 in 1399–1406 to £8,000 in 1407–13: Wright, 'Recovery of Royal Finance', 76–7.

excessive, and the Gloucester parliament complained that the household was continuing to abuse its right of purveyance. Yet the combination of reduced expenditure (attributable in part to Henry's shrinking itinerary) and flexibility in the use of taxation meant that criticism regularly directed at the household during the first half of the reign now subsided. The third reason for satisfaction was the resumption of payment of annuities. After 1406 it was generally annuitants rather than household creditors who were given preference on non-taxative sources of revenue – another beneficial effect of the use of taxation to support the household, for it relieved the pressure on ordinary revenues.[34] For the next two or three years, annuities were paid more regularly and many arrears were cleared, thereby rebuilding trust among the regime's supporters.

It was thus with both vigour and justification that Arundel defended the council's financial policy to the October 1407 parliament, and although the commons quibbled over procedure they granted the one-and-a-half lay subsidies which he requested, to be paid in three instalments between February 1408 and February 1409.[35] In return, the king promised not to request any more lay subsidies until March 1410 and to step up annuity payments, at least 'to those who have deserved it', a refrain which now began to figure increasingly in government rhetoric.[36] With the wool customs also renewed until Michaelmas 1410 and convocation voting one-and-a-half clerical tenths, the council had a clear idea of how much money it had to spend over the next three years, and detailed financial planning could begin. Broadly speaking, the policy of maintaining exchequer control of revenues was continued, although the percentage of cash it received was never as high again as it had been in 1407, with the year from Easter 1408 to Easter 1409 showing an almost exact balance between cash and revenues assigned by tallies.[37] What really mattered, however, was whether tallies would translate into cash, and the fact that fictitious loans accounted for less than £800 during this year indicates that assignment was usually a successful operation and thus that the council was continuing to estimate and allocate resources with care.[38] This is reflected in the order-liness of the issue rolls for these two terms: substantial arrears of annuities

---

[34] *RHKA*, 135–7.

[35] For the 'altercation' with the commons, see above, p. 303.

[36] *PROME*, viii.427–9.

[37] Steel, *Receipt*, 97–8 (£50,710 was received in cash during this year, £51,353 assigned).

[38] However, in the first few months of 1408, before the new subsidies began to come in, there was a crop of fictitious loans totalling over £7,000, which had to be reassigned later in the year (Steel, *Receipt*, 96–8, 457).

and debts of the household from earlier years were cleared, and hardly any sources were overcommitted.[39]

As in the previous year, a review of resources was undertaken during a great council meeting in late January and early February 1408 (although this year there was no moratorium on issues during these months), and the decisions taken then acted upon in March.[40] Naturally, priorities had changed. Under pressure from the staplers, the commons had asked that attention be paid to Calais and the security of the Channel, and their requests were heeded.[41] The reservation of half of the wool subsidy for Calais was extended for another year, and £10,100 was given to the new admiral, the earl of Kent, to sweep the sea of pirates.[42] Prince Henry was given a further £13,890 for Wales, while the Scottish marches and Ireland, having been neglected in 1407, were by now desperate for resources: Prince John and the earl of Westmorland were allocated £9,500 for the former and Prince Thomas £4,666 for the latter. The indenture agreed with Thomas in February 1408, which covered the next three years, specified the individual tax-collectors from whom his current allocations and outstanding debts were to be drawn, as well as his ranking in the order of priorities, an example of the attention to detail now underpinning global budgeting decisions at Westminster.[43]

However, the most radical decision taken by the council in early 1408 was that all sources might now be used to fund the household: £7,000 of its income was to come from the first instalment of the lay subsidy, £4,000 from the wool customs, and all the income from alien priories, episcopal and abbatial vacancies, wards, marriages and other feudal casualties was to be reserved exclusively for its use, existing annuitants excepted.[44] The decision to use lay subsidies for the household seems not to have been controversial, and in November its projected income from this source was

[39] E 403/595 and 596. On 16 Feb. 1409 the council ordered the payment of all arrears of annuities 'to the best of your ability, according to the discretion of you, the treasurer' (E 404/24, no. 292, and see nos. 39, 103, 189, for examples of individual writs for payment of arrears).

[40] E 403/594, 13 Dec. 1407 (summons of great council); the lay subsidy was yielding large sums from 3 Feb. 1408 (E 401/643, 3, 11, 14 Feb.).

[41] The Calais staplers also lobbied the council to maintain their share of the wool subsidy and their monopoly over exports, as well as to preserve the truce with Flanders (POPC, i.305–9).

[42] Kent went to sea but was killed in a raid off the Breton coast in August (below, p. 329).

[43] BL Cotton Titus B. xi (CPR 1405–8, 431–2).

[44] Harriss, 'Budgeting at the Medieval Exchequer', 190; Foedera, viii.510; CPR 1405–8, 408. Harriss, Cardinal Beaufort, 44–6, gives slightly different figures based on warrants (E 404) rather than issue rolls (E 403).

raised to £10,000, although the council simultaneously resurrected the idea of a *certum*, set at £16,000 for the wardrobe and £4,000 for the king's chamber. This was not effective: wardrobe expenditure alone stood at £20,463 in 1408–9, while the chamber devoured another £8,000 and the great wardrobe over £1,500.[45] Nevertheless, the freeing up of ordinary revenues allowed many annuitants' arrears to be cleared during the year and this, combined with the relative reduction of household expenditure, the clearing of some of its debts, the general reliability of assignments and the king's restraint in making grants, meant that, in the absence of military or other emergencies, the council was justified in believing its policy was working.

Early in 1409, therefore, another budget review was held. Calais, Ireland and the household had already been provided for, but following the last half lay subsidy (payable on 2 February) no further direct taxation was due from either laity or clergy during the year, and the mood was cautious. The allocations to Wales and the Scottish marches were reduced by half to around £5,000 each.[46] Yet even these reduced payments soon strained the exchequer, and as revenue dried up during the spring and summer of 1409, fictitious loans once again became a problem, totalling around £12,700 between Easter 1409 and Easter 1410, and there was increased resort to borrowing, mainly from the Londoners.[47] The council continued to try to allocate resources as rationally as possible: following his illness in the spring, Henry begged Arundel to ensure that provision was made for Queen Joan, who always had difficulty securing payment of her 10,000 marks a year dower, and by 1 July Arundel had made the necessary arrangements. The queen now surrendered the letters patent issued to her in 1403 and was instead given a mixed bag of assignments, mainly on the customs and alien priories, totalling some £2,800 (she also received around £1,000 a year from the duchy of Lancaster). Although promised less than in 1403, the strong likelihood is that she would actually receive more. The allocation to

---

[45] For the *certum* of 1404, see above, p. 284;. *RHKA*, 94, 272; *CPR 1408–13*, 35; E 403/606, 20 Nov.; E 404/24, no. 272. The great wardrobe received £1,750 from the exchequer in 1407–8 and £1,593 in 1408–9, and lesser sums from other sources. This did not cover its expenditure: William Loveney left office in May 1408 with debts totalling £4,733 and his successor, Richard Clifford, incurred nearly £2,000 of debts during his first fifteen months (E 101/405/13 and 22). Some of the chamber's money came from the duchy of Lancaster: Rogers, 'Royal Household', 172, 670.

[46] E 403/596, 13 Feb., 1 March. The absence or loss of council records from mid-1408 to mid-1409 makes this process obscure. Prince Henry received £5,204 for Wales between Sept. 1408 and Sept. 1409 (Griffiths, 'Prince Henry, Wales and the English Exchequer', 215).

[47] Steel, *Receipt*, 98–9.

her of revenues from the alien priories was a characteristically pragmatic step. Tiptoft had noted in the parliament of 1406 that the failure to pay her dower meant that Joan was unable to make her expected contribution to the income of the royal household; the alien priories had been reserved for the household, and the new arrangements made in July 1409 must have envisaged that that is what they would be used for. Her expenditure was also being more carefully monitored by now.[48]

Tiptoft's role in stabilizing royal finances in 1407–9 was as influential as Arundel's. For eight months in 1407 he served as both keeper of the wardrobe and chief butler to the king, thus simultaneously controlling the wardrobe's two main spending offices and enabling him to cut expenditure by 20 per cent.[49] In July 1408 he was promoted to the treasurership of the realm, for which he was granted 200 marks a year on top of the usual fee for his 'very good service'.[50] Meanwhile, in late 1407, he married Philippa, widow of Sir Matthew Gournay, as a result of which he became seneschal of Les Landes and constable of Dax in Guyenne.[51] These interests encouraged him to try to reform the exchequer at Bordeaux, for which task he chose Jean de Bourdieu (or Bordili), a Gascon doctor of laws and canon of Bordeaux cathedral. Bourdieu was already the king's procurator-fiscal in Guyenne and lieutenant to the constable of Bordeaux, William Farrington (the duchy's chief financial officer), and in August 1408, a month after Tiptoft became treasurer of England and almost certainly on his initiative, Bourdieu was granted the keepership of the seal of the superior court of Guyenne and asked to carry out an audit of the accounts of the constable and his former lieutenant, Sir John Mitford, sending his report to the exchequer at Westminster. At the same time, all royal officials in the duchy were told not to meddle with the raising of royal revenue but to ensure that it was delivered directly to the constable, who in turn was ordered to make sure these officials were paid first, followed by others with royal grants in accordance with the dates of their grants. What Tiptoft was trying to

---

[48] *Signet Letters*, no. 736; *CPR 1408–13*, 85–7; *PROME*, viii.348, 477–8; DL 28/27/1 and 9. For moving her household from Havering (Essex) to Gloucester in the autumn of 1407, Joan was allocated 100 marks; for moving on from Gloucester to Malmesbury (Wiltshire), 10 marks (E 403/593, 16 Nov.). There is no record of Joan making contributions to the income of the royal household, as queens were expected to do; Philippa of Hainault, wife of Edward III, had paid £3,650 a year to the wardrobe when her household merged with the king's; Anne of Bohemia, wife of Richard II, paid £1,200 a year in the 1390s (*RHKA*, 93–4).

[49] L. Clark, 'John Tiptoft', *ODNB*, 54.832–3.

[50] E 404/24, no. 505 (21 May 1409).

[51] In Sept. 1408 he also became *prévôt* of Entre-deux-Mers (*CGR 1407–9*, nos. 53, 78).

establish in the duchy was a system of centralized revenue collection and rationalized priorities such as he and Arundel had implemented in England since early 1407.[52] He faced opposition, however, for the constable's accounts had never been subject to local audit and Farrington and Mitford reacted angrily to this intrusion on their autonomy. Bourdieu had already crossed swords with Mitford, whom he had replaced as Farrington's lieutenant in January 1408, and whose unorthodox financial transactions were now subjected to close scrutiny, but Tiptoft backed Bourdieu strongly and on 21 August 1409 ordered Farrington to arrest Mitford and bring him to Westminster along with both men's accounts so that they could be properly audited. On the same day, Bourdieu was promoted to the chancellorship of the duchy with power to supervise all income and expenditure, submitting annual accounts to the exchequer at Westminster, and all officials in Guyenne, Farrington included, were ordered to obey him. He remained chancellor of the duchy until the end of the reign and beyond.[53]

Although the impact of these reforms on the finances of Guyenne is unknown, the thrust of the policy is clear. In Ireland too, where, as in Guyenne, there was a local exchequer, attempts were made from early 1407 to establish more control over the collection and disbursement of revenues, although again the effect is unknown.[54] In England, at any rate, it is clear that the reforms introduced by Arundel and Tiptoft made 1408, financially speaking, the best year of the reign. By the autumn of 1409, however, they were running into the sand. Without new grants of direct taxation, competition for resources was creating rivalries and economies were needed: in November an attempt was made to reduce the wardrobe's annual expenditure to £13,333, but when the keeper tried to secure a down payment on this on 22 November, nearly a third of it had to be borrowed from the city of London.[55] The decision in the same month to cut the proportion of the wool subsidy reservation for Calais from a half to a quarter pushed Prince Henry's patience to the limit, for he had assumed the role of champion of the garrison. Within the next fortnight matters came to a head. A council

---

[52] CGR 1407–9, Introduction (by Guilhem Pepin) and nos. 24, 28, 30, 43, 44. The appointment in Sept. 1408 of Adam de Urswick as receiver of revenues at Fronsac was doubtless part of the same programme (no. 45). The 1406 parliament had already passed an ordinance forbidding the granting of any crown revenues in the duchy until the end of the 1407 parliament (no. 9).

[53] CGR 1407–9, 65, 66, 119, 121, 125, 126 (Mitford's unorthodox transactions), 140; Foedera, viii.595–6.

[54] CIRCLE CR 1406–7, no. 3 (25 Jan. 1407); PR 1408–9, no. 96; PR 1409–10, no. 58.

[55] Harriss, Cardinal Beaufort, 48–9; cf. CPR 1408–13, 151. For the issue of £8,618 to Thomas Brounfleet, keeper of the wardrobe, he was given tallies for £5,951 and borrowed £2,666 from London (E 403/602, 22 Nov.).

meeting at Westminster led to a row over the allocation of resources, and on 11 December Tiptoft either resigned or was dismissed from the treasury. He had already sent letters to the customs collectors telling them to send their receipts to the exchequer rather than directly to Calais, but the king, probably urged on by the prince, rather than appointing a new treasurer, issued letters under his signet countermanding Tipftoft's instructions.[56] Parliament had already been summoned to Bristol, perhaps to escape the pressure of the London mercantile and stapler communities, but on 18 December the venue was switched to Westminster. Three days later Arundel resigned the chancellorship. Once again the king did not appoint a replacement but kept the great seal with him for almost a month, during which writs were sealed at his oral instruction.[57] Against the background of this unusual hiatus, a power struggle was played out for control of the crown's executive and resources. The first indication of its outcome came on 6 January 1410, with the appointment as treasurer of the prince's supporter Henry Lord Scrope of Masham, but not until 19 January was the prince's ascendancy confirmed when the king was obliged to countermand the signet letters he had sent to the customs collectors in early December and to place the great seal in the custody of John Wakering, keeper of the rolls of chancery.[58] It took another twelve days for a new chancellor to be appointed, during which time parliament met (on 27 January). The choice of Thomas Beaufort as chancellor four days later marked the definitive collapse of Archbishop Arundel's administration, and the parliament that followed served as midwife to Prince Henry's assumption of power.

[56] These have not survived, but must have ordered the collectors either to bring their takings to the household or to assign them to recipients whom the king specified (*CCR 1409–13*, 25–6, 51; McFarlane, *Lancastrian Kings*, 107–8).

[57] *CPR 1408–13*, 229–35. Over fifty writs were sealed during this time, none of them controversial, several relating to Guyenne and the restitution of goods seized from foreign merchants.

[58] *CCR 1409–13*, 73, 115. Wakering did not relish this role: when asked to keep the great seal again in June 1411 during the twelve-day absence of Thomas Beaufort, he was very reluctant (*CCR 1409–13*, 224–5).

Chapter 21

BETWEEN WAR AND PEACE (1405–1410)

The gradual recovery of royal finance was one of the factors that revived the crown's military fortunes during the middle years of the reign, nowhere more so than in Wales. Despite his setbacks in 1405, Glyn Dŵr's ambition still soared. Such at least is the inference to be drawn from the remarkable manifesto known as the Tripartite Indenture, in which he, Northumberland and Edmund Mortimer bound themselves to stand together against their common enemies (principally, of course, Henry) and, should it transpire that they were 'those persons of whom the prophet speaks', to strive to their utmost to partition 'Greater Britain' between them: Owain would take a much-expanded Welsh principality including several of the border counties, Northumberland everything between the Midlands and Scotland, and Mortimer the rest of England. It is a problematic text, preserved only by one chronicler who dated it to 28 February 1405, but it is hard to see how Northumberland could have been in Wales then, whereas in late February 1406 he and Bardolf had just fled there from Scotland after being warned that they were about to be handed over to the English in return for Scottish hostages.[1] The indenture is probably to be associated with Owain's wider plans for his principality, as reflected in his decision proclaimed at Pennal in March 1406 to sever connections with the Roman papacy, but it was also the last throw of increasingly desperate men. There is nothing to indicate that it circulated widely, and by the autumn, by which time Northumberland and Bardolf had fled to the continent after suffering defeat at the hands of Edward Lord Charlton, it was a dead letter.[2]

---

[1] For the text, see *Giles*, 39–42, with translation in *Welsh Records in Paris*, 116–17. *Giles's* date is supported by Davies, *Revolt*, 166–9 (who elucidates the prophetic lore underpinning it); Matthews dated it to 28 February 1406, supported by Kirby, *Henry IV*, 218, and Wylie, *Henry the Fourth*, ii.408–10. Northumberland and Bardolf were warned to leave Scotland by David Fleming, who was killed on 14 Feb. 1406 (*Scotichronicon*, 61–3, 176).

[2] *Giles* claimed that 'after a short time, this evil bond of friendship was published', but had Henry known about it he would presumably have used it in his indictment of Northumberland and Bardolf.

By now the proactive strategy being pursued by the English was yielding results. Anglesey, a major source of provisions for the rebels, and Ceredigion were largely brought under control by January 1407, Flintshire by April; as the Welsh confidence of 1403–5 ebbed, submissions and defections multiplied.[3] The great council of April 1407 stepped up the pressure: on 12 May, Prince Henry was reappointed as lieutenant of Wales for six months with a force of 600 men-at-arms and 1,800 archers. His first goal was to recover Aberystwyth and Harlech castles, held by Glyn Dŵr's men since late 1404. Cannons of up to four-and-a-half-tons, along with nearly 2,000 lbs (900 kilos) of powder, saltpetre and sulphur, were shipped up the Welsh coast to facilitate the task, although they were not an unqualified success and Aberystwyth's walls mostly withstood the bombardment.[4] Nevertheless, by 12 September, with a blockade in place by land and sea, the Welsh captain of the castle, Rhys Ddu (Rhys the Black), agreed that if not relieved by Glyn Dŵr or his representative by 1 November he would evacuate the castle and perform homage to the English king; in return, Prince Henry swore not to assault the castle in the meantime and to allow Rhys and his fellows to leave unharmed provided they did not destroy the artillery or fortifications.[5]

The dramatis personae of witnesses to the agreement – the chancellor of Oxford University, the duke of York, the earl of Warwick and a dozen other English lords and knights – testified to its significance; even the king hoped to be there in time for the surrender. There was nothing unusual about such pacts in the context of Anglo-French or Anglo-Scottish siege warfare, and it implied a degree of respect for what the rebels had achieved. However, when Owain was told about it he reacted with fury, accusing Rhys and his men of treachery, and once Prince Henry had withdrawn to Gloucester for the parliament he hastened to Aberystwyth and occupied the castle in person, thereby nullifying the agreement. As an act of defiance this was impressive, but it barely held back the tide of English recovery. Within a few months the prince and his gunners were back at Aberystwyth, and in September 1408 the castle fell (although Owain himself was no longer there), whereupon Prince Henry departed for Westminster, leaving the recapture of Harlech to John and Gilbert Talbot.[6] His confidence in

---

[3] Davies, *Revolt*, 123–4. Symbolic of the restoration of order was the foundation by the anglicized Welshman, lawyer and MP David Holbache of Oswestry Grammar School in 1407.

[4] E 403/589, 11 Dec.; E 403/591, 1 June, 23 June; Wylie, *Henry the Fourth*, iii.111–12; one of the cannons, nicknamed *The Messenger*, blew up when fired (Davies, *Revolt*, 253–4).

[5] *SAC II*, 521–7.

[6] E 403/594, 5 March 1408 (£12,178 to the prince for his army in Wales).

them was not misplaced: during the spring of 1409 Harlech too was recaptured, and with it Owain's wife, his son Lionel, two of his daughters and three of his granddaughters, who were all despatched to the Tower. His son-in-law Edmund Mortimer, whose defection in 1402 had so boosted Welsh morale, also perished during the siege,[7] and with him died the last of the alliances from which a few years earlier Owain had hoped to gain so much: France, Scotland, the Percys, the Mortimers – all now quite impotent to come to the old warrior's aid.[8] Valley by valley, the Welsh revolt shrank inexorably back to the north-western heartland whence it had sprung, and although occasional guerrilla raids continued to be launched, by 1409 life in most parts of Wales was returning to normal and English lordship being reimposed; this was now a society in submission.

With submission came its henchman: retribution. There was no reign of terror, although there were some executions, but even persistent rebels such as Henry Don were usually able to secure pardons. The price which the Welsh paid for nearly a decade of defiance came rather from their pockets, for pardons, personal or communal, did not come cheap, and almost every community had to buy one. The county of Carmarthen paid £4,000 between 1407 and 1412, while Brecon handed over £552 in 1410 alone to redeem fines imposed since 1401; the largest individual fines were those demanded of Owain's brother-in-law, John Hanmer, who had been captured in 1405 (£333) and Henry Don, who had led the revolt in Kidwelly in 1403 (£266).[9] The English were certainly not heedless of the fact that such penalization might stir up another revolt, but to them the loss of rents and other perquisites of lordship which they had suffered provided sufficient justification for their imposition. The problem, however, was not only that an already impoverished population was ground down, but also that the economic recovery which might have restored the profitability of English estates in Wales was delayed. The king's own lordship of Brecon, which in the 1390s had usually brought him over £1,000 a year, yielded only about a third of this sum in 1409; a year before this, all the rents in the town of Carmarthen were still being remitted because of the destruction

---

[7] E 403/596, 3 Dec., 13 Feb. (men and guns sent to the siege of Harlech) and 23 May (wages of men formerly at the siege of Harlech). The granddaughters were Edmund's children; a hoard of Owain's possessions was also seized at Harlech (Davies, *Revolt*, 326). Glyn Dŵr's son Griffith, captured in 1405, was kept in Nottingham castle, but moved to the Tower shortly before he died of the plague in March 1411 (*Usk*, 212, 242).

[8] There were hopes of a new Franco-Welsh alliance in 1410, but probably not expectations (Davies, *Revolt*, 195, 214).

[9] Davies, *Revolt*, 299–309; E. Powell, *Kingship, Law and Society: Criminal Law in the Reign of Henry V* (Oxford, 1989), 195–200.

the town had suffered in 1403 and 1405.[10] Retribution also naturally
provided opportunities for corrupt English officials to use threats or worse
to line their own pockets; one who certainly did was Thomas Barneby, the
notoriously venal chamberlain of North Wales.[11] Punitive fines continued
to be imposed during Henry V's reign, and it took not years but decades
for English lordship in Wales once again to realize its potential.

Nor did it help that although the revolt was already languishing by 1409,
it took a long time to die, for it had once again become the type of war to
which the mountains and valleys of Wales were perfectly suited: a hit-
and-run campaign aimed at the destruction of seigneurial resources and
occasional kidnappings.[12] Thus English castles still had to be reinforced
and some communities still had to pay for their security. In November 1409
the earl of Arundel and other Marcher lords were told to repair post-haste
to their lordships and continue the offensive, since their officials were still
making truces with Glyn Dŵr.[13] For Welshmen who had remained loyal to
the crown there was also the danger of revenge attacks: as late as 1412, the
esquire David Gam of Brecon was abducted by former rebels and handed
over to Glyn Dŵr, although he was later freed in return for a ransom.[14]
And although the English border counties suffered little from raiding after
1407–8, the legacy of earlier ravages remained: still in 1411, more than 10
per cent of Shropshire's contribution to the lay subsidy was respited on
account of the destruction it had suffered.[15] As long as Glyn Dŵr remained
at liberty, neither the hope nor the fear that the revolt was over could quite
be extinguished. His last few years were spent as a fugitive with a price on
his head, accompanied by his remaining son Mareddud, and when he died
around 1415, shortly after declining Henry V's offer of a pardon, he was
interred secretly so that his enemies should not desecrate his grave. There
must have been occasions when he could have been betrayed, but his
popular stature ensured that he never was; posterity would resurrect him
as the embodiment of a Welsh nation.[16]

[10] Davies, *Revolt*, 279, 299. By 1413–14, the receipt from Brecon was £691 (DL 28/4/8, fo. 3).

[11] R. Griffiths, 'The Glyndŵr Rebellion in North Wales Through the Eyes of an Englishman', in Ralph A. Griffiths, *Conquerors and Conquered in Medieval Wales* (Stroud, 1994), 123–38.

[12] Davies, *Revolt*, 229–36.

[13] *Foedera*, viii.611.

[14] *SAC II*, 603, 617; *CPR 1408–13*, 406; Davies, *Revolt*, 225–7. Gam died fighting for Henry V at Agincourt.

[15] Watt, 'On Account of the Frequent Attacks', in *Rebellion and Survival*, 66.

[16] Davies, *Revolt*, 325–42.

Scotland's leaders, in contrast, were becoming accustomed to English captivity. On the face of it, the capture of James I in the spring of 1406 put Henry in an enviable position: the two greatest Scottish border magnates (Douglas and Dunbar), the son of regent Albany (Murdoch Stewart), and the earl of Orkney, as well as their king, now resided in England, all of them prisoners except Dunbar who had fashioned his own chains. Like Edward III sixty years earlier, Henry had been handed the opportunity to dictate terms to the Scots, a point made to him by the commons in 1406, who asked him not to surrender his Scottish prisoners lightly.[17]

Hoping to woo, rather than drag, the Scots to the altar of peace, the king now displayed a victor's magnanimity. Scottish students, pilgrims and merchants were granted safe-conducts to visit or trade with England; Albany's glory-seeking nephew Alexander, earl of Mar, came to London to joust with the earl of Kent; the captivity to which the Scottish nobles were subjected was more honourable than custodial; and correspondence between the English king and the Scottish regent was generally respectful or even amicable, stripped clean of the patronizing bluster of overlordship.[18] Much of it naturally concerned the fate of the prisoners. As far as is known, no terms were put forward during Henry's reign for the ransom of the Scottish king, and James believed this to be because Albany did not want him back; the regent was, after all, also the heir presumptive and doubtless had one eye on his own succession.[19] James's frustration and sense of impotence are revealed in his poem *The King's Quair*, in which he

[17] *PROME*, viii.354; however, the commons asked that 'certain castles might be put in pledge' for the earl of Douglas, perhaps hoping that in return for parole further English garrisons could be established north of the border (if that is what they meant). Cf. F. Bériac and C. Given-Wilson, 'Edward III's Prisoners of War: The Battle of Poitiers and its Context', *EHR* 116 (2001), 802–33.

[18] Occasionally Henry referred to Albany as 'governor, as he asserts, of the realm of Scotland' (*Foedera*, viii.479, 609). At first sight gratuitously insulting, this only occurred in instructions to ambassadors which included authority to discuss a final peace as well as a truce, and may in fact be a precaution by the English king against suggestions (for example, from James I) that Albany lacked the authority to negotiate peace on behalf of the Scots; in March 1407 and again in 1409–10 there was talk of a 'final peace', but Arundel advised the king to demand the return of 'the idiot who calls himself King Richard' (*RHL*, ii.153–61, 214–15, 291–4). For the Scottish prisoners, see *Johannis Lelandi Antiquarii de Rebus Britannicis Collectanea*, ed. T. Hearne (67 vols, Oxford, 1715), vi.300–1, which records Henry's visit to Bardney abbey in August 1406 accompanied by two of his sons and the earls of Douglas, Fife (Murdoch) and Orkney, who dined with him and spent the night in the abbey; for the expenses of Scottish prisoners in the Tower or at Windsor, see E 403/589, 10 Dec.; E 404/24, no. 525 (three prisoners with ten servants moved to Windsor castle in May 1409, with half a mark per day for their upkeep); Wylie, *Henry the Fourth*, ii.392–3; Nicholson, *Scotland*, 229–30; *SAC II*, 478–9.

[19] Nicholson, *Scotland*, 246–7, 256; in May 1410 Albany dated a letter to Henry 'in the fifth year of our governorship', a quasi-regal style (*Foedera*, viii.635).

described his imprisonment 'bewailing in my chamber thus alone, despairing of all joy and redemption'. Albany showed more interest in trying to secure the release of his son Murdoch, offering hostages for his parole in July 1407 as well as one of his daughters in marriage to Prince John, although when he was informed that the price could be as high as 50,000 marks the talks lapsed, and in fact Murdoch was not released until 1415. He would pay the price for his father's slighting of his royal nephew: in May 1425, a year after James was unleashed north of the border, he had Murdoch and two of his sons beheaded at Stirling.[20]

The crucial Scottish prisoner apart from the king was the earl of Douglas. As long as George Dunbar also remained in England, Douglas probably felt that his family's domination of southern Scotland was not seriously threatened, but by 1407 Dunbar, short of money and shorn of influence in England, was restless and negotiating with a sympathetic Albany for his repatriation.[21] In March 1407, therefore, Douglas concluded an indenture promising the English king that he and his men would serve Henry 'before all men and against all men', the Scottish king excepted (but not the regent), for the term of his life, and was allowed to return to Scotland on parole.[22] Here his presence soon came to be seen as a threat by Albany, and although Douglas returned to England as agreed, when he obtained another term of parole in April 1408 Albany also sanctioned the return of Dunbar, who disingenuously put it about that he had only defected to the English in order to help destroy the Percys. This was too much for Douglas: although he had indicated to Albany his consent to Dunbar's release, he now became fearful that his rival would rebuild his authority south of the Forth, and when his parole expired at Easter 1409

[20] *Foedera*, viii.544 (July 1407: misrepresented in the syllabus to suggest that Murdoch himself was given safe-conduct), 708 (Dec. 1411), ix.5–6, 40, 48 (April and Sept. 1413); *POPC*, i.323–6; Nicholson, *Scotland*, 231–2, 246–7, 256; M. H. Brown, 'James I, King of Scots', *ODNB*, 29.592–7; S. Boardman, 'Robert Stewart, Duke of Albany', *ODNB*, 52.739–42. Until 1411, Albany referred to James merely as 'the son of the late king'; he was perhaps fortunate to die before James's return; however, he probably did not actively oppose James's return, and there was briefly talk in 1411–12 of the king being ransomed. For *The King's Quair*, see J. Boffey, *Fifteenth-Century Dream Visions: An Anthology* (Oxford, 2003), 90–157 (quote at p. 104).
[21] Brown, *The Black Douglases*, 106–10; Macdonald, 'George Dunbar, Earl of March', *ODNB*, 17.207–10; although granted Somerton castle (Lincolnshire) for his residence in 1402 (*CDS*, iv.124), Dunbar was unhappy in England: in May 1407 he and some forty of his servants were pardoned after a dispute between them and the dean and chapter of Lincoln led to a riot (*Foedera*, viii.481–2).
[22] *Foedera*, viii.478, 483; Douglas had been allowed back to Scotland on parole in 1405, when Henry hoped the Scots might hand over the earl of Northumberland in exchange for him (*SAC II*, 472–3).

he absconded. The indignant English king wrote to Albany demanding his return and even hinting that he might take 'little or right nought' for Murdoch's release as long as Douglas was sent back, but in October Douglas and Dunbar agreed terms with Albany and all that was left to Henry was to rue his misjudgement and fire unchivalric blanks across the border.[23] Douglas's price for consenting to Dunbar's return was the lordship of Annandale; although Dunbar was restored to his earldom of March, he was forced to concede almost undisputed authority south of the Forth to his rival; the 'whorrle-bourlle' (hurly-burly) of his eight-year self-imposed exile had cost him dear.[24]

Henry, too, was by now surveying a policy in ruins. If he had hoped to use the rivalry of the two border earls to put pressure on Albany, it had not worked out. Moreover, the return of their two leading magnates instilled the Scots with the confidence to resume the process of expelling the English cuckoos from their nests. Prince John had written many times to the king and council bemoaning their failure to provide him with the funds to maintain adequate defences on the March: the walls of Berwick had 'mostly collapsed', not least because of the damage inflicted by the king's artillery in 1405; the garrison of Jedburgh was threatening to desert; and that of Fastcastle scarcely dared venture out to forage for fear of ambush.[25] Now he was proved right. Jedburgh was seized while its captain, Robert Hoppen, was in Berwick pleading with Prince John to pay his men's wages; its fortifications were razed under the supervision of Douglas's brother James to prevent it from being held by the English again, and it never was.[26] Early in 1410 Fastcastle also succumbed to a force led by George Dunbar's son Patrick, and, soon after this, another of his sons, Gavin, and a bastard son of Douglas burned the town of Roxburgh, although the castle held out.[27] By the summer it was believed that the Scots were planning an invasion. The English retaliated through Robert Umfraville, lieutenant to Thomas

---

[23] *Scotichronicon*, 73, 182; *Foedera*, viii.536–7 (19 June 1408), 631 (4 April 1410); *POPC*, i.323–6; *CE*, 414. Henry threatened to treat Douglas's hostages 'according to the law of arms', but by May 1411 he seems to have resigned himself to Douglas's escape, perhaps in return for a ransom, and accepted him as an envoy to discuss the truce (*Foedera*, viii.686, 703; Nicholson, *Scotland*, 232).

[24] Brown, *The Black Douglases*, 110–12; Douglas's daughter now married the regent's son.

[25] *RHL II*, 219–24, 228–31; *POPC*, ii.91–4.

[26] It may have been taken in May, and certainly was by December 1409 (*CPR 1408–13*, 231; Nicholson, *Scotland*, 252–3; *Scotichronicon*, 182).

[27] These setbacks did at last spur the council to send enough money to Berwick to pay the garrison's wages: £3,679 was handed over between Nov. 1410 and May 1411, and further money was sent for repairs to the walls of Berwick in March 1412 (Wylie, *Henry the Fourth*, ii. 276–7; iii.275–9; E 404/27, no. 220).

Beaufort as admiral of the north, who led a flotilla of ten vessels manned by 600 men up the Firth of Forth, capturing fourteen ships before returning to Northumberland so loaded with provisions that the Scots called him 'Robin Mendmarket'; after following this up with a raid through Jedworth forest, he was asked to replace Westmorland's son John Nevill as captain of Roxburgh. Shortly after this, talks were arranged to patch up a truce for a few months, but peace was no nearer.[28] Like Edward III, Henry had discovered that the task of converting a trump-filled hand into a winning play was beyond him.

For the English administration in Dublin, the middle years of the reign were shifting and nervy. When the earl of Ormond died in September 1405, his heir was fifteen, and with Prince Thomas and his deputy, Stephen Le Scrope, absent opportunities arose not just for the Gaels but also for those among the Anglo-Irish who resented Ormond's influence to redress the balance of the past few years. Gerald, earl of Kildare, was now chosen as justiciar, and when Thomas, heir to the earldom of Desmond, reached his majority in March 1406, he was allowed his liberties and franchises, simultaneously receiving a pardon for any treasons he had committed (none, as far as is known).[29] Yet Prince Thomas had invested too much in the Ormonds to allow their position to be eroded. Within a month of the third earl's death he had secured the wardship and inheritance of his heir, James the 'White Earl', and after Le Scrope returned in the autumn of 1406 he soon gave the new earl of Ormond effective control of his inheritance, even though he was five years younger than Desmond.[30] The next few years saw the family's position consolidated: when Le Scrope sailed for England once more in January 1408, it was James, now seventeen, who replaced him as deputy, and when Prince Thomas eventually returned to Ireland in August 1408 he imprisoned Kildare and his three sons in Dublin castle, presumably for having flouted James's authority.[31] A month later, Le Scrope died of the plague, so that when Prince Thomas returned to

---

[28] *CPR 1408–13*, 223–4; *Foedera*, viii.639; E 403/606, 9 Dec.; E 403/606, 23 March; E 403/609, 16 Dec.; *Hardyng*, 365–7 (who dates the raid on the Forth to the eleventh year, i.e. before Oct. 1410); *CPR 1408–13*, 223–4; *Foedera*, viii.639.

[29] *CIRCLE PR 7 Henry IV*, nos. 68, 69.

[30] *CIRCLE PR 7 Henry IV*, no. 71, *8 Henry IV*, no. 104.

[31] *CIRCLE PR 9 Henry IV*, no. 105; *Annals of the Kingdom of Ireland*, ed. J. O'Donovan (7 vols, Dublin, 1856), iv.794–5, 799. Marlebergh said that Kildare 'lost all his goods, being spoiled and rifled by the lord lieutenant's men', and was only released after paying a fine of 300 marks (*Ancient Irish Histories*, 22). It is not clear what he or his sons had done to deserve this: Crooks, 'Factionalism and Noble Power', 290–7.

England in March 1409 to be with his father a new deputy had to be found, and it was to another member of the Butler family that he turned, the young earl's half-brother Thomas, prior of the Irish Hospitallers at Kilmainham (Dublin). The White Earl he took with him as a member of his household, first to England and then in 1412 to France, an apprenticeship from which he would emerge to claim a position of dominance among the Anglo-Irish nobility through the first half of the fifteenth century.[32]

Fortunately for the English, the native Irish response during these years was sporadic and uncoordinated. In Louth, internal feuds siphoned off much of the energy of the O'Neills and O'Reillys, while raiding by the O'Connors, O'Donnells, O'Byrnes and the indomitable Art MacMurrough into Meath, Wexford and Kildare between 1405 and 1407 was met by vigorous counter-attacks from the citizens of Dublin and the prior of Connell, one of which yielded a rich haul of rebel heads and banners to be paraded through the city.[33] Eight months later Scrope led an army including the young earls of Ormond and Desmond, first against MacMurrough in Leinster and then against the O'Carrolls and the Burghs of Clanwilliam, who were raiding Ormond's lands in Kilkenny; the ensuing battle of Callan (county Kilkenny) was said to have resulted in the death of 800 Irish and the capture of Walter Burgh. Shortly after Prince Thomas's return to the island in 1408–9 he was wounded in a skirmish at Kilmainham, to which he responded by conducting a campaign into Leinster and holding a parliament at Kilkenny.[34]

Yet all the time the territory under English control was shrinking: several towns were granted exemptions from imposts of one sort or another because they were so ruined by constant raids, and when Scrope summoned a parliament to Dublin in January 1407 it had to be moved to Trim because the city itself was not considered safe. In the summer of 1409, MacMurrough was still being bought off by the commons of Wexford.[35] By June 1410 it was said that all the roads leading out of the four 'loyal counties' (Dublin,

[32] *CIRCLE PR 10 Henry IV*, no. 92; Thomas was in Ireland from 2 Aug. 1408 to 13 March 1409; Kildare was released shortly before he left (*Ancient Irish Histories*, 22). For the White Earl, see E. Matthew, 'James Butler, Fourth Earl of Ormond', *ODNB*, 9.147–9; in February 1412 he was granted two manors in county Kildare for his 'immense service in the king's wars' (*CIRCLE PR 13 Henry IV*, no. 31).

[33] Wylie, *Henry the Fourth*, iii.160–3.

[34] Crooks, 'Factionalism and Noble Power', 297–8. Marlborough said that Thomas 'barely escaped death' from his wound (*Ancient Irish Histories*, 21–2).

[35] *CCR 1405–9*, 178. When MacMurrough died in 1417 the Irish annalist lauded the fact that he had 'defended his province against the English and Irish from his sixteenth to his sixtieth year' (*Annals of the Kingdom of Ireland*, 830–1); for his regular raiding into Wexford, see Cosgrove, *New History of Ireland II*, 543, 552.

Kildare, Meath and Louth) were too dangerous to travel.[36] Despite this, Prince Thomas thought better of returning, and for the remainder of his lieutenancy Prior Butler and Sir Edward Perers carried the burden of responsibility for defending the colony on land while Janico Dartasso attempted to defend its coasts against Scottish and other attackers.[37] What military success the colonists did enjoy was mainly due to the commitment of these deputies and the resilience of the Anglo-Irish community. Prince Thomas's lieutenancy came in for a good deal of criticism, some of it deserved: he spent less than three of his twelve years as lieutenant in Ireland, and although his complaints about underfunding were undoubtedly justified, it is also likely that as his interest in Ireland waned he began to siphon off some of what was given to him to support a princely lifestyle in England.[38] Moreover, his support for the Butlers smacked of partisanship and evidently did not meet with universal approval. In August 1409, shortly after the appointment of Thomas Butler, Prince Henry tried to have his younger brother removed from the lieutenancy, and two years later further questions were raised in the council about the competence of the Dublin administration.[39] Behind these lay the sibling rivalry between the princes that now muddied the trickle of policy seeping forth from Westminster, but the allegations were not followed up, for by this time English eyes were turned towards France.

Between 1404 and 1407, with coastal raiding in the Channel, French offensives against Guyenne and Calais, and the arrival of a French army in Wales, it must have seemed only a matter of time before hostilities with France would erupt into open war. The bushfire conflict in Guyenne, a war

[36] *CIRCLE CR 8 Henry IV*, no. 3; *PR 10 Henry IV*, no. 176; *11 Henry IV*, nos. 99, 102.

[37] Dartasso had been deputy admiral and constable of Dublin since 1401 and became steward of Ulster in 1407; he also led a raid into Ulster in June 1409 which apparently slew eighty Irish rebels (*Ancient Irish Histories*, 23), and a month later was building a ship at Drogheda to resist Scottish raiders (*CIRCLE PR 10 Henry IV*, no. 202). Prior Butler was an active military leader against the native Irish (*CIRCLE PR 12 Henry IV*, no. 14; *13 Henry IV*, no. 56). Edward Perers, a strong supporter of the Butlers, was promoted to 'supervisor' of the keepers of the peace in September 1409; he rebuilt Carlow castle at his own expense and was entrusted in late 1410 with the keeping of Wicklow town and castle, in the midst of rebel-held lands (*CIRCLE PR 9 Henry IV*, no. 108; *10 Henry IV*, no. 208; *11 Henry IV*, no. 18).

[38] G. Harriss, 'Thomas, Duke of Clarence', *ODNB*, 54.284–5; Blacker, 'A Lancastrian Prince in Ireland'. The indenture sealed by Le Scrope in 1406 provided most unusually for his troops to be paid directly from the exchequer rather than from the lieutenant's salary, perhaps because of uncertainty about Prince Thomas's use of his salary: Matthew, 'The Financing of the Lordship of Ireland under Henry V and Henry VI', 104–5; cf. Tiptoft's remarks in 1406 (*PROME*, viii.339.347).

[39] *Annals of the Kingdom of Ireland*, iv.804–5; *POPC*, i.320; Crooks, 'Factionalism and Noble Power', 306–14.

of sieges fought largely by *routiers*, cost the English and their allies ninety-six castles in the duchy in 1405–6 alone – a figure credible enough for Tiptoft to present as a fact to the 1406 parliament – and although Louis of Orléans failed to take Bordeaux or even Bourg, despite a twelve-week siege of the latter in the winter of 1406–7, he continued to harbour hopes of expelling the English. In October 1407 the great castle of Lourdes in the foothills of the Pyrenees, having stood out for nearly two years, was finally lost, sold to the French by its captain Jean de Béarn for 32,500 *écus d'or*, and the French won control of the county of Bigorre.[40] Yet as long as the English held Fronsac on the Dordogne, 'the principal fortress of all Guyenne' according to the mayor of Bordeaux, Sir William Farrington, the Bordelais was secure, and it was to this end that English efforts were now mainly directed.[41] As it turned out, the fall of Lourdes marked the end of four years of French pressure in Guyenne and would be the last significant English loss in the duchy for a generation.

Despite the intensity of hostilities, the thirty-year truce of 1396 remained theoretically in place, although in practice it had to be supplemented by local truces, often of only a few months' duration but usually renewed, which meant that the English government was continuously involved in an interlocking series of negotiations. From early 1406, probably as a result of John of Burgundy's growing influence, hopes of peace and marriage were also revived, and in 1407 the English proposed that Prince Henry be betrothed to Charles VI's daughter Marie, although this foundered when she could not be persuaded to forsake the convent she had entered as a novice at the age of four.[42] The chief obstacle to peace was, as ever, Orléans, who was trying during the autumn of 1407 to undermine the Anglo-Flemish rapprochement upon which Duke John of Burgundy's revenues largely depended, and to block payments from the French treasury to his rival. Whether it was this or simply the accumulation of years of loathing,

[40] *PROME*, viii.339. Henry had ordered 500 marks to be sent to Béarn in April 1407 to try to save Lourdes, but this was not enough (E 404/22, no. 417; Pépin, 'The French Offensives of 1404–1407', 28–30; cf. *RHL*, ii.346–7).

[41] M. Vale, 'The War in Aquitaine', in *Arms, Armies and Fortifications in the Hundred Years War*, ed. A.Curry and M. Hughes (Woodbridge, 1994), 69–82, at pp. 74–8. Fronsac, a royal castle, was held in Henry's reign by either the lieutenant (Rutland), the mayor of Bordeaux (Farrington) or the constable of Bordeaux (Thomas Swynbourne). Yet when Swynbourne died in 1412 arrears of the garrison's wages topped 1,000 marks and in 1414 it was 'in great disrepair' (*CCR 1409–13*, 366).

[42] Philpotts, 'Fate of the Truce', 73–5; Wylie, *Henry the Fourth*, iii.50–1; E 403/591, 15 July; Marie took her final vows at Poissy in summer 1408 (*Saint-Denys*, iv.9).

Burgundy now decided that the king's brother must be eliminated.[43] On the night of 23 November 1407, Louis was visiting Queen Isabeau in her palace close to the Porte Barbette in Paris to console her for the recent loss of a child when a messenger arrived to tell him that the king wished to speak with him urgently. It was a trap. Barely had he stepped into the street when he was set upon by between fifteen and twenty men. 'I am the duke of Orléans,' he cried. 'That is who we are looking for,' they replied, hacking off his left hand, smashing open his skull and stabbing him repeatedly before dragging his corpse on to a rubbish heap. Two days later Burgundy confessed that it was he who had hired the assassins, then fled to Flanders. In March 1408 he returned in arms to Paris, presented an elaborate justification for his action, and received a pardon from the barely sentient Charles VI. This merely inflamed opinion further. To his widow Valentina and son Charles, the blood of Duke Louis cried for vengeance; many others, however, applauded his death, particularly in Paris where he had been detested.[44]

It was against the background of this blood feud which tore the French royal family apart that Anglo-French relations were conducted for the remainder of Henry's reign. Even when sane, Charles VI hardly knew what to do. In July 1408 Burgundy's pardon was revoked, a few months later it was restored; in March 1409 he and the fourteen-year-old Charles of Orléans were publicly reconciled in Chartres cathedral and the king and queen returned to Paris, but the upshot was that the governance of king and kingdom now fell into Burgundy's hands. As for Henry, the removal of Orléans could only strengthen his hand. News of the assassination reached him during the Gloucester parliament, where he happened to be entertaining the French king's ambassadors. Within a week an English embassy had been appointed to discuss terms for a 'true final peace', and a short-term truce had been concluded in Guyenne.[45] Anglo-French relations now improved rapidly. The local truces in Brittany, Flanders and Guyenne were periodically renewed through 1408, a year which saw growing cooperation over the Schism and fewer outbreaks of cross-

[43] Duke John may have planned the murder in June (Famiglietti, *Royal Intrigue*, 60–2). For what follows see *Monstrelet*, i.154; *Saint-Denys*, iii.731–43. The principal assassin was Raoul d'Anquetonville, a man with a personal grudge against Orléans.

[44] R. Vaughan, *John the Fearless* (London, 1966), 66–102. The chronicler of *Saint-Denys*, iv.739, emphasized Orléans's eloquence and charm, but indulgence in vices in his youth.

[45] The truce in Guyenne was extended in April, until September: *Foedera*, viii.504–9, 515–19.

Channel hostilities than at any time since 1401.[46] By September this continuous diplomatic intercourse resulted in a general truce between the two
countries for eighteen months and the renewal of talks about marriage, or
even marriages, between the two royal houses, which by early 1409 had
crystallized into a proposal for a match between Prince Henry and the
French king's youngest daughter Catherine.[47] By now the prince was
stretching his diplomatic wings, and he too favoured marriage as the way
to cement a peace with France – indeed he would eventually marry
Catherine, though not until 1420.[48] The fact that his growing authority in
England coincided with Burgundy's ascendancy in Paris also meant that
Anglo-French diplomacy now became a multilateral affair. Since, and even
before, Orléans's assassination, Henry and Arundel had used the duke of
Berry as their principal contact in Paris, but from the autumn of 1409 it
was increasingly with Burgundy that they dealt.[49] Hence the sumptuous
and widely publicized Anglo-Burgundian jousts held at Smithfield in July
1409 and at Lille in December, probably as a cover for diplomatic
overtures.[50]

Yet it took time to establish trust, and if the autumn of 1409 saw talk of
peace, by early 1410 there was a growing conviction in both England and

---

[46] *Foedera*, viii.504–9, 515, 519 (Guyenne); 511, 530, 548, 614 (Flanders, the duke of
Burgundy); 517 (Picardy); 591 (Brittany). However, skirmishing continued around Calais,
and on 15 September 1408 the earl of Kent, appointed admiral the previous year with a
mandate to sweep the seas of pirates, was killed while attacking the island of Bréhat in an
attempt to pressurize the inhabitants into handing over the portion of Queen Joan's dowry
which they had withheld; he had unwisely removed his helmet during an assault and was
struck through the head by a crossbow bolt (*Giles*, 54; Wylie, *Henry the Fourth*, iii.102–5).

[47] *Foedera*, 530–4, 548–60. Hugh Mortimer, the prince's chamberlain, went twice to France
about a marriage between the prince and Charles's 'second [available] daughter' (E 404/24,
no. 278). When Alexander III became pope, Henry wrote to him urging him to work for
Anglo-French peace, and Alexander duly wrote to Charles VI, but his death shortly afterwards closed this avenue of mediation: BL Cotton Cleopatra E II, fo. 279 (Henry to the
pope, 15 April 1409); BL Add. Ms 30,663, fos. 310–12 (Alexander to Charles VI, 25 July
1409); *CE*, 418; Wilson, 'Anglo-French Relations', 335; Pépin, 'French Offensives of 1404–
1407', 39. The inclusion of Prince Thomas as an ambassador for the first time in December
1407 might indicate that his was one of the possible marriages, but the main object was to
secure a French princess for Prince Henry. Henry Beaufort was chief negotiator (*Foedera*,
viii.585–7, 597).

[48] E 403/596, 19 Oct. 1408 (William Chester, the prince's herald, sent to the French court
with letters for various lords); E 403/599, 23 May 1409 (marriage talks).

[49] For contacts with Berry in 1407–9, see *Signet Letters*, nos. 704, 735, 740, 952; *Saint-Denys*,
i.253; E 404/24, no. 298 (embassy to Berry on 28 Feb. 1409 dealing with *treschargeantes
affaires*); cf. Philpotts, 'Fate of the Truce', 76.

[50] Wilson, 'Anglo-French Relations', 361; Given-Wilson, 'Quarrels of Old Women'; *Giles*,
54–7; *Brut*, ii.369; Schnerb, *Jean Sans Peur*, 501–7.

France that Calais was about to be assaulted.[51] Henry Beaufort, who kept
a closer eye than most on the barometer of Anglo-French enmity, opened
the parliament of January 1410 with just such a warning, and the commons
agreed with him.[52] Had they known of a meeting of Charles VI's council
in Paris in the same month, which heard a catalogue of Henry IV's crimes
and a proposal that open war be declared, their fears would have been
confirmed.[53] Burgundy, now dominant in Paris, was indeed preparing an
assault, but two developments in the spring made him change his plans.
The first was the formation on 15 April 1410 of the League of Gien, a
coalition of Orléanist or Armagnac lords (the dukes of Orléans, Berry and
Brittany and the counts of Alençon, Clermont and Armagnac) sworn to
rid France of those who acted contrary to 'the welfare and honour of the
king and kingdom' – in other words, the duke of Burgundy and his
supporters. Both parties in France now began summoning their retainers.[54]
The second, also in April, was the destruction by fire of the 'enormous
wooden tower' the duke's men had been constructing in the church of
St-Omer as a siege-platform to assault Calais. The monk of Saint-Denis
claimed that the arsonist was a former English prisoner who had failed to
pay his ransom; released and offered 10,000 nobles in return for destroying
the tower, he persuaded one of the carpenters to throw Greek fire on it.
Walsingham gave freer rein to his imagination: the Burgundians planned
to fill their *apparatus mirabilis* with the decomposing remains of snakes, scor-
pions and toads which they had been collecting in jars, believing that when
these were hurled over the walls of Calais the noxious fumes would poison
the inhabitants and allow the besiegers to enter and take it. One of the
town's residents thus volunteered, in return for 140 gold crowns, to go to
St-Omer and burn it. The chroniclers agree that the resulting conflagra-
tion consumed not just the tower but the church and much of the town as
well.[55] Calais, however, was saved.

[51] *Foedera*, viii.586, 589, 593, 601. On 7 Feb. 1410 the king ordered ships to be prepared to
defend Calais since the duke of Burgundy was about to attack it (E 28/23, no. 26). A story
circulating in England was that he had promised to drive the English out of the town in
return for his pardon for Orléans's murder: *SAC II*, 536.

[52] *PROME*, viii.454, 465; *Saint-Denys*, iv.313; *Monstrelet*, ii.33. English defences in Picardy
were reviewed and a new tower above the gate at Calais constructed (E 403/605, 23 June,
31 July). The seneschal of Bordeaux and 400 men going as reinforcements to Guyenne were
captured by men from Harfleur (*Saint-Denys*, iv.313).

[53] *Monstrelet*, ii.54–61; Lehoux, *Jean de France*, iii.163.

[54] Famiglietti, *Royal Intrigue*, 88–90.

[55] *Saint-Denys*, iv.313; *SAC II*, 592–3; *CE*, 417–18, said the French put one of the conspirators to a 'bitter death'.

From the summer of 1399 until the autumn of 1405 Henry had faced military emergencies from every quarter, and the years 1405 to 1409 have something of the feel of clearing up after a storm. That the storm had passed there was no doubt; only in Ireland did hostilities continue at a comparable level to that of Henry's early years. The challenges of the second half of the reign were as much diplomatic as military, though no less intractable for that. Yet progress was made, and the year from mid-1408 to mid-1409 was a time of real optimism. The Welsh revolt effectively ended, there was still hope that the Scottish government in exile might deliver peace on the northern border, and Prince Thomas's return to Ireland – indicative in itself of the easing of tensions elsewhere – offered hope of progress there too. The spirit of cooperation over the Schism that bore fruit in the Council of Pisa also gave new impetus to the Anglo-French peace talks. It was Henry's misfortune that this brief period of détente coincided with the onset of his sickness, but whether he could have capitalized on it even if fit is questionable. Paradoxically, it was Burgundy's unchallenged dominance at the French court during the autumn and winter of 1409–10 that encouraged him to take a more belligerent stance towards England; like Louis of Orléans, he found that control of the government and its resources brought with it the responsibility to uphold the nation's honour and bare his teeth at its familiar enemies. Conversely, when the Armagnacs leagued against him in the spring of 1410, he warmed to the idea of English allies. Talk of peace was revived, and before the end of June the Anglo-French truce was renewed.[56] Looking to the future, the simultaneous rise to power of Prince Henry and Duke John in 1409–10 would inaugurate a new era in Anglo-French diplomacy, but for the next few years, as they struggled to assert themselves, it brought rapid changes of fortune in France, rivalries and differences of opinion in the English council, and a succession of bewildering reversals of policy.

[56] *Foedera*, viii.637, 641–8.

Chapter 22

ALIENS, MERCHANTS AND ENGLISHNESS

It was not only with England's neighbours that tension eased during the middle years of the reign. Relations with its trading partners – Germans, Italians, Castilians – had also suffered, partly from the collateral damage of the Pirate War, partly from the upsurge of anti-alien sentiment in fifteenth-century England.[1] Anti-alien feeling was broadly directed at three categories of foreigner: first and most persistently, alien merchants who came to trade, some of whom formed semi-permanent communities, predominantly in London; secondly, foreigners attached to the royal court; thirdly, foreign religious serving the dependent cells of continental monasteries, the so-called 'alien' priories. Except in respect to the Welsh and Irish, whose inferiority few Englishmen cared to doubt, Henry did not encourage xenophobia. It undermined commerce and thus revenues, and complicated foreign relations. On the other hand, he benefited from the widespread feeling that Richard II had been too eager to please the French and to allow foreign merchants into the London retail trade.[2] Henry could certainly not be accused of Francophilia, however, and although he welcomed foreigners to his court, he presented himself from the start as first and foremost an English king, using the English language to claim the throne and reversing the legend on the great seal from *Rex Francie et Anglie,* as it had read since Edward III claimed the crown of France in 1340, to *Rex Anglie et Francie.*[3] At the heart of his government lay an English affinity and an unequivocally English monarchy (Henry V was the first English king since 1066 to have four English grandparents). The unashamedly jingoistic martial combats

---

[1] This anti-alien sentiment reached a crescendo in the 1450s: *The Views of the Hosts of Alien Merchants 1440–1444,* ed. H. Bradley (London Record Society 46, London, 2012), xi–xvi; A. Ruddock, *Italian Merchants and Shipping in Southampton 1270–1600* (Southampton, 1951), 162–86.

[2] C. Barron, 'Richard II and London', in *Richard II: The Art of Kingship,* 129–54, at pp. 140–2.

[3] W. M. Ormrod, 'A Problem of Precedence', in *The Age of Edward III,* ed. J. Bothwell (Woodbridge, 2001), 133–53, at p. 153.

over which the king presided also heightened nationalistic feeling, as did the enmity from across the Channel and the Welsh rebellion.

There was pressure on the king from the start of the reign to curb foreign privileges. The English staplers and Londoners won a number of concessions in the 1399 parliament, and although Henry insisted that 'friendly' aliens should not be disadvantaged, some Italian merchants considered relocating from London to other ports.[4] That they decided to stay was certainly not due to any moderation of anti-alien sentiment. Suspected not just of enjoying preferential mercantile dispensations but also of spying, piracy, religious irregularity, treasonable conspiracy and even sexual deviance, foreigners were subjected to increasingly strict supervision, both as to where and how they spent their money and where they were permitted to reside.[5] In the 1402 parliament it was enacted that what they earned from imports should not be removed from the kingdom but spent on English exports; eighteen months later a statute was passed requiring all visiting merchants to lodge in English households so that their activities could be monitored by hosts. 'Those who want to oppose this petition', declared its proponents, 'know nothing of the frauds, artifices and deceptions of the alien merchants, through whom the common profit of the realm is destroyed and ruined'; the intention was not to expel all aliens, but to keep specie within the realm, 'to the perpetual benefit of the treasury of this realm of England'.[6] Yet if they did not want to expel all aliens, they certainly wished to be rid of some of them: supporters of the 'antipope' (the Avignon papacy) were to depart forthwith, as were all aliens in the households of the king or queen apart from a few named exceptions; Scotsmen who declined to swear an oath of allegiance to Henry were also to leave, and all Welshmen were to be kept away from the king's person. The January 1404 parliament also passed a statute expelling almost all French monks from their dependent priories in England.[7]

---

[4] *PROME*, viii.39–40 (staplers exempted from having to deposit an ounce of gold at the Mint for each sack of wool exported), 74 (preference to be given to English ships in carrying cargoes. For Henry's general confirmation of privileges to alien merchants see E 28/7, no. 17 (15 Nov. 1399).

[5] *The Views of the Hosts*, xiv–xx. For spying, see below, pp. 411–14. There were rumours that Italians were involved in the 1403 Percy rebellion (Bradley, 'The Datini Factors', 69).

[6] Nine months later, a consolidated petition from 'the merchants of Italy' managed to secure the repeal of some of the more irksome commercial regulations, but their request to have the Hosting Law rescinded met with refusal; the Genoese had also succeeded in 1402 in winning exemption from 'scavage', the subsidy paid for goods brought from Southampton to London (*PROME*, viii.171–2, 213–15, 274–5, 303–5).

[7] *PROME*, viii, 233, 239–40, 243; *SAC II*, 392–3.

By this time, with Breton raiding and piracy at its height, attention had come to focus on the court, with Queen Joan falling under particular scrutiny, and although Henry did his best to mitigate the effect of the 1404 statute for his queen, the virulently anti-alien parliament which met two years later, much influenced by the London mercantile lobby, maintained the pressure. In March, during the first session, the king was asked to remove all Frenchmen and Bretons from the realm. He replied that this would be done as soon as possible, but on 8 May he was required to name a date for their expulsion, which he duly did, first 15 May and then, to allow them time to pay their debts, 24 May. He did, however, exempt any aliens who were lieges of the English crown (Gascons, for example, or those who had sworn allegiance) and it was agreed that certain aliens who were prepared to pay a fine to remain should be allowed to do so; by mid-August more than a hundred such licences had been issued.[8] The commons remained wary, however, and when parliament reconvened in October they insisted that this concession should not extend to those named on a schedule of forty-four persons (mostly Bretons in the queen's service) submitted to the steward of the king's household. The thirty-one articles of December further stipulated that any aliens who were still in England contrary to the ordinance must pay a fine by Easter 1407, or suffer imprisonment and forfeiture of all their goods and chattels.[9]

Despite the king's reputation for generosity to foreigners, those who were attached to his, rather than to the queen's, household attracted little hostility, partly because they were seen as transient (even if in some cases they were not), partly because they were more obviously useful as well as less conspicuous at a court where so many visiting dignitaries were to be found.[10] Around twenty of the king's retained knights were foreigners, and at least

[8] C 49/48, no. 8 (template writ for an alien to remain, agreed in the council on 1 July and proclaimed on 9 July; licensees were to be allowed to keep their goods and chattels in England for life and not to be molested by royal officials); E 401/638, 14 August 1406, records 105 fines from aliens, the largest of £33 from the Genoese Matthew Spicer; no one else paid more than £10 and most ten shillings or less; six cobblers paid twenty pence each.

[9] Walsingham said that Joan's two daughters were expelled, but they might have returned to Brittany because their brother the duke planned to marry them; yet most of the aliens expelled in 1406 were Bretons, leaving about fifteen with the queen. These included her chamberlain, Charles of Navarre, and her secretary, John de Boyas, but she also had non-Bretons in her household: Sir Hugh Luttrell was her steward and Galvano Trenta of Lucca keeper of her jewels (SAC II, 392–3, 474–5; Henneman, Olivier de Clisson, 197–8; Foedera, viii.319, 429; CGR 1402–4, no. 157). The summer and autumn of 1407 saw further restrictions on aliens' right to engage in the London retail trade (PROME, viii.331, 335–7, 351–2, 373; SAC II, 474–5; Lloyd, England and the German Hanse, 110–11).

[10] For Henry's generosity to foreigners, see Kingsford, English Historical Literature, 277 ('Southern Chronicle').

one party of ambassadors was usually in attendance.[11] Knights errant such as Jean de Werchin or the earl of Mar hungered to joust against the best that England could offer, preferably in the king's presence, while Bertolf van der E'me from the Low Countries went one better and engaged in sword play with the king himself, getting his thumb nicked in the process. High status prisoners of war such as the king of Scotland and the earl of Douglas, or impecunious exiles such as Archambaud, count of Périgord, George Dunbar, and William, bishop of Tournai, often accompanied the king, sometimes even to the battlefield.[12] Some foreigners such as the Navarrese esquire Janico Dartasso and the Bohemian knights Roger Siglem, Arnold Pallas and Nicholas Hauberk had served Richard II for many years, but slipped effortlessly into Henry's service and proved loyal and useful – Dartasso in Ireland, Hauberk as a chamber knight, Siglem and Pallas as ambassadors to the empire.[13] Others were valued for their special skills, such as Richard Garner of Piedmont who managed the recoinage of 1411–12, the German gunners who designed and maintained Henry's artillery, or his French, Italian or Portuguese physicians. Two foreigners were especially favoured by the king: the Milanese Francis de Courte, whom Henry knighted and granted letters of denization, and who by 1402 had become a royal chamber knight; and Hartung von Klux from Silesia, whom he had met in 1392–3 and knighted on the Scottish campaign in 1400, and whose active diplomatic career in Henry's service culminated in 1411 with an embassy to Sigismund of Hungary. Five years later, along with Sigismund, von Klux would be elected to the Order of the Garter, but soon after this he returned to Germany where he pursued a fruitful career in the imperial service until his death in 1445.[14] It would have been difficult for the commons or anyone else to gainsay the usefulness to the king of such men.

[11] Between October and December 1402, Henry entertained Byzantine, Spanish and German embassies; in the autumn of 1405, Danish, Scottish and French embassies (E 101/404/21, fos 38–40; BL Harleian MS 319, fo. 41).

[12] E 403/573, 8 May 1402 (Henry wounded E'me's thumb – *pollice* – with a *gladio longo* and gave him an annuity of £10); *Johannis Lelandi*, vi.300. Périgord accompanied the king to Scotland in 1400 (E 403/565, 21 Feb. 1400; E 403/571, 28 Oct. 1400; E 404/16, nos. 773–4, *CDS*, iv.116); for the bishop of Tournai, see E 403, 3 Dec. 1409.

[13] Above, pp. 250–1. (Dartasso); Siglem bought horses for the king at Frankfurt (E 404/15, no. 411; E 404/16, no. 542); for Hauberk and Pallas see E 404/15, 10 Dec. 1399; E 403/567, 5 June 1400.

[14] The king gave Courte two manors in Hampshire in May 1408 to build a chapel, because he 'has no manor or place in England in which to build it' (*CPR 1405–8*, 406). For von Klux, see A. Reitemeier, *Aussenpolitik im Spatmittelalter: Die diplomatiken Beziehungen zwischen dem Reich und England 1377–1422* (Paderborn, 1999), 258–60, 280–3, 497–9; E 403/606, 16 Feb. 1411.

There was, moreover, one alien community that was consistently exempted from the parliamentary acts of expulsion of Henry's reign, and from the additional subsidies sometimes imposed on foreign merchants: the Germans or Hansards.[15] Anglo-Hanseatic trade was at its peak around this time, and generally speaking English kings protected the Hansards; the goods they brought from the Baltic – Rhenish wine, beeswax, beer, furs and skins, timber, amber, copper and iron, grain and much else – were valued, as were their role in the cloth trade (which accounted for 90 per cent of what they exported) and the loans they provided. However, there were times when native pressure was hard to resist, for English merchants resented the privileges granted to the Hansa by Edward III, while Hanseatic merchants resented English attempts to increase their share of Baltic trade.[16] The late 1380s had witnessed the seizure of several ships and the threat of a Hanseatic embargo, but since then relations had calmed. Henry made no attempt at his accession to restrict Hansa privileges, although he did appease the English merchants by reissuing a list of the conditions upon which they had been granted, which included undertakings that English merchants in Prussia would receive similar privileges and that only 'authentic' German merchants – those with letters of accreditation from Hansa towns – be allowed to enjoy them. Hanseatic representatives were also told to come before the king to answer complaints from their English counterparts.[17] Unfortunately the Pirate War soon led to an alarming increase in the number of such cases: sixteen Hanseatic cogs suspected of carrying French or Scottish goods were captured, robbed or destroyed in 1402, a further twenty in 1403, and inevitably there were reprisals against English shipping. In June 1403 Henry wrote to Conrad von Jungingen, Grand-Master of the Teutonic Knights, to invite his ambassadors to England to negotiate a settlement.[18]

Despite the almost competitively polite tone of the correspondence between Henry and Conrad, who had crusaded together in Livonia in the early 1390s, the resulting talks were a struggle. An agreement of October 1403 promised a review of claims and protection until Easter 1404 for

---

[15] *PROME*, viii.337, 351–2; *Giles*, 51–2; *SAC II*, 239.

[16] Lloyd, *England and the German Hanse*, 109–57, 376; P. Dollinger, *The German Hansa*, trans. D. Ault and S. Steinberg (Stanford, 1970), 55–8.

[17] *Foedera*, viii.112; *CPR 1399–1401*, 57; J. Bolton, *The Medieval English Economy 1150–1500* (London, 1980), 306–11; M. Postan, 'Economic and Political Relations of England and the Hanse from 1400 to 1475', in *Studies in English Trade in the Fifteenth Century*, ed. E. Power and M. Postan (London, 1933), 91–153.

[18] *Foedera*, viii.203, 269, 284, 287, 297, 305; BL Stowe 142, fos 4–5; Lloyd, *England and the German Hanse*, 112–16.

merchants on each side, as long as they did not engage in unlicensed trading ventures. However, a spate of outrages in 1404 (a further twenty-two Hanseatic ships captured or robbed) led to the expulsion of English merchants from Prussia by the autumn; there was even talk of a general north European boycott of English trade, though this made little progress.[19] It was thus decided at the October 1404 parliament to send as ambassadors to Marienburg Sir William Esturmy, an expert in northern European diplomacy, the chancery clerk John Kington and the Londoner and former privy councillor William Brampton.[20] They managed to get the ban on English merchants lifted from October 1405, although it was made clear that this was dependent on a satisfactory agreement being reached, but settling the numerous compensation claims took longer.[21] The English claimed 4,535 nobles (£1,512) for Prussian attacks on English shipping; the Prussians countered with a claim of 5,120 nobles for English attacks. This, however, was far from the full extent of Hanseatic grievances. One of the problems in negotiating with the Hansa was that although the towns leagued together when solidarity might further their interests, each also had its own agenda, and before returning the English ambassadors undertook a tour of the Baltic to discover what other claims were being pursued. The Livonians, now subject to the Grand-Master, claimed 8,027 nobles, the merchants of Hamburg 1,117, Bremen 4,414, Stralsund 7,416, Lübeck 8,690, and so forth. Some of the alleged attacks had taken place twenty or more years earlier and there was much room for debate about precise sums, the compensation payable for killings on each side, and those who were responsible. The English not only disputed the sums but also asserted that reciprocal seizures by the men of Stralsund and Greifswald easily covered their losses and that merchants from Rostock and Wismar still had English goods to the value of 32,800 nobles in their possession.

Against this background of claims, counter-claims and sanctions, a settlement was eventually drafted at a meeting held at The Hague (Holland) in August 1407. The English commissioners agreed to pay 8,957 nobles to the Prussians, 22,096 to the Livonians, and 1,372 to the merchants of

[19] *RHL*, i.162–6, 208, 238, 240, 242, 251, 258–64, 371–2, 382, 401; ii.354–62 (summary of the ambassadors' dealings with the Grand-Master and the Hansa); *Foedera*, viii.364; Dollinger, *German Hansa*, 390–1 (English complaints). The chief culprit in Hanseatic eyes was the merchant-pirate John Brandon of Lynn, for whom see below, p. 432.

[20] *Foedera*, viii.395–6, 459, 466–7. Their commission was renewed in November 1406, and again in February 1407 excluding Brampton, who by then was dead; in February 1407 they were also empowered to make an alliance with King Eric of Denmark, Sweden and Norway, Henry's son-in-law.

[21] E 403/585, 26 March 1406 (proclamation of truce); cf. *PROME*, viii.329.

Hamburg, making a total of around £10,800 sterling; during the next year Henry and Ulrich von Jungingen (the new Grand-Master, his brother having died) exchanged letters agreeing the terms.[22] The money was to be paid in six instalments of £1,772 between November 1409 and Easter 1412; English claims for compensation were reduced to just £255 (766 nobles).[23] Naturally matters did not end there. Not all claims had been settled, and it was suggested that, as chancellor, Archbishop Arundel might be asked to consider those still outstanding.[24] Moreover, although the Grand-Master and his Livonian subjects were content with the treaty, the northern Hanseatic towns opposed it, for they stood to gain very little. To some extent, therefore, the English succeeded by playing off different powers within the fragile League against each other, but Henry had also been lucky in his timing, for the Prussians and Livonians were facing the military might of Poland-Lithuania and looking to appease potential allies. Little did it avail them. Disaster struck on 15 July 1410, when Ulrich von Jungingen was killed and hundreds of the Teutonic Order's knights were either slaughtered or captured by a Polish-Lithuanian army at the battle of Grünwald (or Tannenberg). Reactions to this in England were mixed. Walsingham had little sympathy, pointing out that those against whom the knights waged war were themselves Christians. Henry, however, mindful no doubt of his warm reception in Prussia twenty years earlier, wrote to the pope to ask him to use his influence to mitigate the crippling financial penalties imposed by the Polish king who, he alleged, had employed 'Saracens' in his army, which made Henry wary of continuing his payments to the Order in case the money fell into the hands of infidels.[25] This sounds disingenuous, although thus far Henry had done his best to comply with the treaty, handing over the first two instalments of £1,772 each on 3 December 1409 and 1 March 1410.[26] Moreover, payments did not cease, although they slowed: the council noted in March 1411 that £1,772 was

[22] Wylie, *Henry the Fourth*, ii.67–78 and iv.1–21; cf. *PROME*, viii.341.

[23] *RHL*, ii.202, 236–46, 257, 264; *Foedera*, viii.597–9.

[24] This probably explains the survival of several memoranda of claims and counter-claims, relating to Stralsund in particular, surviving in Canterbury cathedral's archives: *Literae Cantuarienses*, ed. J. B. Sheppard (3 vols, RS, London, 1887–9), iii.78–107.

[25] *SAC II*, 594–7; BL Cotton Cleopatra E. ii, fo. 266 (renumbered 279): Henry's letter was dated 24 Nov. 1410. In 1407 Henry was said to have remarked to the Hanseatic envoy Arndt von Dassel that he had spent his 'gadling days' crusading with the Knights and felt himself to be a 'child of Prussia' (Wylie, *Henry the Fourth*, iv.7–9).

[26] *Signet Letters*, no. 726; E 403/602, 3 Dec., 1 March. The second instalment was issued from the exchequer on 1 March 1410, though possibly not handed to the Hanseatic envoys for three months (Lloyd, *England and the German Hanse*, 120–6, who calls the Treaty 'a diplomatic triumph for the English').

needed for 'the men of Prussia', and in February 1412 a further £666 was released. Thus by the time Henry died nearly half the debt had been cleared, but there were no further payments after 1413.[27]

It was not the king's intention that this obligation should fall on the exchequer; merchant communities were responsible for the attacks, and royal officers were directed to levy contributions from them, a task neither popular nor easy. Merchants from Scarborough had to be threatened with imprisonment to persuade them to hand over the 400 marks at which they were assessed, and a new dispute between Boston and Bergen, the Hanseatic hub in Norway, threatened another breakdown in relations and led to the detention of nine Norwegians at Boston, although following undertakings from the Norwegians their men were released in the spring of 1412.[28] Nevertheless, the fact that agreement had been reached in 1407–9 was impressive considering the complexity of the matters under discussion, and Henry continued to do what he could to secure restitution of the Hansards' goods and ships and to uphold their privileges in England. The Pirate War had severely tested this relationship, but goodwill, diplomatic commitment and extrinsic pressure eventually settled a standoff that it was in the interest of neither government to prolong.

The number of Germans who resided continuously in London was around thirty, roughly half the size of the Italian – or 'Lombard' – community in the capital.[29] A hundred years earlier, the Italians had enjoyed great economic power in England, controlling much of the wool trade and acting as bankers to the crown and aristocracy, but with the crash of the major Italian banks in the mid-fourteenth century and the decline of wool exports their influence was much diminished. Even so, they were still both prominent and unpopular: their share of the import market to London was around 30 per cent in the early fifteenth century, and they were second only to the Hansa as exporters of English cloth, in return for which they imported spices, delicacies and fine textiles from the eastern Mediterranean – one of the reasons for their unpopularity, for such luxuries were the preserve of the

---

[27] E 403/609, 23 Feb. 1412; *POPC*, ii.10; Lloyd, *England and the German Hanse*, 125.

[28] *CPR 1408–13*, 62, 308, 319, 321, 383–5, 400. Relations with Bergen were often fraught: it was said that in 1407 they had bound hand and foot one hundred fishermen from Cromer and Blakeney (Norfolk) and drowned them at Vinde Fjord (Norway): *Foedera*, viii.723–4; Wylie, *Henry the Fourth*, iv.11; Lloyd, *England and the German Hanse*, 137–8.

[29] Barron, *London*, 15, 113. Germans lived in the Steelyard on the Thames, Italians in Langbourn and Broad Street; 'Lombards' was often used generically for Italians in England.

rich and seen by some as superfluous.[30] Moreover, as recently as the 1380s some 90 per cent of loans to the crown from aliens (£45,800) had come from Italians.[31] Most of this was advanced by Genoese and Florentine merchants, but from the mid-1390s Anglo-Genoese relations deteriorated. In 1395, encouraged by Philip of Burgundy, Genoa moved its north European staple from Southampton to Bruges; in the following year, the city fell under French domination (Henry's old friend Marshal Boucicault became governor in 1401), and during the Pirate War Genoese carracks and galleys were suspected of aiding the French.[32] Yet there were still Genoese merchants in England, who could be tapped for loans,[33] and in 1405 a Genoese ambassador visited. Perhaps as a result of this, in April 1407 the Genoese were granted the right to sail to England, unload, pick up new cargoes, cross to Flanders and then return to England to unload and reload before sailing back to the Mediterranean, a valuable privilege given the jealousy with which English merchants guarded the cross-Channel trade.[34] Soon after this, however, Anglo-Genoese relations turned sour. In June 1407 a royal sergeant-at-arms was sent to Southampton, the Genoese port of choice, to stop any carrack or galley from Genoa leaving without special licence, and in early 1412 orders were issued not to allow any person to send money or goods out of the country if they were for the use or profit of any Genoese. Behind this lay the complaint of a powerful group of London merchants, who claimed they had been deceived into sailing into Genoa only to find their ships and goods – valued by them at £24,000 – seized. Despite remonstrations from Henry, the Genoese prevaricated, and a month before his death the king gave the Londoners letters of reprisal against any Genoese merchandise they could find up to a limit of £10,000. By this time, they were 'the king's enemies of Genoa'.[35]

Genoese irritation stemmed not merely from the fact that the Londoners were trying to break into the Mediterranean market; they also resented the favours shown by the king to their rivals, the Venetians and Florentines. Henry encouraged Venetian commerce, writing to the Doge four days

---

[30] The *Libelle of Englyshe Polycye* (1436) characterized Italian imports as 'Apes and japes and marmysettes taylede/Nifles, trifles, that litell have avaylede' (Barron, *London*, 113–14).

[31] Steel, *Receipt*, 146–7; W. Childs, 'Anglo-Italian Contacts in the Fourteenth Century', in *Chaucer and the Italian Trecento*, ed. P. Boitani (Cambridge, 1983), 65–87.

[32] Ruddock, *Italian Merchants*, 52–9; *The Views of Hosts*, xi.

[33] In May 1404 they lent the king 1,000 marks, repaid through exemption from customs duties: *Foedera*, viii.358–9.

[34] *CCR 1409–13*, 10, 22.

[35] *Foedera*, viii.420, 717–18, 773–4; *CPR 1408–13*, 461–2; *CCR 1409–13*, 437 (with diatribe against the Genoese); E 403/591, 2 June 1407; Ruddock, *Italian Merchants*, 58–9.

after his accession to assure him that his subjects would be treated 'like our own lieges' in England, and two months later sent £1,000 to Venice to cover the debts left by Thomas Mowbray, who had died there. In 1407, the Venetian Senate noted that the English king was 'most friendly' towards them and voted to allocate two hundred ducats to buy presents for him and Queen Joan.[36] Two years later the Venetians received a licence to bring their 'Flanders Galleys' to compete with the Genoese in the lucrative cross-Channel traffic, although their access to this was only permitted for a year at a time and at the special request of the Doge. Nevertheless, during the last few years of Henry's reign it was renewed annually, although probably not freely, for in October 1409 Venetian merchants paid 2,000 marks to the exchequer as a 'concord' for having evaded customs in the past; the simultaneous receipt of their licence was probably not coincidental.[37] The Venetian presence in London increased markedly during the first third of the fifteenth century.

One role in which the Venetians showed little interest was that of bankers. This niche was occupied by the Florentines, as it had been during the first half of the fourteenth century, although on a much reduced scale. The leading Florentine firm in London comprised the Albertini family, who had been exiled from Florence in 1401 but reacted by setting up profitable businesses in France, Spain and England as well as in several Italian towns. They had acted as Henry's bankers in 1393 and Archbishop Arundel's during his exile in Florence in 1398. However, it was not by lending to kings that they made their money, as the Frescobaldi, Bardi and Peruzzi had done in earlier times, but by acting as agents for Englishmen wishing to transfer money abroad, in particular clerics who needed to make payments to Rome.[38] The commons criticized this traffic, regarding the resulting outflow of specie as scarcely less injurious to the realm than the removal of the profits made by foreign merchants, but as long as England remained a Catholic country Englishmen would continue to seek

---

[36] *Calendar of State Papers Venice*, i.39, 44; E 403/565, 17 Dec. (1399); *RHL*, i.424; cf. Lloyd, *England and the German Hanse*, 119.

[37] *Foedera*, viii.595 (August 1409), 655 (October 1410), 714 (January 1412); E 403/602, 9 Oct. 1409; *Antient Kalendars*, ii.77–8, gives this as £2,000.

[38] G. Holmes, 'Florentine Merchants in England, 1346–1436', *Economic History Review* (1960), 193–208. It was through 'Lombard' merchants that Henry paid Mowbray's debts in Venice (E 403/565, 17 Dec. 1399). After their conquest of Pisa in 1406 the Florentines acquired a port to send ships north, and before the end of Henry's reign some of these visited England; one of their carracks was seized by William Longe in 1411 (*CPR 1408–13*, 317). However, international exchange was their main source of profit in England. Henry did get about £3,000 in loans from the Albertini, mainly in 1406–7 (Ruddock, *Italian Merchants*, 57–8).

papal provisions, go on pilgrimage and engage in litigation at the papal court.[39] In 1409, following the Council of Pisa, it was Filippo Alberti who, along with Richard Whittington, was responsible for collecting nearly £1,000 for the payment of Peter's Pence and procurations to the newly elected Pope Alexander V.[40]

Henry's favourable treatment of the Venetians and Florentines reflected the changing balance of power in Italy: Florence's conquest of Pisa in 1406 and Venice's defeat of Genoa in the War of Chioggia (1378–81) helped to shape the political map of Italy in the fifteenth century, with Venice, Florence and Milan emerging as the great territorial powers in the northern half of the peninsula. Personal contacts – the favourable impression Henry had created at Venice in 1392–3; his and Arundel's prior dealings with the Albertini – strengthened these political bonds, although none of this could mask the decline in Italian influence in England as either bankers or traders since the first half of the fourteenth century.[41]

Iberian merchants also suffered during the Pirate War, although Henry's personal contacts once again helped to limit the fallout, for his sister Philippa was married to João I, king of Portugal (1385–1433), and his half-sister Catherine to Enrique III, king of Castile (1390–1406). Diplomacy with Castile needed to circumvent the Franco-Castilian alliance of 1369 (primarily an anti-English compact) as well as the Schism, for Castile, like France, adhered to the Avignon papacy. Nevertheless, an exchange of embassies in 1400 augured well, and by July 1402 Enrique was addressing Henry as his 'dear and beloved brother, the king of England'.[42] Relations with England's ally Portugal were more straightforward, though not entirely so, since for the Portuguese to welcome Henry's usurpation with too much enthusiasm would have risked antagonizing France and Castile.

[39] PROME, viii.170, 213–14, 436, 446–7, 464. The Libelle would describe the Florentine exchange brokers as 'wiping our nose with our own sleeve' (Harriss, Shaping the Nation, 270).
[40] CPR 1408–13, 101.
[41] Steel, Receipt, 146–7, counted around £5,000 of Italian loans to Henry, but did not include the 1,500 marks from the Genoese and Florentines in May 1404, 500 marks from the Albertini in July 1406, the 2,500 marks from two Lucchese merchants whom Henry encountered on the way to Shrewsbury in July 1403, or perhaps the 1,800 marks advanced by a consortium of Italian merchants in June 1410 (E 401/638, 28 July 1406; E 404/22, no. 278; Foedera, viii.358–9; POPC, ii.114). Loans were also received from Italians in the summer of 1400 (E 403/567, 15 July 1400). Relations with Milan cooled following the death of Henry's friend Duke Gian Galeazzo, and the eruption of his quarrel with the duke's son-in-law, Louis of Orléans, in 1402; nevertheless, they remained cordial, and Henry encouraged the marriage of the earl of Kent to Lucia Visconti in 1407 (cf. RHL II, 21–2).
[42] RHL I, 108.

Yet welcome it they did, and Queen Philippa, to a greater extent than her half-sister, took seriously her role as a bridge between her native and adopted kingdoms.[43] Her husband, the victor of Aljubarrotta, was a forceful and cultured monarch whose friendship Henry cultivated, nominating him in 1400 as the first foreign king to become a Knight of the Garter. By 1403 João was prepared to risk French wrath by recognizing his brother-in-law as king, not just of England but of France as well.[44]

Three years later Enrique of Castile also became a Knight of the Garter. By this time goodwill was sorely needed, for between 1401 and 1403 the Castilians counted around fifty incidents in which their ships or cargoes had been seized by the English.[45] Portugal suffered much less from the Pirate War, although at times English customs officials seized Portuguese goods on the pretext that João had outstanding debts to the English crown dating back to the 1380s.[46] The latter was true, although Henry did not press him for these, and was quick both to forbid such seizures and to help secure restitution of ships and cargoes, as he did with Castilian ships; it was perhaps in recognition of his efforts, as well as to remove any pretext for seizures, that in December 1403 Enrique and João offered to include England in the ten-year truce which they had recently concluded.[47] Henry accepted the offer with alacrity. Not surprisingly, this did not please the French. In the spring of 1404, envoys from Paris reminded Enrique of his treaty obligations and requested ships and men to attack English fleets and ports, but, according to the monk of Saint-Denis, the Castilian king was persuaded by his wife to limit the extent of his aid; in the following year he allowed the adventurer Don Pero Niño to man three galleys to assist the French, but the main Castilian fleet sent north appears to have been under orders simply to trade, despite Niño's attempts to persuade the admiral

---

[43] Although she never returned to England after 1386, she corresponded regularly with her brother and others in England, at times letting her wishes be known with some vigour, as when she helped to secure a pardon for her old friend Bishop Henry Despenser in 1401 (Russell, *English Intervention*, 541–6; J. Geouge, 'Anglo-Portuguese Trade during the Reign of João I of Portugal, 1385–1433', in *England and Iberia in the Late Middle Ages, 12th to 15th Centuries*, ed. Maria Bullon-Fernandez (London, 2007), 121–33, at p. 127; Tiago Faria, 'Court Culture and the Politics of Anglo-Portuguese Interaction in the Letters of Philippa Plantagenet, Queen of Portugal', in *John Gower in Late Medieval Iberia: Manuscripts, Influences, Reception*, ed. A. Saez-Hidalgo and R. F. Yeager (Woodbridge, 2013). Philippa's hand in arranging the earl of Arundel's marriage to her step-daughter Beatrix was also an attempt to strengthen relations (below, p. 449).

[44] *RHL I*, 191.

[45] W. Childs, *Anglo-Castilian Trade in the Late Middle Ages* (Manchester, 1978), 43–6.

[46] *CPR 1408–13*, 234; cf. *Signet Letters*, nos. 691–3.

[47] *Foedera*, viii.312, 345, 351–2; *RHL I*, 191.

otherwise.[48] Undaunted, Niño teamed up with the Orléanist Charles de Savoisy, with whom he spent the summer and autumn raiding the English coast, taking particular pleasure in firing Poole (Dorset), the home of that scourge of French and Castilian shipping, Henry Pay. Yet when the Castilian–Portuguese truce was renewed in December 1405, England was still included.[49]

The later years of Henry's reign were a fruitful time in Anglo-Iberian relations. João did his best to promote good relations with his 'most beloved and most esteemed brother and friend' the English king, and English merchants were welcomed in Lisbon. Philippa's influence was crucial, and it is with justification that she is sometimes seen as instrumental in forging the Anglo-Portuguese alliance which has endured continuously for more than six centuries.[50] In Castile, meanwhile, the death of King Enrique in December 1406 left his infant son Juan as his heir, and for the next decade Queen Catherine and the late king's brother Fernando of Antequera exercised joint regency in the kingdom. Under their influence relations with England continued to improve, and when the Franco-Castilian treaty was renegotiated in 1408 the French, no longer in a position to dictate terms following Louis of Orléans's assassination, recognized Castile's right to make truces for up to a year with the English. Pilgrim traffic to Santiago de Compostella grew, as did trade and friendly intercourse between the two countries, characteristic of which was Henry's suggestion to his sister in 1411 that they exchange sixty letters of safe-conduct to be used by those wishing to visit each other's countries.[51] At one point Catherine also offered herself as a mediator between England and France. This did not happen, nor did the lasting peace sought by both sides, but the truce was renewed without difficulty on an annual basis and further complaints by merchants on each side were dealt with in a cordial fashion.[52] In 1412, Fernando also became king of Aragon. Henry had had few dealings with the Aragonese – a sign in itself of good Anglo-Castilian relations – but Fernando's record of

---

[48] Gutierre Diaz de Gamez, *The Unconquered Knight: A Chronicle of the Deeds of Don Pero Niño, Count of Buelna*, ed. J. Evans (Woodbridge, 2004 reprint), 100, 110, 131; *Saint-Denys*, iii.159.

[49] *Diaz de Gamez, The Unconquered Knight*, 122–3; *Foedera*, viii.425–6.

[50] She and João also fathered the 'Illustrious Generation', which included King Henry the Navigator: Russell, *English Intervention*, 526–48; A. Goodman, 'Philippa of Lancaster, Queen of Portugal', *ODNB*, 44.38–9.

[51] *Foedera*, viii.561–7; Ana Echevarria Arsuaga, 'The Shrine as Mediator', in *England and Iberia in the Late Middle Ages, 12th to 15th Centuries*, ed. Maria Bullón-Fernández (London, 2007), 47–65; *RHL II*, 287; *POPC*, ii.24–6, 118.

[52] *Foedera*, viii.593, 617–21, 703, 705, 721, 770, 772; *RHL II*, 309, 311–12, 318, 326. See C 49/48, no. 12 and *CPR 1408–13*, 474, for a case involving a Spanish cargo seized by John Hauley junior of Dartmouth.

cooperation allowed Henry V to open a diplomatic dialogue with him almost as soon as he came to the throne.[53] Yet the more tangible benefit accruing to Henry V from his father's Iberian policy was the slackening of ties between France and Castile which, despite occasional rumours of hostile intent, played little part in the renewed Anglo-French conflict after 1415.

No single factor accounted for the fluctuations in trade patterns during Henry's reign. Taxation policy, money supply, the state of the foreign markets, industrial growth and decline, weather and disease all played their part. Even so, it is hard not to be struck by the correlation between slump and boom and war and truce. Taxable exports fell by 50 per cent in 1402–3, from an annual average of 15,000 sacks of wool and 43,000 cloths during the first three years of the reign to 10,000 and 27,000, respectively. This was the time when the Pirate War was at its most intense. Two years later exports were still sluggish (12,000 sacks of wool and 22,000 cloths), but in 1405–6, when the Pirate War more or less ended, the numbers rose sharply, to 16,500 and 37,000, respectively. The following year saw another slump, but between 1407 and 1409 recovery resumed, reaching 17,000 sacks of wool in 1408–9 and 36,000 cloths in 1409–10.[54] This was the period which saw the most productive efforts to agree political and mercantile truces, and England's shipping and ports were more secure, as was the revenue accruing to the exchequer. Including tunnage and poundage, the revenue differential between years such as 1402–3 or 1404–5 and 1405–6 or 1408 9 was around £20,000 – between £60,000 and £70,000 in the good years, £40,000 or £50,000 in the bad.[55] Peace meant more money to spend and fewer wars to spend it on; the easing of hostilities and financial recovery were mutually supportive during the middle years of the reign, each feeding off the other.

The government was well aware of this, and Henry did his best to protect foreign trade. Despite this, his reign witnessed an unmistakable hardening of attitudes towards aliens, building on the sharper definition of English nationality which had emerged during the second half of the fourteenth century and encompassing a wider range of restrictions on aliens'

---

[53] *Foedera*, ix.12; in the past England had allied with Aragon at times of tension with Castile.

[54] Carus-Wilson and Coleman, *England's Export Trade*, 122–3, 138.

[55] J. Ramsay, *Lancaster and York* (2 vols, Oxford, 1892), i.150–1, notionally adjusted in line with the comments of M. Ormrod, 'Finance and Trade under Richard II', in *Richard II: The Art of Kingship*, ed. J. Gillespie and A. Goodman (Oxford, 1999), 155–86, at pp. 176–8.

freedom to live and trade as they wished while in England.[56] Commercial, collective or personal concessions, which increasingly included denization, gave foreigners a degree of protection at law, but made little headway against the popular xenophobia of the time. In 1411, a petition was presented to parliament from Gascons who had been driven out of their land by war and forced to resettle in England. Some had married Englishwomen, others had bought property or established businesses, but the English continued to call them aliens 'and many other undesirable names', poor reward for their constant allegiance to the crown. Having nowhere else to go, they begged the king to have their loyalty publicly proclaimed in towns and elsewhere, and to be able to live and work 'as fully as your other lieges born within your said realm of England'. Henry granted their request and ordered letters patent to be issued to them, but this did not make them English, which by common consent was a matter of birthplace and parentage.[57]

Yet compared to the Welsh or Irish, the Gascons could count themselves fortunate. They had not been degraded by the ethnic duality erected in Wales and Ireland during the twelfth and thirteenth centuries, which built on ideas of 'barbarism' and was now enshrined in national legislation.[58] The statutes of 1401–2 proscribed Welshmen not just in Wales but also in England, where they were forbidden to purchase property, carry arms or enjoy borough privileges, while Welsh tenants wishing to remain in England had to provide sureties for good behaviour and swear allegiance to the crown (as, later, did Scots residing in England). Letters from the king demanded enforcement of these laws, and the stalled career of Adam Usk as well as the petition presented by Rees ap Thomas to the parliament of

[56] A. Ruddick, *English Identity and Political Culture in the Fourteenth Century* (Cambridge, 2013), 104–7, 129–30.

[57] *PROME*, viii.536; *Foedera*, viii.719. The later years of Henry's reign saw many letters of denization granted (R. Griffiths, 'The English Realm and Dominions and the King's Subjects in the Later Middle Ages', in *Aspects of Late Medieval Government and Society*, ed. J. Rowe (Toronto, 1986), 83–105, at p. 101).

[58] For anti-Welsh legislation see Davies, *Revolt*, 282–4, and above, p. 188. The 1366 Statute of Kilkenny erecting a cordon sanitaire between English colonists and native Irish was reissued in 1402 and 1409, and the first parliament of Henry V's reign ordered a general expulsion of the Irish from England, although Irish graduates, lawyers, professed religious, 'merchants of good repute' and those who had inheritances in England were excepted: *CIRCLE PR 1401–2*, no. 255; *PR 1402–3*, no. 247 (a man of Irish blood 'freed from all Irish servitude'); *CR 1405–6*, no. 3 (a 'mere Irishman'); *Ancient Irish Histories*, 19, 22; *PROME*, ix.28. See also A. Ruddick, 'English Identity and Political Language in the King of England's Dominions: a Fourteenth-Century Perspective', in *Fifteenth-Century England VI*, ed. L. Clark (Woodbridge, 2006); J. Gillingham, 'Conquering the Barbarians: War and Chivalry in Twelfth-Century Britain and Ireland', *The Haskins Society Journal* 4 (1992), 67–84.

1413 are evidence of their efficacy. In the summer of 1402, random slayings of Welshmen were being reported at Oxford and in the border counties.[59]

The racist laws against the Welsh and Irish went much further than the hosting or commercial restrictions imposed on foreign merchants in the fifteenth century, but even the latter moved well beyond protectionism to tap into a more consciously articulated rhetoric of nationalism. The McCarthyite mentality of Henry's early years contributed to this, especially in the case of Bretons and Frenchmen, but it was the Pirate War that really threatened to undermine England's commercial relations. Fortunately, Henry's personal contacts helped to counteract the bad feeling that followed. It is not a little ironic that it was during the reign of the most widely travelled English king of the later Middle Ages that the 'rampant new Englishness' of the fifteenth century acquired its statutory cutting edge.[60]

---

[59] *PROME*, viii.136–7, 145 (legislation), and ix.11 (Rees ap Thomas); *Usk*, xxi–xxix; BL Add. MS 24,062, fo. 71r (royal letter for enforcement of laws); SC 1/43/61 (slaying of Welshmen).

[60] *The Views of Hosts*, xii (quote).

Chapter 23

ENGLAND, THE PAPACY AND THE COUNCIL OF PISA (1404–1409)

In addition to neighbours and traders, the third major strand in Henry's foreign policy was Anglo-Papal relations. In one sense, this had become easier since the outbreak in 1378 of the Great Schism. Popes, whether Roman or Avignonese, feared losing the support of secular rulers and tried not to antagonize them, which meant inter alia that they were slower to throw their weight behind disputatious clerics, be they primates or parish priests. In the long term, this contributed to the spread of Gallicanism – the movement towards national Churches in which secular authorities arrogated to themselves more of the powers that had once been exercised by either the Papacy or the Catholic hierarchy in the name of a universal Church. Yet the Schism also made international relations more complicated, for it imposed on rulers the moral duty to restore unity to the Catholic Church while simultaneously anathematizing those with whom they had to negotiate in order to do so. Henry certainly wanted to resolve the Schism, but, like other secular rulers, he did not want that resolution to entail reversal of the gains made by the crown in extending its authority over the Church. Among those gains he would have counted the extension of royal justice to include criminal clergy and the limits imposed on the papal right to make appointments to the English Church. It was around such questions that the relationship between kings and their archbishops often turned.

Despite his service and commitment to the Lancastrian regime, Archbishop Arundel never forgot that he was first and foremost the head of the Catholic Church in England. Nothing tested his relationship with Henry as sorely as the execution of Archbishop Scrope. The right of clergy to claim immunity from secular justice was an issue which had caused controversy for centuries, most famously during the quarrel between Henry II and Becket in the 1160s. What was at stake in Henry IV's reign was not benefit of clergy (which covered felonies, and had been relatively clearly defined in the statute *Pro Clero* of 1352) but the vaguer concept of clerical privilege, especially in relation to bishops.[1] What Scrope was accused of in 1405 was treason, and although treason was not clergyable (as the first convocation of the reign acknowledged), it was certainly not customary to put great clerics to death: Alexander Nevill, archbishop of York, and Arundel himself had both been accused of treason, in 1388 and 1397, respectively, but were exiled rather than executed. Nevertheless, convocation in 1399 expressed outrage at the way in which churchmen had been arrested, imprisoned and even hanged on the orders of secular authorities during Richard II's reign, and evidently expected better from Henry.[2]

A test case arose almost immediately: that of Thomas Merks, bishop of Carlisle. Despite pressure from the commons, Henry had been careful in October 1399 not to put Merks on trial in parliament along with the Counter-Appellants (of whose crimes some regarded him as equally guilty), but three months later, when Merks joined the Epiphany rising, he lost patience. Those who committed treason, the bishop was informed in the Tower on 28 January, would be dealt with by the law of the land, clerical immunity notwithstanding; a week later he was condemned to death.[3] This was the first time since the Conquest that a bishop had been sentenced to death in England, and Arundel promptly summoned a meeting of prelates to register its disapproval. Adam Usk attended this meeting: 'more crimes have been committed against prelates in England than in the whole of Christendom', he fulminated, while Arundel reminded the delegates of the case of Thomas de Lisle, bishop of Ely, whom Archbishop Islip (1349–66) had taken by the hand and led away rather than allow him to stand trial in a secular court.[4] Yet Henry had decided to make an example of Merks, and on 15 March wrote to the pope insisting that he be degraded and handed over 'plainly and summarily' to secular justice; if not, the king would proceed as he saw fit. During the summer, however, probably in response to Arundel's pleas, Henry relented, and on 28 November 1400

[1] J. Aberth, *Criminal Churchmen in the Age of Edward III: The Case of Bishop Thomas de Lisle* (Pennsylvania, 1996); L. Gabel, *Benefit of Clergy in England in the Later Middle Ages* (New York, 1964 reprint), 35, 58–9, 122; J. Bellamy, *Criminal Law and Society in Late Medieval and Tudor England* (New York, 1984), 116–17.

[2] *Concilia*, iii.243–5; *Records of Convocation IV*, 204–6 (for treason, see article 55).

[3] Also convicted were Richard II's chaplains, Maudeleyn and Ferriby, executed on 29 January; the ex-primate Roger Walden and the abbot of Westminster were tried but acquitted; Henry Despenser, bishop of Norwich, was imprisoned, but not brought to trial (*SAC II*, 296–8; *CE*, 387; *Foedera*, viii.123; Wylie, *Henry the Fourth*, i.108–9; *Select Cases in King's Bench VII*, 102–5).

[4] *Usk*, 92–4.

Merks was pardoned, although the king made it clear that this was only as an act of special grace, and he was not reinstated to his see.[5]

Yet if Henry eventually drew back from the ultimate sanction in Merks's case, his clemency did not extend to lesser clerics. In February 1401 the Canterbury scribe William Clerk was mutilated and decapitated for disparaging the king; June 1402 saw the hanging of the friars and other clerics for claiming that Richard II was still alive.[6] This was the largest number of clergy executed at one time in England, and again Arundel responded. Three months later in parliament he and his suffragans presented a petition asking the king to confirm *Pro Clero*, specifically including 'treason which does not concern the king or his royal majesty', as well as common theft and highway robbery, among the crimes that ought to be clergyable, since it was an offence to God and a violation of ecclesiastical liberty to sentence clerks accused of these crimes in secular courts. Theft and highway robbery Henry was prepared to concede (thereby clarifying to the clergy's benefit a point which the 1352 statute had left uncertain), but in the case of treason, even if it did not directly concern the king, Arundel was told to consult with his bishops and, before the next parliament, draw up guidelines to ensure that they should not be allowed to purge themselves of their crimes and thus evade proper punishment. If Henry considered these guidelines inadequate, he would devise 'another remedy, in such a way as shall become evident'; in other words, if the clergy did not ensure that treasonous clerks were suitably punished, then he would.[7]

Pending agreement on these guidelines, the issue of clerical immunity receded for a while, perhaps because the king stayed his hand – for example, in the case of the three abbots who conspired with the countess of Oxford in 1404.[8] Then came Scrope's execution. High treason may not have been clergyable, but was Scrope a traitor? The parliament of 1406 had its doubts. Even if he was, did the Court of Chivalry (or possibly just an ad

---

[5] *POPC*, i.115–17 (BL Cotton Cleopatra E. II, fo. 255); *Foedera*, viii.150; *CPR 1399–1401*, 385. He was released on 26 January 1401, the day Canterbury convocation opened (*Select Cases in King's Bench VII*, 105).

[6] *Usk*, 122–3. Clerk was condemned in the court of chivalry, which employed summary procedures. Above, p. 208.

[7] *PROME*, viii.177–9 (cf. *Records of Convocation*, iv.246, 249–51). The clarification relating to common theft and highway robbery focused on the inclusion of the words *communes latrones* and/or *depopulatores agrorum et insidiatores viarum* in indictments against the clergy, for which see Gabel, *Benefit of Clergy*, 58–9, and R. Storey, 'Clergy and Common Law in the Reign of Henry IV', in *Medieval Legal Records in Memory of C. A. F. Meekings*, ed. R. Hunnisett and J. Post (London, 1978), 343, 361.

[8] Above, pp. 262–3.

hoc tribunal of royal *familiares*) have the right to condemn him? Chief Justice Gascoigne had his doubts, and the rapid growth of the archbishop's martyr-cult suggests that many others did too. Was Scrope degraded before trial, as he should have been, or was his archiepiscopal cross simply wrested from his grasp? Such irregularities at once placed Henry on the defensive, and had Arundel not held back from publishing Innocent VII's bull of excommunication, a breakdown in Church–crown relations might have followed. Yet despite his opposition to Scrope's execution, Arundel still tried to save the king from the consequences of his action.[9]

It may be that Henry's hand was forced by retainers who threatened to desert him if Scrope was not put to death, but he had also had enough of clerical opposition to his rule and probably felt that a terrible example was required. Scrope's 'army' had included hundreds, if not thousands, of clerics, and well might the king have wondered what message it would convey to execute an earl for rebellion but to leave a bishop untouched. Yet whether or not his retainers really would have deserted him, those 'knights who never loved the church' were not simply figments of the chroniclers' imagination. It was not just Wyclifites who called for churchmen to be subject to royal justice.[10] On the other hand, Gascoigne's refusal to condemn Scrope represented an approach characteristic of legal opinion in Henry's reign. He and his fellow Chief Justice William Thirning were generally careful to observe the jurisdiction of Church courts, and so, in certain respects, was the king, as indicated by his response to the episcopal petition of 1402.[11] In legal terms, Henry believed himself to be within his rights in executing Scrope, for if it was treason of which he was guilty, it was decidedly treason of concern to the king. Whether it was sensible to do so is a different matter, but the fact that he managed, with Arundel's help, to contain the fallout, probably persuaded him that his show of force had been vindicated. In February 1408, when Lewis Byford, bishop of Bangor, the prior of Hexham, the abbot of Hailes and several monks and chaplains joined Northumberland and Bardolf's last rebellion, Henry

---

[9] Arundel also helped to discourage the development of a martyr-cult at Scrope's tomb in York Minster (D. Piroyanska, 'Martyrio Pulchro Finitus', in *Richard Scrope: Archbishop, Rebel, Martyr*, ed. P. J. Goldberg (Donnington, 2007), 100–13, and C. Norton, 'Richard Scrope and York Minster', in *Richard Scrope Archbishop, Rebel, Martyr*, ed. P. J. Goldberg, (Donnington, 2007), 138–213, at pp. 109–12 and 171–8.

[10] *CE*, 392. *Fasciculi Zizaniorum Magistri Johannis Wyclif cum Tritico*, ed. W. Shirley (RS, London, 1858), 256; *SAC II*, 591; M. Wilks, *Wyclif: Political Ideas and Practice* (Oxford, 2000), 29–31.

[11] Storey, 'Clergy and Common Law', 343–4, 351–2; *PROME*, viii.179.

treated them with circumspection, hanging only the abbot (who was a renegade from his house and was captured in arms) while pardoning the others, although Byford was imprisoned for several months and deprived of his see.[12] Henry had made his point, and by and large he had got away with it.

However, it was not so much the issue of clerical immunity as the Statutes of Provisors, which deprived the papacy of both patronage and revenue, that led to England being described on occasion as a 'disobedient nation'.[13] In theory, the First Statute of Provisors (1351) forbade all papal provisions (appointments) to English benefices, and was given teeth two years later when the Statute of Praemunire outlawed appeals to the Curia. In practice, both Edward III and Richard II allowed limited evasion of the statute when it suited them to do so, although quite sparingly. A second statute in 1390 strengthened the penalties against those who sought provisions from Rome, but in the following year a moderation (soefferance) permitted the king to negotiate individual cases with the pope. What this meant was that he could issue licences to evade the statute or, if he wished, sanction suits against unwelcome provisions. Although it was only agreed for a trial period in the first instance, it gave the crown a loophole too valuable to be discarded and was renewed by Henry IV at the start of his reign.[14]

Yet Henry had to tread carefully, for this was a subject on which many in the commons felt passionately. Initially their hostility had been directed primarily against foreign provisors, who were not merely habitual absentees from their livings (or, if present, suspected of espionage) but also deprived

[12] Wylie, *Henry the Fourth*, iii.153–8; *SAC II*, 530–5; *Foedera*, viii.520, 545; *CPR 1405–8*, 464, 471, 488; *Usk*, xxxv.

[13] W. Lunt, *Financial Relations of the Papacy with England II, 1327–1534* (Cambridge, Mass., 1962), 381–408 (quote at p. 399); P. Heath, *Church and Realm 1272–1461* (London, 1988), 125–33, 213–18, 261–3; Storey, 'Clergy and Common Law', 346–52, 368–80, 408 (appendix of cases under the Statute of Provisors); N. Foulser, 'The Influence of Lollardy and Reformist Ideas on English Legislation *c.*1376–*c.*1422' (unpublished PhD thesis, University of St Andrews, 2004), 67–139.

[14] Henry may have tried to convince the commons to repeal the provisors legislation (perhaps hoping, like Richard, to make a concordat with Pope Boniface), but he was reminded in the parliament of March 1401 that this was not what had been agreed: *PROME*, vii.190, 195; viii.61, 108, 119–20; *POPC*, i.111. In November 1398, Richard II had attempted to strengthen the royal hand, the pope agreeing that he would not appoint bishops contrary to the king's wishes, although that did not mean that he would always provide the king's nominee: R. Davies, 'Richard II and the Church in the Years of Tyranny', *Journal of Medieval History* I (1975), 329–62, at pp. 355–7; this concordat lapsed with his deposition.

the realm of bullion.[15] From around 1390, however, it encompassed English provisors too, and there was growing emphasis on the misappropriation of alms and tithes, which should have been used for charitable purposes, and on the effects of non-residence on pastoral care and hospitality.[16] Yet papal provisions also had their supporters. To Henry, they afforded a useful bargaining tool with Rome, and there was a widespread view, shared by Arundel and the king, that they were the best way to ensure the promotion of deserving university graduates.[17] The problem lay in agreeing who was deserving. Royal clerks competed shamelessly with papal, episcopal and noble protégés, and lawsuits between them, sometimes accompanied by violence, were far from uncommon. Despite prohibitions on seeking benefices at the Curia, it was hard to prevent such disputes. Adam Usk repeatedly sought a bishopric during his four years in Rome (1402–6), thereby infuriating Henry; not surprisingly, he was an advocate of papal provisions.[18] To characterize the problem as essentially a battle between pope, king, nobles and bishops for rights of patronage over the English Church is by no means unjustified, but risks ignoring the insatiable appetites of the clerks who sought that patronage, at times exploiting the legislation, at others evading it.[19]

Given these competing pressures, Henry was aware of the need for self-restraint, and for the first five years of the reign he used his *soefferance* sparingly, granting an average of less than ten licences a year to evade the statute. In June 1402, following discussion in the council, he promised to review the question in the next parliament and to abstain entirely from granting licences thereafter, but by March 1403 he was once again granting them, and two years later the number began to rise alarmingly, to 27 in 1405 and 64 in 1406.[20] This produced a storm of complaints from the commons: reminding the king of his promise, they asked him never in future to grant licences for livings which were already vacant. These, as they pointed out, were the ones that caused disputes, since an English patron was likely already to have presented an alternative candidate.[21]

---

[15] The figure of 20,000 marks or £20,000 was frequently mentioned: Foulser, 'The Influence of Lollardy', 87–8; see also A. Barrell, 'The Ordinance of Provisors of 1343', *HR* 64 (1991), 264–77.

[16] See below, pp. 368–71.

[17] *Concilia*, iii.241–2, 245; Lunt, *Financial Relations*, ii.402; *CPR 1401–5*, 324.

[18] *Usk*, 126–7, 176–7.

[19] Storey, 'Clergy and Common Law', 350–2.

[20] Lunt, *Financial Relations*, ii.402–3, supplemented by Z. El-Gazar, 'Politics and Legislation in England in the Early Fifteenth Century: The Parliament of 1406' (unpublished PhD thesis, University of St Andrews, 2001), 240.

[21] *PROME*, viii.386–91, 398–9.

Henry promised nothing, however, and in October 1407 the commons once again submitted two petitions to the king begging him to uphold the statutes. The king agreed, but only saving his customary prerogatives – in effect, a rebuff. However, the number of licences he issued fell sharply after 1406, to roughly the same level as before 1405, and perhaps as a result the matter was not raised in parliament again.[22]

The likely reasons for the spate of royal licences in 1405–6 were, first, because Henry needed to placate Innocent VII, with whom he was embroiled in a number of disputes over episcopal appointments (to say nothing of the backwash from Scrope's execution), and, secondly, because he was short of money and such licences were a useful form of clerical patronage. Yet throughout his reign Henry showed determination not to allow the Statutes of Provisors to be applied inflexibly. Like kings before him, he wanted the freedom to negotiate individual appointments with the papacy. Nor would he have been insensible to the fact that the provisors legislation proclaimed the Englishness of the English Church and the primacy of royal authority over it. In 1409, during a lawsuit over a prebend at Salisbury, Justice Hankford remarked that 'the pope can do anything' (*papa omnia potest*); 'That was in ancient times,' objected Chief Justice Thirning, 'but I cannot see how he by his bulls can change the law of England.'[23] Henry VIII could not have put it better.

Despite their concern over provisions, the commons generally knew better than to interfere with bishoprics, a more lofty and complex matter.[24] Four parties were involved in filling episcopal vacancies: the dean and chapter of the cathedral in question, whose theoretical right to elect their own bishop was frequently (but not always) overridden; the pope, without whose formal provision to the see no appointment was canonically valid; the primate, who admitted the chosen candidate and received his profession of obedience; and the king, who in practice usually had the greatest influence. All this made for a competitive and confusing situation.

---

[22] *PROME*, viii.433–4, 446–7; Lunt, *Financial Relations*, ii.404.

[23] J. E. Tyler, *Henry of Monmouth* (2 vols, London, 1838), ii.41–5 (judgment went for the crown); Heath, *Church and Realm*, 132, 217.

[24] R. Davies, 'After the Execution of Archbishop Scrope: Henry IV, the Papacy and the English Episcopate, 1405–8', *BJRL* 56 (1977), 40–74.

Table 3 Episcopal translations in the reign of Henry IV[25]

Bangor: Richard Young (1398–1404); Lewis Byford (1404–8, but defected to Glyn Dŵr in 1404); Benedict Nicolls (1408–17)

Bath and Wells: Ralph Erghum (1388–1400); Henry Bowet (1401–7); Nicholas Bubwith (1407–24)

Canterbury: Thomas Arundel (1399–1414)

Carlisle: Thomas Merks (1397–99); William Strickland (1399–1419)

Chichester: Robert Reade (1397–1415)

Coventry and Lichfield: John Burghill (1398–1414)

Durham: Walter Skirlaw (1388–1406); Thomas Langley (1406–37)

Ely: John Fordham (1388–1425)

Exeter: Edmund Stafford (1395–1419)

Hereford: John Trefnant (1389–1404); Robert Mascall (1404–16)

Lincoln: Henry Beaufort (1398–1404); Philip Repingdon (1404–19)

Llandaff: Thomas Peverel (1398–1407); John de la Zouche (1407–23)

London: Robert Braybrooke (1382–1404); Roger Walden (1404–6); Nicholas Bubwith (1406–7); Richard Clifford (1407–21)

Norwich: Henry Despenser (1370–1406); Alexander Tottington (1406–13)

Rochester: William Bottlesham (1389–1400); John Bottlesham (1400–4); Richard Young (1404–18)

St Asaph: John Trevaur (1394–1410, but defected to Glyn Dŵr in 1404); Robert Lancaster (1410–33)

St David's: Guy Mone (1397–1407); Henry Chichele (1408–14)

Salisbury: Richard Medford (1395–1407); Nicholas Bubwith (1407); Robert Hallum (1407–17)

Winchester: William of Wykeham (1366–1404); Henry Beaufort (1404–47)

Worcester: Tideman of Winchcombe (1395–1401); Richard Clifford (1401–7); Thomas Peverel (1407–19)

York: Richard Scrope (1398–1405); Henry Bowet (1407–23)

The episcopal bench which Henry inherited in 1399 consisted largely of Richard II's nominees, although Henry's reinstatement of Arundel to Canterbury in the autumn of 1399, presented to Boniface IX as a fait accompli, established a measure of control as well as making it clear that

[25] Ineffective provisions excluded.

he would not allow Rome to push him around.[26] During the next four years few vacancies occurred, and only one caused controversy. When the see of Bath and Wells fell vacant early in 1400, Boniface provided Richard Clifford, the keeper of the privy seal, while the king proposed his friend Henry Bowet. Deadlock ensued until the fortuitous death in June 1401 of Tideman of Winchcombe, bishop of Worcester, allowed both sides to save face: Clifford went to Worcester, Bowet to Bath and Wells. The vacancy at the latter had lasted eighteen months, hardly ideal from a pastoral point of view, but in the end Henry got his way.[27]

Such obduracy meant that when, in the years 1404–7, nine of England's seventeen bishops died, and three of the four Welsh sees became vacant through either death or defection to Glyn Dŵr – a three-year episcopal casualty rate unmatched during the late Middle Ages – conflict was likely, for this was Henry's chance to reshape the episcopacy. Yet initially things went smoothly. Winchester, the richest see in the country, vacated by William of Wykeham's death, went to the king's half-brother, Henry Beaufort. He was replaced at Lincoln by Henry's friend and confessor, Philip Repingdon, while Hereford, following the death of John Trefnant, was given to Robert Mascall, another of Henry's confessors. Rochester and London, which became vacant in April and August 1404, respectively, proved more problematical. Boniface IX translated Richard Young from Bangor to Rochester, but Arundel refused for nearly three years to admit him, perhaps because the king's first choice was Roger Walden, perhaps in the hope of preventing the papal candidate for Bangor, Lewis Byford, from obtaining that see, for he was suspected of sympathizing with Glyn Dŵr.[28] When London became vacant a few months later, Henry proposed his privy seal keeper, Thomas Langley, while Arundel initially supported Robert Hallum, theologian and chancellor of Oxford University,

[26] As did his admonition to the pope over the latter's over-hasty provision of William Strickland to replace Thomas Merks at Carlisle: R. L. Storey, 'Episcopal Kingmakers in the Fifteenth Century', in *Church, Politics and Patronage in the Fifteenth Century*, ed. R. B. Dobson (Gloucester, 1984), 82–98, at pp. 83–6. For Strickland, see *POPC*, i.115–17, but Henry's rebuke was mainly on procedural grounds, for he did not object to Strickland.

[27] This was the only occasion when parliament spoke up for an episcopal candidate, Clifford, though unsuccessfully (*PROME*, viii.108–12; R. Davies, 'Richard Clifford', *ODNB*, 12.105–7). See also the letter in *ANLP*, no. 289, concerning a debt of 2,000 marks due from Clifford to the Albertini, which states inter alia that he had never had possession of Bath and Wells. The king told Arundel not to write to the pope on Clifford's behalf.

[28] C. Allmand, 'A Bishop of Bangor during the Glyn Dŵr Revolt: Richard Young', *Journal of the Historical Society of the Church in Wales* (1968), 47–56. Young was a member of the Privy Council, crown lawyer and diplomat, and the failure to admit him to Rochester cannot have been on personal grounds (R. Davies, 'Richard Young', *ODNB* online (added May 2007)).

although he later switched to the king's candidate.[29] However, the new pope, Innocent VII (1404–6), ignored them both and provided Walden. Although this had the advantage of freeing up Rochester for Young, neither the king nor Arundel was satisfied, and both sees in practice remained unoccupied.

Matters were further complicated by Scrope's execution on 8 June 1405 and the subsequent excommunication by Innocent of those responsible. Wishing to offend the papacy no further, Henry quickly agreed to accept Walden for London, probably at Arundel's urging. Yet Scrope's death also created a vacancy for England's second archbishopric, and above all the king was determined to have his way at York. Thomas Langley (now chancellor) and Henry Bowet were once again his preferred candidates, and in July the York chapter agreed to elect Langley. The pope prevaricated, however, while Langley himself may have wished to wait until Durham, which he coveted, became vacant. He did not have to wait long: Walter Skirlaw, who had held it for nearly twenty years, died after a long illness in March 1406, and seven weeks later Langley was provided in his place after Bowet (who had also shown interest in Durham, a wealthy and palatine see) agreed to step aside on condition that Langley support his own candidacy at York. Another vacancy at London – which arose when Walden, having enjoyed his temporalities for less than six months, died in January 1406 – might have resolved the situation, but was instead reserved for Langley's successor as privy seal keeper, Nicholas Bubwith, whose claim to a bishopric the king now viewed as urgent. This was on 14 May 1406, the day Langley was provided to Durham, but Innocent VII did not stop there, for, on the same day he also provided Hallum to York. This put Henry in a quandary: he did not lack respect for Hallum – far from it – but with the disturbed state of affairs in the north he needed the two major sees there to be in the hands of men of proven political mettle, not theologians. Arundel, who had supported Hallum, was thus once again persuaded to switch candidates, and in August Henry Chichele and John Cheyne were despatched to Rome to persuade the pope to quash Hallum's provision.[30]

Arriving there, they discovered that Innocent VII had died and that a new pope, Gregory XII, had been elected. This was not necessarily a desadvantage, for Gregory soon fell out with his cardinals over the Schism,

---

[29] *RHL*, i.415–16 (Arundel's face-saving excuse was that he was unaware that Henry was supporting Langley).

[30] SC 1/43/98 is Henry's letter mandating Chichele and Cheyne to go to Rome, but he mentioned that they also had further instructions which should remain secret (and see BL Cotton Cleopatra E. ii, fos. 262–3).

making it more important for him to placate secular rulers. However, he was not yet ready to compromise. The vacancy created when Henry Despenser, bishop of Norwich since 1369, died on 26 August 1406, presented another opportunity, but the chapter quickly elected their vener-able dean, Alexander Tottington, whom the pope confirmed. The king in frustration imprisoned Tottington for several months in Windsor castle, declaring that 'he would never suffer the said bishop-elect to enjoy the episcopal dignity', but faced with capitular election and papal provision there was little he could do – a reminder of the limits to royal masterful-ness.[31] Thus only with the death of Richard Medford, bishop of Salisbury, in May 1407, did it become possible to clear the logjam. This time the government reacted immediately, despatching a messenger within days to the dean and chapter, and the swiftly taken decision to move Bubwith from London to Salisbury (effected by 22 June) undoubtedly met with the approval of both king and archbishop.[32]

This paved the way for the resolution of the outstanding issues between king and pope. In the autumn of 1407 Gregory XII, whose position at the Curia was now too weak to allow him to hold out, agreed to provide Bowet to York. This freed up Bath and Wells, to which Bubwith was now trans-lated (his third see in fifteen months), while Hallum, abandoning his bid for York, was given Salisbury. At the same time, Tottington was released from prison and made his submission to Henry and Arundel during the Gloucester parliament.[33] All this took place in October 1407 as part of an unofficial concordat between king and pope, which also encompassed the withdrawal of Innocent's bull of excommunication. Perhaps for appear-ances' sake, the latter was held over until the spring of 1408, when Chichele, who, along with Cheyne, had spent the past year at the Curia brokering the Anglo-papal deal, was also provided to his first see, St David's; six years later he would succeed Arundel at Canterbury.[34]

[31] ANLP, nos. 316, 344; Davies, 'After the Execution of Archbishop Scrope', 65–7.

[32] These letters 'intimately concerning the estate of the king' bore the seals of Arundel as chancellor, Bubwith himself as treasurer, and Langley as bishop of Durham (E 403/591, 1 June 1407). Bubwith was replaced at London by Richard Clifford, who in turn was replaced at Worcester by Thomas Peverel, both apparently without difficulty.

[33] The professions resulting from most of these promotions and translations in 1407 are to be found in Lambeth Palace Library, Arundel Register, i, fos. 37–42. Richard Young was finally admitted to Rochester on 2 March 1407.

[34] CPR 1405–8, 426; CPL, vi (1404–15), 98 (12 April 1408): to save face, the pope stated that Henry had Scrope executed in order to avoid further violence, and that the archbishop had been judged according to the law. There were no further episcopal casualties in England between 1407 and 1413.

Chichele's appointment also set the seal on a period of turmoil for the Church in Wales. Poor and war-ravaged (both Llandaff and Bangor cathedrals were gutted by fire during Glyn Dŵr's revolt), the Welsh sees were nevertheless sought after as a first rung on the episcopal ladder. Adam Usk tried for both St David's and Bangor, as well as the marcher see, Hereford, while he was in Rome. He eventually accepted Llandaff, but his provision went unrecognized in England since it had been made by the Avignon pope, Benedict XIII, following Glyn Dŵr's decision in March 1406 to defect from Rome.[35] This decision confounded an already confused situation. John Trevaur of St Asaph had defected to Glyn Dŵr in 1404 and had not been replaced, and in 1406-7 the rival popes both provided candidates to Welsh sees, while Lewis Byford, although provided to Bangor by Boniface IX in 1404, was never recognized by the English and eventually joined Northumberland's last rebellion in February 1408; he was then captured and forced to resign. By this time, with Glyn Dŵr's fortunes ebbing, so too were those of the Avignonese candidates, and the appointments of Chichele to St David's, John de la Zouche to Llandaff, and Benedict Nicholls to Bangor, all in 1408, effectively signalled a return to normality – that is to say, bishops provided by Rome and supported by the English king.[36]

By 1407-8, therefore, Henry had, by and large, got the bishops he wanted. Those whose promotion he had especially sought – Beaufort, Bowet, Repingdon, Mascall, Langley, Bubwith – were a mixture of personal friends, spiritual advisers and high-ranking ministers; all were utterly dependable Lancastrians.[37] The king's willingness to face down the pope and other interested parties, especially in securing Henry Bowet's two promotions, says much for his determination to transform the episcopal bench into the clerical arm of the Lancastrian affinity, as well as to ensure that his servants were given the status they needed. Scrope's execution made this more difficult, but filling episcopal vacancies was never straightforward. The ambition of individuals, the patronage of great ecclesiastics (for Arundel, it is clear, did not always follow the king's lead immediately, though he usually did in the end), the obduracy of a cathedral chapter, or

[35] *Usk*, xxvii.

[36] Nicholls succeeded Byford at Bangor; Chichele replaced Guy Mone, who died in 1407; and Zouche replaced Thomas Peverel, who was translated to Worcester. Trevaur continued to support Glyn Dŵr, and not until after his death in 1410 was the situation at St Asaph, in the heart of rebel territory, resolved with the provision of Robert Lancaster.

[37] However, Henry never secured a see for John Prophet, despite trying (Heath, *Church and Realm*, 267).

the claims of even a weakened papacy were all capable of upsetting the king's plans. Such willingness openly to challenge Henry parallels the plain-speaking which he periodically encountered in parliament, even from well-wishers, and resulted in a number of undesirably long vacancies, especially at York – although these were not intolerable to Henry, for they could bring substantial profit in the form of *sede vacante* revenues.[38] Moreover, some prelates probably paid for promotion. An anecdote remembered many years later told how the king once asked Henry Bowet why bishops were no longer translated from their graves after death (in preparation for canonization). Bowet said nothing, but a clerk who overheard the question replied that it was because whereas God used to choose bishops, now kings did; that whereas men used to accept episcopal office reluctantly, now they offered bribes to be promoted; and that whereas bishops used not to be translated from one see to another for larger revenues, now they paid money for the privilege. One, he said, was known to have paid two thousand marks to be translated from his bishopric to an archbishopric. Henry found this amusing, though not Bowet, to whom it referred.[39]

Despite their differences, neither king nor pope wanted an open breach over episcopal appointments. In the case of the Schism, a more fundamental issue was at stake: the integrity of Christendom. Everyone agreed that the Schism was a scandal, making the Church an easy target for heathens and heretics and hindering international peacemaking as well as ecclesiastical reform. Hitherto, English involvement in the quest for unity had been half-hearted. It was the French who had taken the lead, trying to draw Richard II into a scheme to withdraw obedience from the rival popes, and for five years (1398–1403), under Burgundy's influence, unilaterally severing their ties to the Avignon pope, Benedict XIII.[40] During the first two years of Henry's reign, before war and rebellion overwhelmed him, he had attempted to persuade the new emperor, Rupert, to summon a general

---

[38] In 1406 (probably the most lucrative year), 2,000 marks was paid into the king's chamber from the temporalities of York; 1,000 marks to the exchequer from Skirlaw's executors for Durham; and almost £600 in two tranches from London, again to the exchequer (E 401/638, 26 June, 28 July; E 401/639, 24 Oct.; E 403/589, 4 Dec.). The king also exercised his right of appointment while sees were vacant: for example, he made John Prophet dean of York in November 1406 (*CPR 1405–8*, 285).

[39] Gascoigne, *Loci e Libro*, 21–2; cf. Davies, 'After the Execution of Archbishop Scrope', 69.

[40] Above, p. 120. M. Harvey, *Solutions to the Schism 1378–1409* (St Ottilien, 1983), 93–105.

council to resolve the situation, but the escalation of Anglo-French hostilities from 1402 made international cooperation difficult, and the decision by Louis of Orléans in May 1403 to restore French obedience to Benedict seemed for the moment to dash hopes of progress.[41] What altered the situation was the death in rapid succession of two Roman popes, Boniface IX (October 1404) and Innocent VII (November 1406). With criticism mounting, the Roman cardinals swore before each new conclave that whoever was elected would do everything in his power to achieve unity, including resignation if necessary. Innocent VII's pontificate was too brief for him to be put to the test, but eighteen months into Gregory XII's reign it was becoming clear that he had little intention of keeping his promise, and in May 1408 most of his cardinals deserted him. In the same month, with Orléans out of the way, a great council in Paris once again withdrew French obedience from Benedict XIII.[42]

Present at this meeting was Henry IV's representative, William Lord Willoughby. This was not the first sign that the English king was now serious about taking action over the Schism. Cheyne's and Chichele's embassy to the Curia in 1406 included a stop in Paris to try to coordinate a plan of action, and when he discovered that Innocent was dead the king wrote to them again (and to the college of cardinals) expressing the hope that a new conclave might be delayed in the interests of unity. If, however, an election had already taken place, he advised circumspection: 'We would not wish,' he wrote, 'to be either the first or the last in such an important matter' – that is, the question of whether or not to recognize the new pope.[43] By the time his letter arrived, however, it was too late, and for the next fifteen months it probably suited him quite well to deal with an increasingly beleaguered pope, for all the time the momentum for change was building. Henry and Arundel worked closely through this period: if it was the king who took the lead, there is little sign that the clergy resented this.[44] From late May 1408, when Henry heard that Gregory's cardinals had left him, events moved quickly. On 24 June the king ordered the withholding of the payment of papal annates. A few days later, Canterbury and York convocations were summoned to St Paul's and the lords and

---

[41] Harvey, *Solutions to the Schism*, 106–8, 117–23; *PROME*, viii.159.

[42] For Innocent's troubles in Rome, see *Usk*, 204–6; Wylie, *Reign of Henry IV*, iii.1–37, 337–71, describes Gregory's and Benedict's dealings with their cardinals 1406–9; *Monstrelet*, i.255–8, for the Paris council.

[43] E 403/587, 18 May 1406; E. Jacob, *Archbishop Henry Chichele* (London, 1967), 7–8; for Henry's letters, dated 18 January 1407, see *RHL*, i.141–3 and BL Cotton Cleopatra E ii, fos. 262–3.

[44] Harvey, *Solutions to the Schism*, 8, 145, 193–4.

knights of the realm invited to join their deliberations.[45] English interest in the Schism was now awakened, and the meeting on 29 July was well attended. 'Arise! Why do you sleep?' was the theme chosen for the opening address. 'We in the kingdom of England,' declared Arundel, 'have done little as yet to work for union, as a result of which England's reputation has declined.'[46] Conference responded, extending the withholding of annates to all monetary payments, and shortly afterwards the king wrote to Gregory threatening him with a complete withdrawal of obedience if he did not fulfil his oath.[47]

Arundel probably favoured the immediate withdrawal of obedience, but Henry was not yet ready to commit himself. The crucial decision was whether or not to send an English delegation to the general council which the cardinals had summoned to meet at Pisa on 25 March 1409. Henry's caution was well advised: since the autumn of 1407 Gregory had accommodated the king's wishes, and an English decision to attend the council would jeopardize cooperation if matters went awry, as they often did when England and France tried to work together. In August 1408, Gregory made a final attempt to win over the English king, assuring him that he, too, planned to summon a general council and would abide by its decision, but his credibility was spent. The cardinals' riposte was to send Henry's friend, Cardinal-Archbishop Ugguccione of Bordeaux, to the English court. Greeted with pomp and reverence, Ugguccione addressed the enthroned king and a great gathering of nobles and clergy at Westminster on 28–29 October, reminding them of Gregory's broken promises and warning that those who continued to support him would share the perjurer's guilt and be accounted fomenters of the Schism, which was tantamount to heresy.[48] He had already been to Paris and reported that the French intended to go to Pisa. 'The holy college', he concluded, 'urges and pleads with you to show your devotion [and] make provision for the prelates of your realm to attend the said council.' Within two weeks, Henry had made up his mind, although he still wrote to Gregory exhorting him to swallow his pride and

---

[45] Lunt, *Financial Relations*, ii.412–13; Harvey, *Solutions to the Schism*, 133–46; the lords and knights were to communicate with convocation *pro unione ecclesie sancte celebrandum* (E 403/595, 11 July 1408).

[46] *Records of Convocation*, iv.323–5. The upsurge of English interest is reflected in the chronicles, notably *SAC II* and *CE*, which until 1408 had said very little about the Schism, but in 1408–9 said a great deal about it.

[47] BL Harleian Ms 431, fos. 14r–v; *CE*, iii.412.

[48] Ugguccione made a great impression in England (*SAC II*, 538–57; *CE*, 412–13). At his arrival, Henry summoned his retainers to ride in the cardinal's *comitiva*, 'for the king's honour' (E 403/596, 8 Nov.). Ugguccione's retinue included 46 horses (E 404/24, no. 480).

attend as well. To mark this triumph of Anglo-French cooperation, an eighteen-month truce was agreed on 31 October.[49]

Once the decision to go to Pisa had been announced, convocation was summoned to choose the English delegates, but scarcely had it met (on 14 January 1409) when the king fell gravely ill. Arundel, who had been hoping to resign the chancellorship in order to attend, therefore decided not to go, and instead Robert Hallum, now bishop of Salisbury, led the English delegation.[50] It was a deft choice, for Hallum's rhetorical skill and wider vision of what might be achieved earned much respect at Pisa. Precisely what this first general council of the Church for a hundred years could be expected to achieve was, however, an open question. That it would depose Gregory and Benedict was almost a foregone conclusion; that it would then proceed to the undisputed election of a new and mutually acceptable pope was widely anticipated; and in fact both objectives were achieved without difficulty, so that on 26 June 1409 it was announced that Peter Philargi, the Franciscan cardinal-archbishop of Milan, had been elected as Pope Alexander V. This was satisfactory as far as it went, but Hallum and some of the other English delegates – especially Henry Chichele, Thomas Chillenden, prior of Christ Church Canterbury, and Thomas Spofforth, abbot of St Mary's York – hoped that the council would then move on to a discussion of ecclesiastical reform, in anticipation of which Hallum had encouraged the Oxford theologian Richard Ullerston to write a tract as a basis for discussion.[51] Entitled *Petitiones Ricardi quoad Reformationem Ecclesiae Militantis*, this set of sixteen proposals was, at the request of the king's confessor, Roger Coryngham, presented to Henry IV, and it is likely that he approved it.[52] But it was not to be: there was some discussion of reform before the council broke up in early August, but having achieved their main objectives the delegates saw their task as securing recognition for the new pope. Even this, however, proved difficult: since Pisa had recognized Wenzel as emperor, Rupert declined to recognize Alexander as pope, and

[49] *Foedera*, viii.551–60.

[50] *SAC II*, 557–65.

[51] The English sent some thirty-five delegates in all to Pisa, prelates, canonists and civil lawyers, chosen by the convocations and the king. Not all of them were reformist at heart, but most of the leaders were. It is not clear whether Ullerston's tract was actually taken to Pisa, but it was certainly written for *praesens concilium* and was commissioned by Hallum for that purpose (Harvey, *Solutions to the Schism*, 151–65).

[52] After hearing of Alexander's election he wrote to him begging him to continue the council in order to address 'certain detestable abuses': E. Jacob, *Essays in the Conciliar Epoch* (Manchester, 1963), 74–84.

then, by a cruel stroke of luck, Alexander V died suddenly on 3 May 1410. The Schism had not been healed after all.[53]

Ullerston's *Petitiones* are nevertheless a guide to what leading reformers within the English hierarchy believed to be necessary, and what is striking about them is that whereas continental reformers, broadly speaking, were concentrating at this time on reform at the centre (the Curia, papal bureaucracy, the *camera* and its financial apparatus), the emphasis in the *Petitiones* was on reform at the diocesan and parochial levels.[54] It was matters such as appropriations and the disruptive effect of papal dispensations, exemptions and privileges on the spiritual life of dioceses and parishes which constituted the main thrust of Ullerston's argument. Bishops, their ordinaries, and other local people should be consulted, he declared; most appropriations were unnecessary and should be annulled; indeed, the whole question of privileges should be reviewed.[55] Reform at the centre was undoubtedly necessary too: simony was a great evil in Ullerston's view, as were annates, both symptomatic of Curial avarice. Yet the Statutes of Provisors and Praemunire had given the English a shield against claims of papal sovereignty, so it is not surprising that it was with diocesan and parochial matters that English reformers were principally concerned; and they had, in Henry, a king who shared their concern.

Although these issues were discussed at Pisa, probably on Hallum's initiative, little or nothing was done about them. Yet if this was an opportunity missed, and if Alexander V's death subsequently took the shine off its success, the Council of Pisa marked a turning point in the search for a solution to the Schism. It was the first time that a general council of the Church had met without papal summons, and it was the harbinger of its more celebrated successor, the Council of Constance, which met five years later and finally ended the Schism.[56] Especially notable was the role of the great powers, the French and English kings, in making it possible. There was obvious danger in this for the papacy: the risk of increasing state control, of monarchs browbeating popes or legislating to exclude their influence (as the English had done) – the danger, in other words, of national churches replacing a universal Church – and to some extent this happened

[53] Harvey, *Solutions to the Schism*, 184–5.

[54] Jacob, *Chichele*, 10–13; Harvey, *Solutions to the Schism*, 165–73; J. Catto, 'Wyclif and Wycliffism', in *The History of the University of Oxford II: Late Medieval Oxford*, ed. J. Catto and R. Evans (Oxford, 1992), 238–45.

[55] Below, pp. 368–72; for King's Bench overruling a papal privilege, see Storey, 'Clergy and Common Law', 390.

[56] Harvey, *Solutions to the Schism*, 2–3.

in the fifteenth century, so that it was as much Gallicanism as Conciliarism that Pisa heralded. And while Anglo-French cooperation soon evaporated in the heat of political rivalry, this shift in the balance of power between Church and state in England would prove more enduring, evident not simply in the lead taken by Henry IV in the debate over the Schism but also in the question of reform at the national level.

Chapter 24

HERESY, PIETY AND REFORM

Before 1399, Henry and Archbishop Arundel had shared much: high aristocratic birth, exceptional wealth, the empathy of rebellion, exile and restoration. After 1399, it was inevitable that differences would arise between them. As king, Henry wanted the Church not only to serve the spiritual needs of his subjects but also to use its power, wealth and privilege to uphold rather than subvert secular government. This meant principally making loans and granting taxation, acknowledging the king's interests in ecclesiastical appointments and clerical delinquency, and marshalling the Church's influence behind the government. In return, Arundel wanted the king to respect the Church's privileges and property and to help it suppress challenges to doctrinal orthodoxy. Both men also had constituencies to placate: the anticlerical and reformist elements at Henry's court, the doctrinally cautious and the champions of privilege within the ecclesiastical hierarchy. Disagreements between king and Church were common enough in the Middle Ages, and if allowed to escalate could lead to a falling out between king and primate such as had occurred between Henry I and Anselm, Henry II and Becket, John and Langton, or Edward I and Winchelsey. Arundel had already fallen out with one king, Richard II, and there were probably many who expected him to fall out with a second, but personal affection and mutual respect as well as political necessity bound him and Henry together. The fact that they did not fall out played no small part in ensuring that both king and archbishop died in their beds and in office, although the compromises this involved did not come easily.

Issues such as episcopal appointments, the provisors legislation and clerical immunity from secular justice were symptomatic of the widespread belief by the late fourteenth century that the English Church was in need of reform, but how much and by whom were questions which threatened to destabilize the political community from the very start of the reign. To Arundel, the election of John Cheyne as speaker of the commons on 6 October 1399 was anathema, for, as he informed convocation the next day, Cheyne was one of several parliamentary knights known to be inimical to the Church and would not hesitate to publicize its shortcomings. The articles drawn up in convocation a few days later went further: the laity, they claimed, was incorrigibly hostile towards the clergy and planned, under Lollard influence, to bring into parliament new constitutions against the Church, 'which are not in truth constitutions but distractions, or rather they should rightly be called destructions'.[1] A week later Cheyne resigned, ostensibly on grounds of ill health, but in reality because of Arundel's insistence that he was unacceptable; a noteworthy, if minor, early victory for the archbishop.[2]

Convenient as it was to stigmatize them as such, most of those who advocated ecclesiastical reform were not Lollards. Radical beliefs such as the denial of papal authority, wholesale disendowment of clerical temporalities, the rejection of images, cults, pilgrimage, purgatory, clerical celibacy, baptism or even the Eucharistic miracle were the preserve of a Wyclifite rump which twenty years of inquisition and denunciation had effectively marginalized as a lunatic fringe.[3] Far more of a threat to the clerical establishment, because both more numerous and better connected, was the much larger body of faithful who advocated reform but stopped well short of outright Wyclifism. This included many within the Church: the sixty-three articles of the 1399 convocation expressed concern about the standard of the priesthood, the quality of preaching, the taking of excessive fees for wills and notarial instruments, the provision of parochial hospitality (especially when churches had been appropriated) and the misuse of revenues granted to hospitals and chantries.[4] Yet while internal reform was ever a work in progress, there were many laymen who believed that the half-popes of a divided Europe had lost the appetite for meaningful self-examination. This was one reason why Wyclif had insisted that responsibility for reform lay with the secular power, and although it was risky to make this point too openly it was, in practice, what king and parliament had already begun to do. As lay literacy spread and new, more individualistic, modes of religious observance fostered a more critical attitude towards the shortcomings of the clergy, laymen became increasingly involved in ecclesiastical affairs. The Lollard knights of Richard II's court

---

[1] *SAC II*, 220–5; *Concilia*, iii.242; *Records of Convocation IV*, 201 (clause 29).

[2] *SAC II*, 244–5. He claimed that his voice was so frail that it could not be heard, which was no small consideration for a speaker. Cheyne seems to have enjoyed embarrassingly good health for the rest of the reign, however, serving as a privy councillor for six years and as the king's ambassador to France and the Curia.

[3] For Lollardy see Hudson, *The Premature Reformation*; R. Rex, *The Lollards* (Basingstoke, 2002).

[4] *Concilia*, iii.238–45.

were products of this independent-minded class of literate and influential laymen, but for every knight or esquire prepared to risk the tag of Lollardy there were many more who shared some of their views but had no desire to be branded as heretics. Among these were the 'parliamentary knights' or 'knights that never loved the church' who so alarmed both bishops and chroniclers.

Reformation might come in many guises. Monastic reform, an extreme version of which favoured extensive disendowment, also encompassed the less radical notion of shifting resources towards more ascetic orders such as the Carthusians, or more fashionable institutions such as colleges and chantries (as happened with much of the property held by the alien priories).[5] It was the interface between clergy and laity at the parochial level, however, in which parliament showed greater interest. Its principal concern – as witness the growing emphasis in the debate over provisors on issues such as almsgiving and hospitality – was the provision of pastoral and sacramental care by resident parish priests. This is why, beginning in 1394, the commons presented a succession of petitions complaining about pluralism and non-residence by curates, although the king took the view that these were matters for the bishops to deal with. The clamour to reform hospitals also grew louder, leading in 1414 to the first parliamentary petition to place them under closer supervision.[6]

It was the issue of appropriations, however, upon which the commons really chose to bite. By the late fourteenth century, around a quarter of the 9,000 or so parishes in England had been appropriated, mainly by monasteries, giving the latter the right to receive the income of the church in return for appointing a vicar to perform the pastoral functions of the parish priest. The issues this involved were far from simple: parishes depopulated by plague could scarcely maintain a priest, while many Oxford and Cambridge colleges relied heavily on appropriated livings. On the other hand, it was alleged that monks in particular were neglectful of their duties, leading, like non-residence, to the dilapidation of parochial buildings and disregard for the sacraments, preaching, almsgiving and

---

[5] Saul, *Richard II*, 299, 322; A. Tuck, 'Carthusian Monks and Lollard Knights', in *Studies in the Age of Chaucer I: Reconstructing Chaucer*, ed. P. Strohm and T. J. Heffernan (Knoxville, 1985), 149–61; B. Thompson, 'The Laity, the Alien Priories, and the Redistribution of Ecclesiastical Property', in *England in the Fifteenth Century: Proceedings of the 1992 Harlaxton Symposium*, ed. N. Rogers (Stamford, 1994), 19–41.

[6] Above, pp. 352–4, for provisors; *PROME*, vii.274; viii.125, 194, 386 (pluralism and non-residence); viii.192; ix.45–6.

hospitality.[7] The commons' campaign began in 1391 with a statute stating that all licences to appropriate churches must include provision for vicars to be properly endowed, but it was a surge of bulls of appropriation from Boniface IX after 1397 which led them to step up their attacks. In 1401, they asked that no further licences be issued; the king replied that he would consider this further, but in the following year a long-running dispute between the prior of Launceston (Cornwall) and the residents of three parishes appropriated to his house brought the issue to a head.[8] The parishioners claimed that they had no resident ministry, hospitality, or provision for baptisms and burials, even though convocation had recently persuaded the pope to revoke his bulls. Within weeks a statute was passed annulling all appropriations made since 1377 and prohibiting future appropriations unless accompanied by the appointment of a properly endowed and instituted secular and perpetual vicar. Boniface accepted much of this, issuing his own bull on 22 December 1402 confirming that appropriated parish churches be served by secular, rather than monastic, curates, and annulling his own and his predecessors' earlier bulls to the contrary, but although a letter from the king in the following year referred to the 'general revocation of appropriations by the apostle [pope]', in fact matters did not go that far. Nevertheless, Boniface issued no further bulls of appropriation after 1402.[9] There was no doubting the strength of feeling on this subject in England (as in Bohemia, where it was one of the main Hussite grievances). It drew on both a genuine concern for the provision of pastoral care at parish level and popular resentment at the wealth and elitism of the older-established monastic orders, not just from the laity but also from friars and secular clergy.

The campaign against appropriations between 1391 and 1402 represented a striking success for the reformers; not so the simultaneous campaign for disendowment, the most persistent and divisive reformist issue of the time. This was a debate that went back to the old question of whether or not the Church should be permitted to hold property, into

[7] For appropriations (or 'impropriations') see Foulser, 'The Influence of Lollardy', 189–201; W. Jordan, *Philanthropy in England 1480–1660* (London, 1959), 81–2. The sixth article of the 1395 Lollard manifesto severely criticized appropriations, citing the disapprobation of Robert Grosseteste.

[8] The parishes were Liskeard, Linkinhorne and Talland (*PROME*, vii.213; viii.203–4); Storey, 'Clergy and Common Law', 384–90; Heath, *Church and Realm*, 264–5 (Boniface issued 155 bulls of appropriation for England, 130 of them to religious houses and the 'vast majority' between 1397 and 1402).

[9] *SAC II*, 346–9; *ANLP*, no. 282 (June 1403, not 1402); *PROME*, viii.190, 272 (confirmation of January 1404). For a vehement mid-fifteenth century attack on appropriations, see Gascoigne, *Loci e Libro*, 106–15.

which new life was breathed by Wyclif's insistence that it should not.[10] Proposals had been put to parliament in the 1370s and 1380s for the confiscation of a proportion of clerical temporalities, but by marginalizing such views as the work of a radical and arguably heretical fringe, and by omitting mention of them from the official record, it had been possible to ignore them.[11] Yet disendowment in some form was favoured by many moderate as well as radical reformers, and after 1399, sensing a king who might be more sympathetic to their wishes, groups of royal and parliamentary knights renewed their efforts to push it through. The great councils of 1403 and 1405, and the parliaments of October 1404 and 1406, witnessed angry debates between bishops and royal councillors on the issue.[12] The culmination of this campaign came with the Lollard Disendowment Bill presented to the parliament of January 1410, drafts of which had been circulating for at least fifteen years, which proposed the confiscation of the temporalities held – or 'arrogantly plundered' – by all the major monasteries and cathedrals in the realm. Their resources, it suggested, should be redeployed to support the foundation of five (or perhaps fifteen) universities, a hundred almshouses for the support of the poor, and the endowments of fifteen earls, 1,500 knights and 6,200 esquires.[13] Like its precursors, the bill was too radical even to be enrolled on the official parliamentary record. Walsingham described it as the work of 'the accursed company of Lollard knights ... whose aim was to rob the Church of God'. Such diehards tended to characterize the disendowment party as motivated by greed, and the chronic bankruptcy of Henry's government lent plausibility to such arguments, but at its heart lay the age-old desire to strip away the Church's material encumbrances to allow it to focus upon its spiritual mission on earth. Against disendowment stood both those clerics whose communities and careers depended on endowment and the powerful laymen whose ancestors had founded or endowed monasteries as powerhouses of prayer for their and their families' souls. It was monastic wealth against which disendowment was mainly directed.

Also unmistakable were the social concerns underlying the 1410 bill: one of the aims of founding a hundred almshouses (not hospitals, which were

[10] Rex, *The Lollards*, 27–38, 51.

[11] Notably in 1371 and 1385: M. Aston, 'Caim's Castles: Poverty, Politics and Disendowment', in *The Church, Politics and Patronage in the Fifteenth Century*, ed. R. Dobson (Gloucester, 1984), 45–81.

[12] Above, pp. 287–9; *SAC II*, 478–81, 794–9; Wolffe, *Royal Demesne*, 245–7.

[13] *SAC II*, 584–8; *Selections from English Wycliffite Writings*, ed. A. Hudson (Cambridge, 1978), 135–7, 203–7.

to be disendowed) was to allow each town in the realm to support 'all the poor and the beggars who are not able to work for their living because of the requirements of the Statute of Cambridge'. The 'First English Poor Law' passed at the Cambridge parliament of 1388 had placed the onus of feeding the deserving poor on their natal towns. Almshouses were intended to help civic authorities to perform this role, just as the campaigns against pluralism, non-residence, papal provisions and appropriations sought to remedy the decline of pastoral welfare at parochial level.[14] Such concerns resonated with Wyclifite thinking, which emphasized the social, as well as religious, value of pastoral care, the needs of the poor and vagrant, and the importance of education – hence the desire for English translations of the scriptures and the foundation of additional universities. Although most of those who campaigned against appropriations or in favour of disendowment had little option but to disown Wyclif's ideas in public, in fact their attempt to create a more responsive Church in England owed a good deal to him. So too did their desire to make parliament a forum for discussion of ecclesiastical reform – indeed it is striking how much of the legislation of Henry's reign related to the Church, and how often it was Church affairs that provoked the most testy exchanges in parliaments and great councils. This was new, and was resented by most senior clergy, who believed Church reform to be an internal matter, yet it was exactly what Wyclif and his followers had advocated: that it was the moral obligation of the lay power to reform the Church. What parliament was doing was trying to persuade Henry to implement the reforms it wanted, adopting in the process some of the solutions Wyclif had proposed.[15]

Arundel was only too aware of the threat posed by the anticlerical and reformist rhetoric rippling outwards from parliament and court, yet he was far from being the hidebound chief whip often depicted. As a young man, he had mixed with Cambridge-educated canon lawyers who had absorbed the spiritual and eremitical aspirations of mystics such as Richard Rolle; as archbishop of York (1388–96) he had encountered the pastoral reforms introduced by his predecessor John Thoresby (d.1373) to encourage lay men

---

[14] The 1410 parliament ordered all concerned with cure of souls (*curati*) back to their parishes to maintain hospitality, leading to a great exodus from the courts of the king, nobles, bishops and their houses in London (*CE*, 417).

[15] See Wilks, *Wyclif*, 199: 'If Wycliffism meant essentially the assertion of lay supremacy in ecclesiastical matters, then the chroniclers were perfectly entitled to scream that a substantial proportion of all England had become Lollard by 1380'.

and women to take more responsibility for their own salvation.[16] Yet Arundel
also believed in firm direction of the laity by the Church. The line between
orthodoxy and heterodoxy was a fine one and, as Wyclif's followers demonstrated, too personal a religion often led to fragmentation and heresy. The
problem lay in trying to preserve what was best in lay religious enthusiasm
while maintaining the integrity of Catholic liturgy and doctrine. One way
to do this was to control the diffusion of meditative texts, as Arundel did
when in 1411 he approved the publication of the *Mirror of the Blessed Life of
Jesus Christ*, an English translation by Nicholas Love, prior of Mount Grace,
of the pseudo-Bonaventuran *Meditationes Vitae Christi*. Written for 'the edifi-
cation of the faithful and the confutation of heretics', this was a life of
Christ based on the gospels, but with Catholic interpretation (including
anti-Lollard invective) embedded in the narrative.[17]

Arundel saw the combating of heresy as the principal mission of his
primacy.[18] This, convocation was repeatedly told, was the main reason for
its summons. Yet it was a battle that required the support of the secular
authorities, and despite the burning of Sawtry and the passing of *De
Heretico Comburendo* in 1401, the archbishop's reluctance to place himself at
the heart of Henry's government during the next few years left the ecclesiastical hierarchy fighting a rearguard action against calls for disendowment, violations of clerical immunity, and the reformist strictures of
parliament. By late 1406, however, the death of Richard Scrope, disputes
over episcopal appointments, growing pressure to end the Schism, and the
revival of Wyclifism at Oxford – as illustrated by the sermon advocating
disendowment preached by William Taylor, principal of St Edmund Hall,
at St Paul's Cross in November 1406 – persuaded Arundel to take a more
active role.[19] The so-called Statute against Lollards, passed in December
1406, bears his stamp, especially in its condemnation of the disendowment
party and its attempts to control the spread of reformist ideas through
preaching. It also ordered that suspected heretics be brought before the
chancellor, who would decide whether to have them tried in parliament;

[16] J. Hughes, *Pastors and Visionaries* (Woodbridge, 1988), 174–250, and 'Arundel, Thomas',
ODNB, 2.564–10; in 1409 Arundel joined the Carthusian fraternity of Mount Grace; cf. also
I. Forrest, *The Detection of Heresy in Late Medieval England* (Oxford, 2005), 237–9.

[17] Nicholas Love, *The Mirror of the Blessed Life of Jesus Christ*, ed. M. Sargent (Exeter, 2005),
54–7 (Sargent suggests, p. 89, some form of official dissemination of Love's work); W. N.
Beckett, 'Nicholas Love', *ODNB*, 34.502–3.

[18] Wyclif, he declared, was *in mala hora natus* (Lambeth Palace Library, *Arundel Register*, fo.
47r).

[19] Catto, 'Wyclif and Wycliffism', 242–4; *SAC II*, 478–81.

since Arundel was about to become chancellor, this enhanced his authority in the war against heresy.[20]

Wielding his two swords in tandem, Arundel now attacked the Wyclifites head on. As chancellor, he had the notorious Lollard preacher William Thorpe brought before him, interrogated and cast into the archiepiscopal dungeon at Saltwood (Kent), where he probably died.[21] As archbishop, he turned his attention to Oxford University. Arundel had clashed with Oxford over academic privileges and Wyclifite theology during his first convocation as primate in 1397, but ten years on there was still no consensus as to what was permissible. What forced his hand was the emergence around 1406 of a group of freethinking masters such as William Taylor and Peter Payne, both open admirers of 'the great logician' (Wyclif).[22] Summoning convocation to Oxford in November 1407 (the only time during the reign that it met outside London), the archbishop presented to it his much-maligned *Constitutions*, thirteen articles addressing three main issues.[23] First, tighter controls were established over preaching through the issuing of licences, and the exclusion from sermons of controversial topics, especially in relation to the sacraments. Secondly, restrictions were imposed on the teaching of theology at Oxford and Cambridge, including a ban on Wyclif's works (unless vetted by a committee of twelve chosen with Arundel's approval), closer supervision of disputations, and the authorization of monthly enquiries by the principal of each college into the opinions voiced by his scholars. Thirdly, article seven prohibited the translation into English, without authority, of any text of holy scripture, or the reading of any such work in English written during or since Wyclif's time, unless approved by a provincial council. This unwarrantably most famous article was justified on the grounds that scriptural truth was liable to be lost in translation, but it was not nearly as wide-ranging as often pretended and had little effect in the short term. The controls on preaching (articles 1–4) took up a familiar and important strand of anti-Lollard measures, and added the penalty of forfeiture for offenders, which in 1414 would be incorporated in Henry V's

---

[20] *PROME*, viii.361; M. Jurkowski, 'The Arrest of William Thorpe in Shrewsbury and the Anti-Lollard Statute of 1406', *HR* 75 (2002), 273–95. It was unprecedented for an archbishop of Canterbury also to serve as chancellor; in 1396, Arundel had resigned the chancellorship when he became primate. The specious linking of ecclesiastical reformers with those claiming that Richard II was still alive was designed to make the statute doubly acceptable to Henry and his family.

[21] A. Hudson, 'William Thorpe', *ODNB*, 54.675–6.

[22] Lambeth Palace Library, Arundel Register, fos. 44–7; Catto, 'Wyclif and Wycliffism', 232–43; Aston, *Thomas Arundel*, 333.

[23] Printed in *Records of Convocation IV*, 311–18; McNiven, *Heresy and Politics*, 104–7.

statute against Lollards.[24] Of greater importance, even if not entirely novel, was the attempt to muzzle the Oxford masters.[25] It was primarily at the university that the *Constitutions* were directed. (It was more than a year before they were even promulgated outside Oxford.) Yet even here, with the archbishop distracted through 1408 and 1409 by the Schism and the chancellorship, they were only indifferently observed, and the summer of 1409 witnessed further defiance from a group of academics protesting at the restriction of their intellectual freedom.[26]

When Arundel lost the chancellorship on 21 December 1409, the challenge to his authority grew bolder. It may be that the reformists hoped for support from the new chancellor, Sir Thomas Beaufort – the man who had wrestled Archbishop Scrope's cross from his hands at Pontefract in June 1405. It was at any rate to the parliament of January 1410 that the root and branch Disendowment Bill was presented, as well as a petition asking for relaxation of the procedures for the arrest of heretics set out in *De Heretico Comburendo*.[27] Smelling danger, the archbishop reacted as he had in 1401 by taking his stand on the Eucharist. On 1 March, he brought forth from his prison John Badby, a tailor from Evesham (Worcestershire) who, like William Sawtry, had unequivocally denied that the host changed substance into the body of Christ. Disparagement of the Eucharist was a matter about which Arundel felt strongly: at the Coventry parliament of 1404 he had railed to the king after seeing a group of household knights and esquires show 'no more honour to the Body of Christ than they would have shown to a dog's body'.[28] Yet Badby's trial was manifestly opportunistic: like Sawtry, he had already spent a year in prison before Arundel presented him to a tribunal of lords and prelates.[29] Asked if he had changed his mind, Badby replied that he had not, 'If it pleased the reverend fathers'. The Eucharist, he asserted, was of less value than a toad or a spider, which were at least living creatures. At this point, it was claimed, a large black spider appeared on Badby's lips and, resisting his attempts to brush it away, disappeared into his mouth. 'Now we see who it was that taught him to

---

[24] P. Cavill, 'Heresy, Law and the State: Forfeiture in Late Medieval and Early Modern England', *EHR* 129 (2014), 270–95, at p. 276.

[25] There had also been a clampdown on heresy at Oxford in 1382 (McNiven, *Heresy and Politics*, 37–41). In 1401 Arundel investigated Cambridge, but found it untainted by heresy (Hughes, *Pastors and Visionaries*, 247).

[26] McNiven, *Heresy and Politics*, 154–7; Catto, 'Wyclif and Wycliffism', 246.

[27] Above, p. 370; *PROME*, viii.464–5.

[28] *SAC II*, 801 (they had turned their backs on a priest giving the last rites to a dying man).

[29] *SAC II*, 580–3; *Records of Convocation IV*, 362–7; McNiven, *Heresy and Politics*, 199–219; *Foedera*, viii.627.

speak,' exclaimed the archbishop.[30] Condemned on 5 March, the heretic was handed over to the lay power for punishment, although Arundel apparently asked that he be spared the death penalty and unlike some other bishops he seems not to have attended the execution. This took place immediately: Badby was chained to a stake set in a heap of faggots at Smithfield, ringed by a throng including Prince Henry. When the pyre was lit he cried out, and the prince, perhaps thinking that he wished to recant, ordered the flames to be extinguished and offered the blistered martyr a life pension of three pence a day to recant.[31] It was refused, whereupon the fire was rekindled and an obscure tailor from Worcestershire became the second and last heretic of the reign to be incinerated. For those involved (the culprit apart) it was a satisfactory outcome: the prince had publicly demonstrated leadership and orthodoxy, he and Arundel had both, in their different ways, shown a degree of clemency, the procedure for the arrest of heretics was confirmed, and no more was heard in parliament about seizing the Church's temporalities.

Arundel continued to follow up suspicions of heterodoxy for as long as he remained primate, be it at Oxford in 1411 or at Cooling castle (Kent) in 1412–13, where he had already, before Henry IV's death, begun to close in on England's most infamous Lollard, Sir John Oldcastle.[32] It may be that Arundel took Lollardy too seriously, that his determination to extirpate heresy in its various manifestations pushed those who would not abandon their principles into a corner from which Oldcastle's revolt in January 1414 came to seem like the only means of escape.[33] He did, however, succeed from 1407 onwards – at court, at Oxford, in parliament – in wresting back the initiative from the hecklers and sceptics who had so discomfited the ecclesiastical hierarchy during the first half of Henry's reign. For good or ill, he also turned the English Church – through definition, public recantation, the supervision of education and the beginnings of literary censorship – into a more efficient instrument for the enforcement of ecclesiastical discipline. Yet Arundel did not wish simply to silence the reformists. He also wanted to provide conscientious Christians with an alternative: hence the promulgation (in English) of Love's *Mirror*. When the eccentric visionary

---

[30] *CE*, 416–17 (the devil was sometimes compared to a spider in the way he set traps for the unwitting).

[31] Hoccleve, *Regement of Princes*, 11–12.

[32] Below, pp. 488–90 (Oxford).

[33] J. Thomson, 'John Oldcastle, Baron Cobham', *ODNB*, 41.668–72; cf. R. Davies, 'Thomas Arundel as Archbishop of Canterbury 1396–1413', *Journal of Ecclesiastical History* 24 (1973), 9–21, at p. 20 ('Arundel took Lollardy seriously, perhaps too seriously').

Margery Kempe visited him at Lambeth, they had a long interview in his garden, where he spoke to her 'full benignly and meekly', approved her unorthodox manner of living, and granted her requests to choose her own confessor and (most unusually) to receive communion once a week; she left him 'comforted and strengthened in her soul'.[34] Arundel's will, in which he described himself as a 'miserable and unworthy sinner', a 'useless and tepid minister', and asked that his 'fetid, putrid cadaver' be accorded only the plainest of burials, reveals penitence and humility, and suggests that his personal approach to salvation may not always have sat easily with the public pronouncements incumbent on a primate.[35] He knew as well as many of his critics that the Church needed to live up to the standards it set, and that the simple orthodoxy/heterodoxy polarity was really an establishment construct, even if the language he used at times tended to pare the debate to its essentials. His public emphasis on the sacraments was not simply opportunistic, but was consistent with his view of the unifying force of the Catholic mass, with its focus on contemplation of Christ's Passion and the intercessory role of the clergy.

According to Walsingham, Henry rejected the 1410 Disendowment Bill like a 'catholic and orthodox prince', but it was the more spirited opposition of John Norbury ('one man in a thousand . . . who loved the Church with all his heart') that he chose to emphasize. In fact, as the chronicler knew, the king was not always quick to reject calls for disendowment. At Coventry in 1404, Archbishop Arundel, suspecting that Henry sympathized with the plans of John Cheyne and his fellows, had warned him of the fate that awaited kings who despoiled the Church. Henry's reply was reassuring, but by no means unambiguous, and in the end it was the support of a group of temporal lords that scotched the proposals. It may be that Henry found calls for clerical disendowment quite useful: in 1403, 1404 and 1405 they enabled him to put sufficient pressure on convocation to grant clerical tenths.[36] Nor was anyone punished for urging the seizure of the Church's temporalities, not even in 1410, despite the fact that the parliament of 1406 had declared it to be an imprisonable offence.[37]

[34] Her own words; she also wrote warmly of Philip Repingdon, who 'welcomed her dearly', commended her feelings and advised her to write them down, gave her two marks to buy clothes, and was generous in almsgiving: *The Book of Margery Kempe*, ed. B. Windeatt (Woodbridge, 2004), 72, 105–11, 237.
[35] McFarlane, *Lancastrian Kings*, 219–20.
[36] *SAC II*, 380–5, 418–25, 460–3, 591, 795–803.
[37] *PROME*, viii.361–2.

The openness of the debate over ecclesiastical reform during Henry's reign is striking, and behind it lay the belief that reformists could look to the king for support. Some suspected worse: Richard II was reported to have said that if Henry ever became king, 'he would want to destroy the whole of God's holy Church'. Henry flatly denied this (in the 1399 parliament), though he added – significantly – that he hoped to see men chosen as rulers of churches (*rectores ecclesiarum*) who were more worthy of their office than those appointed in his predecessors' times.[38] Three years later the Franciscan Roger Frisby repeated the allegation to his face: 'You never loved the church,' he told the king. 'You disparaged it greatly before you became king, and now you are destroying it.'[39] As the son of John of Gaunt, Henry's orthodoxy might well be open to question, but to be accused of wanting to destroy the Church usually in fact meant wanting to reform it, a desire Henry expressed on more than one occasion.[40] Henry was not, of course, a Lollard, but he almost certainly shared some of their aspirations. Familial influences – not just his father's, but also his first wife Mary's and perhaps his grandfather Henry of Grosmont's – had fostered a questioning attitude to the Church's teaching, and his choice of friends was unlikely to allay the fears of fundamentalists. Men such as John Cheyne and Robert Waterton were well known for their outspokenness on the question of clerical transgressions, yet both remained members of the king's inner circle throughout the reign, as did Philip Repingdon.

An Oxford theologian and early follower of Wyclif, the austere and morally rigorous Repingdon had been obliged to recant his errors during Archbishop Courtenay's purge of academic Lollardy in 1382, since when he had trodden the orthodox path to become abbot of Leicester, a house patronized by the dukes of Lancaster, in 1393. There is no doubting his intimacy with Henry: one contemporary described him as 'the king's very special clerk (*clericus specialissimus regis*)'.[41] In May 1400, Henry helped to arrange his appointment as chancellor of Oxford University, a move which coincided with the revival there of the debates over clerical disendowment and vernacular translation of the

[38] *SAC II*, 248–9.

[39] *CE*, 392.

[40] Above, pp. 363–5, and Jacob, *Conciliar Essays*, 72–5, for his interest in reform at the Council of Pisa.

[41] *RHKA*, 192–3; Repingdon may have shared Henry's exile (*CR*, 126–7, 135). For his letter to Henry of May 1401 and his recantation in 1382, above, p. 208. After the battle of Shrewsbury, Henry sent Repingdon a ring from his finger to show he was alive and had defeated his enemies.

scriptures.[42] In 1404 he became the king's confessor and in 1405 bishop of Lincoln, but, despite his outwardly orthodox stance, Repingdon's *Sermones Dominicales* suggest that he continued to hold views about the Church's shortcomings which more conservative defenders of the faith would have found uncomfortable. Although an active investigator of heterodoxy, he was not a persecutor of heretics; he maintained links with known and suspected Lollards, criticized the worldliness and immorality of the clergy, expressed misgivings about the Church's holding of temporalities, and laid great stress on the alleviation of poverty and the necessity for almsgiving. In other words, he shared the social and religious outlook of the reformers, but chose to work towards reform from within the Church rather than outside it.[43] When told in 1415 to exhume Wyclif's body, he ignored the order. Yet ultimately he seems to have found the contradictions in his position difficult to sustain. In 1419 he retired, thus becoming the first English bishop known to have voluntarily resigned his see. He died five years later, asking that his body be buried naked in a sack in open ground near to his former cathedral, 'there to be food for worms'; that his death be announced by no one but the town crier of Lincoln; and that every farthing of his worldly goods be distributed to the poor.[44] Contempt for the mortal body, the rejection of funereal pomp, and an emphasis on philanthropy and penitence were characteristic of Lollard wills, though by no means restricted to them. Henry IV's will employed similar, though less emphatic, language: he was, he declared, a 'sinful wretch' with a 'sinful soul', and begged God's mercy for his misspent life and his people's pardon for his treatment of them.[45] The resonances between the testamentary language used by the king, his archbishop, and his confessor denote a willingness to push at the boundaries of orthodoxy.

Henry admired and patronized religious orders with an eremitical and meditative tradition such as the Carthusians and the Carmelites. Of the fourteen religious houses to which he donated wine in 1405–6, five were Carthusian. His first two confessors, Hugh Herle and Robert Mascall,

[42] Catto, 'Wyclif and Wycliffism', 238–40; A. Hudson, 'The Debate on Bible Translation, Oxford 1401', *EHR* 90 (1975), 1–18.

[43] S. Forde, 'Social Outlook and Preaching in a Wycliffite *Sermones Dominicales* Collection', in *Church and Chronicle in the Middle Ages: Essays Presented to John Taylor*, ed. I. Wood and G. Loud (London, 1991), 179–91. These sermons were probably not for oral delivery but didactic tracts.

[44] S. Forde, 'Repyndon, Philip', *ODNB*, 46.503–5. In fact he was buried in Lincoln cathedral.

[45] Nichols, *Collection of Wills*, 203; Catto, 'Religion and the English Nobility'; McFarlane, *Lancastrian Kings*, 207–20.

were Carmelite friars, as all of Gaunt's had been. Five of the fifteen men known to have preached before the king during the year 1402–3 were Carmelites, another six Dominicans.[46] At the outset of his reign, Henry showed himself well disposed towards the friars, and although the conspiracies of 1402 and a long-running dispute within the order tested his patience with the Franciscans, he continued to favour the Dominicans (his last confessor, John Tille, was a Dominican).[47] His interest in monasteries, however, was limited, something which was not expected of kings. Richard II and his courtier-nobility had founded a number of Carthusian houses, while Henry V would provide a sumptuous riposte to the idea of disendowment by founding two religious houses (one Carthusian, one Bridgettine) during his first year as king, and later taking a personal interest in the reform of the Benedictine order.[48] Henry IV was not anti-monastic – although he might not have balked at the thought of a degree of monastic disendowment, especially of the older and richer orders – but the foundations with which he actively associated himself were colleges such as the Knolles Almshouse of the Holy Trinity at Pontefract and the college of the Blessed Virgin and All Saints at Fotheringhay (Northants).[49] In both cases he assumed the role of founder from the original patron – Pontefract from Sir Robert Knolles, Fotheringhay from Edmund, duke of York – but in each case he took his role seriously.[50] Henry was involved by 1403 at the

[46] Goodman, John of Gaunt, 241–65; D. Codling, 'Henry IV and Personal Piety', History Today (2007), 23–9; E 101/404/21, fos. 35–7; BL Harleian Ms 319, fos. 40r–v; he also gave Carthusian Mount Grace £100 a year: E 403/571, 11 November.

[47] Forrest, Detection of Heresy, 123; CCR 1396–9, 523–4; Foedera, viii.189; PROME, viii.195–6; CE, 389–94, 403–5; RHL, ii.179. Henry moderated the commons demand to restrict entry to the fraternal orders in 1402.

[48] SAC II, 646, 758–60; one of the few good things that the monk of Evesham could say of Richard II was that he favoured the Benedictines: Vita, 167.

[49] Henry allowed French monks to return to more than thirty alien priories in 1399: A. McHardy, 'The Effects of War on the Church: The Case of the Alien Priories in the Fourteenth Century', in England and her Neighbours 1066–1453: Essays in Honour of Pierre Chaplais, ed. M. Jones and M. Vale (London, 1989), 277–95. He also may have agreed to found three monastic houses as expiation for Scrope's death: N. Beckett, 'Sheen Charterhouse from its Foundation to its Dissolution' (unpublished D.Phil. thesis, Oxford, 1992, 92–101).

[50] Fotheringhay was a joint foundation with Edward of York, the son of Edmund, planned in March 1411 and effected in the November 1411 parliament; it was for a master, twelve chaplains, eight clerks and thirteen choristers – a large college – and endowed mainly with lands from alien priories (PROME, viii.526–32; CPR 1408–13, 358; CPL, vi.190). Pontefract was for a warden, six chaplains and an almshouse for thirteen paupers; originally planned in 1385, it was completed with help from the king shortly after Knolles's death. Henry emphasized in 1408 that 'the king is at present the founder and he and his heirs the dukes of Lancaster will be for ever founders' – the location of the college at Pontefract doubtless determining the insistence on Lancastrian patronage (E 159/182, Brevia, rot. 2d; CPR 1405–8, 182, 297, 319; Calendar of Scrope's Register, i.44; CPR 1408–13, 32, 74).

latest in the endowment of Pontefract college, but his decision in 1411 to act as founder of Fotheringhay and to convert it into a hive of prayer for his and his family's souls was dictated by the brushes with death of his later years, as was the case with the chantry he endowed at St Paul's in December 1408 for the souls of his father and mother and the chantry of St Mary Magdalene, built in 1409–10 on the field of the battle of Shrewsbury. Although Henry had made a vow some years earlier to found a chantry for the souls of those who had died in the battle, and although a little chapel with two chaplains had already been established there for three years, it was the king's illness at the beginning of 1409 which stirred him to action.[51] Lack of resources may have held him back earlier in the reign, but in fact the cuckoo foundations of his later years cost him little.

There was nothing unconventional about Henry's preference for colleges: many more colleges than monasteries were founded by late medieval nobles. They were cheaper to endow, more flexible institutions whose statutes (or 'rule') could be written by the founder and dedicated more exclusively to intercession for his family, and less cut off from the world outside the cloister.[52] On the other hand, the virtues of seclusion, contemplation and asceticism – in other words, being *more* removed from the world – also appealed to many, Henry included: Carthusians and Carmelites apart, he supported several recluses, including Matthew Danthorpe, who founded a chapel at Ravenspur on the spot where Henry landed in 1399, the anchoress Margaret Pensax, and unnamed hermits at Lancaster, Deptford, Bamburgh and Westminster; in 1408 he licensed the excavation from the cliff below Knaresborough of a wayside cave-chapel to Our Lady of the Crag.[53] According to Capgrave, his last words of advice to Prince Henry were to take good and modest men of religion to his heart, especially those who had lived a solitary life of study and prayer.[54]

Conventional piety is not easy to define: individual tastes embraced contrasts, not to say contradictions. Henry certainly had no objections to relics, pilgrimages, shrines or images. When the Byzantine emperor presented him with a piece of the seamless robe of Christ woven by the

---

[51] *CPR 1408–13*, 50–1; Wylie, *Henry the Fourth*, iii.239–43; *Antient Kalendars*, ii.78–9; Priestley, *The Battle of Shrewsbury*, 20–2.

[52] *The Late Medieval English College and its Context*, ed. C. Burgess and M. Heale (Woodbridge, 2008); see especially the chapters by Heale (pp. 67–86) and Burgess (3–27), who suggests that colleges also appealed to national sentiment in an age of warfare.

[53] *CPR 1399–1401*, 209; *Foedera*, viii.296; Abbot Cummins, 'Knaresborough Cave-Chapels', *Yorkshire Archaeological Journal* 28 (1926), 80–8; Wylie, *Henry the Fourth*, iv.144. *Scotichronicon*, 269–75.

[54] *De Illustribus Henricis*, 110–11.

Virgin, he was delighted, and presented half of it to Westminster abbey and the other half to Arundel, who set it in a silver-gilt reliquary, along with a spine from the crown of thorns and a few drops of Becket's blood, and offered it to the high altar of Canterbury cathedral.[55] The king was also instrumental in securing the canonization of John of Bridlington; he visited the shrines at Walsingham and at Canterbury on several occasions, and was the only late medieval English king to have set foot in the Holy Land.[56] His religious observance could not be faulted. When he arrived for a night's stay at Bardney abbey (Lincolnshire) on Saturday 21 August 1406, he knelt and kissed the crucifix, was asperged by the abbot and led to the high altar, heard a hymn and an oration, and kissed the holy relics before retiring; next morning he rose at six, came down to the chapel of St Mary, heard two masses, then followed the procession through the cloister to the choir, where he attended high mass – 'remaining until the end', as the scribe noted – before going to his chamber to dine.[57] He owned the largest illuminated Bible made in medieval England, and may have composed religious music.[58] He took an interest in the worthiness of individual religious and, like his uncle the Black Prince, had a particular devotion to the Trinity, the giver of wisdom, understanding and knowledge.[59] It was his open-mindedness, however – born of a desire to arrive at his own way of understanding – that made his religiosity more than simply conventional, and which explains why he counted Philip Repingdon among his closest friends; why he owned a copy of the Bible in English; why he tried to prevent academic freedom from becoming a casualty of heretical inquisition at Oxford; why he took advantage of his stay at Bardney to peruse the volumes in the monastic library; why Capgrave had met learned men who told him of Henry's interest in ethical questions and theological disputation; and why he was reluctant to close his ears to those who dared to aspire to the creation of a better Church in England.[60]

[55] Lambeth Palace Library, Ms 78 (my thanks to Rob Bartlett for this reference).

[56] *CPR 1401–5*, 248; *CPL*, v.459–60; M. Curley, 'John of Bridlington', *ODNB*, 30.194–6; BL Harleian Ms 319, fo. 27v (visit to Walsingham in 1406); and see above, p. 73.

[57] *Johannis Lelandi*, vi.300.

[58] BL Royal Ms 1 E ix; and see below, p. 388.

[59] Green, *Edward the Black Prince*, 167. Henry was buried in the Trinity Chapel at Canterbury and his memorial service was held on Trinity Sunday. For his interest in individual religious, see, for example, E 28/7, no. 24; SC 1/57/21.

[60] H. Summerson, 'An English Bible and Other Books belonging to Henry IV', *BJRL* 79 (1997), 109–15; *Johannis Lelandi*, vi.300–1; *De Illustribus Henricis*, 108–9. For Henry and Oxford, see below, pp. 488–90.

The king and his archbishop both had to compromise at times, but Arundel gave more ground than Henry. Yet despite his demotion and exile in 1397–9, the English episcopacy did not question Arundel's leadership. The need for secular support in healing the Schism and defeating heresy made compromise inescapable, as did the vulnerability of the Lancastrian regime during its early years, for Arundel was committed to Henry's kingship. As a result, the English Church was increasingly elided with the English state.[61] Similar processes were under way elsewhere, and it was a transformation extending over centuries rather than decades, but Henry IV's reign marked a significant moment in its realization. Nevertheless, Arundel would surely have reckoned that at least he and Henry had prevented England from going down the same road as Hussite Bohemia – which, in 1399, was by no means a foregone conclusion.

[61] Cf. J. Catto, 'Religious Change under Henry V', in *Henry V: The Practice of Kingship*, ed. Harris, 115.

Part Four

LANCASTRIAN KINGSHIP

Chapter 25

THE KING AND HIS IMAGE

The chronicler John Strecche, a canon of Kenilworth priory who saw Henry as a potentially great but flawed king, penned the following portrait of him: 'This King Henry was elegantly built, of great strength, a vigorous knight, brave in arms, wise and circumspect in his youthful behaviour, always fortunate in battle, successful in his deeds and gloriously victorious everywhere, brilliant at music, marvellously learned and most upright in morals.'[1]

Henry's credentials as a warrior were not in doubt; more striking is Strecche's claim for his musicianship. The employment of between four and ten minstrels in his household was no more than would be expected of any great noble, but his gifts to two 'singing clerks' of Gaunt's chapel in 1392 and to an unspecified number of clerks to sing for his younger sons at Kenilworth in 1397–8 are suggestive of an interest in polyphony.[2] Singing was always at the heart of the medieval chapel royal, but the first half of the fifteenth century saw its musical accomplishments reach new heights, supported by a surge in the number of chaplains there and at St George's College, Windsor. Although most of the evidence for this dates from Henry V's reign, it was a process that began under his father, who in turn was influenced both by Gaunt's patronage of noted musicians and by the polyphonic style now in vogue.[3]

---

[1] BL Add. MS 35,295, fo. 262r. The Henry IV section of Strecche's chronicle has not been printed; the Latin reads as follows: *Hic rex Henricus forme fuerat elegantus, viribus fortis, miles strenuus, in armis acer, in omni actu tirocinii sagax et circumspectus, in bello semper fortunatus, in factis felix et victor ubique gloriosus, in musica micans et mirabiliter litteraturis et maxime in morali.*

[2] By 1408–9 Henry had only four minstrels (E 101/405/22, fo. 32); for singing clerks see DL 28/1/3, fo. 3v (1392); DL 28/4/1, fos. 13v–14r (1397–8). For Mary de Bohun's and Joan of Navarre's interest in music, see above, p. 78, and below, p. 421.

[3] By 1402 there were eighteen chaplains in the king's chapel, more than enough for polyphonic pieces. Henry's statutes for Fotheringhay college in 1410–11 stipulated that there should be twelve chaplains, eight clerks and thirteen choristers and that a skilled instructor should be chosen to train them: F. Harrison, *Music in Medieval Britain* (London, 1958), 22, 27. Some of the best polyphonic pieces of this period can now be heard on *Music for Henry V and the House of Lancaster by the Binchois Consort*, director Andrew Kirkman, with

The most compelling evidence for the musical development of the
chapel royal at this time is to be found in the Old Hall Manuscript, a
collection of mainly three-voice mass movements and motets by several
leading composers of the late fourteenth century and early years of the
fifteenth century. Most of these are prefaced by the composers' names, and
two of them (a *Gloria* and a *Sanctus*) are ascribed to 'Roy Henry'. The
manuscript was probably first compiled around 1417–20 for the chapel of
Prince Thomas, by then duke of Clarence, after whose death in 1421 it
passed into Henry V's chapel and further 'layers' were added. Whether
'Roy Henry' was Henry IV or Henry V has been much debated, although
current opinion favours the latter.[4] However, while there is some evidence
for Henry V's musical ability, there is a good deal more for his father's,
not least Strecche's comment.[5] Henry IV is also the first king known to
have paid one of his chaplains, John Bugby, to teach grammar to the boys
(choristers) of his chapel. According to the mid-fifteenth-century *Liber
Regie Capelle*, there were meant to be separate masters for song and
grammar, but instruction in singing and grammar were so closely linked,
the latter being a prerequisite for the former, that Bugby's appointment
may indicate a more serious turn in the chapel's musical aspirations.[6]
However, even if Henry IV was not the composer of these pieces, the
patronage of musicians by his sons, the brilliance of their chapels and the
adventurous musical programmes adopted there and at institutions such as
St George's College, Windsor, are testimony to their upbringing in an

---

text by Philip Weller (CD, Hyperion Records, 2011); I am grateful to Susan Boynton,
Andrew Kirkman and Philip Weller for their help with this section. For numbers of chap-
lains, see R. Bowers, 'The Music and Musical Establishment of St George's Chapel in the
Fifteenth Century', in *St George's Chapel Windsor in the Late Middle Ages*, ed. C. Richmond and
E. Scarff (Windsor, 2001), 171–212, at pp. 177–83. In the 1390s Gaunt was employing the
French composer Henry Pycard: J. Caldwell, *The Oxford History of English Music I* (Oxford,
1991), 119.

[4] M. Bent, 'Old Hall Manuscript', in *New Grove Dictionary of Music and Musicians*, ed. S.
Sadie and J. Tyrrell (2nd edn, 2001), xviii.376–9. The manuscript is BL Add. MS 57,950
('Roy Henry' inscriptions on fos. 12v and 80v); Caldwell, *Oxford History of English Music I*,
114–15. It may be that in a manuscript composed during his son's reign, Henry IV would
have been referred to as 'Roy Henry le pere', or 'le quart'.

[5] Compare Harrison, *Music in Medieval Britain*, 221, who argued for Henry IV as 'Roy
Henry', claiming that 'there is no contemporary evidence for Henry V's musical ability',
but noted that strings were bought in 1397–8 for the future Henry V's zither (*cithara*): DL
28/1/6, fo. 36v.

[6] Bugby was retained in 1401 for £5 a year *pur apprendre et enformer les enfants de notre chapelle
en la science de gramaire* (Wylie, *Henry the Fourth*, iv.208); *Liber Regie Capelle*, ed. W. Ullmann with
a Note on the Music by D. H. Turner (Henry Bradshaw Society 92, Cambridge, 1961), 57,
66; A. Cobban, *The King's Hall within the University of Cambridge in the Later Middle Ages*
(Cambridge, 1969), 19–20, 60–4 (who also noted, p. 186, that John Cooke, one of the Old
Hall composers, was a clerk of the chapel in 1402–3).

ambience that was at the forefront of contemporary musical innovation. A serious interest in serious music became a Lancastrian family habit. With their encouragement, the English chapel royal became famed for its virtuosity, and by the mid-century was admired throughout Europe for the quality of its chant.[7]

The evidence for Henry's literary and educational interests is less equivocal. As well as appointing the first known grammar master in the chapel royal, he was also the first English king known to have appointed a keeper of the king's books, for which two desks were built in the king's new study at Eltham.[8] When there was time, he took the opportunity to read more widely, as at Bardney abbey in 1406. A list of the king's books which ended up in the hands of a London stationer a few years after his death can only represent a fraction of his collection, but affords clues to his literary tastes.[9] His historical works consisted of Higden's *Polychronicon* and a volume of *Smale Cronykles*. A 'book called Gower' was probably either a copy of the *Confessio Amantis*, which the poet had dedicated to him, or the volume of praise poems Gower is known to have presented to the king.[10] The remaining books were religious works: two psalters, one glossed in Greek (although Henry is most unlikely to have known any Greek); a *Catholicon*, a popular Latin grammar and dictionary; a copy of Gregory the Great's *Moralia in Job*, one of the most widely read exegetical works of moral instruction; and two bibles, one in Latin and one in English.[11] Although Henry could read Latin, his ownership of an English bible implies a desire for a more accessible text to allow him to arrive at his own understanding of the Scriptures. Like the *Moralia in Job*, it brings to mind Capgrave's comment that Henry enjoyed discussing ethical questions, and

[7] A. McHardy, 'The Chapel Royal in the Reign of Henry V', in *Henry V: New Interpretations*, 128–56, at pp. 138–42; G. Harriss, 'The Court of the Lancastrian Kings', in *The Lancastrian Court: Proceedings of the 2001 Harlaxton Symposium*, ed. J. Stratford (Donnington, 2003), 1–18, at p. 13.

[8] Ralph Bradfield, keeper of the king's books, was a valet of the royal chamber (Summerson, 'An English Bible', 109–15; *CPR 1408–13*, 470); for Eltham, see below, p. 389.

[9] Passing references to Henry's books include a chest full of books buried by John Holand at Dartington (Devon) and forfeited after his execution in 1400 (E 101/699/25), and a payment to Alice Drax of London for binding some royal books in July 1411 (E 403/608, 23 July).

[10] L. Staley, *Languages of Power in the Age of Richard II* (Philadelphia, 2005), 347.

[11] J. Stratford, 'The Royal Library in England before the Reign of Edward IV', in *England in the Fifteenth Century*, ed. N. Rogers (Stamford, 1994), 187–97; Summerson, 'An English Bible', 115. Henry also borrowed a copy of Gregory the Great's works from Archbishop Arundel (Aston, *Thomas Arundel*, 319n).

his ownership of a silver bookmark suggests that his books did not simply gather dust on the shelves of his desk.[12]

The values of between £5 and £10 given for these volumes indicate that they were illuminated, but they cannot have compared with the luxury manuscripts bought or commissioned by Henry. Two in particular stand out. On his way to the Holy Land in 1393, probably at Venice, he acquired a three-volume antiphonary illuminated in the prestigious Bartolo workshop in Siena which he presented to the Franciscans of Mount Syon at Jerusalem, where it can still be seen.[13] Equally, if not more splendid, was Henry's Great Bible (*Magna Biblia*), illuminated by Herman Scheere and still in the British Library. At 2 ft × 8 in (63 × 43 centimetres), with 350 folios and 166 illuminated initials, it is the largest English bible to have survived from the Middle Ages and may have been intended for readings in the chapel royal.[14] It has several illuminations of St Jerome in his study, showing desks perhaps similar to those built for Henry at Eltham. His son recognized the beauty and value of the volume: in his last will of June 1421, Henry V directed that although it was currently deposited with the nuns of Syon (Middlesex), it was to be returned after his death to the possession of his as yet unborn son. Such sentiments lend support to the argument that it was Henry IV and Henry V, rather than the traditional Edward IV, who were the real founders of the royal library in England.[15] Nor was the care Henry had taken with his sons' education before 1399 allowed to lapse, for shortly after he came to the throne he granted an annuity of ten marks to John Wodehouse to teach grammar to Princes Thomas and John. Monstrelet said that all the king's sons were 'well educated in knowledge' (*bien adrecez en science*).[16]

One chronicler, writing much later, believed Henry also to have been a great builder, but in truth his architectural legacy was inferior to most of his predecessors and successors.[17] Richard II spent about £900 a year on

---

[12] J. Lutkin, 'Goldsmiths and the English Royal Court 1360–1413' (unpublished PhD thesis, Royal Holloway and Bedford New College, 2008), 117. I am grateful to Jessica Lutkin for sending me a copy of her thesis; *De Illustribus Henricis*, 111.

[13] *Treasures of a Lost Art* (Metropolitan Museum of New York, 2003), 58–9. It is displayed in the *Studium Biblicum Franciscanum*, Jerusalem.

[14] BL Royal 1 E IX. It was one of the main display items in the British Library's 2011 exhibition *Royal: The Manuscripts of the Kings and Queens of England*.

[15] As argued by Stratford, 'The Royal Library in England', 193–7.

[16] Somerville, *Duchy of Lancaster*, i.177; *Monstrelet*, ii.337; for their tutors in 1397–9, see above, p. 306. Henry also maintained the usual thirty-two scholars at Cambridge during his reign (E 28/8, no. 6; E 101/405/14, fos. 20–1).

[17] *Johannis Lelandi*, I (2), 310: *in palatiis quae aedificavit rex Henricus nullus in regibus eo gloriosor in diebus suis* (anonymous). Henry completed Richard II's great rebuilding of Westminster Hall

building works, Henry IV £700, and Henry V £1,400, although the figures
for Henry IV and V do not include sums spent on the duchy of Lancaster
houses and castles, which were not placed under the control of sheriffs and
thus separately funded. Henry IV's most important new projects were the
gatehouse of Lancaster castle and the rebuilding of Eltham palace. The
Lancaster gatehouse was begun in 1399 and not completed until late in
Henry V's reign. Paid for by the duchy at the rate of 200 marks a year, it
had two imposing octagonal towers surmounted by projecting battlements
topped off by twin towers with machicolations.[18] In an age known for its
greater emphasis on comfort and less on defensibility, the architect at
Lancaster was clearly under orders not to compromise. Above the central
archway was a niche with a statue of John of Gaunt flanked by shields with
the arms of the king and the prince of Wales – a monument to dynastic
power in the north.

Eltham may have had a moat, a drawbridge, and a 'great wall' (over
which the duke of York was alleged to have planned to climb at Christmas
1404), but it was not a castle. It was Henry's favourite retreat, where he
brought his new queen for eight weeks in 1403 and where he usually spent
Christmas.[19] Barely had he become king when he set in train the building
of a grand new suite of royal apartments to the west of the chapel. In addition to the usual service areas (kitchen, buttery, pantry, scalding-house,
larder, saucery, and a latrine adjoining the moat), this included a new
royal chamber, 38 ft by 18 ft (11.5 × 5.5 metres), parlour, 51 ft by 13 ft (15.5
× 4 metres) oratory and study, all constructed of timber with wainscoted
ceilings, bay windows, stone fireplaces and connecting spiral staircases
(*wyndyngstaires*). Next to the king's chamber there was also a 'secret chamber',
divided by a partition wall (*entreclose*). The windows in his chamber were
glazed with crowns, shields, collars, flowers, birds, beasts and babewyns
alongside the customary *Souvenez vous de moi*, the arms of St George, and
figures of St George, the Trinity and the Salutation of the Virgin.

---

under the direction of his master-mason, Henry Yevele, added a new gate to the palace,
'facing the king's highway, to the west', and built new defensive towers at Calais and
Southampton, the latter stocked with guns; there were, as ever, constant repairs and maintenance; the council noted in 1411 that £1,000 needed to be spent 'for repairing castles and
manors': H. Colvin, R. Allen Brown and A. Taylor, *History of the King's Works: The Middle
Ages* (2 vols, London, 1963), i.199, 532–3; E 403/608, 12 and 15 May 1411; *POPC*, ii.11.

[18] Colvin et al., *King's Works*, ii.69, 2–3.

[19] See Itinerary pp. 542–5. He spent Christmas at Windsor in 1402 and at Abingdon in
1403, probably because Eltham was being reconstructed, but the only time after 1403 that
he was not at Eltham for Christmas was in 1410; he also spent Easter there four times and
paid many other visits. For the duke of York's escapade, above, p. 264.

The king's new study, a place for seclusion and contemplation, had less Lancastrian and more sacred imagery; its seven-light window was filled with the figures of St John the Baptist, St George, Becket, the Trinity, St John the Evangelist and (in the middle, occupying two windows) the Salutation of the Virgin. These were Henry's favourite devotional images: among the New Year gifts he distributed in 1402 were a golden tabernacle of the Trinity garnished with pearls and a sapphire, another with images of the Coronation and Salutation of the Virgin, and a golden tablet of St George on a tower.[20] His study had a 'great desk' on two levels 'to keep the king's books inside', another, smaller desk, and two benches in which books were probably kept as well. He may also have kept his chessboard here.[21] Nearby were separate chambers for the king's confessor and the keeper of his jewels. In 1403, work began on a complementary suite of rooms for Queen Joan, two storeys high and 35 ft (10.668 metres) wide, including a parlour and two withdrawing chambers, one on each floor, with bay windows. By the time this was completed in 1407, at least £1,100 had been spent at Eltham under the supervision of the king's master carpenter, a post held from 1399 to 1404 by Hugh Herland, the man responsible for the hammer-beam roof of Westminster great hall, and thereafter by Thomas Tuttemond.[22] Yet although the new royal apartments at Eltham reveal something of the way Henry spent his leisure, it was also a place for work. Elsewhere in the palace there were individual chambers for officers and friends whose advice the king most frequently sought: John Beaufort (chamberlain), Thomas Erpingham (under-chamberlain), the treasurer of England, the steward, treasurer and controller of the household, John Norbury and Mary Hervy, governess to Henry's younger children. The amenities at Eltham were certainly conducive to relaxation – it had a 'great garden' with vines, a park in which jousts were held to entertain the Byzantine emperor at Christmas 1400, a bath-house and a dancing chamber (*camera tripudiancium*) built by Richard II – but no king could escape the cares of ruling for long.[23]

Government records show just how burdensome those cares were. On average, Henry responded to around fifty or sixty petitions a week. Most of

[20] E 101/404/18, mm. 2, 4.
[21] Colvin et al., *King's Works*, ii.930–7; DL 28/1/4, fo. 17v (chessboard); E 101/502/21 and 23 (desks and glazing).
[22] E 101/496/7; E 28/14, no. 234. For Herland and Tuttemond, see E 404/24, nos. 103, 497.
[23] E 101/502/21.

these were requests for grace or favour: lands, offices, benefices, custodies, pardons for crime, requests for forfeited goods or allowances of timber, venison, even rabbits.[24] More time-consuming financial and judicial decisions would be siphoned off to the council or the justices, but Henry dealt with matters concerning the royal grace in person.[25] Naturally he did not do so unaided. Before petitioners were admitted to the king's chamber, they would already have had to convince the chamberlain or his deputies that theirs was a deserving cause. The quality of the advice the king received mattered greatly, not just from his chamberlains and councillors but also from intercessors. The mediation of intercessors was crucial, and intercession a routine and accepted method of securing royal favour, seen not so much as undue influence (although it could become that) as another way for the king to take counsel.[26] The royal chamber was a crowded arena at times when the king was hearing petitions. It was 'for the quiet and tranquillity of our royal person' that Henry announced in November 1402 that in future he would only deal with petitions on Wednesdays and Fridays, to leave more time for 'our other honest occupations'.[27]

Of these, there were many. Between October 1404 and August 1405, Henry ordered the issue of some 1,500 letters under the great seal and many hundreds more under the privy seal and signet, as well as dealing with 2,500 or so petitions. This was in addition to presiding for six weeks at the parliament of October 1404, holding at least three great councils, conducting negotiations with foreign powers, preparing an expedition to Wales in the spring, spending most of June and July in the north dealing with the risings of Scrope and Northumberland, then returning in August to confront the French expeditionary force in the Welsh marches. This was an age of overwhelmingly personal kingship.

[24] Brown, 'Authorization of Letters under the Great Seal', 125–56; Dodd, 'Patronage, Petitions and Grace', 126, points out that 'grace' could in practice mean back payment for wages still owing; in 1404–5, the payment of annuities became more of an act of grace than a right. When Maude Merlond, a poor *oratrice* from Portugal, asked the king for permission to take one rabbit a week from Sumbury park for her sustenance, the king told her she could take two (E 28/9, no. 73).

[25] G. Dodd, *Justice and Grace: Private Petitioning and the English Parliament in the Late Middle Ages* (Oxford, 2007), 236–7.

[26] Dodd, 'Patronage, Petitions and Grace', 115–16. When the king imprisoned rather than beheaded forty-five men after the Epiphany rising, 'it was said to them that they should sue before the king himself *through their friends* in the meantime in order to have charters of the said king concerning their aforesaid grace and pardon' (E 37/28).

[27] *Foedera*, viii.282; this was endorsed by the commons in the thirty-one articles of 1406 (*PROME*, viii.370); by 1424 it meant that petitions were received on a Wednesday and answered on a Friday (*Select Cases in King's Council*, ed. Leadam and Baldwin, xvi, xix).

Nevertheless, Henry managed to maintain an aura of accessibility, a welcome contrast to the 'kingship of distance' cultivated by his predecessor.[28] Negotiations between the king and speakers in parliament were strongly worded and often exasperating, but they *were* negotiations in a way that the toxic exchanges of Richard's parliaments were not. This 'conversationality' was also one of the characteristics of the poetry circulating amongst the clerks and lawyers who worked in the Westminster offices or the royal household, which was political and critical without being menacing.[29] Whether or not it is literally true that Richard II used to sit on his throne after dinner 'talking to no one but watching everyone', obliging those who caught his eye to bend the knee, it suggests a kingly style far removed from that of Henry IV and Henry V, who preferred after dinner to have a cushion placed on the sideboard in the royal chamber, against which they 'would lean for the space of an hour or more to receive bills and complaints from whomsoever would come'.[30]

Accessibility was one facet of the regal image which Henry projected. John Strecche also claimed of the king that: 'all the people of his realm were so moved by the sight of him that in many towns his face – a sweet sight to his friends, a fearsome one to his enemies – was painted and fashioned in prominent places so that people could always gaze at him and observe his countenance and features'.[31]

The only surviving contemporary statue of the king stands above the east window of Battlefield chapel, Shrewsbury, which does not seem to be the prominent position envisaged by Strecche; nor is Henry known to have commissioned any portrait paintings of himself, unlike Richard II.[32] It may be that what the chronicler meant was that it was the king's supporters who erected images of him, as Henry did for his father at Lancaster, but if so his testimony is uncorroborated. Yet it would be unwise simply to dismiss

---

[28] Saul, *Richard II*, 453–4.

[29] Nuttall, *Creation of Lancastrian Kingship*, 130; note also the almost chatty way in which Henry's parliaments were reported in the *Continuatio Eulogii* (*CE*, 395, 399, 409).

[30] G. Stow, 'Richard II in the *Continuatio Eulogii*: Yet Another Alleged Historical Incident?', *Fourteenth-Century England V*, ed. N. Saul (Woodbridge, 2008), 116–29; Dodd, 'Patronage, Petitions and Grace', 105.

[31] BL Add. MS 35,295, fo. 262r (*Et omni popolo regni sui in visu fuerat affectuosus ita ut eius faciem, amicis dulcem, insidis terribilem, per multas civitates pingeretur et formeretur in locis spectabilibus ut sic quod ad eum sepius posset populus intueri, et eius formam faciei vultumque videre*).

[32] Henry employed four 'king's painters', all Londoners, but their recorded output consisted of banners, shields, the gaily painted royal barges and other such practical tasks: Thomas Gloucester (life appointment from 1400: E 28/8, no. 18); Thomas Prince (annuity of £30 for his office in 1401: E 403/569, 26 March); Thomas Wright and Thomas Kent (E 101/405/22, fo. 30; E 403/612, 20 May); *The Navy of the Lancastrian Kings*, ed. S. Rose (Navy Records Society, 123, London, 1982), 17–18, 82.

it. Propagation of royal imagery focusing on the personal representation of the monarch became more common at this time, and Henry was at the forefront of the trend.[33]

It is in this context that the proliferation of the king's collars and other badges, and the controversy they aroused, needs to be seen. Legislation to restrict the distribution of livery badges had been under discussion for over twenty years. Cheap to manufacture and easy to distribute, badges were powerful symbols of allegiance and hence, in the right circumstances, of factionalism. The first significant attempt to control their distribution was the 1390 ordinance, but the abuse of power by Richard II and the Counter-Appellants in 1397–9 led to much stricter regulations being introduced in the 1399 Statute of Liveries. This prohibited their distribution by lords, and limited the king's distribution of them to members of his household or life retainers of the rank of esquire or above, who, moreover, were only permitted to wear them in the king's presence.[34] In the parliament of 1401, Arnold Savage had tried to go further than this and abolish all livery badges, including the king's. Henry managed to resist this demand, however, and the resulting statute permitted him and Prince Henry to go on distributing badges to their followers of the rank of esquire or above. Yet such special pleading on behalf of the Lancastrian affinity clearly caused unease, and Henry also had to promise not to distribute his lesser livery of the crescent and star to men below the rank of esquire.[35]

Henry showed little sensitivity to these concerns. England after 1399 was flooded with **SS** collars, the dozens proudly displayed on the tomb effigies of lords, knights and esquires affording one indication of their ubiquity, the 192 collars handed out by Henry during his 1399 campaign another.[36] The 200 or so senior members of the king's household, the 250 knights and esquires whom he retained, and many of the peers would have received collars, as did others not formally retained by Henry or employed in his household such as the poet John Gower and Robert Waterton's wife Cecily.[37] In total, the number of persons permitted to wear them could well have

---

[33] J. Watts, 'Looking for the State in Medieval England', in *Heraldry, Pageantry and Social Display in Medieval England*, ed. P. Coss and M. Keen (Woodbridge, 2002), 243–67.

[34] *RHKA*, 236–43; Saul, 'The Commons and the Abolition of Badges', 302–15.

[35] *PROME*, viii.148–9.

[36] DL 28/4/1, fo. 15v; D. Fletcher, 'The Lancastrian Collar of Esses: Its Origins and Transformation down the Centuries', in *The Age of Richard II*, ed. J. Gillespie (New York, 1997), 191–204.

[37] The case of the Scottish esquire Richard Maghlyn is instructive: he was granted a collar in 1408 when he did homage to Henry, but was not formally retained for a further year (*RHKA*, 235).

reached a thousand. The **SS** collar also decorated the initial letter of a royal charter to the town of Gloucester in 1399, the civic sword given to the mayor of Dublin in 1402, and the signet used by both Henry IV and Henry V, although not the new great seal made in late 1406, heraldic badges being considered inappropriate for instruments of state.[38] Items of plate and jewellery distributed by the king were commonly engraved with other Lancastrian motifs such as eagles, swans, greyhounds and even red roses, but it was the **SS** collar that was the hallmark of the dynasty.[39]

Henry seems to have thought that his collars conferred membership of something akin to a chivalric order – in 1400 he gave a ten marks' annuity and a collar to one of his esquires 'so that he may maintain the said order' – and at times disregarded the undertakings he had given. In 1406, for example, he gave a collar to one of his sergeants-at-arms 'notwithstanding the statute [of 1399]', and he continued to have crescents made and presumably therefore distributed.[40] The **SS** collar also became an emblem of English monarchy abroad: eight were sent to his sister Philippa in Portugal in 1401, another six to the Bohemian court in 1405.[41] Many of the collars noted in exchequer accounts were made for the king's use, some of them very ornate and costly: for his wedding in 1403, he paid the London goldsmith Christopher Tyldesley £385 to fashion a gold collar engraved with the motto *Soveignez* and adorned with the letters S and X in enamel, nine large pearls, twelve large diamonds, eight rubies and eight sapphires. A similarly elaborate collar for Queen Joan cost £333.[42] The collars which the king gave to most of his supporters were far simpler, usually costing between six and eight shillings, although some were said to be worth as much as twenty pounds.[43]

Badges aroused strong feelings on both sides. John Gower thought of his collar as a gift from heaven, a mark of loyalty and nobility,[44] but to others, ever since Gaunt began distributing them in the 1370s, they had been seen

---

[38] Henry V also had a second 'signet of the eagle', in use from 1413 (*Signet Letters*, 4, 8; DL 28/4/8, fo. 12v).

[39] See the king's jewel accounts of 1401–3 (E 101/404/18 and 22; also BL Harleian Ms 319, fo. 42r). Henry inherited many artefacts with Richard II's livery signs on them, but often had them reworked before giving them away (Stratford, *Richard II and the English Royal Treasure*, 119).

[40] Walker, *Lancastrian Affinity*, 94–6; E 403/589, 3 Nov. 1406; E 403/605, 28 Sept. 1410.

[41] Lutkin, 'Goldsmiths and the English Royal Court', 155.

[42] E 403/589, 3 Nov. 1406; Lutkin, 'Goldsmiths and the English Royal Court', 155–8.

[43] In 1407, five collars cost £1 13s and thirteen cost £4 4s (E 403/591, 13 and 18 July); in 1403, seven cost £2 13s and twelve cost £4 8s. However, Sir Walter Hungerford valued his collar at £20 (*CPR 1399–1401*, 385).

[44] Fletcher, 'The Lancastrian Collar of Esses', 202.

as inimical to peace and unity. Richard II's purpose in donning his uncle's livery in 1394 may have been to signal the restoration of political harmony, but its effect was quite the opposite, inducing the earl of Arundel to complain about the king's partisanship.[45] At times of tension, badges were seized or hastily discarded. At Bayonne during the revolt of 1400, people wearing Henry's collars were arrested; when the rebel earl of Kent arrived at Sonning (Berkshire) en route for Cirencester in January 1400, he snatched the collars from the necks and the crescents from the arms of those guarding Queen Isabella and cast them away, declaring that they would never be worn in England again.[46] Kent would be dead within a week, but **SS** collars remained ubiquitous both in England and abroad through the first half of the fifteenth century. With time, they doubtless came to be identified with English as much as Lancastrian kingship, but when Edward IV ascended the throne in 1461 they were put away, replaced by Yorkist suns and roses. The **SS** collar never quite seems to have transcended its perception as the badge of a faction.

If the **SS** collar was the chief visual medium used for propagandizing the dynasty, Henry presented his persona as essentially chivalric and martial. Hence the dubbing of forty-six Knights of the Bath on the eve of the coronation. However, it did not escape Froissart's notice that although it was Knights of the Bath who accompanied him to Westminster abbey, the insignia which he himself chose to wear was that of the Garter.[47] Founded by that model of chivalric kingship, Edward III, the Garter provided a ready-made opportunity for the king to demonstrate his commitment to martial ideals. Initially this was problematic, for most of the Knights of the Garter in 1399 were Richard II's nominees and unsympathetic to the usurper, perhaps even considering it their duty to overthrow him. In the event, the attrition rate amongst them during the first six years of the reign was so high – four perished during the Epiphany Rising, another four at the battle of Shrewsbury, and a further ten died of various causes – that by 1405 it had proved possible to reconstitute the Order almost entirely (one reason, perhaps, why the putative 'order' of the Bath failed to flourish).[48] Most of Henry's replacements were unexceptionable. They began with

[45] Above, p. 89.

[46] Vale, *English Gascony*, 37; *SAC II*, 286–7; see also *CPR 1405–8*, 277 (the seizure of one of Thomas Mowbray's collars in 1399) and *CPR 1399–1401*, 385 (the seizure of Walter Hungerford's collar in 1400).

[47] Above, p. 149.

[48] Pilbrow, 'The Knights of the Bath', *passim*.

the king's four sons before alternating between scions of aristocratic houses (Arundel, Warwick, Stafford, Westmorland and Kent), loyal followers with unimpeachable military reputations (Thomas Beaufort, Rempston, Erpingham, Stanley, and Lords Willoughby, Roos, Lovell and Grey) and the kings of Castile, Portugal and Denmark.[49] Nevertheless, the combined effect was to turn England's premier knightly fraternity into an extension of the Lancastrian affinity, for the first criterion for election was always loyalty. This is unsurprising, for the cohesion of the fraternity was severely tested by the Epiphany Rising and the battle of Shrewsbury (all three Percys were Garter knights). By 1405, however, unity had been restored, and henceforth, although political reliability continued to determine election, military reputation carried more weight: Lords Burnell, Charlton, Talbot and FitzHugh had all played key roles in Wales or the north, while Robert Umfraville and John Cornwall were two of the most renowned warriors of their day.[50]

This elision between dynasty and fraternity is symbolized by Henry's presentation in 1401 to the college of St George at Windsor of a set of blue vestments including an orphery decorated with the life of Thomas of Lancaster. He also set in motion the institutionalization of the order that was to gather pace in his son's reign.[51] In 1400, he had the Windsor Tables compiled, a list of members to be displayed in the chapter house. It is possible that the first surviving statutes of the Garter were drawn up in 1402, though more likely that they date from 1415.[52] It must at any rate have been at Henry IV's prompting that in 1399 Canterbury convocation asked that the feast of St George, 'the spiritual patron of all English soldiers', be celebrated as a national feast day.[53] By the latter half of the reign the fame of the company was spreading. The catalyst for the eight-a-side tourney between England and Hainault in 1409 was a letter to the king from Jean de Werchin, seneschal of Hainault, the most famous jouster of his age, asking to be allowed to issue a collective challenge to the Garter knights. Henry interpreted this as a request to take on all twenty-six and

---

[49] Henry was the first king to nominate European rulers for the Garter; all three had close kinship ties to the English royal family, although his choices were also designed to strengthen diplomatic relations.

[50] H. Collins, *The Order of the Garter 1348–1461* (Oxford, 2000), 109–18, 292–3 (list).

[51] R. Barber, *Edward III and the Triumph of England* (London, 2013), 280, 295–6, 468; E 403/571, 9 Dec. 1399; *CPR 1408–13*, 265, 394; *The Inventories of St George's Chapel, Windsor Castle, 1384–1667*, ed. M. Bond (Windsor, 1947), 44.

[52] Collins, *Order of the Garter*, 16 and n. 41.

[53] Henry also had St George represented on his great seal and in his stained glass at Eltham: J. Good, *The Cult of St George in Medieval England* (Woodbridge, 2009), 81.

politely suggested that Werchin restrict himself to one, Sir John Cornwall, who would act as the Order's champion (the first time that the Garter was referred to as an order). In the same year the Veronese knight Pandolf Malatesta challenged the earl of Warwick (KG since 1403) to uphold the honour of the Garter in personal combat.[54] All this was, to be sure, good courtly entertainment, but the fall in the number of Ladies of the Garter during Henry's reign, just ten as opposed to thirty-six under Richard II, was also symptomatic of the renewal of the order's original ideals, which had to some extent been diluted during the last quarter of the fourteenth century.[55]

Henry's reign also witnessed the growth of an *esprit de corps* among the Garter knights. In December 1408 messengers were sent out to summon them to London, for what purpose is not stated, but it can hardly have been for the annual St George's day feast.[56] Two Garter Knights, Lords Willoughby and Roos, jointly founded a guild of the fraternity of St George at Boston.[57] In 1409, the members clubbed together to pay for repairs at St George's Chapel.[58] Most of them must also have contributed to the building of the Hospitaller castle at Bodrum (Turkey), begun in 1404, for of the twenty-two shields of arms of English benefactors encircling that of the king on the north wall of the castle, seventeen belonged to Garter knights.[59] Henry encouraged this spirit of solidarity by attending the festivities at Windsor every year except 1408, when he was in the north clearing up after Northumberland's final rebellion, and by committing large sums to maintain the annual celebrations: in 1411 it was estimated that St George's day would cost £972. Hoccleve's two ballads written in 1414 to 'the most noble King Henry V and the most honourable company of the Garter' reflected the order's reversion under his father to the ideals of Edward III. The policy behind this was not opaque: the growing fame of the Order shone a light on Henry's reputation and reinforced the chivalric values of the aristocracy in general and the Lancastrian affinity in particular, as it continued to do under Henry V, who appointed the first registrar of the Order in 1414 and the first Garter King of Arms three years later.[60] Some, perhaps, thought that the Order and its patron saint were becoming

[54] Collins, *Order of the Garter*, 242–3; Given-Wilson, 'Quarrels of Old Women', 37–8.
[55] Collins, *Order of the Garter*, 92–107, 301–3; no ladies received robes before 1405 or after 1409.
[56] E 403/596, 4 Dec. 1408.
[57] John Milner (personal communication).
[58] *CPR 1408–13*, 267, 315.
[59] R. Dennys, *Heraldry and the Heralds* (London, 1982), 102–3.
[60] *POPC*, ii.11; Collins, *Order of the Garter*, 31–2, 118, 213, 216, 262.

too closely associated with the regime. It is striking that the earl of March, despite reaching his majority in 1412, was never elected, despite (or rather because of) his proximity to the royal family. It is also striking that Archbishop Scrope's 1405 manifesto appealed to St George as the 'special protector and advocate of the kingdom of England' – not just of the king, but also of those who sought to reform the king's government, and who perhaps looked askance at the Lancastrianization of England's national saint.[61]

Rarely did Henry miss an opportunity to remind his subjects of his reputation as a warrior – part of the reason, perhaps, why he continued to proclaim his intention to campaign at home and abroad even after he fell sick. In the autumn of 1405 he was said to be preparing to go to Guyenne, in 1406 to Calais, in 1407 to Wales; in 1408 he led his retainers to Yorkshire to intercept Northumberland and Bardolf, although by the time he got there the revolt was over. In 1411 he was still hoping to lead an army to Calais, in 1412 to Bordeaux.[62] In fact the last time the king took the field was during his 1405 Welsh expedition, but he was reminding his people that he still saw it as his duty to uphold the martial values of English kingship. So, too, the great Christian ideal of crusading. In 1410 he told a Prussian envoy that if he could make peace with France he would like nothing more than to go to Prussia again, and in the meantime would not stop any of his subjects from going. Even as death loomed, he had not abandoned hope of returning to the Holy Land, as foretold at the time of his anointing with Becket's oil.[63] Despite the crusader disaster at the battle of Nicopolis in 1396, there was reason for optimism among Christians at this time. Timur's victory over the Ottoman Sultan Bayezid at Ankara (July 1402) raised the hope that he might be persuaded to join an anti-Muslim alliance, and when the great conqueror followed this up by despatching the Dominican friar John Greenlaw to the west to propose an extension of trading contacts, western rulers responded enthusiastically. Greenlaw had travelled widely in Asia Minor and in October 1400 Pope Boniface had appointed him archbishop of Sultania (Azerbaijan).[64] The French welcomed him, Enrique of Castile sent an embassy to Timur's court, and

[61] Good, *Cult of St George*, 82.
[62] E 101/405/25, m. 2A; E 403/606, 23 March 1411; *SAC II*, 608–10; *POPC*, ii.33, 120; *CPR 1405–8*, 361; *CPR 1408–13*, 321. In August 1411 a council was summoned to discuss the king's plan to go abroad (E 403/608, 28 Aug. 1411).
[63] Lloyd, *England and the German Hanse*, 124; below, p. 516 (Jerusalem in 1413).
[64] *Original Letters*, i.5 5–6; Wylie, *Henry the Fourth*, i.313–15.

Henry gave Greenlaw letters for his friends in the region to try to stir up anti-Muslim sentiment.[65] To the emperor of Abyssinia Henry expressed his joy at the rumour that he planned to recover the Holy Sepulchre from the enemies of the faith, adding that he too had visited Jerusalem and very much hoped to return. Similar letters were sent to the emperors of Trebizond and Constantinople and the king of Georgia. Henry wrote to Timur himself and his son, Miran Shah, thanking them for their support for Christians in the east and congratulating them on the defeat of Bayezid. Greenlaw also carried letters for Michael Steno, doge of Venice, and King Janus of Cyprus, both of whom were friendly towards Henry and would be instrumental in any crusading enterprise.[66]

Henry's response to Timur was in line with that of other Western European monarchs who, especially since Nicopolis, viewed the Ottomans as a real threat to Christianity and anyone who opposed them as a potential ally. In fact Timur was also a Muslim, although more tolerant than some towards Christian merchants and pilgrims, but he died in 1405 and before long the Ottomans renewed their relentless expansion. Nevertheless, Henry continued to offer moral support to crusading orders as far as circumstances permitted and was remembered after his death as a king who fought not just for England but for Christendom.[67] It was 'for love of our Saviour's cross', said Strecche, that he had warred in faraway places against unbelievers, thereby earning much praise. John Capgrave expressed similar sentiments forty years later.[68]

Patronage of duels and tournaments was another way for Henry to keep his chivalric credentials in the public eye. Within a few months of his accession he had arranged for Janico Dartasso and Sir John Cornwall to enter the lists against two followers of Louis of Orléans who had come to England hoping to uphold French national honour but were soundly beaten at

[65] Referred to as the king's eastern correspondence, these letters were in fact endorsed 'Jerusalem' and would be better described as his Jerusalem correspondence (BL Cotton Nero B XI, fos. 172–5, endorsement on fo. 173v). Greenlaw left England in February 1403. The letters are printed in *RHL I*, 419–28.

[66] See the letter to Henry from Queen Anglesia of Cyprus offering to intercede with her brother, the duke of Milan (*RHL II*, 21 Feb. 1405), and the decree of the Venetian Senate in 1407 commenting on Henry's goodwill towards the republic (*Calendar of State Papers Venice*, i. no. 155).

[67] He wrote to Enrique of Castile urging him to support the Hospitallers at Rhodes following a visit by the prior of the Hospital to England in 1410 (BL Harleian MS 431, fo. 12; *Foedera*, viii.654); see also his letter to the pope concerning the Grand-Master of the Teutonic Knights and his support for the building of Bodrum castle (above, p. 397).

[68] BL Add. MS 35,295, fo. 262r; *De Illustribus Henricis*, 99–101.

York.[69] The vitriol accompanying the French challenges of 1401–3 and the English humiliation at Montendre in May 1402 persuaded the king to refrain from further combats, but by 1406 they had resumed, and continued until the end of the reign.[70] Especially notable, not least because they led to resounding English triumphs, were the visit in 1406 of the dashing young Alexander, the Scottish earl of Mar, to joust at Smithfield with the equally dashing young Edmund, earl of Kent, and the week-long eight-a-side combat between England and Hainault in 1409, also at Smithfield, at which the Hainaulters were led by Jean de Werchin but still lost to the English, captained by John Beaufort, by a score of seven to one.[71]

Despite being couched in the language of chivalric brotherhood, there was a sharp jingoistic edge to these challenges. Some combats, however, had a more deadly purpose. Early in 1402 the Hampshire knight Percival Sonday was accused by Yevan ap Griffith Lloyd of treason, and the king ordered that a duel be held at Smithfield; Sonday won and Henry granted him an annuity of forty marks, while his accuser was put to death. Four years later, again accused of treason, Sonday had to fight another duel against the esquire John Walsh; once again he was the victor, while Walsh was immediately drawn to Tyburn and hanged. On 12 August 1407 two citizens of Bordeaux, one of whom had accused the other of incitement to treason, entered the lists at Nottingham in the king's presence, but on this occasion, after they had fought for a while on both horse and foot, the king called a halt, declaring both combatants to have done their duty and discharging them.[72] This was always a king's prerogative, but exercised by Henry in a more chivalric way than Richard had done nine years earlier at

[69] *SAC II*, 302–4. They were Charles de Savoisy and Hector de Pombriant; Walsingham described them as 'arrogant and abusive', but thought one of them to be Italian, perhaps because Sir Richard Arundel did joust with an Italian in the same year. The mayor and aldermen of York erected a chamber for the king, *pour veier certeines poyntz darmes faitz deinz le palaice lerchevesques* (E 101/502/22).

[70] Above, p. 203; *PROME*, viii.102; Given-Wilson, 'Quarrels of Old Women', 37–42; *Giles*, 60. Jousts were held several times a year, mostly at Smithfield: E 101/404/18, mm. 1–2; E 403/571, 22 Nov. 1401, 1 March 1402; E 403/573, 4 April 1402; E 403/591, 1 June 1407; E 403/605, 3 June 1410; E 403/606, 23 March 1411.

[71] *Giles*, 43; *Brut*, ii.369–70; *Great Chronicle of London*, 87; *SAC II*, 478–9; Given-Wilson, 'Quarrels of Old Women', 37–9. The king paid the expenses of Werchin ('the original Don Quijote') and his companions (E 404/24, nos. 533, 538). He also rewarded English knights who went abroad to perform feats of arms, such as John Cornwall in 1409 and Walter Hungerford in 1406 (E 404/24, no. 487; *Foedera*, viii.436).

[72] E 403/571, 1 March 1402; E 403/573, 4 April 1402; *Brut*, ii.368–9; Pepin, 'The French Offensives of 1404–1407', 33; *CGR 1407–9*, no. 25; *Chronicle of London, 1089–1483*, 90.

Coventry. To preside over jousts – a fusion of self-help, regal authority and divine justice – was, in Adam Usk's view, one of the trappings of regality.[73]

If Henry's martial reputation was one of his most exploitable assets, his greatest liability was his questionable assumption of the throne. Even before he became king, chancery and exchequer clerks were being drilled in the art of damage limitation. Documents issued by the administration did not use words such as 'invasion' or 'expedition' to refer to the events of 1398–9. Henry's summer campaign was his 'first arrival' (*adventus*) or 'recent landing' (*applicatio*); the minimal resistance he encountered was 'the malice (*malitia*) of King Richard and other enemies of the lord'. Nor was the term 'exile' used to describe his time in Paris, since it would imply that he had returned unlawfully; rather, he was said to have undertaken a 'certain journey' (*quodam viagio*) or 'crossing to foreign parts' (*transitum versus partes transmarinos*), while his inherited duchy lands were not those which had been confiscated, but those he had held 'before his coronation' (*ante coronacionem suam*). This avoidance of terminology which implied force or illegality on Henry's part was maintained with striking consistency by the new government.[74]

Lancastrian propaganda has long been recognized as both mendacious and effective. To expect it to have been anything other than mendacious would be naïve. It is the business of governments to dissemble; the propaganda of governments is the white noise of history. Yet if the euphemisms and subterfuges employed by Henry to justify his actions did not differ in their essentials from those of his predecessors or successors, the methodical way in which they were carried through was impressive. The thirty-three articles condemning Richard and the text of Henry's claim to the throne, spoken and written in English, reached a wide audience, reproduced in whole or in part by chroniclers summoned to witness the high drama enacted at Westminster in September 1399, and echoed in the work of Chaucer, Gower and popular versifiers. Copies of the *Record and Process*, or something like it, were also sent abroad.[75] Government policies were widely proclaimed and given a disingenuous gloss. The unpopular decision to suspend annuities in 1404 was read out in more than a hundred places up and down the realm, and explained not in terms of insolvency (the real

[73] *Usk*, 176.

[74] See, for example, DL 29/728/11987; SC6/1157/4; DL 28/4/1, fos. 6r, 19r; E 403/564, 6 November; DL 28/1/10, fo. 32v. Richard's administration referred to these events quite differently: see, for example, the chamberlain of Chester's account cited above, p. 133.

[75] J. Scattergood, *Politics and Poetry in the Fifteenth Century* (New York, 1972), 115–16; *Chronicles of London*, 56, 61.

reason) but by the need to distinguish between the deserving and the unde-
serving, a construction designed to appeal to annuitants who used the same
arguments to differentiate those who should be compelled to work, the
able-bodied, from those who could not.[76] Omission might also be propa-
gandist, as with the studied avoidance in government documents of any
discussion of the Mortimer claim: Hotspur was accused of allying with the
Welsh and Scots, of 'calling us Henry of Lancaster and saying that Richard
II is still alive', but no mention was made in government records of his call
to put the earl of March on the throne.[77]

Yet if some historians chose to go on believing Henry's propaganda for
half a millennium or more, it does not follow that his contemporaries did
likewise.[78] Hope, expectation and frustration, ever the handmaids of political change, meant that the language of reform and renewal escaped the
control of its propagators and was taken up by friend and foe alike as the
standard by which to judge the new regime's performance. Time and again
the king's words came back to him in shades of meaning, sometimes querulous or reproachful, sometimes simply baffled. Accusations of Henry's
extravagance, wilfulness and wastefulness, of succumbing to the blandishments of flatterers and ignoring inconvenient truths, even of tyranny – the
substance of his charges against Richard – surfaced early in the new reign
in the petitions of the parliamentary commons, the poetry of advice and
complaint, and the manifestos of his enemies. The framing device used by
the author of *Mum and the Sothsegger*, a poem probably written in 1405, was
that of the narrator's search for someone bold enough to tell the king of
the grievances of his people, because no truth-teller (*sothsegger*) could be
found in the royal household, where all were in thrall to *Mum*, the personification of weak-willed sycophancy.[79] When Henry 'first came to land', his
subjects felt free to complain to him, but now those who did so risked

[76] Nuttall, *Creation of Lancastrian Kingship*, 126; M. Rubin, *Charity and Community in Medieval
Cambridge* (Cambridge, 1986), 68–71.
[77] *Foedera*, viii.313.
[78] See the comments of Clarke and Galbraith, 'Deposition of Richard II', 137.
[79] *Mum and the Sothsegger*, ed. M. Day and R. Steele (EETS, London, 1936). Helen Barr,
The Piers Plowman Tradition (London, 1993), 23, proposed a date of 'shortly after 1409' for the
poem, but early 1405 seems more likely, as its original editors suggested. It certainly dates
from Henry IV's reign and was written after 1402, since it refers to the friars hanged at
Tyburn and to the king's decision in 1402 to hear petitions twice a week (ll. 120, 420, 1672;
Foedera, viii. 282). The reference to licensed and unlicensed preachers (ll. 408–14) is more
likely to refer to the 1401 Lollard Statute than Arundel's *Constitutions* of 1407–9 (*PROME*,
viii.123). There are resonances with the parliament of October 1404, which discussed the
resumption of crown lands and granted generous taxes, thereby helping to restore solvency
to the royal household, but the passage exhorting prelates to counsel the king carries no
reference to the fate of Archbishop Scrope in 1405.

imprisonment or worse, while the parliamentary commons feared the consequences of speaking out.[80] Only in a dream did the narrator find comfort, in the form of an old beekeeper who assured him that ultimately truth would prevail. The poem was by no means inimical to Henry but rather an exercise in loyal criticism larded with complaints about the ills of society and the traditional failings of its orders and estates: monks, friars, bishops, nobles, knights, townsmen and labourers. Yet the central message, that the king lacked someone to tell him the truth, was unmistakable.

Even the supportive John Strecche admitted that Henry 'lost the greater part of the love of his people', because he failed to keep the promises made at his accession. Poets such as the privy seal clerk Thomas Hoccleve and the king's esquire Henry Scogan reflect this loss of trust.[81] Hoccleve's plea for the reinstatement of his annuity was not simply a personal matter; the leit-motiv of monetary fraud running through the *Regement of Princes* (c.1411) also served as a commentary on the government's financial incompetence. Scogan's *Moral Balade*, which was addressed to the king's sons or possibly to the royal household more generally, warned against the dangers of a life of luxury and frivolity. These authors were not outsiders, certainly not enemies of Lancastrian kingship; it was the servants and supporters of the regime who constituted their audience.[82] Yet, needless to say, Henry's enemies also ensured that the language of deceit and mismanagement rebounded on him. The manifestos attributed to the Percys in 1403 and Archbishop Scrope in 1405 echo the *Record and Process* in their talk of harsh taxation, parliamentary manipulation, wasteful government and corrupt counsel.[83] Popular verses in praise of Hotspur and Edmund Mortimer have not survived, nor unsurprisingly has the 'bag' of 'privy prose . . . ballad-wise' referred to in *Mum and the Sothsegger* as bursting with popular opinions on the king's vices and virtues, although echoes of them are to be found in chroni-clers' comments.[84] Popular report, marching with prophecy and dissolving

[80] *Mum and the Sothsegger*, ll. 143–70.

[81] BL Add. MS 35,295, fo. 262r; Hoccleve also emphasized the need for truth-tellers (*Regement of Princes*, 70); E 404/15, no. 115 (£20 annuity to Henry Scogan 'our esquire', 4 Dec. 1399). There is no evidence for the tradition that Scogan tutored the king's sons (cf. D. Gray, 'Scogan, Henry', *ODNB*, 49.313–14).

[82] Nuttall, *Creation of Lancastrian Kingship*, 58–66, 109–22; Scattergood, *Politics and Poetry*, 19–32; G. Dodd, 'Changing Perspectives: Parliament, Poetry and the "Civil Service" under Richard II and Henry IV', *Parliamentary History* 25 (2006), 299–322.

[83] Above (manifestos), pp. 223 and 274.

[84] For example, that in 1401 the people began to grumble against purveyance, or the quip that his decision to tax stipendiary vicars and friars for the first time in 1405 made Henry the first king to have got so many priests to pray for him: *Usk*, 160–1; *SAC II*, 314, 470; *CE*, 389; *Mum and the Sothsegger*, ll. 1343–5.

into rumour, had the potential to inflict real damage on the king, as with the gathering belief that Richard was alive, the Chinese whispers about his undertakings regarding taxation, the martyr-cult focused on Richard Scrope's tomb, or the alleged link between Henry's 'leprosy' and the arch-bishop's death. The suppression in 1401–2 of Welsh minstrelsy (described improbably as 'the cause of the insurrection and rebellion in Wales') and the vain attempts to deny access to Scrope's tomb in York Minster were largely ineffective.[85] Nor was it only among the poor that rumour ran riot: there was, and still is, no certainty as to who was complicit in each of the plots and risings of 1400 to 1405, but the roll-call of those obliged to deny their involvement is testimony to the web of speculation.[86]

Nothing indicates the king's failure to suppress dissent better than his response: the hanging of the friars in 1402, the clampdown on 'vagabonds' spreading rumours, the beheading of the hermit and prophet William Norham at York in 1403.[87] Henry had a keen sense of the power of spec-tacle to create shock and awe, and some of his *coups de théâtre* were jarringly memorable, such as the piecemeal dismemberment of William Clerk at the Tower in 1401, William Serle's stations of the cross from Yorkshire to London in the summer of 1404, the parcelling out of traitors' heads between a dozen or more north-eastern boroughs in the summer of 1405, or the beheading of Archbishop Scrope outside the walls of his city before an audience of prostrate and semi-naked citizenry. Political theatre conveyed a myriad of messages. The bonfire of Richard's blank charters at the London Guildhall in November 1399 was designed to signal the end of government by tyranny. Relatively minor triumphs were celebrated almost like a second Crécy or Poitiers. Following the Epiphany Rising, a parade was led through the city streets to St Paul's by Archbishop Arundel chanting the *Te Deum* in thanksgiving for the sparing of the king's life; the defeat of a Breton raiding party at Dartmouth in April 1404 occasioned another procession, again accompanied by the *Te Deum*, this time to the Confessor's shrine at Westminster, where the king delivered a sermon to

---

[85] *Foedera*, viii.185, 255; *PROME*, viii.211, 362; *SAC II*, 454–6; Raine, *Historians of the Church of York*, iii.291–4; *Signet Letters*, nos. 941, 944. In 1401 a soothsayer, John Kyme, was brought before the council (*Select Cases in Council*, ed. Leadam and Baldwin, xxxiv); the order to the bishop of Lincoln (Repingdon) on 2 January 1406 to search out and imprison soothsayers, magicians and necromancers and, if necessary, bring them before the king was probably more for religious than for political reasons (*Foedera*, viii.427–8; *POPC*, i.288).

[86] An example is the investigation into the abduction of the Mortimer boys (*SAC II*, 430–3).

[87] *Usk*, 122–3; *SAC II*, 380; *CE*, 397.

offer the victory to God.[88] The new great seal cast in late 1406 was iconographically the finest of the late Middle Ages in England, an intricate, yet
integrated, perpendicular reticulation of the patron saints of English
monarchy (Michael, George, Edward the Confessor and Edmund the
Martyr), which also incorporated the change from France Ancient to
France Modern and Prince Henry's arms as prince of Wales, duke of
Cornwall and earl of Chester, a fusion of national and dynastic destiny.[89]
Visibility was one of the salient features of Henry's kingship. By turns
feared and revered, he ensured that royal power could never be ignored.

[88] *Usk*, 89; *SAC II*, 402–5.

[89] The seal was probably used for the first time on 16 Nov. 1406. The change from France
Ancient to France Modern, perhaps prompted by the hope that Prince Henry might marry
a Valois princess, reduced the number of fleurs-de-lys to three: J. Cherry, 'Some Lancastrian
Seals', in *The Lancastrian Court*, ed. Stratford, 19–28, at pp. 20–2; M. Heenan, 'The French
Quartering in the Arms of Henry IV', *The Coat of Arms* 10 (1968–9), 215–21; Bennett, 'The
Royal Succession', in *Rebellion and Survival*, 25; I am grateful to Dr Adrian Ailes for his
comments on Henry's seals.

Chapter 26

COUNCIL, COURT AND HOUSEHOLD

Next after the king in the chain of command, the immediate instruments for the implementation of the royal will, came the council and the household, the latter also serving as the hub around which coalesced the king's court. Although it did not lack political authority, the king's continual or Privy Council was more an executive than a strictly political body.[1] It met almost daily in the Star Chamber at Westminster, usually without the king, although at times of pressure or crisis Henry might summon it to join him elsewhere. When asked to nominate his councillors in parliament, as in 1404 and twice in 1406, Henry gave between seventeen and twenty-two names, but this represented more a pool from which a quorum might be drawn than a list of regular attendees, and in practice business was often transacted by the king's three chief officers – the chancellor (who presided), treasurer, and keeper of the privy seal – often sitting with no more than three or four others; when the king was present, however, numbers could rise to a dozen or even above twenty.[2]

The council's remit was extensive: it heard petitions, advised the king on appointments, military commands and security, debated diplomatic initiatives, helped to plan campaigns, acted as the principal conduit for information between Henry and the Westminster offices, and had the legal power to subpoena witnesses, informants or suspects (heretics, spies, rumour-mongers), to take bonds and oaths and to impose fines or imprisonment, though not corporal or capital penalties. Sensitive cases, some involving the exercise of equitable jurisdiction, were sometimes referred to it, for which the king's legal officers would attend, although its relationship to the

---

[1] There was confusion over terminology, with the Privy (continual) Council sometimes described as the Great Council: *Signet Letters*, no. 258; *PROME*, viii.244–5; Brown, 'Commons and Council'; J. Kirby, 'Councils and Councillors of Henry IV', *TRHS* (1964), 35–65; Brown, *Governance*, 30–42.

[2] Dodd, 'Henry IV's Council', 112; *PROME*, viii.152, 244–5, 338; *POPC*, i.295.

common law was carefully monitored.[3] Its principal responsibility, however, was finance: it negotiated loans (and individual councillors were themselves regular lenders), determined priorities, juggled assignments on local revenues and drew up working budgets.[4] At parliament's request, it was also meant to approve royal grants, leases, wages and expenses: the frequent addition to Henry's grants of the clause 'with the assent of the council' was one way in which he sought to guard against criticism of his generosity.[5]

With the exception of some changes following the 1403 rebellion, the composition of the council was fairly stable through the first seven years of the reign. The three chief officers apart, the bishops who attended most frequently were lawyers such as Richard Young of Bangor and (until they both died in 1404) John Bottlesham of Rochester and John Trefnant of Hereford.[6] More influential than any of these was the dean of Hereford, John Prophet, who had served as clerk of the council under Richard II until dismissed in 1395, was reappointed in 1399, became Henry's secretary in 1402, and then keeper of the privy seal from 1406 to 1415.[7] Archbishop Arundel was also present at a number of meetings during the first year of the reign and was frequently consulted ad hoc during the following three years, but only attended regularly after he was nominated as a councillor in the January 1404 parliament.[8] Of the lay magnates, those most commonly present prior to Shrewsbury were the earls of Northumberland, Westmorland, Worcester and Somerset, but after the fall

[3] Thus a meeting on 8 July 1400 which considered the duchess of Norfolk's claim for dower and an allowance claimed by the bishop of Winchester was attended by eight of the king's justices and sergeants-at-law (C 49/67, no. 24); for the council's judicial work, see *Select Cases before King's Council*, ed. Leadam and Baldwin, Introduction; Brown, *Governance*, 132–4. Dodd identified over 150 petitions submitted to the council between 1399 and 1406 ('Henry IV's Council', 96). The 1399 and 1406 parliaments asked that personal actions not involving the king should be tried by common law, not the council (*PROME*, viii.79, 371). See also the letter from the royal clerk James Billingford to the chancellor in June 1400: 'The king does not intend to seal anything concerning the common law with the seal he has in his own keeping, for which God be praised!' (*CDS*, v, no. 882).

[4] Harriss, 'Budgeting at the Medieval Exchequer', 179–96.

[5] E 404 (warrants for issue), *passim; PROME*, viii.230, 279.

[6] Brown, 'Commons and Council', 30; for Young's role as a councillor see Allmand, 'A Bishop of Bangor'; he replaced Bottlesham at Rochester in 1404.

[7] It was Prophete who inspired the regularization of council record-keeping from the early 1390s, testimony to the council's growing importance as well as important evidence of its composition and activities: Baldwin, *King's Council*, 388–90; A. Brown, *The Early History of the Clerkship of the Council* (Glasgow, 1969), 8–16. He was replaced as king's secretary by William Pilton, former receiver of the chamber (*CPR 1405–8*, 288).

[8] See, for example, E 28/7, no. 70: John Doreward sent from the council to Otford to seek Arundel's advice on whether or not the liberties and franchises of Cork should be confirmed (31 Aug. 1400); Arundel received an annual fee of £200 after 1404 for being a member of the council (E 403/591, 2 May).

of the Percys, Westmorland spent more time in the north and Richard
Grey, John Lovell, Thomas Berkeley and William Willoughby, all peers,
joined Somerset as the senior lay councillors. Following his release from
prison in late 1405 the duke of York also began attending, while the successive appointments as treasurer of William Lord Roos (1403–4) and Thomas
Lord Furnivall, brother of the earl of Westmorland (1404–7), also gave the
council a more secular profile.[9]

It was among the lesser lay members of the council that the greatest
degree of continuity was to be found between 1399 and 1406. Henry relied
heavily from the start of his reign on knights and esquires such as John
Norbury, John Cheyne, Hugh Waterton, John Doreward and John Curson,
and in time they were joined by others: Arnold Savage from late 1402, John
Pelham and John Stanley from 1404.[10] The influence of this knightly bloc
was probably resented by some, and they in turn would not have forgotten
the fate of Bussy, Green and Le Scrope in 1399. Yet Henry's councillors
were more independent-minded than Richard's – as witness Savage's
forthright criticisms when speaker of the commons. It was only in late
1406, when Prince Henry began to flex his muscles, that these knights and
esquires – the king's men rather than the prince's – were relieved of their
duties. The council over which Arundel presided in 1407–9 was more aristocratic though less unified, especially towards the end when the financial
strain began to tell and the king's two eldest sons were vying to exert
influence.

Given Henry's financial and other problems, it is not surprising that
successive parliaments exhorted him to choose his councillors wisely and
nominate them publicly. The first criterion for membership was naturally
loyalty, but the king also valued men of intellectual calibre. Richard Young,
bishop of Bangor and then Rochester, diplomat and member of the
council from 1399 to 1405, was a lawyer of international stature who had
acted as an intermediary between the pope and the emperor and was the
author of several works on the Schism. Archbishop Arundel was a bibliophile whose library at his death was valued at £550, and a friend of the

---

[9] E 403/591, 12 June (duke of York).

[10] During the first eighteen months of the reign, a further group of esquires and London
merchants were also designated as continual councillors (William Brampton, Richard
Whittington, John Shadworth – all Londoners – John Freningham and Thomas
Coggeshall), but they either resigned or were dismissed following the 1401 parliament,
possibly on grounds of 'insufficiency' (Brown, 'Commons and Council', 8). The inclusion
of merchants on the council was novel, although there is little evidence that they
attended regularly; their primary role was probably to help negotiate loans: Baldwin, *King's
Council*, 151.

great humanist chancellor of Florence, Coluccio Salutati. Nicholas Bubwith, by turn king's secretary, privy seal keeper and treasurer, and his friend Robert Hallum co-sponsored a Latin translation of Dante's *Divine Comedy*. Thomas Langley, bishop of Durham, privy seal keeper, chancellor and another bibliophile, reorganized the administration of his palatinate and founded a chantry in Durham cathedral to teach grammar and song to poor children.[11] Nor was it only the king's clerical councillors who left literary remains. Edward, duke of York, passed his time in detention in 1405 by writing *Master of Game*, a translation with additions of the hunting treatise, *Livre de la Chasse*, written by Gaston Phoebus, count of Foix (d.1391), which he dedicated to Prince Henry. John Tiptoft compiled a common-place book into which he inserted 'Tiptoft's Chronicle'; his son, who became earl of Worcester, was a noted humanist scholar.[12]

As well as intellectual breadth, what these men brought to government was a prudent formalism. The council laid stress on good record-keeping – to some extent, perhaps, a response to external pressure, but also the preferred approach of men of a scholarly disposition. John Prophet had kept a journal while clerk of the council in 1392–3, and his example was influential, for in October 1401 his successor, Robert Frye, received forty marks for his 'great labours and work' in writing out the acts of the council in past times.[13] How far back 'past times' stretched is difficult to know, but this may represent an effort to collect and rationalize the records of the council with a view to maintaining them more systematically. Council records are quite full for the first seven years of Henry's reign, and the compilation of formularies by privy seal clerks such as Prophet and Hoccleve implies a methodical approach.[14] The council liked lists – lists of duchy annuitants, of exchequer annuitants, of 'the revenues of the kingdom

---

[11] Harvey, *Solutions to the Schism*, 106–23, 134–6, 142; R. Swanson, 'Robert Hallum', *ODNB*, 24.713–6; C. Fraser, 'Thomas Langley', *ODNB*, 32.500–2. Arundel had befriended Salutati while in exile; they exchanged volumes and Arundel confided to him his fear that his library might be dispersed as a result of his exile. Salutati later wrote to express relief at the recovery of Arundel's books, and in his will of 1414 the archbishop made careful provision for their distribution after his death (J. Hughes, 'Thomas Arundel', *ODNB*, 2.564–10; Aston, *Thomas Arundel*, 318–19).

[12] *The Master of Game*, ed. W. and F. Baillie-Grohman (New York, 1904); York was master of Henry IV's hounds. For Tiptoft, see *HOC*, iv.620–8.

[13] *Pur les grandz labours et travail queux il ad euz et sustenuz entour lescripture des actes du conseil en temps passez* (E 403/571, 28 Oct. 1401; cf. also E 403/578, 6 March 1404; E 403/589, 13 Dec. 1406; E 403/591, 12 June 1407). For Frye (clerk of the council, 1399–1421) and Prophet, see Brown, *The Early History of the Clerkship of the Council*, 4–35.

[14] BL Add. MS 24,062 (Hoccleve's formulary); BL Harleian MS 431 (Prophet's letter-book).

of England'.[15] Meanwhile, in 1402 John Leventhorpe began touring the country gathering archives for his 'great project', the Cowcher Books of the duchy of Lancaster, the massive and indispensable work of reference for the duchy council, which also had rooms at Westminster.[16] Paradoxically, much of the evidence for greater attention to record-keeping comes from the early, financially most difficult, years of the reign, but out of this experimentation grew the systematic budgeting, more measured allocation of resources and stricter control of assignments that characterized the period of recovery after 1406.

The exhortations to Henry to choose his councillors carefully were intended not so much as criticism of either the personnel or the work of the council as an attempt to emphasize its public accountability and independence from the court. Under pressure from the commons to spend taxes on the purposes for which they had been voted, it was not easy for councillors to resist the simultaneous pressure of a king and court whose demands were many and urgent and whose priorities were often different. The lack of a clear distinction between Henry's councillors and his counsellors – those who travelled with the royal household or accompanied him on campaign, and from whom he habitually took informal advice – was part of the problem. Men such as Henry's half-brother and childhood companion John Beaufort, or his under-chamberlain and then household steward Sir Thomas Erpingham, to say nothing of Cheyne, Norbury, Waterton and other intimates of the king, personified a certain ambivalence in the operation of governance: dividing their time between meetings of the council and attendance on the king, they must constantly have found themselves pulled in different directions. Yet the cry of 'evil counsellors' was not much raised during Henry's reign, and there was no question of impeaching or dismissing from court those who resigned in 1401 or 1406. Most of them remained close to the king and continued to undertake important roles. Nevertheless, it was not just the commons who wished to see the council maintain a distance from curial interference which they considered appropriate to its fiscal remit, and that is why there was emphasis on its public accountability. Conflicts of interest were a recurrent concern: many of the clerks of the chancery were also fee'd or employed by members of the nobility during the early years of the reign, but the

---

[15] DL 28/4/1, fo. 31v (duchy annuitants, in duplicate, May 1400); E 403/569, 5 Feb. 1401 (exchequer annuitants); E 403/576, 20 July 1403 (clerks assigned *ad componendum certos rotulos de renencionibus regni Anglie . . . ad quantum dicti renensiones se extendent*, for consideration by king and council).

[16] Somerville, *Duchy of Lancaster*, i.157–60.

commons put a stop to this in 1406 by prohibiting them from serving on anyone else's council 'in opposition to the king'.[17]

One area in which the council's remit expanded during Henry's reign was security. Philippe de Mézières – crusader, polemicist, chancellor of Cyprus and councillor to Charles V of France – was of the opinion that at least one-third of a king's military expenditure should be on espionage.[18] Henry IV never spent more than a fraction of this on spies, but he knew the value of good information, and government documents are full of references to *exploratores* or *espies* sent to Paris, Calais and elsewhere to gather news about enemy intentions.[19] Given that spying has rarely, if ever, been absent from war this is not surprising, but the undeclared and unpredictable nature of the Anglo-French war and the piecemeal Welsh revolt placed a premium on good intelligence. Vigilance was a habit Henry had learned early, in the dangerous 1390s, and which the conspiracies and betrayals of his first few years did nothing to break. In Wales, uncertainty about loyalties was endemic and both sides made constant use of spies, while almost anyone Welsh or with Welsh connections in England was suspect.[20] In 1402, with his career as a crown lawyer stalled because of distrust of Welshmen, the chronicler Adam Usk left for Rome in search of advancement, only to find that even here the king's agents were watching him. 'Adam,' wrote a watchful English clerk at the Curia, 'is reckoned amongst us all, on account of his words, to be in some degree not entirely faultless in relation to Owain Glyn Dŵr, and therefore we do not communicate with him openly about this or any other matter.' Disappointed in his ambitions and shunned by the English at Rome, Usk eventually sought the bishopric he craved from the Avignon pope, but this brought him into contact with the earl of Northumberland and Lord Bardolf, by now refugees in Paris, resulting in

[17] *PROME*, viii.372; C. Smith, 'A Conflict of Interest? Chancery Clerks in Private Service', *People, Politics and Community in the Later Middle Ages*, ed. J. Rosenthal and C. Richmond (Gloucester, 1987), 176–91. During the 1390s at least a quarter of the forty-eight chancery clerks had close connections with Gaunt.

[18] J. Alban and C. Allmand, 'Spies and Spying in the Fourteenth Century', in *War, Literature and Politics in the Late Middle Ages*, ed. C. Allmand (Liverpool, 1976), 73–101, at p. 87.

[19] The usual formulation was 'to discover the intentions and plans of the enemies of the king in France and to inform the king and council of their plans', often including 'with all possible haste'. Those sent were usually obscure (often merely 'a certain messenger'), but might include merchants such as the London goldsmith John Bridd. For examples, see E 403/565, 4 Feb. 1400; E 403/571, 14 March 1402 (Bridd); E 403/585, 27 Feb. 1406; E 403/587, 26 June 1406; E 403/591, 23 June 1407. See also Ford, 'Piracy or Policy', 72; Sumption, *Divided Houses*, 289–91, 579–81; D. Crook, 'The Confession of a Spy, 1380', *BIHR* 62 (1989), 346–50.

[20] Davies, *Revolt*, 164, 223.

1407 in his outlawry, excommunication and deprivation of his benefices. A year later he was offered the chance to redeem himself. If he was prepared to go to Wales and 'pretend to be one of Owain's supporters' – in other words, to spy on Glyn Dŵr – then secretly slip away, the king might see his way to pardoning him: 'and that is what happened,' wrote Usk, 'and it was this promise which saved my life'.[21] Pardoned in March 1411, he returned to England to resume his career.

Usk's journey from watched to watcher casts a thin beam of light into one of the darker corners of early Lancastrian government. Spy-fever was rampant at Westminster, especially during the early years of the reign: there were spies at court, among the alien communities in London, foreign clergy, ambassadorial delegations and even in the royal household, and the king was frequently reminded to be discreet. Some of these allegations were true, for almost anyone sent abroad on official business – diplomats, clerics, merchants, heralds – was expected to keep their ears open for information that might be useful to their masters.[22] Yet if spying on, and by, foreign powers was routine, more worthy of note under Henry was the extension of domestic surveillance, arguably the price paid by a usurper. Informers certainly believed they would be listened to. In 1400, at the time of the Epiphany rising, and again in 1408, after Northumberland's last rebellion, so many informers came forward to accuse neighbours or others against whom they bore grudges that it only made matters worse.[23] However, it could end badly for them. Late in 1405 the approver John Veyse of Holbeach (Lincolnshire) accused fifty-nine heads of religious houses in England of secretly sending money to Glyn Dŵr, and although he was exposed as a liar and drawn and hanged, what is striking is the thoroughness with which his allegations were investigated.[24]

Concern over security encouraged the development of 'a widespread system of public espionage', at the centre of which was the council.[25] Its powers to monitor the comings and goings of the king's subjects had burgeoned since the passing of the anti-papal statutes in the mid-fourteenth century and the inquisitorial role assigned to it by the anti-Lollard measures of the 1380s. Summoning suspects for interrogation was now

---

[21] *Usk*, xxv–xxxii, 238–9.

[22] For allegations of spying and an order to Italians to correspond with their countrymen intelligibly, not by 'ciphers or other obscure figures', see *POPC*, i.182, 288.

[23] *SAC II*, 534–5.

[24] *SAC II*, 464–7; R. Griffiths, 'Some Secret Supporters of Owain Glyndŵr?', *BIHR* 37 (1964), 77–100.

[25] Leadam and Baldwin, *Select Cases in the King's Council*, xxxiv–xxxviii (quote).

routine.[26] When treason was not merely suspected but manifest, as in January 1400 or July 1403, it would have been remiss not to send spies to learn what they could,[27] but the failure to anticipate the Percy rebellion encouraged the adoption of a more proactive role. When Bardolf rode north in the spring of 1405, Lord Roos and Chief Justice Gascoigne were told to follow him. In September 1405, a wayfarer called John Kingsley unwisely prophesied to two esquires whom he met up with near Walsingham (Norfolk) that Glyn Dŵr's power would grow because he paid his followers the wages he promised them. He was reported to the village constables, arrested and placed in Norwich castle to await the king's pleasure.[28] Were his travelling companions agents-provocateurs or merely loyal lieges following the king's order of July 1405 that 'vagabonds' spreading rumours should be arrested?[29] The next year saw a clampdown on sorcerers, sooth-sayers and necromancers, as well as further measures against heretics and rumour-mongers.[30] The net was cast ever wider, creating the opportunity for one enterprising rogue, Walter Forster of East Brainford (Essex), to promise suspects that 'thei shuld be scraped owte of the kynges bokes' in return for payment of a mark; he was brought before the King's Bench for extortion.[31]

Nor was economic espionage neglected, as exemplified by the deposi-tion presented by an obscure vigilante called William Stokes to the king's council in 1411, naming merchants and ship-owners who had evaded customs duties and requesting a commission to set up a surveillance network. It was, he declared piously, the obligation of 'every loyal subject and liege to safeguard and be diligent for the honour, prosperity and profit of the king' – although presumably he was not unaware that rewards were offered to those who reported evasions.[32] England was no police state – the means for that were lacking – but as the English government steadily extended its definition of criminal behaviour in the later Middle Ages it simultaneously extended its reach.[33] Given the obstacles to rapid and

---

[26] Forrest, *The Detection of Heresy*, 35–47; H. Richardson, 'Heresy and Lay Power in the Reign of Richard II', *EHR* 51 (1936), 1–28.

[27] E 403/565, 4 Feb. 1400 (spy sent to Cheshire and Lancashire); E 403/578, 10 Dec. 1403 (Hugh Malpas sent to spy on Hotspur in July).

[28] C 49/48, no. 6; Walker, 'Rumour, Sedition and Popular Protest', 31–2.

[29] E 403/582, 18 July 1405; *SAC II*, 380–1.

[30] *POPC*, i.288.

[31] KB 9/186, no. 47 (2).

[32] Baldwin, *King's Council*, 523–5; *RHL*, ii.303–8.

[33] C. Given-Wilson, 'Service, Serfdom and English Labour Legislation, 1350–1500', in *Concepts and Patterns of Service in the Later Middle Ages*, ed. A. Curry and E. Matthew (Woodbridge, 2000), 21–37.

reliable communication at the time, the information-gathering capabilities of Henry's government are impressive. The price, arguably, was the creation of a 'culture of suspicion', but governments generally mind less about this than do historians.[34]

Separate from the council, though not always as far removed from it as some would have wished, was the king's household. The household existed in order to service the king's domestic, religious and leisure requirements, to advertise his majesty through display and ceremony, to provide him with a mobile treasury (the chamber) and authoritative writing-office (the signet), to guard his person and to act as his personal retinue and command-centre when he went to war.[35] In 1402–3 the number of people receiving fees or robes in the household was 522, in 1405–6 it was 644, although after this the number must have fallen.[36] About 70 per cent of them were sergeants, valets, grooms, carters, huntsmen and falconers, constituting the service (or 'downstairs') element of the household, of whom a hundred or more were valets of the stables caring for its thousands of horses. The other 30 per cent were men of higher status: esquires, sergeants-at-arms, knights and clerks. The topmost rung comprised a dozen or so knights of the king's chamber and the household officers: the steward, chamberlain, keeper of the wardrobe, controller and cofferer; the king's secretary, confessor, almoner, physician and surgeon; the master of the king's horses and the dean of the chapel royal. The king's chamber and chapel formed his household within a household, the private apartments where he slept, prayed, relaxed, took counsel and conducted business.[37] Access to it was controlled by the chamberlains, men of high status and great influence: John Beaufort was chief chamberlain from 1399 to 1410; his under-chamberlains were Thomas Erpingham (1399–1404) and Richard Grey of Codnor (1404–13). Running the hall – the public sphere of the household

---

[34] Forrest, *Detection of Heresy*, 233 (quote).

[35] As the king's personal seal, the signet had special authority: in 1405 the chancellor, treasurer, and privy seal keeper wrote to Henry advising him to send letters under his signet to the bishops to persuade them to exact a tax from stipendiary chaplains, since 'we are quite certain that the bishops, stipendiary chaplains and others will be more willing to accomplish your royal wishes in this matter than they would be by letters under the great or privy seal' (*POPC*, ii.100). However, the signet was never accepted by the exchequer (*Signet Letters*, 3).

[36] *RHKA*, 278. In 1405–6 Queen Joan's household was included. Wardrobe books only survive from 1402–3 and 1405–6, but the decline in expenditure after 1406 and the dismissal of aliens in the 1406 parliament make it likely that numbers were pruned.

[37] 'Relaxing' included gaming, which cost Henry at least £400 in 1405–6 (BL Harleian MS 319, fo. 41v).

– was the responsibility of the steward, a post held by key players such as Thomas Rempston (1399–1401), Thomas Percy (1401–2) and John Stanley (1404–13), who had previously been steward of Prince Henry's household (1402–4). The keeper of the wardrobe was the chief financial officer, sometimes called the treasurer of the household; the controller and cofferer acted as the steward's and keeper's deputies. The chamberlain, steward and keeper were sometimes listed among the half a dozen 'great officers of the realm', a reminder that their political influence and spending power made them accountable to the kingdom as well as the king. The Merciless Parliament saw the execution of Simon Burley and John Beauchamp of Holt, Richard II's chamberlain and steward, as well as several chamber knights.

Henry's ministers did not incur such opprobrium. Rempston, Grey, Norbury and Erpingham (twice) were specifically commended by the parliamentary commons for their good service to king and kingdom. The dismissals of 1401, 1404 and 1406 from the household were not for political graft but for financial or xenophobic reasons. The same holds true for almost all parliamentary criticism of Henry's household: it was too large, its expenditure was out of control, it abused its right of purveyance, and some of its officers were incompetent, but parliament did not talk of it in the terms they had talked of Richard II's household, as a malign influence on the king, manipulating the flow of royal patronage and inclining him towards duplicitous or treasonous policies. Henry was often accused of being too generous, but his patronage was generally seen as even-handed.[38]

Two of the household's four main departments were permanently based in London, the other two itinerated with the king. The former were the great wardrobe, which dealt mainly in textiles and was based at Baynard castle near St Paul's, and the privy wardrobe, which was responsible for the armour, artillery and weaponry stored in the Tower of London. The latter two were the chamber, the king's personal treasury, and the wardrobe of the household, which paid the living expenses of the king and his servants. Chamber accounts were not audited at the exchequer and have not survived, but it is clear that thousands of pounds were usually carried around with the household, in addition to a hoard of plate and jewels, frequently pledged for loans – hence the loss of 'countless treasure and crowns' when the royal baggage train was caught in a flood in 1405.[39] Exchequer and duchy of

[38] Dodd, 'Patronage, Petitions and Grace', 107; Harriss, *Shaping the Nation*, 76.
[39] *SAC II*, 462. The king's chamber (*camera Regis*) had two separate, though related, meanings: (i) the king's private apartments; (ii) the king's privy purse. Two accounts of the receiver of the king's jewels survive (E 101/404/18 and 22), but no overall chamber accounts.

Lancaster liveries to the chamber averaged around £6,600 a year during
Henry's reign, but all sorts of casual revenues and windfalls were also paid
into it – fines, ransoms, forfeitures, *douceurs*, fees for licences or charters, the
profits of episcopal temporalities *sede vacante*, occasional income from alien
priories, and much else.[40] Parliamentary or conciliar recommendations to
reserve some of these sources for the wardrobe were in part an attempt to
stop them being swallowed up by the chamber, for which the king resisted
any suggestion of accountability. However, when the wardrobe was hard
pressed, Henry sometimes authorized the transfer of sums from the
chamber, around £10,000 in 1399–1401 and a further £5,445 between
January 1405 and December 1406.[41]

The wardrobe often struggled for cash, and itineration placed additional strains on it. During the ritual half of the year, the series of solemn
feasts from All Saints at the beginning of November to the Garter festivities at the end of April, the king spent most of his time in London or at
Westminster, retiring for a few days or weeks at a time to Eltham, Windsor
or Hertford, but between spring and early autumn he usually travelled
north or westwards, staying for up to a month at favoured residences such
as Pontefract, Kenilworth, Leicester or Woodstock. It was a way for the
king to show himself to his people, hear complaints, gauge the political
temperature of the shires and keep in touch with his supporters.[42] However,
it also obliged the household to requisition lodgings and supplies as it went,
which often meant abusing its right of purveyance. Four of the five keepers
of Henry's wardrobe ran up debts of £10,000 or more by the time they
demitted office (Tiptoft was the exception). At Henry's death, unpaid bills
of the household amounted to £31,500.[43] The decline in household itineration following the onset of the king's illness in 1408–9 was one reason
for the reduction in its expenditure.

[40] A windfall almost certainly paid to the chamber was a 'new carrack' belonging to Peter
Oliver of Barcelona, captured by seven English balingers and other vessels, the hulk and
rigging of which were valued at 4,000 marks and the master's goods at 1,500 crowns; he was
said to have given these to the king 'as a gift' (E 28/23, no. 15; *Antient Kalendars*, ii.74).

[41] Rogers, 'Royal Household', 371, 670; *RHKA*, 90–2.

[42] When Henry spent a night at Bardney abbey (Lincolnshire) in August 1406, Philip
Repingdon rode across from Lincoln and William Lord Willoughby from Eresby
(Lincolnshire) to speak with him (*Johannis Lelandi*, vi.301). For household itineration, see G.
Harriss, 'Court of the Lancastrian Kings', 15–18.

[43] Thomas Tutbury (1399–1401) left debts of c.£10,300; Thomas More (1401–5) c.£12,000;
Richard Kingston (1405–6) c.£10,700; Tiptoft (1406–8) paid off some of these, but Thomas
Brounfleet (1408–13) left debts of at least £10,000 (*RHKA*, 108–9). For the payment of the
king's debts after his death, see below, p. 522.

The five or six hundred men of the household who received fees and robes comprised only the king's formal domestic establishment, the *domus* or *hostiel du roy*. The number of those 'at court' was often much greater. Nobles, prelates, knights, foreign ambassadors or even rulers, messengers, well-wishers and petitioners all gravitated towards the household, many of them bringing their own servants or retainers with them, often scores of them. Prostitutes, paupers and informers followed it, hoping for business, alms or reward.[44] There must often have been well over a thousand people attached in varying degrees to the household, more than those who lived in most English towns, and it is not difficult to envisage the impact it had on neighbourhoods through which it passed, although naturally it also created opportunities.[45] The household spent a lot of time in and around London, where it had well-established sources of supply for food, wine, cloth and much else, from which the capital's drapers, mercers, grocers and vintners made good profits, providing loans to the crown in return.

The royal bodyguard had been enlarged early in the reign following the Epiphany rising, but when the king went on campaign or faced rebellion, the household evolved into an army. For Henry's Scottish campaign in 1400, the household contingent numbered 244 men-at-arms and 1,227 archers, more than a tenth of the English forces; in March 1405, when he planned to enter Wales, it was 144 men-at-arms and 720 archers.[46] Many of those who came to fight for him were his annuitants and retainers, men who were not in receipt of fees or wages and thus not of the *hostiel*, but the speed with which armies several thousand strong could be mustered was impressive, as demonstrated during the week preceding the battle of Shrewsbury. When the king campaigned in person the household also served as the nerve centre of the army, its officers responsible for musters and logistics as well as commanding detachments and securing towns or castles. When Archbishop Scrope rebelled, it was John Stanley, the steward, and his controller Roger Leche who were sent to York to secure the city ahead of the king's arrival.[47] Men such as Stanley, Rempston, Erpingham and Grey were known not just for military but also for organizational ability. Between them they held several of the crucial strongholds of the realm: Rempston was constable of the Tower, Erpingham of Dover castle,

---

[44] *RHKA*, 60, 69–70.

[45] The assizes held by the clerk of the market of the household to requisition supplies continued to be resented: in 1403 it was said that the weights and measures he used were meant to have been burned in Richard II's reign (KB 9/186/47 (3); cf. *RHKA*, 48–53).

[46] *RHKA*, 63; *CPR 1405–8*, 6.

[47] *CFR 1399–1405*, 310.

Robert Waterton of Pontefract. Windsor was held successively by Hugh Waterton (chamberlain of the duchy of Lancaster) and Stanley, Nottingham by Rempston and then Grey.[48]

As a larger and more amorphous body than the household, the court is less susceptible to definition or quantification. It was the political hub of the realm, a locus of favour, advancement and intrigue. To it came those who sought office or pardon, who hoped to influence policy or lawsuits, or who simply wished to touch greatness or enjoy courtly revels. Usually the court was where the king was, but during the later years of Henry's reign the power centre of the kingdom, and thus arguably 'the court', shifted uncertainly between the king and the prince, whose power-base was the council. Already in February 1409 petitioners were beginning to address themselves not to the king and council but to the prince and the council. When the duke of Burgundy's ambassadors came to England seeking support in the summer of 1411, they approached both the prince and the king, separately.[49]

For most of the reign, however, it was the king who defined the character of his court, and three aspects of Henry's court in particular are worth noting. First, as already noted, it had a reputation for anticlericalism.[50] 'There were at that time,' wrote Walsingham, 'many knights and esquires, especially in the king's household (*familia*), who, instructed in the errors of the Lollards, had among other things little understanding of the Eucharist and the mass.'[51] The number of royal familiars who openly questioned Eucharistic doctrine was probably very small, but the assaults on clerical temporalities at the Worcester councils of 1403 and 1405 and the Coventry parliament of 1404 lent credence to the chronicler's fears. Archbishop Arundel deplored the anticlerical bias of royal intimates such as John Cheyne, Robert Waterton, or Thomas Beaufort, who in June 1405 wrested Richard Scrope's archiepiscopal cross from his grasp before sentencing him to death.[52] Part of the problem was that, when Arundel

[48] *RHKA*, 190–5.

[49] E 28/23, no. 24 (from the earl of Westmorland); below, pp. 493–4.

[50] Above, pp. 377–8.

[51] *SAC II*, 798 (and see pp. 424–6, 590); McNiven, *Heresy and Politics*, 72–8.

[52] *SAC II*, 448–57, 480; the fact that Arundel's own nephew, the young Earl Thomas of Arundel, also sat in judgment on Scrope must also have distressed him. For Cheyne in 1399 and 1404, see above p. 288. In November 1406 at Charing Cross, Robert Waterton demonstrated his contempt for the orthodox preacher Richard Alkerton by offering him a curry-comb, implying that he merely wished to curry favour with prelates; he was master of the king's horses, hence presumably the curry-comb. A royal knight who 'had never loved the Church' told Henry in 1402 that the rumours that Richard was alive would not abate unless the friars were eliminated (*CE*, 392, 407; *SAC II*, 591).

came to court, he was a rather isolated figure. Richard II had been criticized for being overly dependent on clerical advice, and few bishops attended Henry's court as a matter of routine during the early years of the reign, although several were councillors. The king's half-brother Henry Beaufort was a powerful figure, but it was not in the service of the Church that his talents were employed.[53] The churchman personally closest to the king was Philip Repingdon, but his reformist views may not have inclined him to take a stand against the disendowment party. After 1406, with the promotion of Bowet, Langley and Bubwith to bishoprics, and with Arundel holding the chancellorship for three years from January 1407, clerical influence at Henry's court increased. Not, of course, that it was only churchmen who stood up for the Church: the king's friend John Norbury was commended by Walsingham for his vigorous opposition to the Lollard Disendowment Bill in 1410 – although it is telling that the chronicler believed him to be 'one in a thousand'.[54]

The second noteworthy feature of Henry's court was the precedence accorded to the king's family, especially after the downfall of the Percys. Power and high office were now increasingly concentrated in the hands of the king's close relatives and it was made clear in a variety of ways that they constituted almost a separate caste or order at the apex of English society. This did not mean simply the queen and the king's sons; his half-brothers the Beauforts, his brother-in-law Westmorland, and his uncle and cousin, successive dukes of York, also fell within the family circle – although it did not extend further than that.[55] Prince Thomas was steward of England, Prince John constable (after 1403), and Westmorland marshal. England's dominions and marches were parcelled out between them; there was a virtual moratorium on promotions within the peerage which might be seen to challenge their pre-eminence; and as the reign progressed more important posts were concentrated in their hands. Prince Henry replaced Erpingham as constable of Dover castle, while Edward of York replaced Rempston as constable of the Tower after the latter drowned in the Thames in November 1406. The king's sons were first to be dubbed Knights of the Bath on the eve of the coronation, first to be nominated to the Order of the

---

[53] Harriss, *Cardinal Beaufort*, 395–6 ('He had no concern for the defence of the Church's liberties').

[54] Walsingham also commended the duke of York for his pro-clerical stance in 1404 (*SAC II*, 420, 590). The king was godfather to Norbury's son, called Henry, and to John Beaufort's son, also called Henry.

[55] See, for example, the way they were styled as 'our dearest brother', 'our dearest kinsman', etc. in the charter witness lists: Biggs, 'Witness Lists', 414–15.

Garter. There were, of course, rivalries within the royal family, but only in the last two years of the reign did they threaten its stability.

Thirdly, Henry's court was a thoroughly masculine place, where manly qualities were valued and few women were to be found. This may have been a reaction to complaints about the number of noble ladies at Richard II's court, but is more likely to have resulted from a combination of preference and circumstances.[56] Henry's daughters, Blanche and Philippa, were sent abroad to be married aged ten and twelve, respectively. The only other woman apart from the queen who had comparable influence with the king was his ever-supportive mother-in-law Joan, countess of Hereford, a cultured, strong-willed and widely respected woman, to whom he entrusted the arbitration of a number of noble disputes and the upbringing of the heirs of his political enemies; she did not live at court, however, but in Essex, at Pleshey or Rochford.[57] There is nothing to suggest that Henry disliked women: he had affectionate relationships with both his wives as well as his mother-in-law, and treated his stepmother Katherine Swynford with respect and consideration, confirming her jointure from Gaunt, granting her 1,000 marks a year from the honour of Bolingbroke, and according her a fine burial in the Angel Choir of Lincoln cathedral after her death on 10 May 1403.[58] However, the years of campaigning, crusading and exile, and the military exigencies of his early years as king, forged strong bonds with his comrades-in-arms and he seems simply to have preferred male company.

The greatest woman at court was, naturally, the queen, who, even if she neither was, nor was expected to be, the mother of a future king, still had many roles to fulfil: companion, intercessor, symbol, diplomatic buffer, financial burden. As duchess of Brittany (and a princess of the French royal blood), Joan of Navarre had at times intervened effectively in great matters.[59] As queen of England, she had the good sense to cultivate a degree of

---

[56] For ladies at Richard's court, see above p. 100; Richard created thirty-six Ladies of the Garter, Henry created ten, nearly all closely related either to himself or to another Garter knight (Collins, *Order of the Garter*, 79–83, 301–3).

[57] She had custody of Richard de Vere, heir to the earldom of Oxford, and John Mowbray, heir to the earldom of Nottingham, after his brother's execution in 1405; in July 1410 she loaned 500 marks 'in exoneration of' all the taxpayers of Essex (E 403/580, 3 Feb. 1405; E 403/602, 2 Dec. 1409; *POPC*, i.348; *CPR 1408–13*, 216, 220; for arbitration, see *CCR 1409–13*, 305, 395; Sandler, 'The Bohun Women and Manuscript Patronage', 282–3).

[58] DL 29/728/11990, m. 2; A. Goodman, *Katherine Swynford* (Lincoln Cathedral Publications, 1994); Henry also granted her four tuns of wine a year in Nov. 1399 (*CPR 1399–1401*, 58, 408). She lived at Lincoln from 1399.

[59] In 1391, heavily pregnant and carrying her children in her arms, she burst into Duke John's bedchamber one night and threw herself to her knees to beg him to release the royal ambassadors whom he had imprisoned in a fit of temper. She also tried to mediate between him and his mortal foe Olivier de Clisson (*Saint-Denys*, i.724–7).

detachment from court politics, especially following the undeclared war with Brittany in 1403–5 and the bruising criticism of her servants in the 1404 and 1406 parliaments. Occasional references to her influence with the king – on behalf of the countess of Oxford in 1404, for scholars at Oxford or Cambridge, or even to secure a brief truce with Brittany in 1407 – demonstrate little beyond conventional queenly intercession, although she did retain men of political influence such as John Norbury and Thomas Chaucer, and the earl of Westmorland thought it worth paying annuities of between £50 and £100 to her secretary, Anthony Ricz, and the esquires of her chamber, John Periaunt and Nicholas Aldrewich.[60]

Yet if Henry's second marriage was a diplomatic failure, it seems personally to have been a success. One chronicler thought that she and Henry had two stillborn children.[61] Just two years apart in age, Henry and Joan shared an interest in music and almost certainly a mutual affection. Her arrival, wedding and coronation in early 1403 were celebrated in great style, following which she and Henry retired to Eltham for eight weeks.[62] Her relations with her stepchildren were good and her personal conduct unexceptionable. Henry is known to have fathered one illegitimate child before he married Joan, but there is no hint of infidelity once he was married and he was certainly no libertine.[63] He resented the criticism of her followers

[60] C. Ross, 'The Yorkshire Baronage, 1399–1435' (unpublished DPhil thesis, University of Oxford, 1950), 410. These annuities might have been connected with Westmorland's tenure of the honour of Richmond, which was claimed by successive dukes of Brittany. Periaunt was Master of Joan's Horses and his wife Joanna was one of the queen's six ladies-in-waiting, as was Aldrewich's wife Constance (E 101/405/22, fo. 31). The Periaunts were Bretons, but granted letters of denization in 1411–12. Norbury and Chaucer were both esquires of the queen as well as king's servants (*CPR 1408–13*, 144, 283, 298, 368, 460). Ricz was Welsh-born (Rhys) but domiciled in Brittany; he acted as proxy for Joan for her marriage to Henry at Eltham in April 1402 (M. Jones, 'Joan of Navarre', *ODNB*, 30.139–41; *Foedera*, viii.339).

[61] Kingsford, *English Historical Literature*, 282, from a 'Northern Chronicle'.

[62] Among Joan's annuitants was the celebrated composer John Dunstaple, whose music was included in the Old Hall Manuscript (BL Add. MS 57, 950). A. Crawford, 'The King's Burden?: The Consequences of Royal Marriage in Fifteenth-Century England', in *Patronage, the Crown and the Provinces in Later Medieval England*, ed. R. Griffiths (Gloucester, 1981), 33–56, says (p. 35) that the wedding and coronation cost £1,500, but including the embassy to collect her from Brittany it was a lot more than that (for expenses connected with her journey, see E 403/573, 15 July 1402; E 403/574, 19–30 Oct., 22 Feb.). The marriage feast, for which the menu survives, was as lavish as that at the king's coronation (BL Harleian MS 279, fos. 45–6).

[63] Henry's illegitimate son, Edmund Leborde, stated in January 1412 that he was in his eleventh year and was the son of an unmarried man and an unmarried woman. He was thus conceived in 1400 or 1401. He was described as 'son of King Henry, scholar, of the diocese of London', when granted a papal dispensation to proceed to holy orders and receive benefices of any kind once he reached lawful age. The dispensation was granted in consideration of the king's devotion to the pope (John XXIII) and the Roman Church; it is not known what happened to Leborde (*CPL 1404–15*, 314).

and did what he could to mitigate parliament's strictures against them. He built new apartments for her at Eltham, gave her a tower hard by the great gate of Westminster palace to store her muniments and conduct her business, and in March 1403 granted her a dower of £6,666, nearly 50 per cent more than that of Anne of Bohemia.[64] This was hopelessly optimistic, and she also found it hard to secure remittances from her dower lands in Brittany.[65] Henry's inability to live up to his promises to Joan burdened his conscience. The will he drew up when he thought he was dying in January 1409 asked that she be endowed from the duchy of Lancaster, and once he recovered he tried to make proper provision for her, but what she received always fell well short of what she was promised.[66]

Henry's generosity to Joan was symptomatic of a purposefulness, almost wilfulness, in Henry's attitude to the finances of his court and household. Whatever he had, or was thought to have, promised about frugal government in 1399, and despite the chorus of criticism, he was determined that the public face of his monarchy would not suffer by comparison with that of Richard II. Had he and Charles VI arranged a summit, or if the prince had married one of the French king's daughters, Henry would assuredly have made it as splendid an affair as the festivities at Ardres in 1396. This was, after all, a man who had a set of nine matching robes – mantles, tabard, tunics, hat – made from the skins of 12,000 squirrels and eighty ermine.[67] As it was, he spent some £40,000 on the arrivals and departures of Queen Isabella, Queen Joan and Princesses Blanche and Philippa, and great but unquantifiable sums on his and Joan's coronations.[68] His two most distinguished guests were Emperor Manuel in 1400 and Cardinal Ugguccione in 1408. Henry ordered his retainers to ride to Dover to greet and escort them to him, and no expense was spared to impress them. If

---

[64] *RHKA*, 31; *CPR 1401–5*, 473; E 28/14, no. 234 (Eltham chamber); Strohm, *England's Empty Throne*, 153–72.

[65] The exchequer issue rolls record many attempts to pay sums to her, and Crawford, 'The King's Burden', 42–3, lists several additions to her dower between 1403 and 1408, which, however, still left it well short of £6,666. She was obliged to surrender her rights in Brittany in Nov. 1404; the earl of Kent's attack on Brehat in 1408 was an attempt to force the islanders to contribute to her dower (*Giles*, 54).

[66] Nicholls, *Collection of Wills*, 204.

[67] E. Veale, *The English Fur Trade in the Later Middle Ages* (2nd edn, London, 2003), 20.

[68] For expenses connected with Isabella, Blanche and Queen Joan, see *POPC*, i.136, 154 (Isabella); E 403/573, 8 May, and E 403/574, 27–30 Oct. (Joan); E 403/573, 15 and 21 July, 26 Sept. (9,500 marks handed over for Blanche's voyage to Germany, but this was far from the total cost). For Blanche's marriage, the ancient royal prerogative to levy a feudal aid for the king's daughter was revived.

this was the conspicuous consumption that in the eyes of many made the cost of his household 'excessive and outrageous', the king probably considered it money well spent. No king – certainly no usurper – could afford to be thought of as a cheapskate.[69]

Equally to the point, Henry's household servants were close to his heart. Many of them had served him for decades through bad times and good. He tried to prioritize the payment of their fees and annuities and regretted his inability to do so. He remembered them by name in his will, asking that the lowly grooms of his chamber who cared for him night and day through his illness be rewarded, and he remembered them on his deathbed, recalling 'those who have been dear to me' and advising his son to 'cherish their loyalty'.[70] It was the steadfastness of such men upon which his kingship was founded, and he knew it.

[69] The king would have been gratified to see the eulogy of him which Emperor Manuel sent to a friend in 1401: the king of 'Britain the Great', he said, 'overflows with many merits and is bedecked with all kinds of virtues. . . . With his might he astonishes all, and with his sagacity he wins himself friends. . . . And he appears very pleasant in his conversations, gladdening us in all ways and honouring us as much as possible and loving us no less. And, while he has gone to excess in all his negotiations, he seems even to blush a little, supposing himself, alone of all, to fall short of what is needed, so magnanimous is this man' (Barker, *Manuel II Palaeologus*, 178–80); cf. J. Lutkin, 'Luxury and Display in Gold and Silver at the Court of Henry IV', in *Fifteenth-Century England IX*, ed. L. Clark (Woodbridge, 2010), 155–78.
[70] *POPC*, ii.12–13; *Johannis Lelandi*, vi.301; *Political Poems and Songs*, ii.121.

Chapter 27

THE ROYAL AFFINITY AND PARLIAMENTARY POLITICS

To those upon whom its sun did not shine, it might have seemed that the royal court basked in a micro-climate sheltered from the concerns of provincial life. Not so: its force was both centripetal and centrifugal, and leading figures at court were also leading figures in their localities, actively promoting and recruiting for the regime, enforcing the decrees of king or council, arbitrating or suppressing local disputes and keeping an ear out for whispers of discontent. Erpingham in Norfolk, Pelham in Sussex, Rempston in Nottinghamshire, Grey in Derbyshire, Stanley in Cheshire or Robert Waterton in the West Riding of Yorkshire – to cite the best-known examples – helped to keep the shires loyal and to ensure that England remained Lancastrian.[1] There was nothing easy about this, for it was impossible for the king's affinity to represent the interests of all his subjects, and the courtiers and councillors at the heart of it were often hated. William Denton, a monk of Colchester who joined the countess of Oxford's conspiracy in Essex, admitted buying a sword with which to kill 'Coggeshall, Leget, Doreward and others', the local bigwigs whom he believed managed the county on the king's behalf. Thomas Coggeshall and John Doreward were royal councillors, Helming Leget an usher of the king's chamber. His fears were not unfounded: when brought to trial in August 1404, he found Coggeshall and Leget sitting in judgment on him.[2]

Trying to be a king for all his people was especially difficult for a usurper. Richard II had reacted to the political crisis of 1387–8 by retaining around a hundred knights and esquires from up and down the country, most of them prominent members of local gentry society, but during the last two

---

[1] S. Payling, *Political Society in Lancastrian England. The Greater Gentry of Nottinghamshire* (Oxford, 1991), 122–4; N. Saul, *Scenes from Provincial Life. Knightly Families in Sussex 1280–1400* (Oxford, 1986), 70–2; M. Bennett, *Community, Class and Careerism. Cheshire and Lancashire Society in the Age of Sir Gawain and the Green Knight* (Cambridge, 1983), 215–19; Castor, *King, Crown and Duchy*, 64–8, 205–6; Harriss, *Shaping the Nation*, 495; S. Rose, 'A Twelfth-Century Honour in a Fifteenth-Century World: The Honour of Pontefract', in *The Fifteenth Century IX*, ed. L. Clark (Woodbridge, 2010), 39–57.

[2] Wylie, *Henry the Fourth*, i.427–8.

years of his reign his policy had changed direction, focusing almost exclusively on the north-west, from which he recruited over a hundred knights and esquires as well as 600 or more yeomen and archers, the infamous Cheshire bodyguard whose depredations so damaged the king's reputation.[3] On the other hand, his retaining policy between 1389 and 1397 had brought him significant benefits both locally and nationally, and as long as the mistakes of 1397–9 could be avoided this was an approach worth pursuing. Yet Henry's choices were limited, for on becoming king he also inherited from his father a ready-made affinity of knights and esquires whose landed interests were primarily in Yorkshire, Lancashire and the north Midlands, and it was to these men in large part that he owed his throne. The conversion of this Lancastrian affinity into a royal affinity was a work in progress from the start of Henry's reign, and by 1406 the number of king's knights and esquires – excluding those who held positions in the royal household such as the knights and esquires of the chamber – was between 200 and 250, representing perhaps 10 per cent of England's county or upper gentry.[4] Many of these were either his or his father's former supporters, but Henry also showed awareness of the need to broaden his support base: of the sixty-five knights whom he retained during his first year on the throne, twenty-six had also been retained by Richard, most of them from the southern half of the country where loyalty to the new dynasty had shallow roots. In part, this was an attempt to assimilate into the Lancastrian polity those who mattered – those, in other words, whom Richard had also deemed to matter, for assembling an affinity was a process best done by working with, rather than against, the grain of the local establishment – but it was also intended to make the royal affinity look less like the Lancastrian affinity. Henry's separation of the duchy of Lancaster from the crown similarly demonstrated the need to differentiate between his public authority as king and his private interests as duke of Lancaster.[5] However, this did not prove an easy policy to maintain. The leniency he had shown to the Counter-Appellants – contrary to the advice of many of his supporters – backfired, and unsurprisingly Ricardian loyalists continued to feature prominently among rebels and plotters up to, and including, the Percy revolt of 1403. Increasingly, Henry

---

[3] Above, p. 123, and *RHKA*, 203–67 (figures on p. 223).

[4] *RHKA*, 226; Rempston and Erpingham were described as king's knights as early as August 1399, but were certainly not Richard II's knights (*RHKA*, 190).

[5] Prince Henry was in fact made duke of Lancaster in November 1399, although it is clear that it was the king who continued to determine how its resources would be utilized.

found himself driven back to rely on those whom he knew he could trust, which usually meant his pre-1399 partisans.

Although it was most marked in the Lancastrian heartland, the influence of the king's retainers was also disproportionate in many other parts of the country. Indeed there was a sense in which the very concept of a royal affinity, even a broadly based one, sat uneasily with the ideal of the king as leader and defender of the community of the realm, for it created the impression that some were more equal than others. Moreover, whatever may have been his intentions at the start of the reign, Henry made little effort to lower his retainers' profile, as witness his extensive distribution of livery collars.[6] By 1404, his attempts to secure compliant sheriffs, MPs and JPs were also becoming more systematic; the fact that this coincided with the most vociferous complaints (not just from Archbishop Scrope) that he had interfered with parliamentary elections and shrieval appointments was not a coincidence.[7]

Nor was it just knights and esquires retained by the king who were appointed. All sorts of other people – ministers, local officials, tenants, servants, annuitants, or simply well-wishers – had varying degrees of attachment or obligation to his cause, sentiments which fluctuated with time and opportunity; indeed it has proved possible, by aggregating a range of connections between king, court and gentry, to argue that around 50 per cent of sheriffs, 60 per cent or more of JPs, and between 70 and 85 per cent of MPs elected during the first half of Henry's reign had personal incentives of some kind to support Lancastrian kingship.[8] Some obviously mattered a great deal more than others: the influence exerted by a small number of dominant and well-connected individuals was crucial in coordinating political support in their localities. Nevertheless, numbers mattered, for Henry's constant need to raise forces during the first half of his reign, often at short notice, gave him frequent occasion to call out his annuitants and retainers en masse.[9] They certainly saw a great deal more armed service

[6] Above, pp. 393–5. Castor, *King, Crown and Duchy*, 9–19, 191–224, 307–8.

[7] Rogers, 'Household of Henry IV', 596–9; *RHKA*, 251–3; D. Biggs, 'Henry IV and his JPs: The Lancastrianization of Justice, 1399–1413', in *Traditions and Transformations in Medieval England*, ed. D. Biggs, S. Michalove and A. C. Reeves (Leiden, 2002), 59–79.

[8] Biggs, 'Reign of Henry IV', 207–9; see also Dodd, 'Conflict or Consensus', 123, 140–9, whose 'deliberately . . . broad-ranging and inclusive' criteria include membership of the 1402 commissions of the peace, attendance at the great councils of 1401 or 1403, and appointment as a sheriff within a year either side of the parliament in question, in addition to retainers, crown annuitants and officers, duchy officials, and evidence of having been involved in the suppression of rebellion. The conclusions in *HOC*, i.184–238, are more cautious.

[9] Above, p. 284.

in the king's name than Richard II's retainers had done, and the part they played in ensuring Henry's survival was immense – nowhere more so than in Yorkshire, where the king retained twenty-five knights, making him the greatest lord in the county and helping to negate the threat from the Percys.[10]

The military worth of Henry's retainers was demonstrated from the start of the reign. On 13 November 1399, he retained John Cosyn of Cirencester, a former esquire of the duke of Gloucester, with an annuity of £10 for life; two months later Cosyn returned the favour with interest by leading his townsmen in 'manfully (*viriliter*)' capturing and beheading the rebel earls of Kent and Salisbury and Lord Lumley, for which his annuity was immediately increased to 100 marks.[11] More often the role of local enforcer was taken by the sheriff, who had the authority to call out the *posse comitatus*, the shire levy; this is what the king's knight Sir Thomas Rokeby of Yorkshire did to intercept Northumberland and Bardolf in 1408.[12] However, much of the military service undertaken by Henry's knights and esquires was performed further from home. They served in Scotland, in Wales, on ships and in garrisons, in Calais and Guyenne, at Shrewsbury in 1403 and in the north in 1405. Sir John Luttrell's dash from Somerset to Shrewsbury in response to Henry's summons to help him fight Hotspur was the type of forced march repeated time and again by his retainers and annuitants. The sheriff of Northampton, where the king happened to be when he heard of Glyn Dŵr's uprising in September 1400, raised forty men-at-arms and 600 archers in a few days to follow Henry to Wales. Those who failed to answer summonses were denied their annuities and presumably other favours as well.[13] Every man counted, for Henry must have known that some of his retainers, such as Sir Hugh Browe in 1403, Sir John Colville in 1405, or the serial rebel Sir William Clifford, would not remain loyal. In numbers there was safety, or at least hope of it. From the king's point of view, this was unquestionably money well spent.[14]

The incompatible allegiances of men such as Browe, Colville and Clifford raise the question of Henry's control of his affinity. As the son of a man who had once claimed that every lord was capable of keeping his dependants in check, but whose case history suggested otherwise, Henry

---

[10] Ross, 'The Yorkshire Baronage', 426; *RHKA*, 228–30.

[11] *CPR 1399–1401*, 86, 127, 182–3; E 404/16, no. 66.

[12] *SAC II*, 532–3; *Hardyng*, 364.

[13] Castor, *King, Crown and Duchy*, 29–30, for cases of annuities refused for failure to perform military service: E 28/23, no. 9 (John Warwick, sheriff of Northants). Above, p. 231 for Luttrell.

[14] *RHKA*, 228–9.

knew that if his retainers were going to support him, he in turn must support them.[15] Financially this entailed an outlay of around £30,000 a year on fees and pensions, leading to parliamentary and extra-parliamentary vituperation at the 'royal knights' who devoured the king's income so that Henry (as he himself was said to have admitted) 'had nothing while others grew fatter by the year'.[16] Around £8,000–£9,000 of this was met by the duchy of Lancaster, but the corollary was naturally that duchy revenues were unavailable for other needs. Those in receipt of duchy annuities included several of the king's key supporters, and they probably counted themselves lucky, for it was a more reliable source than the exchequer.[17] The arrears that accumulated on exchequer annuities, to say nothing of the stops in 1404–5 and 1410–11, had the potential to cause real political damage to the regime, as Henry and Archbishop Arundel were well aware. Yet it was not merely financially that Henry was beholden to those who kept him on the throne. Politically too they obliged him at times to go against his own better judgment. It was 'those standing around the king', according to one source, who would brook no pardon for Archbishop Scrope; it was 'the king's friends' who insisted that Thomas Percy be executed after the battle of Shrewsbury, despite Henry's wish to spare his life. Individually, such tales may or may not be true, but collectively they add up to a perception of the relationship between the king and his retainers. Whatever his personal views on Church reform, Henry seems to have found it impossible to curb the hard-nosed anticlericalism of some of his supporters, despite the harm it inflicted on the image of his court.[18] Even more damaging in the long run was the king's unwillingness or inability to set limits to their control of local administration and justice. The influence and office which the affinity denied to others was a grievance that festered throughout the reign, coming to a head after the onset of Henry's illness in 1408–9. There were times, especially when it really mattered as in July 1403, when Henry's command and control of his retainers was impressive, but at other times it was not clear who was the

---

[15] *Westminster Chronicle*, 82–3; Walker, *Lancastrian Affinity*, 255–61.

[16] *CE*, 407 (quote).

[17] Castor, *King, Crown and Duchy*, 29. Annuities paid from the South Parts of the Duchy in 1403–4 amounted to £3,000, which included £66 to Erpingham, £200 to Thomas Beaufort, £133 to Willoughby, £20 to Rempston, £24 to Hugh Waterton, £26 to John Cornwall and £666 to Queen Joan; when Wales was included in 1409–10 this rose to £6,210 from the South Parts, although some honours normally accounting among the North Parts were included. Annuities from the North Parts of the Duchy amounted to £5,182 in 1406–7 (including £333 to Queen Joan and £206 to Westmorland), and £5,089 in 1408–9 (DL 28/27/1, 27/3, 27/9 and 27/10).

[18] *CE*, 395, 400; *SAC II*, 376–7, 420–2, 450–3; *Giles*, 45.

lord and who the master, and it required a shift in power at the centre after 1409 to begin to correct the imbalance.[19]

The king's gentry affinity was thus a double-edged sword: crucial to the survival of his regime, it simultaneously subverted his efforts to place himself above faction. There were times when the same could be said of his relations with townsmen, most obviously and dangerously in the case of York. The mayor of York from 1400 to 1405 was William Frost, a relative newcomer to the city, patronized by Henry for his compliance with royal demands. He secured loans and built a warship for the king, ensured that unpopular taxes were collected, and manipulated elections in favour of his supporters, in return for which he received royal grants. However, in February 1405 Frost was overthrown in a civic power struggle, as a result of which his rivals also seem to have taken against the king, and there ensued a period of turmoil culminating in Archbishop Scrope's revolt three months later. Henry's reaction was uncompromising: suspending York's liberties, he first appointed John Stanley as keeper of the city with Frost as his deputy, and then, from August 1405, Frost as sole keeper. One of his tasks was to do what he could to discourage the spread of Scrope's martyr-cult, which did little to endear him to the citizens. Yet when the city's liber-ties were restored in June 1406, Frost was re-elected as mayor, if not at the king's bidding then certainly to his liking. A few months later, when his city sergeants were ejected from office for preventing access to Scrope's tomb, the king wrote demanding their reinstatement.[20]

With around six hundred boroughs in the realm and no permanent crown administration at the local level, it was important for the king to ensure that mayors and other civic officials could be relied upon to do his bidding, but in the case of York his reliance on a narrow and unpopular clique went too far. Fortunately this was not the case with the kingdom's first city. London's pre-eminence among English towns was by this time undis-puted: its population by 1400 was around 40,000 and its taxable wealth at least five times greater than its closest rival, Bristol. Richard II had antago-nized Londoners, stoking merchant rivalries in the 1380s and suspending

---

[19] Below, pp. 479–92.

[20] Liddy, 'William Frost', 79–85; *HOC*, iii.138–40; *Signet Letters*, nos. 520, 944; *Historians of the Church of York*, ed. Raine, iii.291–2 (letter of Thomas Arundel and Thomas Langley, 3 Dec. 1405, to the cathedral chapter saying the king has heard of dissension between the keeper of the city and the cathedral over access to Scrope's tomb and alleged miracles there; both parties are told to desist, and the public should be discouraged from visiting the tomb).

the city's liberties in the 1390s, and they made no effort to save him in 1399. By 1400 the unity of the merchant class had been restored, and Henry went out of his way to placate the citizens, granting them financial privileges and lucrative contracts (especially for cloth and jewellery), including them in spectacular celebrations such as those he laid on for the Emperor Manuel, and making sure that when there was good news to report they were the first to know.[21] In return, Londoners acted as a 'quasi-Bank of England', advancing close to £60,000 to the exchequer over the reign as a whole, roughly half of it provided by the drapers John Hende and Richard Whittington, each of whom personally loaned an average of just over £1,000 a year. This was more than the combined total of around £10,500 loaned by all the other towns in the realm.[22] Hende and Whittington were the most prominent of a small but dominant group of wealthy merchants, also including John Woodcock, Thomas Knolles and Richard Merlawe, whom the king patronized and upon whom he relied to ensure the city's loyalty – as in January 1400, when prompt action by mayor Knolles secured the city against the Epiphany rebels.[23] Each of them served as mayor at least once during the reign, and some also rose to prominence in national politics. Two months into his reign, Henry took the novel step of appointing three Londoners, including Whittington, to his council, and in 1404 three past or future mayors of London were appointed by parliament as treasurers of war.[24] Mercantile, and specifically London mercantile, interests also influenced the protectionist legislation against aliens, and the preference given to Calais among the crown's spending priorities.[25]

London was not only the kingdom's capital but also its busiest port: a third of English wool and a half of English cloth were exported through it, 40 per cent of the country's wine imported and 50 per cent of all tunnage and poundage paid there.[26] Ports required constant vigilance: it was here that ships were impressed, fleets assembled and the customs that contributed more than half of all crown revenue collected. Smugglers had to be

[21] Barron, *London*, 22, 39, 49, 58, 231–41; *POPC*, i.248.

[22] Barron, *London*, 13 (quote); Steel, *Receipt*, 141–6 and 142 n. 1. Especially useful was Londoners' ability to advance substantial sums quickly, as in July 1403 or July 1405: E 403/585, 9 Nov. (loan of £2,695 from John Hende of London on 20 July 1405).

[23] Barron, *London*, 336–7; Steel, *Receipt*, 113, 142–3; *Giles*, 7–9.

[24] Baldwin, *King's Council*, 151; E 403/571, 14 March; Liddy, *War, Politics and Finance*, 137–8; *Signet Letters*, no. 260, 346A. The London mayors who became treasurers of war in March 1404 were John Hadley, Richard Merlawe and Thomas Knolles; Merlawe also served as treasurer of Calais (1407–9).

[25] Above, pp. 333–47.

[26] Barron, *London*, 45, 101.

thwarted, corrupt officials brought to book, and collectors regularly summoned to the exchequer to present their accounts and hand over their takings.[27] Spies, aliens and seditious rumours had to be prevented from entering or leaving the realm; at moments of heightened activity or danger, one of the government's first acts was usually to order every port to be closed.[28] All this made it important to cultivate civic leaders, and in several of the major ports Henry did so. Newcastle was effectively controlled during the first half of the reign by the plutocrat Roger Thornton, 'the Dick Whittington of Tyneside', coal and lead merchant and mayor for five of the first six years of the reign, who is said to have spent 1,000 marks of his own money defending the city against Northumberland's troops in 1405. Henry favoured the town, pardoning its 'loyal and faithful lieges' their ancient debts and raising it to county status, and Thornton's son, Giles, secured a place in the royal household.[29] In Bristol, a strategic port of muster and supply for Wales, Ireland and Guyenne, Henry turned to powerful and wealthy ship-owners such as John Stevens, mayor of the town and staple in 1402–3.[30] Dartmouth (Devon), which provided more ships for the crown during the fourteenth century than any other English port, faced a crisis of loyalty in January 1400 when partisans of John Holand, former duke of Exeter, tried to persuade the townsmen to join the Epiphany rising, but the revolt was nipped in the bud. Henry's most active supporter there was John Hauley, whose thirty-year career as merchant, privateer and fourteen times mayor of the town led to his retention as a king's esquire with an annuity of forty marks and a clutch of lucrative

[27] E 403/578, 10 Dec. 1403 (Frenchman smuggling jewels worth 550 marks out of London); E 403/573, 21 July 1402 and E 403/587, 7 May (measures against corruption at Southampton and Bristol); Signet Letters, no. 58 (collector at Hull accused of concealing 1,600 marks); Steel, Receipt, 90 (corrupt collector at Melcombe); E 403/565, 7 April 1400; E 404/15, no. 26; E 403/587, 7 June (general summonses of collectors to London).

[28] For example, in January and July 1400 (the Epiphany rising and the Scottish campaign): E 403/565, 4 Feb. 1400; E 403/567, 13 July 1400; Signet Letters, no. 154 (July 1403).

[29] E 159/182, rotulus 9d (debts pardoned on 10 August 1405, following the northern uprisings); HOC, iv.596–8; Wylie, Henry the Fourth, ii.255–6; Signet Letters, no. 558; Griffiths, 'Prince Henry, the Exchequer and Wales', 210. Thornton was mayor in 1400–1 and 1402–6; see Prince John's letter passing on his information about the 1405 rebellion (RHL, ii.62–4). One of Thornton's sons also married a daughter of Lord Greystoke.

[30] Stevens was commissioned to gather a fleet to 'attack, capture and destroy' Bretons who were preying on English shipping to Bordeaux in August 1403; to raise troops to resist the Welsh and French in June 1404; to provision the garrisons of South Wales throughout 1404 and 1405; and to muster a force to cross to Ireland in May 1406. In November 1403 Henry gave him twenty marks to be distributed according to his discretion among a group of mariners who had been sent from Bristol to rescue Cardiff castle (Foedera, viii.325–6; E 403/578, 12 Nov.; E 403/579, 17 June; E 403/587, 18 May; Liddy, War, Politics and Finance, 49–50, 55; HOC, iv.474–5).

wardships and other grants.[31] Local leaders such as Hauley and Stevens were enormously useful to Henry, and in return he bolstered their authority. At Lynn (Norfolk), the king intervened first to defend the more powerful (*potentiores*) burgesses from the bullying of Bishop Despenser and then in 1405–6 to uphold their authority against the challenge of the middling and lesser (*mediocres et inferiores*) townsmen. Henry's most useful agent in Lynn was the shipowner and merchant John Brandon, who in 1400 captured the Scottish admiral and was regularly employed by the king to hound Frisian and Scottish pirates in the North Sea. Between 1385 and his death in 1414 he served the town as MP, chamberlain, controller of customs and subsidies and mayor of the town and staple, and the king as a diplomat to the Baltic. He was certainly one of the *potentior* burgesses of Lynn, and probably the *potentissimus*.[32]

Henry had good reason to be well disposed towards townsmen. From the moment of his return to England, even before Richard was deposed, they gave him enthusiastic support in the form of loans and offers of homage, and the speed with which the citizens, not just of London but also of Bristol and Cirencester, acted in January 1400 was crucial in suppressing the Epiphany rising.[33] The refusal of the burgesses of Shrewsbury to admit, or even provision, Hotspur's army in July 1403, and of those of Newcastle to admit his father's forces, was similarly instrumental in foiling the Percy rebellion and, despite strong pressure from Northumberland, the mayors of Newcastle and Berwick would not betray the king in 1405.[34] Their reward was royal support for their local authority. Henry's penchant for patronizing small groups of elite merchants was to some extent a consequence of the increasing concentration of power within a narrowing circle of wealthy, and often interrelated, merchant families in England's late

---

[31] M. Kowaleski, *Local Markets and Regional Trade in Medieval* Exeter (Cambridge, 1995), 29–30, 257 (Dartmouth ships); *HOC*, i.345–8 and iii.328–30; *POPC*, i.233–4; E 403/582, 9 May 1405; Hauley owned twelve ships, but fell out of favour with the king in late 1406 and was imprisoned in the Tower. For the background, see Ford, 'Piracy or Policy'. For Dartmouth and John Holand in 1400, see *CIM*, vii (1399–1422), nos. 88–9.

[32] For Brandon, see *HOC*, ii.336–7. He also helped to organize loans from the town to the king (for example, 500 marks in 1402, 200 marks in 1410). Brandon's chief captives in 1400 were Sir Robert Logan, admiral of Scotland, and David Seton, archdeacon of Ross, King Robert II's secretary (E 403/569, 21 Nov.; cf. *CPR 1399–1401*, 291). He headed the list of burgesses who agreed in 1411 to abide by certain ordinances (C 49/68, no. 3). Cf. Parker, 'Politics and Patronage in Lynn', and A. Goodman, *Margery Kempe and her World* (Harlow, 2002), 24–48.

[33] Above, p. 162; E 403/565, 4 Feb. 1400; *Giles*, 7–9.

[34] Wylie, *Henry the Fourth*, i.358–9 (1403); *SAC II*, 377–9 (1405). See also *SAC II*, 457–9, for the distress of the mayor of Berwick at having been hoodwinked into admitting Northumberland in 1405, and his abject apology to the king.

medieval towns, but it also accelerated that process. It meant too that these mercantile elites were increasingly integrated into the framework of royal government and became more directly accountable to the crown.[35] Naval policy, for example, acquired something of the nature of a joint-stock enterprise between king, parliament and the major ports, with the safe-guard of the sea becoming from the 1370s a subject of intense parliamentary debate and one on which the views of the burgesses carried weight.[36] This reached its height during the Pirate War, culminating in the parliamentary decision in April 1406 that the merchants themselves would raise and man a fleet to protect their trading interests. Although both individuals and ports undoubtedly suffered economic loss and commercial disruption, the alternative, to leave English shipping defenceless, was unthinkable and, despite the fact that it required considerable financial outlay, England's merchants – especially the wealthier sort, who traded internationally – favoured a strong naval policy.

Loans too brought towns, and especially their leading citizens, into a closer relationship with the crown, for repayment was often made through assignments on the customs which they collected, resulting in increased control by the wealthier merchants of customs collection, often through the machinery of the staple.[37] The reward for lending came through the enhanced civic power of the principal lenders and a variety of corporate favours. Norwich, for example, which loaned an average of £90 a year to Henry, including one sum of 1,000 marks soon after his accession, was encouraged by the king to request a new charter, and in 1404 became only the fifth town in the kingdom (after London, Bristol, York and Newcastle) to be granted county status.[38] This entailed the election by towns of their own sheriffs and JPs, who answered not just to the town but also to the king, thus involving leading townsmen in royal, as well as civic, governance. Yet the road to Norwich's charter was a bumpy one, indicative of the competing demands on citizens' loyalties, for Bishop Despenser, fearful of losing his hold over his cathedral city and furious that it had taken the side of his great local rival Thomas Erpingham in a bitter dispute between the

---

[35] Liddy, *War, Politics and Finance*, 211–15 and *passim*. This was especially true of the three greatest towns, London, Bristol and York, all of which had by 1399 been granted county status and thus had sheriffs, JPs and escheators who were royal officials.

[36] Liddy, *War, Politics and Finance*, 43–57. Almost 200 ships from Bristol alone were impressed into royal service between 1350 and 1400.

[37] Liddy, *War, Politics and Finance*, 102.

[38] L. Attreed, *The King's Towns* (New York, 2001), 40–1, 155–7; Liddy, *War, Politics and Finance*, 214–15. Londoners went one better, presenting the king with 1,000 marks as a coronation gift (Barron, *London*, 12).

two men, opposed the grant. Braving their bishop's wrath, the citizens assiduously cultivated Erpingham, paying him a fee of £40 a year and sending gifts of wine, capons and swans to his wife, as well as maintaining his quarrels. Norwich's victory was his victory too, an object lesson in the influence enjoyed by leading courtiers in towns as well as in the shires.[39]

English kings always held the whip hand in their dealings with townsmen: the latter's universally acknowledged social inferiority encouraged and justified such behaviour. Nor did English kings fear civic militias as their continental counterparts did: there was no English equivalent in the fourteenth or fifteenth centuries to the Flemish townsmen's stunning victory against the army of Philip IV at the battle of Courtrai in 1302, or the prolonged armed resistance to their rulers of the citizens of Ghent or Liège, let alone the political autonomy of Florence, Venice or Milan.[40] Yet English kings generally respected borough liberties and did not wilfully interfere in civic affairs. Henry's tendency to rely on small groups of leading citizens certainly ruffled some feathers, but as long as those whom he favoured continued to maintain order, arrange loans, provide ships and mariners to protect overseas trade, provision his armies when required, keep their walls in good repair and deny succour to his enemies, he had little interest in how his patronage affected local rivalries or democratic procedures. Nevertheless, the effect of such a policy was to accelerate the process whereby the merchant oligarchies of England's towns acquired a greater say in national government, which meant that it became necessary to listen to their views. Although even the wealthiest and most powerful merchants could not hope to shape political events in the way that nobles or leading members of the gentry could, they increasingly helped to shape the outcomes of those events.

If it was at court, in the council, and in the counties and towns that the day-to-day politics of the kingdom were conducted, it was in parliament that lords, knights and burgesses came together to sanction or debate policy in a formal setting.[41] Numerically, the largest group in parliament was the burgesses, about 170 of whom usually represented the kingdom's boroughs. Strength in numbers was deceptive, however, for their collective

---

[39] *HOC*, i.525; *PROME*, viii.103–4; Attreed, *The King's Towns*, 42, 113; R. Horrox, 'Urban Patronage and Patrons in the Fifteenth Century', in *Patronage, the Crown and the Provinces in Later Medieval England*, ed. R. A. Griffiths (Gloucester, 1981), 145–66 at 149.

[40] Cf. P. Fleming, *Coventry and the Wars of the Roses* (Dugdale Society, Bristol, 2011).

[41] Ten parliaments were summoned during Henry's reign, most of which lasted between six and eight weeks. The shortest was October 1404 (38 days), the longest 1406 (120 days).

voice was weak compared to that of the knights, let alone the lords. It was certainly the lords and knights who were responsible for the plain speaking that characterized many of Henry's parliaments. For the most part, the outspokenness of speakers such as Savage, Tiptoft or Chaucer focused on the government's financial record, but it was not easy to confine these conversations to fiscal matters and at times there was a reproachful edge to the debate, with each side accusing the other of saying things behind its back. Hence Henry's oft-repeated request for the commons to put their complaints in writing.[42] On the other hand, it was made clear time and again that they had no desire to remove the king. Henry's parliaments, it is worth remembering, were thoroughly Lancastrian in composition: half or more of the knights of the shire had connections (some very close) with the king and court, and although the debates were at times disconcertingly hard-hitting, they lacked the bitter edge of collective fear and personal loathing which had characterized several of the parliaments of Richard's reign. Criticism was offered in the expectation that it would be listened to, not slapped down with threats of arrest or treason. That it came largely from the commons helps to explain this. The lords as individuals doubtless had plenty of advice to offer Henry, both in and out of parliament, and there were rivalries and tensions between some of them, but with the exception of the 1399 parliament, a hangover from the previous reign, they did not bring their feuds into parliament; indeed, they give the impression, even before the battle of Shrewsbury and certainly afterwards, of being unusually united in their support for the crown.

It was this unity of purpose among lords and commons which accounted for the candid nature of parliamentary exchanges, just as it was the closeness to the king of Savage, Esturmy, Tiptoft and Chaucer which gave them the confidence to speak the commons' mind. If they fought Henry all the way, he knew that ultimately they wanted him to succeed, and he knew also that although they would exert whatever pressure they could to bring solvency to the exchequer, they probably would grant him taxation eventually. Their frequent commendations of leading figures such as Erpingham and Norbury, their concern for the promotion of the king's children, and their desire to see the succession to the throne securely established, all indicate their underlying commitment to the Lancastrian dynasty.[43] Their reaction to government insolvency certainly involved the imposition of

[42] C. Given-Wilson, 'The Rolls of Parliament, 1399–1421', in *Parchment and People: Parliament in the Later Middle Ages*, ed. L. Clark (Edinburgh, 2004), 57–72.

[43] *PROME*, viii.291, 303, 348; above, p. 295.

unwelcome restrictions on the king's prerogative, but, faced with the king's illness, their response was not to undermine but rather to shore up the regime. Frustrating as it was for Henry to be made to wait so long for taxation, the temper even of the 1406 parliament was quite different from those of, say, 1385–8 or 1394–7. No magnate faction seized the chance to try to bring down the king or his chief supporters. This was not treasonable opposition in alliance with, or manipulated by, disaffected magnates, but constructive criticism allied to a workable programme of reform.[44] Naturally the commons needed to be wary of the reaction of their constituents to what they agreed or granted: hence the declaration in 1407 that any member of the commons who wished could take away with him and 'make known in his country' a copy of Henry's promise not to demand further direct taxation for three years. Yet with a king who had emphasized from the start of his reign the legitimate role of parliament to engage in meaningful political dialogue with him they knew they were on safe ground.[45] There was something of the feel of a 'Lancastrian party conference' to Henry's parliaments, and it is the prerogative of party conferences to hold their leaders to account.[46]

In addition to ten parliaments, the king also summoned thirty or forty great councils. These were generally attended by up to fifty magnates, prelates, ministers and other advisers of the king, although occasionally they were much larger: to that held at Westminster in mid-August 1401, some 300 people were summoned, mostly knights and esquires selected county by county.[47] The most common venues were Westminster and (until the suppression of the Welsh revolt) Worcester.[48] Their business was often financial, especially raising loans, but they also provided opportunities for focused discussion of major issues of governance, war and diplomacy: that of August 1401, for example, debated the king's plans with regard to

[44] Harriss, *Shaping the Nation*, 500; Harriss, *Cardinal Beaufort*, 34–6; Dodd, 'Changing Perspectives'.

[45] *PROME*, viii.428–9, 448.

[46] Dodd, 'Conflict or Consensus', 136–9; Pollard, 'Lancastrian Constitutional Experiment Revisited' (quote at p. 115).

[47] *POPC*, i.155–64; and *POPC*, ii.98–9, lists over 100 people summoned to a council in 1405–6.

[48] During the first six years of the reign the following great councils have been identified, but there were certainly others: Feb. 1400, Aug. 1401, May 1403, Dec. 1403, Jan. 1405, March 1405 (all at Westminster); Oct. 1400, Oct. 1401, Sept. 1402, Sept. 1403, Sept. 1405 (all at Worcester); March 1401 (Coldharbour, London); Jan. 1404 (Sutton); Aug. 1404 (Lichfield); April 1405 (St Albans); 1404–5, month uncertain (Leicester); Jan. 1402 (in or near London); Maxstoke (date unknown, but see *Signet Letters*, no. 293). See also Brown, *Governance*, 174–5; A. Goodman, 'Richard II's Councils', in *Richard II: The Art of Kingship*, ed. J. Gillespie and A. Goodman (Oxford, 1999), 59–82.

Scotland and Wales, while two months later at Worcester, one of the questions considered was whether the king should conduct the war against Glyn Dŵr in person or commit it to deputies.[49] At times, great councils were used to prepare or complete the work of parliaments: thus the parliament which met on 14 January 1404 at Westminster was preceded by a council at Sutton on 11 January, presumably in an attempt to devise a programme to recommend to the commons, while the parliament which ended on 10 March 1401 was followed a week later by the great council at Coldharbour which, among other things, reviewed and stiffened the anti-Welsh legislation. At other times they were held specifically in order to avoid a parliament, such as that of February 1400 which offered the king loans and military service 'in order to avoid the summoning of a parliament' and the imposition of taxation on 'the common people'.[50] They were also a useful way of affirming support for policy initiatives, as in July 1408 when a great council considered whether to send a delegation to the Council of Pisa. Unlike parliaments, which required forty days for the holding of elections, great councils could be summoned at short notice: for those held at Westminster on 28 May and 11 December 1403, summonses were sent out less than a week beforehand.[51]

Also advantageous from the king's point of view was the fact that he could determine both the membership and the agenda of a great council unencumbered by the formalities and expectations of parliaments. Most of those who attended would probably have been regarded as members of the royal affinity. Yet, like parliaments, they sometimes occasioned fierce debate, as in 1403 and 1405 when the seizure of clerical temporalities was discussed, although generally great councils had more of the character of enlarged sessions of the Privy Council, not making policy so much as testing alternatives and planning ways to implement them. What great councils could not do was grant taxes or make statutes; rarely if ever did Henry summon borough representatives to attend them. Nor does he seem to have made attendance at them a test of political loyalty – indeed the king himself was not always present, especially after he became ill.[52] Despite the uneven documentation of great councils, their frequency suggests that they afforded periodic opportunities to test the political temperature, win support for his plans, or put pressure on those from

[49] Lay Taxes, 77; Giles, 26; Usk, 142–4.
[50] POPC, i.102–6.
[51] E 403/576, 25 May; E 403/578, 7 and 10 Dec.; POPC, ii.81–3.
[52] For the Lambeth great council of 1411, see below, pp. 473–4.

whom more was required, and that Henry welcomed and made extensive use of them.

The king's affinity was impossible to define and equally impossible to ignore. It was the premier power-network in the land, providing the arteries by which governmental authority was explained, distributed and enforced. To disable the king, it would also be necessary to disable his retainers, a point grasped by the Percys. When Northumberland embarked on revolt in 1405, his first move was to try to seize Westmorland, the king's chief agent in the north, his second to seize Robert Waterton, the leading royal retainer in Yorkshire. His aim was to stop them raising the affinity in the north; when this failed, he fled. The earl had good reason to resent the power of the affinity: for a year or more before the battle of Shrewsbury, it had increasingly usurped the authority the Percys had hoped to make their own, probably a deliberate ploy by the king to keep their ambitions in check. Generally speaking, however, Henry was well aware of the need to avoid the charge of factionalism, and it would be unwise to judge popular perception of his affinity solely, or even chiefly, on the evidence of those regions in which Lancastrian retainers were thickest on the ground. Large areas of southern England, the most populous part of the country, had seen little Lancastrian penetration before 1399, and continued to be administered mainly by men who had exercised local authority under Richard. For some of them the revolution was an opportunity, for others an inconvenience, but for very few (after January 1400) was it an incitement to rebellion. It is worth noting that the speakers of Henry's parliaments almost all came from the southern shires.[53] Conversely, it was in the north, where Lancastrian influence was strongest, that the most dangerous challenges to Henry's rule originated. If this suggests on the one hand that it was where the local power of the king's affinity was most deeply entrenched that it was also most deeply resented, it also suggests that elsewhere Henry had managed the process of accommodating local power structures to his regime with some success.

[53] Doreward (Essex); Savage (Kent); Tiptoft (Cambridge); Esturmy (Wiltshire); Chaucer (Oxford); the exception was Henry Retford (Lincolnshire), speaker in 1402.

Chapter 28

NOBLES, REBELS AND TRAITORS

Henry's reliance on his family and affinity was to some extent a consequence of the dearth of active and reliable allies among the aristocracy
during the early years of his reign – which also helps to explain why, especially after the Epiphany rising, he entrusted so much power to the Percys.[1]
When they in turn proved unreliable, it was the Beauforts and their brother-
in-law Westmorland, all four of whom the king routinely referred to as his
brothers, who took their place.[2] John, the eldest of the Beaufort brothers
and the king's chivalric companion in his youth, held the powerful post of
royal chamberlain from the beginning of the reign and in 1401 was made
captain of the town of Calais, although he rarely went there in person; he
also acted as the king's chief emissary, taking Queen Isabella to France in
1401, escorting Princess Blanche to Germany in 1402, and conducting Joan
of Navarre to England in 1403. Until his death in 1410 he was the lay
magnate closest to the king. Bishop Henry Beaufort's acquisition of the
chancellorship in March 1403 enhanced the family's influence; he too was
entrusted with some of the most sensitive diplomatic missions of the reign,
especially to France; wealthy and worldly, he could be relied upon not to
place the needs of the Church above those of the state. Thomas, the
youngest brother, was a soldier and a courtier with a puritanical streak who
served for long periods as admiral and under Prince Henry in Wales, and
was later held up as an exemplar of chivalric *noblesse*; later in the reign he
would act as captain of Calais castle and for two years as chancellor, the first
layman to do so for a quarter of a century. Their sister Joan was married to
Westmorland, a regular councillor before Shrewsbury and thenceforward
the agent of royal power in the north. From mid-1403 until early 1407 it was

[1] The earls of Devon, Oxford and Suffolk were politically insignificant; Warwick died in
1401 and the king's uncle, York, in 1402; much was expected of Stafford and Kent, but they
died in 1403 and 1408, each aged twenty-five, the latter childless, the former leaving a one-
year-old son.
[2] Harriss, *Cardinal Beaufort*, 23–67, and his articles on John, Henry and Thomas Beaufort
in *ODNB*, 4, 625–32 (Henry), 637–8 (John), and 643–4 (Thomas).

the Beauforts above all who held sway in Henry's councils, yet unlike the Percys they never acquired a regional power-base they could call their own. Henry Beaufort may have held the richest see in England, but it was not his 'country', while John and Thomas remained largely dependent on crown service, office, annuities, limited term grants and wardships for their income.[3] Henry IV was not a man to trip on the same stone twice.

Nor did the king show any desire to replenish the ranks of the aristocracy. Reacting to the scorn that had greeted the *duketti* bonanza of 1397 and unwilling to jeopardize his family's exclusivity, Henry bestowed only three great titles in the course of his reign: his eldest son became prince of Wales in 1399, his second son duke of Clarence in July 1412, and his half-brother Thomas Beaufort earl of Dorset in the same month.[4] When it was suggested in the 1402 parliament that John Beaufort resume the marquisate he had forfeited in 1399, he was persuaded to decline it, at the king's urging if not command.[5] Bearing in mind that four dukes, a marquis and an earl were taken down a rank in the first parliament of the reign, Henry thus demoted twice as many great nobles as he promoted.[6] In part this was because the number of peers of baronial rank who were politically active was small (although many more were militarily active). The most important of them was Richard Lord Grey of Codnor, whose family had been summoned to parliament since 1299 and whose ubiquitous service as councillor, admiral, diplomat, commander in Wales and under-chamberlain of the royal household for the last nine years of the reign might well have won an earldom from a less cautious king. He was, in effect, the king's replacement for the earl of Worcester.[7] William Roos, William Willoughby, John Lovell and Thomas Berkeley all served on the council during the first half of the

---

[3] The king originally granted 1,000 marks a year to John Beaufort's son, Henry, whose godfather he was; in Nov. 1404 this was increased to £1,000 and transferred to John himself, until lands could be found 'which are not parcel of the crown' (*CPR 1401–5*, 477; E 403/585, 26 March 1406). Thomas Beaufort's grant of the honour of Wormegay (Norfolk) in 1405 was for life, not in fee (*CPR 1405–8*, 105).

[4] The prince also became duke of Lancaster and Aquitaine and earl of Chester in the 1399 parliament. After John Beaufort's death his earldom of Somerset was kept for his son, but it may have been felt that such a great family ought to be represented by an earl at its head.

[5] On the grounds that marquis was 'an alien name in the kingdom' (*PROME*, viii.164–5).

[6] For the demotions in the 1399 parliament see above, p. 189. Thomas Mowbray should be added to their number, for although not judicially stripped of his dukedom of Norfolk it was denied to his family for twenty-five years (R. Archer, 'Parliamentary Restoration: John Mowbray and the Dukedom of Norfolk in 1425', in *Rulers and Ruled in Late Medieval England: Essays Presented to Gerald Harriss*, ed. R. Archer and S. Walker (London, 1995), 99–116, at pp. 101–2).

[7] He was, however, granted a life annuity of 400 marks in 1409 (*RHKA*, 194).

reign and undertook important military or diplomatic tasks, while Thomas Nevill Lord Furnivall replaced Roos as treasurer for two years before his death in 1407.[8] After 1406 Hugh Lord Burnell, who had campaigned repeatedly with Prince Henry in Wales, also joined the council, swept along with the tide that brought the earls of Arundel and Warwick and other retainers of the prince to Westminster.

Below the level of the baronage Henry also liked to keep men hungry, one result of which was that the first quarter of the fifteenth century witnessed the steepest decline in the number of parliamentary peers of any twenty-five-year period during the later Middle Ages, from 102 to 73.[9] The only case of a new summons to parliament which arguably involved discretion on the king's part was that of John Tuchet, whose first summons in January 1404 was as much a reward for his service at the battle of Shrewsbury and in Wales as a matter of pedigree.[10] Under Edward III or Richard II, men such as Thomas Erpingham, John Stanley and perhaps others would probably have been elevated to the peerage, but despite Erpingham's public commendations in the parliaments of 1404 and 1406, expressly designed to elicit royal generosity, Henry was unmoved.[11] Such self-restraint belies the notion that Henry's experience as a great lord under Richard II led him to adopt a more indulgent approach to the nobility.[12] The liberality for which the king was sometimes held to account by the commons was not exercised in favour of his nobles. What he demanded from them was loyalty and service; what he offered them was the security of tenure denied to him by Richard II – provided they remained loyal.

---

[8] For Berkeley, see *Catalogue of the Medieval Muniments at Berkeley Castle*, ed. B. Wells-Furby (2 vols, Bristol and Gloucestershire Archaeological Society, Bristol, 2004), xl–xli.

[9] K. McFarlane, *The Nobility of Later Medieval England* (Oxford, 1973), 172–6, who tabulated rates of extinction (mainly through forfeiture or failure of male heirs) set against replacements through new summonses to parliament; cf. Harriss, *Shaping the Nation*, 97.

[10] Even this was arguably not a 'new summons': E. Powell and K. Wallis, *The House of Lords in the Late Middle Ages* (London, 1968), 436. Tuchet descended from Joan, sister of Nicholas, Lord Audley (d.1391), but was not summoned until 1404 and died in 1408. John Talbot, John Oldcastle and Hugh Stafford were summoned to parliament in 1410–11 because they had married the daughters of peers, Lords Furnivall, Cobham and Bourchier, respectively.

[11] *PROME*, viii.303, 348; S. Walker, 'Erpingham, Thomas', *ODNB*, 18.512–14. Henry V, following his father's lead, exercised similar care with peerage creations, although in Henry VI's minority the lords were more open-handed.

[12] He issued only six licences to crenellate during his reign, five to royal knights or esquires (including John Stanley and Robert Waterton), the sixth for a house at the entrance to Dartmouth harbour to be fortified against seaborne attack (*CPR 1401–5*, 164, 219, 255; *CPR 1405–8*, 161, 207; *CPR 1408–13*, 160, 232).

For traitors, however, the penalties were dire and becoming direr. The convictions of 1387–8 and 1397–8 occasioned deep unease about the use of treason for political purposes – not merely the process of Appeal, which effectively denied a defendant the ability to defend himself, but also the degradation of great families and their dependants and the feuds and property disputes which ensued. Henry's summary execution of Le Scrope, Bussy and Green at Bristol in July 1399 did nothing to calm these fears, for although (not yet being king) he did not bring treason charges against them, he nevertheless declared their property forfeit by right of conquest, since they were 'destroyers of King Richard and of all his realm'.[13] On what precedent, if any, he based his claim to forfeiture by conquest is not clear. No wonder he had to give assurances at his enthronement that he had no intention of seizing further property through conquest, or that the 1399 parliament was wary, for Henry was after all one of the men behind the first parliamentary Appeal of Treason in 1388. Before the session ended he was also obliged to give undertakings that Appeals would never be introduced to parliament again, that he would keep to the definition of treason set down in the 1352 Statute, and that in matters concerning treason he would act 'in a quite different manner' from Richard II. However, two further requests, that the heirs of convicted traitors of 'ancient ancestry' should be allowed their inheritances both in fee simple and in tail, and that the widows of lords convicted of treason be permitted to sue for dower, merely elicited the response that the existing laws should be observed.[14]

Three months later, confronted by manifest treason in the shape of the Epiphany Rising, Henry tempered his justice with a little mercy, as he had promised to do at his coronation, but not a lot. Since the leaders of the rising – the earls of Huntingdon, Kent and Salisbury, and Lords Despenser and Lumley – had conveniently been lynched, the proceedings at Oxford

[13] *PROME*, viii.89–90, 534–5. John Bussy's son John tried to recover the manors of Silkby and Dembleby (Lincolnshire) on the grounds that they had been enfeoffed by his father on the day he died, but his plea was eventually rejected in 1409 on the grounds that parliament had upheld the king's right to them 'by way of conquest, because the said William Lescrope, John Bussy and Henry Green were destroyers of the said King Richard and of all his realm'. Arundel as chancellor gave this judgment, with the advice of the justices (C 49/68, no. 2).

[14] *PROME*, viii.33, 64, 69. In fact he allowed the widows of John Holand (the king's sister Elizabeth) and Thomas Despenser to sue for dower. Fee simple implied primogenitary heritability of land; tail, or 'entail', limited heritability to direct descendants, and could be further limited, for example, to males ('tail male'); it was frequently employed along with a remainder clause, thus creating additional rights in the estate.

castle on 11–12 January concerned the lesser conspirators.[15] Tried before the steward and marshal of the royal household, about two-thirds of the ninety accused were pardoned, although some were sent to prison for a time. Of the principal culprits, twenty-seven were sentenced to be drawn, hanged and quartered, but only four suffered this fate, the others being simply decapitated to spare them the agonies of a traitor's death.[16] When parliament next met, in January 1401, the lynching of the five lords was confirmed as treason even though they had not been sentenced by due process of law, but only the lands they held in fee simple were forfeited, nothing being said about entailed or enfeoffed lands – that is to say, lands in which others also had rights, either through conditional inheritance grants (entails) or post-mortem trusts (enfeoffments to use).[17] Five years later, however, a statute was enrolled which extended this judgment to include lands which they had enfeoffed to their own use, whether to themselves or to others. This was identical to the sentence imposed on Northumberland and Bardolf in the same parliament (1406). If what the king intended was clarification of their sentence, there is no record of it being discussed in parliament, and it is not clear on what authority Henry amplified the judgment of 1401.[18] This may be why on 28 May 1408, by which time Salisbury's son Thomas was twenty and working his passage towards redemption, the king issued an exemplification of the parliamentary judgment of 1401 confirming that his forfeiture had applied only to lands held in fee simple. This had never been enrolled as a statute.[19]

Albeit that it was not described as such, parliament's decision to condemn the five rebel lords in 1401 was an act of attainder, although the recording of the names of twenty-five lords 'who were present at the said declaration' implies some hesitancy about the procedure.[20] Attainder was not new, but it now acquired a sharper edge in conjunction with the novel

[15] A curious entry in the Year Book for the first year of Henry's reign which records the trial of 'G counte de H' – usually taken to mean John, earl of Huntingdon – for high treason before 'D counte de Westmorland' and the lords at Westminster in January 1400, was fabricated either at the time or later as an example of 'How a Lord shall be Tried by his Peers' and is manifestly a forgery. It is difficult to think that Henry IV's lawyers could have been responsible for such a gross misrepresentation and such errors when the events in question were so recent (*Legal History: The Year Books*, ed. D. J. Seipp at http://www.bu.edu/law/seipp/).

[16] E 37/28, and see above p. 163; one, Sir Alan Buxhull, was acquitted; and for John Ferrour's pardon, see above. p. 29.

[17] *PROME*, viii.109–10.

[18] *Statutes of the Realm*, ii.152 (c.v, Northumberland and Bardolf), 154 (c.xii, the 1400 rebels).

[19] *Foedera*, viii.529.

[20] They were not said to have *agreed* with the decision, as the fifty-seven lords who consented to Richard II's imprisonment in 1399 had done (*PROME*, viii.34–5, 110).

idea of corruption of the blood between those convicted of treason and both their ancestors and their heirs.[21] Henry's reign saw this notion of corruption of traitors' blood become more explicit. Paradoxically, there is no direct evidence that sentences including corruption of the blood were passed at this time; references to it are found only in the petitions for pardon from its implications and the responses to them, suggesting that this 'legal doctrine' may have grown up as a precaution on the part of petitioners rather than by judicial decree.[22] When Thomas Haxey petitioned in 1399 for reversal of the sentence of treason passed on him by Richard II, despite the fact that he had already been pardoned, Henry's response was that he should be 'restored to his name and fame' so that his heirs could inherit from him, since the 1397 judgment had 'interrupted' the blood between him and his heirs and forebears.[23] Within another decade, 'interruption' had become 'corruption', more emphatic though probably not different in legal effect. Thus Ralph Lumley's son John petitioned the 1411 parliament that he might be restored to 'the name and ability' of being the son and heir of his father and his other ancestors, 'notwithstanding that the blood between the said Ralph and the said supplicant [John] was corrupted'. Almost identical wording was used by Ralph Hastings when he petitioned the 1410 parliament for restoration of the lands forfeited by his brother Richard in 1405, and by Ralph, son of Sir Henry Green, in 1411, even though Green's father had not been attainted of treason in 1399.[24] William Lasyngby, a Yorkshire lawyer implicated in the 1405 rising, was that rarity, a traitor who survived. Convicted before Chief Justice Gascoigne but for some reason not executed, he was pardoned his treason in February 1408 at the request of Prince Henry, but still had to petition the 1411 parliament for restoration of his and his descendants' name and ability to sue for return of his forfeited possessions, since his

[21] The word 'attainder' had been used during the fourteenth century in a general way as a synonym for 'condemned' or 'convicted', but now 'by an etymological fancy which warped the meaning of the word', it came to mean the 'tainting' or 'corrupting' of the blood (*Oxford English Dictionary*, i.761–2).

[22] For attainder see J. Bellamy, *The Law of Treason in England in the Later Middle Ages* (London, 1970), 177–205; the first parliamentary example of a *sentence* of corruption of the blood was in 1450 (Jack Cade); see also the bill against the duke of Suffolk (*PROME*, xii.202–3). For corruption of the blood as a 'legal doctrine', see *Henry V: The Practice of Kingship*, ed. G. Harriss (Oxford, 1987), 39.

[23] *PROME*, viii.42 (where 'interruption of the blood' is mentioned in the response to the petition).

[24] *PROME*, viii.478–9, 532–5; *CPR 1408–13*, 195–6. Some lands were restored to John Lumley in 1405, but he was never summoned to parliament; his son Thomas was only summoned from 1461, when at the age of 53 he succeeded in having his grandfather's attainder reversed (Brown, 'Authorization of Letters', 137–8).

attainder had corrupted the blood between him and his heirs and between them and 'all their ancestors'. Ironically, Lasyngby was one of the judges in the treason trials of the Southampton conspirators in 1415.[25]

It may be that these petitions, with their emphasis on the ability of a traitor's descendants to inherit from *any* of their ancestors, were designed to cover all eventualities in a world of increasingly complicated tenurial arrangements.[26] The road to recovery was certainly becoming longer, more complex, and more dependent on royal grace, as exemplified by Thomas Montague's struggle to be treated as his father's heir. Although recognized as earl of Salisbury when he came of age in 1409, he was only restored to the entailed lands his father had held at his death. In 1414 he petitioned for the judgment of 1401 to be overturned, but this was refused; only in 1421, by which time he had been an earl for twelve years and proved his worth to Henry V, was he actually acknowledged as 'heir in blood' to his father and granted inheritance of his lands by right, rather than as an act of grace – the crucial distinction both for him and for his own heirs. Even now, however, Henry V kept the lands held at the time of his forfeiture by Salisbury's father, either jointly or individually to his own use, or which others had held to his use, in fee simple.[27] It is similarly worth noting that when Hotspur's son was allowed the title of earl of Northumberland in 1416 he was not *restored* to his grandfather's earldom but created *de novo*. The judgments of 1403–6 against his father and grandfather were thus upheld and the family's rehabilitation presented as an act of grace.[28]

Acts of attainder – which were often passed against those already dead and in any case precluded any defence – had an unsavoury future ahead of them, and the lords were uneasy about refinements in their interpretation.[29] Whether Henry kept his word not to extend the definition of treason is a moot point. The lords were unwilling to be pushed too far, as they made clear in January 1404 by declaring that Northumberland was only guilty of trespass. The conviction of fifteen friars and others in 1402 for what was in effect treason by words could arguably be construed as falling

---

[25] *PROME*, viii.411, 533–4; *CPR 1408–13*, 54, 353; T. Pugh, *Henry V and the Southampton Plot of 1415* (Gloucester, 1988), 130.

[26] Powell and Wallis, *The House of Lords*, 445–6, argued that corruption of the blood was used to seize entailed lands; if not, it facilitated the process.

[27] *PROME*, ix.42–4, 69–70, 293–6. Thomas's 1421 petition stated that but for the 1401 judgment he 'would have been heir in blood' to his father. For his career, see A. Curry, 'Montague, Thomas, Fourth Earl of Salisbury', *ODNB*, 38.767–9.

[28] Harriss, *Henry V*, 38–40.

[29] Bellamy, *Law of Treason*, 116–17, 136–7, 156–64, 183–5, 204–5; Archer, 'Parliamentary Restoration', 101–2.

within the terms of the 1352 act as 'compassing' or 'imagining' the death
of the king, but treason by words was a grey area and, as the king discovered, jurors were reluctant to convict on such grounds.[30] Yet arguably the
most bizarre extension of the idea of treason came not from the king but
from the commons when they insisted in November 1404 that any person
found to be misappropriating the subsidies granted for war 'shall incur the
penalty of treason'.[31] This was not the same as calling it treason, but it
highlighted another development of Henry's reign, the sentencing to a
traitor's death of men not actually convicted of treason. For his involvement in Gloucester's murder, John Hall was condemned in the first parliament of the reign 'to suffer as harsh a death as could be adjudged or
imposed upon him' – drawn, disembowelled, hanged, beheaded and quartered – though treason was not mentioned.[32]

The spate of conspiracies during the first half of the reign certainly led
Henry to mete out more condign punishments. William Clerk, the Cheshire
scribe who criticized the king with both spoken and written words, does not
seem to have been convicted of treason, but nevertheless had his tongue
and right hand cut off before being decapitated, while the drawn-out
agonies of William Serle were, as the king admitted, more dreadful than
any traitor had suffered before. Harsher penalties also extended to forfeitures: when Hotspur and Worcester were posthumously convicted in the
parliament of January 1404, their entailed and enfeoffed lands were
forfeited, as well as those they held in fee simple, while the lands they held
to the use of others were only excluded following a petition from the
commons.[33] The judgments of 1406 against Northumberland and Bardolf
and the rebel lords of 1400 were also careful to state that none of the lands
which any of them had held to the use of others should be forfeited to the
king and that any grants he had made from such lands were null and void;
these were also probably in response to a common petition.[34]

Yet if the road to recovery for the heirs of traitors was growing longer
and the chances of complete restoration of their ancestors' property diminishing, in practice Henry usually allowed them to rehabilitate themselves:

---

[30] *PROME*, viii.231–2; Strohm, *England's Empty Throne*, 25–7; E. Powell, 'The Strange
Death of Sir John Mortimer: Politics and the Law of Treason in Lancastrian England',
in *Rulers and Ruled in Late Medieval England: Essays Presented to Gerald Harriss*, ed. R. Archer and
S. Walker (London, 1995), 83–97.
[31] *PROME*, viii.289.
[32] *PROME*, viii.88–9.
[33] *PROME*, viii.233, 264: the petition said the lands they held to the use of others were 'on
the point of being forfeited if a remedy is not ordained'.
[34] *Statutes of the Realm*, ii.152–4.

Edmund Holand and Thomas Montague were recognized as earls of Kent and Salisbury, respectively, when they came of age despite their forebears' convictions for treason.[35] The stages of the reconciliation process are exemplified in the case of John Mowbray, son of Henry's old foe and brother of the young earl of Nottingham executed with Archbishop Scrope in 1405. In 1407, aged fifteen, John was placed in the care of the king's mother-in-law, the countess of Hereford, with an allowance of £200 a year for his maintenance; in 1410 he joined the king's household and recovered some of his lands, and in the following year his wardship and marriage were sold for £2,000 to the king's brother-in-law the earl of Westmorland, who married him to his daughter Katherine and restored to him, probably at the king's behest, the title of Earl Marshal which had been such a bone of contention between the two families before 1405. Finally, three weeks before Henry IV's death, John received livery of his lands and was recognized as earl of Nottingham, although he continued to badger Henry V and Henry VI for the restoration of his full rights.[36] Henry IV habitually used trusted members of his family to oversee the rehabilitation of his opponents' heirs: the countess of Hereford had custody of Richard de Vere, heir to the earldom of Oxford, as well as of John Mowbray. John Holand, son of the earl of Huntingdon, was brought up by his mother Elizabeth, the king's sister, while Richard, son of Thomas Despenser, married another of Westmorland's daughters, although he died in 1413 before reaching his majority.[37] However, none of these traitors' heirs recovered their ancestors' lands in full, which tended to make them more dependent on service to the crown to supplement their landed income.

As to the king's conduct of treason trials, this was generally consistent, at least in cases where laymen were involved. The sentences on the Cleveland and Northumberland rebels in July 1405 were given in the Court of Chivalry and according to the law of arms, presided over by the sixteen-year-old Prince John as constable of England. Charges against Northumberland and Bardolf were also first brought in the Court of Chivalry before being

---

[35] Holand, born in 1383, was styled earl of Kent from 1403, but like Montague he did not recover all his family's lands; he died in 1408 (M. Stansfield, 'Edmund Holand, Seventh Earl of Kent', *ODNB*, 27.657–8).

[36] R. Archer, 'John Mowbray, Second Duke of Norfolk', *ODNB*, 39.579–81; although the lordship of Gower, long-disputed between the Beauchamp and Mowbray families, was granted to Warwick in 1405, the grant did not take effect.

[37] John Holand was still under age in 1413, but Henry V restored him to his father's earldom of Huntingdon when he came of age in 1414 (R. A. Griffiths, 'John Holand, First Earl of Huntingdon and Duke of Exeter', *ODNB*, 27.674–6). It is worth noting that none of the heirs of Henry IV's traitors were implicated in the 1415 Southampton Plot.

moved to parliament, which is doubtless also how the earl of Worcester was
dealt with at the battle of Shrewsbury. It was by now the customary way of
conducting treason trials in time of rebellion. When it came to clerics, the
treason trials of Henry's reign aroused more controversy. Archbishop
Scrope was also probably tried, along with the layman Thomas Mowbray,
in the Court of Chivalry, with Sir William Fulthorpe acting as the constable's lieutenant; it was not the procedure per se that Chief Justice Gascoigne
objected to, but the right of the Court of Chivalry to try a man of the cloth,
let alone an archbishop.[38] The fact that a London jury simply refused to
take part in the trial of the friars in 1402, and the prolonged and inconclusive trials in the 1406 parliament, indicate further unease about Henry's
treatment of clerics and suggest that he had not entirely assuaged the fears
expressed about treason in his first parliament. However, he did not put
women to death: the countess of Oxford and Lady Despenser, both of
whom had almost certainly plotted to remove, if not kill, the king, were
each imprisoned for less than a year.

If Richard II had striven to master the aristocracy, Henry IV showed how
they might be mobilized in support of the crown – not by veering capri-
ciously between threats and prodigality, but by firmness, consistency and
partnership. In one respect he was fortunate, for after 1399, with the duchy
of Lancaster now held by the crown, its territorial resources dwarfed those
of any duke or earl, marking a decisive shift in the balance between the
landed power of the crown and that of the nobility. Capitalizing on this,
Henry systematically exalted the power and prestige of his family by
abstaining from new creations, promotions, or grants in fee which might
allow other noble families to establish regional power-bases.[39] The alternative, making them dependent on the crown, naturally came at a price: John
Beaufort's chief source of income was the £1,000 annuity granted to him
in 1404, and such grants placed enormous strain on the exchequer.[40] Yet
Henry made sure that even great nobles of unquestioned loyalty knew their
place. Thomas Fitzalan, earl of Arundel – whose father, Richard, Henry
had colluded in condemning to death in 1397 – took as great a risk as Henry

[38] Keen, 'Treason Trials under the Law of Arms', 85–103; Dunn, *Politics of Magnate Power*,
123; Bellamy, *Law of Treason*, 156–60.
[39] With the lands forfeited by Northumberland in 1405, note the distinction between
those granted to Prince John, which were in tail male, and those granted to Westmorland,
which were for life (*CPR 1405–8*, 40, 50).
[40] The largest exchequer annuities to nobles apart from Beaufort's (above, p. 440) were
Edmund duke of York's 1,000 marks, granted in 1385, and Thomas Percy's 500 marks,
granted in 1399 in return for lands surrendered.

himself when, as an eighteen-year-old, he returned to England in the summer of 1399, but although he was restored to his father's lands and title and made a Knight of the Garter he received little else and lost much. In 1397 Richard II had confiscated not just the Fitzalan lands but also the vast store of cash and valuables accumulated by Thomas's grandfather and stored by his father at Holt castle (Clwyd). Little or nothing of this was returned to him after being removed by Henry in 1399.[41] While still a minor, Earl Thomas also purchased from Henry for 'a sum of gold' the right to marry whom he wished, but within a few years the king, keen to cement the Anglo-Portuguese alliance, pushed him into a marriage with Beatrix, illegitimate daughter of the king of Portugal, for which he was mulcted £1,333.[42] Being obliged in 1405 to concede precedence to the earl of Kent must also have piqued him, for all this was despite years of service in Wales, at the battle of Shrewsbury and helping to suppress the northern risings in 1405, as well as a catastrophic fall in income from his great marcher lordships of Bromfield and Yale, Oswestry, Chirk and Clun. No wonder that the young earl eventually threw in his lot with Prince Henry, who in 1407 retained him for an annual fee of 250 marks; he continued to drift steadily out of the king's and his uncle the archbishop's orbit. His relief when Henry V became king induced him to lend £3,000 to the exchequer in 1414–15, although he had declined to advance loans to Henry IV.[43]

Yet if Henry could be a hard taskmaster, there was no question of a policy of deprivation of the landed nobility; those who remained loyal remained secure, as Henry had promised them in 1399 that they would. It was those who did not who were cut down to size, their families reduced to dependency on royal grace for even a limited measure of recovery. The king – or at any rate the Lancastrian dynasty – enjoyed a high level of

[41] Above, p. 134 and see the king's quittance of Nov. 1402 to John Ikelyngton for surrendering to him £43,964, plus 'a great sum in jewels and valuables', almost certainly seized from Holt castle by Richard in 1397.

[42] The king and queen of Portugal (Henry's sister) wrote to Henry begging him to remit this sum, but he was reluctant to do so. Philippa wrote: 'my most exceeding best beloved brother, you know well that he [Arundel] is now married not at all by his proper inclination, but on the contrary by your commandment, partly at my instance . . .' (*RHL*, ii.92–102). *Original Letters*, i.53, has a letter from the earl to Henry begging pardon for not paying a debt he owed the king because of the great sums he had spent bringing Beatrix to England.

[43] G. Harriss, 'Thomas Fitzalan, Fifth Earl of Arundel', *ODNB*, 19.772–3; Steel, *Receipt*, 189. Earl Richard (d.1376) sometimes loaned £20,000 at a time to Edward III (C. Given-Wilson, 'Richard Fitzalan, Third Earl of Arundel', *ODNB*, 19.768–9). See Arundel's letter to the archbishop asking him not to believe the 'complaints and suggestions' which people were making to him and the king, dated December during 'this present parliament', probably 1411 (*POPC*, ii.117). The prince also retained the earl of Warwick for 250 marks after Warwick returned from the Holy Land in 1410 (Harriss, *Henry V*, 33).

support from most of the nobles after 1403 and from practically all of them after 1405. Henry learned from the mistakes of his early years. It was the combination of a regional power-base with an unparalleled series of military commands, bolstered by influence at court and on the council, which had emboldened the Percys to challenge the king in 1403. Never again was a family permitted to accumulate such power, whatever its status. By birth, the three greatest families in the land apart from the king's were the Beauforts, the Mortimers and the house of York. Each in turn was put firmly in its place. However much the king trusted the Beauforts – and he did – the less than wholehearted confirmation of their act of legitimation in 1407 made it clear that they were not in the line of succession. The earl of March, whose great estates in Wales, Ireland and England and embarrassingly close kinship to the king qualified him for the role of pretender, was never treated in public as a member of the royal family. Although not persecuted, he was watched closely, especially after 1405, and denied the customary honours of a young nobleman of his standing such as election to the Order of the Garter.[44] The grant to Prince Thomas of the dukedom of Clarence in July 1412, shortly before March came of age, was a calculated snub, making it clear that this title, created for Edmund's great-grandfather Lionel and derived from the Mortimer honour of Clare (Suffolk), would not be returning to the family for the foreseeable future. Emasculated by his ancestry, Edmund became a pawn in the intrigues of others, not just the Percys but also the king's cousins, the house of York. As for the latter, if Constanza Despenser's allegations of her brother Edward's complicity in the plot to abduct the Mortimer boys in February 1405 are to be believed, then all three children of Duke Edmund (d.1402) tried at one time or another to unseat the Lancastrian dynasty in favour of March, for it was their younger brother Richard, earl of Cambridge, who was the chief plotter in 1415. What motivated them was surely not a disinterested attachment to the principle of royal primogeniture; more likely, perhaps, that, despite their avowed aims, such scheming was born of a lingering hope that Richard II's desire to pass his throne to Edward might yet be realized.[45] It was always the issue of legitimacy that snapped most doggedly at Henry's heels, and the problem of whom to trust even within the extended royal family never quite went away.

---

[44] Before Prince Henry took charge of them in 1409, John Pelham guarded the Mortimer brothers (E 403/596, 4 Dec. 1408).

[45] Richard was, presumably, assuming that Duke Edmund would by then be dead.

Chapter 29

WAR AND DIPLOMACY

Not all those who cultivated a chivalric reputation also enjoyed battlefield success, but Henry did. He took part in three battles – Radcot Bridge, Vilnius, and Shrewsbury – and three times ended on the winning side. His 'conquest' of 1399 involved little actual fighting, but that was in part because of the speed and boldness of his campaign; in 1403, he again seized the initiative by catching up with Hotspur just nine days after hearing of his uprising. Henry's triumph in 1399 is sometimes attributed largely to Richard's folly, and much of the credit for the battle of Shrewsbury given to Dunbar and Prince Henry, but it is difficult not to think that the king made some of his own luck.

The Welsh revolt was a more intractable affair. Had Henry had the time and money to spend six months or a year in Wales, as Edward I had done, the story might have been different. Henry knew and copied Edward's tactics, marching a circuit around Snowdonia in 1400 and setting up a three-pronged invasion strategy from Chester, Shrewsbury and Hereford in 1402, much as Edward had done in 1277 and 1282–3, respectively. Yet it was only in 1402 that he was able to plan a strategy rather than fight fires. In September 1400 it was North Wales that was ablaze, a year later Carmarthenshire and Cardiganshire, in 1403 Carmarthenshire again, while in 1405 his aims were to halt the Franco-Welsh advance and relieve Coety castle.[1] None of these campaigns lasted more than four weeks, partly because the weather closed in, although it was not by choice that they all fell in September or October. In 1401, 1403 and 1405 Henry's intention was to campaign in Wales earlier in the summer. Even so, the pleas of his supporters in Wales made it clear that they valued his presence there, and it is worth remembering that the year when he did not go, 1404, witnessed the peak of Owain's fortunes: the fall of Harlech, Aberystwyth and Kidwelly, the seizure of Cardiff, and the most intense period of

---

[1] Davies, *Revolt*, 237–46; J. E. Lloyd, *Owen Glendower* (Oxford, 1931), 32–5, 42–4, 54, 73, 104–6.

devastation of Shropshire and Herefordshire.[2] Unfortunately, this was simply not a war that could be won at a stroke, nor was it a war which offered much hope of chivalric glory. Nevertheless, the systematic devastation and pillage practised by his soldiers made survival difficult for the rebels, as well as putting heart into the English settlers and driving Glyn Dŵr's men back from the border counties.

In the first few years of the reign, the English response in Wales was bedevilled by confusion and disagreement as well as lack of funds. The Percys, convinced from an early stage of the need to negotiate with Glyn Dŵr, reckoned the king's insistence on *force majeure* to be pig-headed and Prince Henry's authority over them as irksome, especially after he was made the king's lieutenant at the age of sixteen in March 1403. The political aftermath of the battle of Shrewsbury, the prince's convalescence, and the crown's bankruptcy meant that not until early 1405 was it possible to invest in the strategy which ultimately proved successful: a combination of properly maintained garrisons in the principality and mobile troop concentrations in the marches.[3] This was quite different from the type of war the English were accustomed to fighting in northern France, though not dissimilar to that in Guyenne, which might explain the more pragmatic approach advocated by Hotspur and Worcester, both of whom had served long spells and held high office in the duchy.[4]

Despite this, a decade of warfare in Wales provided the opportunity for strategic developments, the most enduring of which was the growth in the ratio of archers to men-at-arms in English forces. In the 1370s and 1380s the standard mixed retinue for English campaigns to France contained equal numbers of each, but by the time Henry V invaded France in 1415 the norm was three archers to each man-at-arms for mobile land forces and two to one for naval forces and garrisons.[5] Richard II's Scottish and Irish armies of 1385 and 1394 had included around twice and three times as many archers as men-at-arms, respectively. Initially Henry increased the

---

[2] See the letters from John Stanley (*RHL II*, 76–9) and Richard Kingston (*Original Letters*, i.17–19) begging Henry to come to Wales; Watt, 'On Account of the Frequent Attacks', 76–80 (border devastation); at the Worcester council in October 1401 the possibility of Henry returning to Wales was discussed, but it was decided that with winter approaching he needed to return to London (*Giles*, 26).

[3] Eighty-two castles in Wales and its marches were garrisoned by the English during the revolt (Davies, *Revolt*, 248–52).

[4] Worcester spent much time in Guyenne in the 1360s and 1370s, and was seneschal of Poitou; Hotspur was lieutenant of Guyenne in the mid-1390s.

[5] A. Bell, A. Curry, A. King and D. Simpkin, *The Soldier in Late Medieval England* (Oxford, 2014), 262–5.

ratio: for his Scottish campaign of 1400 he had 11,314 archers and just 1,771 men-at-arms, the greatest preponderance of archers (6.5:1) in any medieval English army.[6] The force which Prince Henry maintained on the Welsh border in the summer of 1403 was made up of 2,500 archers and 500 men-at-arms (5:1).[7] These ratios might have been dictated by financial considerations (men-at-arms were paid twelve pence a day, archers six), by the social diversity of retinue captains, or by the belief that longbowmen would be more effective in dealing with difficult terrain and guerrilla skirmishing. On the other hand, it is clear from contemporary accounts of the battles of Humbleton Hill and Shrewsbury that in open-field battles also it was archers who constituted a commander's deadliest weapon, and the consensus within a few years on a ratio of around three to one acknowledged their attritional value in all forms of warfare. This was the ratio adopted for the army led by Clarence to France in 1412, for the Agincourt campaign three years later, and for most of the subsequent expeditions of the Hundred Years War.

Only at the battle of Shrewsbury, where both sides deployed the massed formations of dismounted men-at-arms and archers favoured by English commanders for the previous seventy years, is it possible to get some idea of Henry's battle tactics, but his overall military strategy is a little clearer. He would not have deluded himself that the Scots or Welsh would risk a pitched battle against his more numerous and better-equipped armies,[8] and his campaigns were in part psychological exercises, demonstrating his commitment to the preservation of his dominions and marches, his willingness to hazard his person and his reputation in war, his refusal to abandon those who remained loyal to him and his leadership of his nation in war, as well as to deprive the rebels of equipment and provisions. The military benefits of his 1400 campaign to Scotland are harder to discern, although his thinking was reasonably clear: he hoped to reverse the Scottish recovery of the past thirty years, to capitalize on the defection of George Dunbar, and to impose his authority on a kingdom which thumbed its nose at his claim to overlordship. His refusal to allow his army to plunder and waste the Scottish border counties was a strategic decision born of high

---

[6] A. Curry, A. Bell, A. King and D. Simpkin, 'New Regime, New Army? Henry IV's Scottish Expedition of 1400', *EHR* 125 (2010), 1382–1413; A. Curry, 'After Agincourt, What Next?', in *The Fifteenth Century VII*, ed. L. Clark (Woodbridge, 2007), 23–51.

[7] Worcester's contingent was 200 archers and 40 men-at-arms (E 101/404/24, fos. 1, 4). By 1407 the ratio of the prince's forces in Wales was 3:1 (600 men-at-arms and 1,800 archers: E 403/591, 1 June 1407).

[8] The armies Henry led to Wales were 3,000–4,000 strong.

hopes, but not until the much bloodier affair at Humbleton Hill did they begin to be realized.

Generally speaking, plunder and waste were standard fare in the fighting of the time, but Henry's approach to warfare was not hidebound. One thing his son would have learned much about from him was the guns which he put to such good use at the siege of Harfleur in 1415.[9] Kings of England had acquired cannons from relatively early in the fourteenth century, but Henry IV had a more developed interest in artillery, perhaps as a result of seeing it in action at Vilnius. The king's guns were kept in the privy wardrobe at the Tower, where an inventory from the first year of Henry's reign listed thirty-nine cannons, twenty-three cannon-trunks, over a thousand cannonballs and large quantities of gunpowder, saltpetre and tampions. The men responsible for buying, making and maintaining them were the king's artillerer, William Byker, and his (mainly German) gunners, Antonio Herman, Walter Cook, and John and Gerard Sprong.[10] By February 1405, when Henry Somer replaced John Norbury as keeper of the privy wardrobe, the number of cannons kept at the Tower had fallen to twenty-three, many having been dispersed to where they were needed – Wales, Yorkshire, Guyenne, the Channel coast, and elsewhere.[11] That summer was especially busy, with Wales and the north both regularly needing to have cannons, cannonballs and gunpowder sent to replenish stocks.[12] After 1407, responsibility for the king's cannonry was transferred to the royal chamber, under the care of Gerard Sprong, and more artillery stores were set up around the country: Pontefract was one such repository, and by 1411 Henry had built a new tower with gunloops at Southampton in which to mount the guns needed to defend the harbour approaches.[13]

Whether campaigning in Scotland, Wales, or the north, the king always took his cannons with him, and their impact was considerable. They

[9] *Gesta Henrici Quinti*, ed. F. Taylor and J. Roskell (Oxford, 1975), 36–50.

[10] E 403/567, 13 July 1400 (Byker was replaced by John Albaster in 1407: E 403/591, 2 June); E 403/591, 1 June 1407; E 404/24, no. 403; BL Harleian Ms 319, fo. 52v.

[11] E 101/405/4, which also lists three pellet-guns, lead shot for them, 1,060 cannonballs, 1,522 lbs of gunpowder, 600 lbs of saltpetre, sixteen cannon-trunks and 1,912 tampions (*RHKA*, 84–5). For cannons despatched to Conway, Aberystwyth, Sandwich, Pontefract, and with the duke of Rutland to Guyenne, see Wylie, *Henry the Fourth*, ii.230–4.

[12] E 101/405/10 (file of writs detailing the distribution of the king's guns in 1405).

[13] DL 42/15, fo. 70v; *CPR 1408–13*, 246. This was probably the Catchcold Tower (J. Kenyon, 'Coastal Artillery Fortifications', in *Arms, Armies and Fortifications in the Hundred Years War*, ed. A. Curry and M. Hughes (Woodbridge, 1994), 145–50, at p. 146). Some artillery was still kept in the Tower: in 1409 John Bunting was appointed as keeper of the king's artillery there, replaced by Nov. 1412 by Robert Penford and Baldwin Jacobson (*CPR 1408–13*, 54, 77; E 403/611, 15 Nov.).

certainly helped to secure the surrender of Aberystwyth and Harlech in 1408–9, despite the fact that one of them, the two-ton *Messenger*, blew up when fired at Aberystwyth.[14] They were also instrumental in reducing the northern castles in 1405: shortly after the taking of Berwick, Prince John wrote to his father to say that urgent repairs were needed to its walls, two-thirds of which were ruinous partly as a result of the bombardment inflicted on them by Henry's artillery a few months earlier. The king's own account stated that by the 'good and powerful firing of his cannons, and their great and marvellous blows, the walls of the said castle [Berwick] were battered and broken'.[15] His exultant letter to the council in July 1405 explaining that just seven shots from one of his cannons had brought about the surrender of Warkworth doubtless exaggerated its impact on the outcome of the siege, but his pride in them is unmistakable and evident from early in the reign.[16] In 1402, 10,000 lbs of copper costing £135 were bought at Dinant in the Low Countries to make guns for the king, one of which was nicknamed *The King's Daughter*. Henry was even said to have invented a new 'great cannon' himself, the materials for which cost £25.[17] He also had a 'great gun (*magna gunna*)', said to weigh four-and-a-half tons, which in June 1411 he sent to Spain, perhaps indicative of the sophistication of English cannons at the time.[18] The ship on which it was sent also carried two 'small guns for a ship' made by John Ferkyn – an early reference to the specialized manufacture of shipboard cannons.[19]

The vital role of naval warfare during Henry's reign – not just in the Channel and the North Sea, but also in supplying beleaguered English castles in Wales – also stimulated the king's interest in ships. The great majority of vessels in the crown's pay during the late Middle Ages were requisitioned merchantmen, and although Edward III had owned around forty ships in the 1370s they rarely saw military use and were mostly sold off early in Richard II's reign. By 1399 there were just four ships belonging to

---

[14] E 403/591, 23 June 1407; E 403/596, 13 Nov., 3 Dec. 1408. Davies, *Revolt*, 253. The Welsh captain at Aberystwyth in 1407 had to promise not to remove or disable the cannons he found there (*SAC II*, 526–7).

[15] *POPC*, ii .91 (he also urged that Berwick be restocked with cannons); see *SAC II*, 457–61, for Walsingham's comments on Henry's cannons. He took fourteen with him to Scotland in 1400 (Wylie, *Henry the Fourth*, iv.232).

[16] Keen, 'Treason Trials under the Law of Arms', 95.

[17] Wylie, *Henry the Fourth*, ii.267–9; E 403/594, 17 March 1408; *Issues*, ed. Devon, 307–8.

[18] *Foedera*, viii.694.

[19] *duas parvas gunnas pro navi quas in regno nostro Angliae fecit* (*Foedera*, viii.694). The king's ship, *Le Cristofre*, also carried three cannons (*Navy of the Lancastrian Kings*, 88).

the crown: the *Trinité de la Tour*, *Gracedieu*, *Nicholas*, and *George*.[20] Faced with the need to protect English shipping and ports, Henry initially sought to revive the royal fleet, and on 10 January 1401 ordered towns up and down the country to construct thirty-six balingers and eighteen barges, shallow-draft vessels suitable for coastal and estuarine operations; however, a few weeks later the commissions were repealed because they had been issued without parliamentary assent and contrary to precedent.[21] Thus during the Pirate War the king once again relied heavily on ships owned and skippered by privateers. The combined operations of these early years between the admirals of the northern and southern fleets, who were royally appointed and in charge of operations, and the merchant-privateers who owned, manned and sailed the ships but took their pay and orders from the king's officers, was in effect a public–private partnership for the safeguard of the sea. Henry's admirals were men close to him – Worcester, Rempston, Grey, Thomas Berkeley, Thomas Beaufort – but it was their systematic coopera-tion with the likes of John Hauley, Henry Pay, Mark Mixto, Richard Spicer and John Brandon that gave naval policy its teeth and claws.[22]

However, this did not mean that the king's ships were redundant, and once the Pirate War subsided and the indiscipline of some of the priva-teers began to make them more of a liability than an asset, Henry's desire to revive a royal fleet reasserted itself. His own ships did play a small part in the war, but were more often used to transport members of the royal family.[23] For his personal use on the Thames, Henry had a gold and scarlet barge with a white collared leopard carved on the prow. He also had a 'large ship', presumably a cog or a carrack, which he sent to Brittany to collect Queen Joan in 1403; *Le Holygost de la Tour*, in which he despatched his daughter Philippa to Denmark in 1406; and the *Trinité de la Tour*, which carried the earl of Rutland to Guyenne in September 1401. At least six of Henry's ships were named *de la Tour* – *La Katerine*, *La Godegrace* (or *Gracedieu*), the *Holygost*, *Trinité*, *Sirena* (Siren), and one simply called *La Tour* – for when not in use they were usually berthed on the Thames at Ratcliffe below the

[20] *Navy of the Lancastrian Kings*, 30–4; C. Lambert, *Shipping the Medieval Military* (Woodbridge, 2011), 12–13.

[21] *CCR 1399–1402*, 238–40; *PROME*, viii.106. However the clerk of the king's ships, John Chamberlain, did arrange for one new barge to be built for the king (perhaps by the city of York, unless this was a second) and some others repaired, for £220 (E 403/569, 26 Feb. and 5 March 1401); N. Rodger, *The Safeguard of the Sea: A Naval History of Britain 660–1649* (London, 1997), 68.

[22] Ford, 'Policy or Piracy?'; C. L. Kingsford, *Henry V* (London, 1901), 187–8.

[23] For the king's ships in action in 1401, 1403 and 1405, see *Navy of the Lancastrian Kings*, 32; Wylie, *Henry the Fourth*, ii.101.

Tower, although this was in no real sense a royal dockyard.[24] After 1409 Henry began to acquire more ships, some purchased, some built for him, some as gifts, some as prizes such as his Mediterranean 'great galley' the *Jesus Maria* and a Genoese carrack known simply as *Le Carake*. The appointment in 1408–9 of Thomas Beaufort as admiral of England, Ireland, Guyenne and Picardy – in effect the first Lord High Admiral – also signalled a revival of momentum in naval affairs,[25] and by 1411 responsibility for the king's ships had been entrusted to Helming Leget, usher of the king's chamber, thus bringing them (like the royal cannons) within the king's purview. The construction of the Catchcold tower at Southampton in 1410–11 presaged the use of its harbour as a royal dock.[26]

During the last two years of the reign this process of acquisition began to resemble a policy, encouraged presumably by the prospect of renewed intervention in France. In September 1411 Henry wrote to his sister, the queen of Castile, to ask her if she would sell him her ship the *Santa Maria*, currently lying in San Sebastian harbour, which he had set his heart on (*multum affectat habere*).[27] At the same time, in preparation for his putative voyage to Guyenne, four of his ships were ordered to be got ready: *Le Bernard*, *Le Cristofre*, an unnamed barge, and a carrack, probably *Le Carake*.[28] Although Henry never went to Guyenne, he continued to acquire vessels: in the summer of 1412 he bought the *Thomas* for £266 from Thomas Fauconer, a London mercer, and before his death he had also acquired the *Cog Johan* and at least six other ships. Three of these may have been the galleys for the construction of which William Loveney, who replaced Leget as keeper in March 1412, was ordered in October to cut down 800 oaks at

[24] Wylie, *Henry the Fourth*, ii.287, 449; iv.199, 241; E 404/27, no. 241. Not all ships *de la Tour* were royally owned. In 1405 Prince Thomas was made admiral of a fleet consisting of twenty 'Great ships of the Tower', some of which were Portuguese, twenty barges and twenty balingers, manned by 700 men-at-arms and 1,400 archers (*Foedera*, viii.388–9; Rodger, *Safeguard of the Sea*, 117–18).

[25] Beaufort was appointed admiral of the north and west in September 1408, but his remit was enlarged to cover the whole of England and its overseas dominions in July 1409, the first such all-embracing appointment (*CPR 1405–8*, 467; *CPR 1408–13*, 97, 139). One of Henry's ships was built at Drogheda (Rodger, *Safeguard of the Sea*, 474, 506–7).

[26] Leget was appointed in June 1411 (*CPR 1408–13*, 294, 320; Wylie, *Henry the Fourth*, ii.101). He doubtless accounted in the chamber, which is why no accounts for the king's ships survive for the last two years of the reign. Between 1399 and 1405 John Chamberleyn, clerk of the king's ships, accounted for expenditure of around £700 a year, but after the Pirate War subsided this fell to about £100 a year. In 1409 John Starling became clerk of the king's ships in place of Thomas Elmeton, who held the post from 1405–9 (*CPR 1408–13*, 182). Whether Leget had additional responsibilities, as Keeper rather than Clerk, is unclear.

[27] *POPC*, ii.24–6.

[28] *CPR 1408–13*, 320–1; E 403/608, 28 Aug. 1411 (the council allotted 1,000 marks for their preparation).

Eltham.[29] This re-establishment of a royal fleet was carried forward by
Henry V, who needed to secure the Channel to pursue his ambitions in
northern France.[30] By 1419 there were thirty-six royal ships, some of them
very big such as the *Jesus*, which was around 1,000 tons. The *Gracedieu*, at
1,400 tons was one of the largest ships sailing in northern European
waters,[31] and was also the last ship to be built for an English king for nearly
fifty years. In his will, Henry V asked that some of his ships be sold to pay
his debts, and in fact all but six were soon disposed of, for a total of around
£1,000; his four 'great ships' lingered on for a few years but were abandoned in the 1430s.[32] The reversion to the custom of impressing
merchantmen did not mark the failure of this early Lancastrian experiment in royal fleet building so much as the suspension of active royal
interest in it.

The end of war, as the theorists never tired of repeating, was peace, and
throughout his reign Henry IV was continuously engaged in diplomacy.
On average, he despatched or received about eight embassies a year, of
which over a third were to, or from, France, although between 1402 and
1405 peace talks with the French broke down and meetings were restricted
to discussing infractions of the truce.[33] After 1406, however, a 'perpetual
peace' was once again on the agenda, often in tandem with proposals for
Prince Henry's marriage to a Valois princess. A further 25 per cent of
embassies met with the Scots and around 10 per cent with the Flemish,
although this under-represents the level of Anglo-Flemish diplomacy,
which, in one form or another, was almost continuous between 1402 and
1407. Negotiations with Denmark and the Empire were intense in 1401-2
but fell away once the marriages of Blanche and Philippa had been agreed,
but with the Hansa, Castile and Portugal they continued intermittently

[29] *CPR 1408-13*, 476; E 404/27, no. 426; *Navy of the Lancastrian Kings*, 34, 52-5, 85. Loveney
had served Henry since 1381, went into exile with him in 1398-9, and was keeper of the
great wardrobe 1399-1408; he doubtless accounted in the chamber too. These galleys were
still being constructed when Henry died: J. Wylie and W. Waugh, *The Reign of Henry the Fifth*
(3 vols, Cambridge, 1914-29), ii.372.
[30] The revival of the royal fleet in 1409-13 is sometimes credited to Prince Henry
(Allmand, *Henry V*, 221-2; Rodger, *Safeguard of the Sea*, 130, 143), but there is no evidence for
this assumption and Henry IV's personal interest in ships suggests otherwise.
[31] Henry V also continued to use privateers, for example, Richard Spicer, who in 1417
contracted to provide a fleet for three months for operations in the Channel (Allmand,
Henry V, 224-5). Tonnage at this time related to carrying capacity, not displacement.
[32] The largest ship left by Henry IV to his son in 1413 was the *Cog Johan*, around 220 tons:
Navy of the Lancastrian Kings, 52-5; Rodger, *Safeguard of the Sea*, 68-70.
[33] Information on embassies is mostly taken from *Foedera*.

throughout the reign. Communication with the Papacy was continuous, but mainly conducted by correspondence; in 1406–8, however, with the ending of the Schism in sight, Henry sent John Cheyne and Henry Chichele on a formal embassy to the Curia. Emissaries were also sent to Donald, Lord of the Isles, the duke of Guelders and Sigismund, king of Hungary.

Diplomacy was time-consuming, expensive and frustrating. Months might be spent far from home negotiating a provisional agreement, only for ambassadors to find by the time they returned that circumstances had rendered it obsolete. Cheyne and Chichele arrived in Rome in the winter of 1406–7 to discover that Pope Innocent had died and had to await new instructions; it was while French ambassadors were attending the parliament at Gloucester in November 1407 that news arrived of Orléans's assassination, obliging them to conclude a hasty truce before returning to Paris to assess the situation. Sometimes foreign envoys had to wait for weeks or even months for an audience, as Jean Hangest did at Windsor in the autumn of 1400, or to seek the king in some distant part of the realm where business had taken him, as in the spring of 1408 when a French delegation had to follow Henry to Yorkshire, whither he had gone in the aftermath of Northumberland's last rising.[34] For the most part, however, visiting embassies stayed in or around London, sometimes at one of the royal residences but more often at one of the capital's inns or religious houses.[35] When meetings ended quickly, it was usually a sign of failure: it took just three days at Kirk Yetholm in 1401 for the Scots to make it clear that there was no basis for agreement. However, if the will existed on both sides to reach a settlement, months or even years might be spent talking around obstacles, drafting agreements, reporting back and receiving new instructions. William Esturmy and John Kington spent over a year at Marienburg in 1404–5, while Nicholas Rishton spent the best part of several years at Calais negotiating the mercantile truce with Flanders.

The skill required for such work is self-evident. Henry's most versatile diplomats were Richard Young, bishop of Bangor, and then Rochester, who headed missions to Denmark, Scotland and the Empire as well as negotiating with France, Flanders and the Papacy; and John Cheyne, who accompanied Young to Germany in 1401 to negotiate Princess Blanche's

---

[34] Beds had to be carried both to Gloucester in 1407 and to Yorkshire in 1408 for the French ambassadors: E 101/405/13, m. 3; E 403/595, 11 July.

[35] Three embassies visiting Henry in 1405–6 stayed at the house of the Lyon at Southwark, the house of John Scryveyn in Fleet Street, and the sign of the Bell in Carters Lane (BL Harleian Ms 319, fo. 41v); in 1408–9 ambassadors were accommodated at St Bartholomew's priory in Smithfield, paid for by the king (E 101/405/23, m. 1).

marriage, but was mainly employed on embassies to Paris and Rome. Both men were also privy councillors.[36] Most diplomats were more specialized, steadily building contacts and learning how things worked. When prospects for peace with France seemed bright, as in 1406 and 1409, Henry Beaufort lent weight to the English delegations to Paris, but those more commonly appointed for Anglo-French talks included Cheyne, Chichele, Sir Hugh Mortimer and John Catterick, treasurer of Lincoln; the latter two, both close to Prince Henry, were there in part to represent his interests.[37] Anglo-Flemish talks, which were held mainly at Calais, were usually in the hands of the lawyer Nicholas Rishton and a group of knights, Richard Aston, John Croft, Hugh Lutterell and Thomas Swynburn, while after the fall of the Percys Anglo-Scottish talks were generally conducted by Westmorland, Prince John, Robert Umfraville and Richard Holme, canon of York and king's secretary. Sir William Esturmy and John Kington, canon of Lincoln, were entrusted for years with negotiating with the Empire and the Hansa, although Henry also made good use of a number of German knights with imperial contacts and varying degrees of attachment to the English court. Some of these had served Richard II or Anne of Bohemia in a similar capacity, but this did not prevent them offering their services to Henry after 1399. Especially useful were Roger Siglem, the brothers John and Arnold Pallas, and Hartung van Klux, who between them fostered an atmosphere of goodwill between England and the Empire.[38]

The expertise of lawyers such as Young, Catterick, Rishton and Kington was invaluable – every embassy of importance included at least one – for documents had to be drafted with care to be watertight. The long and repetitive list of questions circulated to crown lawyers and academics in late 1400 establishing the legality of Henry's claim to the residue of King John's ransom was not just for appearance's sake, even if the responses received were probably a foregone conclusion.[39] The legal defensibility or deniability of a diplomatic standpoint depended on the rigour with which it was drafted, which included the citation of authority and precedent – even that of Brutus or Arthur. Diplomats must know their business, for the

[36] Allmand, 'A Bishop of Bangor', 50–3; N. Saul, 'John Cheyne', *ODNB*, 11.376–8; *HOC*, ii.549–52, calls Cheyne 'a diplomat of exceptional ability'.
[37] Mortimer was the prince's chamberlain; as king, Henry V promoted Catterick to the bishoprics of St Davids in 1414, Coventry and Lichfield in 1415 and Exeter in 1419.
[38] Reitemeier, *Aussenpolitik in Spätmittelalter*, 207–64, 496–7. For German knights, see also above, p. 335.
[39] *Usk*, 102–15.

instructions issued to them left room for initiative, as in the king's letter to Chichele and Cheyne seeking their views on the way forward following Innocent VII's death and giving them permission to distribute the jewels entrusted to them as they thought best. Formal instructions were often accompanied by secret oral, or further written, advice setting limits to the discretion allowed them.[40]

Some obstacles could be anticipated, others not. Negotiations with the Danes stalled following a misunderstanding of the conventions for English royal succession, while those with the Hansa and the Flemings were constantly set back by new maritime outrages necessitating the redrafting of calculations for reparation, or threats to break off the talks.[41] Even when terms were agreed, there was no certainty that they would be respected. With Charles VI intermittently insane, Robert III a cipher, James I a prisoner, and the great and powerless empire disputed between Wenzel and Rupert, the early fifteenth century was an age of dysfunctional kingship in north-western Europe, not helped by the fact that much of the diplomacy was conducted between kings who did not recognize each other. Buffeted by the waves of belligerence whipped up by Orléans, Douglas, St-Pol and the freebooters who preyed on the Channel and North Sea ports, there were times when ambassadorial talks barely trod water. In such circumstances, the preservation of the 1396 truce was an achievement, for full-scale war would doubtless have brought even greater horrors, but in practice it was increasingly through local truces and private agreements that hostilities stood the best chance of being checked. Sometimes these were regional, backed by the public authority of powers such as the dukes of Brittany or the towns of Flanders, but often enough, especially in Guyenne and Picardy, they were little more than time-limited abstentions or 'sufferances' between neighbouring lords, garrisons or villages, the aims of which were to allow trade and travel for the next few months or even days, and to preserve the process of negotiation. Made and policed by local officials, these agreements were indicative of the degree to which the decision to continue or suspend hostilities had slipped beyond the reach of

---

[40] BL Cotton Cleopatra E ii, fo. 249 (262); SC 1/43/98 (letter to the chancellor about Chichele's and Cheyne's mission ending *nous volons et vous mandons que vous ne monstrez a nullui la susdite instruction*).

[41] *RHL I*, 119–20. Nicholas Rishton and his colleagues at Calais also objected to the use of French for diplomatic missives by their opposite numbers, which they equated to the 'Hebrew tongue', and tried unsuccessfully to get them to use Latin. The forthright Rishton also described the Privy Council as 'vague, weak and divided' for failing to send him a new commission in 1404, and a few weeks later threatened to return home because his wages had not been paid (*RHL I*, lxxvi, lxxxvi–xci, 357–8, 368, 397).

the central authorities. Diplomacy, like the Pirate War, had something of
the character of a private–public partnership.[42]

Nevertheless, the diplomatic progress of Henry's reign was far from negligible. The marriages of the king's daughters secured the neutrality at worst
of Scandinavia and the Empire; the Franco-Castilian alliance was gently
prised apart, if not ruptured, not least through the intervention of those
excellent allies King João and Queen Philippa of Portugal; the mercantile
truce with Flanders and the final settlement with the Hansa were a long
time in the making, but real achievements for all that, for the Pirate War
had threatened a virtual cessation of commercial traffic in English waters
and created a heap of claims to be resolved. A series of long-term truces
during the later years of the reign – with Scotland and Brittany in particular – also helped to smooth the path towards the hoped-for perpetual
peace with France, consistently the principal aim of Henry's diplomacy.[43]
The fact that peace did not materialize can hardly be laid at the English
king's door, for the bewildering changes of direction in Paris made it difficult to pursue a clear policy even had the English government been able to
agree one. In the circumstances, Henry's diplomatic legacy was propitious:
most importantly, by 1413 much of the entangling undergrowth that had
accumulated since, or even before, 1399 had been cleared, affording Henry
V the luxury, never enjoyed by his father, of being able to focus on the
paramount 'matter of France'.[44]

---

[42] Phillpotts, 'Fate of the Truce', 73–5, 80; Pepin, 'English Offensives', 39–40; Vale, *English Gascony*, 175–9, 218.

[43] An aim strongly supported by Hoccleve (*Regement of Princes*, 194–5).

[44] As have historians of his reign: Keen, 'Diplomacy', in *Henry V*, ed. Harriss, 181–99, deals exclusively with Anglo-French relations; see also Allmand, *Henry V*, xiii and n. 4.

Part Five

THE PENDULUM YEARS 1409–1413

Chapter 30

THE PRINCE'S ADMINISTRATION
(1409–1411)

The parliament of 1406 had marked Prince Henry's entry into politics; that of January 1410 marked his assumption of power. From the spring of 1409, his responsibilities grew apace: constable of Dover castle and warden of the Cinque Ports, guardian to the Mortimer brothers, captain of the town of Calais.[1] Having been betrayed in 1403 by his mentor (Hotspur) and his governor (Worcester), he, like his father, had learned to rely more on his family. The Beaufort brothers now returned to prominence: Henry Beaufort took charge of negotiations with France, while Thomas became chancellor, admiral of England and its dominions, and captain of Calais castle.[2] This did not mean that all those upon whom the king and Archbishop Arundel had relied were jettisoned: Richard Grey retained the trust of all parties until the end of the reign, as did Westmorland, though he remained mainly in the north, patrolling the Scottish marches with Prince John. Yet there was no doubt about the direction in which the pendulum of power had swung.

Tension at court and within the council had been building through 1409, aggravated by the king's illness and renewed financial uncertainty. When Prince Thomas's fee as lieutenant of Ireland was reduced to £4,666 in March 1408, it was made contingent on his going to Dublin and remaining there.[3] Thomas, however, was reluctant to see too much power pass into his

---

[1] *Foedera*, viii.628; *CPR 1408–13*, 57, 202. The prince witnessed two-thirds of royal charters after Sept. 1409; already in Feb. 1409 the earl of Westmorland addressed a petition to 'my lord the prince and the lords of the council' (E 28/23, no. 24).

[2] E 403/599, 23 May, 16 July; E 403/602, 22 Nov.; *Foedera*, viii. 585–7, 597. Thomas Beaufort also remained close to the king until the end of the reign and was 'by the king's mandate . . . attendant about his person' (*CPR 1408–13*, 227; Harriss, 'Thomas Beaufort', *ODNB*, 4.643–4).

[3] BL Cotton Titus B. xi: indenture between the king and Prince Thomas noting that Thomas's fee had been reduced to £6,000 a year in March 1406; this indenture, dated 8 March 1408, was for three years from 1 May; he was also promised £9,000 still owed to him from the previous indenture, but it was endorsed to the effect that if he did not go to Ireland and remain there he would be obliged to repay the money. The council which set these terms was headed by Prince Henry and the indenture drawn up 'at the relation of' Archbishop Arundel.

elder brother's hands while their father still lived, and after arriving back in England in March 1409 showed no desire to return to Ireland, a graveyard of chivalric ambitions. Nor, however, did he wish to relinquish his fee – indeed, in May 1409 he secured £7,666 due to him for his lieutenancy.[4] Prince Henry, exasperated at this dissipation of much-needed resources, suggested in August with the backing of the council that the post be given to Sir John Stanley and that his brother be required to remove his retainers from court so that they would cease to be a burden on the royal household. Although Thomas resisted this, the commons in January 1410 also made it clear that they thought he should take his responsibilities more seriously. Unabashed, he continued to complain about non-payment of his fee, but never went to Ireland again.[5] The autumn of 1409 also saw the eruption of a dispute between the young earl of Arundel, the prince's foremost retainer, and his uncle the archbishop, over hunting and fishing rights on their adjoining lands in Sussex. Such a relatively minor affair should not have been allowed to escalate, but the archbishop would not have forgotten his nephew's role in the condemnation of Richard Scrope and the matter was eventually brought before the king at Holborn and submitted to arbitration by the two chief justices. Although contained, the dispute was symptomatic of the growing assertiveness of Prince Henry and his allies, and the declining authority of the king and the archbishop.[6]

The unusual hiatus between the dismissals of Tiptoft and Arundel, on 11 and 21 December 1409, respectively, and the appointment of replacements, was a sign of indecision at best and more likely of disagreement between the king and the prince over their successors. It was the prince who prevailed.[7] Henry Lord Le Scrope, regarded at this time by Prince Henry as a reliable supporter, became treasurer on 6 January 1410, but not until 31 January, four days after parliament had met, was Thomas Beaufort handed the great seal. His brother the bishop, who had made the opening speech, was in many ways the obvious candidate, but was perhaps too much the exemplar of Caesarean prelacy to which this assembly objected. Thomas

---

[4] E 403/599, 20 May (he had also received £4,266 of arrears in Nov. 1408: E 403/596, 28 Nov.).

[5] POPC, i.319–20, 339; Harriss, *Cardinal Beaufort*, 49; McNiven, *Heresy and Politics*, 151–2. Prince Henry was reluctant to pass money to Thomas, who had to get his father to write begging letters 'from our heart' to the council to give him 'as much as you can' (E 404/26, no. 210; E 404/27, no. 153).

[6] *CCR 1409–13*, 59, 183–5. The award of the justices favoured the archbishop, though with some compromise on each side. Cf. *POPC*, ii.117, a letter from the earl to the archbishop dating from 1406, 1407 or 1411.

[7] McFarlane, *Lancastrian Kings*, 107–8.

was a compromise appointment, acceptable to both king and prince, though less so to Archbishop Arundel.[8] Yet the prince did not have it all his own way. As the taxpayers of England would discover when he came to the throne, he had few inhibitions about asking them to open their purses, and he now began boldly, perhaps too boldly, by asking the commons for a lay and a clerical subsidy to be levied each year without the need for parliamentary consent on each occasion.[9] This was rejected, but its effect was to revive the debate about a long-term solution to the crown's fiscal dilemma. Emboldened by Arundel's dismissal from the chancery, and perhaps hopeful of a sympathetic hearing from the new lay chancellor, a group of MPs now put forward the root-and-branch Disendowment Bill, which would have entailed the largest transfer of landed resources in England between the Conquest and the Dissolution of the Monasteries.[10] This, in turn, led to the burning of John Badby, with whom died the hopes of the disendowment party, but if radical financial remedies were to be discounted there was little option but to return to traditional ones, which in this case meant the grant by the commons of one-and-a-half lay subsidies to be raised at the rate of half a subsidy (c.£18,500) a year until November 1412.[11]

The clearest indication of the prince's ascendancy is found in the complexion of the reshuffled council: the new chancellor and treasurer, Bishop Beaufort, the earls of Arundel and Warwick, Hugh Lord Burnell, Edward Lord Charlton and the future primate Henry Chichele, bishop of St David's, were all men whom he counted as his supporters.[12] In addition to Chichele and Beaufort, the council's clerical ballast was supplied by Bishops Langley and Bubwith and privy seal keeper John Prophet, not the sort of men who ran the country but the sort who made it run. This was the prince's council, and it was he who, following its appointment, informed the parliament of its willingness to serve provided the commons made

[8] *Foedera*, viii.616; Harriss, *Cardinal Beaufort*, 49-51; while chancellor, he received 800 marks a year 'beyond the common fees and wages of the office' (*CPR 1408-13*, 219).

[9] *SAC II*, 590. Walsingham said the annual subsidies were the king's proposal, but given his comments to the parliament, the prince is a more likely candidate; he would make a similar request, when king, to the parliament of May 1421 (Harriss, *Shaping the Nation*, 503; Harriss, *Henry V*, 150-1).

[10] *PROME*, viii.464-5.

[11] *PROME*, viii.476, 482-3.

[12] *PROME*, viii.476. Warwick was in the Holy Land in 1409, but returned to England early in 1410; he and the earl of Arundel joined the council on 2 May 1410, at the end of the parliament (E 404/27, nos. 169, 268). Burnell and Charlton, as well as the two earls, had served extensively in Wales with the prince. Westmorland was asked to serve on the council, but he and Langley claimed to be too busy defending the north and were replaced by Warwick and Chichele; in fact Langley attended frequently in 1410, though Westmorland did not.

adequate provision for it to do so. Shepherded by Speaker Thomas Chaucer, a man with close connections to both the prince and the Beauforts, parliament confirmed the steady leak of authority from king and archbishop to the prince which had characterized the past year, and to set the seal on this transfer of power a restriction was once again placed on the king's freedom to make grants and probably on other facets of his prerogative.[13]

For nearly two years after the January 1410 parliament the prince's council retained effective control of the administration.[14] The king played little part in day-to-day government, although messengers continued to pass between him and the prince on matters concerning the realm, and he continued to respond to petitions and despatch letters to his ministers concerning family matters such as Queen Joan's dower, as well as retaining a selective interest in questions of patronage, judicial and other appointments, religious indiscipline and foreign policy.[15] Between July 1410 and February 1411 he spent six months in the Midlands, mainly at Woodstock, Leicester and Groby, breaking with habit by spending the Christmas season not at Eltham but at Kenilworth, where he stayed for nearly two months. Following a brief visit to Gloucester in May 1411, he remained almost continuously close to London, venturing no further than Windsor and Canterbury, which he visited twice in 1412.[16] Afflicted not just by physical

[13] *PROME*, viii.453, 461. The effectiveness of this restraint in one case is shown by the order from the king to the exchequer dated 26 December 1412 to pay to Richard Cressy, sergeant of the hall, the arrears of an annuity of £34 originally granted to Adam Colton, the king's fruiterer, which Colton was unable to realize 'because of the restraint of such grants by us made in our parliament of the twelfth year'; Colton transferred his annuity to Cressy, his senior, to act as his attorney, but 'nevertheless our chancellor [Thomas Beaufort] did not wish to suffer our letters patent for them to be sealed until the eighteenth day of January last past' [1412, by which time Archbishop Arundel was chancellor and the restraint had been lifted]. Thus the king 'of his special grace' ordered the arrears of the annuity for the period from September 1410 to January 1412, amounting to £55, to be paid to Cressy, 'as attorney of the said Adam'; on 21 Jan. 1413 the annuity was transferred from the exchequer to the ulnager of York (E 404/28, no. 210; *CPR 1408–13*, 370, 453). The restriction imposed in the January 1410 parliament may have covered more than royal grants (below, p. 496).

[14] Council records for these years are intermittent, but indicate that those who attended most frequently were the prince, the two Beauforts, Langley, Bubwith, Chichele, Arundel, Warwick, Le Scrope, Prophet and Burnell (*POPC*, i.331–51). In March 1410 the king granted Prince Henry Coldharbour House as his London residence; he also had a chamber next to the chapel in Westminster palace, overlooking a garden (E 403/603, 20 March; *Foedera*, viii.628).

[15] For example, E 403/608, 23 July (1411), a messenger sent to the king at Leicester, the prior of Ely and the prince at Arundel on urgent business concerning the *statum* of the king and the prince.

[16] See Appendix. For the king's visit to Gloucester in May 1411, see *CCR 1409–13*, 152, and E 403/608, 22 August.

decline but also by personal tragedy – the death of his childhood friend
John Beaufort in 1410 and, devastatingly, of his daughter Blanche, news of
which reached him from Germany in the autumn of 1409 – he spent more
time with Archbishop Arundel, their friendship ripening with age.[17] Prince
Thomas also spent a good deal of time with his father; neither he, nor the
king, nor the archbishop attended the council in 1410–11, and although
Henry appeared at least briefly at the great council at Lambeth in March
1411, a month later he seems to have suffered a relapse. On 16 April he
asked the archbishops and bishops to pray urgently for himself, his sons
and the kingdom, since he was mindful of the great benefits which the
Lord had conferred upon him since he assumed the throne and did not
wish to seem ungrateful to God for saving him from the many perils to
which he had been exposed. His emotional pardons three weeks later to
two minor criminals reiterated these sentiments, and were redolent with
intimations of mortality.[18] He recovered, however, and, never tiring of
chivalric entertainment, presided over jousts at Smithfield and elsewhere
during the summer and still hoped to lead campaigns abroad.[19]

The relaxation of the king's grip was matched by a corresponding
intensification of the rivalry between his two elder sons. Ireland was one
bone of contention between Prince Henry and Prince Thomas, and France
would become another, but familial matters also divided them.[20] The death
of John Beaufort on 16 March 1410 not only deprived the king of his closest
friend among the lay nobility, it also threatened to create a rift between the
Beauforts and the crown, for within five months of John's death his widow,
Margaret Holand, had contracted to marry Prince Thomas. Whether the
king supported the match is not clear – an indication of his shadowy role
in 1410–11. Prince Henry initially supported it, presumably seeing it as a
way to endow his brother without depleting the crown, for Margaret was a

---

[17] See his letters to Arundel signed 'Your true son, Henry', and 'your true friend and child
in God' (*Signet Letters*, nos. 717, 736). Henry was at Lambeth on at least six occasions in 1410
and eight occasions in 1411.

[18] *POPC*, ii.6–13; *Foedera*, viii.679; *CCR 1409–13*, 150; *CPR 1408–13*, 286 (pardons to the
obscure William Compton and Alice Heyward for treason etc., since Henry could see
clearly 'the graces poured upon him [the king] by the Most High King, not by his own
merits, but by His ineffable goodness, and wishes to expend on his subjects the gifts of
grace, and that his affection may have effect, and mutual charity, without which other
things are in vain, may flourish, and his lieges may have more cheerful hearts').

[19] E 403/591, 1 June; E 403/595, 7 July; E 403/605, 3 June; E 403/606, 23 March;
E 403/608, 28 Aug.; E 404/24, nos. 533, 538; *Giles*, 43, 55–60.

[20] For France and Ireland, see below, pp. 493–508.

wealthy woman.[21] Bishop Beaufort, however, whom John had named as his
sole executor, strongly opposed it, especially since, along with his proposed
bride, Thomas also claimed control of her estates, custody of her heirs,
and a sum in cash reputed to amount to £10,000, payable by the bishop.
The danger in such an arrangement was that, if Thomas and Margaret
had children, much of the Beaufort inheritance would in due course pass
out of the family's hands (in fact they did not). The bishop thus tried to
obstruct the marriage, but only managed to delay it for two years, until
May 1412. However, he did eventually persuade Prince Henry to support
his efforts to retain the Beaufort gold, which in turn led to an altercation
between the two princes which required mediation by the lords.[22]

As indicated by the opening exchanges in the January 1410 parliament, the
first concern of the prince's administration was finance. The financial
policy pursued by Arundel and Tiptoft in 1407–9 had been based on clear,
but conservative, principles: the restriction of grants, a reduction in household spending, the issue of a high proportion of cash rather than assignments, the avoidance of over-commitment of resources, the reservation of
half the wool subsidy for Calais, and the honouring of the king's obligations to his annuitants, all of this worked out during budgetary reviews
held early each year. The mercantile and political truces of these years also
meant that wool exports surged, with 15,000 sacks exported in 1407–8 and
over 17,000 (the highest total of the reign) in 1408–9, leading in the latter
year to a total yield to the exchequer from customs and subsidies of around
£65,000–£70,000. Moreover, the November 1407 parliament had granted
three half-tenths and fifteenths to be collected within fourteen months, and
convocation one-and-a-half clerical tenths. In 1410–11 economic circumstances were much less favourable. Cash flow to the exchequer was already
drying up in the second half of 1409, while wool exports slumped to
around 14,000 sacks in 1409–10 and just 11,500 (the second lowest total of
the reign) in 1410–11, reducing the exchequer's income from the customs in
the latter year to around £45,000. A difficult prospect for the council was
made harder by parliament's decision to give £13,333, spread over three
years, directly to the king 'to do with and dispose as you wish'. In return,

---

[21] The deaths of her brothers in 1400 and 1408 left her with much of the Holand inheritance as well as her husband's lands, amounting to c.£1,400 a year (R. Shaw, 'Margaret
Holand', *ODNB*, online). The papal dispensation for the marriage, requested by both
princes, was dated 16 August 1410. Cf. Harriss, *Cardinal Beaufort*, 63–5.
[22] *Giles*, 62, stated that Prince Thomas 'was unable to harass [Bishop Beaufort] beyond
what was reasonable'.

Henry once again promised not to make any new grants until his debts had been paid.[23]

An increase in revenue was thus imperative, and this is what prompted the prince, backed by a new chancellor and treasurer who shared his more robust approach to the maximization of revenue, to ask parliament and convocation for guaranteed direct subsidies each year. In fact, what the commons granted was considerably less than in 1407, for the collection of the three half-fifteenths and tenths they voted was to be spread over two-and-a-half years, with the first not due until November 1410. Other than that, they offered little but complaint: the customs service, they declared, was rife with corruption and evasion and needed to be overhauled. The prince and Henry Le Scrope had already decided, in January, to cancel all existing assignments, change the customs collectors and their seals, and institute a review of payments, but although this secured a few months' respite it also produced a number of uncashable tallies for major creditors such as Prince John and Prince Thomas, and a scramble for new assignments.[24] Le Scrope duly launched a review of customs fraud in the summer of 1410, and orders were issued that 'no one be spared' by the collectors of the lay subsidy, but there was little he could do about the collapse of wool exports. An enquiry was also set up into the king's rights in a number of counties, but its results are unclear.[25] Fortunately, Canterbury convocation granted one-and-a-half clerical tenths and York convocation one.

When parliament ended and the council met in early June for its planning review of the year, its hands were already tied.[26] Parliament had agreed that the proportion of the wool subsidy to be reserved for Calais, of which the prince had become captain on 18 March following John Beaufort's death, would be raised to three-quarters and a total of around £21,500 would be given to the king's household. This left a host of claimants and very little with which to satisfy them. Among them was Prince Thomas, who claimed to be owed £12,205 for Ireland and £1,600 for his captaincy of Guines castle. He was eventually given just £5,016 to cover old debts and

[23] PROME, viii.452–3, 461, 476, 482–3; Carus-Wilson and Coleman, England's Export Trade, 122–3.

[24] CCR 1409–13, 25–6; CFR 1405–13, 162–4; E 403/605, 31 July; POPC, i.333, 339–40.

[25] CPR 1408–13, 182, 228; CFR 1405–13, 179.

[26] POPC, i.331–52. This was the Privy Council, not a great council as in 1407–9. The prince presided, and Henry and Thomas Beaufort, Bishops Langley, Bubwith and Chichele, the earls of Arundel and Warwick, Henry Le Scrope, John Prophet and Hugh Burnell attended. Meetings were held in London, at the Friars Preachers, at Westminster, the bishop of Hereford's house, and at Robert Lovell's house. The retrospective assignment list drawn up in March 1411 may provide a better indication of what was actually paid out (POPC, ii.6–17).

informed that the rest might be forthcoming 'should he perform the cove-
nants agreed in his indentures' – that is, return to Ireland.[27] Prince John and
the earl of Westmorland were regarded as more deserving cases and were
eventually allocated £9,230, although half of this was assigned on the
upcoming lay subsidy.[28] In addition, it was reckoned that £6,241 was needed
to pay a fleet to patrol the seas, £2,550 to send a force to Guyenne along
with £2,666 as a sweetener for the long-suffering Gascon lords, and £4,515
for Wales. This left an overall deficit of around £14,000, so it was decided to
allocate assignments on the first instalment of the lay subsidy, but once this
had been done it transpired that even this source, not due until November,
was already overcommitted by £2,309, and the subsequent tranche would
not be due until November 1411.[29] Loans were needed, and on 14 June
commissioners were appointed county by county, letters being sent under
the great seal to 'lords and other great persons' and under the prince's signet
to abbots, priors, knights and esquires; by late July £8,000 had been brought
into the exchequer, but the total sum borrowed was certainly higher.[30]
Several of the councillors were among the lenders, and they collectively
guaranteed repayment of other loans under their personal seals.[31]

Yet loans were only a stopgap. More radical was the council's order to
the sheriffs and customs collectors on 4 August to stop paying annuities
until Michaelmas, when they were to appear at the exchequer for further
instructions. Ostensibly this was to allow the council time to conduct a
review of annuitants on the basis of merit, but it also bore the stamp of
Prince Henry's belief that annuities, wherever sourced, must be pruned.
He had already cut back annuities from his lands in Cornwall and Chester,
and once he became king he would institute a review of annuitants of both
the duchy of Lancaster and the crown, leading to cuts by the end of his

---

[27] Thomas seems initially to have been promised new tallies for £3,939 to cover assignments which had failed because of the change of customs collectors, but this was later
reduced to £2,666. Yet in March 1411 it was said that he had been given £5,016 from the
wool subsidy before Michaelmas 1410 (*POPC*, i.340, 350; ii.8, 15).

[28] The Scottish marches probably received a maximum of £6,000 (*POPC*, ii.15–16); as
with Ireland, different sums were agreed at different times (*POPC*, i.333–6, 346, 349; ii.8,
15–17). Harriss, *Cardinal Beaufort*, 52–4, arrived at slightly different figures from those given
here; the memoranda are confusing and often contradictory.

[29] *POPC*, i.346 (it was reckoned the first half fifteenth and tenth would yield £18,600 in
November 1410).

[30] *CPR 1408–13*, 204; E 403/605, 23 June; *POPC*, i.343, ii.114; Steel, *Receipt*, 100. Despite its
reservation, Calais needed an immediate injection of £1,400, which treasurer Le Scrope
personally lent to the prince. Tallies for these loans were issued on 23 June, 23 and 31 July,
but would not be cashable for many months.

[31] Henry Beaufort lent £1,000, Bubwith, Le Scrope and the earl of Warwick another
£1,000: *POPC*, i.347–9.

reign of some £12,000 a year.[32] His decision in the summer of 1410 marked a sharp swerve in policy. Archbishop Arundel, wary of the seepage of political goodwill, had prioritized annuities; not so the prince, and in fact the stop on annuities continued through the winter, reinforced by further writs. At the great council which met at Lambeth in March 1411 – the next financial review – it was noted that there was simply no money with which to pay them. The king declared that, if revenue could be increased, he would like his 'loyal and good servants' to have their payments reinstated, and in May a slight relaxation of the stop was announced: annuitants could now be paid from the sheriffs' ordinary revenues (the *corpus comitatus*), though not from any other source; in particular, 'not a penny' was to be paid from any form of taxation, feudal casualties, or the profits of alien priories. This concession was the result of a petition to the king – from whom is not stated, although it would not have lacked support. Thomas Hoccleve, whose annuity as a privy seal clerk had dried up over the winter, appealed in verse to Prince Henry to have his 'smal lyflode' restored. The gloomy poet protested too much: by early July 1411 he was being paid once more, and in February 1412 he received his back payment for the Michaelmas 1410–11 term.[33] He certainly fared a good deal better than many: by the end of the reign, even a man as influential as Henry Lord FizHugh was 750 marks in arrears on a 100-mark annuity.[34]

The stop on annuities in the winter of 1410–11 was unpopular, as was the council's attempt in November to distrain to knighthood all those with more than £40 of land, which was met with indifference by the sheriffs charged with enforcing it and by July 1411 had yielded just £888.[35] Since the proceeds of the half lay subsidy due in November 1410 had all been assigned in the summer, they provided no relief. To its credit, the prince's council did not significantly overcommit resources, for fictitious loans dwindled to around £3,000 during the year following the 1410 parliament.[36] Yet when the Lambeth council met in March 1411, with both king

[32] *Foedera*, viii.651; Harriss, *Henry V*, 163, 168–74; Castor, *King, Crown and Duchy*, 34–6; *RHKA*, 245. By 1422 exchequer annuities had been cut to £12,000 (from £20,000 or more under Henry IV) and the duchy bill from £8,000 to £5,600.

[33] E 403/606, 23 Feb.; E 403/608, 28 May; E 403/609, 26 Feb.; E 404/26, nos. 111, 283, 379; *CCR 1409–13*, 148; Nuttall, *Creation of Lancastrian Kingship*, 84–93; Hoccleve, *Regement of Princes*, 34, 68–9, 157–8, 172–3.

[34] *CPR 1408–13*, 446.

[35] *CCR 1409–13*, 152; *Foedera*, viii 656, 685 (the latter, dated 20 May 1411, ordering the exchequer to punish sheriffs who had neglected to enforce distraint); E 403/606, 9 Dec.; E 403/608, 23 July (the fines, given to the household). This was the first distraint for knighthood for many decades.

[36] Steel, *Receipt*, 100.

and prince present, the various schedules of income and expenditure presented to it made far from happy reading.[37] With the wool customs predicted to yield only around £30,000 in 1410–11, three-quarters of which was earmarked for Calais, only £7,500 was left for military commitments elsewhere, yet by the council's estimation a minimum of £2,666 was needed for Ireland, £8,250 for Guyenne (including the keeping of Fronsac castle) and £8,700 for the Scottish march; and thus, computed the treasurer, 'there is a deficit of £12,125', even before any consideration had been given to paying off earlier debts or funding embassies.[38] A second schedule estimated that the clerical tenth, tunnage and poundage, and the ordinary revenues of the crown would yield a further £18,366, but that the royal household alone would consume £15,280 of this by Michaelmas 1411, while administrative expenses, repairs to royal castles and palaces, the Garter celebrations and other recurrent charges would require a further £7,000.[39] This brought the total deficit to just over £16,000 – and note, the treasurer added, that nothing had been allowed for annuities or for the debts of the household, which were 'very large'. The king, while expressing the wish that payment of annuities be resumed, nevertheless ruled out any reduction in funding for his household or other 'ordinary and necessary charges'. The only cut announced was that no force would be sent to Guyenne, although £2,666 would be sent to the barons there as a reward; this entailed a saving of about £5,000. In fact, further cuts were soon imposed. The allocation for Ireland was trimmed and the Scottish march wardens' rates of pay slashed, while neither Wales nor the defence of the sea received any funding – or at least not until William Longe, taking advantage of an unpoliced Channel, came close enough to shipwrecking the Anglo-Burgundian truce to induce Prince Henry to give admiral Thomas Beaufort £1,000 to hunt him down.[40] The prince's laudable attempt to match expenditure to income meant that England's defence arrangements were becoming threadbare.

[37] *POPC*, ii.6–13. The additional schedule on pp. 14–17 is retrospective, a statement of 'various warrants under the privy seal made and passed, directed to [the exchequer] to be paid'. There are a few additional items from the budgets prepared during the previous year, such as the £4,666 loan repaid to the Londoners (lent in Nov. 1409) and £666 due to Robert Umfraville for his maritime exploits in the north.

[38] In fact the wool customs only yielded *c*.£23,000 (Grummitt, 'Financial Administration', 295, n. 5).

[39] This included £120 for the king's lions in the Tower and £1,772 for the Hanse under the 1407 treaty.

[40] Harriss, *Cardinal Beaufort*, 55; Harriss, *Shaping the Nation*, 534; Griffiths, 'Prince Henry, Wales and the Royal Exchequer', 215; *POPC*, ii.16; E 403/608, 15 May 1411 (£1,000 to Beaufort); Summerson, *Medieval Carlisle*, 402–3. For Longe, see below, pp. 486–8.

The prince's financial policy in 1410–11 was thus markedly different from that of Arundel and Tiptoft in 1407–9, most obviously in the unpopular attempts to increase revenues, the freeze on annuity payments, and the prioritization of Calais. The fact that three-quarters of the wool subsidy, the crown's largest recurrent source of revenue, was committed in advance was an understandable reaction to the mutiny of 1407, and presumably to the short-lived decision in November 1409 to cut the town's allocation from a half to a quarter, but it might have seemed to some to be an overreaction. Given that the decision – which was not on the commons' initiative, but on that of the government – coincided with the prince's appointment as captain of Calais, it might also have been seen as self-serving.[41] In the summer of 1412, when the prince no longer controlled the council, it was said that he was being slandered in Calais because he had failed to distribute all of what he had received to the garrison.[42] This was a time of tension between the prince of Wales, the king and Prince Thomas, and the accusations over the financing of Calais need to be seen in that context; nevertheless, at a time of falling revenues and painful spending cuts, it was perhaps unwise to declare such a large portion of the exchequer's annual revenue to be *hors de combat* as far as other claimants were concerned.

In one respect, however, the prince's financial policy was more conservative than that of Arundel and Tiptoft: this was the question of the coinage. Bullion supply had caused problems for decades, not just in England; much of Europe experienced a bullion famine during the later fourteenth and fifteenth centuries, breeding competition between mints.[43] The parliaments of 1379 and 1381 had considered debasing the gold and silver coins produced at the London and Calais mints, but it was feared that this would lead to unsound currency, and instead various acts were passed over the next twenty-five years attempting to increase the proportion of foreign merchants' import earnings spent on English goods, thereby keeping more specie in the realm.[44] The effect of these was limited, and it was clear that the English coinage remained undervalued by comparison with French or Flemish coins, both of which were debased during the second half of the fourteenth century. Debasement in Flanders, England's chief trading partner, was especially

---

[41] *PROME*, viii.466.

[42] Below, p. 514.

[43] Bolton, *Money*, 228–94.

[44] For the Employment and Hosting acts, see above p. 333; Ormrod, 'Finance and Trade', 166–7; Bolton, *The Medieval English Economy 1150–1500* (London, 1980), 246–7; M. Allen, *Mints and Money in Medieval England* (Cambridge, 2012), 267. I am grateful to Dr Allen for giving me a copy of his paper, 'The English Crown and the Coinage, 1399–1485', ahead of publication.

damaging, since the better prices offered at Burgundian mints drew more and more bullion away from England; during the 1380s Flemish gold coinage was debased by over 50 per cent.[45] The Calais mint closed for lack of business in 1404, and activity at the London mint steadily decreased, its annual output falling from around £18,000 in gold coins and £940 in silver coins in the 1390s to £6,481 in gold and £195 in silver coins between 1403 and 1408. In 1407–8 production fell to £2,170 in gold and just £8 in silver.[46]

By 1409 there had been no recoinage in England for over half a century, but the liquidity crisis, which was at its most acute in that year, persuaded the government that something had to be done.[47] The man asked to do it was the Piedmontese Richard Garner, who had traded in England for many years and on 22 February 1409 was made Master of the Mint at the Tower of London and keeper of the bullion exchange in Lombard Street (the main source of gold for the Mint).[48] As usual, his contract was recorded in an indenture, but in this case, unusually, it was not enrolled; nor did he submit any accounts for the first three years that he held the office, the only gap in a series that runs from the late thirteenth to the mid-fifteenth century. Almost certainly, this was because his contract specified that he would implement weight (though not alloy) reductions in the coins he minted: the gold noble would be reduced from 120 grams to 112.5 grams and the silver penny from 18 grams to 16.1 grams, with corresponding reductions for other coins. No parliamentary sanction had been obtained for this decision, although by custom it should have been. In other words, it was a secret contract. However, it does not seem to have been implemented, perhaps because it was deemed too risky, more likely because of a difference of opinion in the council.[49]

---

[45] Gold was the preferred metal of the wool trade. For the Anglo-Flemish 'war of the gold nobles', see J. Munro, *Wool, Cloth and Gold: The Struggle for Bullion in Anglo-Burgundian Trade 1340–1478* (Brussels, 1972), 43–63.

[46] Allen, *Mints and Money*, 313 and Appendix, Table C.3; N. Mayhew, 'From Regional to Central Minting', in *A New History of the Royal Mint*, ed. C. Challis (Cambridge, 1992), 151.

[47] Bolton, *Medieval English Economy*, 234.

[48] *CPR 1408–13*, 55, 102. It was the master who ran the mint, the nominally superior wardenship being a sinecure. Italians were reckoned to have expertise in recoinage: M. Allen, 'Italians in English Mints and Exchanges', in *Fourteenth-Century England 2*, ed. C. Given-Wilson (Woodbridge, 2002), 53–62. Shortly after this, Garner was granted the right to export 1,200 pieces of tin from the Devon mines, elsewhere than through the staple, each year for seven years, in return for a promise to take half the value of his tin exports in bullion to the mint, and to pay forty marks a year at the exchequer (*POPC*, ii.115–16).

[49] Mayhew, 'From Regional to Central Minting', 172; Allen, *Mints and Money*, 87–8; C. Blunt, 'Unrecorded Heavy Nobles of Henry IV and Some Remarks on that Issue', *British Numismatic Journal* 36 (1967), 106–14, where the indenture, from a Society of Antiquaries Ms, is translated in full.

Garner's indenture was naturally made with the king, but given the state of Henry's health in February 1409 it seems unlikely that it was on his initiative.[50] It was agreed by the council, so presumably the chancellor and treasurer (Arundel and Tiptoft) approved it, but it seems that Prince Henry, whose influence was growing almost daily at this time, was against it. At any rate, there was no attempt to implement it during the prince's ascendancy, and although the coinage was among the items minuted at the council's planning meeting in July 1410, it was not until November 1411, when the prince's council was dismissed, that further action was taken.[51] This time an ordinance was passed with parliamentary authority (though not based on a common petition), and it sanctioned an even larger weight reduction than that proposed in February 1409. By now, with a further Burgundian debasement taking effect in 1409–10, the pressure for a defensive recoinage in England must have been irresistible.[52] The gold noble was accordingly reduced to 108 grams and the silver penny to 15 grams. It was the need to bring the value of English coinage into line with international bullion prices, and thus to remedy 'the great scarcity of money at present in the realm' that prompted the ordinance, and with the price that the London mint could offer for bullion now once again competitive, the effect was electric. In the year from December 1411 to December 1412 the London mint produced gold coins to the value of £149,871 and silver coins worth £2,911; in the following year the respective figures were £138,822 and £5,463.[53] An added benefit was that whereas between 1399 and 1408 the mint had run at a loss, in 1411–13 it made a profit in seigniorage of over £1,500 a year.[54] Yet despite its success, recoinage was still regarded by many with suspicion: the new weights were only agreed for a two-year trial period, and after Henry IV's death Garner had to flee to sanctuary at Westminster abbey, lost his post, and forfeited his possessions – although his weight reductions were retained and remained essentially unchanged until the 1460s.[55] Between November 1412 and September 1417 the mint produced over £450,000 of gold coins, £33,500 of silver coins, and a profit

---

[50] After almost dying around 20–21 January, the king said he had been 'gravely ill' for six weeks: above, p. 305.

[51] *POPC*, i.350, July 1410 (*Item, touchant la gouvernance de la monoye*).

[52] Munro, *Wool, Cloth and Gold*, 61; *PROME*, viii.540.

[53] Allen, *Mints and Money*, 150–1, 285 and Appendix, Table C.3.

[54] Bolton, *Medieval English Economy*, 238; Allen, *Mints and Money*, 199–200 and Appendix, Table D.1; *Giles*, 63, blamed the necessity for a recoinage on debasement by foreigners.

[55] Garner's goods at the Tower, in the city and at Dover castle, were valued by the exchequer in July 1413 (E 403/613, 7 July).

of around £770 a year.[56] This was the money with which the victor of
Agincourt paid his soldiers. Despite the initial reluctance, shared by many
apart from Prince Henry, to embark on a policy traditionally tainted with
the whiff of unsound money, the recoinage of 1411 was a resounding
success, though not for the man who had masterminded it.

[56] Mayhew, 'From Regional to Central Minting', 172–3; Allen, *Mints and Money*, Appendix,
Tables C.3, D.1, and 'Italians in English Mints', 62–3; Allmand, *Henry V*, 387.

Chapter 31

'THE GREATEST UPRISINGS'
(1409–1412)

Finance apart, the most pressing domestic problem facing Prince Henry's administration was disorder. 'Why,' wrote Thomas Hoccleve, 'soffrest thou so many an assemble/ Of armed folk? Wel ny in every shire/ Partye is made to venge her cruel ire.'[1] Henry IV's later years saw lawlessness in parts of England reach epidemic proportions, although this was not so much the mob violence that had marred the post-revolution years as the gentry feuding (or 'fur-collar crime') indicative of a more purposeful flouting of the government's authority. In January 1410 the commons identified ten shires where 'the greatest uprisings have been', and asked that commissions of *oyer et terminer* be sent to deal with them.[2] Apart from Devon, where the immediate cause of concern was a resurgence of the decade-long dispute between Sir Thomas Pomeroy and the Courtenay family over the Chudleigh inheritance,[3] they were all in the north or north Midlands: Cumberland, Westmorland, Northumberland, Yorkshire, Lancashire, Staffordshire, Shropshire, Derbyshire and Nottinghamshire.

Some of these, such as Staffordshire and Derbyshire, were counties rich in duchy lands where periodic visits by the king during the first half of the reign had bolstered his supporters and allowed him to intervene personally in local disputes, but as his energy declined the Lancastrian retainers who had monopolized local government became more exposed to the envy of the disenfranchised.[4] One of those who had suffered not simply through

[1] Hoccleve, *Regement of Princes*, 101.

[2] *PROME*, viii.458; the king said commissions would be sent out if necessary, though little seems to have been done (E. Powell, 'The Restoration of Law and Order', in Harriss, *Henry V*, 175–94). Cf. *CPR 1408–13*, 374, for belated commissions to Yorkshire, Nottinghamshire and Derbyshire.

[3] Above, p. 213. Pomeroy's old foe Philip Courtenay died in 1406, but his second son John continued the fight, and when Pomeroy was elected as MP in the autumn of 1409 he promptly had Sir John Courtenay summoned before the Privy Council to answer for his conduct (*HOC*, iv.109; *CCR 1409–13*, 6–7). John was summoned on 8 Nov. 1409 to appear on the fifth day of the upcoming parliament; cf. Powell, *Kingship, Law and Society*, 201–8.

[4] Castor, *King, Crown and Duchy*, 193–224; C. Carpenter, *Locality and Polity: A Study of Warwickshire Landed Society, 1401–1499* (Cambridge, 1992), 363–72; Powell, *Kingship, Law and*

exclusion from the charmed circle but also from partisan legal judgments was Sir Hugh Erdeswick of Sandon (Staffordshire), who in 1408 teamed up with the brothers Thomas, Robert, William, and John Mynors, an old Lancastrian family that had fallen out of favour, to form a gentry gang bent on targeting duchy officers and tenants. Their preferred victim was Sir John Blount, one of the leaders of the Lancastrian affinity in the north Midlands and, as steward of Newcastle-under-Lyme, the man charged with arresting them. In March 1409 the Erdeswick–Mynors gang tried to abduct Sir John from his mother's house to kill him, and although nothing came of it they now embarked on a campaign to destroy seigneurial resources and drive tenants off duchy lands. They also killed a royal tax-collector and allegedly threatened to break the king's head if he intervened. The king's reaction was to back his retainers to the hilt: the detailed and partisan catalogue of the gang's crimes presented to the 1410 parliament was recast as an indictment, and Erdeswick and his accomplices were told that if they failed to appear to answer it they would, *ipso facto*, be declared guilty.[5] Erdeswick and five of his fellows surrendered and were pardoned in February 1411, but the Mynors brothers were unrepentant. Thomas and Robert were killed by local vigilantes while attacking Wolverhampton church, but William and John pursued the vendetta, blockading Wolverhampton in January 1412 despite having been summoned to appear before the council three months earlier. By May, however, they too had surrendered and received pardons.[6] By now they had made their point. Local government in the north Midlands became more inclusive, and Hugh Erdeswick and the surviving Mynors brothers went on to play important roles in county society – what they had always desired, probably, but had been prevented from achieving by a cartel unwilling to share power or patronage. The belated acknowledgement after 1410 that to use the Lancastrian affinity as the instrument of royal government in the localities was not commensurate with the judicial responsibilities of a king was probably Prince Henry's doing, for he did not have a personal following on the same scale as the king in the north Midlands, and could afford to broaden the base of government there.

Society, 208–16. The death of the young earl of Stafford at Shrewsbury also boosted the power of the king's retainers by removing the chief potential source of alternative lordship in the region.

[5] *PROME*, viii.471–6; *HOC*, iii.29.

[6] *CPR 1408–13*, 275–6, 320, 376, 397; *Crime, Law and Society*, ed. Musson and Powell, 72, 82–4, 203–5. Trouble briefly flared again between Erdeswick and Edmund Ferrers of Chartley in 1413–14.

In neighbouring Nottinghamshire, the most influential figure during the first seven years of the reign was the widely respected Sir Thomas Rempston, steward of the royal household and long-time comrade-in-arms of the king, but following his drowning in 1406 the king's knight, Sir Richard Stanhope, cut loose and began a campaign of intimidation against his neighbours in the north of the county. As with Philip Courtenay in Devon five years earlier, people feared for their lives and limbs if they crossed Stanhope, and although he was removed from the county bench in 1407 this marked only the briefest of checks to a promising criminal career. The incident that brought his activities to a head was a riot following a failed attempt to arbitrate in a property dispute between two gentlemen of the county. Stanhope and five other knights from Nottinghamshire and Derbyshire were committed to the Tower of London on 24 October 1411. Most of them had connections, some close, with Prince Henry, who showed more willingness than his father to discipline his retainers. However, they did not remain in prison for long. Stanhope was released in November and pardoned six months later for any riots or felonies he had committed before December 1411.[7] It was rare for leaders of county society to spend more than a few weeks in prison.

Shropshire probably experienced a higher level of disorder than any other English county during Henry IV's reign, owing partly to Welsh raiding and partly to the emergency measures needed to repel the infiltrators.[8] By far the greatest magnate in the county was the earl of Arundel – lord of Oswestry, Shrewsbury, Chirk, Clun and much else besides – and the king's policy was in effect to entrust its defence to him. This gave his retainers such as John Wele, captain of Oswestry and Shrewsbury castles, Richard Lacon, captain of Clun, and the brothers Robert and Roger Corbet of Moreton Corbet a more or less free hand to plunder the countryside for manpower and provisions as well as to make theoretically treasonous pacts with the rebels. By 1409, many of the county's inhabitants were suffering less from the depredations of the Welsh than from those of the earl's followers. One who certainly did was William Banaster of Hadnall. Banaster was from an old county family on a declining social trajectory, his public service now restricted to holding the escheatorship

---

[7] Payling, *Political Society*, 121–4, 189–93, 214–15; Powell, *Kingship, Law and Society*, 224–8; *CCR 1409–13*, 243; *CPR 1408–13*, 398. Stanhope had become a Knight of the Bath at Henry's coronation.

[8] Powell, *Kingship, Law and Society*, 193–4, 216–24.

early in the reign and occasional appearances as juror or commissioner.[9] Although he had acted as a feoffee together with his near neighbours the Corbet brothers in 1407, his connections with the Arundel affinity were tenuous, and within another year he and the Corbets had fallen out badly over their respective claims to lands in nearby Astley. According to Banaster, on 13 June 1408 Robert and Roger Corbet with a group of armed followers broke into his meadows and trampled his crops with their horses. This was followed by an attack with five hundred armed men on Hadnall manor and an attempt to ambush and kill Banaster as he rode back from Oswestry.[10] In April 1409 the parties agreed to submit their quarrel to the earl of Arundel's arbitration, but this failed after Roger Corbet and eighty of his men 'prepared for war' began terrorizing Banaster's tenants and laid siege for three hours to Hadnall manor, so terrifying his wife that she lost the child she was carrying. One of his servants was killed, another wounded, a third had his house destroyed. Arbitration by Arundel was once again proposed, this time successfully, and on 19 December 1409 the earl and his council delivered their award, but it was not so much a victory for justice as for the earl's retainers. Every one of Banaster's allegations was met either with the response that, according to the earl's information (presumably from the Corbets), Banaster and his servants had also been guilty of using force, 'so that his riot should be set against the other', or a straightforward denial by the Corbets and eleven oath-helpers 'by their faith and with their hands raised'. No compensation or even apology was offered. Banaster, 'out of reverence for my said lord', accepted the award, although he probably had little option.[11] The Corbet brothers were above him, both on the social scale and in the estimation of the earl. Robert and Roger were both 'esquires of the earl of Arundel', and Robert became sheriff, JP and MP for Shropshire. They would be among the earl's foremost supporters in the more serious dispute which broke out in 1413 when John Talbot, Lord Furnivall, began to threaten his dominance in the county.[12]

[9] His grandfather had been MP six times and justice of South Wales in the 1350s and 1360s (VCH Shropshire, iii.235; CPR 1399–1402, 303–4, 416; CPR 1405–8, 339; CCR 1399–1402, 175; CPR 1408–13, 66).
[10] Only Banaster's account of the dispute survives, in the arbitration award of Dec. 1409 (Shropshire Archives Charter D.5791). Cf. K. Towson, 'Greves et Compleyntes: Violence, Disputes and Arbitration in Early Fifteenth-Century Shropshire Gentry Society' (Unpublished MLitt. Dissertation, University of St Andrews, 1997).
[11] The document was endorsed 'to be delivered to William Banaster'. Although the allegations present Banaster's side of the case, the Corbets did not deny the charge of assaulting Hadnall manor, saying they had not intended to harm Banaster's wife or his servants, with the exception of one Ieuan ap Meuric with whom they had a quarrel.
[12] Select Cases Before the King's Bench VII, 227–9.

Until then, however, Arundel and his servants could do more or less as they pleased. The fact that the earl was also Prince Henry's retainer doubtless further emboldened his men, although once he became king, the prince took firmer action. The summer of 1414 saw the arrival of the King's Bench at Shrewsbury, with the duke of York presiding. Shropshire, declared Chief Justice Hankford, was 'rife with homicides and rapes far more than other counties of England' and Henry V was 'deeply concerned about its correction and improvement'. The fact that a kinsman of the Corbets, Sir Robert Corbet of Hadley, was now sheriff did not save them: they, John Wele, Richard Lacon and others were hauled before the council at Westminster in August, briefly imprisoned, and only released after their master, the earl of Arundel, gave pledges for their good behaviour.[13]

In the far north, the situation was complicated by Scottish incursions and the existence of several liberties and franchises where the king's writ did not run, but the real problem here was less the presence of great affinities than the absence of them.[14] The minorities of Thomas Lord Dacre (b.1387) and John Lord Clifford (b.1391), scions of two of the greatest families in Cumberland and Westmorland, respectively, diminished magnate leadership in the west march, while in the east march the prolonged resistance of the earl of Northumberland's castellans between 1403 and 1405 gave ample warning of what it might take to restore the rule of law. Following Northumberland's flight in 1405, royal power was vested in Prince John and the earl of Westmorland, but it was power without roots. The earl of Westmorland had little interest in recruiting a following in Northumberland: his efforts were focused on the North Riding of Yorkshire, especially Richmond, where he tried to build up a concentration of lands and retainers contiguous with his ancestral holdings in Durham.[15] Nor did the king make any real attempt, at least for the moment, either to intrude his supporters into northern society or to reconcile former Percy retainers, with the important exception of Sir Robert Umfraville. Umfraville was a border warlord of impeccable lineage and a former sheriff of Northumberland who, despite being retained by the king

---

[13] Powell, *Kingship, Law and Society*, 222–3; *Crime, Law and Society*, ed. Musson and Powell, 121–2, 185–6.

[14] K. Stringer, 'States, Liberties and Communities in Medieval Britain and Ireland', in *Liberties and Identities in the Medieval British Isles*, ed. M. Prestwich (Woodbridge, 2008), 5–36; M. Holford, 'War, Lordship and Community in the Liberty of Norhamshire', in *Liberties and Identities in the Medieval British Isles*, ed. M. Prestwich (Woodbridge, 2008), 77–97. I am grateful to Jackson Armstrong for his thoughts on northern disorder.

[15] C. Liddy, *The Bishopric of Durham in the Late Middle Ages* (Woodbridge, 2008), 92–101.

in 1402 and remaining loyal in both 1403 and 1405, had risen in the service
of the Percys and continued to be employed by the earl until the latter's
flight to Scotland. He was subsequently entrusted with great responsibilities: captain of several castles, chamberlain of Berwick, diplomat, admiral,
and Knight of the Garter from 1408, he became a totemic figure for the
English borderers.[16] Yet despite his service to the crown, both his later allegiance to the second earl of Northumberland and the admiration expressed
for him by the chronicler John Hardyng, who was brought up in Hotspur's
household, suggest that Umfraville also continued to command the support
of Percy sympathizers, and he may well have been instrumental in recon-
ciling others such as Sir Thomas Gray of Heaton, his brother John, and
John Cresswell, the recalcitrant constable of Warkworth in 1403, who
in February 1409 indented to serve with Prince John at Berwick.[17] Even
Sir William Clifford, acting head of the Clifford affinity in Westmorland
and a Percy diehard who had rebelled three times but always managed to
make his peace with the king, was eventually reintegrated: pardoned his
transgressions and granted the arrears of his annuity in the autumn of
1408, he was allowed in the following year to enter into the inheritance of
his wife Ann (daughter of the rebel Lord Bardolf), and two days after
Henry V's accession he became constable of Bordeaux.[18]

This more inclusive approach to former Percy adherents during the
later years of the reign recognized the fact that the old earl's following
could be neither dismantled nor ignored. Even Northumberland's death in
1408, it was said, merely 'caused hatred to gain strength and greed to rise

[16] *Hardyng*, 365–7, for his famous raid up the Firth of Forth with eight ships and nearly 400
fighting men in 1410, from which he returned with so much booty and provisions that he
came to be known as 'Robin Mendmarket'. He was owed £1,700 for this, but was asked to
take only 1,000 marks, and may initially have agreed to accept this, but later claimed that
he could not sustain such a loss. Since his raid had been such a success, in that there had
been no Scottish raiding on the northern English coasts while he was at sea, he was given
an extra £100 (E 404/26, nos. 211, 380).

[17] H. Summerson, 'Robert Umfraville', *ODNB*, 55.883–5; H. Summerson, 'John
Hardyng', *ODNB*, 25.240–3; C. Kingsford, 'The First Version of John Hardyng's Chronicle',
EHR 1912, 262–82; *Foedera*, viii.479, 703–4; E 403/579, 16 July 1409; E 404/27, no. 434
(chamberlain of Berwick, July 1412); Collins, *Order of the Garter*, 49–50, 117. Umfraville, 'a
jewel for a king' according to Hardyng, spent twenty years as the second earl's deputy in the
marches following the latter's restoration in 1416. For the Grays and Cresswell, see King,
'They Have the Hertes', 152, and A. King, 'Scaling the Ladder: The Rise and Rise of the
Grays of Heaton, 1296–1415', in *North-East England in the Later Middle Ages*, ed. C. Liddy and
R. Britnell (Woodbridge, 2005), 157–73, at pp. 69–71. See also A. King, 'Pur Salvation du
Roiaume: Military Service and Obligation in Fourteenth-Century Northumberland', in
Fourteenth-Century England 2, ed. C. Given-Wilson (Woodbridge, 2002), 13–31.

[18] *CPR 1408–13*, 23, 95–6; E 404/24, no. 39; Bell, Curry, King and Simpkin, *The Soldier in
Late Medieval England*, 34–8.

up in the northern parts', a picture corroborated by Prince John's letters to his father listing the 'armed incursions, robberies, pillages, taking of prisoners, cattle raids . . . and other acts of war' habitually committed in the county.[19] The fact that two further rebellions followed the Percy meltdown in 1403 says more about the state of the north than does their successful suppression. As in Shropshire, it is difficult to distinguish between the effects of cross-border raiding and the escalation of local rivalries, but there is no doubt into which category fell the notorious feud between John Bertram and Sir Robert Ogle. The two men were brothers, descendants of an old and distinguished Northumbrian family, although Bertram, the younger, had taken his grandmother's surname, probably because it was she who had brought Bothal castle into the family. Bothal was the focus of their quarrel. Their father (also Sir Robert) had settled it on his younger son, but following his death on 31 October 1409, before he had even been buried, his elder son collected two hundred men-at-arms and archers and marched with scaling ladders and siege engines to Bothal. Arriving there at midnight on 1 November, ignoring the pleas of two Northumberland JPs who ordered him to desist before retiring in fear of their lives, Ogle besieged the castle for four days until it was surrendered. Buildings and granaries were burned, three of Bertram's servants seized, and goods and chattels to the value of £400 carried away. Robert was still occupying Bothal in February 1410 when the case came before parliament.[20] He was ordered by the lords to evacuate it and appear before the council by May on pain of his life; damages were awarded and his accomplices imprisoned. This was effective in that Bothal was restored to Bertram, but in fact Ogle went almost entirely unpunished and went on to play a leading role in Northumbrian society, as did his brother.

One of the points made by Bertram in his petition was that Bothal was so close to the border that a remedy by recourse to the common law was not practicable. In fact Bothal was some thirty miles from the border, but he seems to have been expressing a viewpoint widely held by Northumbrians, who in the next parliament, that of November 1411, complained that the county was 'so far distant from the law' that royal justices and barons of the exchequer were hardly seen there, allowing

---

[19] *SAC II*, 534–5; C. Neville, *Violence, Custom and Law: The Anglo-Scottish Borderlands in the Later Middle Ages* (Edinburgh, 1998), 104; King, 'They Have the Hertes', 153–7. In Durham and Yorkshire, men such as Bishop Langley, Westmorland's steward Ralph Euer and Robert Waterton (steward of the northern parts of the duchy of Lancaster from 1407) also played important roles, but their influence was little felt on the marches.

[20] *PROME*, viii.469–71; *HOC*, ii.211–12; iii.860.

indictments to be suppressed by royal ministers and maintenance and robbery to flourish.[21] The government's response was that justices should be appointed to make enquiries 'as necessary', but its record in border peacekeeping was not encouraging. Justices of gaol delivery were by now visiting the county only once a year rather than twice, while the system of Marcher law built up during the fourteenth century more or less fell into abeyance following the capture of Douglas in 1402 and the collapse of Percy power between 1403 and 1405. Neither Henry IV nor Henry V showed much interest in reviving it. Only after Douglas's return in 1409 and the renewal of attacks on English garrisons were Prince John's warnings heeded and tentative moves made to revive the March days, but not until 1423–4 was the system fully reactivated.[22] Meanwhile the King's Bench remained at Westminster. Not once during Henry IV's reign did it sit outside the capital, a point driven home when his son took it with him to the Leicester parliament of April 1414 and it held sessions in several Midland counties.[23] Henry V's decision in November 1414 to restore Henry Percy the younger, Hotspur's son, to the earldom forfeited by his grandfather, was also in part driven by the need to restore order. As the new king was acknowledging, it was really very difficult to replace the family that had dominated north-eastern England for nearly a century.[24]

To these slow-burning provincial enmities, the year 1411 added a new spate of outrages closer to home. Except in the sense that it was seen as symptomatic of a more widespread malaise, the ruffianism of a Hugh Erdeswick or a Robert Ogle was, by and large, limited in its impact to the locality in which it was committed, but some crimes had the potential to embarrass the government on a wider stage. Such were those perpetrated by William Longe, the mayor of Rye (East Sussex), and Sir John Prendergast. Longe was a merchant-pirate in the tradition of John Hauley and John Brandon, and had been active in the Channel for several years,

---

[21] *PROME*, viii.548–9.

[22] Neville, *Violence, Custom and Law*, 96–124; H. Summerson, 'Peacekeepers and Lawbreakers in Medieval Northumberland, c.1200–1500', in *Liberties and Identities*, ed. Prestwich, 56–76, at pp. 62–4.

[23] *Select Cases in the King's Bench VII*, lvii–lx. Under Richard II it had held sessions in many different counties.

[24] The parliament of April 1414 saw further complaints of lawlessness in Northumberland (*PROME*, ix.49–50). The second earl of Northumberland held the keeping of the East March of Scotland and Berwick castle from April 1417 until 1434 (R. Griffiths, 'Henry Percy, Second Earl of Northumberland', *ODNB*, 43.704–6; Dunn, *The Politics of Magnate Power*, 127–8). Bower called the second earl 'very friendly' towards the Scots (*Scotichronicon*, 85).

but with the cordon of mercantile truces in place after 1407 there was less tolerance of such behaviour. Despite this, he and Prendergast had many supporters: Walsingham claimed that their attacks on Flemish and Breton fleets brought peace 'on land and sea', and many of those who lived along the Kent and Sussex coast saw them as heroes.[25] Yet when Longe and Prendergast captured two Flemish salt ships in October 1410, they were directly challenging the authority of Prince Henry, not only because he was Warden of the Cinque Ports but also because they were jeopardizing the renewal of the mercantile truce with Flanders and the chances of a political alliance with the duke of Burgundy. English merchants trying to trade with Flanders also blamed them for their troubles.[26]

By the spring of 1411 the two men's defiance was threatening to provoke a diplomatic crisis. If the Anglo-Flemish truce were not renewed by 15 June, English wool and other goods in Flanders would be seized, with disastrous consequences, both for merchants and for the government's customs revenue; the Flemings, however, were demanding justice against Longe and Prendergast before renewing it. The great council of March 1411 thus ordered their arrest, but within a few days they had put to sea again with sufficient strength to seize eighteen ships within a month (sixteen Flemish, one Italian and one Prussian) before returning to Sussex to sell their plundered cargoes, one of their customers being the bishop of Chichester. The infuriated Prince Henry indicted them as traitors, called up the posses of the south-eastern shires and ordered their capture; Longe responded by sailing up the Rother to Smallhythe on 7 May and seizing a ship, the *Juliane*, said to belong to the prince himself. Four days later, with the Anglo-Flemish talks at Calais on the verge of collapse, the prince sent Admiral Beaufort to intercept the pair, with instructions to offer pardons to any of their associates who agreed to desert them.[27] When Beaufort caught up with him, Longe agreed to surrender in return for immunity, but when brought to London he was imprisoned in the Tower, while Prendergast fled to sanctuary at Westminster.[28] This enabled the truce with Flanders to be renewed, but the prince won few plaudits in England for taking a tough line: Walsingham expressed outrage at the treatment of Longe and Prendergast, and although he admitted the truth of some of the charges

---

[25] *SAC II*, 596–9; *HOC*, iii.619–21, claims they had 'the moral backing of the whole English coast'.

[26] *RHL*, ii.297–302; *CCR 1409–13*, 133–4.

[27] *CCR 1409–13*, 210; E 403/608, 15 May (£1,000 to Beaufort to capture Longe 'and other rebels on the sea').

[28] *SAC II*, 596–7; *CPR 1408–13*, 64, 227, 316–18.

against them he claimed that 'all sorts of men' begged the prince not to imprison them. This may well be true, for Prendergast was quickly released, and by May 1412 was once again raiding Normandy and Picardy and ravaging the lands of the king's old foe the count of St-Pol, this time apparently with the government's blessing. Longe secured his pardon in February 1413, a wise precaution with the prince about to come to the throne. On his return to Rye he received a hero's welcome, and three months later was elected to serve the borough in Henry V's first parliament.[29]

The firm action taken by Prince Henry's administration indicated a greater willingness than his father had shown to confront magnate or gentry malefactors, but in some cases the political rivalries at Westminster to which he was a party were also part of the problem. At Lynn (Norfolk), one urban faction looked to Archbishop Arundel, the other to Thomas Beaufort and the prince, to support their mayoral candidates and discipline their opponents, and the tensions between them came to a head in 1411–12 just as rivalry for dominance at Westminster intensified.[30] Although cause and effect are difficult to disentangle, the University of Oxford's defiance of Archbishop Arundel in the summer and autumn of 1411 also reflected divisions at Westminster. After he lost the chancellorship, and once he had seen off the disendowment party in the January 1410 parliament, Arundel took up the fight against heterodoxy with renewed vigour. March and April saw *De Heretico Comburendo* reaffirmed by convocation, the four orders of friars unleashed to preach far and wide against Lollardy, a royal sergeant-at-arms sent to search the houses of four Londoners for suspect books, and an enquiry begun into the activities of a chaplain called John, suspected of spreading heresy while living at Cooling castle (Kent) with Sir John Oldcastle.[31] It was Oxford, however – 'that teeming nest of heresy', according to Usk – that especially concerned Arundel.[32] For the moment, he was prepared to allow the censors authorized by the *Constitutions* to continue their work, until on 26 June 1410 they produced their first report condemning a number of Wyclif's more notorious conclusions.[33] This failed to silence the dissenters, however, while the committee

[29] *SAC II*, 598–9, 602, 616; *CPR 1408–13*, 347, 470.

[30] Parker, 'Politics and Patronage at King's Lynn', in *Rebellion and Survival*, 210–27.

[31] *CPR 1408–13*, 224; *Concilia*, iii.324, 328; *PROME*, viii.456–7; *CE*, 417; *Records of Convocation IV*, 357–8; J. Thomson, 'John Oldcastle', *ODNB*, 41.668–72. The chaplain, John Lay, was later seized as Oldcastle's accomplice; as a peer of parliament, Oldcastle probably promoted the Disendowment Bill in 1410.

[32] *Usk*, 248–9; Catto, 'Wyclif and Wycliffism', 247–52.

[33] *SAC II*, 570–9 (wrongly dated by Walsingham to 1409). For Arundel's *Constitutions*, see above, p. 373.

grew ever more unpopular: in October 1410 the king ordered the punishment of those who had made up 'opprobrious words and rhymes' about its
members.[34] Weathering the scorn, they managed by March 1411 to
complete their investigation, a copy of which, proscribing 267 of Wyclif's
conclusions, was sent to Arundel for approval. This was accompanied by
the burning of Wyclif's books at Carfax in the heart of the city.

Still Arundel was not satisfied, and on 23 June 1411 he ordered every
scholar at the university, whatever his standing, to take an oath on the
gospels to shun heterodox texts and opinions; any who resisted were to be
brought before him in person to explain why they should not be punished
as upholders of heresy.[35] He also announced his intention to conduct a
visitation of the university. Visitations were often controversial, this one
unusually so. Thomas Prestbury, who as chancellor of the university had
publicized Arundel's decision, was forced to resign, and was replaced by
Richard Courtenay. Courtenay was a protégé of Prince Henry, with whom
he enjoyed the kind of intimacy that Philip Repingdon had with the king,
but his failure to discipline known dissenters such as Peter Payne and
William Taylor when chancellor of the university in 1406 rendered him
suspect in the archbishop's eyes.[36] With the prince in the ascendant at
Westminster, he now wrote to the king, citing a papal bull of 1395 granting
the university exemption from visitation, adding that his scholars were
sworn to disperse rather than lose their liberties. Henry pointed out that the
validity of the bull was disputed, but promised to protect the scholars' legitimate privileges, and a few days later he wrote to Arundel asking him to
restrict his visitation to cases of heresy and suggesting they discuss the
matter in person.[37] By this time, however, Arundel was on his way to
Oxford, where, on 7 August, he encountered violent opposition – including
an audacious threat from Courtenay to excommunicate him for infringing
the university's liberties – and was forced to withdraw. Oxford was in
turmoil, its scholars and masters divided between the two camps, the citizens mainly supporting the archbishop against the university officials,
meetings that began as debates ending as riots, and even reports of fatalities

[34] *Signet Letters*, no. 745 (22 October 1410). It was also about this time that Peter Payne, the
most outspoken dissenter, was promoted to principal of St Edmund Hall (F. Smahel, 'Peter
Payne', *ODNB*, 43.208–13).
[35] *Records of Convocation IV*, 372–3, where it is dated to June 1410, but 1411 (the date on the
document) is surely correct (Catto, 'Wyclif and Wycliffism', 248).
[36] R. G. Davies, 'Courtenay, Richard', *ODNB*, 13.684–5.
[37] *Signet Letters*, nos. 749, 751 (15 and 24 July).

(although whether anyone died is not clear).[38] The king ordered both parties to appear before him.

The outcome of this arbitration, held on 9 September 1411, was Courtenay's resignation, but despite a royal mandate a few days later forbidding the scholars to re-elect him, this is exactly what they did. Such defiance hints at the expectation of support in high places.[39] The king, however, was furious, his initial inclination to strike a balance between the defence of academic freedom and the authority of his archbishop weakening in the face of the university's recalcitrance – even if in fact the scholars were far from united in supporting Courtenay. Fortunately, parliament had been summoned to meet on 3 November, and within two weeks a compromise was agreed, although it was more to the archbishop's than the university's taste. His right to visit Oxford was upheld, the 1395 bull rejected, Courtenay wrote an apologetic letter of submission and, most importantly, the university agreed henceforth to forswear Wyclifite conclusions; to save face, however, the scholars were allowed to re-elect Courtenay as their chancellor. It was said that Prince Henry brokered this compromise, thereby sparing the blushes of his favourite clerk. Eighteen months later, he would nominate Courtenay to the first bishopric to fall vacant after he came to the throne, that of Norwich in April 1413.[40]

William Longe's barefaced defiance of the prince and the Oxford scholars' refusal to bow to the authority of the English primate hint at a contagious disregard for the sanctions of the law in the later years of Henry's reign, but the most shocking breach of the peace to come before the parliament of 1411 involved none other than a royal justice. Sir Robert Tirwhit, Justice of the King's Bench, was alleged to have brought five hundred armed men to Wrawby (Lincolnshire) on 3 October 1411 to overawe a love-day called to settle a dispute between his tenants and those of William Lord Roos.[41] Since it was Chief Justice Gascoigne who was due to arbitrate, he could bear witness to the ambush, and Tirwhit made no attempt to deny it, admitting his folly and placing himself at the king's mercy. Archbishop Arundel (a friend of Roos) and Richard Lord Grey were asked to resolve the matter, which they did by awarding that Tirwhit admit his guilt, apologize to all involved, accept Gascoigne's decision, and provide

[38] *Usk*, 244–5; Wylie, *Henry the Fourth*, iii.442–9.
[39] *Signet Letters*, nos. 753–5; Catto, 'Wyclif and Wyclifism', 247–53.
[40] *PROME*, viii.523–6; *CPL* vi.303–4.
[41] *PROME*, viii.519–22; the dispute was about turf-cutting and hay-mowing on neighbouring properties; accompanying Roos to Wrawby were Henry Lord Beaumont and Thomas Lord Warre.

two fattened oxen, twelve fattened sheep and two tuns of Gascon wine for a love-day with Roos and his men. Remarkably, Tirwhit remained a Justice of the King's Bench for the remaining twenty years of his life. It may have been this case, or simply the general rise in disorder, which prompted the passing of a Statute of Riots introducing more stringent procedures for dealing with violent assemblies or 'routs', the initiative for which came from the government rather than the commons. Its provisions included an enhanced role for the Privy Council, both in ensuring that JPs and sheriffs apprehended offenders and in determining punishments.[42] It was probably the prince who was behind this. His first two parliaments as king complained much about the failure to suppress lawlessness during the later years of his father's reign, and the second of them passed a more stringent Riot Act.[43]

The roots of disorder were different in different parts of the country, for each region had its own political complexion, but it was the withdrawal of the king's personal involvement (especially in the north Midlands) following the onset of his illness that proved crucial in changing the balance of power. Until then he had been prepared, like the earl of Arundel in Shropshire, to delegate local control to his retainers and uphold their quarrels when necessary. This was understandable, for there was manifestly a limit to Westminster's reach, and peacekeeping was often more effective at a local level, but there was also manifestly a limit to the ability of kings and magnates to discipline their retainers. The concerns expressed in the later parliaments of the reign indicate that the upsurge of violence shocked even those inured to the routine intimidation and feuding of the propertied classes. Constant vigilance on the king's part was required to maintain an acceptable level of order. Prince Henry was less tolerant of the peccadilloes of members of his father's affinity, who by now were coming to be seen more as the problem than the solution. He did not have the personal rapport or shared history which the king had with many of his leading retainers. To be sure, the prince needed his retainers, but he did not need them as much as his father did.[44] Yet he too was reluctant to invoke the full rigours of the law against criminals of gentry or noble status, not even a man such as William Longe who had flagrantly flouted his personal

---

[42] The livery legislation was also re-enacted in 1411 (*PROME*, viii.547–8, 558).

[43] *PROME*, ix.57–61; Musson and Powell, *Crime, Law and Society*, 126, 140; *Select Cases in the King's Council*, ed. Leadam and Baldwin, xxxi.

[44] This is one reason why he cared less than the king about the payment of annuities (above, pp. 472-3).

authority. Until it could be demonstrated that royal justice was more effective than local self-help, their usefulness to the government would continue
more often than not to save them from the consequences of their actions.
At times, the scale of the violence practised by men such as Philip
Courtenay, Robert Ogle, the Erdeswick–Mynors gang or the Corbet
brothers in effect amounted to private warfare, yet hardly ever did they
spend more than a few weeks in prison, after which pledges would be
taken, pardons granted, love-days or other rituals of reconciliation enacted,
and, it was hoped, their reintegration into local society launched. This was
the point of pardons, which were not so much a sign of weakness as a
useful social tool. In addition to individual pardons, Henry IV issued six
general pardons during his reign, sometimes to mark notable moments in
his life, such as his accession (November 1399) or his fear of approaching
death (January 1409), but more often as a way to try to re-establish law and
order, as in March 1401 or December 1411. Henry V issued one in April
1413 to celebrate his coronation.[45] Being non-discriminatory, general
pardons were seen as a fairer way to exercise the royal prerogative of
mercy. Acts of grace on the king's part, they reasserted his authority and
proclaimed the re-establishment of peace as the priority, rather than the
creation of new feuds or grudges, inviting those who had offended back
into the fold and giving them a stake in the upholding of the law (as
happened in the case of Erdeswick, Ogle, Tirwhit and others). There was,
naturally, room for debate about the balance between mercy and retribution, but in a society that relied so heavily on magnates and gentry to
govern the localities, there were also realistic expectations about what
could be achieved.

---

[45] *Foedera*, ix.3; H. Lacey, *The Royal Pardon* (York, 2009), 179 and *passim*; Powell, *Kingship,
Law and Society*, 229–46. General pardons were also issued in November 1403, on the queen's
initiative, and January 1404, to draw a line under the Percy revolt. They also raised revenue,
for individual charters still had to be sued out for payment of a fee.

Chapter 32

BURGUNDIANS, ARMAGNACS
AND GUYENNE (1411–1413)

In the spring of 1411 the long-threatened civil war between Armagnacs and Burgundians broke out in France, and the appearance in England of ambassadors from both sides seeking support opened a new era of opportunity for Anglo-French diplomacy and English arms. First to arrive, at the end of April, were envoys from the dukes of Orléans (Charles, son of Duke Louis), Berry and Brittany and the count of Armagnac, but whatever they offered Henry it was evidently not enough, and after nine days they returned to France.[1] Two months later, French royal emissaries operating under Burgundy's instructions crossed to England offering Duke John's eldest daughter in marriage to Prince Henry; in return they wanted an expeditionary force to fight alongside the Burgundian army. The king, however, was more concerned with the threat posed to Calais by the massing of both sides' troops in Picardy and Artois.[2] He did not rule out the possibility of helping the Burgundians in the future, but for the moment 'he would none men give them', instead advising the envoys to tell their master to conciliate Orléans, whom he had wronged by procuring his father's murder.[3] In the middle of August the king announced his intention to lead an expedition in person to save Calais and its marches from 'certain enemies of France, who are hastening thither with their whole power'; his ships, retainers and annuitants were to be ready by 23 September. A council was summoned on 28 August to discuss the king's plans.[4] In the meantime, Duke John's envoys had also spoken with Prince Henry, whom they found

---

[1] They were in England from 30 April to 9 May (E 404/26, no. 374; Allmand, *Henry V*, 48–50). For the terms 'Armagnac' (Orléanist) and 'Burgundian', see *Saint-Denys*, iv.446; *Monstrelet*, ii.102.

[2] Vaughan, *John the Fearless*, 90.

[3] *Great Chronicle of London*, 90 (quote); *Saint-Denys*, iv.474–7; A. Tuck, 'The Earl of Arundel's Expedition to France, 1411', in *Rebellion and Survival*, 228–39; *SAC II*, 598–601.

[4] *CCR 1409–13*, 166, 240–1; Wylie, *Henry the Fourth*, iv.37–40; E 403/608, 28 Aug. The commission to the keeper of the king's ships on 15 July made no mention of his plan to go abroad. The preparation of royal barges to go to Guyenne in September was not for an expedition by the king in person (*CPR 1408–13*, 320–1).

more receptive, and who persuaded his father at least to explore their offer.[5] The king's response, dated 1 September, was cagey; the English envoys were to find out what Burgundy was prepared to offer in terms of land and jewels along with his daughter, whether he was prepared to bear the cost of any expedition, who was to be excluded or included in the alliance, and, crucially, whether he was willing to help with the recovery of Guyenne. Their remit was limited to discussion of a marriage and nothing was to be agreed until they had reported back to the king. These were, explicitly, the prince's proctors, and it was the prince's retainer, Thomas earl of Arundel, who headed the embassy.[6] Yet already Prince Henry had decided to take matters into his own hands, and when Arundel crossed the Channel on 26 September he took 200 men-at-arms and 800 archers, a force which doubled in size once reinforcements arrived.[7] What the king intended as an embassy had thus metamorphosed into an army, almost certainly contrary to his wishes, for on 6 September he had still been planning to go abroad himself.[8] It was, as contemporaries observed, the prince who 'sent forth' Arundel to fight alongside Duke John.[9] English government records make no mention of the campaign, which was financed out of the prince's estate revenues backed by the promise of repayment from the Burgundian *chambre des comptes*.

During the autumn Armagnac troops had been converging on Paris, forcing Duke John to retire northwards, so that it was not in Paris but in Arras that Arundel and Burgundy joined forces on 3 October.[10] By this time Saint-Denis, spiritual home of the French monarchy, and the vital bridge across the Seine at Saint-Cloud, were in Armagnac hands, and they were threatening the capital from both the north and the west. On

[5] *Giles*, 60–1, and *Brut*, ii.371, say they approached only the prince for help, but the Great Chronicle of London says they only went to the prince after being refused help by the king; *CE*, 419, says they approached the king and does not mention the prince.

[6] *POPC*, ii.19–24; *Foedera*, viii.698–9. The other envoys were Bishop Chichele, Sir Francis de Courte, Hugh Mortimer and John Catterick.

[7] Lehoux, *Jean de France*, iii.243–4. Some of these were the prince's retainers, and the force may have been larger than this: J. Milner, 'The English Enterprise in France in 1412–13', in *Trade, Devotion and Governance: Papers in Later Medieval History* (Stroud, 1994), 80, says 800 men-at-arms and 2,000 archers.

[8] The great wardrobe made around seventy banners, pennons, standards and gytons of the king's arms, some red and blue, others black and white, for his ships before the campaign was abandoned (E 101/405/25, m. 2A).

[9] *CPR 1408–13*, 32; *Brut*, ii.371; *Great Chronicle of London*, 90; *Giles*, 61.

[10] Duke John's enemies claimed he had offered to hand four Flemish ports to the English, to do homage to Henry for Flanders and help him secure Normandy and Guyenne, but the monk of Saint-Denis did not believe this (*Saint-Denys*, iv. 476–7, 522–5); when John met with English representatives at Peronne on 26 Sept., they asked for help to recover Guyenne (Tuck, 'The Earl of Arundel's Expedition', 231–2).

23 October, however, Burgundy and Arundel returned to Paris and on 9 November their army, along with a contingent of Parisians, launched a night attack on Saint-Cloud and recaptured the bridge, following which Charles of Orléans's troops abandoned Saint-Denis and drew back from the capital, leaving it in Burgundian hands.[11] English chroniclers claimed that Arundel's men were principally responsible for the victory, as well as for saving several prisoners from summary execution, while the monk of Saint-Denis gave most of the credit to the Parisians.[12] The English were certainly well treated: Arundel was twice invited to dine with King Charles and Duke John at the Louvre, and his men were paid as promised in Burgundian gold. Burgundy's hold on power was now stronger than ever. Armagnacs in Paris were proscribed and before Christmas a brief campaign led by the dauphin drove their garrisons out of several towns south of the city. By this time Arundel had returned to England, having enhanced his reputation and encouraged Prince Henry's belief that he had backed the right horse, but in fact the success of the Anglo-Burgundian alliance sowed the seeds of its own demise, for the Armagnacs were now desperate.

Henry's reaction to his son's presumption was to issue writs on 21 September for a parliament to meet on 3 November.[13] There was no financial rationale for a parliament, for the grant of the wool customs would not expire for another year, the third half subsidy granted in 1410 was not due for collection until November 1412, and the king had agreed not to ask for further taxation until then. Nor was there any discussion of foreign affairs, or if there was it was not recorded on the roll; presumably the prince's behaviour made it too delicate a topic. Yet there was no sign of repentance from Prince Henry, quite the contrary. Convinced that his father was acting too cautiously, he and Bishop Beaufort now tried to persuade him to abdicate on the grounds that he was too debilitated to govern effectively. Henry retorted that he would govern for as long as he drew breath, and on 5 November, despite the frailty that had prevented him from attending the opening three days earlier, came to Westminster to reassert his authority.[14]

---

[11] Between 600 and 900 Armagnac knights and esquires perished at Saint-Cloud (*Saint-Denys*, iv.524–7, 560; *Journal d'un Bourgeois de Paris*, ed. A. Tuetey (Paris, 1881), 15–17).

[12] Despite his contempt for the Armagnac troops, the French chronicler was horrified that Duke John had allied with the 'mortal enemies' of France (*SAC II*, 601–3; *Saint-Denys*, iv.554–7; *Brut*, ii.371; *Hardyng*, 368).

[13] *PROME*, viii.511–58.

[14] *CPR 1408–13*, 346; *CE*, 420–1, says the prince and Beaufort were supported by many lords, and places the incident at the end of the reign, but *Giles*, 62–3, more plausibly

His response to the choice as speaker (for the third parliament in a row) of
Thomas Chaucer was to tell him that he had no intention of permitting
'any kind of novelty', but would exercise his liberties and franchises in the
same way as any of his predecessors had done; the restraint imposed on
the king eighteen months earlier was annulled and on 30 November the
prince's councillors were dismissed, albeit with royal gratitude.[15] No new
council was formally appointed, but those who sat on it for the next fifteen
months were the king's nominees. Sir John Pelham, a Lancastrian retainer
for the past twenty-five years, displaced Henry Le Scrope as treasurer,
Archbishop Arundel embarked on his fifth term as chancellor, and the
earls of Arundel and Warwick, the Beauforts and Lord Burnell made way
for the reliably royalist William Lord Roos and Henry Bowet.[16] Moreover,
although there was no question of asking for a fifteenth and tenth, the
commons did grant the king a subsidy of one-third of a pound on every
£20 of landed income, convocation granted half a clerical tenth, and wool
and cloth exports recovered strongly after two sluggish years.[17] Henry was
also allocated £13,333 to be spent as he wished, and wasted no time in
procuring a down payment of £4,000 of this from the exchequer.[18] The
grant was doubtless meant to appease the king, who was in no mood for
mulishness. On the last day of the session, 19 December, Speaker Chaucer
ventured to ask him if there was truth in the rumour that he harboured
ill-will towards some members of the commons, assuring him that they
were his 'faithful lieges and humble subjects'; Henry rather grudgingly
'granted and allowed' Chaucer's request and issued a general pardon 'in
those places where it seems necessary'. The prince contented himself with
the observation that had the commons been more generous in the spring
of 1410 his council would have been able to do more.[19]

---

associated it with this parliament. Beaufort's part in the attempted coup was remembered
fifteen years later (*PROME*, x.290).

[15] The prince was given 1,000 marks for his work on the council in 1409–11 (E 403/609,
18 Feb.).

[16] Le Scrope was dismissed on 20 Dec. and Pelham took office three days later; Arundel
became chancellor on 6 Jan. 1412, the same day that the new council took office. Both
were replaced as soon as Henry V became king. Westmorland and Bishop Langley
were summoned to Westminster in January, but probably then returned north (E 403/609,
16 Dec., 22 Jan., 6 Feb.).

[17] 17,000 sacks of wool and 33,000 cloths in 1412–13, compared to 12,000 and 20,000 in
1411–12; *CFR 1405–13*, 243 (clerical tenth).

[18] *PROME*, viii.518–19; E 403/609, 22 Jan., 4 Feb. Collection of the £20 land tax began
in early January, but it only yielded £1,388 (*CPR 1408–13*, 378; *Lay Taxes*, 78–9).

[19] *PROME*, viii.513–14, 517, 519, 539; *CCR 1409–13*, 311; E 403/609, 22 Jan.

Although the prince no longer attended the council once parliament ended, he did not withdraw from public affairs, for Burgundy had no intention of letting his advantage slip. Early in 1412 he sent another embassy to England, headed by the bishop of Arras, to pursue the question of a marriage alliance.[20] Meetings were held in February with both the king and the prince, and when they returned to Paris in March, full of optimism following the welcome they had received, an English delegation led by Henry Chichele went with them.[21] Yet already the ground was being cut from under Duke John's feet, for on 24 January the chief Armagnac lords – the dukes of Orléans, Berry and Bourbon and the counts of Armagnac and Alençon – had sealed a joint letter to Henry recognizing him as king of England and offering to do whatever was in their power to restore the duchy of Guyenne to him in return for military support against Burgundy.[22] Inevitably, their offer was seen by many in France as treason, which may explain why the duke of Brittany, who a few months earlier had been attached to the Armagnac cause, now opened separate negotiations with the English king.[23] Yet the Armagnacs were in a corner: they had all been proscribed as traitors; Burgundy controlled Paris, the king and the dauphin; and even a small force such as Arundel's had shown what a difference English military help might make. Any hope that the Armagnacs' approach could be kept secret proved futile. Rumours reached Paris within a few weeks, and shortly before Easter one of their envoys was captured in Normandy and the documents he was carrying read out to the French king's council. Burgundy sent ships to intercept the Armagnac envoys, but Henry despatched Lord Grey to escort them safely across the Channel. By the time the Anglo-Armagnac talks began in earnest at the beginning of May, the enraged Duke John was planning a more robust response.[24]

Despite the alarm expressed by some chroniclers at the apparent English volte-face in the spring of 1412, and despite the warnings of Emperor Sigismund, Prince Henry and, apparently, Queen Joan not to become embroiled in France,[25] there is nothing surprising about Henry's reaction to the Armagnac offer. The bottom line of his policy towards France had always been to maintain English lordship in Guyenne and to keep control

[20] *Foedera*, viii.712, 721; E 404/27, no. 165.
[21] *Monstrelet*, ii.232–3; Wylie, *Henry the Fourth*, iv.64, 211; E 404/27, no. 221.
[22] *Foedera*, viii.715–16.
[23] *Signet Letters*, no. 760.
[24] *Foedera*, viii.718, 726; *CPR 1408–13*, 428; *Monstrelet*, ii.236–41; *Signet Letters*, no. 957.
[25] J. Milner, 'The English Commitment to the 1412 Expedition to France', in *The Fifteenth Century XI*, ed. L. Clark (Woodbridge, 2012), 9–23, at pp. 14–15; Allmand, *Henry V*, 50–4.

of Calais and its hinterland. He had no interest in leading a *chevauchée* through France in the manner of Edward III. Whenever he announced his intention to campaign abroad, it was either to 'rescue' Calais or to 'recover his right' in Guyenne. Around Calais and its marches, despite much skirmishing, his reign had seen the English successfully maintain their lines, but in Guyenne the French assaults of 1403–7 had led to a steady erosion of the territory under English control. The support of the Armagnac lords – including Berry, the French king's lieutenant in Guyenne – now presented Henry with the opportunity to reverse these losses. Speed was of the essence, however, for Burgundy's reaction to what he saw as his betrayal by the English was to plan his own expedition to Guyenne.[26] Even as the talks were in progress, Henry was preparing to go to the duchy in person. On 10 April he issued orders in London and Calais prohibiting his subjects from going to France to fight for either side, since he would soon need all the men he could muster for his own campaign; three weeks later ships were requisitioned, and on 16 May the king's annuitants were summoned to join him by 15 June to recover Guyenne and reduce its inhabitants to obedience.[27]

On 18 May the Anglo-Armagnac Treaty of Bourges – actually negotiated in London – was concluded. Sworn on the French side by the envoys of the dukes of Berry, Orléans and Bourbon and the count of Alençon, and on the English side by Henry and his four sons, it provided for the duchy of Guyenne to be restored to the English king and his heirs 'as fully and freely as any of his predecessors had held it', together with around 1,500 strongholds which the Armagnac lords and their vassals held in the duchy. Twenty named castles were to be handed over at once, the rest they would either conquer or 'aid in the conquest thereof' at their own expense. The dukes of Berry and Orléans would continue to hold the counties of Poitou, Angoumois and Périgord until their deaths, whereupon they would revert to Henry or his successor; the count of Armagnac (who also swore to abide by the treaty) would continue to hold four castellanies in Rouergue in perpetuity, but would do homage for them to the English king. In addition, the French lords offered their children and other relatives in marriage according to Henry's discretion, with their lands, treasure and goods to help prosecute his quarrel, and their friends – 'well nigh all the nobility of France', they declared – as his well-wishers and abettors. Both sides

[26] Berry refused to accept his dismissal from the lieutenancy of Guyenne in October 1411 (Famiglietti, *Royal Intrigue*, 101, 105; Wilson, 'Anglo-French Relations', 474–5; *Foedera*, viii.737; Vale, *English Gascony*, 61; Lehoux, *Jean de France*, iii.265).

[27] *CPR 1408–13*, 427, 429; *CCR 1409–13*, 273, 328, 339; *Foedera*, viii.733; *Monstrelet*, ii.247.

forswore any confederacy or alliance with Burgundy or his kinsmen, and Henry agreed to provide an English force of 1,000 men-at-arms and 3,000 archers to resist Duke John; it was to proceed as soon as possible to Blois, its wages for the first two months paid by Henry and for the next three by the Armagnacs.

Territorially, therefore, the treaty more or less reverted to the terms agreed at Brétigny, but it differed crucially from what had been agreed in 1360 in that nothing was said about Guyenne being separated from the French crown, or about the French king resigning his sovereignty and *ressort*. This was what allowed the Armagnac lords to insist at the outset that they recognized Henry's hereditary right to the duchy, but 'by helping to deliver the same to him and his heirs they do not in any way break or renounce their fealty (*in nullo offendunt seu laedunt eorum fidelitatem*)' – that is, their fealty to Charles VI. By omitting any mention of the French king they were implicitly recognizing his continued sovereignty over Guyenne; as a consequence, were they unwilling to refer to Henry as king of France? Disagreement over this issue was reflected in the different texts of the treaty. The 'Final Concord' preserved in the English archives described Henry as king of England and France. It was said to have been sealed at Bourges on 18 May, but this could not have been possible, since on that day the Armagnac envoys were in London swearing to a different copy which they took back with them. This referred to Henry only as 'king of England and duke of Guyenne'. The Final Concord was clearly copied from the latter and 'king of England and France' inserted by a chancery clerk, either through habit or – more likely – because this was the royal style on which Henry insisted.[28] The English king expressed delight with the treaty: 'How welcome is this moment, the day we have longed for,' he told Archbishop Arundel. 'Let us enjoy God's bounty and go to France to obtain with a little negotiation the land that is ours by right!'[29] The truth, as he well knew, was that only by agreeing to sweep under the carpet the most intractable issue in Anglo-French diplomacy of the past fifty years – not the English claim to the French throne, but sovereignty over Guyenne – had it proved possible to draft terms to which both sides could put their seals.[30] Neither party can

---

[28] The texts are in *Foedera*, viii.738, 742, and copied, with the same difference in style, on the Gascon Roll (*CGR 1409–13*, nos. 126–7; *Monstrelet*, ii.257). The Final Concord was, for the English, the official copy of the treaty, sealed with six laces of silk and green wax (*CCR 1409–13*, 282). The letter of the Armagnac lords dated 24 January (*Foedera*, viii. 715–16) also referred to Henry only as king of England and duke of Guyenne.

[29] *SAC II*, 608–11.

[30] Nine months later the lords of Armagnac and Albret, who still took some notice of the treaty, 'protested and reserved that homage will be done [for them] for the entire duchy of

have believed that the Treaty of Bourges would stick, but it suited their short-term interests to pretend that it might, and, as it turned out, both drew some profit from it.

Even before the treaty was sealed, the king had been persuaded that his body would not bear the strain of a military campaign and had instead appointed Prince Thomas to command it.[31] Yet his commitment to the recovery of Guyenne was undimmed, for this is what he had seen from the start as the prize for intervention in the French civil war – 'to cross the sea, God willing, to the parts of Guyenne, there to recover and retain our heritage of our duchy of Guyenne from the hands of our enemies, adversaries and rebels who for a long time have held it against us'.[32] All was now directed to this end, beginning with the neutralization of the threat from other potentially hostile powers, which meant taking steps to ensure that truces were in place. The duke of Burgundy was clearly a lost cause, but that did not mean that his allies and dependants were, and on 16 May Henry wrote to the burgomasters of Ghent, Bruges and Ypres asking them not to break the Anglo-Flemish truce, despite the differences between him and their lord. The Flemings replied cautiously that they had no intention of doing so, but must obey Duke John; although not entirely satisfied with this, Henry was able on 11 June to announce that the truce had been renewed for five years.[33] John V of Brittany, eager to avoid war in his duchy, was by now as keen as Henry to convert the annual truces in place for the last five years into something more permanent. Embassies thus passed regularly between England and Brittany during 1411, resulting in the agreement of a ten-year Anglo-Breton truce from 1 January 1412. This was reissued on 23 April, and efforts made during the spring and summer to

---

Guyenne to the king of France at the due time, as he was in entire and peaceful possession of the same, and that sovereignty should be reserved to him. And that at the present, and always, the said count and lord [Armagnac and Albret] should have their *ressort* and right of appeal to the said king' (Vale, *English Gascony*, 64–5).

[31] *SAC II*, 610. Prince Thomas's indenture was dated 8 June (*Foedera*, viii.745), but his command was probably decided by 11 May and certainly by 26 May: P. McNiven, 'Prince Henry and the English Political Crisis of 1412', *History* 65 (1980), 1–18, at p. 9; *CPR 1408–13*, 373.

[32] E 404/27, no. 433 (quote). It was always as 'the recovery of our right in Guyenne' that Henry described the campaign (*Foedera*, viii.745; *POPC*, ii.19–20, 120; *CPR 1408–13*, 403, 418, 421; *RHL*, ii.333; *CE*, 419).

[33] *Foedera*, viii.737; *RHL*, ii.314; E 28/23, no. 48. A milder version of Henry's letter is in *POPC*, ii.28–30, but since the *Foedera* letter was seen by *Monstrelet*, ii.260–2, this version must have been sent. For appointment of conservators, see *CPR 1408–13*, 423, 432–3.

enforce it.[34] Scotland also needed to be removed from the equation. Anglo-Scottish relations had eased since the upsurge of violence in late 1409 and 1410, partly because, like Henry, the duke of Albany had more pressing matters to cope with. On 24 July 1411, the long-simmering feud between Albany and Donald, Lord of the Isles, came to a head at the battle of Harlaw (Aberdeenshire), where Donald inflicted heavy losses on the regent's men, led by the earl of Mar.[35] Although the outcome of Harlaw was not conclusive, a lengthy cessation of hostilities now suited both England and Scotland, and in December 1411 a truce 'from the river Spey to the Mount of St Michael' was agreed to last until Easter 1418. The day before the Treaty of Bourges was sealed, Prince John and Westmorland were told to make sure it was once again proclaimed in the borders.[36] This did not stop the earl of Douglas from seeking to challenge English preten-sions if he could, but it did oblige him to find new ways of doing so: in the spring of 1412 he was in Paris, negotiating to lead 4,000 Scotsmen to fight with the Burgundians.[37]

With truces in place for five years with Flanders, six years with Scotland and ten years with Brittany, the English administration worked at full pace to ensure the success of Prince Thomas's expedition. Of the promised 1,000 men-at-arms and 3,000 archers, half were recruited by Prince Thomas himself, the other half roughly equally by his two fellow commanders, the duke of York and Thomas Beaufort, former and future

[34] A dispute with Burgundy over internal Breton matters had led John V to join the League of Gien in 1410, but his relations with John the Fearless were soon repaired (Henneman, *Olivier de Clisson*, 206; Vaughan, *John the Fearless*, 247; G. Knowlson, *Jean V, Duc de Bretagne, et l'Angleterre* (Rennes, 1964), 68–75; E 404/27, no. 238). Early in 1412 there was even talk of a separate Anglo-Breton peace (*CPR 1408–13*, 428, 432–3, 473–4, 476; *Foedera*, viii.727, 732, 744 (safe conduct for Queen Joan's son, Gilles de Bretagne, to visit England, 20 May 1412, but by July he was dead of dysentery at Auxerre); *Monstrelet*, ii.296; M. Jones, *Between France and England: Politics, Power and Society in Late Medieval Brittany* (Aldershot, 2003), vii.5, n. 23.

[35] The dispute between Donald and Albany centred on the succession to the earldom of Ross. It is possible that the captive King James encouraged Donald to challenge Albany, for whom he had no love: in August 1407 Hector Maclean, the nephew of the Lord of the Isles, came to London to talk first with King Henry and then with King James (*CDS*, iv.144, no. 698; I am also grateful to Steve Boardman for his comments on this question). James did not lack influence in Scottish affairs during his captivity, as witness his support in 1411 for the foundation of the University of St Andrews, that intellectual beacon of the north (Nicholson, *Scotland*, 241–3). Donald submitted to Albany in 1412, but when James returned in 1424 he awarded the earldom of Ross to the Lord of the Isles, perhaps indicative of his intentions thirteen years earlier. Hector Maclean died at Harlaw (Nicholson, *Scotland*, 234–7; *Scotichronicon*, 184).

[36] *CCR 1409–13*, 340; *Foedera*, viii.703–4, 737.

[37] Lehoux, *Jean de France*, iii.297.

lieutenants of Guyenne.[38] All those who could be were persuaded to loan sums for shipping and advance wages, and by 9 July at least £16,600 had been raised, even though it meant mortgaging the final instalment of the lay subsidy due in November. Nearly a third of this sum (£6,666) came from Londoners, the rest mainly from bishops, heads of religious houses, royal clerks and towns. Archbishop Arundel led the way with a loan of 1,000 marks, an example to all.[39]

That the archbishop and Prince Thomas supported the king's policy is beyond doubt. Not so Prince Henry. His responsibilities as captain of Calais, constable of Dover, and Warden of the Cinque Ports meant that his priorities and strategic vision differed from the king's, while his experience in office in 1410–11 gave him an understanding of the importance of the Flemish wool trade to English crown finances. He was, naturally, as keen as his father or brother to recover Guyenne, but in his view an alliance with the Armagnac lords was more likely to endanger the duchy by inciting Charles VI and Burgundy to attack it (for, as the Treaty of Bourges made clear, the Armagnac lords held much land there), while the chances of an Anglo-Armagnac pact delivering on its promises were not high. Irritated as he was by the events of the past few months, the prince was not simply being obstructive: he genuinely believed his father's policy in the spring of 1412 to be wrong-headed, and between January and March 1412 he remained closely involved in the negotiations with Burgundy, doing what he could to persuade the king to conclude an alliance with Duke John. However, the argument went against him. He did not, as one chronicler claimed, react by immediately withdrawing from court and setting off on a tour of the country to recruit supporters.[40] On 20 May, two days after the Treaty of Bourges was concluded, he and his three brothers (but especially he) promised, in the presence of the Armagnac envoys at Westminster, to uphold its terms and to refrain from making any alliance with Burgundy, his children or his kinsmen.[41] However, he could not hide his disappoint-

---

[38] Milner, 'The English Commitment', *passim*.

[39] *POPC*, ii.31–2, gives the sums borrowed, whereas those recorded in *CPR 1408–13*, 421–2, and *Foedera*, viii.760–7, were assignments for repayment from the instalment of the lay subsidy due in November 1412, which were not always for the full value of the loan. Florentine and Venetian merchants contributed £533, and the king added 200 marks of his chamber money (E 403/611, 10 Dec. 1412, repayment). As well as the sums mentioned in these sources, Prince Thomas was assigned £2,270, and the duke of York £1,150, which they had borrowed to make preparations (*CPR 1408–13*, 403). These sums are included in the £16,600.

[40] *Giles*, 63.

[41] *Foedera*, viii.743.

ment, or indeed his shame, and on 31 May he wrote to Duke John explaining that the offer made by the Armagnac lords had simply been too good for the king to refuse, and although he himself had been eager to pursue the idea of a Burgundian marriage (as he had told the duke's envoy Jean Kernezn when he saw him), he now had no choice but to disengage from any alliance with the duke; indeed he was obliged, in the interests of recovering the rightful heritage of the English in Guyenne, to defend the Armagnacs against anyone who opposed them. The earl of Arundel, equally if not more embarrassed (for Duke John's treatment of him and his men had been exemplary), wrote on the same day in much the same terms. He reminded Duke John of the speed with which he and the prince had reacted to his plea for help the previous autumn, thanked him for his generosity and assured him that he had done what he could to promote the marriage of his daughter. However, like the prince, his lord and master (*domini mei singularissimi*), he was now irrevocably bound by the king's treaty with the Armagnacs and could not enter into any agreement without the approval of his superiors.[42] Both prince and earl had been whipped into line.

Despite the prince's disappointment at the outcome of the negotiations, it seems that during the initial planning stages of the 1412 campaign, when his father still hoped to lead it in person, he either intended or was encouraged to accompany him.[43] However, by 26 May at the latest it had been decided that Prince Thomas would lead the English army, and in early June Prince Henry left Westminster, perhaps in frustration, perhaps to seek support. Walsingham said that the king's friends were sowing discord between father and son, at which he took offence. There could obviously be no question of the heir to the throne serving under his younger brother's command, but whether Prince Henry requested, or was at any point offered, command of the expedition is not clear.

What is clear is that it was the army of Guyenne that prompted the open letter he wrote from Coventry on 17 June.[44] In this, the prince claimed that his father had asked him to accompany him on campaign but had

[42] B. Pocquet du Haut-Jussé, 'La Renaissance Littéraire autour de Henri V, Roi d'Angleterre', *Révue Historique* 224 (1960), 329–38.

[43] *POPC*, ii.33–4 (A memorandum detailing the financial arrangements for the campaign, emphasizing the need for loans to be raised, thus probably late May, before they were raised, rather than July as catalogued; it mentions men and archers going with 'My lord the prince in the company [of] the lord king'; 'Monseigneur le Prince' was always Prince Henry, never Prince Thomas).

[44] *SAC II*, 610–15. The prince witnessed a charter at Westminster on 1 June (McNiven, 'Prince Henry and the English Political Crisis', 8–16).

limited the number of men whom he could bring, a decision which made it impossible for him either to serve him honourably or to ensure his own safety. He had thus asked for permission to consult with his kinsmen and friends with a view to recruiting additional retainers, and this was what had brought him – with the king's knowledge and consent – to Coventry. He had no army with him, nor was he stirring up popular discontent (that is to say, he was not acting as Archbishop Scrope had). Nevertheless, certain 'children of iniquity, disciples of dissension, supporters of schism, instigators of wrath and originators of strife, who . . . desired, with serpentine cunning, to attack the proper order of the royal succession' were spreading lies to the effect that the prince, 'longing for the crown of England with murderous desire', was raising a rebellion to seize the throne for himself. They were also accusing him of trying to impede the departure of the campaign to Guyenne, thereby creating the impression that civil war was imminent. In fact, the prince protested, nothing was closer to his heart than the recovery of Guyenne and the crown's other rights and inheritances, a cause to which he would devote himself 'as effectively as power is granted to me to do so'. As for his loyalty to his father, it was 'as great as filial humility can express'. All this was, he declared, 'the unfeigned truth of our innermost heart', and his purpose in setting it down was to ensure that the truth be known.

Although Walsingham said this letter was despatched to 'almost every part of the realm', the Latin in which it was composed – learned, obscure, legalistically repetitive, as favoured by the Lancastrian chancery for its *pièces justificatives* – hardly made it appropriate as a popular manifesto, and as the prince made clear two weeks later when he arrived in London to 'make more manifest' the truth of what he had written, its intended audience was really the king. On 30 June the prince took up his lodgings with Thomas Langley, bishop of Durham and royal councillor, at St Martin in the Fields. The large and exalted retinue accompanying him ('much people of lords and gentles') was not intended as a military threat, but probably to remind his father of the strength of his following in the country.[45] A day or two later he came into the king's presence where, according to Walsingham, he asked for one thing only, the punishment of those who had been traducing him. The king 'seemed to assent' to this, but told his son that if proceedings were to be brought they should be delayed until parliament next met.[46] A more fanciful account of their meeting was preserved a

[45] *Chronicle of London from 1089 to 1483*, 94 (quote).
[46] *SAC II*, 615.

hundred years later in *The First English Life of Henry V*, apparently based on the recollections of James, earl of Ormond, who was in London at the time, preparing to sail to Guyenne. According to this, the prince sought an interview with his father because whisperers had persuaded the king that he wished to usurp the crown. Thus, 'disguising himself' (dressing up) in a blue satin gown pierced by multiple eyelets from each of which hung, by a silk thread, the needle used to make it, and with a **SS** collar on his arm, he came to Westminster with 'a great company of lords' and asked to speak to his father in private. When the king had been carried through on his litter to a secret chamber where only three or four others were present, he asked his son what concerned him. Prince Henry began by protesting his undying loyalty and insisting that there was no truth in the rumours that he wished to replace his father; indeed, if there was any person in the world whom the king feared, he would see it as his duty to punish that person, 'thereby to erase that sore from your heart'. Then, having assured his father that he had prepared himself for this moment by confessing himself and receiving communion, he held out a dagger, saying, 'I desire you here before your knees to slay me with this dagger, [for] my life is not so desirous to me that I would live one day that I should be to your displeasure, [and] I clearly forgive you my death'. The king, overcome with compassion, wept copiously, cast the dagger away, embraced his son, and assured him that, whatever anyone said to him, he would henceforth trust him absolutely. Thus was Prince Henry restored to his 'former grace and favour'.[47]

Whatever the truth of the matter, it is clear that a degree of reconciliation followed this meeting, but the prince can hardly have been satisfied with its outcome.[48] No parliament was summoned to try those who had slandered him, and there was no sign of the favouritism being shown to his younger brother being modified. It was this that rankled most with Prince Henry. Hardyng said that when the king had discharged him from the council, he had replaced him with Thomas, whereupon Prince Henry's 'wrath and wilful head' led to a quarrel between the brothers which was

---

[47] *The First English Life of Henry the Fifth*, ed. C. Kingsford (Oxford, 1911). McFarlane, *Lancastrian Kings*, 111, dated this story to the prince's second visit to London in late September (see below, p. 514), but Ormond was in France by then, and Kingsford's early July date (p. xxv) is to be preferred. Although the *Chronicle of London* placed the king at Clerkenwell at the beginning of July, it would have been quite easy for him to come to Westminster to meet the prince; it is suggestive (though not definitive) that letters patent were dated at Westminster by the king on 3 July (*CPR 1408–13*, 410–12).

[48] The first version of Hardyng's chronicle stated that 'The Prynce came into his magnificence/Obeyand hole with all beyvolence/Unto the Kyng, and fully were accorde/ Of all maters of which thay were discorde' (*First English Life*, xxii–xxiii).

only resolved after the king forced his eldest son to submit.[49] John Strecche employed biblical analogy to make the point. When he made Thomas duke of Clarence, said Strecche:

> He gave him his paternal blessing and in his manner confirmed all his goods to him, and he placed his other lords beneath him, weeping and kissing and declaring, 'Just as Isaac the patriarch in his old age blessed Jacob his son with fatherly affection, so now I bless you. And I pronounce you the favoured one, and fortunate in war.' As a result of which great fortune was bestowed on Thomas, a most noble prince and knight.[50]

The chronicler's meaning was unmistakable. Jacob was the son who had usurped his brother Esau's birthright by duping their blind father Isaac into giving him rather than Esau his paternal blessing: 'Be lord over thy brethren, and let thy mother's sons bow down to thee.' When Esau discovered what Jacob had done, he swore vengeance, but Isaac said to him that for the moment he must serve his brother, but that 'when thou shalt have the dominion, thou shalt break his yoke from off thy neck'.[51]

Henry was far too practical to contemplate making Thomas his heir, a step which would almost certainly have plunged the fledgling Lancastrian dynasty into civil war. Nevertheless, the summer of 1412 witnessed a dangerous escalation of the rivalry between the king's two eldest sons, and the fact that it was at exactly this time that the financial settlement consequent on the marriage of Thomas and Margaret Beaufort was being worked out provided another bone of contention to add to the prince's resentment at his dismissal from the council, his brother's new-found prominence, and the reversal of his Burgundian policy.[52] Yet it is most unlikely that Prince Henry was asking for drastic action to be taken against Thomas; it was the court whisperers at whom his ire was levelled. His objective was to reassert his authority as heir to the throne, which had been severely dented during the past eight months.

---

[49] *Hardyng*, 367.

[50] BL Add. MS 35, 295, fo. 264r (*cui paternalem dedit benedictionem et eidem modulo suo omnia bona stabilivit et eius dominos ceteros subiecit, flendo et osculando ita dicens, 'Sicut Ysaac patriarcha Jacobum filium suum in senectute benedixit effectu paternali, ita iam te benedico, et faustum te constituo et fortunatum in bello'. De quo nobilissime Thoma principe et militia fortunatissimo*). Thomas's charter of creation as duke called him *praecarissimus filius* (Milner, 'The English Commitment', 16).

[51] *Genesis*, 27.

[52] Prince Henry had initially supported Thomas's betrothal, but by the time they married in May 1412 he had thrown his weight behind Bishop Beaufort's efforts to preserve what he could of the family's fortune from Thomas's grasp: *Giles*, 62; Harriss, *Cardinal Beaufort*, 64–5; above, pp. 469–70.

By 3 July, when the king moved from Clerkenwell to the bishop of London's palace, the immediate battle of wills was over, but it was the king, not the prince, who had reasserted his authority. Henry may have softened the blow by making some concessions to his son. A detachment under the prince's retainer the earl of Warwick was sent to reinforce Calais soon after this, and on 1 August a writ was issued for the arrest of Prior Butler, deputy lieutenant of Ireland. Prince Henry had long criticized his brother's governance of Ireland and was ever an advocate for Calais.[53] But on the issues that really mattered he was overborne. Any hopes he still entertained that the Guyenne campaign might be suspended or diverted were quashed (according to the well-trained Burgundian spy Jean Kernezn, the king persuaded the prince to 'change his mind') and arrangements for the army's departure gathered speed.[54] On 5 July, to enhance his authority for the campaign, Thomas Beaufort was made earl of Dorset, following which the king moved down the Thames to Rotherhithe where, between 8 and 10 July, a council was held to finalize plans.[55] On 9 July, Thomas was made duke of Clarence – again, to enhance his authority and to put him on a par with the French dukes and with his second-in-command, the duke of York. The next week saw the settlement of the outstanding issues between him and Bishop Beaufort over his wife's dowry, which, although it involved compromise on each side, was broadly in Thomas's favour.[56] Although Prince Henry remained at St Martin in the Fields until 11 July, he played no part in any of this. He witnessed neither the promotion of Dorset nor that of Clarence, nor the appointment of the latter as the king's lieutenant of Guyenne (of which the prince was, nominally, the duke).[57] On the day

<hr/>

[53] CPR 1408–13, 373; Monstrelet, ii.302. Wavrin, Chroniques, i.154, said that Warwick brought 2,000 men to Calais (for Calais, see also Foedera, viii.771). For the suggestion that Bishop Langley mediated between the king and the prince, see Milner, 'The English Commitment', 18.

[54] Kernezn told his master that the prince 'had been trying for several days to prevent the departure of his brother, although at the request of his father he had changed his mind' (Saint-Denys, iv.657). For Kernezn (also Carmin, Kerneau, Carnehen, Carnyan), see Pocquet du Haut-Jussé, 'La Renaissance Littéraire', 336 n. 2; E 403/611, 23 Nov. 1412 (his expenses as ambassador), and Foedera, viii.729 (safe-conduct to come to England ostensibly to joust with Sir Richard Arundel, 14 April 1412).

[55] Arrears of pay were now sent to Guyenne for the restive garrison of Fronsac: POPC, ii.30–3 (£2,300); CCR 1409–13, 366; E 404/27, no. 392 (1,000 marks).

[56] CPR 1408–13, 414–16, 420 (general pardon to Bishop Beaufort as executor of his brother's will, 13 July), 422–3 (grant of John Beaufort's lands to Thomas and Margaret, 16 July); Bishop Beaufort retained part of his fortune, but agreed to pay 200 marks a year to support his brother's children, who were to be brought up in Thomas and Margaret's household (Harriss, Cardinal Beaufort, 64–5).

[57] Chronicle of London 1089–1483, 94; Foedera, viii.758–60 (appointment and powers as lieutenant).

he left London, orders for the muster were issued, and Clarence, York, Dorset and their captains set off for Southampton. Delayed by a contrary wind, it was not until 1 August that the fleet of fourteen ships set sail, only to be blown back into harbour three days later. A second attempt was successful, and around 10 August the English army disembarked, auspiciously, at Saint-Vaast-la-Hougue on the Cotentin peninsula of Normandy where, sixty-six years earlier, Edward III had landed his army for the campaign that would climax at the battle of Crécy.[58]

The despatch of a 4,000-strong army to France within twelve weeks of the Treaty of Bourges was no mean organizational feat, but it was not quick enough. France was already on a war footing, and once Charles VI and Burgundy saw which way the wind was blowing they raised an army and marched due south from Paris to Bourges. Their priority was to bring the Armagnac lords to obedience; after that it was said that they planned to march on Guyenne (thereby confirming Prince Henry's fears). On 11 June they arrived before Bourges, where the duke of Berry was ensconced with the main Armagnac force, and laid siege to the town. After a month during which heat, thirst and dysentery debilitated both camps, the king and Burgundy faced a dilemma: to await the arrival of the English and the likelihood of a pitched battle, or to offer terms which, inescapably, would include pardoning the Armagnac 'Judases'. By 12 July they had chosen the latter, and the septuagenarian duke of Berry, who had moved residence seven times during the siege to avoid the cannonballs fired from Burgundy's great guns, swiftly accepted. In return for renouncing the Treaty of Bourges, agreeing to cooperate with the king and Burgundy against Clarence, and promising not to make any further alliance with the English, the Armagnac lords were readmitted to the fold and their confiscated lands and titles restored to them.[59] If this news did not reach Clarence before he sailed, he would have heard it as soon as he landed, but he chose to ignore it and, having made short work of a substantial French force waiting in the Cotentin to repel him, set off through Normandy towards the Loire.[60] Meanwhile, the now united French lords had moved to Auxerre where, on 22 August, at a grand and solemn convocation in the church of

[58] The likely date is 10 August, but up to 15 August is possible (Milner, 'The English Commitment', 10). In addition to York and Dorset, Clarence was accompanied by the earls of Oxford, Suffolk and Ormond, and the king's brother-in-law, Sir John Cornwall.

[59] Lehoux, *Jean de France*, iii.270, 281–2; *Monstrelet*, ii.270–88; *Saint-Denys*, iv.685–713 ('Judas' at p. 685); Famiglietti, *Royal Intrigue*, 105–10.

[60] *English Chronicle*, ed. Marx, 40.

Saint-Germain, presided over by the Dauphin Louis since Charles VI was suffering one of his 'absences', assurances of peace and reconciliation were exchanged. Clarence's army, they all agreed, must be removed from France; the problem was how.

The English army, reinforced by six hundred Gascons who had been at Bourges, was by now in Anjou, ravaging the countryside as it went.[61] As early as 22 July, the Armagnac lords had written to the English king and his sons explaining that King Charles had been 'greatly displeased' at the Treaty of Bourges and had ordered them to repudiate it, as a result of which they would not be able to honour their commitments; they enclosed a copy of Charles's letter, dated the previous day.[62] Although this was obviously a blow to Clarence, it did not need to, and did not, deflect him from his purpose. Not all the signatories to the Treaty of Bourges accepted its repudiation: the count of Alençon, who had greeted the English warmly and whose lands they had already begun to restore, absented himself from Auxerre, and it soon became clear that he, Orléans, Armagnac and Albret hoped to reach an accommodation with Clarence which would obviate the ravaging of their southern lordships.[63] By 16 September the English had reached Blois, where heralds from the duke of Berry arrived with letters, but since these were addressed to the English king and Prince Henry, Clarence declined to accept them. His self-righteous reply averred disbelief at the idea that Berry would dishonour his word and claimed that had the English king not received such promises from the Armagnacs he would have been minded to ally with the Burgundians. This was probably true, but his confidently expressed expectation that Berry would still come to Blois so as to 'mind his faith and loyalty' was bluff.[64]

What was clear from Clarence's letter was that he had no intention of going home quietly, if at all. His army had been promised payment, and had already shown what it would do to get it. When the French lords protested that they had no money, the citizens of Paris retorted that it was up to those who had invited the English in to pay them to go away. Each day they remained, the catalogue of their atrocities lengthened: burning, looting, killing, kidnapping, destroying towns and churches, they spent two

[61] *Monstrelet*, ii.291–2.
[62] *RHL II*, 322. The letters were from Berry, Orléans, Bourbon and Albret. Also enclosed was a letter to the same effect from Burgundy, although he had sworn that he had no alliances with the English that required repudiation.
[63] Wavrin, *Chroniques*, i.154; Famiglietti, *Royal Intrigue*, 110.
[64] *RHL II*, 328.

months inflicting great evils (*grans maulx*) on the lands around the Loire.[65] By mid-October the Armagnac lords had bowed to the inevitable and opened negotiations, resulting on 14 November in an agreement at Buzançais (between Bourges and Poitiers) whereby, in return for agreeing to leave the kingdom of France by 1 January, the English would receive 210,000 *écus d'or* (£40,000). Whether 'the kingdom of France' included Guyenne was a moot point, as elusive in the agreement at Buzançais as in the Treaty of Bourges. Pledges were given in the form either of treasure and jewels, especially by the famously wealthy and discerning duke of Berry, or of hostages, including Orléans's eight-year-old brother John, count of Angoulême, who would spend the next thirty years in England before being released.[66] The French king gave the English a safe-conduct to Bordeaux, and the monk of Saint-Denis reported that once they had been promised what they wanted and set off, they 'behaved on their march more moderately than the French'. They arrived at Bordeaux on 11 December.[67]

Now began Clarence's real mission. Broadly speaking, the landed power of the Armagnac lords lay in central and southern France, including a swathe of territories encircling the Bordelais: Poitou was the duke of Berry's, Angoumois and Périgord were held by Orléans, Armagnac and Albret by their respective counts. This was what had enabled them to make a plausible case for the English recovery of the duchy in the Treaty of Bourges, and what now made it imperative for the future security of Guyenne that some accommodation be reached with them. When Clarence and Orléans met at Buzançais on 14 November, in addition to the published pact ending hostilities they had also agreed a personal bond of brotherhood-in-arms.[68] Orléans may have hoped that this would soften the terms of his brother's captivity, but it was principally a safeguard against a new Anglo-Burgundian alliance; for Prince Thomas, it held out the hope of a free hand in Guyenne. On 17 December, having settled into his lodgings at the archiepiscopal palace, the new lieutenant of Guyenne, acting on his

[65] Milner, 'The English Enterprise', 85; *Saint-Denys*, iv.721.

[66] Wilson, 'Anglo-French Relations', 452; *Choix de Pièces Inédites*, ed. Douët-d'Arcq, i.359. The English would evidently have accepted 150,000 *écus* had cash been available at once. For Berry's surrendered treasure, which included a great bejewelled gold crucifix containing a nail from the cross, and which never came back to France, see Milner, 'The English Enterprise', 87. Clarence reserved 178,000 *écus* for himself and his retinue, dividing the rest between his captains (J. Bolton, 'How Sir Thomas Rempston Paid His Ransom', *Fifteenth-Century England VII*, ed. L. Clark (Woodbridge, 2007), 104).

[67] *Saint-Denys*, iv.721; Vale, *English Gascony*, 62; Lehoux, *Jean de France*, iii.288.

[68] *Choix de Pièces Inédites*, ed. Douët-d'Arcq, i.359.

father's behalf, summoned the count of Armagnac to do homage for his fiefs, as he had promised to do at Bourges, in return for which he was offered confirmation of his privileges. Armagnac resisted this, but he and Albret did draw up an agreement with Clarence on 13 February 1413 making it clear that, although they still regarded Charles VI as sovereign lord of the duchy, they also recognized Henry IV as rightful duke of Guyenne. In other words, they maintained the stance that they had implicitly adopted in the Treaty of Bourges.[69] It was also reiterated that Henry IV would not support the duke of Burgundy against Berry, Orléans, or their allies, and that he would come to the aid of the Armagnacs if the French king attacked them.

This qualified and conditional salvage operation on the Treaty of Bourges was an encouraging start for Clarence, but its success would depend on the removal by military force of the threat from Burgundy and his supporters.[70] This, too, Clarence set about with a will, reducing to English obedience a host of towns in the vicinity of Bordeaux.[71] The French marshal in Guyenne, Jacques de Heilly, attacked Soubise but was driven off with heavy losses, captured and shipped to England; survivors from his army returned to Paris to beg for reinforcements.[72] Information reaching Paris in January indicated that the English were encountering little resistance in Guyenne and were thus able to campaign with moderation, persuading the duchy's inhabitants to recognize Henry's lordship 'as if they were securely ensconced in London surrounded by their compatriots', and that once spring came round they would take every town and castle in the region; unless a large French force was committed to the field, it would be exceedingly hard to stop them. At the meeting of the Estates-General in Paris on 30 January 1413, a barrage of invective was directed at the government's incompetence and corruption; under orders from the

[69] Compare Vale, *English Gascony*, 63–8, who interpreted the omission of explicit reference to sovereignty differently, arguing that the 13 February agreement represented a 'profound moderation' of their stance since Bourges. The Armagnac lords' insistence that they were not breaking their fealty to Charles VI suggests otherwise.

[70] Among whom was the count of Foix, who had been appointed Captain-General of Guyenne by Charles VI in February 1412, a challenge both to English authority and to his old foe the count of Armagnac.

[71] Wylie, *Henry the Fifth*, i.116–18, 129, 134; *Monstrelet*, ii. 305. Clarence's attorney was asked in mid-October to send £500 worth of military equipment to Bordeaux, and the king sent £224 worth of bows, bowstrings and arrows in the following month (Milner, 'English Enterprise', 85; E 403/611, 15 Nov.). Pope John XXIII asked Henry IV to allow Clarence to come to Italy to fight for him in the winter of 1412–13, but Henry replied that he must stick to his task in Guyenne (*CE*, 420).

[72] *Saint-Denys*, iv.733–47; *SAC II*, 616–18.

count of Armagnac, it was told, many lords were continuing the war in the south and, by leaguing with the English, threatening to 'destroy the kingdom'.[73] There was no money to stop them, however, and April and May saw Paris engulfed by the Cabochien uprising and the renewal of the suicidal power struggle at the French court.

The revitalization of the crown's authority in Guyenne attracted little attention in England. Overshadowed by the domestic drama of Henry IV's death and Henry V's accession, its achievement was underestimated and its purpose misunderstood by many.[74] Henry IV had no interest in 'helping the Armagnacs' or 'helping the Burgundians' beyond what could be won in return. The choice facing the English government in 1411–12 was the prioritization of Calais or Guyenne. The upshot, Clarence's expedition, shocked and shamed the French. This was the first major English campaign in France for a quarter of a century, and the sight of Clarence's army marching virtually unchallenged from Normandy to Bordeaux, being handed a Danegeld of £40,000, and then settling in to enforce its claim to Guyenne, revived the reputation of English arms abroad and struck terror into the French.[75] Not everything went the way of the English, but despite Clarence's return to England to attend his father's memorial service in June, they and their allies continued to recover ground in Saintonge, Angoumois and the Bordelais under the new lieutenant, the earl of Dorset, whom Henry V continued to support, both morally and financially.[76] By the time a year-long truce was agreed in February 1414, Henry IV's decision to focus on Guyenne had been vindicated and the crown's position in the duchy was immeasurably stronger than it had been two years earlier.[77] This was one reason why Henry V was able to focus his attention on the war in the north of France.

---

[73] Famiglietti, *Royal Intrigue*, 112–14; Lehoux, *Jean de France*, iii.293–7; *Monstrelet*, ii.307–33.

[74] *Hardyng*, 369, was upbeat about the 'great honour' acquired by Clarence and his men, and the continuator of the *Polychronicon*, viii.547, thought that Clarence 'set the country [Guyenne] at peace and rest', but *CE*, 420, said that Clarence returned with 'little honour'; Walsingham passed no verdict on the camapaign's outcome.

[75] Milner, 'The English Enterprise', 82–5.

[76] E 403/613, 18 Sept. 1413 (£5,600, plus 500 sheaves of arrows sent to Dorset 'for the safekeeping and governance of the duchy'); Henry V consulted the Treaty of Bourges in May 1415 (*Antient Kalendars*, ii.84).

[77] Wylie, *Henry the Fifth*, i.134–5; *CGR 1413–14*, nos. 7, 9, 37, 58; Vale, *English Gascony*, 68–75. Sir John Blount's defence of Soubise against (it was said) 4,000 Frenchmen, and the capture of many French lords by Dorset at Montendre in August 1413, were especially noted by chroniclers (*Chronicle of London 1089–1483*, 95–6; *SAC II*, 616–18; Dorset's esquire, who brought news of the capture of French lords at Montendre and elsewhere, was given £20 by Henry V: E 403/613, 18 Sept.).

Chapter 33

FATHER AND SON II (1412–1413)

The king's reassertion of his authority in the autumn of 1411 and his pursuit of the recovery of Guyenne in the following year took place against a background of terminal decline in his health. By now, said Strecche, Henry's body had been committed to his doctors; by early 1412 he could no longer walk or ride without pain and was horribly disfigured.[1] The shrinking of his life is mirrored in his itinerary: after visiting Gloucester in May 1411 he remained in and around London, never venturing further than Windsor or Canterbury. Much of his time was spent with Archbishop Arundel. He was at Lambeth palace on nine occasions during the last two years of his life, in addition to periods at Merton Priory, Stratford abbey, and the archbishop's manors of Croydon and Mortlake. From 22 February to 10 April 1412, despite the decisions awaiting resolution at Westminster, he spent six weeks at Canterbury.[2] It may have been Becket's healing powers that brought him there, but he was probably also preparing for death, for it was in Arundel's cathedral that he wished to be buried. Penitence and reconciliation weighed heavily on his mind, and there is probably some truth in the reports that he hoped, even planned, to end his days in Jerusalem, however impractical the idea. The commission to William Loveney, keeper of the king's ships, to fell 800 oaks in Eltham park for the construction of three new galleys for the king's use can hardly have been with France in mind, for it was issued on 1 October 1412, long after his plan to go to Guyenne was abandoned and two months after Clarence sailed.[3]

---

[1] BL Add. Ms 35, 295, fo. 264v; *SAC II*, 608–9; *Usk*, 242–3. Henry's physician from 1408, David Nigarellis, died in 1412; the king was attended in his last years by Thomas Morstead, surgeon, Elias de Sabato of Bologna, and Peter de Alcobaça from Portugal (*CPR 1408–13*, 233, 363, 391–2, 410; Mortimer, *Fears*, 382–3).

[2] See Itinerary (Appendix). Prince Thomas was at Canterbury on 4 April (*CIRCLE PR 1411–12*, no. 23).

[3] *CPR 1408–13*, 476 (*tribus galeis de novo faciendo ad opus nostrum*: C 66/387, m. 13d); *Brut*, ii.372 (copied by *Polychronicon*, viii.547 and many later sources), said that in his last year the king made great galleys, hoping to sail to Jerusalem; Strecche said he announced this plan to the February 1413 parliament (below, p. 515). However, it would have been more usual to travel overland to Venice and sail from there.

The disagreements that had marred the summer refused to settle, not least because the heavy borrowing for Clarence's campaign, the grant of such a paltry tax in the 1411 parliament, and increased spending on the royal household were once again fuelling competition for resources.[4] Burgundian partisans were threatening Calais, and Prince Henry – who could be forgiven for wondering why, if Clarence was in France, he should continue to receive his fee as lieutenant of Ireland – was worried that the town was under-funded. His hand strengthened by the collapse of the Treaty of Bourges, the prince thus came to London again on 23 September 'with a huge people'. If the later story that an attempt was made to assassinate him is to be believed, it probably dates from this time. The alleged incident took place in the Green Chamber at Westminster, where a spaniel sniffed out a man hiding behind a hanging in the room where the prince was staying. Interrogated by the earl of Arundel, the intruder claimed to have been sent by Bishop Beaufort to kill the prince; he was tied in a sack and cast into the Thames. The fact that this tale was repeated to the parliament of 1426 lends it some credibility, although the bishop's involvement is scarcely believable.[5]

Better documented are the allegations against the prince concerning misappropriation of funds for Calais. The prince was being slandered in the town because, although he had received 'great sums' to pay the garrison, he had failed to distribute them to the soldiers. Suspicion also fell on Robert Thorley, who had been reappointed as treasurer of Calais when the prince took power in December 1409. Two 'rolls of paper' were thus brought in to the council for consideration, and although it was agreed that these demon-strated the prince's innocence, the matter did not end there. Further accounts were called for, Thorley was briefly imprisoned, and at a council meeting on 21 October at Merton Priory the king insisted that in future payments to Calais must pass through the exchequer to ensure proper scrutiny.[6] Two days later, all the customs collectors were ordered to bring their proceeds directly to the exchequer, despite the fact that it had been agreed in the previous parliament to reserve three-quarters of the proceeds for Calais.[7] Yet if the

---

[4] For the 1411 tax, see above, p. 496; household expenditure rose from an annual average of £17,110 in 1410–11 to £19,707 during the last eighteen months of the reign (*RHKA*, 272).

[5] C. Kingsford, *Chronicles of London* (Oxford, 1905), 78, 91–2, 299; *PROME*, x.312.

[6] *Chronicle of London 1089–1483*, 95; *POPC*, ii.34–40; *CCR 1409–13*, 366. The king said Thorley was not to 'meddle' with any receipts or payments until further notice. Reginald Curteis, former victualler of Calais, secured a pardon in November (*CPR 1408–13*, 454).

[7] *CCR 1409–13*, 367, 373–4; when the order was repeated later, it was said that the king planned to use the money 'for the advantage of the realm' (ibid., 387). The prince reasserted the three-quarters reservation with payments to Thorley of £15,000 during the last three weeks of his father's life (E 403/610, 1, 17 and 20 March).

reservation for Calais of such a large proportion of the wool customs remained controversial, so, too, was Prior Butler's conduct of Irish affairs, especially since he had failed to respond to the summons issued to him in August. On 20 November 1412 this was repeated more peremptorily, for 'the king's will is not to leave such contempt unpunished', but still he failed to appear. He and Prince Thomas were both replaced at the start of the new reign.[8]

It was now a year since parliament had met, and on 1 December writs were issued for a meeting at Westminster on 3 February 1413, although whether the king would live to see it was uncertain.[9] Shortly before Christmas he again fell gravely ill, although he recovered in time to celebrate the festive season at his accustomed retreat, Eltham, 'with as much joy as he could summon'.[10] He spent the next month moving – or being moved – between Greenwich, Mortlake and Lambeth before returning to Westminster early in February. Here he spent the last six weeks of his life, rousing himself one last time to address his subjects. Although no official roll survives of the proceedings of the February 1413 parliament, it certainly met: a draft of the speaker's protestation was preserved, and the burgesses elected for Salisbury brought back an ordinance passed there concerning clothmaking.[11] Henry did not attend the opening session – it was Arundel, as chancellor, who accepted the speaker's protestation – but according to Strecche the king did later appear 'publicly before all the people' to explain that, God willing, it

[8] *POPC*, ii.35; *CCR 1409–13*, 401. The treasurer of Ireland, William Allington, was in England in the autumn (*CIRCLE PR 1412–13*, no. 12).

[9] *CCR 1409–13*, 406; *CPR 1413–16*, 38.

[10] *SAC II*, 619.

[11] I am grateful to Linda Clark (*History of Parliament*) for these references, of which I was unaware at the time of editing *PROME*, viii.514. The draft speaker's protestation is printed in *Parliamentary Texts of the Later Middle Ages*, ed. N. Pronay and J. Taylor (Oxford, 1980), 197–201. Internal evidence indicated that it must date from 1413, 1447, 1487 or 1504, although 1447 was soon ruled out. The editors suggested 1504, but it is much more likely to be 1413, for the text survived in a commonplace book belonging to John Whittocksmead, a burgess from Somerset who sat in twelve parliaments between 1427 and 1472, whose father and grandfather had been elected on several occasions between 1361 and 1410, and who died in 1482–3 (Linda Clark, 'Whittocksmead, John', forthcoming in the *History of Parliament 1422–1461*). The protestation is one of the earliest examples of the recording of parliamentary business in English, along with the first surviving commons' bill in English in 1414. The responses to the speaker were given in Latin by the chancellor (Arundel), presumably because the king was ill. The protestation is more verbose and deferential than the usual formula recorded on the rolls, consisting of two parts: (i) a request on account of his unworthiness for a different person to be elected, which was refused; (ii) acceptance of the office and a request to enjoy the same privileges as former speakers, including royal favour and the support of his fellow members, to which the chancellor responded that this should be enrolled in the usual manner. For the ordinance on clothmaking, see *The First General Entry Book of the City of Salisbury 1387–1452*, ed. D. Carr (Wiltshire Record Society 54, Trowbridge, 2001), no. 118.

was his intention 'to restore the Holy Cross to the hands of Christians', in order to accomplish which he asked for aid to be made available to him; 'having said which, he immediately exacted for his proposed expedition a tenth from the clergy and a fifteenth from the people in parliament, and withdrew'.[12] Three months later, in Henry V's first parliament, the knights and burgesses elected in February claimed to have remained at Westminster at their own cost until it was dissolved following the king's death, and asked the new king to grant payment of their expenses. A record of the parliament's proceedings would certainly have been kept, but once Henry IV died its acts, including the taxes granted, were nullified.[13]

Various accounts were preserved of conversations at Henry's deathbed, focusing on two themes: a homily from the king to the prince, and a request from his confessor, John Tille, to repent of his misdeeds. Tille, a Dominican friar, had been Henry's confessor since 1411.[14] According to Capgrave's English chronicle, certain lords who were present asked him to induce the king to repent for three things in particular: the death of Richard II, the death of Archbishop Scrope, and his 'wrong title' (usurpation) of the crown. For the first two, replied Henry, he had written to the pope and received absolution; as for the third, there was no remedy to be had, 'for my children will not suffer that the regality go out of our lineage'.[15] The dying king's advice to his son found its way into a number of sources, some written within a decade of Henry's death, others much later. Common sentiments were expressed, but with variations. Capgrave and Elmham made the king emphasize the transience of all earthly things, the need to love and fear God, and to be strong in adversity and modest in victory.[16] Capgrave added that he advised the prince to take a wise confessor who was not afraid to offer him salutary warnings (in the manner of Tille, or of Repingdon), that he should especially value holy men who had led a solitary life of prayer, and that he should eschew idleness and dedicate himself to God and his realm. Strecche endorsed much of this, adding an exhortation from the king to the prince to act righteously in his judgements and love his brothers. The last point was taken up and expanded a century later in the *First English Life*, which had the king say that he feared that after his

[12] BL Add. MSS 35, 295, fo. 264v–265r.

[13] *PROME*, ix.18.

[14] Codling, 'Henry IV and Personal Piety', 27; *CPR 1408–13*, 452.

[15] Capgrave, *Chronicle of England*, 302–3 (written around 1460).

[16] *De Illustribus Henricis*, 110–11; *Political Poems and Songs*, ii.120–2 ('Letter of King Henry IV to His Son').

death 'some discord' might arise between Princes Henry and Thomas, for they were both 'of so great stomach and courage'. The prince replied that he would love and honour his brothers above all men so long as they remained true to him, but if they conspired or rebelled against him, 'I assure you that I shall as soon execute justice upon any one of them as upon the worst and most simplest person within your realm'. The king was 'marvellously rejoiced in his mind' to hear this and launched into a peroration on the virtues of swift and impartial justice, fear of God and the love of his people as the keys to a tranquil and glorious reign.[17] Several of these accounts end with the king bestowing his paternal blessing on the prince.

The sickness that had wasted Henry's body had now run its course. He was, said Capgrave, 'all sinews and bones'; Usk described him as 'cruelly tormented with festering of the flesh, dehydration of the eyes and rupture of the internal organs'. Strecche went further, describing the king's body as 'completely shrunken and wasted by disease . . . his flesh and skin eaten away [and] all his innards laid open and visible . . . apart from those which had been wrapped and bandaged'.[18] Such putrefaction might have been caused by the skin disease which had afflicted him for years, or by circulatory problems (such as blocked arteries) cutting off the blood supply to parts of his body. Death finally released him on 20 March, after he collapsed in Westminster abbey, having gone there to make an offering at the shrine of Edward the Confessor. Comatose, he was laid on a pallet and carried to the high and spacious Jerusalem chamber in the abbot's lodging, where he was placed in front of the fire.[19] Presently he revived and asked his chamberlain where he was; when told that the chamber was called Jerusalem he declared that his time had come, that it had been prophesied that he would die in Jerusalem, and that now he would yield himself up to God. Strecche reported his last words as, ' "Now I hope to see God in the land of the living, and under His most gentle mercy I await my death." ' And thus 'King Henry gave up his life to the Saviour'.[20]

[17] First English Life, 13–15.

[18] Usk, 242–3; De Illustribus Henricis, 111; BL Add. MSS 35, 295, fos. 26v–265r (corpus suum ex nimia tunc infirmitate decoctum et tabefactum, consumptis carnibus et cutis . . . omnia alia interiora sui corporis visum fuerant patefacta . . . eius membra ligata et involuta).

[19] Polychronicon, viii.547; Brut, ii.372; CE, 421. Elmham called it the Bethlehem chamber (Political Poems and Songs, ii.122) but all other sources call it Jerusalem, presumably because of its wall-paintings. The chamber is at the west end of the abbey, 36 x 18 ft, and had a fireplace in the east wall: A. J. Kempe, 'Some Account of the Jerusalem Chamber in the Abbey of Westminster', Archaeologia 26 (1836), 432–45. It now contains two busts, of Henry IV and Henry V, with the inscriptions: 'Here died King Henry IV', and 'Here Henry V became king'.

[20] Above, Introduction, p. 1, for a different version of the king's last words.

Although the many stories surrounding Henry's last days and death
grew in the telling, they carried within them elements of truth and reflect
contemporary perceptions. That his confessor should have attended his
master's deathbed was to be expected, and whether or not Tille advised
Henry to beg God's forgiveness for his usurpation and the deaths of Scrope
and Richard II, it was such matters that contemporaries thought ought to
have been on the dying king's mind.[21] If there is a familiar ring to the
advice he offered his son, there is no doubting Prince Henry's presence at
Westminster during the final weeks of his father's life, and it is easy to
imagine that they conversed on a number of occasions. The concerns
raised in the king's speeches resonate not just with traditional advice literature such as mirrors for princes, but also with the concerns of the moment
such as the disagreements between his sons. That Henry died in a chamber
called Jerusalem is beyond doubt; that he actually planned to travel to
Jerusalem is not, but the intention, or at least hope of doing so, was real
enough, and the association between the Holy Land and the king's last
days was a reminder of what to many continued to mark him out as a truly
Christian king: his years of pilgrimage and crusading.

In the will he dictated on 21 January 1409, Henry had asked to be buried in
Canterbury cathedral, 'after the discretion of my cousin the archbishop of
Canterbury', and although this must have been superseded by a second will
the king evidently did not change his mind about his place of burial.[22] A
number of considerations influenced his choice of Canterbury over
Westminster, not least the fact that space was running out in St Edward's
chapel, where seven royal tombs already formed a horseshoe around the
Confessor's shrine, and an eighth – that of Richard II and Anne of Bohemia
– had stood empty and reproachful for fifteen years.[23] Henry might have
usurped Richard's throne, but he could hardly usurp his grave, whereas to
have himself buried in a less conspicuous place than the king he had
deposed might have seemed impolitic. Yet these problems were not insu-

---

[21] Following his account of Henry's death, Strecche included a long passage on
Archbishop Scrope and his miracles (BL Add. MSS 35,295, fo. 265r).

[22] Henry's first will appointed Prince Henry as his sole executor, but after his death his
executors were said to be Archbishop Bowet, Bishop Langley, John Pelham, Robert
Waterton and John Leventhorpe, with Prince Henry and Archbishop Arundel as supervisors (Nichols, *Collection of Wills*, 203–7; *CPR 1413–16*, 54).

[23] The tombs were: Edmund Crouchback, Edward I, Henry III, Eleanor of Castile,
Philippa of Hainault, Edward III, Richard II with Anne of Bohemia, and King Sebert of
the East Saxons, placed there in 1307: P. Binski, *Westminster Abbey and the Plantagenets* (New
Haven, 1995), 123, 147, 195.

perable – Henry V later found a convenient spot for his tomb just east of the shrine – and there must also have been positive reasons to prefer Canterbury, notably the lure of burial next to the shrine of Thomas Becket, a more prestigious, if less royal, saint than the Confessor. That it was Becket's oil that had anointed Henry as king and that his tomb would be within the Trinity chapel, mirroring his lifelong Trinitarian devotion, were probably decisive.[24] Henry's tomb on the north side of Becket's shrine would also complement that of the Black Prince, England's lost warrior king and another devotee of the Trinity, on the south side; moreover, he would be surrendering his soul to the care of his friend Archbishop Arundel, whose 'true son' and 'child in God' he had declared himself to be.[25]

Details of the king's interment are lacking, although the insertion of the current *ordo* for the burial of English kings, *De Exequiis Regalibus*, into the register of Archbishop Bowet, one of Henry's executors, suggests that an attempt was made to follow the usual procedure.[26] According to this, the corpse was washed, rubbed down with balsam and spices and then embalmed, which meant replacing the brain, viscera, heart and other internal organs with oils and ointments to prevent putrefaction. Once embalmed, the *ordo* prescribed that it should be clothed in a tunic stretching to the heels, then a royal mantle. The beard was to be carefully arranged on the chest, the head and face covered with a silken handkerchief, a crown or diadem placed on the head, the hands covered with gloves decorated with orphreys, and a gold ring placed on the middle finger of the right hand. A gilded orb was then to be placed in the right hand, into which a golden rod surmounted by a cross was inserted, with the cross lying on the dead king's chest, while the left hand held a gilded sceptre extending upwards as far as the left ear. Finally, the shins and feet were to be covered with silken stockings and slippers.

In Henry's case, it was later discovered that his body had been wrapped five times round in leather and sealed in a leaden shroud before being placed in an elm-wood coffin so large that it had to be packed with

---

[24] Wilson, 'The Tomb of Henry IV', 181–90. The placing of John Beaufort's tomb in Canterbury in 1410 suggests that the precise location of Henry's tomb had already been chosen, for Beaufort was originally placed at the foot of what would be the king's tomb before being moved around 1440 to the Holand Chapel. Henry's will opens with the words 'In the name of God, father and son and Holy Ghost, three persons and one God'; for his devotion to the Trinity, see above, p. 381.

[25] *SAC I*, 32–3 (Black Prince); *Signet Letters*, nos. 717, 736 (quotes).

[26] *Fabric Rolls of York Minster*, ed. J. Raine (Surtees Society 35, 1858), 192. This version of the funeral *ordo* dates from 1360–70: C. Given-Wilson, 'The Exequies of Edward III and the Royal Funeral Ceremony in Late Medieval England, *EHR* 124 (2009), 257–82.

hay-bands to prevent it shifting; since this shroud was moulded to human shape, the regalia (assuming they were included) must have been placed beside it in the oversized coffin. The cortege then proceeded by barge, accompanied by a torchlight procession which included the new king, his brothers, and other lords and prelates, down the Thames to Gravesend and overland from there to Canterbury, where it was buried next to Becket's shrine.[27] All this was probably done by the end of March, certainly before Henry V's coronation on 9 April, and was paid for by the transfer of a relatively modest 500 marks from the duchy of Lancaster to Thomas Brounfleet, treasurer of the dead king's household.[28]

Once Henry V's first parliament had met (15 May to 9 June) and Clarence had returned from Guyenne, a memorial service was held in Canterbury cathedral – appropriately, on Trinity Sunday (18 June).[29] Henry V and his brothers arrived in Canterbury on 16 June, and on the following day the king hosted a banquet.[30] A great iron *herce* (candle-frame) costing £200 and constructed by Simon Prentout, wax-chandler of London, was erected between the choir and the high altar, around which burned ten dozen torches.[31] These *herces* could reach as high as the vault, and were also known in France as *chapelles ardentes*. Henry's was draped with forty pennons (*gytons*), other hangings (*valances*) painted with images, and encircled by barriers covered with black cloth, within which the chief mourners stood or knelt. The pennons and hangings were provided by Henry IV's painters, Thomas Kent and Thomas Wright, who also made ninety banners 'with all their stuff' on which were painted 'the arms of all the Christian kings and other great men of the various kingdoms of the world', each of which cost half a mark.[32] For a pilgrim, warrior and crusader of international renown, the connotations were unmistakable.

[27] *Brut*, ii.372 (but the barge went to Gravesend, not Faversham; Wylie, *Henry the Fourth*, iv.111–13).
[28] DL 28/4/8, fo. 11v (500 marks for the *sepulturam* of Henry); Wylie, *Henry the Fifth*, i.2; E 403/612, 20 May; *CPR 1413–16*, 64; *Foedera*, ix.14.
[29] This was not the burial, although it may have been thought of as Henry's 'public' funeral (it is referred to as Henry's *anniversarium* or *exequiarum*: E 403/612, 20 May, 27 June).
[30] Wylie, *Henry the Fifth*, i.47–8.
[31] This was painted by Thomas Gloucester of London, the king's painter. In addition to the 120 torches *ad ardendum circa herceam*, it had many more candles and other adornments (*una cum toto lumino de cera et toto alio apparatu ad dictam herceam pertinentem*) (E 403/612, 20 May; *CPR 1413–16*, 64; *Foedera*, ix.14).
[32] *xc vexillorum cum toto estuffamento pro eisdem de armis omnium regum Christianorum et alium procerum diversorum regnorum mundi* (E 403/612, 20 May; E 403/614, 15 Nov.).

Henry V's personal contribution to the memorial service on 18 June was a gilded head, probably a reliquary, studded with pearls and precious stones, which cost him £160 and which he offered at Becket's tomb. That evening he gave a banquet to mark the feast of the Trinity, but these were his last acts beyond the obligatory minimum to honour the memory of the father to whom he owed his throne.[33] Indeed Henry V spent considerably more money on the reburial of Richard II in Westminster abbey in December 1413 than he did on his father's exequies, a point not lost on contemporaries.[34] It was not he but Queen Joan who commissioned the monument to her and her husband erected over Henry's grave a decade or so after his burial.[35] Their alabaster effigies were probably made in the workshop of Thomas Prentys and Robert Sutton at Chellaston (Derbyshire). The tester above them carefully integrated their heraldry, one shield of each of their arms and, in the middle, a third impaling their arms, set against repeating lines of Henry's motto, *Soverayne*, and Joan's, *A Temperance*, alternating with badges of Henry's crowned eagles and Joan's ermines (Joan's first husband, John IV of Brittany, had founded the order of the ermine in 1381). Each of the shields was encircled by a **SS** collar 'fastened' by an eagle in flight. The tomb chest had alabaster angels also holding arms of England and Navarre. Gazing up at the tester, side by side with their heads on pillows supported by angels, were placed the figures of the king and queen in their robes of state, she wearing a prominent **SS** collar. His figure is considerably larger than hers, a naturalistic detail confirmed by the respective sizes of their leaden shrouds. Henry's face – stern and pudgy – also seems naturalistic, and is the closest thing we have to a likeness of the king, possibly based on

[33] *pro uno capite de auro ad formam capitis hominis ornato perlis et lapidibus preciosis per ipsum dominum regem ad tumbam sancti Thome Cantuariensis in propria persona oblato* (E 403/612, 4 July); my thanks to Julian Luxford for his comments on this. The banquet cost £98 (Wylie, *Henry the Fifth*, i.47).

[34] This began with Henry V borrowing from Canterbury the banners which had been hung at his father's funeral to re-use them for Richard's reburial. More torches, banners and gytons and a hearse were ordered, 'new work' undertaken at Westminster, and the remarkable sum of 1,000 marks (not 100, as in *Issues*, ed. Devon) was distributed to paupers along the route taken by Richard's corpse from Langley to Westminster. Walsingham said Henry V 'declared that he ought to show as much veneration for Richard as he would to his very own father'; he had visited Langley at the start of his reign (E 403/613, 4 May; E 403/614, 8 Nov., 11 Dec., 27 Jan., 19 Feb.; *Issues*, ed. Devon, 325–32; *SAC II*, 634–7).

[35] C. Wilson, 'The Medieval Monuments', in *A History of Canterbury Cathedral*, ed. P. Collinson, N. Ramsay and M. Sparks (Oxford, 1995), 451–510, at pp. 498–506; Wilson, 'The Tomb of Henry IV', 181–90. M. Duffy, *The Royal Tombs of Medieval England* (Stroud, 2003), suggested that Henry V was more likely to have commissioned his father's tomb, but there is no reference to this in any royal record, whereas references in royal records to Edward III's, Richard II's and Henry V's tombs are numerous.

a death mask.[36] The panels at either end depict the martyrdom of Becket and the Coronation of the Virgin by the Trinity. It was doubtless the fact that Henry was buried in the cathedral that also led to the incorporation into the late fifteenth-century stained glass of the north-west transept of an image of St Thomas holding a small phial, the oil with which he and his successors were anointed.[37]

His burial apart, the most pressing charge laid by Henry IV on his executors was the payment of his debts, especially those of his household, but this arrangement was soon overturned. On 15 May 1413, the opening day of parliament, by which time his debts had been calculated at £16,666, his executors (Henry Bowet, Thomas Langley, John Pelham, Robert Waterton and John Leventhorpe) renounced execution of his will on the grounds that his goods were insufficient to cover his debts, and agreed instead that the goods be given to Henry V, who in return would pay £16,666 over four years to the executors, under the supervision of Archbishop Arundel.[38] This money would then be used by the executors to pay the debts. This was done on Henry V's initiative, and it was he who benefited from the arrangement. However, Arundel's death in February 1414 removed the one person who might have held the new king to his word, and in fact by the time Henry V died nine years later he had passed no more than £4,000 in total to the executors. As a result, a new committee had to be appointed in the parliament of 1422 to oversee the work, although the fact that Henry V had also left debts of around £14,000 complicated the process. Nevertheless, with an administration more sympathetic to royal creditors, it proved possible to clear Henry IV's account by 1429 and largely to clear Henry V's by 1432.[39]

A further charge laid upon Henry's executors was the endowment of a perpetual chantry for two priests to pray for his soul in Canterbury

[36] Wilson, 'The Medieval Monuments', 502, calls it 'pudgy, ill-looking'; Duffy, *Royal Tombs*, 202. Joan's effigy was added after her death in 1437.

[37] Wilson, 'The Tomb of Henry IV', 190.

[38] E 404/29, no. 3; *PROME*, ix.9–10; *CPR 1413–16*, 54. The king's real debts were much higher than this; those of his household alone have been estimated at £31,000, although some of these may have been discounted. Arundel had been appointed by the dead king as one of the supervisors of his will, along with the then prince; once the executors renounced execution of the will, it devolved upon the archbishop as diocesan ordinary.

[39] *CPR 1422–9*, 188–9 (by which time the debt was said to be £17,333, but still only £4,000 received from Henry V); Wylie, *Henry the Fifth*, i.27, thought Henry V to have been 'immensely the gainer' from the renunciation by Henry IV's executors, and although it was probably not as bad as it looked (that is, £16,666 worth of goods for a mere £4,000), the transaction was clearly done at the new king's behest. He doubtless intended to pay off his father's debts, but preferably not during his lifetime (Roskell, *Commons in the Parliament of 1422*, 113–20).

cathedral. Since Henry V had made it clear that his father's pious bequests were only to be funded once his debts had been paid, this chantry was never endowed, even though the chapel to house it was constructed around 1440. Instead, it was left to others such as the faithful Bowet to endow chantries for Henry IV.[40] Henry had also asked that Queen Joan be endowed from the revenues of the duchy of Lancaster. Given the difficulties already experienced in making up her dower, it is not surprising that no new assignment of duchy lands was made to her, although she did continue to receive revenues at a respectable level from both the duchy and the crown.[41] Before 1413, Henry V's relationship with his stepmother had been good, and for the next six years it remained so, but in September 1419 he suddenly ordered her arrest on suspicion of planning his death by means of witchcraft, and all her lands and possessions were seized. Although her imprisonment was far from harsh, she remained under arrest for nearly three years, during which time she was supported by a grant of between 1,000 and 1,500 marks a year from the exchequer, leaving the king with a net profit of over £5,000 a year from her dower lands. Charges were never brought against her, and it is clear that the accusation of witchcraft was simply an excuse for Henry V to apply the proceeds of her lands to his wars. Shortly before his death he shamefacedly ordered her release, and she spent the remaining fifteen years of her life wealthy and unmolested.[42] Henry V learned many things from his father, but filial duty was not one of them.

Four centuries later, in curious circumstances, the face of Henry IV was glimpsed one last time. In his *History of the Martyr Richard Scrope*, written a few years after Henry's death, a supporter of the archbishop called Clement Maydestone wrote a passionate attack on the king into which he incorporated a morality tale he claimed had been told to his father, Thomas Maydestone, by a man who came to dine at Hounslow priory in April 1413. The unnamed visitor said that he had accompanied the king's coffin on its journey down the Thames from Westminster, but that when the barge was between Barking and Gravesend a violent storm blew up, so he and two

---

[40] Wilson, 'The Medieval Monuments', 503; *CPR 1413–16*, 51; Raine, *Fabric Rolls of York Minster*, 274.

[41] From 1415, however, as the king's needs grew, Joan lost some of her lands, such as Hertford castle (replaced only with King's Langley manor), alien priories taken into the king's hands in 1414, and lands restored to the earl of Northumberland in 1415 (Somerville, *Duchy of Lancaster*, i.175; *CPR 1413–16*, 164–7, 351).

[42] A. Myers, 'The Captivity of a Royal Witch: The Household Accounts of Queen Joan of Navarre, 1419–1421', in *Crown, Household and Parliament in Fifteenth-Century England*, ed. C. Clough (London, 1985), 93–134; Jones, 'Joan of Navarre', *ODNB*, 30.139–41.

other men opened the coffin, cast the body into the river – it being considered bad luck to have a corpse on board – then resealed the lid and continued on their way, the storm having subsided as soon as the body hit the water; thus, he said, the coffin buried in Canterbury cathedral was empty. That anyone should admit to so heinous a deed when the dead king's son was on the throne was, of course, preposterous. Nevertheless, on 21 August 1832, to get to the truth of the matter, the dean of Canterbury permitted a group of clerics and other interested parties, including George Austin, the cathedral's surveyor, and the Reverend John Spry, one of its prebendaries, to examine Henry's tomb.[43] After removing the marble pavement, they found the coffin lid, 'of very rude form and construction', about a third of the length of which projected beyond the monument to the west. On top of this, directly below the monument, was a leaden shroud presumed to hold the remains of Queen Joan, which they left untouched. Unable to remove the coffin lid because most of it was under the monument, they decided to saw through it, and once a piece had been removed they found the chest to be stuffed with hay-bands, on top of which was 'a very rude small cross, formed by merely tying two twigs together', which fell to pieces when handled. Packed amongst the hay-bands was Henry's leaden shroud, 'moulded in some degree to the shape of a human figure', which it was clear had never been disturbed. This too they sawed through, removing 'an oval piece of the lead about seven inches long and four inches over at the widest part', which in turn revealed a leather wrapper which, they soon discovered, was wound five times around the king's body. According to the Reverend Spry, the leather was:

> firm in its texture, very moist, of a deep brown colour and earthy smell. These wrappers were cut through and lifted off; when, to the astonishment of all present, the face of the deceased king was seen in complete preservation. The nose elevated, the cartilage even remaining, though, on the admission of the air, it sunk rapidly away, and had entirely disappeared before the examination was finished. The skin of the chin was entire, of the consistence and thickness of the upper leather of a shoe, brown and moist; the beard thick and matted, and of a deep russet colour. The jaws were perfect, and all the teeth in them, except one fore tooth, which had probably been lost during the king's life. The opening of the lead was not large enough to expose the whole of the features,

---

[43] Kempe, 'Some Account of the Jerusalem Chamber in the Abbey of Westminster', to which is appended 'An Examination of the Tomb of King Henry IV' by the Rev. J. Spry.

and we did not examine the eyes or forehead. But the surveyor stated that when he introduced his finger under the wrappers to remove them, he distinctly felt the orbits of the eyes prominent in their sockets. The flesh upon the nose was moist, clammy, and of the same brown colour as every other part of the face. Having thus ascertained that the body of the king was actually deposited in the tomb, and that it had never been disturbed, the wrappers were laid again upon the face, the lead drawn back over them, the lid of the coffin put on, the rubbish filled in, and the marble replaced immediately.

If the presence of the body gives the lie to Maydestone's improbable tale, the fact that only a small section of the lead and not much of the coffin lid were cut away leaves other questions unanswered. Henry's state of preservation makes it clear that his corpse was embalmed, and the elevated nose cartilage dispels the rumours of leprosy, but the rough-hewn coffin, 'rude' little cross of twigs and lowly hay-bands seem a far cry from what was expected, indeed prescribed, for a king. The fact that no regalia are mentioned does not mean that they were not there, but the impression remains that Henry was rather hastily, and perhaps not very grandly, buried. On the other hand, he may not have wished to be buried with great pomp. He was, he said in his will, a 'sinful wretch', with a 'sinful soul, the which had never been worthy to be man but through [God's] mercy and His grace; which life I have misspent'. Unlike some of his contemporaries, he did not use his will explicitly to reject funereal pomp, but nor did he make provision for candles, mourners, funeral robes and suchlike, as Edward III and Richard II had done and as Henry V would do.[44] Archbishop Arundel, however, another 'most miserable and most unworthy sinner', had asked for the most lowly burial for his 'foetid and putrid cadaver', and it was at his discretion that Henry was buried. If anyone knew the king's true wishes, it was he.

[44] Given-Wilson, 'Exequies of Edward III'. Henry V made arrangements for an elaborate and expensive funeral and chantry monument (Duffy, *Royal Tombs*, 207–15).

CONCLUSION

It may well be true that 'Henry Bolingbroke would have been a happier man if, like his father John of Gaunt, he had lived and died as duke of Lancaster', but that was not a luxury Richard II was prepared to allow him.[1] Insecure and vindictive, Richard had come to the conclusion by the mid-1390s that the house of Lancaster presented a challenge to the fullness of his kingship, a threat magnified in the king's mind by the lack of personal empathy between him and Henry, and the history of conflict between him and both Gaunt and his son during the 1380s. Nor, it must be said, had Gaunt and Henry gone out of their way to allay the king's fears. The immensity of Lancastrian power, built up over a century, solidified by social and political developments during the second half of the fourteenth century and thrust to the forefront of national politics by the lack of active kingship in the 1370s and 1380s, was not something they tried to hide. Richard initially responded by constructing an affinity of his own and a court party from which Gaunt and Henry were excluded, but when in 1398–9 the opportunity arose to disassemble the Lancastrian edifice, he could not resist it.

The revolution of 1399 brought the best out of Henry. Purposeful and ruthless – as he had to be – he initially secured the throne almost without opposition, but soon discovered that the kingship of a usurper was qualitatively different from that of a legitimate monarch. Even with kings as manifestly unsuitable as Edward II or Richard II, it took ten or fifteen years for baronial exasperation to turn to talk of deposition and twenty for the threats to be realized; Henry was on the throne for just three months before the first attempt to unseat him. The soldierly qualities for which he was renowned, allied to a quiet strength of character which before 1399 had been subordinated to that of his father, now served him well. Yet early misjudgements cost him dear. By 1403, the power he had entrusted to the Percys, combined with the evaporation of the hopes attending Richard's

[1] Pugh, *Southampton Plot*, 26 (quote).

removal, brought him to the brink of disaster. Popular revulsion at the death of Archbishop Scrope – Henry's second great mistake – marked the nadir of his reign and his reputation.

His response was both practical and tactical. He elevated his family to a position of unchallenged dominance in the realm, a process entailing close management of the nobility, implacability towards traitors and relentless propagation of his dynasty and its destiny. The deeper state he created made extensive use of spies and informers. He militarized the royal household and surrounded himself with a protective shield of retainers. Yet armour-plated kingship came at a price. There was resentment throughout the reign at the public power enjoyed by the king's retainers, and a sense that Henry was as much the prisoner as the master of his affinity. Only during the last few years of the reign did Prince Henry begin to rein them in.

In the shires and boroughs this power was mediated through the offices of sheriff, mayor and justice of the peace; at Westminster, it manifested itself in the composition of the Privy Council and parliament. Under the twin pressures of financial insolvency and royal incapacity, the role of the council was formalized, reflected in its better record-keeping and responsibility for financial planning as well as its enhanced role in matters such as security and law enforcement. Under Prince Henry in 1410–11, it became an alternative locus of power in the realm, but with active kingship its role was more administrative than political. Parliament, in contrast, was by definition a political body. The rumbustious atmosphere of many of Henry's parliaments was to some extent deceptive, for although they were argumentative they were not threatening to the king. The habitual mood was of querulous disappointment. Yet the atmosphere also betokened a genuinely competitive forum for interest groups: it meant that proceedings focused on the best means to achieve the 'good and abundant governance' desired by the commons rather than the collision of factions, and it helped the government to avoid the charge of cronyism. The fact that many of the commons were closely – and their speakers very closely – connected to the king could well have lent plausibility to such a charge, but in reality it was often the king's most committed supporters who were his fiercest parliamentary critics.

This criticism focused on the question of solvency, the essence of good and abundant governance. The fact that the joint efforts of king, council and parliament only briefly came close to achieving it (in 1407–9) is attributable to several factors: the high cost of protecting England's shipping and ports, defending its marches and dominions and suppressing rebellions; the simultaneous collapse of revenues from those dominions, so that

colonies or outposts which had once produced a profit or at least enjoyed
a degree of self-sufficiency were now a constant drain on resources; the
decline by around 20 per cent during the first quarter of the fifteenth
century in the exchequer's income from indirect taxation; and the increase
by roughly the same percentage in the domestic charges of government –
household, affinity and administration – charges which the king viewed as
politically imperative but which also reflected the extravagance of a youth
who had never known insufficiency. Yet fiscal innovation was unwelcome
in late medieval England: the experimentation of 1404–6 proved barren,
the reversion to traditional methods after 1407 more productive.[2] Despite
this, the government's credit never quite ran out, although as time went by
it found itself increasingly reliant for loans on a narrowing circle of
Londoners, ministers, councillors and other committed supporters, whose
influence on policy grew accordingly.

Henry's overriding foreign policy consideration was always France, his
aims reasonably consistent. He wanted a lasting peace, preferably sealed
by the marriage of Prince Henry to a French princess; failing that, he
wanted to preserve the truce for as long as possible; the minimum require-
ment was to retain Guyenne and Calais, because a usurper who mislaid his
empire would struggle for credibility. The fact that Henry was able to
pursue broadly the same foreign policy towards France as Richard II had
done without incurring the same opprobrium is explicable in part by the
fact that it took a man untainted with the whiff of Francophilia to pursue
a credible policy of peace with the national enemy. In the event, the
barrage of hostility from Louis of Orléans and his acolytes soon led to the
collapse of meaningful peace talks, while the slide towards civil war in
France after 1407 made the outcome of negotiations increasingly unpredictable. It did, however, eventually allow Henry to take the initiative, and
in so doing to reveal what lay closest to his heart – the retention of Guyenne,
to which he had a recent Lancastrian, as well as a long-standing royal,
claim. Yet in general the steadily deflating rhetoric of Henry's diplomacy
is a measure of the puncturing of his ambition: the extravagant language
of overlordship which so irritated the Scots during the first three years of
the reign all but vanished thereafter, and although he continued to style
himself 'king of France' (as did his successors until the nineteenth century)
this was irrelevant to the real diplomacy of the reign.

<hr />

[2] Harriss, *Shaping the Nation*, 59–61; M. Ormrod, 'England in the Middle Ages', in *The Rise
of the Fiscal State in Europe, c.1200–1815*, ed. R. Bonney (Oxford, 1999), 42.

The connections between the Welsh revolt, the upsurge of resistance in Ireland, and the hostility of the Scottish magnates (until checked at Humbleton Hill) are not easy to pinpoint, but what they obviously shared was ambivalence towards the imperial pretensions of a king whose authority was challenged even in his homeland. The Mortimer following, even the Mortimer name, probably lent an air of legitimacy to the king's opponents in Ireland; they certainly did in Wales. Here and on the northern marches landed and military power had become concentrated in fewer and greater hands during the fourteenth century, and when trust was lost, as with the Percys in 1402–3, the consequences were correspondingly greater.[3] Yet the defeat of the Percys only created another dilemma: how to govern (or defend) the north without them? It was a problem replicated elsewhere. The dominions Henry inherited in 1399 constituted a ramshackle and unruly empire, governed by separate laws, customs and languages and ruled under a miscellany of titles – lord of Ireland, duke of Guyenne, or even, in the case of the Channel Islands, duke of Normandy.[4] In practice, the king's hold on them was dependent on the support of enough people in each whose interests were served by upholding and exploiting the privileges and powers the crown could offer them: the Butlers in Ireland, the gated communities of Wales, the Gascon lords who feared French domination, the townsmen of Calais, Dublin and Bordeaux whose prosperity depended on commerce with the mother country.[5] That the offices, annuities and grants which secured their compliance tended with time to become hereditary meant that the distinction between public and private authority in England's dominions became blurred, and although Henry held on to his empire there was a growing sense that English rule was exercised in the conditional tense. Clarence's 1412–13 campaign achieved its goal in the medium term, but within another forty years Guyenne would be lost, English administration would be reduced to a 'lytell cornere' of Ireland, and, against a background of collapsing marcher revenues, a native Welsh squirearchy was increasingly usurping the lands and offices of its former masters.[6]

Conflict resolution displayed similar tendencies, with international truces routinely supplemented by local agreements, which in practice stood

[3] M. Brown, *Disunited Kingdoms: People and Politics in the British Isles 1280–1460* (Edinburgh, 2013), 237–47.
[4] Ruddick, 'English Identity and Political Language'; Griffiths, 'The English Realm and Dominions'.
[5] Davies, *Revolt*, 221–2; Vale, *English Gascony*, 53; *New History of Ireland II*, ed. Cosgrove, 534–5; Frame, 'Lordship Beyond the Pale', 5–18.
[6] Harriss, *Shaping the Nation*, 517–27; Scattergood, *Politics and Poetry*, 38 (quote).

the best chance of securing a respite from war. Individuals and communities desperate to save their homes, families and livestock resorted constantly to private compacts with their tormentors, frequently accompanied by protection money. In theory, treaties with rebels or enemies of the English crown – terrorists in modern parlance – were treasonable; in practice the king usually had little option but to sanction them, acknowledging his inability to protect his subjects from the 'hard war' inflicted on them.[7] Characteristic of such agreements was the double marriage contract in April 1410 between the children of Janico Dartasso and John (Eòin) Mór, younger brother of Donald, Lord of the Isles. From an English point of view, its aim was to bring peace to Ulster, for Mór had pursued his interests there with vigour and stood in need of a royal pardon, which Henry granted him at the same time as he licensed the marriages.[8] Yet this compact between a footloose Navarrese adventurer, who through service and marriage had acquired a stake in Irish political life, and the brother of a Highland chieftain who barely noticed the Scottish king's authority except to flout it – a private treaty born of an attempt to solve a public problem – was far from untypical of some of what passed for international diplomacy in this age of dysfunctional kingship. Henry simply lacked the resources to govern his empire effectively. More than £70,000 was passed from the exchequer to Prince Henry between 1401 and 1413 to suppress the Welsh revolt, and at least an equivalent sum lost in seigneurial revenues as a result of the disorder.[9] Yet the commons were not always sympathetic to the king's problems. Reluctant to grant taxation for what they construed as rebellion, they argued that the way to deal with 'barefooted buffoons [the Welsh]' or 'wild Irishmen' was for the lords who held estates there to remain in their castles and defend them. When the king told the parliament of January 1404 that, as well as having to safeguard Calais and the seas, he was effectively at war in Wales, in Scotland, in Ireland and in Guyenne, they replied, 'These things do not trouble England much.'[10] Their England could be a little place.

There was a certain irony in this, for one of the consequences of the accession of a duke of Lancaster was that England became a more

---

[7] See his pardon to the tenants of Whittington (Shropshire) in 1408 (*CPR 1408–13*, 30; cf. Davies, *Revolt*, 234–6).

[8] For these negotiations, see *CPR 1408–13*, 183, 190; Walker, 'Janico Dartasso', 44; S. Kingston, *Ulster and the Isles in the Fifteenth Century* (Dublin, 2004), 43–4, 51–2, 60, 166, 190; Wylie, *Henry the Fourth*, iii.164–8; *CDS*, iv.145; *Foedera*, viii.527.

[9] The real cost was higher still (Davies, *Revolt*, 259–61).

[10] *CE*, 399 (*Isti non inquietant multum Angliam*). For the commons' unwillingness to fund the Welsh war, see *PROME*, viii.423, 427, 459–60. Cf. *Brut*, ii.357 ('wild Irishmen').

geographically integrated nation. When Richard II journeyed to the north of his kingdom, it had something of the feel of a state visit; when Henry did so, it was more like a homecoming. Northern knights now outnumbered southern ones in the royal affinity, while northern magnates and prelates – the Percys, Westmorland, Langley, Roos, Bowet – enjoyed great influence at Westminster.[11] Not that integration was necessarily welcome: the rising associated with the name of Archbishop Scrope suggests that the 'problem of the north' went a good deal deeper than Percy disaffection. Yet equally noteworthy is the lack of a corresponding 'problem of the south' during the reign of the first Lancastrian king, at least after January 1400. The decapitation of several great southern magnate affinities during the Epiphany rising probably had something to do with this, but so did Henry's efforts to build relationships with Londoners and former followers of Richard II in the southern shires.[12]

Henry's personality was, on the whole, well suited to kingship. He kept his friends close and his enemies afraid. Steely and watchful, not to say sly, he also had an easy charm and a wry wit that gave him an aura of accessibility and helped him to work through diplomatic problems, although at times obstinacy clouded his judgement. His refusal to talk to Glyn Dŵr in 1401–2 cost him dear. On the other hand, his championing of chivalric values allowed him to make close friendships with like-minded knights and nobles, and his militant piety won him many plaudits. A dutiful son and a faithful and attentive husband, he drew strength and comfort from his family. He had an erratic compassion – for women, for paupers – which sat rather incongruously with his savagery towards traitors, but stemmed in part from a religiosity based on something deeper than contractual obligation.[13] There were, as he knew, sins he had committed that only God could forgive. Cultured, educated and sceptical, he encouraged the English Church to take its pastoral role seriously, promoted men of learning to his council, took more than a passing interest in guns, music and theological

[11] *RHKA*, 227–33.

[12] It was a southern chronicler who claimed that, despite constantly raising taxes, the king was always greatly loved (*amantissimus*) by his people (Kingsford, *English Historical Literature*, 277).

[13] For example, he granted two pence a day to Isabella Taylor of London, who had seven children but had gone blind and could not support her family (E 403/571, 17 Oct. 1401; E 404/27, no. 387); two rabbits a week to the 'poor oratrice' Maude Merlond to feed herself, when she asked for one (E 28/9, no. 73); and six pence a day to Matthew Flint, 'tooth-drawer', to enable him to practise his art for 'any poor lieges of the king who may need it in the future without receiving anything from them' (*CPR 1399–1401*, 255).

disputation, and fathered a royal family which was one of the most cultivated in English history.

Of the king's friends, the one who did most to ensure his survival was
Archbishop Arundel, an outstanding public servant whom Henry came to
think of as a spiritual father-figure.[14] Throughout the reign, this political alliance that grew into a wary but sincere friendship was at the heart of
England's affairs. As primate, Arundel stamped his authority on the English
Church from the moment of his restoration, but his experience of secular
government also gave him an understanding of the needs of the crown, and
there were doubtless some members of his flock who saw his commitment to
Henry's kingship as the alliance of the shepherd and the wolf.[15] Yet his situation was a difficult one, for without the king's support he stood little chance
of defeating Lollardy or healing the Schism – and royal support came at a
price. Driven by instinct, as well as by a vocal reformist group at court and
in parliament, Henry played on the fears of the ecclesiastical hierarchy to
bring the English Church under closer secular control and, through parliament, to introduce a limited measure of reform. Arundel in turn played on
the king's fear of radical-inspired sedition and took his stand on fundamen-
talist Christian doctrine, a tactic that occasionally served him well. More
often, however, he was forced to give ground. Privately, he and Henry were
probably not that far apart in their devotional preferences, and they could
take equal credit for the fact that, despite what each saw as undue provocation, the public alliance of Church and crown held fast. The crushing of
Oldcastle's revolt in January 1414 sealed that alliance, a fitting culmination to
Arundel's primacy, which ended with his death a month later.

Henry's most significant achievement was the restoration of the consensual style of politics practised by Edward III, but overborne by Richard II.
Such an assertion is naturally subject to caveats, the most obvious being
that consent was generally sought within restricted circles – though certainly
not as restricted as during the 1390s. The difference was palpable. No
longer was parliament the plaything of royal or magnate faction, veering
giddily between servile acquiescence and violent antipathy to the king
and his supporters. Whatever reverses and frustrations Henry suffered in

[14] Cf. 'yowre true frend and chyld in God', 'your trewe sone Henrye' (*Signet Letters*, nos.
717, 736). Arundel was fourteen years older than Henry.
[15] See, for example, the letter of Arundel to Henry of 7 Dec. 1404 apologizing for the fact
that the convocation just ended had failed to sanction the king's demand for a subsidy from
stipendiary chaplains, swearing that he had done his best to secure this despite unanimous
opposition, recommending to the king that the diocesans should put pressure on the chaplains directly, and offering to expedite this if king and council were in agreement (BL
Cleopatra Ms E ii 252 (265).)

parliament, he did not threaten or intimidate the commons; he held his nerve and acknowledged the limitations of royal power. From the time that he first came out in opposition to Richard II, he demonstrated a consistency of character and principle, born of a belief in government by consent. That did not mean that he surrendered his prerogative; he insisted from the start of his reign that the rights and powers he inherited from Richard II were diminished not a jot, and it was upon this assumption that he and his successors acted. It is not just the kingship of Henry IV but also that of Henry V, Edward IV, Henry VII and Henry VIII which gives the lie to the idea that the deposition of 1399 – not, after all, the first royal deposition in medieval England – led to a lasting curtailment of monarchical power in England.

Henry IV's great misfortune was to become sick just at the moment when he appeared to have won his dynasty a measure of security. Despite the imprecision of contemporary descriptions, there is enough correlation between them to indicate that Henry suffered from more than one medical condition. The skin disease – perhaps psoriasis – mentioned in 1387–8, 1399 and 1405 probably grew more acute as he aged, and the *graunde accesse* he suffered in 1406 is likely to have been a prolapsed rectum. His collapse in the summer of 1408 was probably a coronary thrombosis, resulting in blocked arteries and steadily increasing problems with blood circulation, leading eventually to necrotic ulcers which, by the last year of his life, seem to have turned gangrenous (the 'festering' or 'putrefaction' mentioned by Usk and Strecche). During the last months, perhaps years, of his life, Henry must have endured great pain, retaining his regnal power until the end only through a ferocious effort of will. Yet what followed the onset of his illness vindicated his rule. That there were rivalries and policy disagreements was inevitable, but they were contained (unlike in France), and in general the collective willingness of the extended Lancastrian clan to place the preservation of royal authority above personal interests was impressive. This was the moment that witnessed the coalescence of that familial system of government – revolving around the prince and future king, his brothers, his uncles Henry and Thomas Beaufort, Westmorland, and adopted sons such as Chichele, Erpingham, Tiptoft and Langley – which for the next twenty-five years, through Henry IV's illness, Henry V's absences, and Henry VI's minority, worked to ensure the survival of the Lancastrian dynasty into the second half of the fifteenth century.[16]

[16] J. Catto, 'The King's Servants', in *Henry V: The Practice of Kingship*, ed. G. Harriss (Oxford, 1987), 75–95, at pp. 81–2.

Henry V's stunning victories in France cemented and strengthened this coalition, and although its cohesion was tested by the enmity of Humphrey of Gloucester and Henry Beaufort, and depleted by natural wastage through the 1420s – Clarence died in 1421, the king in 1422, Westmorland in 1425, Thomas Beaufort in 1426, Erpingham in 1428 – broadly speaking, it held until the death of Bedford (Prince John) in 1435 and the coming of age of Henry VI a year later. What followed destroyed it: the rise of a court party centred on the duke of Suffolk, financial collapse, humiliation abroad and above all the ineptitude of Henry VI. By the time the last of Henry IV's sons, Humphrey, died or was murdered in 1447, he had come, almost unthinkably, to be seen as an enemy, even a traitor, to the Lancastrian regime. Meanwhile the special relationship between the dynasty and its original heartland had been allowed to atrophy, and by the time the Wars of the Roses began at St Albans in 1455, the descendants of men who had fought and died for Henry IV and Henry V were as likely to be followers of the duke of York.[17] By the spring of 1461, two centuries after its foundation, the house of Lancaster had lost its duchy, its affinity and its crown.

---

[17] Castor, *King, Crown and Duchy*, 40–9, 305–12; R. Storey, 'The North of England', in *Fifteenth-Century England 1399–1509*, ed. S. Chrimes, C. Ross and R. A. Griffiths (Manchester, 1972), 129–44, at p. 138.

EPILOGUE

THE PLACE OF THE REIGN OF HENRY IV IN ENGLISH HISTORIOGRAPHY

Over the centuries since Henry IV's death, debate about the longer-term significance of his reign has focused broadly on two questions: first, the belief that the revolution of 1399 was the root cause of civil strife in the fifteenth century, especially the Wars of the Roses; second, the extent to which Henry's usurpation, justified as it was by the necessity to oust a tyrannical king, succeeded in introducing a less autocratic (or more 'constitutional') form of government to England.

Central to the first question is the enormous influence of Shakespeare's History plays. Although perhaps not originally conceived as such,[1] Shakespeare's eight *Histories*, spanning the period from Richard II to Richard III, embodied what was seen during the sixteenth century as the orthodox overview of fifteenth-century history, namely, that the Wars of the Roses had their origin in the deposition of Richard II and were not healed until Henry VII ascended the throne in 1485 and, a few months later, married Elizabeth of York, thereby uniting the houses of York and Lancaster and restoring political harmony – a view encapsulated in the title of Edward Hall's *The Union of the Two Noble and Illustre Famelies of Lancastre and Yorke, beeyng long in Continual Discension for the Croun of this Noble Realme* (1548). In its neatest formulation, this 'Tudor Myth' assigned exactly a hundred years to this age of blood and political deformity, beginning with the battle of Radcot Bridge (1387), at which 'Henry of Lancaster' first took up arms against his sovereign, and ending with the battle of Stoke (1487), which scotched the last significant Yorkist threat to Henry VII's throne.[2] This overarching framework naturally allowed for differences of emphasis: whereas Yorkist-leaning historians laid the blame squarely on the shoulders of Henry IV's act of opportunism in 1399 and saw him and

---

[1] *Henry VI Parts I, II and III*, and *Richard III*, the 'first tetralogy' covering the years 1422–85, were written in the early 1590s, whereas *Richard II, Henry IV Parts I and II*, and *Henry V*, the 'second tetralogy' covering 1398–1422, in the late 1590s.

[2] M. Aston, 'Richard II and the Wars of the Roses', in *The Reign of Richard II*, ed. F. Du Boulay and C. Barron (London, 1971), 280–317, at p. 301.

his successors as the 'three wrong kings', Lancastrian sympathizers were more concerned to show that even if Richard II's deposition was a personal tragedy, his continuance in office would have led to national tragedy. The Tudors, whose claim to the throne came through the Lancastrian line (via the Beauforts), particularly stressed their own role in healing the schism.

These tensions are reflected in Shakespeare's *Richard II*. Broadly speaking, the first half of the play portrays Richard as a whimsical autocrat who brings ruin upon himself, but once the king is captured (Act 3, Scene 3), the emphasis shifts towards showing how difficult are the choices facing a ruler and how dangerous will be the consequences of usurpation. 'The blood of English shall manure the ground', warns the bishop of Carlisle, 'And future ages groan for this foul act . . . And in this seat of peace tumultuous wars/Shall kin with kin and kind with kind confound.'[3] The doubts thus raised, and the brutal act of regicide with which the play ends, evoke growing sympathy for the fallen king. The second half of *Richard II* thus prefigures *Henry IV Parts I and II*, in which the dreadful consequences of usurpation constitute the principal theme, exemplified not just by the wearying sequence of rebellions and conspiracies Henry faces, but also the riotous disobedience of his eldest son, God's punishment for his (and England's) original sin. As in *Julius Caesar*, the deeply problematical question of the morality of rebellion lies at the heart of the plays – not so much the personal morality of 'Bullingbrook' (although that is certainly not ignored) as the political circumstances, if any, that might justify the violent overthrow of an anointed ruler, tyrannical or not. This was a question with powerful contemporary resonance in the 1590s. Elizabeth I's famous 'I am Richard II. Know ye not that?' was not simply a rhetorical conceit. John Hayward's history of *The First Part of the Life and Raigne of King Henrie the IIII* (1599) was suppressed by the Privy Council and the author imprisoned for three years for 'making this time seem like that of Richard II' and daring to imply 'that it might be lawful for the subject to depose the king'. The early stage productions and editions of Shakespeare's *Richard II* wisely omitted the deposition scene in Act Four, which first appeared in the 1608 Quarto edition.[4] Despite the fact that Shakespeare was reworking a theme that, through Polydore Vergil, Edward

---

[3] *Richard II*, 4.I.136–47.
[4] W. Chernaik, *The Cambridge Introduction to Shakespeare's History Plays* (Cambridge, 2007), 95–6.

Hall and Raphael Holinshed, had characterized a century of Tudor historiography, it still required circumspection.

The enduring popularity of Shakespeare's work, reaching a new peak in this quatercentenary of his death, has meant that audiences have continued, and continue to this day, to be influenced by his version of the Tudor Myth and, to a lesser or greater degree, to ingest the view of the revolution of 1399 as the catalyst to a century of conflict.[5] Needless to say, the morality of rebellion remains as problematical as ever, but few historians of late medieval England nowadays subscribe to the view that the Wars of the Roses originated in the revolution of 1399, seeing them rather as the consequence of the manifold failures of Henry VI's kingship in the 1440s and 1450s. Yet there was no doubting the perceived relevance of the Tudor Myth in the seventeenth century. Both the Civil War of the 1640s and the Glorious Revolution of 1688 provided the occasion for new histories of the Wars of the Roses, pointing out their relevance to contemporary issues and carrying the story back to the reign of Richard II.[6] The Reformation and the prominence of religious dissension through the seventeenth century added fuel to the debate. As the king during whose reign the burning of heretics was believed to have been introduced, Henry IV was also denounced for having nipped in the bud England's early inclination towards Protestantism, with the civil strife of the fifteenth century seen by some Protestant polemicists as divine punishment for his impunity. Even John Foxe understood that to present Richard II as an advocate of Wyclifism was stretching the point, but that did not stop him from pointing out that Richard was 'no great disfavourer' of Wyclifites, 'neither was he so cruel against them as others that came after him', by which he meant principally Henry IV, who was 'altogether bent to hold with the pope's prelacy ... the first of all English kings that began the unmerciful burning of Christ's saints for standing against the pope', as a result of which his reign was 'full of trouble, of blood and misery'.[7] The heretic-burning Thomas Arundel naturally also excited the wrath of Foxe and other reformers, inducing Archbishop Cranmer who ordered the destruction of his predecessor's chantry chapel in Canterbury cathedral. Not until the

---

[5] Hence, in part, the special popularity of the second tetralogy, although the dramatic contrasts they encompass – the tragic Richard, the 'immortal Falstaff', the heroic but ambivalent Henry V – also account for much of their appeal. There were nearly three times as many references to Falstaff as to any other Shakespearean character in the seventeenth century (Chernaik, *Shakespeare's History Plays*, 125, and, for *Henry V*, 147–67).

[6] Aston, 'Richard II and the Wars of the Roses', 286–7.

[7] Aston, 'Richard II and the Wars of the Roses', 291–7.

nineteenth century did Arundel's reputation begin to recover (as witness the sympathetic Lambeth Palace portrait), although it still bears the scars of centuries of vilification.

From the mid-seventeenth century, as English monarchy began to acquire a more constitutional feel, interest in the reigns of Richard II and Henry IV shifted accordingly. In the view of some parliamentarians of the 1640s, it was the establishment of the parliamentary committee of 1398, undermining as it did the legitimate role of parliament, which revealed the true measure of Richard's autocracy. What, though, did Henry IV do to restore 'constitutional' rule? Despite growing interest in the origins of the constitution, not until Bishop Stubbs propounded his thesis of 'Lancastrian Constitutionalism' in the second half of the nineteenth century was a fully formulated answer to this question put forward. Stubbs saw constitutionalism largely in terms of the relationship between crown and parliament. The Lancastrian epoch (1399–1461), he declared, saw 'the trial and failure of a great constitutional experiment, a premature testing of the strength of the parliamentary system', which demonstrated 'an instinctive looking towards a greater destiny'. Henry IV came to power as the advocate of constitutional monarchy and 'ruled his kingdom with aid of a council such as he had tried to force on Richard II, and yielded to his parliaments all the power, place and privilege that had been claimed for them by the great houses which he represented'. Nowhere was this more apparent than in the parliament of 1406, which 'seems almost to stand for an exponent of the most advanced principles of medieval constitutional life in England'. Here was a king who 'acted on the principles which he had professed as a subject', and as a result managed to 'withstand and overcome any amount of domestic difficulty'. Stubbs conceded that this did not make him a strong king: indeed, he went on, it may have been the very 'weakness of central power' during his reign that created the conditions for constitutional rule. Yet, whatever his failings, Henry could not be accused of hypocrisy, and his son and grandson followed his example: the house of Lancaster 'reigned constitutionally', but fell 'by lack of governance'. The Yorkists, on the other hand, reigned unconstitutionally, 'stronger but not sounder' than the Lancastrians, demeaning parliament, levying arbitrary taxation, maintaining armed forces and perverting the law with their 'judicial cruelties'. Whereas the Lancastrians had acted on 'the hereditary traditions of the baronage', the Yorkists acted on 'the hereditary traditions of the crown'; and although the Yorkists failed to destroy the constitution, 'the nation needed rest and renewal, discipline and reformation, before it could enter into the enjoyment of its birthright'.[8]

This classic exposition of 'Whig history' – the overarching view of England's story as a stately progression towards limited monarchy and parliamentary democracy – was in tune with its age, a time of parliamentary reform and imperial self-confidence, and although Lancastrian Constitutionalism was declared moribund well before the mid-twentieth century, it has taken a long time to die, not least because of its influence on the higher education curriculum. Yet its weaknesses are all too apparent. Leaving aside the problems associated with notions such as the 'hereditary traditions' of crown or baronage, Whig or constitutional history placed far too much emphasis on the relationship between crown and parliament and on the role of the commons in parliament. Parliaments were only in session about 10 per cent of the time during the late Middle Ages, and if there is no disputing their importance or the expanding role of the commons, they were still many centuries away from incorporating the day-to-day realities of English political life. To be fair, Stubbs was explicitly writing a *constitutional*, not a political, history, but he mistook parliament's constitutional authority for political power and showed little evidence of understanding the massive gulf between fifteenth-century and nineteenth-century political society.[9] Doggedly checking off the milestones on his pre-planned route, he seems barely to have noticed the surrounding scenery.

It is the attempt to sketch in this scenery during the last half-century and more that has replaced the Whig interpretation of English history. Broadly speaking, this has taken three directions: first, biographical or prosopographical studies of individuals or groups as a way of understanding the motivation of key political actors and of seeing political history from below and within as well as from above; second, regional studies designed to elucidate the workings of local political society and the two-way relationship between government and the localities; third, closer study of political ideas and language in order to reveal the common framework of assumptions that underlie political action. At the heart of this lies not only the desire to understand political mentalities but also the recognition that the late medieval polity was increasingly inclusive and multi-layered. To return to a point made in the Introduction, the expansion of government in the

---

[8] W. Stubbs, *The Constitutional History of England in its Origin and Development* (fifth edn, 3 vols, Oxford, 1896), iii.1–294 (quotes at pp. 2, 5, 8, 59, 74, 274, 276, 280–94).

[9] G. Harriss, 'The Medieval Parliaments', *Parliamentary History* 13 (1994), 206–26, at p. 207.

late Middle Ages was bound to open up more fault-lines: the more questions the king asked of his subjects, the more demands he made of them, the more of them at more levels he drew into the governmental process, then the more they would become politicized and the more occasions there would be for negotiation, disagreement or resistance. Rather than mistaking this for evidence of the breakdown of effective government, it should rather be seen as 'a price to be paid for the development of a cohesive and generally successful political order'.[10]

Like most books, this one is a product of its age and reflects the influence of modern historiography. The interpretations of K. B. McFarlane and his pupil and successor G. L. Harriss underlie much of the recent historiography of late medieval England and continue to influence most of the work on the political history of the period, mine included. Modern scholars working specifically on Henry IV's reign whose work I have found especially useful include A. L. Brown (on government), Simon Walker (on political society and rebellion), Gwilym Dodd (on parliament and the council), Jenni Nuttall (on political language and propaganda), Rees Davies (on the Welsh revolt), Peter Crooks (on Ireland and empires), Guilhem Pepin (on Guyenne), Helen Castor (on the Lancastrian affinity), Christian Liddy (on towns), Peter McNiven (on heresy), Margaret Harvey (on the Schism) and Jeremy Catto (on religiosity).[11] Yet engagement with modern historiography should not entail wholesale rejection of earlier views of the significance of Henry IV's reign. Although the Tudor Myth has long been discarded, the 'abiding moral and political uncertainties created by Henry IV's act of perjured usurpation' and refracted through Shakespeare's *Histories* continued to resonate through his reign and beyond, and the question of whether it was his governance that made people question his title or vice versa admits of no easy answer.[12] Moreover, whatever terminology one chooses to employ – constitutional, consensual, contractual – it is hard to avoid the sense that Henry's kingship was qualitatively different from Richard II's. In part this was a question of character, in part of policy, in part of circumstances; the difference manifested itself in the king's relationship with his nobles, with his affinity, with gentry, townsmen and civil servants, as well as in the language of parliaments and contemporary

---

[10] S. Walker, *Political Culture in Later Medieval England*, ed. M. Braddick (Manchester, 2006), 11 (Introduction by G. L. Harriss, but quoting Walker).

[11] Full references can be found in the Bibliography. I have also made extensive and fruitful use of the superbly researched biographies in *The House of Commons 1386–1421*, and in the *Oxford Dictionary of National Biography*.

[12] Walker, *Political Culture*, 11 (quote).

literature. Credit for this has not always been given where it is due. The conspiracy of approval enveloping Henry V has been slow to recognize the solidity of his father's legacy, a historiographical distortion extended almost by default to the unwarranted assumption that the prince was responsible for most of the good things that happened during the later years of the reign. In some cases this was true, but in most it was not. On the scale of the possible for a usurper, Henry IV's achievement ranked high. Unlike his son, he is not remembered as a great king, but it is not impossible to imagine that, given different circumstances, he could have been.

APPENDIX: HENRY IV'S ITINERARY
1399–1413

1399

*c.*June 30, Henry's Landing from France at Ravenspur (Spurn Head, Humberside). July 1 Bridlington. *c.*July 7 Pickering. July 9 Knaresborough. July 13–14 Pontefract. July 15–16 Doncaster. July 20 Leicester. July 23 Coventry. July 24 Warwick. July 25–26 Gloucester. July 27 Berkeley. July 28–31 Bristol. Aug. 1 Usk. Aug. 2 Hereford. Aug. 3 Leominster. Aug. 4 Ludlow. Aug. 5–6 Shrewsbury. Aug. 7 Prees. Aug. 8 Coddington. Aug. 9–19 Chester (but *c.*12–13 Holt castle, Clwyd; Aug. 16 Flint castle). Aug. 20 Nantwich. Aug. 21 Newcastle-under-Lyme. Aug. 22 Stafford. Aug. 23–24 Lichfield. Aug. 25–26 Coventry. Aug. 27 Daventry. Aug. 28 Northampton. Aug. 29 Dunstable. Aug. 30–31 St Albans. Sept. 1 Westminster. Sept. 2–21 London (Bishop of London's palace; Hospitaller priory, Clerkenwell). Sept. 22 Hertford. Sept. 26 Waltham. Sept. 27–29 London. **September 30 Henry's Enthronement at Westminster**. Oct. 1–Nov. 21 Westminster. Dec. 20 Hertford. Dec. 25–31 Windsor.

1400

Jan. 1–3 Windsor. Jan. 4 London. Jan. 5 Hounslow Heath. Jan. 11–13 Oxford. Jan. 15 London. Feb. 26 Eltham. March 16 Eltham. April 8 Eltham. May 20–21 Westminster. May 27 St Albans. June 14 Clipstone. June 20–25 Pontefract. July 2–16 York. July 18 Northallerton. July 20 Darlington. July 23–Aug. 7 Newcastle. Aug. 8–12 Fenwick. Aug. 15 Haddington. Aug. 18–21 Leith. Sept. 2 Newcastle. Sept. 3–4 Durham. Sept. 6 Northallerton. Sept. 8–9 Pontefract. Sept. 11–12 Doncaster. Sept. 19 Northampton. Sept. 22 Coventry. Sept. 23 Lichfield. Sept. 26 Shrewsbury. Oct. 8 Bangor. *c.*Oct. 10 Mawddy. Oct. 15 Shrewsbury. Oct. 19 Evesham. Oct. 24–29 Windsor. Nov. 12 Westminster. Nov. 21–27 Hertford. Dec. 4 Hertford. Dec. 20 Hertford. Dec. 21 London. Dec. 25–31 Eltham.

1401

Jan. 1–6 Eltham. Jan. 22–March 10 Westminster. March 22 Eltham. March 26–April 11 Leeds (Kent). April 19 Windsor. May 7 Easthampstead. May 19 Easthampstead. May 20–26 Wallingford. June 2–4 Evesham. June 5–14 Worcester. June 21 Wallingford. June 24 Windsor. June 25–27 Westminster. July 12 Farnham. July 19–20 Selborne. July 26 Bishop's Sutton. July 26 Southampton. Sept. 2–10 Windsor. Sept. 29–30 Evesham. Oct. 1 Worcester. Oct. (*c.*2–14 Oct., dates lacking) Brecon, Llandovery, Carmarthen, Strata Florida Abbey, Welshpool. Oct. 15 Shrewsbury. Oct. 18 Shifnal. Oct. 27–28 Worcester. Nov. 1 Westminster. Nov. 3–13 Hertford. Dec. 1 Windsor. Dec. 11–13 Hertford. Dec. 17 Tower of London. Dec. 25–31 Eltham.

1402

Jan. 1–27 Eltham. Feb. 24 Westminster. March 10 Eltham. April 3 Eltham. April 28 Windsor. May 14–24 Berkhamstead. June 16 Kennington. June 25 Berkhamstead. June 30 Market

Harborough. July 5 Lichfield. July 23 Lilleshall. July 26 Lichfield. July 29 Burton on Trent. Aug. 1 Tideswell. Aug. 4–5 Ravensdale (Derbyshire). Aug. 7 Tideswell. Aug. 15–17 Nottingham. Aug. 22–26 Lichfield. Aug. 30 Kenilworth. *c.*2–16 Sept. in Wales (dates lacking). Sept. 20 Daventry. Sept. 22 Westminster. Sept. 26 Berkhamstead. 30 Sept.–26 Nov. Westminster (but Oct. 8, 22, 29–1 Nov. Eltham). Nov. 27–Dec. 2 Eltham. Dec. 3–9 Tower of London. Dec. 5 Barnet. Dec. 6 St Albans. Dec. 9–22 Berkhamstead. Dec. 23–31 Windsor.

1403

Jan. 1–6 Windsor. Jan. 7–9 Easthamstead. Jan. 9–20 Reading. Jan. 20–27 Farnham. Jan. 28 Clarendon. Jan. 31 Exeter. Feb. 4–9 Winchester. Feb. 10 Bishop's Sutton. Feb. 11 Farnham. Feb. 12 Guildford. Feb. 13 Kingston. Feb. 14–24 Eltham. Feb. 24–March 3 Westminster. March 3–15 Eltham. March 16 Rochester. March 20 Ospringe. March 22 Canterbury. March 27–April 28 Eltham (but 19 April Westminster). April 28–May 9 Windsor (but 6 May Chertsey). May 10–18 Easthamstead. May 19–30 Henley on the Heath. May 31 Kennington. June 3–19 Windsor. June 20–22 Tower of London. June 23–25 Windsor. June 25–27 Kingston. June 27–July 3 Kennington. July 4 Waltham. July 5 Hertford. July 6 Hitchin. July 7–8 Newenham. July 9 Higham Ferrers. July 10 Market Harborough. July 11 Leicester. July 12–13 Nottingham. July 13–14 Derby. July 15 Burton on Trent. July 16–18 Lichfield. July 19 Stafford. July 20–22 Shrewsbury. July 23–24 Lilleshall. July 25 Stafford. July 25–26 Lichfield. July 27 Burton on Trent. July 28 Derby. July 29 Nottingham. July 30 Mansfield. Aug. 1 Blyth. Aug. 2 Doncaster. Aug. 3–6 Pontefract. Aug. 7 Rothwell Haigh (Tadcaster). Aug. 8–12 York. Aug. 13–15 Pontefract. Aug. 16 Doncaster. Aug. 17 Worksop. Aug. 18–19 Nottingham. Aug. 20 Leicester. Aug. 21 Lutterworth. Aug. 22 Daventry. Aug. 23–31 Woodstock. Sept. 1 Evesham. Sept. 2–10 Worcester. Sept. 11–18 Hereford. Sept. 19 Michaelchurch. Sept. 20 Brecon. Sept. 21 Devynock. Sept. 24–29 Carmarthen. Oct. 3–6 Hereford. Oct. 7–14 Gloucester. Oct. 17–27 Bristol. Oct. 29–Nov. 14 Cirencester. Nov. 16–22 Westminster. Nov. 23–30 London. Dec. 9 Coventry. Dec. 18 Westminster. Dec. 23–31 Abingdon.

1404

Jan. 1–6 Abingdon. Jan. 11 Sutton. Jan. 14–March 20 Westminster (but Feb. 8 Tower of London). March 31–April 6 Eltham. April 6–15 Westminster. May 5 St Albans. May 8 Woburn. May 16–20 Leicester. May 25–June 1 Nottingham. June 6 Castle Donington. June 8–12 Nottingham. June 13 Worksop. June 14 Doncaster. June 17–21 Pontefract. July 6–10 Pontefract. July 11 York. July 14 Pontefract. July 19 Wressle. July 26 Leicester. Aug. 7 Rockingham. Aug. 8 Drayton. Aug. 11 Pipewell Abbey. Aug. 14–21 Leicester. Aug. 22–29 Lichfield. Sept. 1–27 Tutbury (but Sept. 13–25 Ravendale). Sept. 28–9 Maxstoke. Oct. 6–Nov. 14 Coventry. Nov. 16–18 Kenilworth. Nov. 29–Dec. 1 Barnet. Dec. 4–9 Tower of London. Dec. 12 Hertford. Dec. 21–22 Tower of London. Dec. 24–31 Eltham.

1405

Jan. 1–6 Eltham. Jan. 9–15 Westminster. Jan. 19–27 Eltham. Jan. 30–31 Tower of London. Feb. 2 Westminster. Feb. 3 Eltham. Feb. 9 Tower of London. Feb. 14 Kennington. Feb. 15 Windsor. Feb. 17–March 9 Westminster. March 10 Barnet. March 11 St Albans. March 11–17 Berkhamstead. March 18 Barnet. March 19–20 Westminster. March 26 Canterbury. March 27 Sittingbourne. March 30 Tower of London. April 2–5 St Albans. April 6–11 Berkhamstead. April 16–23 Windsor. April 24 High Wycombe. April 25–26 Oxford. April 27–28 Woodstock. April 29 Chipping Norton. April 30 Evesham. May 1–12 Worcester. May 14–23 Hereford. May 24–26 Worcester. May 27 Hatfield (Worcestershire). May 28 Derby. May 30–June 1 Nottingham. June 2 Doncaster. June 3–4 Pontefract. June 6–8 York. June 9–16 Ripon. June 17 Thirsk. June 18 Northallerton. June 19–21 Durham. June 21–25 Newcastle. June 27 Widdrington. July 1–2 Warkworth. July 8 Worthington. July 10–12 Berwick. July 12 Warkworth. July 14 Alnwick. July 15–17 Newcastle. July 18–20 Durham.

July 20–22 Raby. July 22–23 Northallerton. July 23–29 Pontefract. Aug. 3 Newstead. Aug. 4–14 Nottingham. Aug. 15–19 Leicester. Aug. 20–31 Worcester. Sept. 3–10 Hereford. *c.*12–25 Sept. in Wales (Coety castle, date lacking). Sept. 29–30 Hereford. Oct. 1 Bromyard. Oct. 2–6 Worcester. Oct. 7 Alcester. Oct. 8–Nov. 2 Kenilworth. Nov. 3–5 Daventry. Nov. 6–7 Stony Stratford. Nov. 8 Barnet. Nov. 9–21 Tower of London. Nov. 23–Dec. 3 Westminster. Dec. 4–6 Tower of London. Dec. 7–20 Hertford. Dec. 21 Waltham. Dec. 22 Tower of London. 23–31 Dec. Eltham.

1406

Jan. 1–6 Eltham. Jan. 7–17 London. Jan. 18–28 Westminster (Jan. 24 at earl of Northumberland's hostel). Jan. 29 Waltham. Jan. 30–Feb. 4 Hertford. Feb. 5 Waltham. Feb. 6–19 Tower of London. Feb. 20–25 Hertford. Feb. 26 Waltham. Feb. 27–April 7 Westminster. April 8–20 Eltham. April 21 Greenwich. April 22–23 Kingston. April 24–29 Windsor. April 29 Kingston. April 30 Westminster. May 1–July 5 London (Bishop of Durham's house, Dowgate; but 15, 22 and 24 May, 7 and 19 June at Westminster). July 6 Waltham. July 7–9 Hertford. July 10–15 Tower of London. July 16 Waltham. July 17–19 Hertford. July 20 Berksway. July 21 Babraham. July 22–23 Bury St Edmunds. July 24–25 Thetford. July 26 Wymondham. July 27–29 Norwich. July 30 Cawston. July 31–Aug. 1 Walsingham. Aug. 2–3 Castle Rising. Aug. 4–11 Lynn. Aug. 12 Wisbech. Aug. 13 Gedney. Aug. 14–15 Spalding. Aug. 16 Boston. Aug. 19 Revesby. Aug. 20 Horncastle. Aug. 21–22 Bardney. Aug. 23–25 Lincoln. Aug. 26 Newark. Aug. 27 Bottesford. Aug. 28 Melton Mowbray. Aug. 29–Sept. 5 Leicester. Sept. 6 Market Harborough. Sept. 7–8 Northampton. Sept. 9 Stony Stratford. Sept. 10 Dunstable. Sept. 11–12 St Albans. Sept. 13 Barnet. Sept. 14–30 London. Oct. 1 London (earl of Northumberland's hostel). Oct. 2–4 Westminster. Oct. 5–11 Merton. Oct. 12–29 Westminster. Oct. 30 Waltham. Oct. 31–Nov. 1 Hertford. Nov. 2 Waltham. Nov. 3–Dec. 23 Westminster. Dec. 24–31 Eltham.

1407

Jan. 1–7 Eltham. Jan. 8 Tower of London. Jan. 13–17 Merton Priory. Jan. 30 Westminster. Feb. 7 Hertford. March 18–April 8 Hertford. April 23 Windsor. May 9–23 Windsor. May 28 Rotherhithe. June 1 Waltham. June 22–28 Leicester. July 7–Aug. 16 Nottingham. Aug. 17 Newstead. Aug. 18 Worksop. Aug. 19–22 Pontefract. Aug. 24–Sept. 1 Rothwell Haigh (Tadcaster). Sept. 5–6 York. Sept. 8 Faxfleet. Sept. 11–13 Beverley. Sept. 14 Bridlington. Sept. 16–21 York. Sept. 22 Cawood. Sept. 29 Worksop. Sept. 30 Nottingham. Oct. 4 Repton. Oct. 10–16 Evesham. Oct. 22–Dec. 5 Gloucester. Dec. 8 Cirencester. Dec. 10 Evesham. Dec. 11 Gloucester. Dec. 14 Windsor. Dec. 18 Westminster. Dec. 25–31 Eltham.

1408

Jan. 1–11 Eltham. Jan. 12 Merton. Feb. 20 London. Feb. 21 Westminster. March 2 St Albans. March 12 Leicester. March 16 Nottingham. March 18 Pontefract. March 20 Rothwell Haigh. March 26 York. March 26–April 6 Wheel Hall. April 7–8 Selby. April 8–30 Pontefract. May 3 Newstead. May 8–12 Leicester. May 21–24 Windsor. May 26 Sutton. May 29–31 Tower of London. June 1–July 12 Mortlake. July 14–22 Hertford. July 23–29 London. Aug. 16 Waltham. Sept. 2 Westminster. Sept. 7 London (Hugh Waterton's hostel). Sept. 19 Windsor. Nov. 1 Southwark (Bishop of Winchester's hostel). Nov. 12 Westminster. Nov. 15 London (Hugh Waterton's hostel). Nov. 28–Dec. 10 King's Langley. Dec. 17 London (Hugh Waterton's hostel). Dec. 24 Lambeth. Dec. 25–31 Eltham.

1409

Jan. 1–12 Eltham. Jan. 21–March 12 Greenwich. March 17–April 10 Eltham. May 1–8 Sutton. May 9 Windsor (Birdsnest Lodge). May 20 Windsor (castle). June 1–6 Windsor (castle). June 27 Windsor (Birdsnest Lodge). July (dates lacking) London (Archbishop of York's hostel; St. Bartholomew's Priory, Smithfield). July 5 Westminster. July 22 Westminster. July 23 London (Bishop of Ely's hostel, Holborn). July 24 Havering-atte-Bower. Aug. 4 Windsor. Aug. 15 Westminster. Aug. 20 Sutton. Aug. 22 Beauregard. Aug. 27 Bagshot. Sept. 3 Romsey. Oct. 3 Windsor. Oct. 4 London (Bishop of Ely's hostel, Holborn). Oct. 5 Windsor. Oct. 22 Westminster. Nov. 11 Westminster. Nov. 14 St Albans. Nov. 20 Berkhamstead. Nov. 23 Stony Stratford. Nov. 23–25 Northampton. Dec. 2–4 Leicester. Dec. 4 Groby. Dec. 15 Northampton. Dec. 21–23 Westminster. Dec. 25–31 Eltham.

1410

Jan. 1–19 Eltham. Jan. 25–27 Westminster. Feb. 13 Lambeth. March 4 Westminster. March 19 Lambeth. April 3 Beauregard. April 8 Lambeth. April 10 Windsor. April 12 Sutton. April 15–20 Windsor. April 24–26 Lambeth. May 2 Westminster. May 11–12 Lambeth. May 14 Windsor. May 20 Westminster. May 25–27 Windsor. May 27–28 Lambeth. May 29–June 9 Windsor. May 16–28 Sonning. June 26–July 10 (dates lacking) Henley, Tetsworth, Thame. July 10–Aug. 20 Woodstock. Aug. 22 Dadlington. Aug. 28 Daventry. Sept. 6–20 Leicester. Sept. 15 Bilton. Sept. 21 Oakham. Sept. 24–27 Leicester. Oct. 12–Nov. 11 Groby. Nov. 23–Dec. 3 Leicester. Dec. 6–8 Groby. Dec. 9–14 Leicester. Dec. 20 Coventry. Dec. 25–31 Kenilworth.

1411

Jan. 1–Feb. 16 Kenilworth. Feb. 22 Dunstable. March 15–19 Lambeth. April 1–2 Beauregard. April 9–28 Windsor (but April 20 Beauregard). May (dates lacking) Gloucester. May 4 Lambeth. May 8 Rotherhithe. May 12–13 Lambeth. May 15 Rotherhithe. May 16 Westminster. May 18–28 Rotherhithe. June 9–13 Stratford Abbey (Essex). June 15 Lambeth. June 19–Aug. 6 Stratford Abbey. Aug. 11 Lambeth. Aug. 18 Beauregard. Aug. 20 Stratford Abbey. Aug. 21 Beauregard. Aug. 26 Rotherhithe. Aug. 28 Lambeth. Aug. 29–Sept. 1 Rotherhithe. Sept. 3–7 Lambeth. Sept. 8 Stratford Abbey. Sept. 9–26 Lambeth. Sept. 27 Beauregard. Sept. 28 Windsor (Birdsnest Lodge). Sept. 29–Oct. 2 Beauregard. Oct. 6–26 Windsor. Nov. 2 Beauregard. Nov. 5–Dec. 19 Westminster. Dec. 25–31 Eltham.

1412

Jan. 1–12 Eltham. Jan. 13–22 Stratford Abbey. Jan. 28 Charlton. Feb. 1–7 Eltham. Feb. 12–18 Tower of London. Feb. 18 Eltham. Feb. 22–April 10 Canterbury. April 16 Tower of London. April 26 Westminster. April 28 Windsor. May 5 Beauregard. May 18 London. May 23–24 Stratford Abbey. June 28 London. June 30–July 3 Clerkenwell. July 3–8 London (Bishop of London's palace). July 8–10 Rotherhithe. July 11 Westminster. July 15 Fulham. July 17 Croydon. July 19 Rotherhithe. July 20 Croydon. July 30–Aug. 1 Fulham. Aug. 1–12 London. Aug. 18 Fulham. Aug. 26 London. Sept. 12 Tower of London. Sept. 15–19 Canterbury. Oct. 11–28 Merton. Nov. 3 Croydon. Nov. 4–5 Merton. Nov. 6–30 Croydon. Dec. 1 Merton. Dec. 1–23 Croydon. Dec. 25–31 Eltham.

1413

Jan. 1–24 Eltham. Jan. 25 Lambeth. Jan. 28 Mortlake. Jan. 30–31 Eltham. Feb. 5 Greenwich. Feb. 21–March 20 Westminster. **March 20, Death of Henry IV at Westminster**.

BIBLIOGRAPHY

MANUSCRIPT SOURCES

Classes of documents consulted in The National Archives, Kew, London

C 47	Chancery, Miscellanea
C 49	Chancery, Council and Parliament
C 53	Chancery, Charter Rolls
C 66	Chancery, Patent Rolls
DL 27	Duchy of Lancaster, Deeds
DL 28	Duchy of Lancaster, Accounts Various
DL 29	Duchy of Lancaster, Ministers' Accounts
DL 37	Duchy of Lancaster, Chancery Rolls
DL 42	Duchy of Lancaster, Miscellanea
E 28	Exchequer, Council and Privy Seal Records
E 37	Exchequer, Court of the Marshalsea
E 101	Exchequer, King's Remembrancer, Accounts Various
E 159	Exchequer, King's Remembrancer, Memoranda Rolls
E 175	Exchequer, Parliamentary and Council Proceedings
E 361	Exchequer, Enrolled Wardrobe and Household Accounts
E 401	Exchequer, Receipt Rolls
E 403	Exchequer, Issue Rolls
E 404	Exchequer, Warrants for Issue
KB 9	Court of King's Bench, Ancient Indictments
SC 1	Special Collections, Ancient Correspondence
SC 8	Special Collections, Ancient Petitions

Other manuscript repositories consulted

Arundel Castle, Arundel
Bodleian Library, Oxford
Borthwick Institute, York
British Library, London (Additional, Cotton, Harleian and Stowe collections)
Lambeth Palace Library, London
Shropshire Archives, Shrewsbury
Trinity College Library, Dublin

PRIMARY SOURCES

Ancient Irish Histories: The Works of Spencer, Campion, Hanmer and Marleburrough, ed. J. Ware (2 vols, Dublin, 1809)
Anglo-American Legal Tradition (online resource)
Anglo-Norman Letters and Petitions, ed. M. D. Legge (Anglo-Norman Text Society 3, Oxford, 1941)

Anglo-Scottish Relations 1174–1328: Some Selected Documents, ed. E. Stones (Oxford, 1965)

'Annales Ricardi Secundi et Henrici Quarti', in *J. de Trokelowe et anon, Chronica et Annales*, ed. H. Riley (RS, London, 1866)

Annals of the Kingdom of Ireland, ed. J. O'Donovan (7 vols, Dublin, 1856)

Anonimalle Chronicle 1333–1381, ed. V. H. Galbraith (Manchester, 1927)

Antient Kalendars and Inventories of the Treasury of His Majesty's Exchequer, ed. F. Palgrave (3 vols, London, 1836)

Arderne, John, *Treatise of Fistula in Ano*, ed. D'Arcy Power (EETS 139, London, 1910)

Black Book of Winchester, ed. W. Bird (Winchester, 1925)

Book of Margery Kempe, ed. B. Windeatt (Woodbridge, 2004)

Bower, Walter, *Scotichronicon*, ed. D. Watt, viii (Aberdeen, 1987)

Brut, or Chronicles of England, ed. F. Brie (2 vols, EETS, vols 131, 136, London, 1906–8)

Calendar of Ancient Deeds in the Public Record Office

Calendar of Charter Rolls in the Public Record Office

Calendar of the Close Rolls in the Public Record Office

Calendar of Documents Relating to Scotland, ed. J. Bain, G. Simpson and J. Galbraith (5 vols, Edinburgh, 1881–1986)

Calendar of Fine Rolls in the Public Record Office

Calendar of Gascon Rolls 1399–1413, ed. G. Pepin (online resource, 2014)

Calendar of Inquisitions Miscellaneous

Calendar of Inquisitions Post Mortem

Calendar of Irish Chancery Letters (CIRCLE), Close Rolls and Patent Rolls, ed. P. Crooks (online resource, 2012)

Calendar of Papal Letters

Calendar of the Patent Rolls in the Public Record Office

Calendar of the Register of Richard Scrope, Archbishop of York 1398–1405, ed. R. Swanson (Borthwick Texts and Calendars, 2 vols, 1981, 1985)

Calendar of State Papers Milan I, 1385–1618, ed. A. Hinds (London, 1912)

Calendar of State Papers Venice I, 1202–1509, ed. R. Brown (London, 1864)

Catalogue of the Medieval Muniments at Berkeley Castle, ed. B. Wells-Furby (2 vols, Bristol and Gloucestershire Archaeological Society, Bristol, 2004)

Chaucer Life-Records, ed. M. Crow and C. Olson (Oxford, 1966)

Chaucer, *The Book of the Duchess*, ed. H. Phillips (Durham and St Andrews Medieval Texts, 1982)

Choix de Pièces Inédites Relatives au Règne de Charles VI, ed. L. Douët-d'Arcq (2 vols, SHF, Paris, 1863)

Chronica Monasterii de Melsa, ed. E. Bond (3 vols, RS, London, 1866–8)

Chronicle of Adam Usk 1377–1421, ed. C. Given-Wilson (Oxford, 1997)

Chronicle of John Hardyng, ed. H. Ellis (London, 1812)

Chronicle of London from 1089 to 1483, ed. N. Nicolas and E. Tyrell (London, 1827)

Chronicles of London, ed. C. L. Kingsford (Oxford, 1905)

Chronicles of the Revolution 1397–1400, ed. C. Given-Wilson (Manchester, 1993)

Chronique d'Enguerran de Monstrelet 1400–1444, ed. L. Douët-d'Arcq (6 vols, SHF, Paris, 1858)

Chronique du Religieux de Saint-Denys 1380–1422, ed. M. Bellaguet (6 vols, SHF, Paris, 1839–52)

Chronique de la Traïson et Mort de Richart Deux Roy Dengleterre, ed. B. Williams (London, 1846)

Chronographia Regum Francorum, ed. H. Moranvillé (3 vols, SHF, Paris, 1891–7)

Complete Peerage, by G. E. Cockayne, ed. V. Gibbs (12 vols, London, 1910–59)

Concilia Magnae Brittaniae et Hiberniae, ed. D. Wilkins (3 vols, London, 1737)

Coronation of Richard III, ed. A. Sutton and P. Hammond (Gloucester, 1984)

Crime, Law and Society in the Later Middle Ages, ed. A. Musson with E. Powell (Manchester, 2009)

Deposition of Richard II, ed. D. Carlson (Toronto Medieval Latin Texts, Toronto, 2007)

Deposition of Richard II, ed. T. Wright (Camden Society, London, 1838)

Diplomatic Correspondence of Richard II, ed. E. Perroy (Camden Third Series 48, London, 1933)

Duo Rerum Anglicanum Scriptores Veteres viz Thomas Otterbourne et Johannis Whethamstede, ed. T. Hearne (2 vols, Oxford, 1732)

English Chronicle 1377–1461, ed. W. Marx (Woodbridge, 2003)

English Coronation Records, ed. J. Wickham Legg (London, 1901)

Eulogium Historiarum sive Temporis, vol. 3 (*Continuatio Eulogii*), ed. F. Haydon (RS, London, 1863)

Expeditions to Prussia and the Holy Land made by Henry Earl of Derby in the Years 1390–1 and 1392–3, ed. L. Toulmin Smith (Camden Society, New Series 52, London, 1894)

Fabric Rolls of York Minster, ed. J. Raine (Surtees Society 35, Durham, 1858)

Fasciculi Zizaniorum Magistri Johannis Wyclif cum Tritico, ed. W. W. Shirley (RS, London, 1858)

First English Life of Henry the Fifth, ed. C. Kingsford (Oxford, 1911)

First General Entry Book of the City of Salisbury 1387–1452, ed. D. Carr (Wiltshire Record Society 54, Trowbridge, 2001)

Foedera, Conventiones, Litterae, etc., ed. T. Rymer (20 vols, London, 1727–35)

Froissart, Jean, *Chroniques*, ed. S. Luce (17 vols, SHF, Paris, 1869–1919)

Froissart, *Oeuvres*, ed. Kervyn de Lettenhove (25 vols, Brussels, 1867–77)

Froissart, Jean, *Chronicles of England, France, Spain and the Adjoining Countries*, ed. and trans. T. Johnes (2 vols, London, 1848)

Froissart, *Chronicles*, ed. G. Brereton (Harmondsworth, 1968)

Gascoigne, Thomas, *Loci e Libro Veritatum*, ed. J. Rogers (Oxford, 1881)

Gesta Henrici Quinti, ed. F. Taylor and J. Roskell (Oxford, 1975)

Gower, John, *Confessio Amantis*, ed. R. Peck (Toronto, 1980)

Great Chronicle of London, ed. A. Thomas and I. Thornley (Gloucester, 1983)

Gutierre Diaz de Gamez, *The Unconquered Knight: A Chronicle of the Deeds of Don Pero Niño, Count of Buelna*, ed. J. Evans (Woodbridge, 2004 reprint)

'Histoire de Charles VI, Roy de France, par Jean Jouvenal des Ursins', in *Choix de Chroniques et Mémoires sur l'Histoire de France*, ed. J. Buchon (Paris, 1838), 323–573

Historia Anglicana Thomae Walsingham, ed. H. Riley (2 vols, RS, London, 1863–4)

Historia Mirabilis Parliamenti 1386, Per Thomam Fovent, ed. M. McKisack (Camden Miscellany 14, London, 1926)

Historia Vitae et Regni Ricardi Secundi, ed. G. Stow (Philadelphia, 1977)

Historians of the Church of York and its Archbishops, ed. J. Raine (3 vols, RS, London, 1879–94)

Historical Collections of a Citizen of London, ed. J. Gairdner (Camden Society, New Series 17, London, 1876)

Hoccleve, Thomas, *The Regement of Princes*, ed. F. Furnivall (EETS, London, 1897)

Incerti Scriptoris Chronicon Angliae de Regnis Trium Regum Lancastriensium, ed. J. Giles (London, 1848)

Inventories of St George's Chapel, Windsor Castle, 1384–1667, ed. M. Bond (Windsor, 1947)

Issues of the Exchequer Henry III to Henry VI, ed. F. Devon (London, 1837)

Johannis Capgrave Liber de Illustribus Henricis, ed. F. Hingeston (RS, London, 1858)

Johannis Lelandi Antiquarii de Rebus Britannicis Collectanea, ed. T. Hearne (6 vols, Oxford, 1715)

John of Gaunt's Register 1371–1375, ed. S. Armitage-Smith (2 vols, Camden Third Series 20 and 21, London, 1911)

John of Gaunt's Register 1379–1383, ed. E. Lodge and R. Somerville (2 vols, Camden Third Series 56 and 57, London, 1937)

John Leland's Itinerary, ed. J. Chandler (Stroud, 1993)

Journal d'un Bourgeois de Paris, ed. A. Tuetey (Paris, 1881)

Kirkstall Abbey Chronicles, ed. J. Taylor (Thoresby Society, York, 1952)

Knighton's Chronicle 1337–1396, ed. G. Martin (Oxford, 1995)

'Le Livre des Faicts du Bon Messire Jean le Maingre dit Boucicaut', in *Collection Complète de Mémoires Relatifs à l'Histoire de France*, ed. M. Petitot, vols 6–7 (Paris, 1819)

Liber Regie Capelle, ed. W. Ullmann with a Note on the Music by D. H. Turner (Henry Bradshaw Society 92, Cambridge, 1961)

Literae Cantuarienses, ed. J. B. Sheppard (3 vols, RS, London, 1887–9)

Love, Nicholas, *The Mirror of the Blessed Life of Jesus Christ*, ed. M. Sargent (Exeter, 2005)

Major Latin Works of John Gower, ed. and trans. E. W. Stockton (Seattle, 1962)

Master of Game, ed. W. and F. Baillie-Grohman (New York, 1904)

'Metrical History of the Deposition of Richard the Second', ed. J. Webb, *Archaeologia* (1823), 55–176

Minor Latin Works of John Gower, ed. R. F. Yeager (Kalamazoo, 2005)

Mum and the Sothsegger, ed. M. Day and R. Steele (EETS, London, 1936)

Music for Henry V and the House of Lancaster by the Binchois Consort, director Andrew Kirkman, with text by Philip Weller (CD, Hyperion Records, 2011)

Navy of the Lancastrian Kings, ed. S. Rose (Naval Records Society 123, London, 1982)

Original Letters Illustrative of English History, ed. H. Ellis (4 vols, London, 1824–7)

Oxfordshire Sessions of the Peace in the Reign of Richard II, ed. E. G. Kimball (Oxfordshire Record Society 53, Banbury, 1983)

Parliament Rolls of Medieval England 1275–1504, ed. P. Brand, A. Curry, C. Given-Wilson, R. Horrox, G. Martin, M. Ormrod, S. Phillips (16 vols, Woodbridge, 2005)

Parliamentary Texts of the Later Middle Ages, ed. N. Pronay and J. Taylor (Oxford, 1980)

Political Poems and Songs, ed. T. Wright (2 vols, RS, London, 1859–61)

Political Songs of England from the Reign of John to that of Edward II, ed. T. Wright (Camden Old Series 6, London, 1839)

Polychronicon Ranulphi Higden, Monachi Cestrensis, ed. C. Babington (9 vols, RS, London, 1865–86)

Proceedings and Ordinances of the Privy Council of England, ed. N. Nicolas (vols 1–2, Record Commission, London, 1834)

Records of Convocation, ed. G. Bray (10 vols (Canterbury), Woodbridge, 2006)

Recueil des Actes de Jean IV, Duc de Bretagne, ed. M. Jones (2 vols, Paris, 1983)

Register of Thomas Appleby of Carlisle, ed. R. Storey (Canterbury and York Society 96, Woodbridge, 2006)

Registrum Johannis Trefnant, ed. W. Capes (Canterbury and York Society 20, 1916)

Royal and Historical Letters during the Reign of Henry the Fourth, ed. F. Hingeston (2 vols, RS, London, 1860–65)

St Albans Chronicle: The Chronica Maiora of Thomas Walsingham, ed. J. Taylor, W. Childs and L. Watkiss (2 vols, Oxford, 2003, 2011)

Scrope and Grosvenor Controversy, ed. N. Nicolas (2 vols, London, 1832)

Select Cases in the Court of King's Bench VII, ed. G. Sayles (Selden Society, London, 1971)

Select Cases before the King's Council 1243–1482, ed. I. Leadam and J. Baldwin (Selden Society, London, 1918)

Selections from English Wycliffite Writings, ed. A. Hudson (Cambridge, 1978)

Signet Letters of Henry IV and Henry V, ed. J. Kirby (London, 1978)

Statutes of the Realm (11 vols, Record Commission, 1810–28)

Treasures of a Lost Art (Metropolitan Museum of New York, 2003)

Views of the Hosts of Alien Merchants 1440–1444, ed. H. Bradley (London Record Society 46, London, 2012)

Wavrin, Jean, Collection of the Chronicles and Ancient Histories of Great Britain, ed. W. Hardy (6 vols, RS, London, 1864–91)

Welsh Records in Paris, ed. T. Matthews (Carmarthen, 1910)

Westminster Chronicle 1381–1394, ed. L. Hector and B. Harvey (Oxford, 1982)

SECONDARY SOURCES

Aberth, J., *Criminal Churchmen in the Age of Edward III: The Case of Bishop Thomas de Lisle* (Philadelphia, 1996)

Alban, J. and Allmand, C. 'Spies and Spying in the Fourteenth Century', in *War, Literature and Politics in the Late Middle Ages*, ed. C. Allmand (Liverpool, 1976), 73–101

Allen, M., *Mints and Money in Medieval England* (Cambridge, 2012)

Allen, M., 'Italians in English Mints and Exchanges', in *Fourteenth-Century England 2*, ed. C. Given-Wilson (Woodbridge, 2002), 53–62

Allmand, C., *Henry V* (New Haven, 1997)

Allmand, C., 'A Bishop of Bangor during the Glyn Dwr Revolt: Richard Young', *Journal of the Historical Society of the Church in Wales* (1968), 47–56

Ambuhl, R., *Prisoners of War in the Hundred Years War: Ransom Culture in the Late Middle Ages* (Cambridge, 2013)

Archer, R., 'Parliamentary Restoration: John Mowbray and the Dukedom of Norfolk in 1425', in *Rulers and Ruled in Late Medieval England: Essays Presented to Gerald Harriss*, eds R. Archer and S. Walker (London, 1995), 99–116

Archer, R. and Walker, S. eds, *Rulers and Ruled in Late Medieval England: Essays Presented to Gerald Harriss* (London, 1995)

Aston, M., *Thomas Arundel* (Oxford, 1967)

Aston, M., 'Richard II and the Wars of the Roses', in *The Reign of Richard II*, eds F. Du Boulay and C. Barron (London, 1971), 280–317

Aston, M., 'Caim's Castles: Poverty, Politics and Disendowment', in *The Church, Politics and Patronage in the Fifteenth Century*, ed. R. Dobson (Gloucester, 1984), 45–81

Attreed, L., *The King's Towns* (New York, 2001)

Autrand, F., *Charles VI: La Folie du Roi* (Paris, 1986)

Baldwin, J., *The King's Council in England during the Middle Ages* (Oxford, 1913)

Barber, R., *Edward III and the Triumph of England* (London, 2013)

Barker, J., *Manuel II Palaeologus (1391–1425): A Study in Late Byzantine Statesmanship* (New Brunswick, 1969)

Barr, H., *The Piers Plowman Tradition* (London, 1993)

Barrell, A., 'The Ordinance of Provisors of 1343', *HR* 64 (1991), 264–77

Barron, C., *London in the Later Middle Ages: Government and People, 1200–1500* (Oxford, 2004)

Barron, C., 'Richard II and London', in *Richard II: The Art of Kingship*, eds J. Gillespie and A. Goodman (Oxford, 1999), 129–54

Bean, J., 'The Percies and their Estates in Scotland', *Archaeologia Aeliana* 35 (1957), 91–9

Bean, J., 'Henry IV and the Percies', *History* 44 (1959), 212–27

Beckett, N., 'Sheen Charterhouse from its Foundation to its Dissolution' (unpublished DPhil thesis, Oxford, 1992)

Bell, A., 'Medieval Chroniclers as War Correspondents during the Hundred Years War: The Earl of Arundel's Naval Campaign of 1387', in *Fourteenth Century England VI*, ed. C. Given-Wilson (Woodbridge, 2010), 171–84

Bell, A., Curry, A., King, A. and Simpkin, D., *The Soldier in Late Medieval England* (Oxford, 2014)

Bellamy, J., *The Law of Treason in England in the Later Middle Ages* (London, 1970)

Bellamy, J., *Criminal Law and Society in Late Medieval and Tudor England* (New York, 1984)

Bellamy, J., 'The Northern Rebellions in the Later Years of Richard II', *BJRL* 47 (1964–5), 254–74

Bennett, M., *Community, Class and Careerism. Cheshire and Lancashire Society in the Age of Sir Gawain and the Green Knight* (Cambridge, 1983)

Bennett, M., *Richard II and the Revolution of 1399* (Stroud, 1999)

Bennett, M., 'Edward III's Entail and the Succession to the Throne, 1376–1471', *EHR* 113 (1998), 580–609

Bennett, M., 'Prophecy, Providence and the Revolution of 1399', in *Prophecy, Apocalypse and the Day of Doom: Harlaxton Medieval Studies XII*, ed. N. Morgan (Donington, 2004), 1–18

Bennett, M., 'Henry IV, the Royal Succession and the Crisis of 1406', in *The Reign of Henry IV: Rebellion and Survival, 1403–1413*, eds G. Dodd and D. Biggs (York, 2008), 16–27

Bent, M., 'Old Hall Manuscript', in *New Grove Dictionary of Music and Musicians*, eds S. Sadie and J. Tyrrell (2nd edn, 2001), xviii.376–9

Bériac F. and Given-Wilson, C., 'Edward III's Prisoners of War: The Battle of Poitiers and its Context', *EHR* 116 (2001), 802–33

Biggs, D., *Three Armies in Britain* (Leiden, 2006)

Biggs, D., 'The Reign of Henry IV: The Revolution of 1399 and the Establishment of the Lancastrian Regime', in *Fourteenth Century England I*, ed. N. Saul (Woodbridge, 2000), 195–210

Biggs, D., 'Henry IV and his JPs: The Lancastrianization of Justice, 1399–1413', in *Traditions and Transformations in Medieval England*, eds D. Biggs, S. Michalove and A. C. Reeves (Leiden, 2002), 59–79

Biggs, D., 'Royal Charter Witness Lists for the Reign of Henry IV, 1399–1413', *EHR* 119 (2004), 407–23

Biggs, D., 'An Ill and Infirm King: Henry IV, Health, and the Gloucester Parliament of 1407', in *The Reign of Henry IV: Rebellion and Survival*, eds G. Dodd and D. Biggs (York, 2008), 180–209

Binski, P., *Westminster Abbey and the Plantagenets* (New Haven, 1995)

Binski, P. and Panayotova, S., eds, *The Cambridge Illuminations* (London, 2005)

Blacker, B., 'A Lancastrian Prince in Ireland', *History Ireland* (1998), 22–6

Blair, C. and Delamer, I., 'The Dublin Civic Swords', *Proceedings of the Royal Irish Academy* (1988), 87–142

Blunt, C., 'Unrecorded Heavy Nobles of Henry IV and Some Remarks on that Issue', *British Numismatic Journal* 36 (1967), 106–14

Boardman, S., *The Early Stewart Kings: Robert II and Robert III, 1371–1406* (East Linton, 1996)

Boffey, J., *Fifteenth-Century Dream Visions: An Anthology* (Oxford, 2003)

Bolton, J., *The Medieval English Economy 1150–1500* (London, 1980)

Bolton, J., 'How Sir Thomas Rempston Paid His Ransom', *Fifteenth-Century England VII*, ed. L. Clark (Woodbridge, 2007), 102–18

Bothwell, J., *Falling from Grace* (Manchester, 2008)

Bowers, R., 'The Music and Musical Establishment of St George's Chapel in the Fifteenth Century', in *St George's Chapel Windsor in the Late Middle Ages*, eds C. Richmond and E. Scarff (Windsor, 2001), 171–212

Bradley, H., 'The Datini Factors in London', in *Trade, Devotion and Governance: Papers in Later Medieval History*, eds D. Clayton, R. Davies and P. McNiven (Stroud, 1994), 55–79

Bridbury, A. R., *Medieval English Clothmaking: An Economic Survey* (London, 1982)

Brown, A., *The Early History of the Clerkship of the Council* (Glasgow, 1969)

Brown, A., *The Governance of Late Medieval England 1272–1461* (London, 1989)

Brown, A., 'The Commons and the Council in the Reign of Henry IV', *EHR* 79 (1964), 1–30

Brown, A., 'The Reign of Henry IV: The Establishment of the Lancastrian Regime', in *Fifteenth-Century England*, eds S. B. Chrimes, C. Ross and R. A. Griffiths (Manchester, 1972), 1–28

Brown, A., 'The Authorization of Letters under the Great Seal', *BIHR* 37 (1964), 125–56

Brown, A., 'The Latin Letters in MS. All Souls 182', *EHR* 87 (1972), 565–73

Brown, A., 'The English Campaign in Scotland', in *British Government and Administration: Studies presented to S. R. Chrimes*, eds H. Hearder and H. Loyn (Cardiff, 1974), 40–54

Brown, M., *The Black Douglases 1300–1455* (East Linton, 1998)

Brown, M., *Disunited Kingdoms: People and Politics in the British Isles 1280–1460* (Edinburgh, 2013)

Bueno de Mesquita, D., 'The Foreign Policy of Richard II in 1397: Some Italian Letters', *EHR* 56 (1941), 628–37

Burgess, C. and Heale, M., eds, *The Late Medieval English College and its Context* (Woodbridge, 2008)

Burgess, C. and Heale, M., eds, *The Late Medieval English College and its Context* (Woodbridge, 2008)

Caldwell, J., *The Oxford History of English Music I* (Oxford, 1991)

Carlton, D., *The Deposition of Richard II* (Toronto, 2007)

Carpenter, C., *Locality and Polity: A Study of Warwickshire Landed Society, 1401–1499* (Cambridge, 1992)

Carus-Wilson, E. and Coleman, O., *England's Export Trade 1275–1547* (Oxford, 1963)

Castor, H., *The King, the Crown, and the Duchy of Lancaster* (Oxford, 2000)

Catto, J., 'Religion and the English Nobility in the Later Fourteenth Century', in *History and Imagination*, eds H. Lloyd-Jones, V. Pearl and B. Worden (London, 1981), 43–55

Catto, J., 'The King's Servants', in *Henry V: The Practice of Kingship*, ed. G. Harriss (Oxford, 1987), 75–95

Catto, J., 'Wyclif and Wycliffism', in *The History of the University of Oxford II: Late Medieval Oxford*, eds J. Catto and R. Evans (Oxford, 1992)

Catto, J., 'The Prayers of the Bohuns', in *Soldiers, Nobles and Gentlemen. Essays in Honour of Maurice Keen*, eds P. Coss and C. Tyerman (Woodbridge, 2009), 112–25

Cavill, P., 'Heresy, Law and the State: Forfeiture in Late Medieval and Early Modern England', *EHR* 129 (2014), 270–95

Chernaik, W., *The Cambridge Introduction to Shakespeare's History Plays* (Cambridge, 2007)

Cherry, J., 'Some Lancastrian Seals', in *The Lancastrian Court: Proceedings of the 2001 Harlaxton Symposium*, ed. J. Stratford (Donington, 2003), 19–28

Childs, W., *Anglo-Castilian Trade in the Late Middle Ages* (Manchester, 1978)

Childs, W., 'Anglo-Italian Contacts in the Fourteenth Century', in *Chaucer and the Italian Trecento*, ed. P. Boitani (Cambridge, 1983), 65–87

Chrimes, S. and Brown, A., *Select Documents of English Constitutional History 1307–1485* (London, 1961)

Christiansen, E., *The Northern Crusades: The Baltic and the Catholic Frontier 1100–1525* (London, 1980)

Clark, J., 'Thomas Walsingham Reconsidered: Books and Learning at Late Medieval St Albans', *Speculum* 77 (2002), 832–60

Clarke, M. and Galbraith, V., 'The Deposition of Richard II', *BJRL* (1930), 125–81

Cobban, A., *The King's Hall within the University of Cambridge in the Later Middle Ages* (Cambridge, 1969)

Codling, D., 'Henry IV and Personal Piety', *History Today* (2007), 23–9

Collas, E., *Valentine de Milan, Duchesse d'Orléans* (Paris, 1911)

Collins, H., *The Order of the Garter 1348–1461* (Oxford, 2000)

Colvin, H., Allen Brown, R. and Taylor, A., *History of the King's Works: The Middle Ages* (2 vols, London, 1963)

Coote, L., *Prophecy and Public Affairs in Later Medieval England* (York, 2000)

Cosgrove, A., ed., *New History of Ireland II: Medieval Ireland 1169–1534* (Oxford, 1987)

Cox, R., 'A Law of War? English Protection and Destruction of Ecclesiastical Property during the Fourteenth Century', *EHR* 128 (2013), 1381–417

Crawford, A., 'The King's Burden'?: The Consequences of Royal Marriage in Fifteenth-Century England', in *Patronage, the Crown and the Provinces in Later Medieval England*, ed. R. A. Griffiths (Gloucester, 1981), 33–56

Crook, D., 'The Confession of a Spy, 1380', *BIHR* 62 (1989), 346–50

Crook, D., 'Central England and the Revolt of the Earls', *BIHR* 64 (1991), 403–10

Crooks, P., 'Factions, Feuds and Noble Power in the Lordship of Ireland, c.1356–1496', *Irish Historical Studies* 35 (2007), 425–54

Crooks, P., 'Representation and Dissent: "Parliamentarianism" and the Structure of Politics in Colonial Ireland', *EHR* 125 (2010), 1–34

Crooks, P., 'State of the Union: Perspectives on English Imperialism in the Late Middle Ages', *Past and Present* 212 (2011), 3–42

Crooks, P., 'Factionalism and Noble Power in English Ireland, c.1361–1423' (unpublished PhD thesis, Trinity College, Dublin, 2007)

Cummins, Abbot, 'Knaresborough Cave-Chapels', *Yorkshire Archaeological Journal* 28 (1926), 80–8

Curry, A., 'After Agincourt, What Next?', in *The Fifteenth Century VII*, ed. L. Clark (Woodbridge, 2007), 23–51

Curry, A. and Hughes, M., eds, *Arms, Armies and Fortifications in the Hundred Years War* (Woodbridge, 1994)

Curry, A., Bell, A., King, A. and Simpkin, D., 'New Regime, New Army? Henry IV's Scottish Expedition of 1400', *EHR* 125 (2010), 1382–413

Curtis, E., 'Janico Dartas: Richard II's "Gascon Esquire": His Career in Ireland, 1394–1426', *Journal of the Royal Society of Antiquaries of Ireland* 63 (1933), 182–205

Davies, R. G., 'Some Notes from the Register of Henry de Wakefield, Bishop of Worcester, on the Political Crisis of 1386–88', *EHR* 86 (1971), 547–58

Davies, R. G., 'Thomas Arundel as Archbishop of Canterbury 1396–1413', *Journal of Ecclesiastical History* 24 (1973), 9–21

Davies, R. G., 'Richard II and the Church in the Years of Tyranny', *Journal of Medieval History* I (1975), 329–62

Davies, R. G., 'After the Execution of Archbishop Scrope: Henry IV, the Papacy and the English Episcopate, 1405–8', *BJRL* 56 (1977), 40–74

Davies, R. R., *The Revolt of Owain Glyndŵr* (Oxford, 1995)

Davies, R. R., *Lordship and Society in the March of Wales 1282–1400* (Oxford, 1978)

Davies, R. R., *Lords and Lordship in the British Isles* (ed. B. Smith, Oxford, 2009)

Dennison, L., 'British Library, Egerton MS 3277: a Fourteenth-Century Psalter-Hours and the Question of Bohun Family Ownership', in *Family and Dynasty in Late Medieval England*, eds R. Eales and S. Tyas (Donington, 2003), 122–55

Dennys, R., *Heraldry and the Heralds* (London, 1982)

Devine, M., 'The Dog that did not Bark: Richmondshire and the 1405 Rebellion', in *Richard Scrope: Archbishop, Rebel, Martyr*, ed. P. J. Goldberg (Donington, 2007), 45–63

Dillon, D., 'Remarks on the Manner of the Death of King Richard II', *Archaeologia* (1840), 75–95

Dobson, R., *The Peasants' Revolt of 1381* (London, 1970)

Dodd, G., *Justice and Grace: Private Petitioning and the English Parliament in the Late Middle Ages* (Oxford, 2007)

Dodd, G., 'Richard II and the Transformation of Parliament', in *The Reign of Richard II*, ed. G. Dodd (Stroud, 2000), 71–84

Dodd, G., 'Conflict or Consensus: Henry IV and Parliament, 1399–1406', in *Social Attitudes and Political Structures. The Fifteenth Century Series* 7, ed. T. Thornton (Stroud, 2001), 118–49

Dodd, G., 'Henry IV's Council', in *Henry IV: The Establishment of the Regime 1399–1406* (York, 2003), 95–115

Dodd, G., 'Changing Perspectives: Parliament, Poetry and the "Civil Service" under Richard II and Henry IV', *Parliamentary History* 25 (2006), 299–322

Dodd, G., 'Patronage, Petitions, and Grace: The Chamberlains' Bills of Henry IV's Reign', in *The Reign of Henry IV: Rebellion and Survival, 1403–1413*, eds G. Dodd and D. Biggs (York, 2008), 105–35

Dodd, G., ed., *Henry V: New Interpretations* (York, 2013)

Dodd, G. and Biggs, D., eds, *Henry IV: The Establishment of the Regime 1399–1406* (York, 2003)

Dodd, G. and Biggs, D., eds, *The Reign of Henry IV: Rebellion and Survival 1403–1413* (York, 2008)

Dollinger, P., *The German Hansa*, trans. D. Ault and S. Steinberg (Stanford, 1970)

Du Boulay, F., 'Henry of Derby's Expeditions to Prussia 1390–1 and 1392', in *The Reign of Richard II*, eds F. Du Boulay and C. Barron (London, 1971), 153–72

Duffy, M., *The Royal Tombs of Medieval England* (Stroud, 2003)

Dugdale, W., *Monasticon Anglicanum* (6 vols, London, 1846–9)

Dunn, A., *The Politics of Magnate Power* (Oxford, 2003)

Dunn, A., 'Henry IV and the Politics of Resistance', in *Fifteenth-Century England III*, ed. L. Clark (Woodbridge, 2003), 5–23

Dunn, A., 'Loyalty, Honour and the Lancastrian Revolution: Sir Stephen Scrope of Castle Combe and his Kinsmen, c.1389–c.1408', in *Fourteenth Century England III*, ed. M. Ormrod (Woodbridge, 2004), 167–83

Echevarria Arsuaga, A., 'The Shrine as Mediator', in *England and Iberia in the Late Middle Ages, 12th to 15th Centuries*, ed. Maria Bullón-Fernández (London, 2007), 47–65

Ehlers, A., 'The Crusade of the Teutonic Knights against Lithuania Reconsidered', in *Crusade and Conversion on the Baltic Frontier 1150–1500*, ed. A. Murray (Aldershot, 2001), 21–44

El-Gazar, Z., 'Politics and Legislation in England in the Early Fifteenth Century: The Parliament of 1406' (unpublished PhD thesis, University of St Andrews, 2001)

Famiglietti, R., *Royal Intrigue: Crisis at the Court of Charles VI* (New York, 1986)

Faria, T., 'Court Culture and the Politics of Anglo-Portuguese Interaction in the Letters of Philippa Plantagenet, Queen of Portugal', in *John Gower in Late Medieval Iberia: Manuscripts, Influences, Reception*, eds A. Saez-Hidalgo and R. F. Yeager (Woodbridge, 2013)

Fleming, P., *Coventry and the Wars of the Roses* (Dugdale Society, Bristol, 2011)

Fletcher, C., *Richard II: Manhood, Youth and Politics, 1377–1399* (Oxford, 2008)

Fletcher, C., 'Narrative and Political Strategies at the Deposition of Richard II', *Journal of Medieval History* 30 (2004), 323–41

Fletcher, D., 'The Lancastrian Collar of Esses. Its Origins and Transformations down the Centuries', in *The Age of Richard* II, ed. J. Gillespie (Stroud, 1997), 191–204

Ford, C., 'Piracy or Policy: The Crisis in the Channel, 1400–1403', *TRHS* 29 (1979), 63–78

Forde, S., 'Social Outlook and Preaching in a Wycliffite *Sermones Dominicales* Collection', in *Church and Chronicle in the Middle Ages: Essays Presented to John Taylor*, eds I. Wood and G. Loud (London, 1991), 179–91

Forrest, I., *The Detection of Heresy in Late Medieval England* (Oxford, 2005)

Foulser, N., 'The Influence of Lollardy and Reformist Ideas on English Legislation *c.*1376–*c.*1422' (unpublished PhD thesis, University of St Andrews, 2004)

Fowler, K., *The King's Lieutenant: Henry of Grosmont, First Duke of Lancaster, 1310–1361* (London, 1969)

Frame, R., *The Political Development of the British Isles* (Oxford, 1990)

Frame, R., 'Lordship Beyond the Pale: Munster in the Later Middle Ages', in *Limerick and South-West Ireland: Medieval Art and Architecture* (British Archaeological Society Transactions 34, Leeds, 2011), 5–18

Gabel, L., *Benefit of Clergy in England in the Later Middle Ages* (New York, 1964 reprint)

Gardner, A., *Alabaster Tombs of the Pre-Reformation Period in England* (Cambridge, 1940)

Geouge, J., 'Anglo-Portuguese Trade during the Reign of João I of Portugal, 1385–1433', in *England and Iberia in the Late Middle Ages, 12th to 15th Centuries*, ed. Maria Bullón-Fernández (London, 2007), 121–33

Giancarlo, M., *Parliament and Literature in Late Medieval England* (Cambridge, 2007)

Gillespie, J., 'Thomas Mortimer and Thomas Molineux: Radcot Bridge and the Appeal of 1397', *Albion* 7 (1975), 161–73

Gillespie, J. and Goodman, A., eds, *Richard II: The Art of Kingship*, (Oxford, 1999)

Gillingham, J., 'Conquering the Barbarians: War and Chivalry in Twelfth-Century Britain and Ireland', *The Haskins Society Journal* 4 (1992), 67–84

Given-Wilson, C., *The Royal Household and the King's Affinity* (New Haven, 1986)

Given-Wilson, C., *The English Nobility in the Late Middle Ages* (London, 1987)

Given-Wilson, C., *Chronicles* (London, 2004)

Given-Wilson, C., 'The King and the Gentry in Fourteenth-Century England', *TRHS* 37 (1987), 87–102

Given-Wilson, C., 'Richard II, Edward II, and the Lancastrian Inheritance', *EHR* 109 (1994), 553–71

Given-Wilson, C., 'Service, Serfdom and English Labour Legislation, 1350–1500', in *Concepts and Patterns of Service in the Later Middle Ages*, ed. A. Curry and E. Matthew (Woodbridge, 2000), 21–37

Given-Wilson, C., 'Chronicles of the Mortimer Family, 1250–1450', in *Family and Dynasty in Late Medieval England*, eds R. Eales and S. Tyas (Donington, 2003), 67–86

Given-Wilson, C., 'Legitimation, Designation and Succession to the Throne in Fourteenth-Century England', in *Building Legitimacy. Political Discourses and Forms of Legitimacy in Medieval Societies*, ed. I. Alfonso, H. Kennedy and J. Escalona (Leiden, 2004), 89–105

Given-Wilson, C., 'The Rolls of Parliament, 1399–1421', in *Parchment and People: Parliament in the Later Middle Ages*, ed. L. Clark (Edinburgh, 2004), 57–72

Given-Wilson, C., 'The Coronation of Richard II', in *Ceremonial de la Coronacion, Uncion y Exequias de los Reyes de Inglaterra*, ed. E. Ramirez Vaquero (Pamplona, 2008), 195–227

Given-Wilson, C., 'The Quarrels of Old Women: Henry IV, Louis of Orleans, and Anglo-French Chivalric Challenges in the Early Fifteenth Century', in *The Reign of Henry IV: Rebellion and Survival, 1403–1413* (York, 2008), 28–47

Given-Wilson, C., 'The Exequies of Edward III and the Royal Funeral Ceremony in Late Medieval England', *EHR* 124 (2009), 257–82

Given-Wilson, C., 'The Earl of Arundel, the War at Sea, and the Anger of Richard II', in *The Medieval Python*, eds R. Yeager and T. Takamiya (New York, 2012), 27–38.

Given-Wilson, C., 'Richard II and the Higher Nobility', in *Richard II: The Art of Kingship*, eds J. Gillespie and A. Goodman (Oxford, 1999), 107–28

Goldberg, P. J., ed., *Richard Scrope: Archbishop, Rebel, Martyr* (Donington, 2007)

Good, J., *The Cult of St George in Medieval England* (Woodbridge, 2009)

Goodman, A., *The Loyal Conspiracy* (London, 1971)

Goodman, A., *John of Gaunt* (Harlow, 1992)

Goodman, A., *Katherine Swynford* (Lincoln Cathedral Publications, 1994)

Goodman, A., *Margery Kempe and her World* (Harlow, 2002)

Goodman, A., 'Richard II's Councils', in *Richard II: The Art of Kingship*, eds J. Gillespie and A. Goodman (Oxford, 1999), 59–82

Gransden, A., *Historical Writing in England II* (London, 1982)

Green, D., *Edward the Black Prince* (Harlow, 2007)

Grierson, P., 'The Origins of the English Sovereign and the Symbolism of the Closed Crown', *British Numismatic Journal* 33 (1969), 118–34

Griffiths, R., 'Prince Henry, Wales and the Royal Exchequer, 1400–1413', *Bulletin of the Board of Celtic Studies* 32 (1985), 202–15

Griffiths, R., 'Prince Henry and Wales', in *Profit, Piety and the Professions in Later Medieval England*, ed. M. Hicks (Gloucester, 1990), 51–61

Griffiths, R. A., *Conquerors and Conquered in Medieval Wales* (Stroud, 1994)

Griffiths, R. A., 'Some Secret Supporters of Owain Glyndŵr?', *BIHR* 37 (1964), 77–100

Griffiths, R. A., 'The English Realm and Dominions and the King's Subjects in the Later Middle Ages', in *Aspects of Late Medieval Government and Society*, ed. J. Rowe (Toronto, 1986), 83–105

Griffiths, R. A., 'The Glyndŵr Rebellion in North Wales through the Eyes of an Englishman', in *Conquerors and Conquered in Medieval Wales* (Stroud, 1994), 123–38

Grummitt, D., 'The Financial Administration of Calais during the Reign of Henry IV, 1399–1413', *EHR* 113 (1998), 277–99

Guard, T., *Chivalry, Kingship and Crusade: The English Experience in the Fourteenth Century* (Woodbridge, 2013)

Hall, E., *The Union of the Two Noble and Illustre Families of Lancastre and York* (London, 1542)

Harrison, F., *Music in Medieval Britain* (London, 1958)

Harriss, G., ed., *Henry V: The Practice of Kingship* (Oxford, 1987)

Harriss, G., *Cardinal Beaufort* (Oxford, 1988)

Harriss, G., *Shaping the Nation: England 1360–1461* (Oxford, 2005)

Harriss, G., 'Political Society and the Growth of Government in Late Medieval England', *Past and Present* 138 (1993), 28–57

Harriss, G., 'The Medieval Parliaments', *Parliamenary History* 13 (1994), 206–26

Harriss, G., 'The Court of the Lancastrian Kings', in *The Lancastrian Court: Proceedings of the 2001 Harlaxton Symposium*, ed. J. Stratford (Donington, 2003), 1–18

Harriss, G., 'Budgeting at the Medieval Exchequer', in *War, Government and Aristocracy in the British Isles c.1150–1500: Essays in Honour of Michael Prestwich*, eds C. Given-Wilson, A. Kettle and L. Scales (Woodbridge, 2008), 179–96

Harvey, M., *Solutions to the Schism 1378–1409* (St Ottilien, 1983)

Heath, P., *Church and Realm 1272–1461* (London, 1988)

Heenan, M., 'The French Quartering in the Arms of Henry IV', *The Coat of Arms* 10 (1968–9), 215–21

Henneman, J., *Olivier de Clisson and Political Society in France under Charles V and Charles VI* (Philadelphia, 1996)

Holford, M., 'War, Lordship and Community in the Liberty of Norhamshire', in *Liberties and Identities in the Medieval British Isles*, ed. M. Prestwich (Woodbridge, 2008), 77–97

Holmes, G., *The Estates of the Higher Nobility in Fourteenth-Century England* (Cambridge, 1957)

Holmes, G., 'Florentine Merchants in England, 1346–1436', *Economic History Review* (Second Series 13, 1960), 193–208

Horrox, R., 'Urban Patronage and Patrons in the Fifteenth Century', in *Patronage, the Crown and the Provinces in Later Medieval England*, ed. R. A. Griffiths (Gloucester, 1981), 145–66

House of Commons 1386–1421, ed. J. Roskell, C. Rawcliffe and L. Clark (4 vols, History of Parliament, Stroud, 1992)

Hudson, A., *The Premature Reformation* (Oxford, 1988)

Hudson, A., 'The Debate on Bible Translation, Oxford 1401', *EHR* 90 (1975), 1–18

Hughes, J., *Pastors and Visionaries* (Woodbridge, 1988)

Jacob, E., *Essays in the Conciliar Epoch* (Manchester, 1963)

Jacob, E., *Archbishop Henry Chichele* (London, 1967)

Johnston, D., 'Richard II's Departure from Ireland, July 1399', *EHR* 98 (1983), 785–805

Jones, M., *Ducal Brittany 1364–1399* (Oxford, 1970)

Jones, M., *Between France and England: Politics, Power and Society in Late Medieval Brittany* (Aldershot, 2003)

Jordan, W., *Philanthropy in England 1480–1660* (London, 1959)

Jurkowski, M., 'The Arrest of William Thorpe in Shrewsbury and the Anti-Lollard Statute of 1406', *HR* 75 (2002), 273–95

Jurkowski, M., Smith, C. and Crook, D., eds, *Lay Taxes in England and Wales 1188–1688* (Kew, 1998)

Kaminsky, H., 'The Politics of France's Subtraction of Obedience from Pope Benedict XIII, 27 July 1398', *Proceedings of the American Philosophical Society* 115 (1971), 366–97

Keen, M., 'Treason Trials under the Law of Arms', *TRHS* (Fifth Series 12, 1962), 85–103

Keen, M., 'Diplomacy', in *Henry V: The Practice of Kingship*, ed. G. Harriss (Oxford, 1987), 181–99

Kempe, A., J. 'Some Account of the Jerusalem Chamber in the Abbey of Westminster', *Archaeologia* 26 (1836), 432–45

Kenyon, J., 'Coastal Artillery Fortifications', in *Arms, Armies and Fortifications in the Hundred Years War*, eds A. Curry and M. Hughes (Woodbridge, 1994), 145–50

King, A., 'Pur Salvation du Roiaume: Military Service and Obligation in Fourteenth-Century Northumberland', in *Fourteenth-Century England 2*, ed. C. Given-Wilson (Woodbridge, 2002), 13–31

King, A., 'They have the Hertes of the People by North: Northumberland, the Percies and Henry IV, 1399–1408', in *Henry IV: The Establishment of the Regime*, eds G. Dodd and D. Biggs (York, 2003), 139–59

King, A., 'Scaling the Ladder: The Rise and Rise of the Grays of Heaton, 1296–1415', in *North-East England in the Later Middle Ages*, eds C. Liddy and R. Britnell (Woodbridge, 2005), 157–73

King, A., 'Sir William Clifford: Rebellion and Reward in Henry IV's Affinity', in *The Fifteenth Century IX: English and Continental Perspectives*, ed. L. Clark (Woodbridge, 2010), 139–54

Kingsford, C., *English Historical Literature in the Fifteenth Century* (Oxford, 1913)

Kingsford, C., *Henry V* (London, 1901)

Kingsford, C., 'The First Version of John Hardyng's Chronicle', *EHR* 27 (1912), 262–82

Kingston, S., *Ulster and the Isles in the Fifteenth Century* (Dublin, 2004)

Kirby, J., *Henry IV of England* (London, 1970)

Kirby, J., 'Councils and Councillors of Henry IV', *TRHS* (Fifth Series 14, 1964) 35–65

Knowlson, G., *Jean V, Duc de Bretagne, et l'Angleterre* (Rennes, 1964)

Kowaleski, M., *Local Markets and Regional Trade in Medieval Exeter* (Cambridge, 1995)

Lacey, H., *The Royal Pardon* (York, 2009)

Laidlaw, J., 'Christine de Pizan, the Earl of Salisbury and Henry IV', *French Studies* 36 (1982), 129–43

Lambert, C., *Shipping the Medieval Military* (Woodbridge, 2011)

Larson, A., 'Are all Lollards Lollards?', in *Lollards and Their Influence in Late Medieval England*, eds F. Somerset, J. Havens and D. Pitard (Woodbridge, 2003), 59–72

Lehoux, F., *Jean de France, Duc de Berri* (3 vols, Paris, 1966)

Liddy, C., *War, Politics and Finance in Late Medieval England: Bristol, York and the Crown 1350–1400* (Woodbridge, 2005)

Liddy, C., *The Bishopric of Durham in the Late Middle Ages* (Woodbridge, 2008)

Liddy, C., 'William Frost, the City of York and Scrope's Rebellion of 1405', in *Richard Scrope: Archbishop, Rebel, Martyr*, ed. P. J. Goldberg (Donington, 2007), 64–85

Linehan, P., *History and the Historians of Medieval Spain* (Oxford, 1993)

Lloyd, J. E., *Owen Glendower* (Oxford, 1931)

Lloyd, T., *England and the German Hanse 1157–1611* (Cambridge, 2002)

Lunt, W., *Financial Relations of the Papacy with England II, 1327–1534* (Cambridge, MA, 1962)

Lutkin, J., 'Luxury and Display in Gold and Silver at the Court of Henry IV', in *Fifteenth-Century England IX*, ed. L. Clark (Woodbridge, 2010), 155–78

Lutkin, J., 'Goldsmiths and the English Royal Court 1360–1413', (unpublished PhD thesis, Royal Holloway and Bedford New College, 2008)

Lydon, J., 'Ireland: Politics, Government and Law', in *A Companion to Britain in the Later Middle Ages*, ed. S. Rigby (London, 2009), 335–56

Macdonald, A., *Border Bloodshed. Scotland, England and France at War, 1369–1403* (East Linton, 2000)

McFarlane, K., *John Wycliffe and the Beginnings of English Nonconformity* (Oxford, 1953)

McFarlane, K., *Lancastrian Kings and Lollard Knights* (Oxford, 1972)

McFarlane, K., *The Nobility of Later Medieval England* (Oxford, 1973)

McHardy, A., 'The Effects of War on the Church: The Case of the Alien Priories in the Fourteenth Century', in *England and her Neighbours 1066–1453: Essays in Honour of Pierre Chaplais*, eds M. Jones and M. Vale (London, 1989), 277–95

McHardy, A., 'De Heretico Comburendo, 1401', in *Lollardy and the Gentry in the Later Middle Ages*, eds M. Aston and C. Richmond (Stroud, 1997), 112–26

McHardy, A., 'John Scarle: Ambition and Politics in the Late Medieval Church', in *Image, Text and Church, 1380–1600. Essays for Margaret Aston*, eds L. Clark, M. Jurkowski and C. Richmond (Toronto, 2009), 68–93

McHardy, A., 'The Chapel Royal in the Reign of Henry V', in *Henry V: New Interpretations*, ed. G. Dodd (York, 2013), 128–56

Mackman, J., 'Hidden Gems in the Records of the Common Pleas: New Evidence on the Legacy of Lucy Visconti', in *The Fifteenth Century VIII*, ed. L. Clark (Woodbridge, 2008), 59–72

McNiven, P., *Heresy and Politics in the Reign of Henry IV* (Woodbridge, 1987)

McNiven, P., 'The Cheshire Rising of 1400', *BJRL* 52 (1969–70), 375–96

McNiven, P., 'The Betrayal of Archbishop Scrope', *BJRL* 54 (1971), 173–213

McNiven, P., 'The Scottish Policy of the Percies and the Strategy of the Rebellion of 1403', *BJRL* 62 (1979–80)', 498–530

McNiven, P., 'Prince Henry and the English Political Crisis of 1412', *History* 65 (1980), 1–18

McNiven, P., 'The Problem of Henry IV's Health', *EHR* 100 (1985), 747–72

McNiven, P., 'Rebellion, Sedition and the Legend of Richard II's Survival in the Reigns of Henry IV and Henry V', *BJRL* 76 (1994), 93–117

Maddicott, J., *Thomas of Lancaster 1307–1322* (Oxford, 1970)

Maddicott, J., *Law and Lordship: Royal Justices as Retainers in Thirteenth and Fourteenth Century England* (Past and Present Supplement 4, Oxford, 1978)

Matthew, E., 'The Financing of the Lordship of Ireland under Henry V and Henry VI', in *Property and Politics in Later Medieval English History*, ed. A. Pollard (Gloucester, 1984), 97–115

Mayhew, N., 'From Regional to Central Minting', in *A New History of the Royal Mint*, ed. C. Challis (Cambridge, 1992), 83–178

Milner, J., 'The English Enterprise in France in 1412–13', in *Trade, Devotion and Governance: Papers in Later Medieval History*, eds D. Clayton, R. Davies and P. McNiven (Stroud, 1994), 80–101

Milner, J., 'The English Commitment to the 1412 Expedition to France', in *The Fifteenth Century XI*, ed. L. Clark (Woodbridge 2012), 9–23

Morgan, P., *War and Society in Late Medieval Cheshire 1277–1403* (Chetham Society, Manchester, 1987)

Morgan, P., 'Henry IV and the Shadow of Richard II', in *Crown, Government and People in the Fifteenth Century*, ed. R. Archer (Stroud, 1995), 1–32

Mortimer, I., *The Fears of Henry IV* (London, 2007)

Mortimer, I., 'Richard II and the Succession to the Crown', *History* 91 (2006), 320–36

Mott, R., 'Richard II and the Crisis of July 1397', in *Church and Chronicle in the Middle Ages: Essays Presented to John Taylor*, ed. I. Wood and G. Loud (London, 1991), 165–77

Munro, J., *Wool, Cloth and Gold: The Struggle for Bullion in Anglo-Burgundian Trade 1340–1478* (Brussels, 1972)

Murray, A., ed., *Crusade and Conversion on the Baltic Frontier 1150–1500* (Aldershot, 2001)

Myers, A., 'The Captivity of a Royal Witch: The Household Accounts of Queen Joan of Navarre, 1419–1421', in *Crown, Household and Parliament in Fifteenth-Century England*, ed. C. Clough (London, 1985), 93–134

Myres, J., 'The Campaign of Radcot Bridge in December 1387', *EHR* 42 (1927), 20–33

Neville, C., *Violence, Custom and Law: The Anglo-Scottish Borderlands in the Later Middle Ages* (Edinburgh, 1998)

Neville, C., 'Scotland, the Percies, and the Law in 1400', in *Henry IV: The Establishment of the Regime, 1399–1403*, eds G. Dodd and D. Biggs (York, 2003), 73–94

Nichols, J., *A Collection of All the Wills of the Kings and Queens of England* (Society of Antiquaries, London, 1780)

Nicholson, R., *Scotland: The Later Middle Ages* (Edinburgh, 1974)

Nicol, D., 'A Byzantine Emperor in England: Manuel II's Visit to London in 1400–1401', *University of Birmingham Historical Journal* 12 (1969–70), 204–25

Nightingale, P., *A Medieval Mercantile Community: The Grocers' Company and the Politics and Trade of London 1000–1485* (London, 1995)

Nordberg, M., *Les Ducs et la Royauté* (Uppsala, 1964)

Norton, C., 'Richard Scrope and York Minster', in *Richard Scrope: Archbishop, Rebel, Martyr*, ed. P. J. Goldberg (Donington, 2007), 138–213

Nuttall, J., *The Creation of Lancastrian Kingship* (Cambridge, 2007)

Nuttall, J., '*Vostre Humble Matatyas*: Culture, Politics and the Percys', in *The Fifteenth Century V*, ed. L. Clark (Woodbridge, 2005), 69–83

Oliver, C., 'A Political Pamphleteer in Late Medieval England: Thomas Fovent, Geoffrey Chaucer, Thomas Usk, and the Merciless Parliament of 1388', in *New Medieval Literatures VI*, eds D. Lawton, R. Copeland and W. Scase (Oxford, 2003), 167–93

Ormrod, M., *Edward III* (New Haven, 2011)

Ormrod, M., 'Finance and Trade under Richard II', in *Richard II: The Art of Kingship*, eds J. Gillespie and A. Goodman (Oxford, 1999), 155–86

Ormrod, M., 'England in the Middle Ages', in *The Rise of the Fiscal State in Europe, c.1200–1815*, ed. R. Bonney (Oxford, 1999)

Ormrod, M., 'A Problem of Precedence', in *The Age of Edward III*, ed. J. Bothwell (Woodbridge, 2001), 133–53

Ormrod, M., 'The Use of English: Language, Law and Political Culture in Fourteenth-Century England', *Speculum* 78 (2003), 750–87

Ormrod, M., 'The Rebellion of Archbishop Scrope and the Tradition of Opposition to Royal Taxation', in *The Reign of Henry IV: Rebellion and Survival, 1403–1413*, eds G. Dodd and D. Biggs (York, 2008), 162–79

Palmer, J., *England, France and Christendom 1377–1399* (London, 1972)

Palmer, J., 'The Parliament of 1385 and the Constitutional Crisis of 1386', *Speculum* 46 (1971), 477–89.

Palmer, J., 'The Historical Context of the *Book of the Duchess*: a Revision', *Chaucer Review* 8 (1974), 253–6

Palmer, J., 'The Authorship, Date and Historical Value of the French Chronicles on the Lancastrian Revolution', *BJRL* 61 (1978–9), 145–81, 398–421

Paravicini, W., *Die Preussenreisen des Europäischen Adels* (2 vols, Sigmaringen, 1989–95)

Park, G., *The English Traveller to Italy I: to 1525* (Rome, 1954)

Parker, K., 'Politics and Patronage in Lynn, 1399–1416', in *The Reign of Henry IV: Rebellion and Survival, 1403–1413*, ed. G. Dodd and D. Biggs (York, 2008), 210–27

Payling, S., *Political Society in Lancastrian England. The Greater Gentry of Nottinghamshire* (Oxford, 1991)

Pearce, E., *William de Colchester, Abbot of Westminster* (London, 1915)

Pépin, G., 'The French Offensives of 1404–1407 against Anglo-Gascon Aquitaine', in *Soldiers, Weapons and Armies in the Fifteenth Century*, eds A. Curry and A. Bell (Woodbridge, 2011), 1–40

Phillpotts, C., 'John of Gaunt and English Policy towards France', *Journal of Medieval History* 16 (1990), 363–86

Phillpotts, C., 'The Fate of the Truce of Paris, 1396–1415', *Journal of Medieval History* 24 (1998), 61–80

Pietresson P., de Saint Aubin, 'Documents inédits sur l'installation de Pierre d'Ailly à l'évêché de Cambrai en 1397', *Bibliothèque de l'Ecole des Chartes* 113 (1955), 121–39

Pilbrow, F., 'The Knights of the Bath: Dubbing to Knighthood in Lancastrian and Yorkist England', in *Heraldry, Pageantry and Social Display in Medieval England*, eds P. Coss and M. Keen (Woodbridge, 2002), 195–218

Piroyanska, D., 'Martyrio Pulchro Finitus', in *Richard Scrope: Archbishop, Rebel, Martyr*, ed. P. J. Goldberg (Donington, 2007), 100–13

Pistono, S., 'Henry IV and Charles VI: the Confirmation of the Twenty-eight-year Truce', *Journal of Medieval History* 3 (1977), 353–65

Pistono, S., 'The Diplomatic Mission of Jean de Hangest, Lord of Hugueville, October 1400', *Canadian Journal of History* 13 (1978), 193–207

Pocquet, B., du Haut-Jussé, 'La Renaissance Littéraire autour de Henri V, roi d'Angleterre', *Revue Historique* 224 (1960), 329–38

Pollard, A., *Late Medieval England 1399–1509* (Harlow, 2000)

Pollard, A., 'The Lancastrian Constitutional Experiment Revisited: Henry IV, Sir John Tiptoft and the Parliament of 1406', *Parliamentary History* 14 (1995), 103–19

Post, J., 'The Obsequies of John of Gaunt', *Guildhall Studies in London History* (1981), 1–12

Postan, M., 'Economic and Political Relations of England and the Hanse from 1400 to 1475', in *Studies in English Trade in the Fifteenth Century*, ed. E. Power and M. Postan (London, 1933), 91–153

Powell, E., *Kingship, Law and Society: Criminal Law in the Reign of Henry V* (Oxford, 1989)

Powell, E., 'The Restoration of Law and Order', in *Henry V: The Practice of Kingship*, ed. G. L. Harriss (Oxford, 1987), 175–94

Powell, E., 'The Strange Death of Sir John Mortimer: Politics and the Law of Treason in Lancastrian England', in *Rulers and Ruled in Late Medieval England: Essays Presented to Gerald Harriss*, eds R. Archer and S. Walker (London, 1995), 83–97

Powell, J. E. and Wallis, K., *The House of Lords in the Middle Ages* (London, 1968)

Prestwich, M., ed., *Liberties and Identities in the Medieval British Isles* (Woodbridge, 2008)

Priestley, E., *The Battle of Shrewsbury 1403* (Shrewsbury, 1979)

Pugh, T., *Henry V and the Southampton Plot of 1415* (Gloucester, 1988)

Ramsay, J., *Lancaster and York*, (2 vols, Oxford, 1892)

Reitemeier, A., *Aussenpolitik im Spätmittelalter: Die diplomatiken Beziehungen zwischen dem Reich und England 1377–1422* (Paderborn, 1999)

Rex, R., *The Lollards* (Basingstoke, 2002)

Richardson, H., 'Heresy and Lay Power in the Reign of Richard II', *EHR* 51 (1936), 1–28.

Richardson, H. and Sayles, G., 'Parliamentary Documents from Formularies', *BIHR* 12 (1934), 152–4

Risk, J., *The History of the Order of the Bath* (London, 1972)

Rodger, N., *The Safeguard of the Sea: A Naval History of Britain 660–1649* (London, 1997)

Rogers, A., 'The Political Crisis of 1401', *Nottingham Medieval Studies* 12 (1968), 85–96

Rogers, A., 'Henry IV and the Revolt of the Earls', *History Today* 18 (1968), 277–83

Rogers, A., 'The Royal Household of Henry IV' (unpublished PhD thesis, University of Nottingham, 1966)

Rose, S., 'A Twelfth-Century Honour in a Fifteenth-Century World: The Honour of Pontefract', in *The Fifteenth Century IX*, ed. L. Clark (Woodbridge, 2010), 39–57

Roskell, J., *The Commons in the Parliament of 1422* (Manchester, 1954)

Ross, C., 'The Yorkshire Baronage, 1399–1435' (unpublished DPhil thesis, University of Oxford, 1950)

Ross, J., 'Seditious Activities: The Conspiracy of Maud de Vere, Countess of Oxford, 1403–4', in *Fifteenth-Century England III: Authority and Submission*, ed. L. Clark (Woodbridge, 2003), 25–41

Rubin, M., *Charity and Community in Medieval Cambridge* (Cambridge, 1986)

Ruddick, A., *English Identity and Political Culture in the Fourteenth Century* (Cambridge, 2013)

Ruddick, A., 'English Identity and Political Language in the King of England's Dominions: A Fourteenth-Century Perspective', in *Fifteenth-Century England VI*, ed. L. Clark (Woodbridge, 2006)

Ruddock, A., *Italian Merchants and Shipping in Southampton 1270–1600* (Southampton, 1951)

Russell, P., *The English Intervention in Spain and Portugal in the Time of Edward III and Richard II* (Oxford, 1955)

Sandler, L., *Gothic Manuscripts 1285–1385* (2 vols, Oxford, 1986)

Sandler, L., 'The Lichtenthal Psalter and the Manuscript Patronage of the Bohun Family', *Studies in Medieval and Renaissance Art History* 38, London, 2004)

Sandler, L., *Illuminators and Patrons in Fourteenth-Century England: The Psalter and Hours of Humphrey de Bohun and the Manuscripts of the Bohun Family* (London, 2014)

Sandler, L., 'Lancastrian Heraldry in the Bohun Manuscripts', in *The Lancastrian Court: Proceedings of the 2001 Harlaxton Symposium*, ed. J. Stratford (Donington, 2003), 221–32

Sandler, L., 'The Bohun Women and Manuscript Patronage in Fourteenth-Century England', in *Patronage, Power and Agency in Medieval Art*, ed. C. Hourihane (Princeton, 2013), 275–96

Saul, N., *Scenes from Provincial Life. Knightly Families in Sussex 1280–1400* (Oxford, 1986)

Saul, N., *Richard II* (New Haven, 1997)

Saul, N., 'The Commons and the Abolition of Badges', *Parliamentary History* 9 (1990), 302–15

Saul, N., 'Richard II and the Vocabulary of Kingship', *EHR* 110 (1995), 854–77

Saul, N., 'John Gower: Prophet or Turncoat?', in *John Gower, Trilingual Poet. Language, Translation and Tradition*, eds E. Dutton, with J. Hines and R. F. Yeager (Woodbridge, 2010), 85–97

Scattergood, J., *Politics and Poetry in the Fifteenth Century* (New York, 1972)

Schnerb, B., *Jean Sans Peur, Le Prince Meurtrier* (Paris, 2005)

Sherborne, J., 'Perjury and the Lancastrian Revolution of 1399', *Welsh History Review* 14 (1988), 217–41

Siberry, E., 'Criticism of Crusading in Fourteenth-Century England', in *Crusade and Settlement*, ed. P. W. Edbury (Cardiff, 1985), 127–34

Simms, K., 'The Ulster Revolt of 1404 – an Anti-Lancastrian Dimension?', in *Ireland and the English World in the Late Middle Ages: Essays in Honour of Robin Frame*, ed. B. Smith (Basingstoke, 2009)

Small, G., *Late Medieval France* (Basingstoke, 2009)

Smith, B., *Crisis and Survival in Late Medieval Ireland* (Oxford, 2013)

Smith, C., 'A Conflict of Interest? Chancery Clerks in Private Service', in *People, Politics and Community in the Later Middle Ages*, eds J. Rosenthal and C. Richmond (Gloucester, 1987), 176–91

Somerville, R., *History of the Duchy of Lancaster I* (London, 1953)

Staley, L., *Languages of Power in the Age of Richard II* (Philadelphia, 2005)

Staley, L., 'Gower, Richard II, Henry of Derby and the Business of Making Culture', *Speculum* 75 (2000), 68–96

Steel, A., *Receipt of the Exchequer 1377–1485* (Cambridge, 1954)

Storey, R., 'Clergy and Common Law in the Reign of Henry IV', in *Medieval Legal Records in Memory of C. A. F. Meekings*, eds R. Hunnisett and J. Post (London, 1978), 342–408

Storey, R., 'The North of England', in *Fifteenth-Century England 1399–1509*, eds S. Chrimes, C. Ross and R. A. Griffiths (Manchester, 1972), 129–44

Storey, R., 'Episcopal Kingmakers in the Fifteenth Century', in *Church, Politics and Patronage in the Fifteenth Century*, ed. R. Dobson (Gloucester, 1984), 82–98

Stow, G., 'Richard II in the *Continuatio Eulogii*: Yet Another Alleged Historical Incident?', in *Fourteenth-Century England V*, ed. N. Saul (Woodbridge, 2008), 116–29

Stratford, J. ed., *The Lancastrian Court: Proceedings of the 2001 Harlaxton Symposium* (Donington, 2003)

Stratford, J., *Richard II and the English Royal Treasure* (Woodbridge, 2012)

Stratford, J., 'The Royal Library in England before the Reign of Edward IV', in *England in the Fifteenth Century*, ed. N. Rogers (Stamford, 1994), 187–97

Stretton, G., 'Some Aspects of Medieval Travel', *TRHS* Fourth Series 7 (1924), 77–97

Strickland, M. and Hardy, R., *The Great Warbow* (London, 2005)

Stringer, K., 'States, Liberties and Communities in Medieval Britain and Ireland', in *Liberties and Identities in the Medieval British Isles*, ed. M. Prestwich (Woodbridge, 2008), 5–36

Strohm, P., *England's Empty Throne 1399–1422* (London, 1998)

Strohm, P., 'The Literature of Livery', in P. Strohm, ed., *Hochon's Arrow: The Social Imagination of Fourteenth-Century Texts* (Princeton, 1992), 179–86

Strong, R., *Coronation. A History of Kingship and the British Monarchy* (London, 2005)

Stubbs, W., *The Constitutional History of England in its Origin and Development* (fifth edn, 3 vols, Oxford, 1896)

Summerson, H., *Medieval Carlisle. The City and the Borders from the Late Eleventh to the Mid-Sixteenth Century* (Cumberland and Westmorland Antiquarian and Archaeological Society, 2 vols, Kendal, 1993)

Summerson, H., 'An English Bible and Other Books Belonging to Henry IV', *BJRL* 79 (1997), 109–15

Summerson, H., 'Peacekeepers and Lawbreakers in Medieval Northumberland, c.1200–1500', in *Liberties and Identities in the Medieval British Isles*, ed. M. Prestwich (Woodbridge, 2008), 56–76

Sumption, J., *Divided Houses: The Hundred Years War III* (London, 2009)

Taylor, C., 'Weep thou for me in France'. French Views of the Deposition of Richard II', in *Fourteenth Century England III*, ed. M. Ormrod (Woodbridge, 2004), 207–22

Thompson, B., 'The Laity, the Alien Priories, and the Redistribution of Ecclesiastical Property', in *England in the Fifteenth Century: Proceedings of the 1992 Harlaxton Symposium*, ed. N. Rogers (Stamford, 1994), 19–41

Thornton, T., 'Cheshire: The Inner Citadel of Richard II's Kingdom?', in *The Reign of Richard II*, ed. G. Dodd (Stroud, 2000), 85–96

Towson, K., '"Hearts Warped by Passion": The Percy–Gaunt Dispute of 1381', in *Fourteenth Century England III*, ed. M. Ormrod (2004), 143–52

Towson, K., '*Greves et Compleyntes*: Violence, Disputes and Arbitration in Early Fifteenth-Century Shropshire Gentry Society' (unpublished MLit. dissertation, University of St Andrews, 1997)

Tuck, A., *Richard II and the English Nobility* (London, 1973)

Tuck, A., 'Carthusian Monks and Lollard Knights', in *Studies in the Age of Chaucer I: Reconstructing Chaucer*, ed. P. Strohm and T. Heffernan (Knoxville, 1985), 149–61

Tuck, A., 'Henry IV and Europe: A Dynasty's Search for Recognition', in *The McFarlane Legacy. Studies in Late Medieval Politics and Society*, ed. R. Britnell and A. Pollard (Stroud, 1995), 107–25

Tuck, A., 'Henry IV and Chivalry', in *Henry IV: The Establishment of the Regime, 1399–1406* (York, 2003), 55–71

Tuck, A., 'The Earl of Arundel's Expedition to France, 1411', in *The Reign of Henry IV: Rebellion and Survival, 1403–1413* (York, 2008), 228–39

Turville-Petre, T., *The Alliterative Revival* (Cambridge, 1977)

Tyerman, C., *England and the Crusades* (Chicago, 1988)

Tyler, J., *Henry of Monmouth* (2 vols, London, 1838)

Vale, M., *English Gascony* (Oxford, 1970)

Vale, M., 'The War in Aquitaine', in *Arms, Armies and Fortifications in the Hundred Years War*, ed. A. Curry and M. Hughes (Woodbridge, 1994), 69–82

Vaughan, R., *John the Fearless* (London, 1966)

Veale, E., *The English Fur Trade in the Later Middle Ages* (2nd edn, London, 2003)

Victoria History of the Counties of England (London, Institute of Historical Research, 1899)

Walker, S., *The Lancastrian Affinity 1361–1399* (Oxford, 1990)

Walker, S., *Political Culture in Later Medieval England*, ed. M. Braddick (Manchester, 2006)

Walker, S., 'Letters to the Dukes of Lancaster in 1381 and 1399', *EHR* 106 (1991), 68–79

Walker, S., 'Rumour, Sedition and Popular Protest in the Reign of Henry IV', *Past and Present* 166 (2000), 31–65

Walker, S., 'The Yorkshire Risings of 1405: Texts and Contexts', in *Henry IV: The Establishment of the Regime, 1399–1406*, ed. G. Dodd and D. Biggs (York, 2003), 161–84

Walker, S., 'Janico Dartasso: Chivalry, Nationality and the Man-at-Arms', in *Political Culture in Later Medieval England*, ed. M. Braddick (Manchester, 2006), 115–35

Watt, H., '"On Account of the Frequent Attacks and Invasions of the Welsh": The Effect of the Glyn Dŵr Rebellion on Tax Collection in England', in *The Reign of Henry IV: Rebellion and Survival, 1403–1413*, ed. G. Dodd and D. Biggs (York, 2008), 48–81

Watts, J., *The Making of Polities: Europe 1300–1500* (London, 2009)

Watts, J., 'Looking for the State in Medieval England', in *Heraldry, Pageantry and Social Display in Medieval England*, ed. P. Coss and M. Keen (Woodbridge, 2002), 243–67

Watts, J., 'The Pressure of the Public on Later Medieval Politics', in *The Fifteenth Century IV, Political Culture in Late Medieval Britain*, eds L. Clark and C. Carpenter (Woodbridge, 2004), 159–80

Wilks, M., *Wyclif: Political Ideas and Practice* (Oxford, 2000)

Williams-Jones, K., 'The Taking of Conwy Castle, 1401', *Transactions of the Caernarvonshire History Society* 39 (1978), 7–43

Wilson, C., 'The Tomb of Henry IV and the Holy Oil of St Thomas at Canterbury', in *Medieval Architecture and its Intellectual Context: Studies in Honour of Peter Kidson*, eds E. Fernie and P. Crossley (London, 1990), 181–90

Wilson, C., 'The Medieval Monuments', in *A History of Canterbury Cathedral*, eds P. Collinson, N. Ramsay and M. Sparks (Oxford, 1995), 451–510

Wilson, F., 'Anglo-French Relations in the Reign of King Henry IV of England, 1399–1413' (unpublished PhD thesis, McGill University, 1973)

Wolffe, B., *The Royal Demesne in English History* (London, 1971)

Wright, E., 'Henry IV, the Commons and the Recovery of Royal Finance in 1407', in *Rulers and Ruled in Late Medieval England*, eds R. Archer and S. Walker (London, 1995), 65–82

Wright, S., *Martyrium Ricardi Archiepiscopi* (Catholic University of America, 1997)

Wylie, J., *History of England under Henry the Fourth* (4 vols, London, 1884–98)

Wylie, J. and Waugh, W., *The Reign of Henry the Fifth* (3 vols, Cambridge, 1914–29)

INDEX

Abberbury, Richard, 58 n.41
Aberystwyth, Aberystwyth castle, Wales, 192, 218, 240, 242, 318, 451–2
Abyssinia, emperor of, 399
Adam Usk, *see* Usk, Adam
Agenais, France, 258, 259
Agincourt, battle of, 14, 478
Agneta, servant, 80 n.19
Aire-sur-l'Adour, France, 259
Alain, Herbelain, 62–3 n.6
Albany, Robert Stewart, duke of (d.1420), 167–70, 197–200, 214–15, 218, 307 n.18, 321–3, 501; Murdoch Stewart, earl of Fife, son of, 199–200, 214, 321–3; captured at Humbleton Hill, 200; death, 322
Albaster, John, 454
Albert of Hapsburg, duke of Austria, 74
Alberti Bank, of Florence, Alberti family, 74, 341 n.38, 342, 356 n.27; Filippo, 342; Matteo, 74
Albret, Charles I, count of, 256–7, 258, 502, 509–12
Alcobaça, Peter de, 513 n.1
Aldrewich, Constanza, 421 n.60
Aldrewich, Nicholas, 421
Alençon, John I, count of, 330, 497, 498, 509
Alexander V, pope, 329 n.47, 363–4
Alfonso XI, king of Castile, 148
Alice, daughter of Henry de Lacy, earl of Lincoln, 12, 13, 15
aliens in England, 292, 294, 332–47, 460
Aljubarrota, Portugal, battle of, 39, 343
Alkerton, Richard, 418 n.52
Allerthorpe, Laurence, 181, 206, 211–12
Allington, William, 515 n.8
Alnwick, castle, Northumberland, 267, 270, 271
Anglesey, Wales, 134, 190, 219 n.17, 240, 242, 318
Anglesia, queen of Cyprus, 300 n.66
Angoulême, John, count of, 510

Angoumois, France, 498, 510, 512
Angus, George Douglas, earl of, 200
Annandale, Scotland, 216 n.2, 323
Anne of Bohemia, queen of England, 30, 32, 37 n.7, 42, 46, 55 n.31, 62 n.3, 99, 152 n.7, 164 n.28, 176 n.10, 422, 460; death of, 96; tomb, 518
annuities, royal, 175, 178, 212, 283, 300, 311–12, 427–8, 472–4
Anquetonville, Raoul d', 328 n.43
Anselm, saint, 366
Appleton, William, 29
Aquitaine, France, 63, 97 n.35; *see also* Guyenne
Aragon, Aragonese, 344–5
Arderne, John of, 293
Ardres, France, 98–9, 422
Armagnac, Armagnac lords, 493–500 n.30, 502, 509–12
Armagnac, Bernard, count of, 257, 259, 330, 509–12
Armeston, William, 81
Arnald, esquire, 30
Arnauld of Gascony, 40 n.20
Arras, bishop of, 497
Arthur, legendary king of the Britons, 90 n.12, 460–61
Arundel castle, 27, 44 n.35
Arundel, earls of, 19 n.20, 25 n.7
Arundel, John d', 25 n.7
Arundel, Richard, 400 n.69, 507 n.94
Arundel, Richard Fitzalan, earl of (d.1397) conflict with Richard II, 38, 42–3, 44–6, 48–52, 55, 57–9; expedition to Brittany, 58; dismissed from office of admiral, 59; seeks reconciliation with Richard, 60; 89–90, 101–3; arrested and tried for treason, 102–6; death, 106, 188, 448–9
Arundel, Thomas (Fitzalan), bishop of Ely, archbishop of York, archbishop of Canterbury (1353–1414), 40–1, 51, 102–3 n.15, 115, 124, 127, 134–40, 141, 142, 147, 149–52, 160, 162, 177 n.16,